The Bloomsbury
Companion
to Spinoza

Other volumes in the series of Bloomsbury Companions:

THE BLOOMSBURY
COMPANION
TO SPINOZA

GENERAL EDITORS

Wiep van Bunge
Henri Krop
Piet Steenbakkers
Jeroen van de Ven

Bloomsbury Companions

B L O O M S B U R Y
LONDON • NEW DELHI • NEW YORK • SYDNEY

Bloomsbury Academic
An imprint of Bloomsbury Publishing Plc

50 Bedford Square	1385 Broadway
London	New York
WC1B 3DP	NY 10018
UK	USA

www.bloomsbury.com

Bloomsbury is a registered trade mark of Bloomsbury Publishing Plc

First published in 2011 by Continuum

British Library Cataloguing-in-Publication Data
A catalogue record for this book is available from the British Library.

ISBN: HB: 978-0-8264-1860-9
       PB: 978-1-4725-3272-5
       ePDF: 978-1-4725-3362-3
       ePub: 978-1-4725-2760-8

Library of Congress Cataloging-in-Publication Data
A catalogue record for this book is available from the British Library.

Typeset by Newgen Imaging Systems Pvt Ltd, Chennai, India
Printed and bound in Great Britain

CONTENTS

INTRODUCTION

Today, Baruch or Benedict de Spinoza (1632–77) is widely considered to be one of the greatest philosophers who ever lived. Despite his early death at the age of forty-four, his stature and reputation now equal those of contemporaries such as Thomas Hobbes (1588–1679), René Descartes (1596–1650), John Locke (1632–1704), Gottfried Wilhelm Leibniz (1646–1716) and Pierre Bayle (1647–1706), who all lived much longer. Apart from his expulsion in 1656 from the Portuguese-Jewish community of Amsterdam and his recorded anger over the assassination, in 1672, of the Grand Pensionary of Holland Johan de Witt and his brother Cornelis, the story of his life seems relatively uneventful. His biography testifies first and foremost to the philosopher's total commitment to his work. Spinoza's correspondence, consisting of some eighty odd letters to and from the Dutch philosopher, is largely concerned with the details of his philosophy. Hence, much of Spinoza's life remains in the dark and research into the particulars of his biography continues to inspire the experts. We know much more about the details of the lives of Hobbes, Descartes, Locke, Leibniz and Bayle than we do about Spinoza's and they all produced much more voluminous Collected Works.

Spinoza's *Tractatus theologico-politicus*, published anonymously in 1670, has recently enjoyed considerable scholarly attention, yet to most contemporary readers Spinoza is still essentially the author of a single masterpiece, the *Ethics*, published posthumously in 1677. The *Ethics*, however, composed in Latin and modelled on Euclid's *Elements*, has always been regarded as an exceptionally difficult book, if only on account of the austerity of its language and its geometrical method. Up to this day it has given rise to diverging and even conflicting interpretations, as has the issue of the precise relationship between the *Ethics* and Spinoza's other works.

Following the format of this series, the opening section provides an overview compiled by Jeroen van de Ven of the documentary evidence now available relating to Spinoza's life. This chronicle aims to be complete, and it clearly shows the many lacunae still facing every potential biographer. The next section, on the influences on Spinoza's thought, was edited by Piet Steenbakkers. It does not claim to deliver a complete picture of all the sources at work in Spinoza's philosophy, but we feel it would be folly even to attempt supplying such an exhaustive list. More often than not Spinoza is silent about his sources, but then he was no humanist scholar: as a follower of the newly created Cartesian school in philosophy he attached small importance to traditional scholarly erudition and so he may not always have felt the need to clearly indicate where his ideas came from or how they related to those of other thinkers.

The appeal Spinoza's works held and still hold for many readers should not hide from view the widespread revulsion his ideas also incited. We now know that from a very early stage Spinoza was admired across the length and breadth of Europe, but the large majority of his early readers were appalled by his 'atheism', his 'materialism' and his 'fatalism'. From the 1670s onward dozens of 'refutations' were published, and the section Early Critics, compiled by Wiep van Bunge, provides an anthology of some of the objections raised against Spinozism as a comprehensive philosophy. Opinions will vary as to the effectiveness of much of the polemical energy vested in dismantling Spinoza's philosophy, but we feel the opposition to Spinozism remains an important and fascinating aspect of its presence in early modern philosophy.

The largest section fell under the responsibility of Henri Krop. The Glossary contains a rich collection ranging from short notes to minor essays on the concepts which together make up Spinoza's thought. By spelling out Spinoza's conceptual vocabulary, or rather by having a wide variety of experts do so, we hope to be able to shed new light both on the origins and inner logic of Spinozism as well as on its details. Fortunately, the contributors to this particular section disagree on several aspects of Spinoza's thought. As a consequence a multi-faceted picture emerges, which we hope will serve to provoke further reflection.

The next section is the work of Piet Steenbakkers. His Synopses provide a summary of Spinoza's writings, including the ones less familiar even to the experts such as Spinoza's Hebrew Grammar. The final section, a short essay on the history of Spinoza scholarship, was written by Wiep van Bunge. As editors we have also written many of the entries brought together in this volume, but we have constantly tried to keep the kaleidoscopic nature of this project intact, for this book was edited by Dutchmen, but co-written with a host of colleagues and friends from the Netherlands, Belgium, France, Italy, Switzerland, Finland, the United States and Canada.

Despite the quiet and brevity of his life as well as his relatively small output, Spinoza continues to inspire philosophers, historians, scientists but also laymen without any professional interest in Spinoza. We hope this Companion may help to stimulate further reflection and research on the Dutch philosopher's life and work.

The Editors

ACKNOWLEDGEMENTS

The editors would like to thank the Continuum International Publishing Group for its support of this project. Rudi Thoemmes and Merilyn Holme in particular have been a great help. So have been Bart Leeuwenburgh of the Erasmus University and, again, Michiel Wielema for his editorial assistance. Michiel has saved us from many mistakes. Although this Companion has become a very different book from *The Dictionary of Seventeenth and Eighteenth-Century Dutch Philosophers* (2003), it was a great pleasure to have so many members of the *équipe* responsible for the publication of the *Dictionary* willing and able to produce this 'sequel'. Our Rotterdam colleague Paul Schuurman, co-editor of the *Continuum Companion to Locke* (2010), was always at hand to lend advice. His stimulating example has helped us to finish this project. Of course we owe the greatest debt to our contributors, for without Mark Aalderink, Roberto Bordoli, Bert Bos, Laurent Bove, Filip Buyse, Thomas Cook, Herman De Dijn, Hans Gribnau, Michael Hampe, Jonathan Israel, Chantal Jaquet, Paul Juffermans, Olli Koistinen, Frank Mertens, Jon Miller, Pierre-François Moreau, Gianluca Mori, Jan Noordegraaf, Tammy Nyden, Miriam van Reijen, Tamar Rudavsky, Han van Ruler, Donald Rutherford, Marin Terpstra, Tad Schmalz, Leen Spruit, Theo Verbeek and Rienk Vermij the *Bloomsbury Companion to Spinoza* would not have been complete.

The Editors

ABBREVIATIONS

In this work the following abbreviations are used:

A. WORKS OF SPINOZA

G   Spinoza, *Opera*, ed. C. Gebhardt (Heidelberg: Winter, 1925; repr.1972), 4 vols. (This is the reference edition, quoted by volume, page, line numbers. Thus, G IV, 95:12 = vol. IV, p. 95, line 12.)

Adn   *Adnotationes ad Tractatum theologico-politicum*

CG   *Compendium grammatices linguae Hebraeae*

CM   *Cogitata metaphysica*

E   *Ethica* (followed by part and component)

Components: al = aliter; ax = axioma; aff = affectuum definitio; app = appendix (for E4, app1 means caput 1 of the appendix); c = corollarium; def = definitio; dem = demonstratio; exp = explicatio; lem = lemma; p = propositio; post = postulatum; praef = praefatio; s = scholium.

Ep   *Epistolae*

KV   *Korte verhandeling van God, de mensch en deszelvs welstand*

PPC   *Renati Des Cartes Principia philosophiae*

TIE   *Tractatus de intellectus emendatione* (followed by section numbers as introduced by Bruder 1844, in Arabic numerals)

TP   *Tractatus politicus*

TTP   *Tractatus theologico-politicus*

B. WORKS OF DESCARTES

AT: *Œuvres de Descartes*, ed. Ch. Adam & P. Tannery, 2nd ed. (Paris, 1965–83; [1]1897–1910)

Meditationes   *Meditationes de prima philosophia*

PA   *Passiones animae / Les Passions de l'âme*

PP   *Principia philosophiae*

C. OTHER SEVENTEENTH-CENTURY AUTHORS

Burgersdijk, F. *Idea philosophae moralis*:	Franco Burgersdicius, *Idea philosophiae moralis, ex Aristotele maxima parte excerpta, & methodice disposita*, Lugduni Batavorum, ex officina Elzeviriana, 1624.
Burgersdijk, F., *Institutiones Logicae*:	Franco Burgersdicius, *Institutionum logicarum libri duo, decreto illustriss. ac potentiss. dd. ordinum Hollandiæ et West-Friesiæ, in usum scholarum ejusdem provinciae, ex Aristotelis praeceptis nova methodo ac modo formati, atque editi, Editio secunda, ab auctore multis locis emendata*, Lugduni Batavorum, apud Abrahamum Commelinum, 1634.
Burgersdijk, F., *Institutiones Metaphysicae*:	Franco Burgersdicius, *Institutionum metaphysicarum libri II, Editio altera, priori correctior*, Lugduni Batavorum, apud Hieronymum de Vogel, 1642.
Heereboord, A. *Meletemata*:	Adrianus Heereboord, *Meletemata philosophica, in quibus pleraeque res metaphysicae ventilantur, tota ethica ... explicatur, universa physica per theoremata & commentarios exponitur, summa rerum logicarum per disputationes traditur*, Editio nova, Amstelaedami, sumptibus Henrici Wetstenii, 1680.
Hobbes, Th. *De cive*:	Thomas Hobbes, *Elementa philosophica de cive*, Amsterodami, apud Ludovicum Elzevirium, 1647.
Hobbes, Th. *De corpore*:	Thomas Hobbes, *Elementorum philosophiae sectio prima De corpore*, Londini, excusum sumptibus Andreæ Crook,1655. Contains: the *Computatio sive logica* and *De Motu*.
Hobbes, Th. *De homine*:	Thomas Hobbes, *Elementorum philosophiae sectio secunda De homine*, Londini, typis T.C. sumptibus Andr. Crooke, 1658.
Hobbes, Th. *Leviathan*:	Thomas Hobbes, *Leviathan, sive De materia, forma, & potestate civitatis ecclesiastiae et civilis*, Amstelodami, apud Joan. Blaeu, 1668.

D. SEVENTEENTH-CENTURY DICTIONARIES

Chauvin	Etienne Chauvin, *Lexicon philosophicum... ita tum recognitum & castigatum; tum varie variis in locis illustratum, tum passim quammultis accessionibus auctum & locupletatum, ut denuo quasi novum opus in lucem prodeat...*, Leeuwardiae, excudit Franciscus Halma, 1713; 1a ed.: Rotterdam, 1692.
Goclenius	Rudolphus Goclenius, *Lexicon philosophicum, quo tanquam clave philosophiae fores aperiuntur*, Frankfurt, 1613.
Micraelius	Johannes Micraelius, *Lexicon philosophicum terminorum philosophis usitatorum*, Jena, 1653; 2a ed.: Stettin, 1661, 1662.

LIST OF CONTRIBUTORS

Mark Aalderink
Department of Philosophy
Utrecht University
The Netherlands

Roberto Bordoli
Professor, Department of Philosophy
Universita degli Studi di
Urbino Carlo Bo
Italy

Bert Bos
Professor, Department of Philosophy
Leiden University
The Netherlands

Laurent Bove
Professor, UFR de Philosophie et
Sciences Humaines et Sociales
Université de Picardie Jules
Vernes
Amiens
France

Wiep van Bunge
Professor, Faculty of Philosophy
Erasmus University Rotterdam
The Netherlands

Filip Buyse
École Doctorale de Philosophie
Université de Paris 1, Panthéon-
Sorbonne
France

Thomas Cook
Professor, Department of Philosophy
and Religion
Rollins College
Winter Park, FL
USA

Herman De Dijn
Professor Emeritus, Institute of
Philosophy
Catholic University of Leuven
Belgium

Hans Gribnau
Professor, Faculty of Law
Leiden University
and Senior Lecturer, Faculty of Law
Tilburg University
The Netherlands

Michael Hampe
Professor of Philosophy,
Department of Humanities, Social and
Political Sciences
ETH-Zürich
Switzerland

Jonathan Israel
Professor, Institute of
Advanced Studies
Princeton, NJ
USA

Chantal Jaquet
Professor, École Doctorale de
Philosophie
Université de Paris 1,
Panthéon-Sorbonne
France

Paul Juffermans
Lecturer, HOVO Brabant
Seniorenacademie
Tilburg University
The Netherlands

Olli Koistinen
Professor, Department of Philosophy
University of Turku
Finland

Henri Krop
Senior Lecturer, Faculty of Philosophy
Erasmus University Rotterdam
The Netherlands

Frank Mertens
Department of Philosophy
University of Ghent
Belgium

Jon Miller
Associate Professor,
Department of Philosophy
Queen's University
Kingston, Ontario
Canada

Pierre-François Moreau
Professor, Département des Sciences
Humaines
École Normale Supérieure des
Lettres et Sciences Humaines de Lyon
France

Gianluca Mori
Professor, Faculty of Letters and
Philosophy
Università degli Studi del Piemonte

Orientale Amedeo Avogadro
Vercelli
Italy

Jan Noordegraaf
Senior Lecturer, Faculty of Letters
Free University of Amsterdam
The Netherlands

Tammy Nyden
Assistant Professor, Department of
Philosophy
Grinnell College
Grinnell, IA
USA

Miriam van Reijen
Lecturer, AVANS Hogeschool
Breda
The Netherlands

Tamar Rudavsky
Professor, Melton Center for Jewish
Studies
The Ohio State University
Columbus, OH
USA

Han van Ruler
Professor, Faculty of Philosophy
Erasmus University Rotterdam
The Netherlands

Donald Rutherford
Department of Philosophy
University of California, San Diego
La Jolla, CA
USA

Tad Schmalz
Professor, Department of Philosophy
University of Michigan
Ann Arbor, MI
USA

Leen Spruit
Lecturer, Faculty of Letters and
Philosophy
Università La Sapienza Roma
Italy

Piet Steenbakkers
Professor, Faculty of Philosophy
Erasmus University Rotterdam
and Senior Lecturer, Department of
Philosophy
Utrecht University
The Netherlands

Marin Terpstra
Lecturer, Faculty of Philosophy
Radboud University Nijmegen
The Netherlands

Jeroen van de Ven
Boxtel
The Netherlands

Theo Verbeek
Professor Emeritus, Department of
Philosophy
Utrecht University
The Netherlands

Rienk Vermij
Assistant Professor, Department of the
History of Science
University of Oklahoma
Norman, OK
USA

1

LIFE

Spinoza's Life and Time.
An Annotated Chronology
Based Upon Historical Documents

The heading of each entry in this chronology provides (if known) both the date and, when applicable, the location of a historically documented event in the life of Spinoza, in italics. Dates in the chronology are given according to the Gregorian calendar, unless otherwise indicated. If relevant, a date is followed by the equivalent of the Jewish calendar. In some cases, the date of a historical event or letter is designated according to both the Gregorian ('New Style') and Julian calendars ('Old Style' (OS)), when discussing events that took place in those parts of the Dutch Republic or countries that adhered to the 'Old Style'. Conjectural dates, places and facts are always put between square brackets.

References to Spinoza's published correspondence (published letters (88) and all (lost) missives (37), in Latin and Dutch) are given according to the chronological numbering (Ep) introduced by Van Vloten and Land (1882–3) and to the original standard edition of Carl Gebhardt (1925, 1985, abbreviated G). Reconstructed letters postulated from

evidence in the correspondence or from other historical sources have been assigned a unique code entirely based on their dating (year, month and day) according to the Gregorian calendar. When unknown, the month or day is given as '00'. The mathematical symbols < or > in front of a letter code indicate a dating respectively 'before' or 'after'. Letter codes are followed by an asterisk if a letter has been reconstructed (e.g. 1663.01.11*). Standard reference works that have been used more than once in this study are specified in the list of abbreviations and reference works. In the seventeenth century, names were often spelled in a variety of ways. Dutch family names are given in the common form. Topographical names are indicated in their local form unless there is a more common equivalent in English. Dutch institutions and technical terms are given in italics if there is no satisfactory English equivalent.

The present chronology, modelled after the chronologies of the lives of Leibniz, Husserl and Hobbes (Müller and Krönert, 1969; Schuhmann, 1977 and Schuhmann,

1998), is a heavily reduced version of a forth-coming comprehensive historical survey that aims to render available the documentary sources of the life, writings, intellectual networks and earliest reception of Spinoza covering the time frame to 1680 (Van de Ven, 2014/2015).

1. PROLOGUE: ORIGIN AND FAMILY RELATIONS

[VIDIGUEIRA], NANTES, AMSTERDAM: 1587/88–MID-JULY 1631

After Philip II, King of Spain (1527–98), conquered Portugal in 1581, the Inquisition spread rapidly throughout the Iberian Peninsula, accusing thousands of Marranos (or New Christians) of secretly practising Judaism. In due course, many Portuguese crypto-Jews are obliged to flee their country, making their home in other cities throughout Europe. Many of these refugees settle in the French town of Nantes (Brittany), attracted by the city's relative religious freedom, blooming trade and commerce. The grandparents of Spinoza also seek refuge in Nantes from the rigours of the Inquisition in the Iberian Peninsula. The young Michael d'Espinosa (the philosopher's father) is amid these Portuguese refugees. Very likely, he is born the second son of the wealthy merchant Pê(d)ro Roiz Rodrigues Espin(h)osa (alias Isaac de Espinosa, c. 1550/60–1627) and his wife Mor (Maior) Alvares (b. 1550/60), who fled from South Portugal (Vidigueira) to Nantes in early 1605 (cf. Borges Coelho, 1987, vol. 1, p. 411). If Pê(d)ro and Mor are indeed the parents of Michael, the latter had two siblings: an older brother, named Fernando, and one sister,

Maria Clara. When at the beginning of the seventeenth century the majority of the Portuguese Jews in Nantes choose to convert to Roman Catholicism, the Sephardim community in the city gradually diminishes. In that same time frame, many Portuguese Jews from Nantes commence relations with Portuguese-Israelite communities in the newly founded (1578) Dutch Republic in Amsterdam, the leading maritime city in the world and one of the few places in Europe where Jews are not hindered from practising Judaism privately. Around 1615, French communication networks with the Amsterdam Sephardim community quickly grow tighter as a result of the brutal expulsion of the remaining Jewish population from Nantes. In the same year, the Dutch States General (Dutch central assembly in permanent session in The Hague) makes the settling of the Sephardim Jewry in the United Provinces legal. Six years later, sometime before late October 1621, members of the Espinosa family finally leave Nantes to settle in Amsterdam. They probably find lodgings in the Vlooienburg quarter near the adjacent Breestraat, where most Sephardim Jews in this period make their home. The newcomer Michael d'Espinosa works as a successful immigrant merchant, particularly in the profitable import-export business of subtropical fruit. After the death (1627) of his first wife, Rachel de Espinosa, Michael marries Hanna Deborah d'Espinosa (the philosopher's mother) in 1628.

1587 OR 1588, [VIDIGUEIRA, PORTUGAL]

Exact date unknown
'Michael de Espinose' is born in the small city of 'Vidiger', which may be identified as the Portuguese town of Vidigueira. The birth year of Michael d'Espinosa can be calculated

2

from several legal documents in the town archives of Amsterdam (see for instance Vaz Dias and Van der Tak, p. 11, III, 1a, c).

1621, NANTES, [AMSTERDAM, VLOOIENBURG QUARTER]

Before Thursday 28 October
Members of the Espinosa family leave Nantes, either willingly or forced, to settle in [Amsterdam]. Documentary evidence for the early presence of members of the Espinosa family in the city is contained in the burial registers of *Beth Haim*, the Portuguese-Israelite cemetery in the village of Ouderkerk aan de Amstel, which have been preserved in the Amsterdam town archives. According to the so-called 'Livro de Bet Haim do Kahal Kados de Bet Yahacob' (a register containing the regulations, decisions, income and revenue of the *Beth Haim* cemetery of the Portuguese-Jewish congregation *Bet(h) Jacob*, see Pieterse, 1970) a child 'from the house of Isaac de Espinoza' (Michael's father, Pê(d)ro Roiz Rodrigues Espin(h)osa) was buried in Ouderkerk on Thursday 28 October 1621/13 Kislev 5382 (Vaz Dias and Van der Tak, p. 4, I, B).

[1622, OR EARLY 1623, AMSTERDAM, VLOOIENBURG QUARTER]

Exact date unknown
Michael d'Espinosa marries his [paternal] cousin, Rachel de Espinoza (fl. 1622/23–7). Very likely, they registered their intention to marry at the old medieval town hall of Amsterdam on the Dam square (until 1652). In due course, the mandatory banns of their forthcoming marriage were publicly posted for three consecutive weeks. As no marital records have survived from that era, the exact date of the marriage

(1620, cf. Meinsma, p. 56, 1622 or early 1623) between Michael and Rachel is unknown.

1627, (AMSTERDAM, VLOOIENBURG QUARTER), OUDERKERK AAN DE AMSTEL

Sunday 21 February (5 Adar 5387)
Death of Rachel de Espinosa. She is buried (row 9, no. 18) on the same day at the Portuguese-Israelite cemetery *Beth Haim* ('Livro de Bet Haim', Walther and Czelinski, 2006, vol. 1, p. 187, no. 14). Michael commemorates the death of his wife by contributing one (Carolus) guilder (or florin, the equivalent of 20 *stuivers* (or patars) or 320 *penningen*) to the Sephardim community in Amsterdam (Walther and Czelinski, 2006, vol. 1, p. 188, no. 16).

Friday 8 October
Michael d'Espinosa works as an entrepreneur in Amsterdam. It is unclear how and when exactly he entered into business, but it is by no means unreasonable to suppose that he learned his managerial skills in and around the trading firm of his father or family. On 8 October 1627, 'Michiel Despinosa about 38 years of age', together with Mendo Lopes (fl. c. 1577–1627) and Jorge Fernandes Canero (fl. c. 1596–1627), signs a legal document, written in Dutch, before the notary public Sibrant Cornelisz (fl. 1616–38) in Amsterdam to confirm the identity of the Portuguese merchant Diego da Silva (fl. 1570–1629) (Vaz Dias and Van der Tak, p. 11, III, 1a). Michael's ability to understand Dutch must have been very limited and it is almost certain that he regularly needed the help of others to have documents written in Dutch translated for him into Spanish. That is proven in two legal statements (16 August and 8 October 1652) which he still needed to have translated for

him by both a family member and a servant (see Walther and Czelinski, 2006, vol. 1, pp. 234–6, nos. 56–7).

c. 1628, AMSTERDAM
[VLOOIENBURG QUARTER]

Exact date unknown
Michael d'Espinosa marries in second wedlock Hanna Deborah d'Espinosa. She is the daughter of Baruch Senior (fl. 1598–1619) and Maria Nunes Garces (c. 1577–after 1638) (if they are indeed her parents), who both left Portugal to settle in the city of Amsterdam as early as 1598. Michael and Hanna in all probability officially registered their intention to marry at the town hall of Amsterdam.

[c. 1629], AMSTERDAM
[VLOOIENBURG QUARTER]

Exact date unknown
Birth of Spinoza's sister, Mirjam d'Espinosa (c. 1629–50).

1631, AMSTERDAM
[VLOOIENBURG QUARTER]

February
A son named Isaac is born from Michael d'Espinosa's marriage with Hanna Deborah d'Espinosa. This is therefore the philosopher's elder full brother – a fact for which so far no conclusive evidence was available. The date of his birth can be inferred from the postscript to one of the autograph manuscripts with Hebrew sermons delivered by the Amsterdam rabbi Morteira, now preserved in the Library of the Rabbinical Seminary in Budapest (MS 12 'Giv'at Sha'ul', 5 vols; see Saperstein, 2005): 'The sermon I delivered in the year 5391 (1631) on the day of the celebration of

the son of the honourable Michael Espinosa' (MS 12 'Giv'at Sha'ul', vol. 2, fol. 177v (Exod. 35.21), quoted in Saperstein, 2005, p. 9). Isaac d'Espinosa attended the Amsterdam Talmud Torah School at the Houtgracht sometime in 1637, until the age of 13 or 14, together with his brother Bento. Isaac died on 24 September 1649. No further biographical particulars are known about him.

Tuesday 15 July
Michael d'Espinosa works in the import-export business of subtropical fruit in Amsterdam. According to a legal document of 15 July 1631, Michael together with a certain Philips Pelt holds the keys of a warehouse at the Prinsengracht, in which such goods as sugar, Brazilian wood and candied ginger were stored (Vaz Dias and Van der Tak, p. 53, a). In the affidavit, made by the notary public Daniel Bredan (fl. 1623–4) in Amsterdam, two men declare that they transported goods to the weighing house from the warehouse at the Prinsengracht on 27 May and 18 June 1631.

2. BIRTH AND EARLY CHILDHOOD

AMSTERDAM: LATE NOVEMBER 1632–AUGUST 1636

We have very little and only fragmentary information about the early upbringing of the young Spinoza. He is born the [second] son of Michael d'Espinosa and his second wife, Hanna Deborah d'Espinosa, in Amsterdam on 24 November 1632. Since no archival records of Spinoza's birth in the municipal archives of Amsterdam have survived, the exact address where he is born remains unclear. The oldest, most reliable source claiming Spinoza to be born in

Amsterdam is the anonymous preface to the philosopher's posthumous works (1677). The Lutheran minister Johannes Nicolaus Colerus (1647–1707), Spinoza's eighteenth-century biographer, adds to this that he was born at the Burgwal, near the old Portuguese Church (Colerus, 1705, see Walther and Czelinski, 2006, vol. 1, p. 98). Spinoza has four siblings: Isaac, Mirjam, Rebecca and Gabriel.

LATE 1632, AMSTERDAM
[VLOOIENBURG QUARTER]

Wednesday 24 November
Spinoza is born the [second] son of Michael d'Espinosa and Hanna Deborah d'Espinosa, most probably in a house in the Vlooienburg quarter. According to Colerus, that house was a 'vraay Koopmans huis op de Burgwal naast de Oude Portugieze Kerk' (a handsome Merchant house at the Burgwal next to the Old Portuguese Church) (Walther and Czelinski, 2006, vol. 1, p. 98). Another short biography (1747) by Johannes Monnikhoff (1707–87) adds to this that the philosopher was born 'op de Hout-gragt, naast de oude Portugeesche Kerk...in een fraaij Koopmans huijs: waar voor in het Jaar 1743 een nieuwe gevel, en in die 't oprechte Tapijthuis is gezet' (at the Houtgracht, next to the old Portuguese Church...in a handsome Merchant house: which in the year 1743 was furnished with a new façade with the name 't oprechte Tapijthuis') (Walther and Czelinski, 2006, vol. 1, p. 172). Research has clearly established that Spinoza may have been born in the house described, though the name ''t oprechte Tapijthuis' (the true Carpet house) dates from the middle of the eighteenth century (Vaz Dias and Van der Tak, 1982, pp. 172–5). Summing up, there is no historical evidence to confirm the claims made by Colerus and Monnikhoff.

[Wednesday 1 December]
The young Spinoza is ritually circumcised (Nadler, 1999, p. 42). During this (undocumented) circumcision ceremony ('Brit milah' or 'Bris'), which officially initiates him into the Sephardic community, Spinoza receives the name Bento (Baruch, or 'the Blessed').

AFTER 1632, AMSTERDAM
[VLOOIENBURG QUARTER]

Exact date unknown
Sometime after 1632, two other children from Michael d'Espinosa's second marriage are born: Rebecca (fl. 1632–95) and Gabriel d'Espinosa (alias Abraham d'Espinosa, fl. 1632–64).

1633, AMSTERDAM
(VLOOIENBURG QUARTER)

Friday 2 December
A legal document, made by the notary Bredan, confirms that 'Mr Michel despinosa Portuguese merchant of this city' is living with his family 'in a house here in Vlooienburg'. From this document, we also learn that he is active in the long-distance trade of raisins. The deed concerns the receipt of 50 small barrels of raisins from Malaga, which apparently did not arrive in good condition in Amsterdam (Vaz Dias and Van der Tak, p. 11, III, 2a).

1634, AMSTERDAM
[VLOOIENBURG QUARTER]

Thursday 29 June
The Jewish-Moroccan merchant David Pallache (fl. 1626–50) signs a legal document before the notary public Daniel Bredan. In an effort to clear some of his debts, Pallache in this document transports a

carrier with its complete cargo to both Michael d'Espinosa and the brothers Pieter and Wijnant Woltrincx (Vaz Dias and Van der Tak, p. 53, b).

1636, AMSTERDAM
[VLOOIENBURG QUARTER]

August
Michael d'Espinosa is officially registered as an independent entrepreneur (Vlessing, 1997, p. 21). He is also mentioned as one of the *Parnassim* of the Portuguese-Jewish congregation *Bet(h) Jacob* (Vaz Dias and Van der Tak, p. 15, III, 4a) for the period 1636–7. This is an indication that he acquired respect and status in the Amsterdam (Sephardim) community.

3. FORMAL EDUCATION AND INTELLECTUAL TRAINING

AMSTERDAM: 1637–MID-SEPTEMBER 1654

The life of the young Spinoza is marked by periods of mourning as well as celebration. As a young child, he experiences the death (1638) of his mother, Hanna Deborah d'Espinosa, but also the third marriage (1641) of his father Michael with Hester de Espinosa. Somewhere around Spinoza's thirteenth birthday (1645) the Espinosa family celebrates his *bar mitzvah*. During his teenage years, Spinoza is again confronted with distressing and sad events involving people who were very close to him: the death of his brother Isaac (1649), the death of his sister Mirjam (1651), and, finally, the passing away of his father Michael (1654).

We possess but very little information about Spinoza's formal schooling in Amsterdam. Almost certainly, he attends the Amsterdam *Talmud Torah* School (more commonly known as *Ets Haim* School) at the Houtgracht (c. 1637) together with his brother Isaac until the age of 13 or 14, giving him a solid training in the Hebrew Bible and Jewish commentaries. There is however no documentary evidence to support this claim. Nevertheless, there is little reason to doubt that Spinoza attended the *Talmud Torah* classes, as his father was repeatedly chosen as one of the principal administrators (1635, 1636, 1642 and 1643) of this primary public school for the education of Jewish boys (cf. Vaz Dias and Van der Tak, p. 15, III, 4c). In addition, Spinoza is mentioned as a member of the society *Ets Haim* ('Tree of Life') of the *Ets Haim* School (1637). Next to nothing is known about Spinoza's upbringing and occupations in the ten-year period until 20 April 1655, when his name is mentioned in the notarial records of Amsterdam in relation to a financial business conflict of the trading firm which he took over from his father in the early spring of 1654. So we may assume that Spinoza came into business through the trading firm of his father. Historical facts about Spinoza's early intellectual training are also lacking. It is plausible that he was a pupil at the Latin School of the notorious free-thinker Franciscus Affinius van den Enden (1602–74) sometime in the mid-1650s, but there is no independent historical evidence to support this. War is declared by English Parliament on the United Provinces on 10 July 1652 (First Anglo-Dutch War, 1652–1654).

1637, AMSTERDAM
[VLOOIENBURG QUARTER]

Exact date unknown
Spinoza presumably receives his formal education at the *Ets Haim* School at the Houtgracht. Together with his brother, Isaac, he is mentioned as a member of the society

Ets Haim of the *Ets Haim* School (Vaz Dias and Van der Tak, p. 26, V, 1). The philosopher's name was later struck out, perhaps due to his subsequent ban from the unified Portuguese-Jewish congregation *Talmud Torah* in 1656. This is the earliest historical document known referring to the young Spinoza.

1638, AMSTERDAM [VLOOIENBURG QUARTER] AND OUDERKERK AAN DE AMSTEL

Thursday 8 June
The Amsterdam *schepenbank* (local Dutch court of law) appoints Michael d'Espinosa and Ruy Gomes Frontera (fl. 1622–38) to step in for a certain Diego Cardozo Nunes (fl. 1624–47) as official trustees for the bankrupt estate of the recently deceased Pedro Henriques (d. before 1639) (Vaz Dias and Van der Tak, pp. 53–4, g). Another record on this same matter in the Amsterdam archives is dated 26 January 1639 (Vaz Dias and Van der Tak, pp. 54, h).

Tuesday 8 September
Michael d'Espinosa and his second wife Hanna Deborah are seriously ill and confined to bed in their house in the Vlooienburg quarter. That is confirmed in a legal document of 8 September 1638 made by the notary Jan Warnaertz (fl. 1621–45) at their house at the request of a certain Simon Barkman (fl. 1638–46). The deed concerns the refusal of a 'wisselbrief' (a bill of exchange, an unconditional order in writing (by the drawer) to pay a fixed sum of money at a nominated time to a nominated person, or to the bearer or holder of the bill) by Michael and Hanna Deborah 'because of the illness' (Vaz Dias and Van der Tak, 1982, pp. 187–8, Annex 1). That bill of exchange (worth 1,600 Taler and 34 copper coins) was

initially nominated by the deceased Henriques to a certain Lopo Nunes. Apparently, Michael, Henriques's estate trustee, took over the debt and agreed to make payment to Nunes through 'Simao Barquman' on 21/31 August 1638 (Walther and Czelinski, 2006, vol. 1, pp. 220–1, no. 48).

Friday 5 November (28 Cheshvan 5399)
Death of Hanna Deborah d'Espinosa. The philosopher's mother is buried on the same day at the Portuguese-Israelite cemetery *Beth Haim* (Vaz Dias and Van der Tak, p. 3, I, A).

1641, AMSTERDAM (VLOOIENBURG QUARTER)

Exact date unknown
The business finances of Michael d'Espinosa's trading company are growing vigorously. His credit balance in the Amsterdam *Wisselbank* runs in five months to the impressive sum of 28,052 Dutch guilders and 88 *penningen* (about 300,000 euro nowadays).

Sunday 28 April
Michael d'Espinosa marries in third wedlock Hester de Espinosa. According to the Amsterdam marriage registers, the newly-wed couple was living in the 'Vloijenburgh' quarter (Vaz Dias and Van der Tak, p. 22, III, 11b).

1642, AMSTERDAM [VLOOIENBURG QUARTER]

Saturday 1 February
The finances of Michael d'Espinosa's trading firm begin to grow rather problematical as compared to the far more prosperous year 1641. The credit balance of his account in the *Wisselbank* has now diminished to the sum of 1,323 Dutch guilders (now approximately 15,000 euro) ('Balansboek', Vaz Dias and Van der Tak, p. 55).

1644, AMSTERDAM [VLOOIENBURG QUARTER] AND OUDERKERK AAN DE AMSTEL

Monday 25 April

Michael d'Espinosa enters into a Portuguese trading contract with Francisco Lopes d'Azevedo (fl. 1614–41). Also involved in the business agreement is the London-based merchant and shipping magnate Antonio Fernandes Carvajal (c. 1590–1659) (Vaz Dias and Van der Tak, p. 54, n).

[1645 OR 1646], AMSTERDAM [VLOOIENBURG QUARTER]

Exact date unknown

The young Spinoza leaves the *Ets Haim* School sometime in [1645 or 1646]. In the same period, he is to celebrate his *bar mitzvah* in the newly built Portuguese *Talmud Torah* synagogue at the Houtgracht. The ceremony in the Amsterdam synagogue is not documented.

[AFTER 1645–1646], AMSTERDAM [HOUTGRACHT]

Exact date unknown

We may assume that Spinoza, after leaving the Amsterdam *Ets Haim* School, enters the business trade, learning his managerial skills in and around the trading firm of his father or family. Apart from that, almost nothing is known about his intellectual training as a young man after his formal education at the *Ets Haim* School. According to Colerus, he was first tutored on a daily basis in Latin by a 'Hoogduitsch Student', most likely a tudesco, a German Jew of Ashkenazi extraction (Walther and Czelinski, 2006, vol. 1, p. 100), but this claim is not supported by any documentary evidence. After that, according to the same source, he was tutored

by 'that notorious Teacher and Physician Frans van den Ende', who may be identified as the free-thinker Franciscus van den Enden. There is, however, no independent historical evidence to confirm that Spinoza entered Van den Enden's Latin School. Contacts between Spinoza and Van den Enden have not been documented. An early documentary source suggesting that Spinoza learned Latin from the 'ex Jesuit' Van den Enden is a report on the life and works of Spinoza submitted by the Dutch vicar apostolic Johannes Baptista van Neercassel (1626–86) to the Supreme Sacred Congregation of the Roman and Universal Inquisition (or Holy Office of the Inquisition, the supreme Roman Catholic tribunal for the whole world founded in 1542) submitted on 9 September 1678 (Orcibal, 1949, p. 464, Annex 11; see also Bayle in Walther and Czelinski, 2006, vol. 1, p. 61).

1649, AMSTERDAM [VLOOIENBURG QUARTER] AND OUDERKERK AAN DE AMSTEL

Friday 24 September (18 Tishrei 5410)

Death of Spinoza's brother, Isaac d'Espinosa. He is buried at *Beth Haim*, probably on the same day.

1651, AMSTERDAM (HOUTGRACHT) AND OUDERKERK AAN DE AMSTEL

Wednesday 19 July

The Spinoza family lives in a rented house at the Houtgracht in the Amsterdam Vlooienburg quarter. According to the property tax register (concerning the so-called 'achtste penning', the 8th penny) of Amsterdam the house, owned by one Willem Kick, is located somewhere 'achter de Bree straet, nae d'oude Stadt' (behind the Breestraet, near the old city). According to the same source, Michael d'Espinosa pays the tax of 16 guilders and five *stuivers* for the renting of Kick's house (Vaz Dias and Van der Tak, p. 12, III, 2b).

Wednesday 6 September (*20 Elul 5411*)
Spinoza's sister Mirjam d'Espinosa (who died in childbirth) is buried at *Beth Haim* (Vaz Dias and Van der Tak, p. 3, I, A).

**1652, AMSTERDAM (HOUTGRACHT)
AND OUDERKERK AAN DE AMSTEL**

Friday 7 June
The Spinoza family, according to the Amsterdam property tax register, is still living in a house at the Houtgracht owned by Kick (Vaz Dias and Van der Tak, p. 12, III, 2b).

Wednesday 23 October
Hester de Espinosa, Spinoza's stepmother, makes her will before the notary Jan Volkertsz Oli in her house (at the Houtgracht). In her written will, Hester is referred to by her Portuguese name as well as by her Jewish family name ('s.ra giomar de soliz alias Hester d'Espinoza'). According to the document, in which she appoints her husband Michael as her legal heir, she is bedridden and so weak that she is even unable to sign her own testament (Vaz Dias and Van der Tak, 1982, pp. 188–9, Annex 2).

Thursday 24 October (*22 Cheshvan 5413*)
Death of Hester de Espinosa. She is buried at *Beth Haim*, most likely on the same day (Vaz Dias and Van der Tak, p. 3, I, A).

1653, AMSTERDAM (HOUTGRACHT)

Thursday 3 July
The Spinoza family is still living in a rented house at the Houtgracht owned by Kick (Vaz Dias and Van der Tak, p. 12, III, 2b).

**1654, AMSTERDAM [HOUTGRACHT]
AND OUDERKERK AAN DE AMSTEL**

Saturday 28 March (*10 Nisan 5414*)
Michael d'Espinosa dies in [Amsterdam]. The philosopher's father is buried in Ouderkerk, probably on the same day (Vaz Dias and Van der Tak, p. 3, I, A). Spinoza is 21 years old; according to Dutch law, he is legally still a minor.

[12] September (*1 Tishrei 5415*)
'Baruch d'Espinosa' is mentioned for the first time as *Jahid* in the journal of the *Gabay* (treasurer) of the unified Portuguese-Jewish community *Talmud Torah*. The entries in this register concern his bi-annual communal payments (the obligatory *fintas* or *impostas*, a fixed contribution, and the voluntary *promesas*, to be paid at Pesah (Passover) and Rosh Hashanah, the Jewish New Year) to the Sephardim community for two years (1654–6) (Vaz Dias and Van der Tak, 1982, p. 190).

4. ENTREPRENEURSHIP, EXPULSION AND EARLIEST WRITINGS

AMSTERDAM: APRIL 1655–EARLY AUGUST 1659

After Michael d'Espinosa's sudden death in late March 1654, Spinoza at the age of 21 takes over the family firm, very likely in partnership with his younger brother Gabriel. From 1654, Spinoza is mentioned several times as an entrepreneur in legal deeds in the Amsterdam town archives. Two years later, between 23 and 28 March 1656, the Supreme Court of Holland officially releases him from having accepted his father's estate. In this way, he can escape from Michael d'Espinosa's financial obligations after the latter had become the trustee of the insolvent estate of the Portuguese-Jewish merchant Henriques. Only four months later, on 27 July 1656, the *Mahamad* officially bans Spinoza from the *Talmud Torah* synagogue at the Houtgracht. Though several discoveries have been made recently concerning Spinoza's family firm and its bankruptcy, his problematic relations with the Portuguese-Jewish community in Amsterdam as well as the actual reasons for his excommunication remain unclear up to this day. Biographical information is very sparse about the crucial years following Spinoza's expulsion until the spring of 1661. Evidently, Spinoza in this clouded period is standing at the crossroads of his old life as an entrepreneur in the Amsterdam Sephardim community, and a new life as an original, independent thinker, optician and natural scientist, well versed in the Cartesian system and frequenting radical Cartesian 'circles'. Very likely, he remains in Amsterdam for most of this time prior to his moving to the village of Rijnsburg (close to Leiden) somewhere [before 29 July 1661]. The only information about Spinoza from that period known to us is that he meets an Augustine friar from Spain, Tomás Solano y Robles (c. 1627–after 1659), in Amsterdam in the course of late 1658 or early 1659. Then, sometime between November 1658 and mid-January 1659, he also makes the acquaintance of one captain Miguel Pérez de Maltranilla (c. 1625–after 1659). Shortly afterwards, in early August 1659, both Spaniards testify before the Inquisition tribunal in Madrid that they encountered many Jews while in Amsterdam, Spinoza and a physician named Juan de Prado (c. 1614–after 1665) amongst others. Both Spaniards specifically label Spinoza a 'good philosopher',

but also an apostate and atheist. In this same period, Spinoza composes his earliest writings, his unfinished *Korte verhandeling van God, de mensch en deszelvs welstand* and *Tractatus de intellectus emendatione*.

1655, AMSTERDAM [HOUTGRACHT]

Wednesday 17 November

Spinoza signs a legal document before the public notary Lock concerning the transportation of a 'wisselbrief' to a Portuguese merchant in Amsterdam, named Joseph Francis. He also signs this document for 'Sʳ Gabriel de Espinosa sijn broeder & Compagnon' (Mr Gabriel de Espinosa his brother & Companion) in the following manner: 'Bento y gabriel despinoza'. In the document, Spinoza and his brother convey and sell a bill of change (worth 876 Portuguese crusades and 79 'groot') to Joseph Francis, who apparently is not present during the transaction. (Vaz Dias and Van der Tak, pp. 31–2, V, 9).

Sunday 5 December (6 Kislev 5416)

Spinoza donates the sum of six guilders to the unified Portuguese-Jewish congregation *Talmud Torah* (Vaz Dias and Van der Tak, p. 32, V, 9). The offer to support the poor (*nedabah*, or voluntary offering) seems to indicate that Spinoza is still an active and a loyal member of the Amsterdam Sephardim community.

1656, AMSTERDAM [HOUTGRACHT]

March (Nisan)

Spinoza offers the payment (the voluntary *promesas*) of 12 *stuivers* (Vaz Dias and Van der Tak, 1982, p. 190).

Thursday 16 March

The 'Heeren Weesmeesteren' (Lords Orphan Masters) of the Amsterdam *Weeskamer*

(Orphan chamber) appoint Louis Crayers (1623–88) as legal custodian of 'Bento d'Espinosa' (Vaz Dias and Van der Tak, pp. 32–3, V, 10).

[Before Thursday 23 March]
Crayers, legal custodian of 'Bento d Spinosa minderjarige naegelaeten soon van Michael de Spinosa' (Bento d Spinosa underaged orphaned son of Michael de Spinosa) informs the Supreme Court of Holland in a legal deed that his pupil fully renounces the estate of his father. Crayers turns to the Supreme Court to relieve Spinoza officially from the debts of his father's estate and from any legal action he has already taken with regard to this property. In this way, Spinoza is able to escape from his father's financial obligations to the creditors of the insolvent estate of Henriques, of whom Michael had become the trustee on 8 June 1638 (see Vlessing, 1997, pp. 19–20). A rather serious accusation in this deed is that Michael did not give his son the appropriate part of the inheritance after the death of his second wife. In the deed, Crayers puts forward Spinoza as a preferential creditor of Michael's estate based on his claim on the goods of his deceased mother (Vaz Dias and Van der Tak, pp. 32–3, V, 11).

Thursday 23 March
The Supreme Court of Holland, Zeeland and West-Friesland officially releases Spinoza from having accepted his father's estate (Vaz Dias and Van der Tak, p. 32, V, 11).

Thursday 27 July (6 Av 5416)
The Amsterdam *Mahamad* officially places Spinoza under the ban (*herem*) of the unified community *Talmud Torah* ('Escamoth' (register of rules and regulations), Vaz Dias

and Van der Tak, 1982, p. 164, V, 12, p. 170). As the matter stands, many key questions remain about Spinoza's problematic relations (if any) with the Sephardim community as well as the exact reasons for his sudden expulsion. The *herem* imposed on him may very well relate to the bleak financial situation of his father's estate, rather than to the philosopher's opinions in matters of religious revelation as is often assumed. For the writ, a ritualistic formula which seems to have been derived from late thirteenth- or early fourteenth-century Venice, is in fact extremely vague, mentioning 'abominable heresies' and 'monstrous deeds' without any further explanation. So much is clear: there are no archival sources, testimonies or writings whatsoever to confirm or prove that Spinoza had any deviant ideas or publicly preached at the time (see Vlessing, 1997, p. 15; Walther and Czelinski, 2006, vol. 1, pp. 262–3, no. 73).

1658, AMSTERDAM [HOUTGRACHT]

Between Wednesday 21 August 1658 and Friday 21 March 1659
Spinoza makes the acquaintance of the Augustine friar Solano y Robles, who found his way to Amsterdam where he waits for a ship to sail back to Spain. So apparently the philosopher is still living in Amsterdam. Sometime between November 1658 and 14 January 1659, Spinoza also meets the infantry captain Miguel Pérez de Maltranilla, one of Solano y Robles's fellow travellers (cf. Revah, 1959, p. 32). Nothing precise is known about their relations, except that they met in Amsterdam and discussed matters of religion. Pérez de Maltranilla travelled back to Spain on 14 January 1659, while Solano y Robles set sail on 21 March 1659.

1659, [AMSTERDAM, HOUTGRACHT]

Friday 8 August

After his return to Spain, Solano y Robles is interrogated by the Inquisition in Madrid on the conversion to Judaism of the Spanish actor and musician Lorenzo Escudero (fl. 1659–1683). The Inquisition court however takes a much broader interest and also asks the Spanish monk to provide details about his contacts in Amsterdam. Solano y Robles testifies that he met many Jews in Amsterdam, specifically referring to his encounter with the physician De Prado and Spinoza, 'whom he thinks is born in one of the cities of Holland, because he studied in Leiden and is a good philosopher'. The Madrid Inquisition report is the only known source to imply that the philosopher might have attended Leiden University before August 1658. We know with certainty that Spinoza did not officially matriculate as a student in Leiden, for his name is not mentioned in the official matriculation register of Leiden university. If we assume however that Spinoza may have taken private classes (for instance philosophy lessons under the supervision of Arnold Geulincx (1624–69)) there, it could perhaps be explained why he settled in early 1661 in the village of Rijnsburg, which is in the close vicinity of Leiden. Both De Prado and Spinoza, according to the Madrid interrogation record, had professed in a private meeting that they were banned from the Sephardic community for their atheistic preferences and their belief that the soul dies together with the body, claiming to believe in God only philosophically (Revah, 1959, pp. 32 and 64, Annex 2).

Saturday 9 August

One day later, Pérez de Maltranilla is also heard on the Escudero affair by the Inquisition in Madrid. While staying in Amsterdam, he testifies, he made the acquaintance of several Jews in the house of a physician, called Joseph Guerra. There, he also met Michael Reynoso (fl. 1614–55), a physician from Seville, and a certain Samuel Pacheco, a confectioner from Seville who made a living in the trade of chocolate and tabacco. He also claims to have spoken with two apostates, Juan de Prado and Spinoza (Revah, 1959, pp. 32–3, 66–8, Annex 2).

5. OUTSIDE THE WALLS OF THE LEIDEN ACADEMY

[AMSTERDAM], RIJNSBURG: MID-MAY 1661–MID-APRIL 1663

Spinoza's reputation as an original thinker begins to spread after his expulsion (27 July 1656) from the Portuguese-Jewish community in Amsterdam sometime in the early 1660s. The dissemination of his views among a group of admirers in Amsterdam presumably starts with the *Tractatus de intellectus emendatione*. In the early 1660s, Spinoza establishes close relations and enters into a correspondence with several of these admirers: the writer and medical doctor Lodewijk Meyer (1629–81), the Mennonite merchant Simon Joosten de Vries (1633/34–67), Pieter Balling (fl. 1647–64) and, presumably, Jan Rieuwertsz Sr (c. 1617–87), one of the most productive publishers and bookdealers in Amsterdam at this time. Many insiders of this talented study 'circle' are free-thinkers and non-academic radical Cartesians. Meanwhile, Spinoza is also composing another treatise, elaborating his own philosophical system of what would eventually become his posthumously published *Ethics*. At this stage, however, he still plans to present his philosophy in a discursive form, surviving in a Dutch translation of his unfinished *Korte verhandeling van God, de mensch en des zelvs welstand* (the lost original was written in Latin), which he reworked in the geometrical style as late as 1665.

Five years after his expulsion from the synagogue, Spinoza finally leaves Amsterdam. He settles in a small house in Rijnsburg, where he will stay from the summer of 1661 until late April 1663. The philosopher never reveals his motives for moving there, and the exact date (sometime [before 29 July 1661]) remains unknown, too. In this period, Spinoza studies the New Philosophy of René Descartes (1596–1650), Francis Bacon (1561–1626) and Thomas Hobbes (1588–1679) as well as the textbooks of various neoscholastics, such as Franco Petri Burgersdijk (1590–1635), Adriaan Heereboord (1614–61) and Bartholomeus Keckermann (1573–1609). Also, he is in close contact with a young Leiden student, named Johannes Casearius (c. 1642–77), whom he teaches Descartes's *Principia philosophiae*. To all appearances, Spinoza in this Rijnsburg period seems already a luminary of some renown who even attracts the attention of the international Republic of Letters. In the same interval, the first (indirect) reference by the Danish anatomist Olaus Borrichius (1626–90) is made to Spinoza not only as an atheist, but also as an optician manufacturing glasses and microscopes. Between the second half of 1660 and 1662, he makes the acquaintance of the Danish natural scientist and theologian Niels Stensen (1638–86), with whom he shares an interest in Cartesianism and human anatomy. Sometime before 29 July 1661, he receives a visit from the German scholar

Henry Oldenburg (c. 1615–77), one of the founding fellows of the British 'invisible college' of natural philosophers (the precursor of the Royal Society). Almost instantly upon his arrival in London, Oldenburg enters upon a lively philosophical exchange of letters with Spinoza starting 26 August 1661. Through Oldenburg as intermediary Spinoza communicates with the British naturalist Robert Boyle (1627–91). With Boyle he discusses the nature of experiment, particularly his *Certain Physiological Essays*, an account of experiments with pure nitre or saltpetre (the powerful fertilizer potassium nitrate KNO_3). In this way, Oldenburg becomes an important conduit for Spinoza into the world of science and the supranational Republic of Letters'. Their correspondence, a portion of which seems to circulate among Spinoza's friends, also yields information about the philosopher's own experimental work on nitre performed in Rijnsburg.

1661, [AMSTERDAM, HOUTGRACHT], RIJNSBURG [KATWIJKERLAAN]

[Before Friday 29 July], Amsterdam, Rijnsburg
From Amsterdam, Spinoza moves to Rijnsburg, where he takes up residence at the house (at the Katwijker Laantje or Kwakkel-, or Paradijslaantje, nowadays Spinozalaan 29, the house now known as the 'Spinozahuis') of a local surgeon, Herman Homan. The exact date of Spinoza's definitive departure is unknown, but it must have been sometime [before 29 July 1661]. In his early Rijnsburg period, Spinoza receives a visit from the diplomat and natural philosopher Henry Oldenburg, discussing with him various philosophical subjects, viz. God, the attributes extension and thought and their

differences, body and soul, as well as Cartesian and Baconian philosophy (cf. Oldenburg to Spinoza, Ep 1, G IV, 5–6).

Friday 26 August (16 OS)

Almost three weeks after his return to London, Henry Oldenburg dispatches a letter to Spinoza (Ep 1, G IV, 5–6), inviting him to start a philosophical correspondence. Oldenburg asks Spinoza to write to him on the distinction between extension and thought as well as the weaknesses in Cartesian and Baconian philosophy. Furthermore, he promises Spinoza to send him a copy of a pending publication 'by an English nobleman, a man of extraordinary learning' (i.e. Boyle), entitled *Certain Physiological Essays*. Oldenburg's letter of 16/26 August 1661, the earliest surviving letter of Spinoza's correspondence, marks the beginning of his long friendship with the young Dutch philosopher. They remained close (epistolary) friends until Spinoza's death in early 1677, exchanging at least 31 letters (with enclosures) over the period from 26 August 1661 to 11 February 1676.

Early September [Rijnsburg]

Spinoza replies to Oldenburg's letter of 16/26 August 1661. In his reply (Ep 2, G IV, 7–9), he brings up the definition of God, the relation between substance and God, without answering Oldenburg's questions concerning his distinction between the attributes extension and thought. Furthermore, Spinoza propounds three propositions on substance. In his letter, he also encloses 'a clear and concise proof' of his theory of substance, arranged 'in geometrical fashion' (*more geometrico*). The enclosure itself is lost, but can be reconstructed. The stage of these philosophical views expounded in this letter to Oldenburg is a mixture between his *Korte verhandeling*

van God, de mensch en deszelvs welstand and what would later become his *Ethics*. The second part of his letter revolves around the defects in the philosophy of Descartes and Bacon concerning the conflict between free will and reason as the basis of all error.

Saturday 10 September

Olaus Borrichius, travelling in the region of Leiden, in his diary quotes the testimony of a certain Daniel Langermann from Hamburg, which may be interpreted as a veiled reference to Spinoza. Borrichius in his diary refers to someone who is almost an atheist, and 'who has left Judaism and become a Christian'. That atheist, who is living in the vicinity of 'Rensberg' (Rijnsburg), does not bother about the Old Testament, the Koran, nor Aesop's fables, but on the other hand he presents absolutely no harm to others, spending his time manufacturing glasses and microscopes (Borrichius, 1983, vol. 1, p. 128; see also Klever, 1989, p. 314).

Saturday 24 September, Rijnsburg

During Olaus Borrichius's trip to Katwijk aan Zee, Valkenburg and Rijnsburg, a German physician named Menelaus provides him with some striking details about Spinoza. According to Borrichius's travel diary, Spinoza, 'who had left Judaism and become a Christian', is living in Rijnsburg. The latter supposedly excels in Cartesian philosophy, even superseding some of Descartes's distinct ideas. Borrichius also stresses the fact that Spinoza's ideas even surpass the work of the Amsterdam mathematician Johannes Hudde (1628–1704), who appended a tract called 'De forkeren' to Descartes's *Geometria* (i.e. the second Latin edition of Descartes's *Géométrie* (1637), see Descartes, 1996, VI, 367–485). This much is clear, the information recounted to Borrichius by Menelaus seems to confirm the reputation Spinoza enjoyed as an expert of some note in Cartesian philosophy in his early Rijnsburg period (Borrichius, 1983, vol. 1, p. 128; see also Klever, 1989, p. 314).

1661 OR 1662, RIJNSBURG [KATWIJKERLAAN], [LEIDEN]

Exact date unknown
After moving to Rijnsburg, Spinoza makes the acquaintance of the young Danish intellectual Niels Stensen sometime between the second half of 1660 and 1662, either in Rijnsburg or in Leiden very likely. Their encounter is confirmed in a lengthy document ('Libri prohibiti circa la nuova filosofia dello Spinosa' (Forbidden books centering around the new philosophy of Spinosa)), which Stensen later submitted in Rome to the Supreme Sacred Congregation of the Holy Office (4 September 1677). In the document, Stensen testifies that he was on familiar terms with Spinoza 'some fifteen or sixteen years ago' during the time (after 27 July 1661) he was studying medicine in Leiden. Spinoza, 'whose doctrines very much confused me', was of Jewish extraction, but he had no specific religious belief. Stensen furthermore asserts that Spinoza had studied for the rabbinate for some time and was in contact with a 'certain' Van Enden, who ultimately may be held responsible for his deviant, atheistic views. Also, Descartes's philosophy exerted a very profound influence on Spinoza's thinking (Totaro, 2000, p. 100; Totaro, 2002, Appendix, p. 33). What is biographically the most intriguing in the report is Stensen's claim that Spinoza daily attended his anatomical dissections of the brain of various animals, which he performed 'to find the seat of the principle of motion and the source of the human feelings' (Totaro, 2000, p. 100; Totaro, 2002, Appendix, p. 33).

AFTER 1661, [RIJNSBURG, KATWIJKERLAAN]

A manuscript copy in Latin of Spinoza's *Korte verhandeling van God, de mensch en deszelvs welstand* circulates among his friends and followers in [Amsterdam] very likely (cf. Akkerman, 2005, p. 230).

JANUARY–EARLY APRIL 1663, RIJNSBURG [KATWIJKERLAAN], THE HAGUE

Saturday 24 February, Rijnsburg
From Amsterdam, Simon Joosten de Vries writes a letter to Spinoza in Rijnsburg (Ep 8, G IV, 38–41). Firstly, De Vries apologizes for not visiting him there, because the wintry weather prevented him from doing so. Then he expresses some jealousy about 'your companion Casuarius' (i.e. Johannes Casearius), who 'dwells beneath the same roof and can converse with you during breakfast, lunch and on walks'. So apparently Casearius shares lodgings in Rijnsburg with Spinoza. More importantly, De Vries's letter yields explicit information about the circulation of Spinoza's earliest writings among a small group of admirers in Amsterdam. He writes to Spinoza that his 'circle' recently resumed its meetings to discuss his writings on a regular basis. One member does the reading, gives his explanation of the passage and then continues with a demonstration of Spinoza's propositions. When they disagree, they make a note of it and write to Spinoza for more clarification and guidance to defend the truth against 'those who are religious and Christian in a superstitious way'. De Vries in his letter also raises questions about the nature of definition, axiom and postulate. To all appearances they read an early instalment of the first part of the *Ethics* rather than the *Korte verhandeling van God, de mensch en deszelvs welstand*.

6. EXPANDING THE SCHOLARLY NETWORK

VOORBURG, SCHIEDAM: LATE APRIL 1663– MID-JUNE 1665

Sometime after 20 April 1663, Spinoza settles in the small village of Voorburg (close to The Hague) for unknown reasons. He rents rooms in the Kerklaan (nowadays known as Kerkstraat) at the house of a painter called Daniel Harmensz Tydeman (fl. 1654–77), until moving to The Hague between early September 1669 and mid-February 1671. In his new dwelling, he intensively works on a geometric presentation of Descartes's *Principia philosophiae* to which he appends an annex containing his own metaphysical views. Gradually, Spinoza's international network of relations with intellectuals and writers is expanding. He also remains in close contact with Oldenburg and in all likelihood writes a letter to Robert Boyle. He keeps in touch with his friends in Amsterdam, in particular Rieuwertsz Sr and Meyer, to whom under Spinoza's own direction he entrusts the entire project of editing, correcting, printing and publishing his *Renati des Cartes Principia philosophiae*. Since Rieuwertsz Sr. had no printing office, he hired the Amsterdam typographer Daniel Bakkamude to typeset the work for him. Shortly after having published the work in the late summer of 1663, he disseminates a (lost) treatise on rainbows amongst friends for study purposes. With Willem van Blijenberg (1632–96), a Dordrecht grain broker and amateur philosopher, Spinoza enters into a correspondence on several issues in his reworking of Descartes's *Principia* as well as on a variety of other philosophical and theological topics. He is also in direct communication with the medical doctor Johannes Bouwmeester (1634–80), Jarig Jelles (1619/20–83) and Pieter Balling; the latter very probably translated Spinoza's *Renati des Cartes Principia philosophiae* into Dutch, a book published in 1664. The book was not typeset by Bakkamude, but by another printer named Aaltsz. Meanwhile, Spinoza is also composing another treatise, expanding his own philosophical system into what would eventually become his posthumously published *Ethics*. In 1665, he decides to present his philosophy in the geometrical style rather than the discursive form he had preferred earlier.

Between late December 1664 and mid-February 1665, Spinoza temporarily leaves Voorburg to stay at 'Langen bogert' ('The Long Orchard'), the home of the Mennonite merchant Alewijn Jacobsz Gijse (c. 1627–83) in the vicinity of the small trading port of Schiedam (close to Rotterdam), probably to escape from the plague that is sweeping through The Hague and its region. In the spring of 1665, Spinoza is in direct communication with one of the greatest men of science in Europe at that time, Christiaan Huygens (1629–95). They may have met each other either in the residence of the Huygens family at the Plein in The Hague (called 'Domus') or in their country house 'Hofwijck' (south east of The Hague), located very close to Spinoza's residence at the Kerklaan in Voorburg. With Huygens, he actively shares his enthusiasm for a variety of subjects: astronomy, the laws of motion and, most importantly, practical optics and the fabrication of lenses. In all likelihood, Spinoza is also introduced to Christiaan's older brother Constantijn (1628–97) and to their famous father, the renaissance virtuoso Constantijn Huygens (1596–1687), who both maintain a keen interest in optics.

1663, Voorburg (Kerklaan), Amsterdam

After Friday 20 April, Voorburg, Amsterdam
Spinoza leaves the village of Rijnsburg to settle in Voorburg, where he rents rooms in the house of the painter Daniel Tydeman in the Kerklaan. Soon afterwards, he visits Amsterdam. It is not known for how long Spinoza remains there, but on 26 July 1663 he is back in Voorburg again, where he is visited by some of his 'friends' (cf. Spinoza to Oldenburg, Ep 13, G IV, 63–9). He now works intensively on what would become his first book, *Renati des Cartes Principia philosophiae*, an exposition of Descartes's *Principia*, 'demonstrated in geometric style', to which he appends a lengthy annex containing the *Cogitata metaphysica*, which deal with contemporary neoscholastic metaphysics.

Thursday 26 July, Voorburg
Spinoza writes a short letter (Ep 12A, Offenberg, 1975) to his confidant Meyer to provide him with instructions for the completion of *Renati des Cartes Principia philosophiae*. The letter is a reply to Meyer's (lost) letter which he received on 25 July 1663 about corrections in the manuscript of that work. It shows that the philosopher takes an active interest in the printing of his text.

Friday 27 July (17 OS)
From [Voorburg], Spinoza writes a letter to Henry Oldenburg (Ep 13, G IV, 63–9). The first part of the letter contains details about the genesis of *Renati des Cartes Principia philosophiae* and the order in which the work was originally composed (second part, first part, the *Cogitata metaphysica*, Meyer's preface). Firstly, Spinoza informs Oldenburg about his moving to Voorburg (after 20 April 1663) and his visit to Amsterdam. While in Amsterdam, 'some of my friends' requested him to provide them with a treatise containing a short account of the second part of Descartes's *Principia* 'demonstrated in a geometrical style', which he had previously dictated to a certain young man (his Rijnsburg companion Johannes Casearius) to whom he did not wish to reveal his own thoughts. At the request of these friends, he also completed an account of the first part of Descartes's *Principia* according to the same method; he finished this account in two weeks. His friends then asked his permission to publish the whole work. Most willingly, he gave them permission under the condition that one of them (Lodewijk Meyer) should correct the style 'in my presence' and also add a short preface to warn readers 'that I do not acknowledge everything in the treatise as my own opinion'. To supervise Meyer's work was why he stayed in Amsterdam for some time. Spinoza then explains to Oldenburg why he gave permission to publish his treatise. He promises his correspondent to send him either his forthcoming book or a written summary of his work 'which is now in the press'.

Friday 3 August
From Voorburg, Spinoza writes to Meyer (Ep 15, G IV, 72–3). He sends him his (marginal) corrections to the preface to *Renati des Cartes Principia philosophiae*, which he has received through Simon Joosten de Vries. To all appearances, a portion of Spinoza's exposition of Descartes is already typeset whereas other parts of the work are still in the process of printing. He also expects his friend to mention in his preface the fact that many of his own demonstrations in fact differ from Descartes's. Furthermore, Spinoza urges Meyer to delete the entire part Meyer specifically wrote against an otherwise

unidentified scholar, whom he sees as a windbag and sardonically labels as 'that petty man'. He promises Meyer to convey to him the printed sheets with the scholium to proposition 27 (starting on p. 75) of the second part of *Renati des Cartes Principia philosophiae*, which must absolutely be reset by the printer wih his new corrections and additions.

After Friday 3 August

The Amsterdam bookseller Jan Rieuwertsz Sr publishes *Renati des Cartes Principia philosophiae*, the first book that appeared openly under Spinoza's own name in his lifetime. The precise publication date of this quarto edition is not known, but the date *post quem* is Spinoza's letter to Lodewijk Meyer of 3 August 1663. It is abundantly clear that Meyer edited *Renati des Cartes Principia philosophiae* and the *Cogitata metaphysica* rather heavily according to Spinoza's explicit instructions (cf. Steenbakkers, 1994, p. 20). The work, according to Spinoza's own testimony, is published 'for the benefit of all men'. The preface to it is composed by Meyer. Spinoza's lifelong friend, Johannes Bouwmeester, is credited with having composed the laudatory poem 'Ad librum'. Appended to the work is an annex containing the *Cogitata metaphysica*. The manuscript of the work itself has been lost. As was shown by Gerritsen (1980; see also Gerritsen, 2005, p. 255), the main text of the Latin work was typeset from a case (dated 1663) from which were also set seven editions of works authored by the poet Joost van den Vondel (1587–1679). One of these is also typographically linked with a Vondel text set with a different case used by the Amsterdam printer Thomas Fonteyn (fl. 1630–61) between 1659 and 1662. Typographical research has now shown that

the printer who did typeset Spinoza's digest of Descartes was Daniel Bakkamude (Jagersma and Dijkstra, 2014).

After mid-August

In all likelihood, Spinoza is spending a portion of his time in the study of light and colours, an aspect of mathematical physics. Shortly after publishing his *Renati des Cartes Principia philosophiae*, he disseminates another treatise concerning rainbows among the 'circle' of friends in Amsterdam (Akkerman and Hubbeling, 1979, no. 9, pp. 112–13). The manuscript and text of the work have been lost.

1664, VOORBURG (KERKLAAN), SCHIEDAM (AT THE 'LANGEN BOGERT')

Exact date unknown

Sometime in 1664, Rieuwertsz Sr publishes *Renatus des Cartes Beginzelen der wysbegeerte*, the Dutch adaptation of *Renati des Cartes Principia philosophiae*, under Spinoza's full name. The work, augmented and revised in many places by its author most likely, was translated from Latin into the vernacular by someone who signed his name as 'P.B.'. Presumably, the person responsible for this translation was Spinoza's friend Pieter Balling, although there is no historical evidence to support that claim. The preface to the work is composed by Meyer. The work contains the Latin dedicatory poem 'Ad librum' attributed to Bouwmeester (I.B.M.D.), plus two other Dutch poems. One is a free translation of this dedicatory poem, the other poem is signed by 'H. Van Bronchorst, M.D.', who can be identified as the Cartesian physician Hendrik van Bronchorst (1636–78) from Amsterdam. The book was printed by the Amsterdam typographer

Aaltsz (Jagersma and Dijkstra, 2014). The manuscript of the work has also been lost.

Friday 12 December
From [Dordrecht], the grain broker and amateur philosopher Willem van Blijenberg writes a letter to Spinoza (Ep 18, G IV, 79–85). The letter is enclosed in another (lost) letter of Van Blijenberg dated 21 December 1664 (Van Blijenberg to Spinoza, 1664.12.21*). Spinoza, according to his own testimony, receives the packet on 26 December 1664 while staying at the homestead of the Mennonite merchant Alewijn Gijse close to the village of Schiedam (cf. Spinoza to Van Blijenberg, Ep 19, G IV, 86–95). The letter of 12 December 1664 marks the beginning of the exchange between Spinoza and Van Blijenberg, who was an enthusiastic reader of *Renati des Cartes Principia philosophiae*. Van Blijenberg's letter of 12 December 1664 is the first known reaction to Spinoza's *Renati des Cartes Principia philosophiae* and the *Cogitata metaphysica*.

Before Friday 26 December, Schiedam
Spinoza departs from Voorburg to stay three or four weeks in the vicinity of Schiedam at the homestead of Gijse (cf. Spinoza to Van Blijenberg, Ep 19), called the 'Langen bogert' ('Long orchard'). The reason for the philosopher's short stay there is very likely an attempt to diminish chances of infection from the plague that swept through The Hague and its region. Gijse's home was situated outside Schiedam (cf. Van Blijenberg to Spinoza, Ep 20, G IV, 96–125) in Oud-Mathenesse. Although Spinoza, according to his own testimony, planned to stay in Schiedam for almost an entire month, he only returns to Voorburg after 19 February 1665.

1665, Schiedam (at the 'Langen bogert'), Voorburg (Kerklaan), Amsterdam

Friday 13 March, Voorburg
From Voorburg, Spinoza writes a letter to Van Blijenberg (Ep 23, G IV, 144–52) in response to the latter's objections and questions of 19 February 1665. In this reply, Spinoza presses his own arguments against Van Blijenberg's objections to his axioms of God and also answers three moral questions. His answers to Van Blijenberg's second question (whether stealing, in relation to God, is as good as righteousness) reveals the intriguing fact that the philosopher is now working on a treatise titled *Ethics*, 'which I have not published yet'. This is the first known occurrence of the title of Spinoza's exposition of his own philosophical system and also the first direct reference to his plans to put the *Ethics* into the press.

[May], [Amsterdam]
Spinoza, who is presumably still in Amsterdam, answers Henry Oldenburg's letter of 28 April 1665. His reply to Oldenburg (Ep 26, G IV, 159) clearly indicates that he is now in close communication with Christiaan Huygens. Spinoza in his letter reacts to Huygens's information that Boyle is still alive and that the latter's treatise on colours has been newly printed. Huygens is willing to lend him his own copy of that treatise, 'if I understood English', Spinoza says, so the letter clearly demonstrates that he was unable to read English. Spinoza also informs Oldenburg that Huygens owns a copy of 'the book of microscopic observations'. Without doubt, that book is Robert Hooke's *Micrographia* (1665). Spinoza's letter also yields information about the contents of his other conversations with Huygens. Apparently,

they discussed a great variety of subjects, in particular issues of astronomy such as microscopes and Italian telescopes that were used to observe the eclipses of Jupiter and a shadow on Saturn (causing the image of a ring). Another subject was Descartes's explanation concerning the question why Saturn's satellites do not move.

7. PRACTISING PHILOSOPHY, CRAFTSMAN OF SCIENCE

Voorburg: September 1665–Late 1670

In early September 1665, while lodging at Tydeman's house in the Kerklaan in Voorburg, Spinoza works intensively on the *Tractatus theologico-politicus*, which slows down and influences the earlier exposition of his own philosophical system in the *Ethics*. Meanwhile, he continues his epistolary friendship with Oldenburg in London, with whom he discusses a wide range of subjects, ranging from philosophy, books and anatomical observations by Oxford scientists to the Second Anglo-Dutch naval war. In mid-December 1665, his exchange with Oldenburg is interrupted for an interval of approximately ten years. In the mid-1660s, contacts between Spinoza and Christiaan Huygens seem to become more intense. With him, he discusses various scientific matters, particularly their personal pursuits in the field of optics. Moreover, Huygens gives Spinoza access to the manuscript of his *Dioptrics*. In early 1666, Spinoza is also in contact with Johannes Hudde, who has some fame in practical optics, producing microscopes and constructing telescope lenses. A letter of (June) 1666 to Hudde clearly indicates that Spinoza is spending a portion of · his time manufacturing lenses. Apart from optics matters, Spinoza's correspondence from this period also proves that he divides his time between various subjects, such as the calculus of probabilities and alchemy.

Relatively little is known with certainty about the philosopher's personal life in the period between late March 1667 and 1670. No correspondence survives from 1668 and 1670, but we must surmise that Spinoza worked on the text of the *Tractatus theologico-politicus*. The only palpable evidence that he is also continuing his optical work on (telescopic and microscopic) lenses can be found in his own personal correspondence and in the missives exchanged between Christiaan and Constantijn Huygens. To all appearances, Spinoza is also collaborating with Hudde in researching and manufacturing (telescopic) lenses, and, maybe, a refracting telescope. Another letter from this period (5 September 1669) to his close friend Jelles indicates that Spinoza devises an experiment in fluid mechanics. It is uncertain when Spinoza leaves Voorburg to settle in The Hague. That must be sometime after dispatching his letter to Jelles of 5 September 1669 and before early February 1671.

In the early spring of 1670, Spinoza causes a stir in the United Provinces with the publication (late 1669 or early 1670) of the *Tractatus theologico-politicus*, an uncompromising vindication of the liberty to philosophize against the encroachments of organized religion. Though contemporary politics are only touched upon in the preface and epilogue, public reactions are extremely hostile and the treatise remains the object of vituperation for many decades. The first known official response to the *Tractatus theologico-politicus* is dated 8 April 1670. Almost immediately upon publication, both the contents and impact of this work are intensely debated in various meetings of local consistories, regional *classes* as well as provincial synods (the three-tiered system of the Dutch Reformed Church). As a result, the *Tractatus theologico-politicus* and its anonymous author are ranged among the worst enemies of Christianity. In addition, Spinoza's *Tractatus theologico-politicus* swiftly attracts the attention of prominent thinkers both in the Dutch Republic and abroad, provoking great controversy amongst intellectuals, among them Jacob Thomasius (1622–84), Gottfried Wilhelm Leibniz (1646–1716) and Hobbes. After the publication of the *Tractatus theologico-politicus*, the philosopher takes up his *Ethics* again.

1665, VOORBURG (KERKLAAN)

[Between Sunday 13 September and Sunday 20 September]
From [London], Oldenburg replies to Spinoza's letter of 4 September 1665. In his response (Ep 29, G IV, 164–5) he discusses the Latin edition of Boyle's treatise upon colours and refers to Kircher's *Mundus subterraneus*. Oldenburg also informs Spinoza that Boyle is about to put an account of his research into the origin of forms and qualities in the press. Accordingly, he refers to Spinoza's project on 'angels, prophecy and miracles', a work of which he urges his correspondent to outline the plan and object in his next letter. Oldenburg's intriguing remark concerns the early origins of Spinoza's *Tractatus theologico-politicus*. He also relates the latest scientific news communicated to him in a letter by the Danzig astronomer Johannes Hevelius (1611–87). That news concerns his *Cometographia* (a twelve-volume study upon two recent comets and sunspots) and his pending *Prodromus cometicus*. Oldenburg terminates his letter by asking Spinoza to express the view of the Dutch

on Christiaan Huygens's invention of the pendulum clock and its use in finding longitude at sea. He also longs for the latest news about Huygens's achievements in dioptrics and on motion.

Friday 20 November, Voorburg
From Voorburg, Spinoza writes a lengthy letter (Ep 32, G IV, 169–76) to Oldenburg. The first subject of the letter is the coherence of each separate part of nature with nature itself and other parts in relation to the universe. Furthermore, the letter proves that Spinoza is still in close contact with Christiaan Huygens, for he provides Oldenburg with some detailed information about Huygens's works on optics. Other subjects are his own criticism of one of Descartes's rules of bodily motion and the precise date of Huygens's migration to France. As regards Huygens's machine for grinding lenses, Spinoza continues, the latter is also able to craft special moulds for grinding and polishing lenses. Being a skilled, experienced optician himself, Spinoza suspects the contraption to be quite useless, for he reckons that a free hand brings much safer and better results in polishing lenses on spherical plates. This is the first known historical document confirming the fact that Spinoza is actually spending a part of his time grinding lenses. Many key questions about his interest in practical optics remain to be answered. A question of major importance is who trained him in the delicate skills of lens grinding and polishing glass. In the mid-1660s only a very small group of intellectuals in the United Provinces took a keen interest in the laborious job of grinding and polishing (telescopic) lenses. It is also unclear when exactly Spinoza took up the craft of lens making. If we assume Borrichius's account of 10 September 1661 to be reliable it may even have been as early as 1661. Likely candidates for initially having

introduced him to the exacting craft and maybe also having trained him are evidently the Huygens brothers, who took up lens grinding (of object glasses) in 1654. Another possible candidate is the Amsterdam mathematician Hudde, who in his own time enjoyed much fame in optics. On the other hand, Spinoza may also have learned the technical skills from professional opticians working in and around The Hague. A letter of [18] December 1665 to Spinoza is the last known to have been exchanged between Spinoza and Oldenburg for the next ten years. Spinoza does not restart their correspondence before April/May 1675.

1666, VOORBURG (KERKLAAN)

[June]
Spinoza replies to Hudde's (lost) letter of 19 May 1666. The subject of the second part of the letter (Ep 36, G IV, 183–7), practical optics, indicates that Spinoza is spending a large portion of his time manufacturing lenses. According to his own testimony, he is seriously considering to have crafted some new moulds for grinding lenses ('slijpschuttels') and so he welcomes Hudde's advice on that matter. He has doubts however about the use of polishing convex-concave lenses, which cause spheric aberration. Convex-plane lenses (bulging outwards) on the other hand, as he has calculated, seem to be more useful to him (to produce a telescopic effect). In this context, Spinoza brings up a treatise of Hudde ('your small Dioptrics'), the directions of which he follows for his own calculations of refraction. Hudde's treatise may be identified as his *Specilla circularia* (1656). This leaflet on convex-concave lenses (recently discovered, see Vermij and Atzema, 1995) demonstrated that aspherical lenses have no advantages (cf. Dijksterhuis, 2004, p. 71).

1667, THE HAGUE AND VOORBURG (KERKLAAN)

Thursday 30 September
Christiaan Huygens writes to his brother Constantijn from Paris. One of the main issues of his letter is the technical improvement upon the object lens (or object glass, the primary lens that receives the first light rays from the object observed) and the eyepiece lens (an ocular lens or lenses at the eye end) of a so-called 'Campanine' telescope (a refracting, optical telescope which solely uses an arrangement of lenses). From this letter, it appears that in this time frame Constantijn spends a portion of time on practical optics. Although he works alone on the improvement of the 'Campanine' telescope, he is in direct contact with Spinoza and 'Monsieur Hudde', with whom he seems to communicate about the object lenses of telescopes. For in his writing Christiaan urges his brother to convey to him the dimensions of the 'ouverture' (aperture, the diameter of the main optical lens of the telescope) calculated by 'Spinoza and Mister Hudde' for a telescope measuring 40 'pieds' (Huygens, *Œuvres complètes*, vol. 6, p. 151). In short, the letter clearly indicates that Spinoza is actively working on the fabrication of (telescopic) lenses), and maybe even on the construction of a refracting telescope for either astronomical, terrestrial or maritime use, in close collaboration with Hudde. Up until recently relatively little specific was known about the work done by Spinoza in the field of practical optics. The philosopher's own 'dioptrical' letters as well as the correspondence on optics exchanged between the Huygens brothers (from early September 1667 to 1670) were the only independent historical sources to assess Spinoza as a craftsman in lens making so far. A newly

found historical document (1717) confirms that Spinoza was also actively involved in the construction of refracting telescopes, as was already suggested in the Huygens correspondence (see Christiaan Huygens to Constantijn Huygens Jr, 30 September 1667, 6 April and 11 May 1668). That important historical document concerns an inventory of scientific instruments in the 'Friedensteinische Kunstkammer' at the ducal court of the German town of Gotha (west of Erfurt). The Dukes of Sachsen-Gotha, Ernst I called the 'Pious' in particular, held one of the largest collections of astronomical telescopes of their time at their residence, the Friedenstein castle. Their collection included several telescopes built by the famed Augsburg optician Johann Wiesel (1583–1662) and the Polish astronomer Johannes Hevelius amongst others (Keil, 1999). One of the telescopes detailed in the inventory is 'a Dutch tube made by Spinoza' (Keil, 1999, p. 77). The Friedenstein inventory does not provide any information for deciding whether Spinoza constructed the telescope entirely by himself or that he only ground the set of its five glasses. The fact that the inventory specifically lists the name of each individual telescope builder makes it quite valid to assume that Spinoza also signed (one of) these lenses (as was the habit of the Huygens brothers). Spinoza's telescope seems not to have been made for astronomical use, as all Dutch astronomical telescopes had only two glasses (a large convex object glass and a convex ocular glass, cf. Zuidervaart, 2007, p. 27). Altogether, it remains completely unknown how and when the 'Dutch tube' came into the possession of the Dukes of Sachsen-Gotha. Ernst I may well have obtained the complete instrument or only the set of five lenses during Spinoza's lifetime. It is also possible that his grandson, Frederic II (reigning from 1691 onwards), purchased either the telescope or the lenses set after the philosopher's death in early 1677. If we consider the possibility that one of them only acquired the set of five lenses, the seven drawtubes (made of material such as cardboard, vellum, wood or metal plate) of the instrument may well have been manufactured by a local German craftsman. The five separate lenses were thence cleverly arranged and fitted in the drawtubes afterwards. Of course, this is all a matter of pure speculation. By the end of the eighteenth century, the instrument was no longer in the Friedenstein collection (cf. Keil, 1999, p. 78). Yet the Friedenstein inventory clearly establishes that Spinoza was an optician and lens maker of some repute in his own day.

Friday 4 November
From Paris, Christiaan Huygens writes to his brother Constantijn on his work on practical optics and the subject of lens polishing. He informs his brother that 'the Jew of Voorburg' finishes his lenses with the help of an 'instrument' and this renders them very excellent. Christiaan therefore wonders why Constantijn is not applying a similar apparatus. If Spinoza will continue his work on the manufacture of 'des grands verres' (large lenses, more precisely object lenses) Christiaan urges his brother to keep him fully informed about the philosopher's achievement (Huygens, *Œuvres complètes*, vol. 6, p. 158).

1668, VOORBURG (KERKLAAN)

Friday 11 May
Christiaan Huygens writes a letter to Constantijn from Paris. The subject is again optics. Christiaan confirms Spinoza's conclusion that smaller object lenses in microscopes

23

deliver much more distinct image results in magnifying objects than larger lenses are able to do (see also Christiaan Huygens to Constantijn Huygens Jr, 14 October 1667, *Œuvres complètes*, vol. 6, p. 155). Undoubtedly, this outcome must have some sort of logical explanation, but neither Spinoza nor he himself is able to give a sufficient reason for that phenomenon (Huygens, *Œuvres complètes*, vol. 6, p. 213). Christiaan, in the same letter, also gives a description of his 'new method', in this case the application of a small concave lens in an eyepiece to reduce spherical aberration of the convex lens in the objective lens. He expects his brother not to pass this secret to the 'Israelite'. Through him opticians like Hudde or others may hopefully also learn about this method (Huygens, *Œuvres completes*, vol. 6, p. 215). Nothing is further known about any contacts between Spinoza and the Huygens brothers until early May 1674, when the philosopher meets Christiaan personally either in The Hague or in Voorburg (cf. Constantijn Huygens Sr to Oldenburg, 1 May 1676, Oldenburg, *Correspondence*, vol. 12, pp. 255–6).

1669, VOORBURG (KERKLAAN), [AMSTERDAM, THE HAGUE]

Thursday 5 September, Voorburg
From Voorburg, Spinoza writes to Jarig Jelles (Ep 41, G IV, 202–6). The subject of the letter is an account of Spinoza's experimentation into the nature of fluid dynamics (or hydrodynamics) following a conversation with Jelles, who also sent him a letter (now lost) on the matter on an earlier occasion (1669.09.05*). Spinoza's letter to Jelles demonstrates that he conducted a fluid-dynamics experiment. In the experiment, he focused on the pressure and the velocity of

water flowing in a specially built model of lockable horizontal and vertical wooden tubes. Spinoza used an improvised leverage pump to measure the velocity of the water flowing in the model, 'because I had no pendulum clock at hand'.

After Thursday 5 September, Voorburg, The Hague
Spinoza moves from Voorburg to The Hague. He never reveals his motives for settling there, and the exact date is unknown too. It must have been sometime after dispatching his letter to Jelles of 5 September 1669 (see Ep 41), but before 17 February 1671, when writing his first known letter from The Hague to Jelles (see Ep 44, G IV, 227–9). The philosopher first rents a room in the house of the widow of the lawyer Willem van der Werve, at the Stille Veerkade most likely. Sometime later, he rents a room on the second floor at the back of the house of the painter Hendrik van der Spijck (fl. 1667–after 1715) at the (nowadays 'Gedempte') Paviljoensgracht (nos. 72–4) (formerly Burgwal), opposite the Dubeletstraat.

Fall, [Amsterdam, Voorburg or The Hague]
Presumably, Spinoza spends some portion of his time in Amsterdam to supervise the printing process of his *Tractatus theologico-politicus* and to deliberate with his publisher, Rieuwertsz Sr. Nothing is known about the preparations of the printing of the work, which is published in late 1669 or in the first months of 1670. Rieuwertsz Sr did not own a press in 1669 or in 1670 and there are strong arguments indicating that Israel de Paull did the printing for him (Jagersma and Dijkstra, 2014). After his trip to Amsterdam, Spinoza returns to his residence in either Voorburg or to his new lodgings in The Hague.

1670, [Voorburg or The Hague]

Before Tuesday 8 April, Voorburg or
The Hague

Spinoza anonymously publishes his *Tractatus theologico-politicus*. The publisher's name on the title-page of this carefully disguised Latin quarto edition, Henricus Künraht (in other editions also spelled as 'Künrath'), is a fiction and most certainly an alias for Rieuwertsz Sr, while the place of publication is falsely declared to be 'Hamburg'. The printer's device on the title-page of the treatise was first used by Rieuwertsz Sr and Fonteyn in 1650 and it was still in use in 1682. There is no independent historical evidence to establish an exact publication date of the *Tractatus theologico-politicus*, but the date *ante quem* is formed by the records of the Reformed *kerkenraad* (Reformed consistory, local church council) of Utrecht, which condemns the work in a meeting on 8 April 1670. Similar evidence is found in a work of the Utrecht theologian Frans Burman (1628–79), entitled *Burmannorum pietas* (1700). The publication date of the *Tractatus theologico-politicus* proposed by Burman is sometime 'in the year 69, or was put into print in 70'. (Burman, 1700, p. 204, quoted in Bamberger, 1961, pp. 9 and 28).

Tuesday 8 April

Public reactions in the United Provinces to the *Tractatus theologico-politicus* are extremely hostile from the start, identifying its anonymous author as an outright atheist and condemning the book as dangerous to orthodox Christian religion. The first known official response to the treatise by the Dutch Reformed Church authorities is that of 8 April 1670, when the outraged Utrecht *kerkenraad* reports on the work, urging the city's Burgomasters to consider appropriate

measures against the treatise (Utrecht *kerkenraad* transactions, 8 April 1670, Walther and Czelinski, 2006, vol. 1, p. 287, no. 88).

Thursday 8 May

Soon after the publication of the *Tractatus theologico-politicus*, rumours about Spinoza's controversial treatise reached Protestant Germany and responses to the work there were similar to the reactions of the local church authorities in the United Provinces. The first intellectual to raise his voice against the book is the Leipzig professor of eloquence Jacob Thomasius. In an academic lecture programme ('Programma', 8 May 1670) published later that year in a work called *Adversus anonymum*, Thomasius indirectly refutes the *Tractatus theologico-politicus* as a threat to religion and society, denouncing its naturalism, contractualism and libertinism. Surprisingly, Thomasius seems to be already aware that Spinoza, 'a Jewish apostate and a formal atheist', is the originator of this work (Thomasius and Thomasius, 1693, p. 571). Thomasius also suspects that the anonymous treatise appeared in Amsterdam, and not, as its title-page falsely declares, in Hamburg. The German theologian is also the first to suggest a direct affinity between the *Tractatus theologico-politicus* and the work of the English philosophers Herbert of Cherbury (1583–1648) and Hobbes (Freudenthal, 1899, p. 192, no. 4).

Friday 9 May

The condemnation of the *Tractatus theologico-politicus* by the Utrecht *kerkenraad* (8 and 11 April 1670) was soon followed by violent reactions in other towns (Leiden, Haarlem, Amsterdam, The Hague, Schieland). On 9 May 1670, the Leiden *kerkenraad* warns against the publication of a 'Notorious libellous work', named 'Tractatus Theologico Politicus'. The consistory also decides that they are to request the Leiden Burgomasters 'that the same is to be seized and banned' (Leiden *kerkenraad* transactions, 9 May 1670, art. 4, Walther and Czelinski, 2006, vol. 1, p. 288, no. 90).

Between Tuesday 15 July and Friday 25 July
The violent response to the *Tractatus theologico-politicus* by local Dutch Reformed consistories and *classes* is soon echoed by strong religious reactions of the provincial synods. The first official response called forth by the treatise is given by the Synod of South Holland. One of the issues discussed during the synod's gathering in the summer of 1670 is the printing and selling of the treatise. The South Holland Synod roundly condemns the treatise, urging the gathered ministers to persuade the local magistrates to guard against it and suppress the work. The synod also resolves to appoint some representatives to inform the Court of Holland about this suspect work (South Holland Synod resolutions, 15–25 July 1670, art. 10 (ad art. 13, South Holland Synod of 1669), *Acta der particuliere synoden*, 1908–16, vol. 4, p. 531).

8. BUILDING A REPUTATION FOR CONTROVERSY

VOORBURG, THE HAGUE: 1671–LATE DECEMBER 1676

Sometime between early September 1669 and mid-February 1671, Spinoza leaves Voorburg to settle in The Hague, for reasons unknown. First, he rents a room in a house at the Stille Veerkade, but later on he takes his lodgings in a street nearby, in the house of the painter Hendrik van der Spijck at the (nowadays 'Gedempte') Paviljoensgracht, still standing today. His *Tractatus theologico-politicus* rapidly becomes notorious in the Dutch Republic, Germany and England. As his treatise provokes furious reactions in official assemblies of the Reformed Church and the Églises Wallonnes (the Dutch Walloon Church), Spinoza begins to worry about being accused of overtly preaching atheism with disguised arguments. In addition, many scholars, such as Lambert van Velthuijsen (1621/2–85), his former Leiden friend Stensen and another erstwhile companion, Albert Coenraadszn Burgh (1650–1708) (both converts to Roman Catholicism), also declare Spinoza a threat to piety and society, rejecting the work as atheistic and totally abhorrent to Christian religion. Although many critics attack the treatise, the work continues to be attentively read and newly printed editions ([1672], 1673, 1674) seem to find easy circulation both in the Dutch Republic and abroad. Due to a relatively mild political climate in the United Provinces, the Supreme Court of Holland, Zeeland and West-Friesland officially bans the work only in a placard of 19 July 1674.

By the early 1670s, Spinoza's writings and networks seem to have established firmly his overall reputation of a talented mathematician and optician as well as an audacious, controversial free-thinker outside academe. As Spinoza's fame soon reaches a higher pitch, his philosophical views also attract the attention of influential intellectuals abroad. In October 1671, Leibniz, who is aware of Spinoza as a commentator on Descartes and as the clandestine author of the *Tractatus theologico-politicus*, cautiously tries to contact the philosopher by writing him a letter (22 April 1671) on the safe topic of optics. In

February 1673, Spinoza also receives a letter from the theologian Johann Ludwig Fabritius (1632–96) inviting him to take up the chair of philosophy in Heidelberg, an offer which he turns down decidedly. During Louis XIV's so-called 'Dutch War' (April 1672–78/9), Spinoza meets the military governor Johann Baptista Stouppe (1624–92/1700) in the French army headquarters in the occupied town of Utrecht sometime between 25 and 28 July 1673, following an earlier invitation of the French military commander Louis II de Bourbon (1621–86), the famous Prince of Condé ('le Grand Condé' or 'le Héros'). We do not know whether Spinoza played a role during the occupation of Utrecht, nor what the purpose of his visit was. The only independent documentary evidence we have confirms that Spinoza did travel to Utrecht and met Stouppe sometime between 25 and 28 July 1673.

During the 1670s, Spinoza maintains his relations with his longtime friends Jelles, Hudde and Rieuwertsz Sr, while strengthening new contacts with many other intellectuals, viz. Johannes Georgius Graevius (1632–1703), Ehrenfried Walther von Tschirnhaus (1651–1708), Georg Hermann Schuller (1650/1–79), Pieter van Gent (fl. 1640–93/4) and Van Velthuijsen. In September 1674, he enters into a lengthy discussion with a legal scholar from Gorinchem, Hugo Danielsz Boxel (1607/12?–1680?), on apparitions, spirits and ghosts. In May 1675, Spinoza also renews his correspondence with Oldenburg after a ten-year interval, probably induced by the visit of the young German intellectual Tschirnhaus to London. Some months later, in late July 1675, he completes the *Ethics* and makes preparations for its publication in Amsterdam. Deterred by increasing hostility and rumours that he is about to put a work into print that seeks to show that there is no God, Spinoza decides

to cancel the publication immediately upon his arrival in Amsterdam. Another project probably commenced between 1670 and 1675 is the *Compendium grammatices linguae Hebraeae*, a Hebrew grammar presumably intended for the private use of friends, which was to remain unfinished. Between 1675 and 1676, Spinoza begins to compose new additional notes which he plans to include in a revised edition of the *Tractatus theologico-politicus*. He presents (25 July 1676) an annotated copy of his treatise in his own handwriting to a Leiden law student from Pomerania, Jacobus Statius Cleefman (fl. 1646/7–75). In the second half of 1676, he embarks upon a new project, his unfinished *Tractatus politicus*. Finally, in late November 1676, the philosopher receives a visit from Leibniz in The Hague with whom he intensively discusses various subjects, particularly his arguments for the existence of God as propounded in his *Ethics*.

1671, VOORBURG AND THE HAGUE

Before Monday 16 March
After the fierce reactions of the Dutch provincial synods, new attempts are made at a high political level to place the *Tractatus theologico-politicus* under an official ban in the opening months of 1671. Representatives of the North Holland Synod deliberate with the Grand Pensionary (a sort of secretary-general) of Holland (Johan de Witt, 1625–72) on Spinoza's treatise. Shortly afterwards, they communicate to him several extracts from the work together with a request urging the Supreme Court of Holland, Zeeland and West-Friesland to ban the *Tractatus theologico-politicus* (cf. North Holland Synod transactions, 16 March 1671, art. 37, Walther and Czelinski, 2006, vol. 1, p. 296, no. 100, see also Walther and Czelinski, 2006,

vol. 1, p. 292, no. 97). De Witt in his capacity as Grand Pensionary was directly involved in the joint efforts of the North and South Holland Synods to petition the suppression of the *Tractatus theologico-politicus* on a province-wide basis. Claims however that the republican-minded Grand Pensionary would deliberately have hindered and slowed down the prohibition of Spinoza's treatise are actually not supported by any documentary evidence (cf. Israel, 2001, pp. 275–6).

Thursday 5 October
Leibniz has been informed about the full identity of the anonymous author of the *Tractatus theologico-politicus* in a letter (22 April 1671) from the Utrecht professor of history and rhetoric Johannes Georgius Graevius. Then, in the fall of that same year, Leibniz decides to make an effort to come into contact with the Dutch philosopher, hoping to draw Spinoza into a correspondence. On 5 October 1671, he sends Spinoza a highly complimentary letter (Ep 45, G IV, 230–1) on the issue of optics. In the first part of his letter Leibniz politely invites Spinoza to express his view about his *Notitia opticae promotae*, a long section from his work on motion, *Hypothesis physica nova*. With the letter, he sends two copies of the tract as an enclosure (cf. Ep 46, G IV, 231–3). Furthermore, Leibniz in his letter brings up the book *Prodromo*, in which the Italian Jesuit Francisco Lana de Terzi (1631–87) expresses his views on optics. Another work discussed in the letter is a work by 'Johannes Oltius' (i.e. Johannes Heinrich Ott), called 'Cogitationes Physico-Mechanicas de Visione', about the use of a lathe for lensgrinding and the solution of the problem of spheric aberration. In the postscript to this letter, Leibniz finally encourages Spinoza to write back to him through the intermediary of one of his correspondents, 'the esteemed legal scholar Diemerbroeck', who may be identified as Johannes van Diemerbroeck (fl. 1668–81). He also promises Spinoza to send him a printed copy of his *Hypothesis*, if he desires this work. Leibniz in his letter makes no mention whatsoever of the *Tractatus theologico-politicus*.

Before Monday 2 November
Spinoza's erstwhile Leiden friend, Niels Stensen, writes an 'open letter' of justification (Ep 67A, G IV, 292–8) trumpeting his conversion to Roman Catholicism. Stensen composed his 'open letter' four years after his conversion on 2 November 1667 (see Totaro, 2002, p. 36). This document, entitled 'Nicolas Stenonis ad nova philosophiae reformatorem de vera philosophia epistola', was published as part of a four-part collection (*Ad virum eruditum*) of missives with religious reflections in 1675. Although lacking the name of an addressee, Stensen's text is unquestionably intended for Spinoza, to whom he indirectly refers as 'a man once rather familiar to me'. The bulk of Stensen's text, the first document originating in Italy that shows full interest in Spinoza's ideas, is altogether a brazen attack on 'your book of which others have told me that you are the author', which undoubtedly is the *Tractatus theologico-politicus*. It is unknown whether Spinoza was aware of Stensen's booklet and if his former Leiden companion ever dispatched this text in the form of a letter from Italy to the philosopher (cf. Christofolini, 2008). This may explain why the philosopher never wrote a response to this attack.

Monday 9 November
Spinoza replies to Leibniz's letter on optics of 15 October 1671, dispatching his learned response (Ep 46, G IV, 231–3) on 8 December

1671. Firstly, Spinoza asks for a clarification about Leibniz's remarks on the exact size of 'the aperture of the glasses' (the object lenses of refracting telescopes most likely) and the correction capability of his newly invented 'pandochal' (all-receiving) lenses compared with circular and large convex lenses as propounded in Leibniz's *Notitia opticae promotae*. In addition, he asks his correspondent to provide him with a copy of his 'Physical hypothesis' (Leibniz's *Hypothesis physica nova*), for the work is not for sale in The Hague. In the postscript to this letter, Spinoza informs Leibniz that his proposed intermediary, Diemerbroeck, does not live in The Hague. He will therefore dispatch his letters via the ordinary mail carrier and asks him to think of someone else in The Hague who may act as a trustworthy intermediary of their correspondence. Finally, Spinoza promises Leibniz to send him a copy of the *Tractatus theologico-politicus* in return for his offer to send him his *Hypothesis* if the work has not reached him as yet. Spinoza's reply is the last known letter of their brief epistolary exchange.

1672, [THE HAGUE]

June

In the Franco-Dutch war, Louis XIV and Jean Baptiste Colbert (1619–83) wanted France to take over the supremacy in the European economy from the Dutch Republic. As a result, a secret treaty between France and England was signed in the port of Dover in May 1670 with the aim of isolating the United Provinces. Two years later, in April 1672, Louis XIV's army invades the southern bishopric of Liège (Lüttich) towards the United Provinces. In June, the troops of the Prince of Condé cross the Rhine, thus beginning the invasion of the United Provinces. In

the same month, the French armies gain complete control over the Provinces of Gelderland and Utrecht, capturing eastern cities like Arnhem and Nijmegen and the central Dutch town of Utrecht (13 June 1672).

1673, THE HAGUE (STILLE VEERKADE OR PAVILJOENSGRACHT), UTRECHT

Thursday 16 February

As Spinoza's fame increases, his philosophical views also attract the attention of intellectuals abroad. From Heidelberg, he receives a letter from the Calvinist theologian Johann Ludwig Fabritius (Ep 47, G IV, 234–5), writing on behalf of the Elector Palatine, Karl Ludwig (1619–80). In his letter, he forwards an official invitation from his master to accept the chair of philosophy (and mathematics) at Heidelberg University. The invitation may very well have been initiated by the French writer Urbain Chevreau (1613–1701) when visiting the Heidelberg court, but there is no independent evidence to support that hypothesis. In his *Chevraeana*, the latter gives a detailed account of the events preceding the invitation and claims that he was the one who promoted the mathematical work of Spinoza during his stay in Heidelberg. After inspection of some chapters of Spinoza's *Renati des Cartes Principia philosophiae*, Chevreau continues, the Elector Palatine took the decision to approach Spinoza about the chair of philosophy at Heidelberg University through Fabritius. The monarch's only condition was that Spinoza would not interfere with religious matters in the Rhenish Palatinate (Chevreau, 1700, vol. 2, pp. 105–6, see Walther and Czelinski, 2006, vol. 1, p. 305, no. 109). Fabritius had clearly opposed Karl Ludwig's choice to invite Spinoza for a professorship to Heidelberg. Since Fabritius was in the service of the Elector Palatine, he obeyed however, 'but with a clean conscience' (Heidegger, 1697, p. 74), because he had to approach Spinoza not for a professorship in theology, but in philosophy and mathematics. Finally, Fabritius came up with an ingenious solution in his letter of invitation of 16 February 1673, namely that Spinoza was to be given the liberty to philosophize to the extent that this would not interfere with religious matters in the Rhenish Palatinate. Thus, his letter was in fact a stratagem to curb Spinoza. It was to be expected that such a limited and offending invitation would never be accepted by the philosopher.

Thursday 30 March
Spinoza answers Fabritius's letter of invitation of 16 February 1673. In his response (Ep 48, G IV, 235–6), he politely turns down Karl Ludwig's offer of a professorship in philosophy in Heidelberg (see also Jelles and Meyer's preface to Spinoza's posthumous works, no. 7, Akkerman and Hubbeling, 1979, pp. 112–13). The reason he gives is that he does not know within what limits the freedom to philosophize should be contained if the established religion is not to be disturbed.

Between Tuesday 4 May and Friday
19 May
The high-ranking Swiss officer Jean Baptiste Stouppe, who holds headquarters in Utrecht since late November 1672, composes his *La religion des Hollandois* between 4 and 19 May 1673. The work, a purely programmatic pamphlet on the various aspects of civil and religious life in Holland organized in six letters addressed to a Swiss Protestant theology professor (whose name is not mentioned in the pamphlet; Freudenthal, 1899, p. 293, identifies him as Professor Hommel in Bern), was ordered by Louis XIV (cf. Feer, 1882, p. 80) to justify the French occupation of the United Provinces. Stouppe especially

wonders whether the country invaded by Louis XIV is truly Protestant given the fact that many religions, sects and convictions exist and thrive in that state. *La religion des Hollandois* also contains the first known French reaction to Spinoza's *Tractatus theologico-politicus*. Stouppe strongly criticizes Dutch theologians for not refuting Spinoza's treatise (Stouppe, *La religion des Hollandois*, p. 65, letter 3).

[Between Tuesday 25 July and Friday
28 July], The Hague, Utrecht
The French military commander Louis II de Bourbon, his son Lieutenant-General Henri III Julius de Bourbon (1643–1709) and his close friend and confidant François-Henri de Montmorency-Bouteville (1628–95) make their Joyeuse Entrée in Utrecht, either on 21 April (cf. Cohen, 1925–6, no. 6, p. 62) or 8 May 1673 (cf. Duc d'Aumale, 1889–96, vol. 7, p. 383). The French commander, according to several sources (Colerus, Morales, Buissière, [Lucas], Stouppe, Leibniz), summoned Spinoza to his presence at his army headquarters while in Utrecht. Colerus furthermore states that the military governor of Utrecht Stouppe even provided the philosopher with a passport to visit the occupied town. The biographer also asserts that the officer wanted to enter into a correspondence with the philosopher (see Walther and Czelinski, 2006, vol. 1, p. 128). Another account of the philosopher's visit is produced in a letter of Stouppe's elder brother, Pierre-Alexandre (1620–1701), the military governor of Utrecht. A letter by Pierre-Alexandre Stouppe (written before 25 July 1673) to the Utrecht professor of history and rhetoric Johannes Georgius Graevius proves that his brother Jean Baptiste Stouppe was the linchpin in the (secret) plan to summon Spinoza to Utrecht (Van de

Ven, 2014). In his letter, addressed to Condé and dated 28 July 1673, Pierre-Alexandre explicitly claims that Spinoza was summoned to the French army headquarters in Utrecht 'at the request of my brother'. When arriving in Utrecht, Spinoza had informed his brother Johann Baptista about the news that the effigy of 'the Lord of Montbas' (i.e. Colonel Jean de Barthon), who was court-martialled in November 1672, had been hanged 'last Tuesday' (Cohen, 1926, p. 70). De Barthon's effigy was symbolically 'hanged' for public display on a gallows in The Hague on 25 July 1673. That event, according to Pierre-Alexandre's letter to Condé, had been discussed by Spinoza with his brother Johann Baptista during his visit to Utrecht. If we accept Pierre-Alexandre's letter as a more reliable historical document than the incomplete and conflicting information in Colerus's and [Lucas's] biographies plus the two early eighteenth-century testimonies gathered by Pierre Desmaizeaux (1666?–1745) (see Walther and Czelinski, 2006, vol. 2, p. 36), Spinoza must have either witnessed or heard rumours about De Barthon's public disgrace in The Hague, leaving soon afterwards for Utrecht to meet up with Johann Baptista Stouppe on 26, 27 or 28 July 1673. The latter then informed his elder brother Pierre-Alexandre, who recounted the story of his brother's meeting with Spinoza to Condé in his letter of 28 July 1673. In short, this account not only provides a more accurate date for Spinoza's visit to the French camp, but it also makes it plausible that the philosopher did indeed visit Utrecht shortly after 25 July 1673. However, it is highly unlikely that he met Condé, for the French General had left Utrecht for Grave on 15 July 1673. Although the details in Pierre-Alexandre's letter to Condé historically seem to be rather

consistent, we may simply conclude by stating that it is certain that Spinoza accepted Stouppe's invitation and that he indeed went to the French army headquarters (Van de Ven, 2014–2015).

Before Friday 8 December
A new Latin octavo edition of Spinoza's *Tractatus theologico-politicus* is printed and bound in one volume with the text of Meyer's *Philosophia S. Scripturae interpres*. In the same time frame, three other disguised octavo editions of these two treatises are also brought into circulation under different aliases, false titles and fictitious printers' names. The first, supposedly written by the Spanish physician Enríquez de Villacorta, is entitled *Opera chirurgica omnia*. The second imprint, *Operum historicorum collectio prima (secunda)*, is presented as having been composed by the Leiden humanist Daniel Heinsius (1580–1655). The third disguised edition, allegedly written by the famed Leiden anatomist Franciscus de le Boë Sylvius (1614–72) is published under the title *Totius medicinae idea nova*. Nothing further is known about the printing process of these editions nor about Spinoza's involvement in the publication. The exact date of all four publications is also unknown.

1674, THE HAGUE (STILLE VEERKADE OR PAVILJOENSGRACHT)

Thursday 19 July
Due to the changed political climate in the United Provinces after William III came to power as Stadholder of Holland and Zeeland in the calamitous 'Rampjaar' (Disaster Year) 1672, the Reformed provincial synods finally manage to have Spinoza's *Tractatus theologico-politicus* placed under an official ban. On 19 July 1674, the Supreme Court of

Holland, Zeeland and West-Friesland issues a public placard by order of William III aimed to prevent the printing, distribution and public sale of Hobbes's *Leviathan*, the *Bibliotheca fratrum polonorum*, Meyer's *Philosophia S. Scripturae interpres* as well as Spinoza's *Tractatus theologico-politicus* (Walther and Czelinski, 2006, vol. 1, pp. 315–16, no. 117).

Friday 14 September
Hugo Boxel, the former pensionary of Gorinchem, writes a short letter to Spinoza on apparitions and spirits or ghosts (Ep 51, G IV, 241–2). Accordingly, he refers to the belief in spirits held by many contemporary theologians and philosophers and to the numerous tales about ghosts, which seem to suggest that they may be real. Boxel inquires whether Spinoza believes in ghosts, inviting him to express his view on this matter, expecting however that the philosopher's response will be negative. The letter of 14 September 1674 marks the beginning of a series of six letters exchanged between Boxel and Spinoza on apparitions and spirits or ghosts.

1675, THE HAGUE (STILLE VEERKADE OR PAVILJOENSGRACHT) AND AMSTERDAM

Saturday 5 January
Ehrenfried Walther von Tschirnhaus writes a letter to Spinoza (Ep 59, G IV, 268–70). Firstly, Tschirnhaus asks Spinoza when he will deliver his 'method' of directing reason in seeking out unknown truths as well as his general principles in physics, directly referring to the subsidiary theorems in the second part of the *Ethics*, more particularly, which in his opinion will solve many difficulties in physics in an easy manner. So the letter

proves that by now Tschirnhaus has had access to the text of the *Ethics*. Next, Tschirnhaus invites Spinoza to give him a definition of motion and an explanation of that definition. Tschirnhaus refers to 'our encounter' during which 'you pointed out to me the method you adopt in seeking out truths as yet unknown'. The letter thus confirms that there has been a personal meeting between Tschirnhaus and Spinoza in The Hague sometime before 5 January 1675.

[April/May]
Spinoza resumes his long-interrupted exchange with Oldenburg after a silence of almost ten years. The philosopher sends Oldenburg a copy of his *Tractatus theologico-politicus*, which for some reason never reaches his correspondent (cf. Oldenburg to Spinoza, Ep 61, G IV, 271–2). We may assume that Spinoza sent him the package together with an accompanying letter, which is now lost (1675.[04/05].00*).

End of the first week in May
Tschirnhaus, travelling from France to England, is now intensively studying the *Ethics*, for in the letters he exchanges with Georg Hermann Schuller he asks him to approach Spinoza for a clarification of certain difficulties in the first part of the work (cf. Schuller to Spinoza, Ep 63, G IV, 274–6). This request proves that Tschirnhaus journeyed to England with a manuscript copy of the *Ethics* in his bags. In the same period, Oldenburg dispatches a (lost) letter (1675.[05].00*) from London to Spinoza to thank him for the copy of the *Tractatus theologico-politicus* (which, however, apparently had never reached him). In that (lost) letter, Oldenburg propounds his negative opinion about the work. It is unknown whether there is a connection between Spinoza's initiative

of sending a copy of the *Tractatus theologico-politicus* to London in [April/May] 1676 and Tschirnhaus's travels to England.

Friday 21 June
The Reformed *kerkenraad* of The Hague warns (cf. The Hague *kerkenraad* resolutions, art. 5) against the spreading of 'the highly godless opinions of Spinoza'. The consistory urges its members to observe a high degree of vigilance to find out 'whether any other book written by him is about to be printed' and to investigate its potential danger. The warning almost certainly concerns rumours about the philosopher's plan to publish his *Ethics* (Walther and Czelinski, 2006, vol. 1, p. 320, no. 121).

Monday 22 July
From London, Oldenburg writes to Spinoza (Ep 62, G IV, 273) in reply to the philosopher's (lost) letter of 5 July 1675. Oldenburg answers Spinoza that he has learned from his (lost) letter of 5 July 1675 about his desire to publish 'your five-part treatise', undoubtedly the *Ethics*. So the letter makes it clear that Spinoza by this time had finished the work and was preparing to have it printed.

After Monday 22 July, The Hague, Amsterdam
Spinoza travels to Amsterdam to see the manuscript of his *Ethics* (cf. Spinoza to Oldenburg, Ep 68, G IV, 299) through the press. Just before leaving The Hague, he receives Oldenburg's letter of 22 July 1675 (see Ep 62, G IV, 273). Upon his arrival in Amsterdam, the philosopher begins to worry seriously about being accused of preaching atheism and about the increasing hostility towards his philosophy. Rumour has it that he is soon to put a work into print denying God's existence. Certain theologians have

now lodged complaints with the Prince of Orange and the magistrates. 'Stupid Cartesians' are constantly denouncing his opinions and writings in order to defend themselves against sympathizing with his standpoints. Spinoza decides to postpone the publication of his *Ethics* (cf. Spinoza to Oldenburg, Ep 68) and to wait and see what will happen. Nothing further is known about Spinoza's trip to Amsterdam, but most certainly he saw Rieuwertsz Sr to discuss with him the publishing of the *Ethics*. It is unknown whether some portions of the work were already typeset at the time of his stay in Amsterdam.

Tuesday 3 September
From [Florence], Albert Coenraadszn Burgh writes a letter to Spinoza (Ep 67, G IV, 280–91) on his recent decision to convert to Roman Catholicsm. In the introductory part, Burgh refers to his promise 'to write to you, if anything worthy of note should occur on my travels'. The introduction of Burgh's letter stresses that they were still in contact shortly before the latter's departure from the Netherlands to Italy in 1673. In his letter, Burgh writes about his personal motivation for joining the Roman Catholic Church. He also gives his decidedly negative opinion about Spinoza's 'true' philosophy, which he thinks will only amount to 'illusion' and 'chimera'. In his view, Spinoza's philosophy is as unsure and futile as are all other philosophies. Next, he refers to 'your book, to which you have given that impious title' (i.e. *Tractatus theologico-politicus*), accusing his correspondent of purposely confusing philosophy and theology. He also rigidly denounces Spinoza's interpretation of Scripture and any doubts about its sacrosanct truth, preaching to him to acknowledge the infallible truth of Roman Catholicism in order to avoid eternal damnation.

[September/October]
From [The Hague], Spinoza writes a reply to Henry Oldenburg's letter of 22 July 1675. In his response (Ep 68, G IV, 299), Spinoza refers to his visit (after 22 July 1675) to Amsterdam to prepare the printing of his *Ethics* and his decision to postpone publication. The second part of the letter to Oldenburg yields explicit information on his intentions to publish a second, revised edition of the *Tractatus theologico-politicus* in the near future.

Before Thursday 14 November
Tschirnhaus writes a (lost) letter (text unknown) from Paris to Georg Hermann Schuller. The contents of the letter are known exclusively from Schuller's letter to Spinoza of 14 November 1675 (see Ep 70, G IV, 301–3). Tschirnhaus informs Schuller about his occupations and encounters in Paris, where he met Christiaan Huygens, Leibniz and others. One of the issues of Tschirnhaus's letter concerns his objections against certain propositions in the first part of the *Ethics* (see Tschirnhaus to Spinoza, Ep 65, G IV, 279, Spinoza to Tschirnhaus, Ep 66, G IV, 280), so apparently he is still spending time studying Spinoza's unpublished work. Tschirnhaus also requests Schuller to ask for the philosopher's permission to allow Leibniz access to his manuscript copy of the *Ethics*.

Late 1675 or early 1676
From [The Hague], Spinoza replies to the letter of Burgh, dated 3 September 1675, in reaction to his announcement to convert to Roman Catholicism (see Ep 67, G IV, 280–91). Spinoza starts his letter (Ep 76, G IV, 316–24) by expressing his unbelief that Burgh has actually joined the Roman Catholic Church. He refers to 'other causes to which you once gave your approval' when

speaking about Stensen, 'in whose footsteps you now follow'. Spinoza counters the arguments in Burgh's letter to embrace Roman Catholic faith, referring to the period when 'you worshipped an infinite God by whose efficacy all thing absolutely are started and preserved'. Another issue is Burgh's criticism of Spinoza's philosophy. In fact, Spinoza declares, he does not pretend that he has found the best philosophy, but simply knows that he understands the true philosophy, namely 'in the same way that you know that the three angles of a triangle are equal to two right angles'. In turn, he reproaches Burgh for having given no reasonable grounds for his faith whatsoever. He finally calls upon Burgh to do away with superstition and to acknowledge reason. Spinoza ends his letter by defending himself against Burgh's objection to the fundamental principle of his *Tractatus theologico-politicus*, namely to give up the sacrosanct status of Scripture and to understand the Bible through itself alone. Finally, the philosopher invites Burgh to read his account closely and study the history of the Christian church, which, he surmises, will bring him back to reason.

1676, THE HAGUE (STILLE VEERKADE OR PAVILJOENSGRACHT)

Before Saturday 25 July
In his lodgings in [The Hague], Spinoza spends some time composing supplementary notes to his *Tractatus theologico-politicus* (cf. Akkerman, 2005, pp. 210–36). In the course of time, he enters these *Adnotationes* (Spinoza, 1802) into the margins of a personal copy of the treatise.

Saturday 25 July
In [The Hague], Spinoza receives a visit from a young German law student, Jacobus Statius

Cleefman. The contact with the latter must have been of some importance, for the philosopher presents him with a copy of the first printing of his *Tractatus theologico-politicus*. That copy, now preserved in Haifa, not only contains a dedication on the title-page, but also five marginal supplementary notes (pp. 2, 70, 93, 116 and 117) in the philosopher's own handwriting.

Second half of 1676
Spinoza works intensively on a theory of politics, which will finally become his unfinished *Tractatus politicus*. In this work, the philosopher is to discuss three different forms of state government, i.e. monarchy, aristocracy and democracy. When composing the treatise on politics, Spinoza receives a (lost) letter from a close friend (> 1676. 07.00*). Nothing is known about the contents of his friend's letter, but Spinoza's answer (Ep 84, G IV, 335–6) in any case seems to suggest that they were on a very firm footing at that time. Biographically most important is that Spinoza's letter proves that the unidentified friend is the one who had encouraged him to write a theory of politics.

Between Sunday 18 October and Thursday 29 October
After a four-year stay in Paris, Leibniz finally returns to Germany via a circuitous route to take up his new post as counselor and personal librarian in Hanover. After his departure from Paris (4 October 1676), he travels to Calais to embark on a ship for a brief second visit to England. After the crossing, he meets Oldenburg in London (after 18 October 1676). Nothing is known about their conversations, but they may well have spoken about Leibniz's imminent visit to Spinoza. During one of their meetings, Leibniz may

also have copied out three recent letters of Spinoza to Oldenburg (Ep 73, G IV, 306–9, Ep 75, G IV, 311–16 and Ep 78, G IV, 326–9). In addition, Oldenburg hands him a (lost) letter for Spinoza (> 1676.10.18*), which Leibniz however never forwards to the philosopher for reasons unknown (cf. Oldenburg to Leibniz, 22 February/4 March 1677). Leibniz plans to travel to the United Provinces in the first week of November 1676, but severe storms prevent his ship from sailing out of Fort Sheerness (cf. Müller and Krönert, 1961, p. 45).

[Between Wednesday 18 November and Saturday 21 November]
Leibniz makes some forays to Haarlem, Leiden and Delft, where he makes the acquaintance of the famous naturalist Antonie van Leeuwenhoek (1632–1723). Soon thereafter, he also travels to The Hague (cf. Müller and Krönert, 1961, p. 46) where he finally meets Spinoza (Leibniz, 1734, p. 231; Leibniz to Count Ernst von Hessen-Rheinfels, 4/14 August 1683; Leibniz, AA, 2:1, p. 535; Leibniz to Jean Gallois, 1676/77, Walther and Czelinski, 2006, vol. 1, p. 331, no. 139). Leibniz's visit to Spinoza must have taken place sometime [between 18 and 21 November 1676] (cf. Müller and Krönert, 1961, p. 46). Leibniz and Spinoza discuss various issues, ranging from the assassination of the Dutch politicians Johan and Cornelis de Witt (1672), Descartes's theory of motion, the 'characteristica universalis', to the arguments to demonstrate the existence of God. During their conversation, Leibniz writes down his ontological argument for God's existence (Leibniz, AA, 2:1, pp. 426–8, no. 131) on a slip of paper. Spinoza also gives Leibniz access to (some parts of) his manuscript of the *Ethics* (cf. Schuller to Leibniz, 16/26 February 1677, Leibniz, AA, 2:1, p. 304; 3:2, p. 46). This also

becomes evident from Leibniz's critical remarks on Spinoza's ontological argument on the same piece of paper (quoted in Leibniz, AA, 2:1, p. 428, no. 131, see also Leibniz, AA, 6:3, pp. 578–80).

9. FATAL DISEASE, SUDDEN DEATH AND FUNERAL

The Hague: January–Late February 1677

Sometime in late 1676 or early 1677, Spinoza suffers from the physical consequences of some advanced incurable disease. Shortly before his death in late February 1677, the philosopher spends a portion of his time working on a naturalistic theory of politics, a tract that will eventually become his unfinished *Tractatus politicus*. On 6 February 1677, Spinoza's health condition is reported by Schuller to be deteriorating rapidly due to 'inherited' *phthisis* (tuberculosis). Then, unexpectedly, Spinoza dies in his rooms in Van der Spijck's house in The Hague on Sunday 21 February 1677. On the same day, a provisional, general inventory of the assets of his estate is drawn up by the notary Willem van den Hove (1650/51–after 1684). According to Spinoza's biographer Colerus, the philosopher did make some last arrangements by asking Van der Spijck to convey his *Ethics* safely to the Amsterdam bookseller and publisher Jan Rieuwertsz Sr upon his death with the aim of having it published. Rieuwertsz Sr confirms the arrival of Spinoza's writing box in a letter to Van der Spijck (25 March 1677), so we may assume that the latter shipped off Spinoza's writing box with all his papers from The Hague to Amsterdam in the weeks following the philosopher's death.

The greater part of the events surrounding his last hours and death are shrouded in mist and we have only a few indications about the primary cause of the philosopher's death. Although various sources (1677, 1680, 1703 and 1705) are at our disposal, they are for the greater part erratic, fragmentary, partly conjectural and incomplete, offering conflicting information or simply gossip. In the days following Spinoza's sudden death, his landlord Van der Spijck in collaboration with the philosopher's closest friends prepare for the funeral and make the necessary memorial service arrangements. On 25 February 1677, the funeral ceremony for Spinoza is held in the Nieuwe Kerk at the Spui in The Hague.

1677, The Hague (Paviljoensgracht)

Saturday 6 February
From Amsterdam, Schuller reacts to a (lost) letter of Leibniz of 18 January 1677. He relates to his correspondent that Spinoza's health is deteriorating rapidly due to 'inherited' *phthisis*. Schuller clearly worries that the philosopher will die soon as a consequence of his *phthisis* (Leibniz, AA, 3:2, p. 37).

Sunday 21 February
At the age of 44 Spinoza dies in his rooms on the second floor of the house of his landlord Van der Spijck at the Paviljoensgracht in The Hague. The supposed time of his sudden death, 'at three o'clock', is given by Colerus (Walther and Czelinski, 2006, vol. 1, p. 158), who could rely on the testimonies of Spinoza's landlord and landlady, but that claim is not supported by any historical evidence. Colerus reports that a physician, 'L.M.', was with Spinoza when he died; the presence of a physician is also mentioned in an anonymous manuscript from 1678 to 1679 (see

Steenbakkers, Touber and Van de Ven), and Schuller tells Leibniz in a letter that he was the one who attended Spinoza. The exact circumstances, however, of Spinoza's death cannot be reconstructed with certainty (cf. Steenbakkers, 1994, pp. 34–5). The only palpable historical documentation on the events surrounding Spinoza's final day is produced in a legal inventory made by the notary Willem van den Hove on Sunday 21 February 1677, confirming the exact date and place of death (Walther and Czelinski, 2006, vol. 1, pp. 336–7). Immediately upon Spinoza's death, Van den Hove was charged by Van der Spijck to draw up a provisional, general inventory of the assets of Spinoza's estate. To all appearances, Spinoza failed to produce any written document to indicate his last will. Colerus, however, quoting the testimony of Van der Spijck, asserts that Spinoza did make some (verbal) arrangements with his landlord to have his *Ethics* printed. According to Colerus, Van der Spijck had testified to him that the philosopher had asked him to convey his writing box to Rieuwertsz Sr in Amsterdam immediately upon his death (Colerus, see Walther and Czelinski, 2006, vol. 1, p. 140).

Between Sunday 21 February and Thursday 25 March

From The Hague, Van der Spijck conveys Spinoza's 'writing box' to Amsterdam. Its precise contents ('Writings and letters' (Colerus, see Walther and Czelinski, 2006, vol. 1, p. 140)) are not known. The date *ante quem* of the sending of the writing box from The Hague is a (lost) letter of Rieuwertsz Sr to Van der Spijck of 25 March 1677 confirming the arrival of Spinoza's desk in good order.

Thursday 25 February

Spinoza's burial takes place in the Nieuwe Kerk at the Spui in The Hague (Colerus; see

Walther and Czelinsky, 2006, vol. 1, p. 162. Six horse-drawn carriages with many prominent people follow the coffin. According to the burial register of the 'rentmeester' (the steward of the financial resources) of the Nieuwe Kerk, Spinoza was buried in a so-called 'huirgraft' (a hired vault, no. 162) ([Wichers], 1889, pp. 56–7), close to the grave of the Grand Pensionary of Holland, De Witt. The vault, according to the same register of the 'rentmeester', was subsequently cleared in the years 1738, 1766, 1786 or 1809 (cf. Wildeman, 1893, pp. 120–1). The philosopher's vault may thus have been cleared as early as the late 1730s, but also later. His remains were in all likelihood scattered around the Nieuwe Kerk.

10. ESTATE AND LEGACY, INQUIRIES FROM ROME

THE HAGUE: LATE FEBRUARY–DECEMBER 1677

The weeks and months following Spinoza's death and burial are focused on the legal arrangements around his estate and, more importantly, on the publication of his written legacy. On 2 March 1677, an official inventory of Spinoza's household goods and private library, made by Van der Spijck and witnessed by Rieuwertsz Sr, is authenticated by the notary Van den Hove. In late March 1677, Van der Spijck starts a judicial procedure to recover the costs advanced for Spinoza's living, rent and burial from the philosopher's legal heirs, i.e. his sister Rebecca d'Espinosa and his nephew Daniel de Carceris. The legal case is closed when both Rebecca and Daniel sign a deed (30 September 1677) in Amsterdam, in which they officially and fully renounce their claim on the estate of their deceased brother and uncle. On 4 November 1677, Spinoza's possessions, particularly his books, optical instruments and grinding tools, are sold at a public auction in Van der Spijck's house in The Hague.

Probably immediately upon Spinoza's death on 21 February, but certainly before 25 March 1677, Van der Spijck ships off Spinoza's writing box with all his papers to Rieuwertsz Sr in Amsterdam. Soon thereafter, a dedicated group of the philosopher's closest confidants embark on the prestigious and hazardous project of publishing all his works and correspondence in two separate language editions. Friends considered to be involved in the joint effort of editing, translating and printing the posthumous works are Meyer, Van Gent and Bouwmeester (*B.d.S. Opera posthuma*), Jelles, Rieuwertsz Sr (*De nagelate schriften van B.d.S.*) and the professional translator Jan Hendriksz Glazemaker (1619/20–82). Schuller seems to have had access to Spinoza's papers, but his role in the printing of the posthumous works remains unclear. The entire editorial process is more or less hurriedly completed between late February and 27 July 1677, when a Latin edition of the posthumous works and a Dutch rendering are conveyed to an unidentified printer who works for Rieuwertsz Sr in Amsterdam. The actual technical process of the typesetting, the proofreading and the printing of Spinoza's posthumous works is completed sometime between late July and 31 December 1677.

In [late August or September] 1677, Roman Catholic officials begin a search for more information on Spinoza's life and works, in order to investigate whether his writings could imperil the purity of religious doctrine. Spinoza's erstwhile Leiden friend, Stensen, may well have been the instigator of that orchestrated search. The date *post quem* of the inquiry is a visit (around [21 August] 1677) to Stensen in Rome by 'a foreigner of Lutheran religion', who may in all likelihood be identified as Tschirnhaus. That visitor shows Stensen a manuscript copy of an unpublished work by Spinoza, which is undoubtedly his *Ethics*. Stensen then hurries to alert the Roman Catholic authorities about the pending danger of the work by handing in a report on Spinoza to the Supreme Sacred Congregation of the Holy Office of the Inquisition (4 September 1677). Alarmed by rumours about the existence of an atheistic manuscript compiled by Spinoza, the Congregation's prefect and Grand Inquisitor Francesco Barberini (1597–1679) orders (18 September 1677) the vicar apostolic of the *Missio Hollandica*, Van Neercassel, to dig up more information on Spinoza's life and works. On 25 November 1677, Van Neercassel provides Barberini with more detailed information on Spinoza which he had gathered in the Dutch Republic. He obtained this information through his network of contacts and informants (a Roman Catholic theology student named Martinus Henricus de Swaan (1651–1713), his brother Jan de Swaan (d. after 1677), an unknown rabbi, a candidate in Arminian theology called 'Mister Wandelmannus' and an unidentified Socinian amongst others) in Amsterdam and The Hague. While continuing his search, Van Neercassel sends Barberini a copy of the *Tractatus theologico-politicus* through the intermediary of the Roman Catholic Internuncio in Brussels, Sébastien Antoine Tanara (1650–1724), on 28 November 1677. Spinoza's posthumous works leave the press in December 1677, and distribution starts in January 1678.

1677

Friday 26 February (16 OS)
From Amsterdam, Schuller writes to Leibniz in response to a (lost) letter of mid-February 1677. One of the issues in Schuller's letter is the autograph manuscript copy of the *Ethics*, which 'you saw at his house' ([between 18 and 21 November 1676]). Schuller writes to Leibniz that the 'autograph' of the *Ethics* is now up for sale at the price of 150 guilders. He therefore urges his correspondent to convince his master Johann Friedrich, Duke of Brunswick-Lüneburg-Calenberg (1625–79), to purchase the autograph manuscript for his Hanover library (Leibniz, AA, 3:2, p. 46; Steenbakkers, 1994, p. 15). This important statement is relevant for the history of the hazardous editorial process of the posthumous works, but we must approach it with care, since it is not supported by any other historical evidence. Apart from the author's copy, we have no evidence of how many transcripts of the *Ethics* were actually in circulation. That there must have been several copies of the work written out by various people is explicitly confirmed in the preface to the posthumous works (Akkerman and Hubbeling, 1979, no. 74, pp. 146–7). All in all, the only copy we know of with certainty is the manuscript that Tschirnhaus carried around in his bags in England, France and Italy between July 1675 and mid-1679. The existence of that copy (the Vatican codex Vat.lat. 12838; Spruit and Totaro, 2011) is confirmed in several letters to and from Spinoza. Spinoza's writing box, conveyed by Van der Spijck to Rieuwertsz Sr in Amsterdam on or shortly after 21 February (and at any rate before 25 March 1677), may have contained not only the original autograph manuscript of the *Ethics,* but also a manuscript copy (and maybe even a fair-copy) of the work (see Steenbakkers, 1994, pp. 55–8).

[Before or on Tuesday 2 March]
Rebecca d'Espinosa and her stepson Daniel de Carceris request the town secretary of The Hague, Anthony de Veer (1643–1716), for official permission to have a notary public draw up an inventory of the estate of their deceased brother and uncle. In the same period, Rieuwertsz Sr is present in The Hague and signs as witness to two notarial deeds in connection with the legal inventory of Spinoza's estate made by the notary Van den Hove (cf. Colerus, see Walther and Czelinski, 2006, vol. 1, p. 140).

Tuesday 2 March
Secretary De Veer signs a legal document in which he gives official permission to Rebecca d'Espinosa and Daniel de Carceris to have an inventory made of the estate of their deceased brother and uncle. In the same document, De Veer also instructs Van der Spijck to give a public officer full access to the assets of his deceased lodger (Walther and Czelinski, 2006, vol. 1, p. 339, no. 149). Apparently, Rebecca d'Espinosa and Daniel de Carceris agreed with Van der Spijck that he would further supervise the work surrounding the making of the inventory. For on the same day, Van der Spijck requests the notary Van den Hove in The Hague to investigate and break the door seals of the room in which are stored Spinoza's grinding device, his tools for grinding glass and a bookcase with books. He had locked this room immediately upon the philosopher's death in the late afternoon or evening of 21 February 1677 (Walther and Czelinski, 2006, vol. 1, p. 340, no. 150). After Van den Hove has broken the seals on the door to Spinoza's room and confirmed that these were all intact, he then authenticates an inventory of Spinoza's possessions, which to all appearances was drawn up by Van der Spijck (see Walther and Czelinski, pp. 341–59,

no. 151). The inventory includes common household goods, but also a list of Spinoza's books (160) and a brief description of Spinoza's instruments and material for grinding lenses and building telescopes (Walther and Czelinski, 2006, vol. 1, p. 358, no. 151).

Monday 29 March

From Amsterdam, Schuller dispatches a letter to Leibniz, which is a reply to a (lost) letter of Leibniz of mid-March 1677. Schuller, who temporarily lives in the house of his friend Van Gent, tells his correspondent that he is much relieved by the fact that he has not yet informed 'his Prince' (i.e. Johann Friedrich of Brunswick-Lüneburg-Calenberg) about his earlier offer to purchase the autograph manuscript of Spinoza's *Ethics* (see Schuller to Leibniz 16/26 March 1677). Confidently, Schuller then points out to Leibniz that there has been a radical change of plan since he has now accommodated the differences of opinions amongst Spinoza's friends about what should be ultimately done with the philosopher's written legacy. As a result, Schuller continues, he is now determined to have Spinoza's manuscripts published for the public benefit in their entirety, not only the *Ethics*, but also his other surviving writings as well as his exchange of letters. To prevent the project from being nipped in the bud, he urges Leibniz to tell nobody about it, 'not even the friends'. According to Schuller's own testimony, he now has in his possession the autograph manuscripts (cf. Meinsma, 1896, p. 443) or copies (cf. Steenbakkers, 1994, p. 60) of the (unfinished) *Tractatus de intellectus emendatione*, Spinoza's letter to Henry Oldenburg of [April] 1662 (see 1662.[04].00 (Ep 6)), the (unfinished) *Tractatus politicus* and an unknown number of letters (Leibniz, AA, 2:1, pp. 476–7; 3:2, pp. 52–3). Schuller's letter to Leibniz of 29 March 1677 is thus the

first historical document revealing the plan of a dedicated group of friends to publish Spinoza's philosophical writings posthumously. To all appearances, Schuller has firsthand knowledge of the project and is in close contact with that group. Still, there are no concrete indications of his direct involvement in the editorial process and Schuller's limited contribution should probably be assessed rather as organizational (cf. Steenbakkers, 1994, p. 63), mediating and facilitating.

Tuesday 30 March

In The Hague, Van der Spijck signs a power of attorney before the notary public Libertus Loeff (1647–1704), in which he grants one Robbert Smedingh from Amsterdam the legal authority to act on his behalf and to recover for him the costs made for Spinoza's living and funeral (Walther and Czelinski, 2006, vol. 1, p. 364, no. 153). Van der Spijck in the deed mandates Smedingh to summon Spinoza's legal heirs Rebecca d'Espinosa and Daniel de Carceris before the commissioners of *kleine zaken* (smaller claims) to recover all his expenses (now approximately 6,000 euro). Spinoza's biographer Colerus makes mention of this power of attorney and he recounts the fact that Spinoza's sister Rebecca came to Van der Spijck's house to announce herself as legal heir to her brother's estate with a view to claiming his property, but he adds to this that she refused to pay the costs of the funeral and other remaining debts of her brother (Colerus, see Walther and Czelinski, 2006, vol. 1, p. 166–8). The sum advanced by Van der Spijck for the lodging and funeral of Spinoza is not mentioned in the power of attorney, but we learn from another legal document of 8 July 1677 that the sum he demanded from Spinoza's legal heirs was 250 guilders, 14 *stuivers* and two *penningen* (now approximately 2,500 euro).

Thursday 8 July

Van der Spijck files an official statement of claim with the *vierschaar* (municipal court) of The Hague to take appropriate legal measures against the collective legal heirs of Spinoza. Van der Spijck's statement is repeated on 23 September and 13 October 1677 (see Walther and Czelinski, 2006, vol. 1, resp. p. 370, no. 159, p. 372, no. 161). The final verdict of the *vierschaar* is unknown, but in all likelihood the case was unsuccessfully closed since Spinoza's heirs had officially renounced the estate of their brother and uncle in a disclaimer of 30 September 1677. In addition, Van der Spijck's legal representative Johan Louckers, the procurator of the municipal *vierschaar*, will have given official permission to his client to sell the estate publicly to pay for the debts owed by Spinoza.

Tuesday 27 July (17 OS)

Schuller writes to Leibniz to announce that all of Spinoza's posthumous works have now been conveyed to the printer. The philosopher's works, according to the letter, will be simultaneously published in Latin and Dutch (Leibniz, AA, 3:2, p. 202). Schuller's letter to Leibniz is the earliest historical document on the progress of the editorial labour by the group of friends that prepared Spinoza's writings for the press. From Schuller's letter it becomes clear that most of the work on the texts for the *Opera posthuma* and their translation for *De nagelate schriften* was done sometime between the first preparations in late March (see Schuller to Leibniz, 29 March 1677) and their completion in late July 1677. Biographically the most important issue is who were involved in editing Spinoza's posthumous works. As the matter now stands, Meyer and maybe also Van Gent are to be considered responsible for the Latin edition. Spinoza's friend Bouwmeester may also have

been involved in the editing project, but there is no conclusive historical proof for this as yet (cf. Steenbakkers, 1994, p. 17). As for the role of Schuller (who by late March 1677 possessed the bulk of the autograph manuscripts or copies of Spinoza's writings), there are no concrete indications for his direct involvement in the editing project of the posthumous works and his contribution (if any) will have been mostly organizational (cf. Steenbakkers, 1994, p. 63). The preface to the posthumous works was authored by Jarig Jelles and was presumably translated into Latin by Meyer (cf. Akkerman and Hubbeling, 1979, p. 105; see also Pierre Bayle to Theodorus Jansonius ab Almeloveen, 7 March 1686, Deckherr, 1686, pp. 387–8). The people involved in editing *De nagelate schriften*, the Dutch twin of the Latin edition, were presumably Jelles, Glazemaker and Rieuwertsz Sr (see [Duijkerius], 1991, p. 195). The *Opera posthuma* and *De nagelate schriften* consist of the following parts: preface, *Ethics*, *Tractatus politicus*, *Tractatus de intellectus emendatione* (both unfinished) and the edited version of Spinoza's correspondence (75 letters). In addition, the Latin edition includes the (unfinished) *Compendium grammatices linguae Hebraeae*. According to the preface to the posthumous works, particularly the *Ethics* was printed at the philosopher's own request. None of the proofs of the writings and correspondence are known to have survived.

August

Spinoza's erstwhile Leiden companion Stensen receives a visit from 'a foreigner of the Lutheran religion' in Rome. According to Stensen's own testimony, that foreigner showed him 'a manuscript without saying to him from whom it originated', of which Tschirnhaus revealed later on that it was authored by Spinoza (cf.

Totaro, 2000, p. 101; Totaro, 2002, Appendix, p. 33). The meeting between the Lutheran traveller and Stensen must be dated sometime in August 1677, shortly before or after the latter's nomination (21 August 1677) to the difficult post (on the request of Johann Friedrich, Duke of Brunswick-Lüneburg-Calenberg) as vicar apostolic in the northern mission fields at the ducal court in Hanover. The date *ante quem* for the encounter is 4 September 1677, when Stensen hands in his report to the Holy Office of the Inquisition, in which the reference to his meeting with the unknown foreigner is made. The name of the Lutheran foreigner is not mentioned, but very probably he must be identified as the young German intellectual Tschirnhaus. During his Grand Tour, the latter spent time in Rome from mid-April 1677 (see Tschirnhaus to Leibniz, 17 April 1677) to 10 April 1678 and there is historical evidence to confirm that he made the acquaintance of Stensen in August 1677. Since Tschirnhaus is known to have journeyed in England, France and Italy (between July 1675 and mid-1679) with a manuscript copy of the *Ethics* in his bags (cf. note by Leibniz made in 1676, AA, 6:3, p. 384), we may assume that this was in fact the very manuscript he had shown to the Danish convert. Stensen somehow succeeded in obtaining the manuscript copy from Tschirnhaus. He later decided to submit it (23 September 1677) to the Holy Office of the Inquisition (Spruit and Totaro, 2011, pp. 2, 11–12). There certainly remain some questions surrounding Tschirnhaus's conduct during his encounter with Stensen in August 1677. Why did Tschirnhaus give Stensen access to Spinoza's *Ethics*? Stensen may have taken in Tschirnhaus (who was aware of Spinoza's warning not to show his *Ethics* too hastily to others, see Spinoza to Schuller, Ep 72, G IV, 304–5) by telling him that he once had been on friendly terms with Spinoza when studying medicine in Leiden in

1661 or 1662. And did Tschirnhaus also tell Stensen about Spinoza's death and about the preparations for publishing his philosophical legacy? It is unknown if Tschirnhaus had already acquired information about the editing of the posthumous works. If Tschirnhaus did tell Stensen, one can imagine that the latter hastened to inform the Roman Catholic authorities about the pending publication of the *Ethics* by submitting his report on 4 September 1677.

Saturday 4 September
In Rome, Stensen signs and submits his report to the Holy Office of the Inquisition. The aim of the report is to supply information on the dangers of the 'new philosophy' of 'a certain Spinosa in Holland'. The widely spread 'disease' of this dubious philosophy must be opposed with every possible remedy to prevent further infection and contagion and to provide suitable treatment to those already poisoned (Totaro, 2000, p. 100; Totaro, 2002, Appendix, p. 33). After a short account of his personal contacts with Spinoza in Leiden or Rijnsburg in 1661 or 1662, Stensen provides details about the philosopher's writings, 'some under his own name, others without a name'. Some years ago, he adds to this, he took the occasion to write Spinoza a letter, which he had published under the title 'Ad novae philosophiae reformatorem de vera philosophia epistola' (Ep 67a). To his knowledge, the philosopher also completed 'certain manuscripts' which he eventually decided not to have printed after warnings from his confidants (Totaro, 2000, pp. 100–1; Totaro, 2002, Appendix, p. 33). Stensen seems to be well informed about Spinoza's writings, both published and unpublished. He recounts his encounter with the Lutheran foreigner, who showed him one of the philosopher's manuscripts, presumably

the *Ethics* (Totaro, 2000, pp. 101; Totaro, 2002, Appendix, p. 33). Stensen continues his account with a harsh critique of Spinoza's philosophical views, particularly his theory of divine substance and its attributes. Lastly, he provides information about Spinoza's supporters and followers. All of them, he states, were specialists in mathematics and took a keen interest in Descartes. They studied either in the United Provinces or in England where they had been infected by Spinoza's mistakes. Even if they did not actively support the philosopher's errors, Stensen holds them at least responsible for spreading them further (Totaro, 2000, p. 102; Totaro, 2002, Appendix, p. 34). Stensen ends his report by stressing that the 'evil' must have spread widely, since Spinoza frequently received letters from as far away as England. He also recalls that a foreigner stayed in the philosopher's house to have a better understanding of his views. Stensen furthermore refers to a discourse he once had with someone in Holland, which fully proved to him that the principles in the manuscript were already widely spread among heretics, but not, as far as he could remember, among Roman Catholics (Totaro, 2000, p. 103; Totaro, 2002, Appendix, p. 35). The 'frequent letters from England' referred to by Stensen undoubtedly concern the philosopher's correspondence with Oldenburg in the early 1660s. His assertion about the visit of a foreigner to Spinoza may also relate to Oldenburg. Stensen's report marks the beginning of a more or less systematic search for incriminating information about Spinoza to find out whether he could be a threat to Roman Catholic doctrines. In mid-March 1679 Spinoza's correspondence, his *Ethics*, the *Tractatus theologico-politicus* and the *Tractatus politicus* are placed on the Index of prohibited books. Nothing is known about

Stensen's precise role in the targeted search by the Holy Office of the Inquisition in mid-September 1677, but we may assume that he provided the names of people in the Dutch Republic that could be helpful as informants or intermediaries in the Roman inquiries.

Sunday 12 September
Van der Spijck signs a legal document before the notary public Matijs van Lievendael (fl. 1671–81) in The Hague. In the deed, he appoints Johan Louckers, the procurator of the municipal *vierschaar*, to act as his legal representative in his statement of claim (filed with the *vierschaar* on 8 July 1677) against Spinoza's legal heirs, Rebecca d'Espinosa and Daniel de Carceris, to recover the payment of charges and debts advanced by him for the philosopher's living, rent and burial.

Saturday 18 September
From Rome, Cardinal Barberini, prefect of the Holy Office of the Inquisition, dispatches a letter of instruction to the Dutch vicar apostolic Van Neercassel. Barberini informs his correspondent that other cardinals in the Holy Office warned him about 'a manuscript book on matters of atheism by Spinosa', undoubtedly the *Ethics*. The Jewish author of that manuscript, according to Barberini, is supposed to have published other works in which he endangers the purity and the fundamentals of the Roman Catholic doctrine and Church. He orders Van Neercassel to investigate if the rumours reported to him are correct, to find out whether the manuscript has already been sent to the press and, if so, to procure a copy of it. He also charges Van Neercassel to purchase copies of all other works of that same author and to redirect these instantly to Rome together with all other information that could be relevant in any way (Orcibal, 1949, p. 460, Annex 2).

Barberini's decision to have Van Neercassel start an investigation into Spinoza's writings and life had some practical advantages. Van Neercassel was in charge of the Holland Mission and in that capacity he could rely on a cohesive network of Roman Catholic communities and clerics throughout the Reformed Northern Netherlands. In addition, Van Neercassel also had his seat in Amsterdam, which must have been rather efficient at tracking down people in the Dutch centre of liberal thought and printing who might know more about the philosopher's works. Shortly after the receipt of Barberini's letter, Van Neercassel went into action, recruiting two relatives of (his later successor) the Oratorian Petrus Codde to assist him in his inquiries about Spinoza. They were the devout young Roman Catholic student of theology Martinus Henricus de Swaan and his brother Jan de Swaan, an influential merchant working in Amsterdam (cf. Van Neercassel to Martinus de Swaan, 31 October 1677), whom Van Neercassel must have chosen for their zealous commitment to the Roman Catholic faith as well as for their network of contacts.

Thursday 30 September
Rebecca d'Espinosa and Daniel de Carceris sign a document in which they officially and fully renounce their legal rights and claims to the estate of their brother and uncle (Walther and Czelinski, 2006, vol. 1, p. 371, no. 160). The official renouncement of Spinoza's estate should not be linked directly to the statement of claim (8 July 1677) filed by Van der Spijck with the *vierschaar* in The Hague against Spinoza's legal heirs to recover the costs of his funeral and other remaining debts. From the start, so it seems, the relatives suspected that the estate of their deceased brother and uncle might be laden with debts. That becomes evident first of all from their state-

ment of 30 May 1677 before a lawyer of the Supreme Court, that they will only accept the deceased's estate without the liability to debts beyond the assets descended. The unwillingness of his relatives to accept unconditionally financial responsibility for the funeral and estate of Spinoza is also expressed in the account by Colerus.

[Tuesday 28 September/Saturday 2 October]
Schuller informs Leibniz on the progress made in the printing of Spinoza's posthumous works. In his letter, he tells his correspondent confidentially that the work is now near completion and that it will be sold to the public within a fortnight. Schuller also says that the work will most certainly upset theologians who will seek ways to have it banished as soon as possible (Leibniz, AA, 3:2, p. 239).

Saturday 16 October
Van Neercassel dispatches a letter to the Vatican diplomatic envoy Tanara in Brussels. In his letter, he assures his correspondent that all his and Barberini's letters were transmitted to him in good order. The Dutch vicar apostolic tells Tanara that he wrote to Barberini to inform him about the 'Jew' Spinoza, who is the author of the *Tractatus theologico-politicus*. In addition, he informs the papal envoy that he will now continue his search for facts about Spinoza's 'morals and writings' in the towns of Amsterdam and The Hague, which may indicate that he is aware of where the philosopher lived (Orcibal, 1949, p. 460, Annex 2).

Tuesday 26 October (16 OS)
From Amsterdam, Schuller writes to Leibniz. He promises to send him a copy of Spinoza's posthumous works immediately upon publication (Leibniz, AA, 3:2, p. 264).

Sunday 31 October
Van Neercassel writes a letter to his inform-
ant De Swaan. He points out that the name
of the 'heir' of Spinoza's written legacy may
perhaps be uncovered by someone whom he
describes as 'your rabbi'. That qualification
indicates that De Swaan (or his brother Jan)
must have had contacts with people
within the Portuguese-Israelite community of
Amsterdam. Van Neercassel furthermore
turns his correspondent's attention to 'a candidate in Arminian theology', known to
'Mister Wandelmannus', who could be useful
in contacting a Socinian. Through the intermediary of this Remonstrant theology student it may be possible to find out whether
Spinoza left any other writings behind
(Orcibal, 1949, pp. 460–1, Annex 4). The
person referred to by Van Neercassel as
'Mister Wandelmannus' may be identified
as the Roman Catholic priest Johannes
Wandelman (before 1657–1686) from
Amsterdam. The names of the rabbi and the
Arminian theology candidate are not given in
Van Neercassel's letter to De Swaan.

Thursday 4 November
Two days after the announcement in the
newspapers of Amsterdam and Haarlem,
Spinoza's estate is sold at a public auction in
the house of his landlord Van der Spijck at
the Paviljoensgracht in The Hague. That is
confirmed in an inventory of auction results
made on 4 November 1677, part of which is
quoted by Colerus. The inventory, according
to the biographer, was made by a property
auctioneer, called Rykus van Stralen. Van der
Spijck must have given Colerus access to the
administration of the entire financial estate
settlement when the latter was preparing the
philosopher's biography in the early eighteenth century. During these preparations,
Colerus carefully studied the 'Boel-cedulle'

of 4 November 1677, for in his biography he
provides detailed information about the
prices and results (430 guilders and 13 *stuivers*) of the public auction of Spinoza's personal belongings (see Walther and Czelinski,
2006, vol. 1, pp. 168–70). There are strong
indications that the public sale of the philosopher's property was not supervised and run
by the aforementioned Van Stralen, as
Colerus assumes, but by a qualified 'vendue-
meester' (head auctioneer) from The Hague,
called Pieter de Graef (fl. 1672–8). That is
confirmed in a legal deed in the business
archives of De Graef concerning the results
of the public auction of Spinoza's estate.
According to the account, a small portion
(30 pounds, 13 *schellingen* and eight *penningen*) of that total was rightfully reserved
for Hendrick van der Spijck (Freudenthal,
1899, p. 173, no. 78, see also Walther and
Czelinski, 2006, vol. 1, p. 374, no. 165).

Friday 5 November (26 October OS)
Schuller dispatches a letter to Leibniz to
inform him that the printing of Spinoza's
posthumous writings is ready, except for the
index. He promises his correspondent to send
him some copies immediately upon publication (Leibniz, AA, 3:2, p. 264).

Thursday 25 November
From Utrecht, Van Neercassel sends a letter to
Barberini. Van Neercassel informs his
correspondent that inquiries among Christians
and Jews have failed to uncover the existence
of any suspect manuscript or book written by
Spinoza that may harm the Roman Catholic
faith. The author, according to his information,
passed away in the 'summer' (sic), and had left
all his writings to a Mennonite and Socinian
bookseller in Amsterdam, called 'Joannes
Rieuwerze'. The latter, according to Van Neercassel, had assured him that he is only aware

of some handwritten meditations on Descartes's *Principia* (i.e. *Renati des Cartes Principia philosophiae*). The only work published by Spinoza known to him, according to Rieuwertsz's information, is the *Tractatus theologico-politicus*. Van Neercassel ends his account of Spinoza by assuring his correspondent that he will immediately spring into action against any danger threatening Roman Catholic doctrines (Brom, 1911, p. 152).

Sunday 28 November
Van Neercassel writes a letter to Tanara in Brussels. Along with this letter, he sends him a copy for Barberini of the 'treatise of the Hebrew Spinosa', which in all likelihood is the *Tractatus theologico-politicus*. Tanara in turn must have redirected the work to Barberini in Rome (Orcibal, 1949, p. 462, Annex 6).

Friday 31 December (21 OS)
Schuller informs Leibniz in a letter that Spinoza's posthumous works are now printed. He expects that they will be sold soon after the start of the new year. Again, he assures his correspondent that he will be one of the first to receive a copy of the book (Leibniz, AA, 3:2, p. 304).

11. EPILOGUE: POSTHUMOUS WORKS, EARLY REACTIONS, BAN AND INDEX

1678–9

Spinoza's posthumous works, issued in two separate (Latin and Dutch) editions by the Amsterdam publishing firm of Rieuwertsz Sr, are offered for public sale in the first weeks of January 1678. Just as his anonymous

Tractatus theologico-politicus had provoked mixed reactions from intellectuals and theologians, the philosopher's posthumous writings immediately cause a storm of fierce sentiments in the United Provinces and beyond. Almost instantly his *Ethics* meets with opposition in various outraged assemblies of the Reformed Church. The first known official reaction is the condemnation by the Leiden *kerkenraad* (4 February 1678). One week later, the Leiden Burgomasters take the decision to seize copies of the posthumous writings in the local bookshops. Alarmed by the Leiden deputies, the Grand Pensionary of Holland, Gaspar Fagel (1634–88), informs the States of Holland on 17 March 1678 about the complaints submitted by the North and South Holland Synods concerning the dissemination of the *Opera posthuma*. Finally, after many intensive debates and internal deliberations the Supreme Court of Holland, Zeeland and West-Friesland decides to suppress the posthumous works in an official placard on 25 June 1678.

In the same period, the head of the *Missio Hollandica*, Van Neercassel, continues to dig up detailed information on Spinoza in the United Provinces. A vital role in the process of informing Rome about Spinoza is played by Tanara, the papal envoy in Brussels. Another important figure is the papal diplomat Lorenzo Casoni (1643–1720), to whom Van Neercassel sends a lengthy report on the philosopher's life and works (9 September 1678). Four days later, Van Neercassel forwards to him a copy of the posthumous works with the request to redirect the package to Barberini in Rome. Soon thereafter, in early 1679, the Holy Office of the Inquisition officially places most of Spinoza's works on the Index of prohibited books.

The provincial ban issued by the Dutch civil authorities forbids the printing, distribution, sale and translation of Spinoza's posthumous works in the latter part of the seventeenth century and throughout the entire eighteenth century. Neither that ban, however, nor the decision of Rome to place almost all the philosopher's writings on the Index, can prevent the growing dissemination of Spinoza's ideas among both admirers and opponents. His writings continue to be read, circulated and translated during the early Enlightenment. This can be measured by the amount of newly printed editions of the *Tractatus theologico-politicus*. Apart from editions in Latin ([1678]), renderings in both French ([1678]), English (1689) and Dutch (1693, 1694), clandestinely published with false titles and imprints, still find easy distribution for many decades. The profound impact of the provocative ideas of Spinoza in Europe diminished around 1730, but immediately prior to the French Revolution interest in Spinoza again intensified.

1678

Between Saturday 1 January and Monday 24 January

Barely eleven months after Spinoza's death and burial, his posthumous works are offered for public sale in a Latin language trade edition and in a Dutch language counterpart, both in quarto format, unbound and in sheets, as was the practice in those days. Details about the number of print runs of both editions are unknown. There is no independent historical evidence to establish an absolute publication date for the two editions, but we know from Schuller's letter to Leibniz of 21/31 December 1677 that their publication was scheduled soon after the start of the new year. The date *ante quem* is established by a reaction to the publication of the posthumous works in a letter by Graevius to Nicolaas Heinsius (1620–81) writ-

ten on 24 January 1678. In the two language editions, the philosopher's name is purposely suppressed into a monogram: *B.d.S. Opera posthuma*; *De nagelate schriften van B.d.S.* (see Akkerman and Hubbeling, 1979, no. 10, pp. 112–13). It appears from the preface that there had been deliberations with Spinoza about the printing of the *Ethics*, which he desired to be published anonymously. The friends who prepared the two language editions also omitted the place of printing (Amsterdam), and the name of the publisher (Rieuwertsz). Recent typographical research has proven that the work was typeset by the Amsterdam printer Israel de Paull (Jagersma and Dijkstra, 2014). Around 1680, an unidentified artist produced a copper engraving of Spinoza (usually referred to as the 'Opera portrait'), which was bound into some copies of the *Opera posthuma* (cf. Ekkart, 1999, p. 13, no. 7).

Monday 3 January

From [Brussels], Tanara writes to Van Neercassel. The letter concerns Tanara's reply to the receipt of a copy of the *Tractatus theologico-politicus* forwarded to him by Van Neercassel on 28 November 1677. He most certainly reacts in his letter to rumours that Spinoza's posthumous works were to be published in the United Provinces soon. Tanara in his letter urges the Dutch vicar apostolic to continue his search in the United Provinces for facts relating to Spinoza, particularly to find out whether the philosopher has recently published another book (Orcibal, 1949, p. 462, Annex 7).

Monday 24 January

From Utrecht, the humanist Johannes Georgius Graevius writes to the noted classicist and poet Nicolaas Heinsius in Vianen. In his letter, he informs his correspondent about the fact that a 'detestable' book on 'moral doctrine and the soul' by Spinoza is now published in the United Provinces together with his other posthumous works. The letter, quoted in Burman's *Sylloge epistolarum a viris illustribus scriptarum*, is the first known historical document referring directly to the publication of the philosopher's posthumous writings, and more particularly, to the *Ethics* (Burman, 1727, vol. 4, p. 475).

Friday 4 February
Reactions to the publication of the posthumous works are hostile from the start. The first known official response by the Reformed Church authorities, dated 4 February 1678, is given by the Leiden *kerkenraad*. The gathering condemns the atheistic contents of the '*Opera posthuma* of one B.D.S.' (Leiden *kerkenraad* resolutions, 4 February 1678, Walther and Czelinski, 2006, vol. 1, p. 380, no. 171). In due course, the outraged *kerkenraad* instructs its representatives to take further steps to ban 'that harmful and poisonous book' (Leiden *kerkenraad* resolutions, 4 February 1678, Walther and Czelinski, 2006, vol. 1, p. 380, no. 171). The assigned deputies report to the Leiden consistory about their actions on 11 February 1678.

Friday 11 February
The *kerkenraad* of Leiden is further informed by its deputies about their efforts to have the city's Burgomasters ban Spinoza's posthumous works from the local bookshops. According to the *kerkenraad* resolutions, the Burgomasters had informed them that they had finally decided to seize the book and to request the States of Holland to consider an official interdict (Leiden *kerkenraad* resolutions, 11 February 1678, Walther and Czelinski, 2006, vol. 1, pp. 381, no. 172). On

the same day, the *kerkenraad* of The Hague asks its members to guard against 'the newly published Books of Spinosa, both in Latin, and in Dutch'. The Council also decides to instruct the Reformed minister David Amya (fl. 1678–1711) of the local church at The Hague to urge the Supreme Court of Holland to take further measures to ensure 'that the distribution of the said books is to be stopped as much is possible' (The Hague *kerkenraad* resolutions, 11 February 1678, Walther and Czelinski, 2006, vol. 1, p. 382, no. 173).

Saturday 25 June
Shortly after 16 April 1678, the States committee on suspect books, consisting of deputies from Leiden and States delegates specially charged with matters of theology, renders its judgement about a total interdiction of Spinoza's posthumous works in the province of Holland and West-Friesland. Most likely, their spokesman was the city's pensionary Pieter Burgersdijck (c. 1623–91) (cf. North Holland Synod resolutions, 1 August 1678, ad art. 5, North Holland Synod of 1677, Walther and Czelinski, 2006, vol. 1, p. 392, no. 180). Acting on the committee's advice, the States of Holland and West-Friesland by order of Stadholder William III issue an official placard to stop the printing, distribution, sale and translation of the philosopher's writings. The title of the decree, printed by Jacobus Scheltus, runs as follows: *Placaet van de Heeren Staten van Hollandt ende West-Vrieslant, tegens het Boeck geintituleert B.D. Spinosa Opera Posthum. In date den vijff-en-twintighsten Junij 1678* (*Placard of the Lords States of Hollandt and West-Vrieslant, Against the Book Entitled B.D. Spinosa Opera Posthum. On the Date 25 June 1678*) (Walther and Czelinski, 2006, vol. 1, pp. 385–6, no. 177).

*Between Monday 11 July and Saturday
23 July*

The resolutions of the provincial Synod of South Holland of mid-July 1678 offer an instructive insight into the efforts of the Dutch Reformed Church authorities to influence the special States commission (installed on 17 March 1678) in their decision-making to suppress suspect books. During a meeting in Leiden, the South Holland delegates inform the Synod about their earlier efforts to strive for a ban on 'harmful books', in particular 'the books of B.D.H. opera posthuma (undoubtedly of Spinosa)'. According to their account, they had approached the 'Fiscael' (Advocate General) of the Supreme Court of Holland together with the deputy of the *kerkenraad* of The Hague, David Amya (cf. The Hague *kerkenraad* resolutions, 11 February 1678, Walther and Czelinski, 2006, vol. 1, p. 382, no. 173), requesting the seizure of all copies of these suspect works. In due course, the Advocate General had advised them to submit their complaints directly to the Supreme Court of Holland. Accordingly, they had confronted the Court with various dreadful passages from Spinoza's writings and finally handed in a report with their religious objections. On the same day, according to the Synod's deputies, the Supreme Court had decided to raid the bookshops in The Hague immediately and to seize all copies of the posthumous works. The deputies state that they had also forwarded the passages (in Dutch translation) from Spinoza's works to the Grand Pensionary (i.e. Gaspar Fagel), which were subsequently redirected to some members of the States of Holland (the States' delegates charged with theological matters in the special States commission on suspect books very probably). In conclusion, the States had then decided to give out a placard against the philosopher's posthumous works (South Holland Synod resolutions, 11–23 July 1678, art. 9 (ad art. 16 and 17, South Holland Synod of 1677), *Acta der particuliere synoden van Zuid-Holland 1621–1700*, vol. 5, pp. 236–7). The resolutions indicate that the South Holland Synod had also engaged several theology professors to add weight to the attempts of its delegates to influence the decision-making of the States committee on suspect books from the sidelines. According to this source, one of these professors was the Leiden Cartesian theologian Christoph Wittich (1625–87) (Walther and Czelinski, 2006, vol. 1, p. 390, no. 179).

1679

Monday 13 March

Following the considerations and conclusions in the report on Spinoza submitted by the vicar apostolic Van Neercassel, the Roman Holy Office of the Inquisition in a decree officially condemns the philosopher's *Epistolae*, his *Ethics,* the *Tractatus theologico-politicus* and the *Tractatus politicus*, for corrupting the morals of Roman Catholic doctrine. The Holy Office places the works on the Index of prohibited books (*Index librorum prohibitorum Innoc. XI*, quoted in Walther and Czelinski, 2006, vol. 1, p. 397, no. 184). On 29 August 1690, the Holy Office officially places Spinoza's entire *Opera posthuma* on the Index of prohibited books (*Index librorum prohibitorum Leonis XIII*).

APPENDIX: EDITIONS AND TRANSLATIONS OF SPINOZA'S WRITINGS

Seventeenth Century

1. B. de Spinoza, *Renati des Cartes Principia philosophiae* (Amsterdam: J. Rieuwertsz, 1663). 4°, 78 fols, [16] 1–141, figures (see J. Kingma and A.K. Offenberg, pp. 4–5, no. 1). 100 copies known.

2. B. de Spinoza, *Principia: Renatus des Cartes Beginzelen der wysbegeerte* (Amsterdam: J. Rieuwertsz, 1664). 4°, 93 fols, [6] 1–101 [2] 109–168, figures (see Kingma and Offenberg, pp. 5–6, no. 2). 13 copies.

3. *Tractatus theologico-politicus* (Hamburg [Amsterdam]: H. Künraht, 1670). T1. 4°, 124 fols, [12] 1–233 [3], list of errata, without corrections. P. 104 misnumbered as 304 (see Kingma and Offenberg, p. 8, no. 3). 15 copies.

4. *Tractatus theologico-politicus* (Hamburg [Amsterdam]: H. Künraht, 1672). T2. 4°, 123 fols, [12] 1–233 [1], list of errata, corrections (pp. 8, 22, 39, 41, 95, 121). P. 42 misnumbered 24; 207 as 213; 161 Cap. XVI misprinted XIV; signature (*)3 as (*)4 (see Kingma and Offenberg, pp. 8–9, no. 4). 19 copies.

5. *Tractatus theologico-politicus* (Hamburg [Amsterdam]: H. Künraht, 1670 [1672?]). T2a. 4°, 124 fols, [12] 1–233 [3], list of errata, corrections (pp. 8, 22, 39, 41, 95, 121). P. 42 misnumbered 24; 207 as 213; 161 Cap. XVI misprinted XIV; signature (*)3 as (*)4 (see Kingma and Offenberg, p. 9, no. 5). 10 copies.

6. (F. Henriquez de Villacorta), *Opera chirurgica omnia* (Amsterdam: J. Paulli, 1673). Disguised edition of the *Tractatus theologico-politicus*. T3V. 8°, 180 fols, [24] 1–136 [1]; 110 fols, [18] 1–182 [20] (see Kingma and Offenberg, p. 12, no. 8). 4 copies.

7. (D. Heinsius), *Operum historicorum collectio prima (secunda)*, (Leiden: I. Hercules, 1673). Disguised edition of the *Tractatus theologico-politicus*. T3H. 8°, 180 fols, [24] 1–336 [1]; 110 fols, [18] 1–182 [20], (see Kingma and Offenberg, pp. 12–13, no. 9). 26 copies.

8. (F. de le Boe Sylvius), *Totius medicinae idea nova* (Amsterdam: C. Gratianus, 1673). Disguised edition of the *Tractatus theologico-politicus*. Printed together with: L. Meyer, *Philosophia S. Scripturae interpres* (Amsterdam, 1666). T3S. 8°, 178 fols, [22] 1–334; 110 fols, [18] 1–182 [20] (see Kingma and Offenberg, pp. 13–14, no. 10). 5 copies.

9. *Tractatus theologico-politicus* (Hamburg [Amsterdam]: Kunraht, 1673). Together with the *Philosophia S. Scripturae interpres*. T3T. 8°, 180 fols, [22] 1–334 [4]; 110 fols, [18] 1–182 [20] (Kingma and Offenberg, pp. 14–15, no. 11). 5 copies.

10. *Tractatus theologico-politicus* (n.p. [Amsterdam?], 1674). *Ab Authore longè Emendatior*. Printed together with the *Philosophia S. Scripturae interpres*. T3E. 8°, 180 fols, [20] 1–334 [4]; 109 fols, [18] 1–182 [20] (see Kingma and Offenberg, pp. 15–16, no. 13). 54 copies.

11. B.d.Ş., *Opera posthuma* (n.p. [Amsterdam]: [J. Rieuwertsz], 1677). 4°, 404 fols, [41] 2–264 [1] 266–354 [1] 356–392 [2] 395–614 [34] 1–112, figures (see Kingma and Offenberg, pp. 26–7, no. 24). 167 copies.

12. B.d.S., *De nagelate schriften* (n.p. [Amsterdam]: [J. Rieuwertsz], 1677). 4°, 270 fols, [48] [1] 2–300 [1] 302–403 [2] 406–446 [2] 449–666 [2], signature Nn3 misprinted N3, p. 265 misprinted

165, figures (see Kingma and Offenberg, pp. 27–8, no. 25). 45 copies.

13. *Tractatus theologico-politicus* (Hamburg [Amsterdam]: H. Künrath, n.d. [after 1677]). T4. 4°, 123 fols, [12] 1–233 [1], p. 130 misprinted 830 (see Kingma and Offenberg, p. 10, no. 6). 12 copies.

14. *Tractatus theologico-politicus* (Hamburg [Amsterdam]: H. Künrath, n.d. [after 1677]). T5. 4°, 123 fols, [12] 1–233 [1], p. 192 misnumbered 92 (see Kingma and Offenberg, p. 10, no. 7). 11 copies.

15. *La clef du santuaire par un sçavant homme de nôtre siecle* (Leiden: P. Warnaer, 1678). Disguised edition of the *Tractatus theologico-politicus*. X1. 12°, 312 fols, [32] 1–531 [31] 1–30 (see Kingma and Offenberg, pp. 17–18, no. 13). 11 copies.

16. *Reflexions curieuses d'un esprit des-interessé sur les matieres les plus importantes au salut, tant public que particulier* (Cologne: Cl. Emanuel, 1678). Disguised edition of the *Tractatus theologico-politicus*. X2. 12°, 312 fols, [32] 1–531 [21] 1–30 (see Kingma and Offenberg, p. 18, no. 14). 20 copies.

17. *Traitté des ceremonies superstitieuses des juifs tant anciens que modernes* (Amsterdam: J. Smith, 1678). Disguised edition of the *Tractatus theologico-politicus*. X3. 12°, 312 fols, [32] 1–531 [31] 1–30 (see Kingma and Offenberg, pp. 18–19, no. 15). 29 copies.

18. *La clef du sanctuaire par un sçavant homme de nôtre siecle* (Leiden: P. Warnaer, 1678). Disguised edition of the *Tractatus theologico-politicus*. Y1. 12°, 313 fols, [33] 1–531 [31] 1–30 (see Kingma and Offenberg, p. 19, no. 16). 2 copies.

19. *La clef du sanctuaire par un sçavant homme de nôtre siecle* (Leiden:

P. Warnaer, 1678). Disguised edition of the *Tractatus theologico-politicus*. Y2. 12°, 313 fols, [32] 1–531 [31] 1–30 (see Kingma and Offenberg, p. 20, no. 17). 18 identified copies, but many more unidentified copies known.

20. *La cléf du sanctuaire par un sçavant homme de nôtre siecle* (Leiden: P. Warnaer, 1678). Disguised edition of the *Tractatus theologico-politicus*. Y3. 12°, 313 fols, [33] 1–531 [31] 1–30 (see Kingma and Offenberg, pp. 20–1, no. 18). 1 copy.

21. *Reflexions curieuses d'un esprit des-interessé sur les matieres les plus importantes au salut, tant public que particulier; Traitté des ceremonies superstitieuses des juifs tant anciens que modernes* (Cologne/Amsterdam: Cl. Emanuel/J. Smith, 1678). Disguised edition of the *Tractatus theologico-politicus*. Y4, Y5. 12°, 312 fols, [32] 1–531 [31] 1–30 (Kingma and Offenberg, pp. 21, no. 19). 22 copies, but many more unidentified copies known.

22. *Miracles, no Violations of the Laws of Nature*, ed. Ch. Blount (London: R. Sollers at the King's Arms and Bible, 1683). In the main a paraphrase into English of the sixth chapter of the *Tractatus Theologico-Politicus*. With extracts of Hobbes's *Leviathan* and T. Burnett's *Telluris theoria sacra* (London, 1681). 8°, [6] 1–531 [6]. 4 copies.

23. *A Treatise Partly Theological, and Partly Political* (London, 1689). First translation of the *Tractatus theologico-politicus* into English. 8°, 241 fols, [30] 1–452 [31], p. 130 misprinted as 120 (see Kingma and Offenberg, p. 22, no. 20). 35 copies.

24. *De rechtzinnige theologant, of godgeleerde staatkundige verhandelinge*

(Hamburg (Amsterdam): H. Koenraad, 1693). First translation into Dutch of the *Tractatus theologico-politicus*. 4°, 194 fols, [28] 1–360, signature B3 misprinted as A3, p. 204 misprinted 203 (see Kingma and Offenberg, p. 24, no. 22). 14 copies.

25. *Een rechtsinnige theologant, of godgeleerde staatkunde.* Revised reprint of *De rechtzinnige theologant* (Bremen: H.J. von der Weyl, 1694). 4°, 156 fols, [20] 1–289, signature [Ii3] misprinted as [Ii3, p. 191 misprinted as 199 (see Kingma and Offenberg, pp. 24–5, no. 23). 8 copies.

Eighteenth Century
26. *An Account of the Life and Writings of Spinosa. To Which is Added, an Abstract of His Theological Political Treatise* (London: W. Boreham at the Angel in Pater-Noster-Row, 1720). Reprint of the English translation of Colerus's Spinoza biography together with an abstract of the *Tractatus theologico-politicus*. 8°, 50 fols, [5] 2–27 [1] 29–96 (see Kingma and Offenberg, pp. 22–3, no. 21). 8 copies.

27. *A Treatise Partly Theological, and Partly Political* (London, 1737). Second reprint of the English translation of the *Tractatus theologico-politicus*. 8o, [30] 1–452. 7 copies.

28. B.v.S., *Sittenlehre widerleget von dem beruehmten Weltweisen unserer Zeit Herrn Christian Wolf* (Frankfurt/Leipzig, 1744). First German translation of Spinoza's *Ethica* by Johann Lorenz Schmidt. 8°, 389 fols, [3] 4–6 [1] 8–56 [3] 430 339–340 341–540 [1] 542–598 [3] 4–128 (see Kingma and Offenberg, pp. 28–9, no. 26). 13 copies.

29. *Tractatus de primis duodecim Veteris Testamenti libris: in quo ostenditur eos omnes ab uno solo historico scriptos fuisse: deinde inquiritur quisnam is fuerit, et an huic operi ultimam manum imposuerit, idque ut desiderabat, perfecerit* (London, 1763). Extract from the eighth and ninth chapters of the *Tractatus theologico-politicus*. 8°, 52 pp. 9 copies.

30. B. de Spinoza, *Zwey Abhandlungen ueber die Kultur des menschlichen Verstandes und ueber die Aristokratie und Demokratie* (Leipzig: in der Schönfeldschen Handlung, 1785). First German translation of the *Tractatus de intellectus emendatione* and the *Tractatus theologico-politicus*. Preface by S.H. Ewald. 8°, 204 fols, [5] VI–XVI [1] 2–96 [1] 2–32 [1] 34–54 [1] 56–71 [1] 73–212 [1] 214–248 (249–255) [1], p. 222 misprinted 122, pp. 249–255 misprinted 257–263 (see Kingma and Offenberg, p. 29, no. 27). 16 copies.

31. B. de Spinoza, *Philosophische Schriften* (Gera: Chr.Fr. Bekmann, 1787–93). Publication in two volumes of a German translation of Spinoza's posthumous works. 8°, 244 fols, [5] IV–XXII [8] [1] 2–456; 123 fols, [3] II–LXII [1] 2–182 p. 67 misprinted 6; 151 fols, [3] 2–299 (see Kingma and Offenberg, pp. 30–1, no. 28). 19 copies.

32. B. de Spinoza, *Philosophische Schriften* (Leipzig: A.Fr. Böhme, 1796). Reprint of the edition of 1787. 8 copies.

BIBLIOGRAPHY
First Editions of Spinoza's Works
B. de Spinoza, *Renati des Cartes Principia philosophiae* (Amsterdam, 1663).
B. de Spinoza, *Renatus des Cartes Beginzelen der wysbegeerte* (Amsterdam, 1664).
[B. de Spinoza], *Tractatus theologico-politicus* (n.p. (Amsterdam), 1670).

Various editions. Published in 1673 under three different aliases and with false titles: F. Henriquez de Villacorta, *Opera chirurgica omnia* (Amsterdam, 1673); D. Heinsius, *Operum historicorum collectio prima (secunda)* (Leiden, 1673); F. de le Boe Sylvius, *Totius medicinae idea nova* (Amsterdam, 1673).

B.d.S. [B. de Spinoza], *De nagelate schriften* (n.p. (Amsterdam), 1677). Also available as digital publication on the website of the Digitale Bibliotheek voor de Nederlandse Letteren (http://www.dbnl.org/tekst/spin003nage01_01/).

———, *Opera posthuma* (n.p. (Amsterdam), 1677). Facsimile edition: *Opera posthuma: Amsterdam 1677: riproduzione fotografica integrale, complete photographic reproduction*, eds P. Totaro, et al. (Macerata: Quodlibet, 2008). Reproduction of a copy preserved in Rome, Biblioteca dell'Accademia Nazionale di Lincei e Corsiniana (67 D 19). The *Opera posthuma* are also available as digital publication (http://posner.library.cmu.edu/Posner/books/book.cgi?call=199_S75O) on the websites of the Carnegie Mellon University (Pittsburgh), Posner Collection and the Herzog August Bibliothek (Wolfenbüttel).

Reference Works

Freudenthal, J., *Die Lebensgeschichte Spinozas in Quellenschriften, Urkunden und nichtamtlichen Nachrichten* (Leipzig: Von Veit, 1899). Rev. and augm. by M. Walther and M. Czelinski as: *Die Lebensgeschichte Spinozas* (2006).

Huygens, Chr., Œuvres complètes: Correspondance (1638–1684), *vols 1–8 and 22 (The Hague: Nijhoff, 1888–1950). Also available as digital* publication on the website Gallica (Bibliothèque nationale de France).

Kingma, J. and A.K. Offenberg, *Bibliography of Spinoza's Works up to 1800* (Amsterdam: Amsterdam University Library, 1977). Offprint from *Studia Rosenthaliana*, no.11 (1977) pp. 1–32.

Leibniz, G.W., *Sämtliche Schriften und Briefe* (Darmstadt: Reichl, 1923–), quoted as AA.

Meinsma, K.O., *Spinoza en zijn kring. Historisch-kritische studiën over Hollandsche vrijgeesten* (The Hague: Nijhoff, 1896; repr. Utrecht: Hes, 1980).

Oldenburg, H., *Correspondence*, eds A.R. Hall and Marie Boas Hall, 13 vols (Madison, Milwaukee and London: University of Wisconsin Press; Mansell; Taylor and Francis, 1965–85).

Steenbakkers, P., *Spinoza's Ethica from Manuscript to Print. Studies on Text, Form and Related Topics* (Assen: Van Gorcum, 1994).

Vaz Dias, A.M. and W.G. van der Tak, *Spinoza, mercator & autodidactus. Oorkonden en andere authentieke documenten betreffende des wijsgeers jeugd en diens betrekkingen* (The Hague: Nijhoff, 1932). Repr. with many additions in: 'Spinoza. Merchant & Autodidact. Charters and Other Authentic Documents Relating to the Philosopher's Youth and His Relations', *Studia Rosenthaliana*, no. 16 (1982), pp. 105–95.

Walther, M. and M. Czelinski, *Die Lebensgeschichte Spinozas. Lebensbeschreibungen und Dokumente. Zweite, stark erweiterte und vollständig neu kommentierte Auflage der Ausgabe von Jakob Freudenthal 1899* (Stuttgart-Bad Cannstatt: Frommann-Holzboog, 2006).

Primary Sources

Acta der particuliere synoden van Zuid-Holland 1621–1700, ed. W.P.C. Knuttel, 6 vols (The Hague: Nijhoff, 1908–16). Also available as digital publication on the website of the Institute of Netherlands History (http://www.inghist.nl/retroboeken/actazh/).

Borrichius, O., *Itinerarium 1660–1665*, ed. H.D. Schepelern, 4 vols (Copenhagen: Reitzel/Brill, 1983).

Boyle, R., *Certain Physiological Essays, Written at Distant Times, and on Several Occasions* (London, 1661; rev. and augm. edn, London, 1669).

Brom, G., *Archivalia in Italië belangrijk voor de geschiedenis van Nederland: Rome. Vaticaansche Bibliotheek*, vol. 2 (The Hague: Nijhoff, 1911).

Burman, F. Jr, *Burmannorum pietas, gratissimae beati parentis memoriae communi nomine exhibita a Francisco Burmanno, adjiciuntur mutuae Cl. Limburgii & Fr. Burmanni epistolae* (Utrecht, 1700).

Burman, P., *Sylloge epistolarum a viris illustribus scriptarum*, 5 vols (Leiden, 1727).

Chevreau, U., *Chevraeana ou diverses pensées d'histoire, de critique, de érudition et de morale*, 2 vols (Amsterdam, 1700).

Colerus, J., *Korte, dog waarachtige levensbeschryving van Benedictus de Spinosa, uit autentique stukken en mondeling getuigenis van nog levende personen, opgestelt* (Amsterdam, 1705; repr. The Hague: Nijhoff, 1880; The Hague: Nijhoff), 1910.

Deckherr, J., *De scriptis adespotis, pseudepigraphis, et supposititiis conjecturae cum additionibus variorum* (Amsterdam, 1686).

Descartes, R., *Principia philosophiae* (Amsterdam, 1644).

———, *Œuvres*, eds Ch. Adam and P. Tannery, 11 vols (Paris: Cerf, 1897–1913; new edn, Paris: Vrin, 1964–71; repr. Paris: Vrin, 1996).

[Duijkerius, J.], *Het leven van Philopater, opgewiegt in Voetiaensche talmeryen, en groot gemaeckt in de verborgentheden der Coccejanen* (Groningen [Amsterdam], 1691). Edited by G. Maréchal: J. Duijkerius, *Het leven van Philopater & Vervolg van 't leven van Philopater* (Amsterdam: Rodopi, 1991). Also available as digital publication on the website of the Digitale Bibliotheek voor de Nederlandse Letteren (http://www.dbnl.org/auteurs/auteur.php?id=duij002).

———, *Vervolg van 't leven van Philopater. Geredded uit de verborgentheeden der Coccejanen, en geworden een waaragtig wysgeer* (Groningen (Amsterdam), 1697). Published as: J. Duijkerius, *Het leven van Philopater & Vervolg van 't leven van Philopater*, ed. G. Maréchal (Amsterdam: Rodopi, 1991). Also available as digital publication on the website of the Digitale Bibliotheek voor de Nederlandse Letteren (http://www.dbnl.org/auteurs/auteur.php?id=duij002).

Heidegger, J.H., *Historia vitae et obitus Ludovici Fabricii, sanctae memoriae theologi, & consultoris ecclesiastici archapalatini celeberrimi...* (Zürich, 1697).

Hevelius, J., *Cometographia, totam naturam cometarum ... exhibens ... acc. omnium cometarum historia, notis et animadversionibus locupletata, iconibus aeri incisis illustrata* (Danzig, 1668).

———, *Prodromus Cometicus, quo historia, cometae anno 1664 exorti cursum, faciesq[ue] diversas capitis ac caudae accurate delineatas complectens* (Danzig, 1665).

Hooke, R., *Micrographia: or Some Physiological Descriptions of Minute Bodies Made by Magnifying Glasses. With*

Observations and Inquiries Thereupon (London, 1665; repr. London, 1667).

[Hudde, J.], *[Specilla circularia, sive quomodo per solas figuras circulars fieri possint omnis generis specilla, tam microscopia quam telescopia, eundem [planè] effectum habentia, aut saltem quam proxime accedentem ad eorum, quae per ellipsicas aut hyperbolicas figuras]* (n.p., 1665).

Kircher, A., *Mundus subterraneus in XII libros digestus; quo divinum subterrestris mundi opificium, mira ergasteriorum naturae in eo distributio* (Amsterdam, 1664; repr. Amsterdam, 1665).

Lana de Terzi. Fr., *Prodromo overo saggio di alcune inventioni nuove premesse all'arte maestra* (Brescia, 1670).

Leibniz, G.W., *Hypothesis physica nova: quae phaenomenorum naturae plerorumque causae ab unico quodam universali motu, in globo nostro supposito, neque Tychonicis, neque Copernicanis aspernando, repetuntur* (Mainz, 1671).

———, *Essais de théodicée sur la bonté de Dieu, la liberté de l'homme et l'origine du mal*, 2 vols (Amsterdam, 1720; rev. repr. Amsterdam, 1734; repr. Paris: Aubier, 1962; repr. Paris: Garnier-Flammarion, 1969).

[Lucas, J.M.], *La vie et l'esprit de mr Benoit de Spinosa* (Amsterdam, 1719; repr. Hamburg, 1735).

[Meyer, L.], *Philosophia S. Scripturae interpres: exercitatio paradoxa, in quâ, veram philosophiam infallibilem s. literas interpretandi normam esse, apodicticè demonstratur, & discrepantes ab hâc sententiae expenduntur, ac refelluntur* (Eleutheropoli (Amsterdam), 1666; repr. Halle, 1776).

Ott, J.H., *Cogitationes physico-mechanicae de natura visionis* (Heidelberg, 1670).

Pieterse, W.Chr., *Livro de Bet Haim do Kahal Kados de Bet Jahacob* (Assen: Gemeente Amsterdam, Stadsarchief, 1970).

Socinus, F., et al., *Bibliotheca fratrum Polonorum, quos unitarios vocant...* (Irenopoli [Amsterdam], 1668).

Spinoza, B. de, *Benedicti de Spinoza adnotationes ad Tractatum theologico politicum*, ed. Chr.G. von Murr (The Hague, 1802).

———, *Opera quotquot reperta sunt*, eds J. van Vloten and J.P.N. Land, 2 vols (The Hague: Nijhoff, 1882–3).

———, *Opera*, ed. C. Gebhardt, 5 vols (Heidelberg: Winter's Universitätsbuchhandlung, 1925, 1985).

———, *Korte verhandeling van God, de mensch en deszelvs welstand*, ed. F. Mignini (L'Aguila: Japadre Editore, 1986).

——— *Tractatus theologico-politicus/Traité théologico-politique*, ed. F. Akkerman et al. (Paris: Presses Universitaires de France, 1999).

Stensen, N., *Ad virum eruditum, cum quo in unitate S.R.E. desiderat aeternam amicitiam inire. Epistola detegens illorum artes, qui suum de interprete s. scriptura errorem sanctorum patrum testimonio confirmare nituntur* (Florence, 1675).

[Stouppe, J.B.], *La religion des Hollandois, representée en plusieurs lettres écrites par un officier de l'armée du roy, a un pasteur & professeur en theologie de Berne* (Cologne, 1673; Paris, 1673).

Thomasius, J., *Adversus anonymum, de libertate cogitandi...P.P. Dominica rogationum d. 8 Maji anno MDCLXX* (Leipzig, 1670). Also published in Thomasius and Thomasius, 1693, pp. 571–81.

Thomasius, J. and Chr. Thomasius, *Dissertationes LXIII. Varii argumenti magnam partem ad historiam philosophicam & ecclesiasticam pertinentes. Antea a beato autore in*

Academia Lipsiensi intra quadraginta circiter annos per modum Programmatum separatis foliis publicatae (Halle, 1693).

Secondary Literature

Akkerman, F., '*Tractatus theologico-politicus*: texte latin, traductions néerlandaises et *Adnotationes*', in F. Akkerman and P. Steenbakkers (eds), *Spinoza to the Letter* (2005), pp. 209–36.

——, and H.G. Hubbeling, 'The Preface to Spinoza's Posthumous Works 1677 and its Author Jarig Jelles (c.1619/20–1683)', *Lias. Sources and Documents Relating to the Early Modern History of Ideas*, no. 6 (1979), pp. 103–73.

——, and P. Steenbakkers, *Spinoza to the Letter. Studies in Words, Texts and Books* (Leiden and Boston: Brill, 2005).

Aumale, Duc d', *Histoires des Princes de Condé pendant les XVIe et XVIIe siècles*, 7 vols (Paris: Lévy, 1889–96).

Bamberger, F., 'The Early Editions of Spinoza's Tractatus Theologico-Politicus. A Bibliohistorical Examination', *Studies in Bibliography and Booklore*, no. 5 (1961), pp. 9–33.

Borges Coelho, A., *Inquisição de Évora. Dos primórdios A 1668*, 2 vols (Lisbon: Caminho, 1987).

Cristofolini, P., 'La Lettera di Stensen: un falso autore', *Historia philosophica*, no. 6 (2008), pp. 141–4.

Cohen, G., *Le séjour de Saint-Évremond en Hollande et l'entrée de Spinoza dans le champ de la pensée française* (Paris: Champion, 1925). Also published in *Revue de la littérature comparée*, no. 5 (1925), pp. 431–54, no. 6 (1926), pp. 28–78 and 402–23.

Dijksterhuis, F.J., *Lenses and Waves. Christiaan Huygens and the Mathematical Science of Optics in the Seventeenth Century* (Dordrecht: Kluwer, 2004).

Ekkart, R., *Spinoza in beeld. Het onbekende gezicht* (n.p. [Voorschoten]: Het Spinozahuis, 1999).

Feer, L., 'Un pamphlet contre les Hollandois', *Bulletin de la Société de l'Histoire du Protestantisme français*, vol. 31 (1882), pp. 80–91.

Gerritsen, J., 'Vondel and the New Bibliography', in A.R.A. Croiset van Uchelen (ed.), *Hellinga Festschrift/feestbundel/mélanges: Forty-Three Studies in Bibliography Presented to Prof. Wytze Hellinga on the Occasion of His Retirement from the Chair of Neophilology in the University of Amsterdam at the End of the Year 1978* (Amsterdam: Israel, 1980), pp. 205–15.

—— , 'Printing Spinoza – Some Questions', in F. Akkerman and P. Steenbakkers (eds), *Spinoza to the Letter* (2005), pp. 251–62.

Israel, J.I., *Radical Enlightenment: Philosophy and the Making of Modernity 1650–1750* (Oxford: Oxford University Press, 2001).

Jagersma, R. and T. Dijkstra, 'Uncovering Spinoza's Printers by Means of Bibliographical Research', *Quaerendo*. Forthcoming (2014).

Keil, I., 'Die Fernrohre von Herzog Ernst I, dem Frommen, von Sachsen-Gotha', *Beiträge zur Astronomiegeschichte*, no. 2 (1999), pp. 70–9.

Klever, W.N.A., 'Burchard de Volder (1643–1709): A Crypto-Spinozist on a Leiden Cathedra', *Lias. Sources and Documents Relating to the Early Modern History of Ideas*, no. 15 (1988), pp. 191–241.

——, 'Spinoza and Van den Enden in Borch's Diary in 1661 and 1662', *Studia Spinozana*, no. 5 (1989), pp. 311–25.

Müller, K. and G. Krönert, *Leben und Werk von Gottfried Wilhelm Leibniz. Eine Chronik* (Frankfurt am Main: Klostermann, 1969).

Nadler, S., *Spinoza. A Life* (Cambridge: Cambridge University Press, 1999).

Offenberg, A.K., *Brief van Spinoza aan Lodewijk Meijer, 26 juli 1663* (Amsterdam: Universiteitsbibliotheek, 1975). Also published as: 'Letter from Spinoza to Lodewijk Meijer, 27 July 1663', in S. Hessing (ed.), *Speculum Spinozanum* (London: Routledge/ Kegan Paul, 1977), pp. 426–35, and in *Philosophia. Philosophical Quarterly of Israel*, no. 7 (1977), pp. 1–13.

Orcibal, J., 'Les Jansénistes face a Spinoza', *Revue de littérature comparée*, no. 23 (1949), pp. 440–68.

Revah, I.S., *Spinoza et Dr. Juan de Prado* (Paris and The Hague: Mouton, 1959).

Saperstein, M., *Exile in Amsterdam: Saul Levi Morteira's Sermons to a Congregation of 'New Jews'* (Cincinatti: Hebrew Union College Press, 2005).

Schuhmann, K., *Husserl-Chronik. Denk- und Lebensweg Edmund Husserls* (The Hague: Nijhoff, 1977).

——, *Hobbes une chronique. Cheminement de sa pensée et de sa vie* (Paris: Vrin, 1998).

Spruit, L. and P. Totaro (eds), *The Vatican Manuscript of Spinoza's Ethica* (Leiden/ Boston: Brill, 2011).

Steenbakkers, P., J. Touber and J. van de Ven, 'A Clandestine Notebook (1678–79) on Spinoza, Beverland, Politics, the Bible and Sex', *Lias: Journal of Early Modern Intellectual Culture and its Sources*, 38:2 (2011), 41–181.

Totaro, P., 'Documenti su Spinoza nell'Archivio del Sant'Uffizio dell'Inquisizione', *Nouvelles de la République des Lettres*, no. 1 (2000), pp. 95–128.

——, '"Ho certi amici in Ollandia": Stensen and Spinoza – Science Verso Faith', in K. Ascani et al. (eds), *Niccolò Stenone (1638–1686): anatomista, geologo, vescovo. Atti della seminario organizatto da Universitetsbiblioteket i Tromso e l'Accademia di Danimarci, lunedì 23 ottobre 2000* (Rome: 'L'Erna' di Bretschneider, 2002), pp. 27–38.

Van de Ven, J.M.M., '"Crastinâ die loquar cum Celsissimo principe de Spinosa". New Perspectives on Spinoza's Visit to the French Army Headquarters in Utrecht in Late July 1673' *Intellectual History Review*. Forthcoming (2014).

——, *Spinoza. Facts in Focus. An Intellectual Chronology of the Life and Times of Benedictus de Spinoza Based upon Historical Documents*. In preparation (2014/2015).

Vermij, R. and E.J. Atzema, 'Specilla Circularia: An Unknown Work by Johannes Hudde,' *Studia Leibnitiana*, no. 27 (1995), pp. 104–21.

Vlessing, O., 'The Excommunication of Baruch Spinoza. A Conflict Between Jewish and Dutch Law', *Studia Spinozana*, no. 13 (1997), pp. 15–47.

[Wichers, L.], 'De grafplaatsen van de De Witten en Spinoza in de Nieuwe Kerk', *Jaarboekje Die Haghe*, no. 1 (1889), pp. 53–7.

Wildeman, M.G., 'Nog iets over de grafplaatsen van de De Witten en Spinoza in de Nieuwe Kerk', *Jaarboekje Die Haghe*, no. 5 (1893), pp. 117–21.

Zuidervaart, H.J., *Telescopes From Leiden Observatory and Other Collections 1656–1859. A Descriptive Catalogue* (Leiden: Museum Boerhaave, 2007).

Jeroen van de Ven

2

INFLUENCES

INTRODUCTION

In his writings Spinoza hardly ever refers to authorities. Such an appeal to external testimonies would be out of place in the synthetic argument of the *Ethics*, but he does not, as a rule, document his sources in his other works either. This reluctance to buttress an argument with quotations is part of a rhetorical strategy (Lagrée, 2005). It does not mean that Spinoza started from scratch. His thought emerged under the influence of and in reaction to philosophical traditions. Given the paucity of known facts about Spinoza's life, and his own reticence about sources, any assessment of the influences that contributed to his philosophical development must remain tentative. H.A. Wolfson notoriously claimed that 'if we could cut up all the philosophic literature available to [Spinoza] into slips of paper, toss them up into the air, and let them fall back on the ground, then out of these scattered slips of paper we could reconstruct his *Ethics*' (Wolfson, 1934, vol. 1, p. 3). In spite of the impressive scholarship displayed in Wolfson's hefty and still precious study, this reductionist approach does not do justice to Spinoza's philosophy (cf. Gueroult, 1968, p. 442). Nor does it contribute to an understanding of the sources of Spinozism.

There are a few philosophers whose influence on Spinoza is beyond dispute: Descartes, Maimonides. Even then, it remains difficult to assess what they contributed to his own thought. As will become clear from the following contributions, adopting another philosopher's terminology and assumptions did not mean that Spinoza agreed with them. One way of responding to a formative intellectual tradition is to transcend and undermine it, by developing the implications of a certain position and transforming it into an entirely different theory.

In this section a number of sources of Spinoza's thought will be presented and their impact explored: Jewish philosophers (Maimonides, Crescas, Abrabanel, Menasseh ben Israel and Delmedigo), Descartes, Stoicism, the seventeenth-century neo-scholastics Burgersdijk and Heereboord, and Spinoza's teacher Van den Enden. The list is far from exhaustive. Thus, there are no entries on Giordano Bruno (1548–1600), Uriel da Costa (c. 1583–1640) or Arnold Geulincx (1624–69). For all three of them, good arguments may be (and have been) given why they could have influenced Spinoza's thought, but so far no evidence has been produced that they actually did (for Bruno, see Spruit, 2008; for Da Costa: Osier, 1983, especially pp. 77–97, and Nadler, 2001, pp. 165–73; for

Geulincx: Van Ruler, 2006). Similarly, no entries on scholasticism have been included, apart from those on Burgersdijk and Heereboord. Spinoza certainly knew and read scholastic sources, and turned them to advantage (Coppens, 2003; *Spinoza and Late Scholasticism*, 2008). Bar Burgersdijk and Heereboord, however, it is impossible to determine what his sources were. The situation is somewhat different for Machiavelli, Francis Bacon and Hobbes. They are occasionally mentioned by Spinoza, he had works by these authors on his bookshelves, and there are similarities that reveal influences of some sort. For Bacon, the connection is superficial. Spinoza did study Machiavelli intensively, and mentions him with respect in the TP (5.7, 10.1). Yet the extent of Machiavelli's influence is unclear, and it is difficult to distinguish between direct and indirect sources here: Spinoza was also acquainted with the work of Pieter and Johan de la Court, who may have been intermediaries in the connection between Spinoza and republican Machiavellian thought (Steenbakkers, 2010, pp. 44–5, Morfino, 2002, p. 260; for Machiavelli and Spinoza, see also Gallicet Calvetti, 1972). Hobbes and Spinoza knew each other's works, and in the TTP Spinoza obviously reacts to the *Leviathan* (Verbeek, 2003). Here again, however, it is not evident what Spinoza had read of Hobbes and how the influence is to be assessed (see *Spinoza and Hobbes*, 1987; and in particular Schuhmann, 2004).

Spinoza was acquainted in a general way with the major philosophical currents of Antiquity. An affinity between his views and Stoicism has often been postulated; an entry is here included on Stoic aspects of Spinoza's philosophy. Plato and Aristotle are hardly ever mentioned by Spinoza, and when he does refer to them, it is to express his dislike

(Ep 56). Yet this does not imply that his own philosophy is not in any way indebted to (neo-)Platonism and Aristotelianism. One important source for neo-Platonic elements in his work is the Renaissance philosopher Abrabanel, known as Leone Ebreo (see Gebhardt, 1921). He will be dealt with in the contribution on Jewish influences. There are no signs that Spinoza studied Plato's works, but a passage in CM 2.7 shows that he did read Aristotle (Manzini, 2009). In spite of Spinoza's explicit praise of Epicurus and Lucretius (Ep 56), so far little research has been done into Epicurean elements in his philosophy (Moreau, 2006). Correspondences between Spinoza and scepticism, on the other hand, have been explored, notably by Richard Popkin (1979).

Inevitably there will be gaps in any survey of the sources that may have influenced Spinoza. This part of the *Companion* focuses on the most obvious philosophers and currents, while acknowledging that other choices would have been defensible. The reader who wants to pursue different tracks will find suggestions for further reading in the bibliography.

BIBLIOGRAPHY
Ayers, M., 'Spinoza, Platonism and Naturalism', in M. Ayers (ed.), *Rationalism, Platonism and God* (Oxford: Oxford University Press, 2007), pp. 53–78.
Coppens, G. (ed.), *Spinoza en de scholastiek* (Leuven and Amersfoort: Acco, 2003).
Gallicet Calvetti, C., *Spinoza lettore del Machiavelli* (Milan: Università Cattolica del Sacro Cuore, 1972).
Gebhardt, C., 'Spinoza und der Platonismus', *Chronicon Spinozanum*, no. 1 (1921), pp. 178–234.

Gueroult, M., *Spinoza I. Dieu (Éthique I)* (Hildesheim: Olms, 1968).

Lagrée, J., 'La citation dans le Traité théologico-politique', in F. Akkerman and P. Steenbakkers (eds), *Spinoza to the Letter: Studies in Words, Texts and Books* (Leiden: Brill, 2005), pp. 107–124.

Manzini, F., *Spinoza: Une lecture d'Aristote* (Paris: Presses Universitaires de France, 2009).

Moreau, P.-F., *Problèmes du spinozisme* (Paris: Vrin, 2006), pp. 15–26.

Morfino, V., *Il tempo e l'occasione: l'incontro Spinoza-Machiavelli* (Milan: LED, 2002).

Nadler, S., *Spinoza's Heresy: Immortality and the Jewish Mind* (Oxford: Oxford University Press, 2001).

Osier, J.-P., *D'Uriel da Costa à Spinoza* (Paris: Berg, 1983).

Popkin, R.H., *The History of Scepticism from Erasmus to Spinoza* (Berkeley: University of California Press, 1979), pp. 229–48.

Ruler, H. van, 'Geulincx and Spinoza: Books, Backgrounds and Biographies', *Studia Spinozana*, no. 15 (1999; published 2006), pp. 89–106.

Schuhmann, K. (2004), 'Methodenfragen bei Spinoza und Hobbes: Zum Problem des Einflusses', in K. Schuhmann, *Selected papers on Renaissance Philosophy and on Thomas Hobbes*, ed. P. Steenbakkers and C. Leijenhorst (Dordrecht: Kluwer), pp. 45–71.

Spinoza and Hobbes. Special issue of *Studia Spinozana*, no. 3 (1987).

Spinoza and Late Scholasticism. Special issue of *Studia Spinozana*, no. 16 (2008).

Spruit, L., 'Bruno en Spinoza: substantie en gelukzaligheid', in C. van Heertum (ed.), *Libertas philosophandi: Spinoza als gids voor een vrije wereld* (Amsterdam: In de Pelikaan, 2008), pp. 166–182.

Steenbakkers, P., 'Spinoza leest Machiavelli', in A.C. Klugkist and J. van Sluis (eds) *Spinoza: zijn boeken en zijn denken* (Voorschoten: Uitgeverij Spinozahuis, 2010), pp. 35–54.

Verbeek, Th., *Spinoza's Theologico-political Treatise: Exploring 'the Will of God'* (Aldershot: Ashgate, 2003).

Wolfson, H. A., *The Philosophy of Spinoza*, 2 vols (Cambridge, MA: Harvard University Press, 1934).

P. Steenbakkers

BURGERSDIJK, Franck Pieterszoon (1590–1635)

Burgersdijk had an influence on Spinoza through the philosophical manuals in which he offers a methodically ordered epitome of neo-scholastic learning. In the seventeenth century, these manuals were widely used in the Protestant universities. Adapting the *Corpus Aristotelicum* to the humanist method, they fulfilled the demands of the early modern teaching of philosophy as required by the religious and civil authorities in Protestant countries.

Franck Pieterszoon Burgersdijk (Burgersdicius) was born in 1590 at De Lier, near Delft. In 1610 he matriculated at Leiden University, where he attended public lectures on Greek, physics and theology, as well as private lectures given by Gomarus and Voetius, who was to become the informal leader of strict Calvinism between 1640 and his death in 1676. In 1614, Burgersdijk went to the Protestant Academy of Saumur, where he studied theology, again under Gomarus. In 1619 he was appointed professor of logic in Leiden, filling one of the vacancies caused by the purges of the university after the Synod of Dordt. From 1620, he also taught ethics.

Burgersdijk's teaching raised the level and the status of philosophy in the Dutch universities. His manuals covered the whole of philosophy, and transformed it from a propaedeutic discipline into a body of knowledge independent of theology and philology. Only a month after the delivery of his inaugural address he presided over a disputation that rejected the doctrine of the double truth and defended the inalienable rights of philosophy with respect to theology. Burgersdijk, who adopted Aquinas's view of the relationship between these disciplines, argued that although theological dogma may exceed the limits of human reason, philosophy as such is free from error. That is why the pagan Aristotle was the greatest philosopher. In the same vein, Burgersdijk fully acknowledged the authority of Iberian neo-scholasticism and of other Roman Catholic philosophers. Wundt's and Dibon's suggestion that Burgersdijk attempted to create a Calvinist philosophy is therefore to be rejected. The predominance of this attitude towards philosophy also contributed to the rapid acceptance of Cartesianism in the Dutch Republic. Burgersdijk lectured on physics as well, and in 1628 he exchanged the chair of moral philosophy for that of physics. In 1630, in his capacity as rector of Leiden university, he enrolled Descartes as student of mathematics. Burgersdijk died on 8 February 1635.

Burgersdijk's most successful work was his manual of logic, which went through many reprints throughout the seventeenth century, and was used by Spinoza for his exposition of the concept of causality. The recommendations of the national Synod of Dordt to the States General included a call for reforming the Latin Schools and the teaching of logic and rhetoric. The school regulations promulgated in 1625, the so-called *Schoolordre* ('School order'), demanded an outline of logic and a full-scale textbook on that subject. Both books were commissioned from Burgersdijk.

Burgersdijk's textbook of metaphysics, *Institutionum metaphysicarum libri II*, was published posthumously. That Spinoza knew this manual well and made good use of it, albeit critically, in developing his own terminology is attested by a number of implicit references in KV, E and CM. Trendelenburg (1867, pp. 317–25) noted that Spinoza's division of the efficient cause in KV 1.3 and E1p16–18 is taken from Burgersdijk's *Institutiones logicae* 1.17. In his pioneering study 'Spinoza und die Scholastik' Freudenthal showed that Spinoza extensively used Burgersdijk's *Institutiones metaphysicae* in his CM. After observing that Spinoza adopted the dichotomy of metaphysics in a general and particular part from Burgersdijk and late scholasticism in general, he points out that in CM 2 Spinoza deals with almost the same attributes of God as does Burgersdijk, be it in a slightly different order, viz. eternity, unity, immensity, immutability, simplicity, life, intellect, will, power, creation and concurrence (CM 2.1–11). In Burgersdijk we find: necessity, unity, eternity, immensity, simplicity, immutability, life and intellect, will and power, creation and concurrence (Freudenthal, 1887, p. 110). Both Freudenthal and

Coppens explain Spinoza's interest in late scholasticism as a result of the inadequacies of the theology of Descartes, who never 'wrote a well structured theology', and thus failed to offer an adequate treatment of the divine attributes (Coppens, 2004, p. 19). It should be noted, however, that Spinoza often refers to Burgersdijk in a polemical vein. Thus, though Burgersdijk's theory of inter-mediate being (*Institutiones metaphysicae* 1.3) is crucial for his metaphysics, Spinoza dismisses it curtly in CM 1.1, and Burgers-dijk's proofs of God's attributes in *Institu-tiones metaphysicae* 2.6–7 come in for sarcastic commentary twice: 'We have often wondered at the futile arguments by which some have sought to establish the unity of God' (CM 2.2); and 'when authors deal with God's *Immensity*, they seem to ascribe quan-tity to him...which is most absurd.'

BIBLIOGRAPHY

Primary Sources

Idea philosophiae naturalis, sive methodus definitionum et controversiarum (Leiden, 1622, 1643, 1652; Dutch trans. A.L. Kók, Amsterdam, 1648).

Idea philosophiae moralis, sive compendiosa institutio (Leiden, 1623; Oxford, 1631).

Institutionum logicarum libri II decreto D.D. Ordinum Hollandiae et West-Frisiae, novâ methodo ac modo formati, atque editi (Leiden, 1626, 1637, 1648, 1651, 1653; Dutch trans. A.L. Kók, Amsterdam, 1646; English trans. as *Monitio Logica or an Abstract and Translation of Burgersdicius his Logick*, London, 1697).

Collegium physicum disputationibus XXXII absolutum (Leiden, 1632, 1650, 1664;

Dutch trans. A.L. Kók, Amsterdam, 1648).

Institutionum logicarum synopsis, sive rudimenta logica (Leiden, 1632, 1637, 1646, 1659, 1661, 1716; Dutch trans. A.L. Kók, Amsterdam, 1646).

Institutionum metaphysicarum libri II (Leiden, 1640, 1651, 1653, 1657, 1675).

Idea oeconomicae et politicae doctrinae (Leiden, 1644, 1723).

Secondary Literature

Bos, E.P. and H.A. Krop (eds), *Franco Burgersdijk (1590–1635): Neo-Aristotelianism in Leiden* (Amsterdam: Rodopi, 1993).

Coppens, G., 'Spinoza et la conception scolastique de Dieu dans le contexte hollandais', in Chantal Jaquet (ed.), *Les Pensées Métaphysiques de Spinoza* (Paris: Sorbonne, 2004), pp. 19–36.

Dibon, P.A.G., *La philosophie néerlandaise au siècle d'or: L'enseignement philosophique dans les universités à l'époque précartésienne (1575–1650)* (Paris and Amsterdam: Elzevier, 1954), pp. 99–136.

Freudenthal, J., 'Spinoza und die Scholastik', in *Philosophische Aufsätze Eduard Zeller gewidmet* (Leipzig: Fues's Verlag, 1887), pp. 85–138.

Ruestow, E.G., *Physics at 17th and 18th-Century Leiden* (The Hague: Mouton, 1973), pp. 14–33.

Trendelenburg, A., *Historische Beiträge zur Philosophie III* (Berlin: Bethge, 1867).

Wundt, M., *Die deutsche Schulmetaphysik des 17. Jahrhunderts* (Tübingen: Mohr, 1939), pp. 87–9.

H. Krop

DESCARTES, René (1596–1650)

Note – This section incorporates substantial parts, at times *verbatim*, of the account of Descartes's life and works as given in Verbeek 2003, with the generous permission of the author.

Descartes is the philosopher to whom Spinoza is most indebted. Even though he never was a Cartesian in any strict sense, the impact of the French philosopher is unmistakable. Spinoza owned Descartes's works (in several editions) and he may have had access to a manuscript of the then as yet unpublished *Regulae ad directionem ingenii*. As his own works testify, he studied Cartesianism attentively, perceptively and critically. Throughout Spinoza's philosophical development, the heritage of Descartes is omnipresent – from the terminology, issues and approaches in Spinoza's early works (the epistemology in TIE, the inventory of the passions in KV, the metaphysics in PPC and CM) to the sincere esteem for and incisive critique of Descartes in his mature philosophy (E3praef, E5praef). The intellectual environment in which Spinoza moved was thoroughly Cartesian. For his friends and many of his correspondents, Descartes's achievements constituted the frame of reference for all matters philosophical and scientific. In the second half of the seventeenth century, Dutch Cartesianism, in its many shades and varieties, was a robust and most influential current – more so than anywhere else (Thijssen-Schoute, 1950). As Verbeek put it: Descartes spent the greater part of his life in the country, discussed his projects mainly with his Dutch friends (among them Beeckman, Huygens, Golius, Reneri, Regius), and almost all his works were conceived, written and printed in the Netherlands; his philosophy was discussed and taught at Dutch universities right from the start, and Dutch philosophers made Cartesianism part of the intellectual and academic tradition in philosophy; Dutch translations of all of Descartes's works gave him a large popular audience (Verbeek, 2003, p. 258). For a philosopher like Spinoza, Cartesianism inevitably was the most important formative influence.

René Descartes (in Latin: Renatus Cartesius) was born on 31 March 1596 in La Haye (now named Descartes) in Touraine. He was presumably destined to follow his father's career and become a lawyer. He was sent to the Jesuit college of La Flèche, then to the University of Poitiers, where he obtained a degree in Law in 1616. After a period of indecision Descartes headed for the Netherlands, presumably at the beginning of 1618, and took service in the army of Maurice of Nassau in Breda. Towards the end of 1618 he met Isaac Beeckman, with whom he discussed questions of mathematics, music and harmony, and the law of falling bodies.

In Germany, where he travelled for the two following years, Descartes had a dream which he interpreted as both a divine command and a confirmation of his intuition of a general science of quantity and proportion, in relation to which other mathematical sciences (arithmetic, geometry, algebra, music, etc.) would be no more than applications. After travels in Italy and a sojourn in Paris, where he worked on optics and mathematics and wrote an unfinished book on method, the *Regulae ad directionem ingenii*, Descartes returned to the Netherlands, briefly in October 1628, then definitively in the spring of 1629. In the next five years, he lived in Franeker, moved to Amsterdam, Deventer and back to Amsterdam again. He worked on algebra, dioptrics, metaphysics, 'meteorology' (all natural phenomena between the earth and the moon) and general physics. Meanwhile he became friends with various Dutch personalities: Henricus Reneri (1593–1639), professor of philosophy in Deventer and Utrecht, Jacob Golius, professor of oriental languages and mathematics at the university of Leiden, Constantijn Huygens (1596–1678), the personal secretary of the Stadholder, and David le Leu de Wilhem (1588–1658), a rich and influential sponsor. All tried to persuade Descartes that he should go back on his decision never to publish anything. Descartes began writing a text, consisting of three 'essays', on dioptrics, meteors and geometry, preceded by a general 'discourse on method' (the part we usually refer to as *Discours de la méthode*). It was published in 1637 in Leiden. Descartes had included a summary of his metaphysics in the *Discours*, but its briefness created confusion and provoked criticism. He began writing an elaborated version, which gradually developed into the *Meditationes de prima philosophia*. Descartes hoped to make the acceptance of his views easier by including six sets of 'objections and replies'. The book was published in 1641 in Paris. Louis Elzevier (1604–70) of Amsterdam offered to produce a second edition, which was ready in January 1642. By that time Descartes had become involved in a conflict over his philosophy at the university of Utrecht. Theses submitted by his friend, the professor of medicine Henricus Regius, aroused the anger of the theological faculty, especially of Voetius, who was also the university's *rector magnificus*. A row broke out which ended with a formal condemnation of 'new philosophy' and the relegation of Regius to the medical faculty. In about the same period the Jesuits, in particular Pierre Bourdin (1595–1653), submitted objections to the *Meditations* which Descartes found futile. Accordingly, Descartes used the second edition of the *Meditations* to include, not only the objections of Bourdin, with his replies, but also an open letter to the Provincial of the Jesuits in Paris to complain about Bourdin, whom he tried to dissociate from his order, as well as about Voetius. These *Seventh Objections and Replies* and the *Letter to Dinet* were printed as an 'appendix' to the *Meditations* and published in the spring of 1642. Now it was Voetius's turn to be furious. He engaged Schoock to undertake his defence, which the latter did by writing the *Admiranda methodus* (1643; see also Descartes and Schoock, 1988). Descartes initially ascribed the authorship to Voetius and started writing a reaction. It resulted in an open letter to Voetius (the *Epistola ad Voetium*).

Even before finishing the *Meditations* Descartes had started a different project, viz. the publication of the principles of his philosophy. The plan was to a certain extent polemical: Descartes wanted to include a refutation of scholastic philosophy. Supplementary motives were that the book would give Descartes's philosophy a didactic format. What eventually came out of it was a systematic presentation of Descartes's own philosophy in four parts: (1) metaphysical and cognitive principles; (2) the principles of nature (laws of motion, etc.); (3) the structure of the universe (celestial physics); (4) an explanation of physical phenomena such as fermentation, magnetism, etc. Parts on plants, animals and man were planned but could not be realized because of Descartes's lack of empirical and experimental data. The work, which was called *Principia philosophiae*, was published in 1644. A French translation by Claude Picot, which deviates from the Latin original on some important points, came out in Paris in 1647.

The correspondence with Princess Elisabeth of Bohemia, which started in 1643, was the occasion of Descartes's last work, *Les Passions de l'âme*. The more precise occasion was her request for an exact 'definition' of the passions. The text was published in 1649. Meanwhile Descartes had left the Netherlands for Sweden. However, the lessons in mathematics Queen Christina required him to give her in the early morning hours (5 a.m.) proved fatal to Descartes. On 11 February 1650 he expired in the arms of the French ambassador, Chanut, presumably from pneumonia.

It is unknown how and when Spinoza became acquainted with the new philosophy in general and Descartes's works in particular. The philosophy taught at the Jewish school he attended, *Ets Haim*, focused on commentaries of the Torah, Mishna and Talmud. This is where he studied Maimonides and other medieval thinkers. There he may have encountered the works of classical and Renaissance philosophers, too. The earliest known letter to Spinoza, written by Henry Oldenburg in August 1661 (Ep 1), refers to a discussion they had about the philosophies of Descartes and Bacon. In his reply (Ep 2), Spinoza explains his objections: Descartes and Bacon have no knowledge of the first cause and origin of all things, nor of the true nature of the mind, nor of the true cause of error. He specifically criticizes Descartes's notion of the free will, which in his view is a mere mental construct (*ens rationis*). This topic surfaces again and again in the correspondence (Ep 21, 57, 58). In his preface to the PPC (1663) Lodewijk Meyer explicitly mentions the free will as one of the issues in which Spinoza departs from Descartes (cf. also Ep 15). Meyer himself can be considered a Cartesian (Thijssen-Schoute, 1954), but his *Philosophia S. Scripturae interpres* (1666) shows that the term applies only in a very loose sense. Meyer sees not only his own *Interpres* but also the – then still unpublished – philosophy of Spinoza as a radical expansion of the Cartesian programme. This is why Meyer, in the epilogue to his book, announces the publication of Spinoza's *Ethica* as a further development of the Cartesian project (Meyer, 1666, final page, unnumbered).

In this very broad and liberal interpretation, Cartesianism was a matter of sharing notions and a rational method rather than a set of well-defined philosophical tenets. It could thus include thinkers like Meyer and Spinoza, in spite of their rejection of positions dear to Descartes himself: unlike the French philosopher, Meyer and Spinoza refused to leave God and the soul to theology, but turned these into eminently philosophical issues instead. Faced with the *odium theologicum* provoked by the publication of such works as Meyer's *Interpres*, Spinoza's TTP and Hobbes's *Leviathan*, 'stupid Cartesians' in the Netherlands were eager to dissociate themselves from Spinoza, as the latter complained in a letter to Oldenburg (Ep 68). Reformed orthodoxy, however, kept suspecting that ultimately Cartesianism and Spinozism were of a kind. The case was very explicitly stated half a century later by Johannes Regius, in his *Cartesius verus Spinozismi architectus* (1719): all Spinozists had initially started out as Cartesians, and the Cartesian system would collapse unless it adopted Spinozistic principles, in particular the identification of God and the world and the concomitant necessity of natural laws. There may have been some truth in Regius's stepping-stone theory, but it certainly did not hold for Spinoza himself.

What, then, is the extent of Descartes's influence on Spinoza? In order to answer this question, it should be kept in mind that Spinoza and Descartes found themselves in very different philosophical contexts. Descartes's reluctant involvement with metaphysics was motivated by his search for certain knowledge, which – as he saw it – required a radical separation of the physical and the mental realms, a God who had freely created a law-governed world, and a free will in human beings that would account for the emergence of error. Spinoza's starting point was an ethical issue: the place of human beings within nature as a whole – how does everything interconnect, and what does that entail for human behaviour? Making use of a basically Cartesian metaphysical framework of substance, attributes and modes, Spinoza came to conclusions squarely opposite to those reached by Descartes. If substance is 'nothing other than a thing which exists in such a way as to depend on no other thing for its existence', then 'there is only one substance which can be understood to depend on no other thing whatsoever, namely God', as Descartes himself had observed (*Principia* 1.51). Spinoza takes this definition of substance to its logical conclusion: God is the only substance, and everything else must exist *in* substance, that is to say as a mode of substance. This overturns Cartesian metaphysics: God cannot be a creator, and his causality can only be an immanent one. The fundamental disagreement between Descartes and Spinoza is also mirrored in the clashing structures of the *Meditations* and the *Ethics*. Descartes starts with doubt (for which there is no room in Spinoza's theory: Mason, 1993), continues with the human mind, and then moves on to the existence of God. The rest follows – culminating in the existence of the physical world and the (qualified) reliability of human knowledge of that world. Spinoza's trajectory is the reverse: starting from God, from whose essence all things must necessarily follow (E2praef), he moves on to the human mind. What follows is the underpinning not of knowledge, but of ethics.

If Spinoza's reception of Cartesian metaphysics is predominantly a negative one – adopting the terminology and some of its basic assumptions only in order to reject its consequences – he generally seems to accept Descartes's physics. Though he occasionally (Ep 31, 32, 81) criticizes the rules of collision set forth in *Principia* 2.46–52, Spinoza does adopt them, apparently without reservation, not only in his PPC (2p24–31), but also in the so-called physical excursus after E2p13 (see Van der Hoeven, 1973).

Cartesian epistemology, with its emphasis on clear and distinct perceptions, and its opposition between imagination and the pure intellect, undergoes a considerable transformation in the philosophy of Spinoza. The importance Spinoza attaches to the uses of the imagination (in the chapters on prophecy in the TTP, and in his theory of the affects in E3–4) and his un-Cartesian account of the origins of error make his epistemology distinctly different, in spite of the similarity in terminology.

In the course of his philosophical development, Spinoza changed his mind about the psychological theories propounded by Descartes in *Les Passions de l'âme*. Whereas the inventory of the passions presented in this work and the bulk of their descriptions were more or less directly imported into the KV, Spinoza offers an entirely new theory of the affects in E3. As a corollary of his critique of the Cartesian doctrine of the affects, Spinoza also dissociates himself from what he designates as the Stoic view that passions can be controlled (E5praef). The Stoic example he gives is that of two dogs undergoing a different training; it was taken from Descartes's *Passions* 1.50. The theory of the pineal gland as the connection between body and soul, which Descartes had put forward in *Les Passions*, is analysed and repudiated in E5praef. Spinoza's critique here is intimately connected with his view of the unity of body and mind.

Summing up: Spinoza's philosophy would have been unthinkable (in a strong sense) without the legacy of Descartes. Yet the two systems are incompatible: however much Spinoza's thought owed to Descartes's, it cannot be reduced to a variety of Cartesianism.

BIBLIOGRAPHY
Primary Sources
Descartes, R., *Œuvres de Descartes*, ed. Ch. Adam and P. Tannery, 11 vols (Paris: Cerf, 1897–1913).
———, *The Philosophical Writings of Descartes*, trans. John Cottingham et al., 3 vols (Cambridge: Cambridge University Press, 1985–91).
Descartes, R. and M. Schoock, *La Querelle d'Utrecht*, ed. Th. Verbeek (Paris: Les impressions nouvelles, 1988).
Meyer, L., *Philosophia S. Scripturæ interpres: Exercitatio paradoxa* (Amsterdam, 1666).
Regius, J., *Cartesius verus Spinozismi architectus* (Franeker, 1719).
Schoock, M., *Admiranda methodus novae philosophiae Renati Des-Cartes* (Utrecht, 1643).

Secondary Literature
Brunschvicg, L., 'Descartes,' in idem, *Spinoza et ses contemporains*, 4th ed. (Paris: Presses Universitaires de France, 1951), pp. 153–93.
Clarke, D.M., *Descartes: A Biography* (Cambridge: Cambridge University Press, 2006).
Cottingham, J., *Cartesian Reflections: Essays on Descartes's Philosophy* (Oxford: Oxford University Press, 2008).
Descartes – Spinoza. Special issue of *Les études philosophiques*, no. 71 (2004).
Gueroult, M., *Spinoza, I: Dieu (Éthique, I)* (Paris: Aubier-Montaigne, 1968), pp. 529–56.
———, *Spinoza, II: L'Âme (Éthique, II)* (Paris: Aubier-Montaigne, 1974), pp. 619–25.
Hoeven, P. van der, 'Over Spinoza's interpretatie van de cartesiaanse fysica, en de betekenis daarvan voor het systeem der *Ethica*', *Tijdschrift voor filosofie*, no. 35 (1973), pp. 27–86.
Mason, R. V., 'Ignoring the Demon? Spinoza's Way with Doubt', *Journal of the History of Philosophy*, no. 31 (1993), pp. 545–64.
Moreau, P.-F., 'Spinoza et Descartes,' in idem, *Problèmes du spinozisme* (Paris: Vrin, 2006), pp. 32–50.
Specht, R., 'Spinozas Umgestaltung der Grundthesen Descartes',' in idem, *Innovation und Folgelast: Beispiele aus der neueren Philosophie- und Wirtschaftsgeschichte* (Stuttgart-Bad Cannstatt: Frommann-Holzboog, 1972), pp. 137–84.
Spinoza and Descartes. Special issue of *Studia Spinozana*, no. 10 (1994).
Thijssen-Schoute, C. L., 'Le Cartésianisme aux Pays-Bas', in E.J. Dijksterhuis et al. (eds), *Descartes et le cartésianisme hollandais* (Paris: Presses Universitaires de France/Amsterdam: Éditions

Françaises d'Amsterdam, 1950),
pp. 183–260.

Thijssen-Schoute, C. L., *Lodewijk
Meyer en diens verhouding tot
Descartes en Spinoza* (Leiden:
Brill, 1954).

Verbeek, Th., 'Descartes', in W. van Bunge
et al. (eds), *The Dictionary of Seventeenth
and Eighteenth-Century Dutch
Philosophers* (Bristol: Thoemmes, 2003),
pp. 254–60.

P. Steenbakkers

ENDEN, Franciscus van den (1602–74)

Franciscus van den Enden was baptized on
6 February 1602, in Antwerp, where he
attended the Augustinian College and the
Jesuit College. In 1619 he entered the Jesuit
noviciate in Mechelen. He studied philosophy at Leuven and grammar at Antwerp, and
then served as a teacher at different Jesuit
colleges in Flanders. In 1629 he returned to
Leuven to study theology, but on 15 May
1633 he was dismissed from the order for
unclear reasons. Van den Enden then apparently became an associate of the Spanish
Austin Friar Bartlomé de los Rios y Alarcon,
propagator of Marian devotion and, as con-
fessor to the Infanta Isabella, a powerful figure at the Brussels court. Sometime between
1637 and 1641 Van den Enden obtained a
degree in Medicine, but it is not known
where. In this period Van den Enden also
became involved in the art trade of his
younger brother, the famous Antwerp print
publisher Martinus van den Enden I.

In 1640 Van den Enden married Clara
Maria Vermeeren in Antwerp. They had

seven children, of whom only three daugh-
ters reached maturity. In the middle of the
1640s Van den Enden and his family moved
to Amsterdam. There he frequented artists'
circles, set up his own art shop and acted as
a publisher, mainly of prints, including
images of canonized Roman Catholic mar-
tyrs. In 1650, very likely prompted by the
recent tensions between Stadholder William
II and the States of Holland, he also published at least one political pamphlet, *Korte
verthooninghe* (Brief demonstration), which
had been written in the 1580s by François
Vranck to defend the sovereignty of Holland
and West-Friesland against the rule of the
Earl of Leicester. Spinoza referred to this
pamphlet in TTP 18, in the same context.
When in 1652 Van den Enden's art shop
went bankrupt, he probably went back to
teaching.

The first evidence that Van den Enden ran
a Latin School dates from February 1654,
when his pupils performed parts of Virgil's
Aeneid for the marriage of Cornelia van
Vlooswijk, the daughter of one of the Amsterdam Burgomasters. Among Van den Enden's
pupils were Nicolaes and Johan van Vloos-
wijck, Romeyn de Hooghe, Pieter Rixtel,
Jan van Elslandt, Albert Burgh, Theodoor
Kerckring, and Benedictus de Spinoza. Van
den Enden became most closely associated
with Kerckring, who became his son-in-law,
and who was involved in the conspiracy
against Louis XIV that would cost Van den
Enden his life.

Between 1665 and 1667 Van den Enden
became acquainted with some discontented
French nobles. In 1671, probably at their
instigation, he moved to Paris. There he
opened another Latin School, the *Hôtel des
Muses*. In 1672 Van den Enden married
Catharina Medaens, and in that same year –
the Dutch 'Year of Disaster' – the French

invaded the Republic. This calamity probably prompted Van den Enden to push ahead with the bold enterprise that would cost him his life. Together with le Sieur de Rohan and De Latréaumont, he plotted to assassinate Louis XIV, kidnap the Dauphin, stir up a rebellion in Normandy and install a 'free republic' in France. The popular revolt did not come off and all the conspirators were soon seized, tortured, and brought to trial. On 6 December 1674 Van den Enden was hanged.

Many claims have been made about the relationship between Van den Enden and Spinoza. There is no scholarly agreement about the time they met each other (Meinsma, 1980, p. 124; Von Dunin Borkowski, 1933, vol. 1, p. 249; Gullan-Whur, 1998, pp. 59–60; Israel, 2001, p. 169 and particularly Israel, 2002, p. 130). On the basis of what is known, though, Spinoza can be associated with reasonable certainty with Van den Enden's school only in the years 1657 and 1658 (Akkerman, 1980, pp. 3–10). Taking into account that in the spring of 1658 Spinoza probably played one of the more complex roles in the Latin performance of Terence's *Eunuchus*, he must by then have mastered Latin sufficiently. As Van den Enden was able to prepare his pupils for university in two years, this suggests that Spinoza entered the school at the latest at around the time he was excommunicated (July 1656).

It remains unclear if Van den Enden influenced Spinoza in adopting a naturalistic world view. Van den Enden's conventionally religious *Philedonius* (1657) seems to suggest that it was the other way around. Scholars have claimed that Van den Enden introduced Spinoza to the modern philosophy of Descartes, Galileo, Gassendi, Hobbes, Bacon, Bruno and Machiavelli (e.g. Nadler, 1999, p. 111), but there is no indication that he did.

Van den Enden may have acquainted Spinoza with the works of the brothers De la Court, but this may have been due to Johannes Bouwmeester and Jacob Vallan as well (Mertens, 2008, p. 80, note 26).

Bedjai and Klever simultaneously discovered that two anonymously published political pamphlets, *Kort Verhael van Nieuw Nederland* (1662) and *Vrye Politijke Stellingen* (1665), were written by Van den Enden. They inferred from these texts that Van den Enden's influence on Spinoza was very substantial, but the content of the pamphlets does not warrant such a claim. A few specific statements in the *Vrye Politijke Stellingen* indicate that Van den Enden by 1665 was familiar with Spinoza's views: for instance that all the 'promises, threats and miracles' of Jesus should be interpreted as an accommodation to 'the nature and requirement of the common Jewish People', that people foolishly pretend 'to be the first cause of their knowledge and actions', and that '*imagining, believing* and *clear knowledge*' are three forms of 'knowledge' (Van den Enden, 1665, pp. 28, 41, 44). Further analysis suggests that in these instances Van den Enden was influenced by Spinoza (Mertens, 1994, pp. 730–4). Van den Enden's political ideas may have had an indirect influence on Spinoza, as some of his thoughts, including his central principle 'evengelijkheit' (equality), are clearly present in two publications by Pieter Balling, a Collegiant friend of Spinoza (Balling, 1663, pp. 2–4 and Balling, 1664, pp. 3–5). It is unlikely, however, that such an influence on Spinoza would have occurred during the first half of the 1660s, as Spinoza in this period showed little interest in politics. Spinoza's *Tractatus theologico-politicus* (1670) and *Tractatus politicus* (1677) clearly demonstrate that by the late 1660s Spinoza had become deeply immersed in political theory. These works allow a more detailed comparison between his thought and that of Van den Enden. Both defend democracy as the best form of government, insist on religious toleration and the dominance of the state over the church, and argue that freedom of speech is the best way to prevent a state from becoming unstable. Nevertheless, the way in which they reach these conclusions is not identical, as they differ considerably in their analysis of human beings and society. Spinoza's equation of 'right' and 'power', for instance, is entirely absent in Van den Enden's much more morally defined political theory. Van den Enden's positive views on the state of nature, as exemplified in his 'virtuous Indian', are not reflected in Spinoza's negative, more Hobbesian, conception of the state of nature.

Despite these differences, there are some basic ideas about a republican state and about the relation between state and church that Van den Enden and Spinoza have in common with a circle of radical friends, including Pieter Balling, Lodewijk Meyer and Adriaan Koerbagh. The written evidence also seems to suggest that they still had some friends in common as late as the 1670s (Kerckring, 1670, pp. 68, 178, 199–200 and De Koeckoecx-zangh, 1677, p. 10). If they stayed in touch after Van den Enden's move to Paris, it is likely that Spinoza was aware of his former master's conspiracy against Louis XIV. When word reached the Dutch Republic that the plotters had been apprehended, and when eventually the news arrived that they had been executed in front of the Bastille, this must have saddened Spinoza, although – as in all other such cases – no written records are known that can confirm this.

BIBLIOGRAPHY
Primary Sources
Anonymous, *De Koeckoecx-zangh van de nachtuylen van het Collegie Nil Volentibus Arduum, huylende met eenen naare geest: Dr. Ruysch en Boeckelman zijn de beest, of een blyeyndende zamenspraak tusschen een doctor, proponent, en poeet* (Zwolle, n.d. [1677]).
[Balling, P.], *Verdediging van de Regering der Doopsgezinde Gemeente* (Amsterdam, 1663).
———, *Nader verdediging van de regering der doopsgezinde gemeente* (Amsterdam, 1663).
Enden, F. van den, *Philedonius. Tonneelspel; slaande op de woorden des wijzemans: In alle uwe werken gedenk uwe uitersten, en ghy zult in der eeuwigheit niet zondigen* (Amsterdam, 1657).
[Enden, F. van den], *Kort Verhael van Nieuw-Nederlants Gelegentheit, Deughden, Natuerlijke Voorrechten, en byzondere bequamheidt ter bevolkingh* (n.p. [Amsterdam], 1662).
———, *Vrye politijke stellingen, en consideratien van staat, gedaen na der ware christenens even gelijke vryheits gronden; strekkende tot een rechtschape, en ware verbeeteringh van staat, en kerk* (Amsterdam, 1665).
Kerckring, D., *Specilegium anatomicum, continens observationum anatomicarum rariorum centuriam unam: nec non osteogeniam foetuum* (Amsterdam, 1670).
Pels, A., *Gebruik én misbruik des tooneels* (3rd edn, Amsterdam, 1718).

Rios y Alarcon, B. de los, *Phoenix Thenensis e cineribus rediviuus* (Antwerp, 1637).

———, *De Hierarchia Mariana libri sex* (Antwerp, 1641).

Rixtel, P., *Mengel-rymen* (Haarlem, 1669).

[Vrancx, F.], *Korte verthooninghe van het Recht by den Ridderschap, Edelen ende Steden van Hollandt ende West-vrieslant* (Amsterdam, 1650).

Secondary Literature

Akkerman, F., *Studies in the Posthumous Works of Spinoza: On Style, Earliest Translation and Reception, Earliest and Modern Edition of Some Texts* (Ph.D. thesis, Groningen, 1980).

Bedjai, M., 'Métaphysique, éthique et politique dans l'œuvre du docteur Franciscus van den Enden (1602–1674). Contribution à l'étude des sources des écrits de B. de Spinoza', *Studia Spinozana*, no. 6 (1990), pp. 291–313.

Borrichius, O., *Itinerarium 1660–1665*, ed. H.D. Schepelern, 4 vols (Copenhagen: Reitzel/Brill, 1983).

Dunin Borkowski, S. von, *Spinoza*, 4 vols (Münster i.W.: Aschendorffsche Verlagsbuchhandlung, 1933–6).

Gullan-Whur, M., *Within Reason. A Life of Spinoza* (London: Jonathan Cape, 1998).

Israel, J.I., *Radical Enlightenment. Philosophy and the Making of Modernity 1650–1750* (Oxford: Oxford University Press, 2001).

———, 'Philosophy, Commerce and the Synagogue: Spinoza's Expulsion from the Amsterdam Portuguese Jewish Community in 1656', in J. Israel and R. Salverda (eds), *Dutch Jewry. Its History and Secular Culture (1500–2000)* (Leiden, Boston and Köln: Brill, 2002), pp. 125–39.

Klever, W., 'Proto-Spinoza Franciscus van den Enden', *Studia Spinozana*, no. 6 (1990), pp. 281–8.

Meininger, J.V. and G. van Suchtelen, *Liever met wercken, als met woorden; de levensreis van doctor Franciscus van den Enden. Leermeester van Spinoza, complotteur tegen Lodewijk de Veertiende* (Weesp: Heureka, 1980).

Meinsma, K.O., *Spinoza en zijn kring. Historisch-kritische studiën over Hollandsche vrijgeesten* (The Hague: Nijhoff, [1896]; repr. Utrecht: HES, 1980).

Mertens, F., 'Franciscus van den Enden: tijd voor een herziening van diens rol in het ontstaan van het spinozisme?', *Tijdschrift voor filosofie*, no. 56, (1994), pp. 718–38.

———, 'Spinoza's Amsterdamse vriendenkring: studievriendschappen, zakenrelaties en familiebanden', in C. van Heertum (ed.), *Libertas philosophandi: Spinoza als gids voor een vrije wereld* (Amsterdam: In de Pelikaan, 2008), pp. 68–81.

Nadler, S., *Spinoza. A Life* (Cambridge: Cambridge University Press, 1999).

Vries, Th. de, *Spinoza. Beeldenstormer en wereldbouwer* (Amsterdam: Becht, n.d. [c. 1980]).

———, *Spinoza. Biografie* (Amsterdam: De Prom, 2003).

F. Mertens

HEEREBOORD, Adriaan (1614–61)

For Spinoza, Heereboord's work was one of the sources from which he learned about contemporary neo-scholasticism. It is, in principle, even possible that Spinoza attended Heereboord's lectures in Leiden if he already lived in Rijnsburg before the middle of 1661, but there is no evidence that he did. Though Heereboord continued and developed the neo-scholastic teaching of Franco Burgersdijk, whose pupil he was, he is also credited with the introduction at Leiden university of the philosophy of Descartes, of whom he was an ardent admirer. His part in the conflicts over Cartesianism eventually made his position in the university untenable. The situation was severely aggravated by his irascible, violent character and by the alcoholism that marked his life.

Adriaan Heereboord was born in Leiden on 13 October 1614. He matriculated at Leiden university as a student in philosophy and theology in 1629. In 1641 Heereboord was appointed professor *extra ordinem* in philosophy in Leiden, charged particularly with the teaching of logic. In the next year he became *subregent* (deputy dean) of the *Statencollege,* a theological college for bursaries of the States of Holland. In 1644 he accepted the chair of ethics. Heereboord's Cartesian sympathies became manifest towards the end of 1643. On 8 January 1644 Descartes wrote in a letter (AT, vol. 4, pp. 76–8): 'Heereboord declares himself more openly for me...than Regius has ever done.' Even so, there were few open clashes before 1647, when Revius, Heereboord's superior at the *Statencollege*, started a series of disputations against Cartesian philosophy. In the row that followed, Heereboord intervened several times. Not only did he

provide Descartes with the information necessary for writing his letter to the governors of Leiden university, he also wrote his own 'Letter to the governors' (contained in the *Meletemata*), in which he provides a detailed account of the conflict. Meanwhile the sordid facts of his private life were meted out in several pamphlets by his brothers-in-law, Pieter and Johannes de la Court, who later became known as writers on political theory. In 1652 it was decided that Heereboord was no longer capable of fulfilling his academic duties, although he continued to preside over some disputations until the end of his life. He died on 17 June 1661.

Heereboord's main work is a voluminous manual of metaphysics. Its title, *Meletemata philosophica,* recalls Descartes's metaphysics – *meletemata* is Greek for *meditationes.* Though too unwieldy to be a suitable textbook, it remained in print long after Heerboord's death. Heereboord also edited Burgersdijk's manual of metaphysics and annotated the latter's short logic, and provided new editions of the traditional metaphysical works of other philosophers.

In 1644, Heerebord had students debating Cartesian theses, such as that 'all things are true which we perceive clearly and distinctly' and 'the cause of all error is the will'. In the following year, in a public lecture he called Descartes 'the morning-star' who had 'disclosed the secrets of nature, uncovered the key to philosophy, and revealed the way to unshakeable truth'. Some years later, Heereboord described the French philosopher as 'the greatest luminary of all philosophers, guard and saviour of truth, philosophy and the freedom of thought' (*Epistola ad curatores,* 11 and 13). Yet it would be a mistake to describe his philosophical position simply as Cartesian: he sympathizes with other new philosophers (such as Ramus and Bacon) too. Moreover, his – qualified – plea for Cartesianism seems to follow from his humanism and Calvinism. Time and again Heereboord denounced scholasticism for its barbarism and impiety. In his 1641 inaugural address he divided the history of philosophy into an old and a new period. During the Middle Ages, monks concealed the truth behind obscure words and transformed philosophy into an inaccessible labyrinth. Only when Erasmus, Petrarch and Agricola claimed the 'Socratic' freedom to philosophize, was scholasticism brought to ruin. Since intellectual and religious freedom coincide, humanism paved the way for the reformation of the Church. The mind has to be liberated from prejudices and from all innate or acquired 'idols'. This liberation is possible only if we make use of a certain method, and – following Descartes – apply the example of the mathematicians to learning as a whole (*Epistola ad curatores*, 14). In the Preface to Spinoza's PPC, Lodewijk Meyer, who graduated under Heereboord, emphasized the need to apply the geometrical method to philosophy as well.

Although Heereboord acquired the reputation of a staunch Cartesian, he continued to teach the 'old' philosophy himself, because the 'new' philosophy was unable to replace traditional philosophy completely, since it covered only physics and lacked an ethics. Therefore philosophy has to be 'eclectic'.

Heereboord is one of the very few sources explicitly mentioned by Spinoza, viz. in a remarkable quote from Heereboord's *Collegium Ethicum* 1.10 in CM 1.2. Heereboord there deals with the intellect as the moving principle of the will. Like Spinoza, he rejected the conventional notion of the will's indifference, held by the 'Jesuits and the Remonstrants'. Apparently Spinoza overlooked the counterfactual nature of Heereboord's

argument and uses it in a different context, namely the identity of will and intellect.

Spinoza used many traditional metaphysical terms, such as substance, attribute, affection, mode and modification, but his source for these (with the exception of modification) may well have been Descartes. There are several examples in Spinoza's work of terminological influences whose sources cannot be identified with certainty. Thus, the division of causes in E1p16–18 and KV 1.3 may derive from Burgersdijk, but it also occurs in Heereboord's work. Again, *finis cujus causa* (E4def7) is used by Heereboord in his disputation on the final cause (*Meletemata* 2.23); the pair of concepts *in suo genere* and *absolute* is used by Burgersdijk and Heereboord in *Institutiones logicae* 1.17; and the pair *natura naturans – natura naturata* (KV 1.8–9; CM 2.7, 2.9; Ep 9; E1p29s; E1p31) occurs in many sources, among them Heereboord's *Collegium Physicum* 2. Borrowings, however, may also serve polemical purposes. Thus in E1app, Spinoza uses the scholastic distinction between *finis indigentiae* and *finis assimilationis*, taken from *Meletamata* 2.24, only to reject it.

BIBLIOGRAPHY
Primary Sources
Sermo extemporaneus de rectâ philosophicè disputandi ratione (Leiden, 1648).
Philosophia naturalis, moralis, rationalis (Leiden, 1654).
Hermeneia logica, seu synopseos logicae Burgersdicianae explicatio (Leiden, 1650, 1651,1652, 1658, 1663, 1666, 1670, 1676, 1680, 1694).
Meletemata philosophica maximam partem metaphysica (Leiden, 1654, 1659, 1664, 1665, 1680).

Secondary Literature

Coppens, G., 'Spinoza et la conception scolastique de Dieu dans le contexte hollandais', in Chantal Jaquet (ed.), *Les Pensées métaphysiques de Spinoza* (Paris: Sorbonne, 2004), pp. 19–36.

Freudenthal, J., 'Spinoza und die Scholastik', in *Philosophische Aufsätze Eduard Zeller gewidmet* (Leipzig: Fues's Verlag, 1887), pp. 85–138.

Robinson, L., *Kommentar zu Spinozas Ethik* (Leipzig: Meiner, 1928).

Verbeek, Th., *Descartes and the Dutch* (Carbondale: Southern Illinois University Press, 1992).

———, 'Descartes and Some Cartesians', in T. Sorell (ed.), *The Rise of Modern Philosophy* (Oxford: Clarendon Press, 1993), pp. 167–96.

H. Krop

JEWISH PHILOSOPHICAL INFLUENCES: MAIMONIDES, CRESCAS, ABRABANEL, MENASSEH BEN ISRAEL, KABBALAH, DELMEDIGO

In this entry will be examined those Jewish thinkers who helped to frame Spinoza's intellectual life. In particular Maimonides, Crescas, Abrabanel, Menasseh ben Israel and Delmedigo will be discussed. Spinoza attended the *Talmud Torah* School in Amsterdam up through at least the fourth grade (roughly age fourteen) and presumably excelled in his studies in Jewish law (*halakha*) and Hebrew. That Spinoza read works in Jewish philosophy, including medieval Jewish commentaries, is undeniable. From the list of books in Spinoza's estate, we know that he owned a number of Jewish philosophical texts, including works of Maimonides, Abrabanel and Delmedigo (Freudenthal, 1899, pp. 160–4). From this listing, we can assume that Spinoza was at least aware, if not already reading, such works as Maimonides's *Guide of the Perplexed*, Crescas's *Light of the Lord* (*Or Adonai*), Abrabanel's *Dialoghi d'Amore*, and works by Delmedigo. Scholars have argued over whether any of these works might have contributed to Spinoza's ultimate apostasy. Gebhardt (1987) for example has argued that it was Abrabanel's book that inspired Spinoza to leave the synagogue. Nadler (2001) maintains that it was Spinoza's denial of personal immortality, a doctrine discussed extensively in Jewish thought, that played the key role in his excommunication. Jonathan Israel, on the other hand, has argued that it was Spinoza's public repudiation of the fundamentals of Rabbinic Judaism that led to the excommunication (Israel, 1985, pp. 162–74). According to Israel, the individual most apt to have guided the young Spinoza in a heretical and radical direction was his Latin master Franciscus van den Enden.

Just as the question whether his repudiation of basic Jewish beliefs or practices led to Spinoza's *herem* is beyond the scope of this section, so too is the related question of the extent to which the mature Spinoza was influenced by Jewish philosophical works. Let me suggest, though, that like his Jewish forebears, Spinoza is engaged in the quest to reconcile Aristotelian metaphysics with broader cosmological and theological concerns, and like his Jewish predecessors, he recognizes the importance of reconciling theological and philosophical paradigms of thought. We can infer from his autobiographical comments in his early *Short Treatise*, and his *Treatise on the Emendation of the Intellect*, that he was engaged in a long intellectual struggle from an early age. It is not unlikely that his engagement with his Jewish predecessors contributed to this struggle.

MOSES MAIMONIDES (C. 1135–1204)

Influential philosopher, Talmudist, and physician, Maimonides is unarguably one of the greatest figures in the medieval Jewish period. His works consist in a conjunction of philosophic inquiry and halakhic authority. In his major philosophical work *Moreh Nevukhim* (*Guide of the Perplexed*), Maimonides applies Aristotelian principles of mathematics and logic to religious doctrines in such ways that his intended audience, the devout religious who also admire science and law, could potentially assuage their intellectual 'perplexities'. He engages in extensive biblical hermeneutics, reading Aristotelian and Neoplatonic themes into Scripture, in an attempt to reconcile disparate elements in religion and philosophy. Spinoza amplified Maimonides's critical tendencies in his *Theological-Political Treatise*. Spinoza's tactic, however, is exactly opposed to that of Maimonides: whereas Maimonides tried to find evidence of philosophical nuggets in Scripture, Spinoza argued that this search was useless. For this reason Maimonides comes under particular attack by Spinoza (see Pollock, 1880; Chalier, 2006). Spinoza frequently cites Maimonides by name, often to disagree with him. For example, he quotes at length a passage from the *Guide* in which Maimonides writes why he does not accept the eternity thesis, only to attack Maimonides on this point. In general, Spinoza attacks Maimonides's use of philosophical exegesis of the Bible as 'noxious, useless and absurd' (TTP 7.21, TTP 15).

Despite Spinoza's disdain for Maimonides's hermeneutical method, there is no question that he was very much influenced by Maimonides (see Dienstag, 1986). In his magisterial study of Spinoza, H.A. Wolfson has argued that 'it is only Maimonides and Descartes...that can be said to have had a dominant influence upon the philosophic training of Spinoza and to have guided him in the formation of his own philosophy' (Wolfson, 1934, vol. 1, p. 19). Other modern scholars to argue systematically for a distinctive Maimonidean influence on Spinoza were Roth and Pines. Leon Roth in his *Spinoza, Descartes and Maimonides* presented Spinozism as a Maimonidean critique of Cartesianism, arguing that often 'Maimonides and Spinoza speak throughout with one voice' (Roth, 1924, p. 144). Pines too, in his introduction to Maimonides's *Guide*, argued for a direct influence of Maimonides on Spinoza (in Maimonides, 1963, pp. xcvi, xcviii, c). More recently, Harvey (1981, p. 155) has argued that 'the fundamental elements of Maimonides's philosophy recur as fundamental elements in Spinoza's'. He lists several such fundamental elements, arguing that these elements are unique to Maimonides, and not found in other medieval authors.

Several of these influences are worth noting. Epistemologically, both Maimonides and Spinoza maintain a sharp distinction between intellect and imagination, arguing that this distinction allows a further parallel between true/false on the one hand, and good/evil on the other. It is by virtue of the imagination alone, they argue, that we fall into error (*Guide* I:2; E2p40–2). Both Spinoza and Maimonides emphasize that imagination must *not* be confused with intellect (*Guide* I:73 princ10 and TIE 84; see Ravven 2001). In contradistinction to Descartes, both maintain that the imaginative faculty is a bodily faculty, and again, in contradistinction to Descartes, that the imagination is unable to conceive the incorporeal (*Guide* I:73; TIE 89).

The implications of this distinction between intellect and imagination are important when we turn to moral claims. Both Maimonides and Spinoza argue that good and evil, as opposed to true and false, are not intellectual concepts, but rather are notions that arise as a result of the act of the imagination. Good and evil reflect pragmatic conditions and do not indicate anything positive in reality. As Harvey puts it, 'according to the Maimonidean-Spinozistic definitions of "good" and "evil",...the question of what things are to be considered good or evil is at bottom a subjective one, that is, it is relative to our own intents, targets, and *exemplaria*' (Harvey, 1981, p. 158; *Guide* III:13; E4praef; KV 1.10). This is not to say that either Maimonides or Spinoza is a moral relativist; on the contrary, both present a clear articulation of what they take to be the end of human endeavour. But from a meta-ethical perspective, the terms good and evil have no definitive meaning. The relativism of moral terms can be contrasted with the propositions of mathematics and physics, which we can know through the science of demonstration (*Guide* I:73; E2p44). Maimonides relegates knowledge of good and evil to the level of 'popularly accepted notions' (*Guide* I:2), whereas Spinoza identifies knowledge of good and evil with the lowest epistemological level of knowledge of the 'first kind' associated with opinion or imagination; good and evil are 'entia, non rationis, sed imaginationis' (E2p40s2, E2p41, E4p68). Both writers point out that theoretically (although such a person does not exist in fact) an individual ruled entirely by intellect, and not at all by his affections, would not entertain the

notions of good and evil; such terms would be either meaningless or redundant. Finally, both Maimonides and Spinoza use the Garden of Eden story to confirm their position (*Guide* I:2 and E4p68; see also TTP 4, Ep 19).

Another parallel between Maimonides and Spinoza lies in their mutual rejection of teleology: the view that the universe has any final end outside of itself or God, or that the universe was created for the sake of humans (*Guide* III:12, III:13; E1app). Both allude to Proverbs 16:4 to support the anti-anthropocentric view, Maimonides explicitly and Spinoza implicitly. Both argue that believing in anthropocentrism is at the bottom of the erroneous search for teleological explanations of the universe. As Harvey points out, this similarity is particularly striking inasmuch as Maimonides's strong anti-teleological views had no parallel in the medieval literature; nor were these anti-teleological sentiments shared by Descartes (see Gueroult, 1968, pp. 399–400; Harvey, 1981, p. 164; Wolfson, 1934, vol. 1, pp. 400–40).

Furthermore, Maimonides's God is very close in idea to Spinoza's attribute of thought; Pines suggests that what Spinoza does is add the attribute of extension to the God that he inherited from Maimonides (see Maimonides, 1963, p. xcviii). Consider Maimonides's famous statement in *Guide* I:68, wherein he develops the Aristotelian idea that God is the Knower, the Known and the Knowledge itself – 'He is the Intellect [*ha-Sekhel*], the intellectually cognizing Subject [*ha-maskil*] and the intellectually cognized Object [*ha-muskal*], and these three notions in Him, may He be exalted, are one single notion in which there is no multiplicity' (Maimonides 1963, I:68; see Aristotle, *Metaphysics* XII:7, 1072b 19–23; 1075a 10–11).

Spinoza alludes to this statement in E2p7s – 'a mode of extension and the idea of that mode are one and the same thing, but expressed in two ways. Some of the Hebrews seem to have seen this, as if through a cloud, when they maintained that God, God's intellect, and the things understood by him are one and the same'. In this passage, Spinoza is developing the logical implication of Maimonides's own position, namely that if in fact God is both knower and known, and extended space is intellectually cognized by God, then God, being identical with the objects of His thought, must be extended. However, Maimonides is loath to attribute body or corporeality to God, reminding his readers repeatedly in *Guide* 1:35 that God 'is not a body', on the grounds that attributing to God corporeality compromises God's unity (since body is divisible). Thus Spinoza, in attributing extension to God, pushes Maimonides's statement to its logical conclusion (see Fraenkel, 2006).

HASDAI CRESCAS (C. 1340–C. 1410)

Catalonian philosopher, rabbi, statesman and amateur poet, Crescas studied philosophy and Talmud under Rabbi Nissim ben Reuben Gerondi. Serving as secretary of the Jewish community in Barcelona, Crescas became the local authority on Talmudic law, and was asked by King Peter IV of Aragon to adjudicate cases concerning Jews. Philosophically his interests lay in distinguishing the fundamental beliefs, or religious concepts, that follow analytically from his view of the nature of the Torah. In his major work, *Or Adonai (Light of the Lord)*, Crescas argues that the Torah is a product of voluntary action from God. In an attempt to weaken Aristotle's hold upon Jewish philosophy, and to uphold the basic dogmas of Judaism,

Crescas subjects Aristotle's physics and metaphysics to a trenchant critique.

Crescas's influence upon Spinoza is undeniable, and he is one of the few Jewish philosophers mentioned by name by Spinoza. In letter 12, Spinoza refers to Crescas as 'a certain Jew, called Rab Ghasdaj', referring to Crescas's argument for God's existence. Crescas's main work *Or Adonai* adumbrates many of the themes found in Spinoza's work. For example, Crescas and Spinoza both reject the view of infinite extension being made up of measurable parts; both hold matter to be eternal, the act of creation consisting in the ordering of matter; the material world participates in the Divine nature. One of the most striking aspects of Spinoza's ontology is the doctrine of infinite extension. Wolfson has already noted that Spinoza's discussion in letter 12 of the indivisibility of infinite extension involves many details that reflect Crescas's own discussion in *Or Adonai* (Wolfson, 1934, vol. 1, p. 265). Both Crescas and Spinoza establish the existence of an infinite by positing an incorporeal quantity. What Crescas calls incorporeal extension or vacuum logically corresponds to what Spinoza calls extended substance or the attribute extension; what Crescas calls corporeal extension corresponds to Spinoza's particular modes of extension (see Wolfson, 1934, vol. 1, p. 281; Rudavsky, 2001).

Most interesting, however, is the thoroughgoing determinism found in both systems. In *Or Adonai* Crescas lists six fundamental doctrines: God's knowledge of particulars, Providence, God's power, prophecy, human choice, and the purposefulness of the Torah. Against his predecessor Gersonides (1288–1344), Crescas affirms God's knowledge of future contingents, even those determined by human choice. He then argues that human freedom is only apparent and not genuine: humans think they are free because they are ignorant of the causes of their choices. Human responsibility for action lies not in the actual performance of the action, but rather in the agent's acceptance of an action as his or her own. The feeling of joy an agent feels at acquiescing to certain actions, e.g. fulfilling the commandments, is the reward for that action. Wolfson (1934, vol. 1, p. 308) has noted the importance of Crescas's discussion for understanding Spinoza's own determinism, both with respect to his view of God as a 'free cause' and to human choice. Although both Crescas and Spinoza deny that any event can be called contingent, Crescas's brand of determinism nevertheless differs from that of Spinoza in that Crescas upholds teleology, whereas Spinoza in E1app rejects any talk of final causes. Both Crescas and Spinoza suggest that the 'consciousness of freedom' may be an illusion: we think we are free because we are ignorant of the causes of our actions (see *Or Adonai* II.5.3; E2praef, E2p35s, E3p2s). Nevertheless, whereas Spinoza refutes the commonly accepted view among the medievals that 'nature does nothing in vain', Crescas (unlike his predecessor Maimonides) is loath to give up this teleological picture of nature as a whole.

JUDAH ABRABANEL
('LEONE EBREO' C. 1460–AFTER 1523)

The work of Abrabanel represents an excellent example of the fusion of Hebraic thought with Ficino's revival of Greek philosophy. Son of the philosopher Isaac Abrabanel, Judah was born in Lisbon and spent much of his youth studying under his father. He was friendly with scholars of the Platonic Academy in Florence, and served as the physician to the Spanish viceroy, Don Gonsalvo de Córdoba. Judah wrote his major dialogue

Dialoghi di Amore with the interlocutors representing the epitome of platonic lovers. In this work, he constructs an allegory between two Jewish courtiers, Philo and Sophia, in order to illustrate the importance of the philosophical love of God. (For details of Judah Abrabanel's work, see Tirosh-Rothschild, 1997, pp. 522ff.) Philo has explained to Sophia the origins of love, which raises the more general question of when love was born: was it produced from eternity or was it created in time? Philo immediately connects this question with the issue of the origin of the universe, which leads to a summary of the three regnant positions on the creation of the universe – that of Plato, that of Aristotle, and that of Moses. In the course of explaining why on the Aristotelian model the universe is eternal, Philo alludes to the view that time must likewise be eternal, 'for any given instant is in reality the end of past time and the beginning of the future, and there can be no instant which is the first and the beginning of time. Time is therefore eternal and without beginning' (Leone Ebreo, 1937, p. 280). Philo then attempts a reconciliation of Platonic theory with Mosaic law and Kabbalah, applying this reconciliation to the doctrine of love.

The full extent of Abrabanel's influence upon Spinoza has remained an issue of contention. Wolfson has argued that 'Leo Hebraeus' influence upon Spinoza has been unduly exaggerated' (Wolfson, 1934, vol. 2, p. 277), and suggests that many of the supposed influential passages are not unique to Abrabanel and can be traced to many other later medieval works. We do know however that Spinoza owned a copy of Abrabanel's *Dialoghi di Amore* in his library, in a Spanish translation. Many of the themes in this work reappear in Spinoza. In his early work *Short Treatise*, Spinoza reiterates the general theme of *Dialoghi di Amore*, namely the intellectual love of God to be aspired. He distinguishes two types of love (stressed as well by Abrabanel): the directing of love on a corruptible, or upon an eternal, object. Spinoza argues that our love ought to be directed to that which is 'eternal and incorruptible' which thing he identifies with God, or 'what we take to be one and the same thing, the Truth' (KV 2.5). Love, he says, is a union with an object that our intellect judges to be good; by that 'we understand a union such that the lover and loved come to be one and the same thing, or to form a whole together' (KV 2.5).

MENASSEH BEN ISRAEL (1604–57)

Spinoza's own teacher Menasseh ben Israel was born in 1604 (possibly in Madeira). When he was still a child, his family settled in Amsterdam, where he became a printer, establishing Holland's first Hebrew press in 1626. In 1632 Menasseh ben Israel published a work called *The Conciliator* in which he tried to explain all the apparently contradictory passages in Scripture; as a result of this work, many leading Christian thinkers came to regard him as a spokesperson for Jewish thought to the Christian world. Menasseh learned about Jewish mystical and Kabbalistic thought from Rabbi Aboab Hererra, as well as from Delmedigo, who was in Amsterdam in the 1620s. In 1650 Menasseh published his best known work, *The Hope of Israel*, in Spanish, Latin, English, Hebrew, and later in Dutch, a statement of the importance of the reappearance of the Lost Tribes of Israel for messianism. He then became involved in the movement of the English millenarians, who were convinced that the Second Coming was imminent, and depended upon the admission of the Jews to England. He died in Middelburg on 2 November 1657.

Menasseh's work *Nishmat Hayyim*, published in 1651, was devoted to the nature of the soul. It was written in part in response to Uriel da Costa, whose polemical treatises denying the immortality of the soul led to his excommunication. In this work, following the tradition of his Amsterdam peers, Rabbis Mortera, Aboab and Moses Raphael d'Aguilar, all of whom had published treatises on the soul, Menasseh supported a view of personal immortality (see Nadler 2001 for details of these works). Menasseh argued that the doctrine of immortality is fundamental to belief in other Jewish tenets, such as belief in God's existence, the divine origin of the Torah, and reward and punishment. Like his teacher, Spinoza focuses upon the doctrine of immortality of the soul as well, although it should be noted that he does not use the term immortality to express the survival of part of the mind. The only time that the term 'immortal' (*immortalis*) appears in the *Ethics* is in 5p41s: 'if someone, because he sees that the Mind is not eternal, or immortal (*vel, quia videt Mentem non esse aeternam seu immortalem*), should prefer to be mindless'. Spinoza's famous discussion of the eternity of the mind, which is couched against the backdrop of what the human mind can know, is summed up in E5p23, 'The human Mind cannot be absolutely destroyed with the Body, but something of it remains which is eternal'.

KABBALAH

So far I have tried to emphasize some of the motifs and texts that might have influenced the young Spinoza. This overview is by no means exhaustive, and in fact we might have noted other influences in Jewish thought.

Take, for example, Spinoza's ambivalence toward Kabbalah. On the one hand he dismisses the Kabbalists (see TTP 9). However, in other contexts he uses a tone of respect to talk about 'ancient Hebrew opinions and traditions', referring possibly to earlier Kabbalistic notions, which were eventually supplanted by the modern Kabbalah (see E2p7s; Ep 21; see also Brann, 1967).

JOSEPH SOLOMON DELMEDIGO (1591–1655)

Another possible influence is Delmedigo, who visited Amsterdam in 1626. He was befriended by Spinoza's teacher Menasseh ben Israel, who published, among other works, Delmedigo's *Sefer Elim*. Ruderman has emphasized Delmedigo's tendency, along with that of his mentor Galileo, to understand the natural world outside the framework of Aristotelian physics; it is this tendency that is aligned with Delmedigo's interest in Kabbalah and Neoplatonic thought (see Ruderman, 1995, p. 134). In his *Sefer Elim*, a work that discusses in great detail Galileo's scientific theories, Delmedigo describes the 'strange astronomy', as well as the dangers inherent in this new astronomy, which challenged the reigning metaphysics (Delmedigo 1864; see Levine 1983, pp. 208–9; for a survey and discussion of Delmedigo's work, see Barzilay, 1974; Ruderman 1995, pp. 118–52). The very style of *Elim* is reminiscent of Galileo's dialogues. Delmedigo places in the mouth of Moshe Metz a thorough critique of the philosophical foundations of the old astronomy (*Elim*, pp. 48–62, esp 54ff). As Barzilay puts it, 'in no other part of Yashar's writings does one come across such an unprecedented, all-out assault on the basic concepts of ancient and medieval metaphysics, in general, and astronomy, in particular, as in this relatively short tract' (Barzilay, 1974, p 153).

But can we trace an actual influence between Delmedigo and Spinoza? While we do know that Spinoza had a copy of at least one of Delmedigo's works in his library (*Abscondita Sapientae*), it is not clear whether Spinoza had access to *Elim* as well; all we have in Freudenthal's listing of Spinoza's library holdings is a reference to an unnamed 'rabbinical mathematical work'. D'Ancona offers compelling evidence to suggest that not only was this a reference to *Sefer Elim*, but that very likely Spinoza had read the work carefully (d'Ancona, 1940). D'Ancona for example argues that difficulties in understanding certain features of part one of the *Short Treatise* – such as the ordering of its subject matter – testify to an influence of Delmedigo's work on Spinoza. For example, he argues that the twelfth question of Zerach bar Natan to Delmedigo, which is divided into seven paragraphs, bears 'an unmistakably close relation' to the first chapters of the *Short Treatise*, especially the order and division of chapters (d'Ancona, 1940, p. 35) More recently, Jacob Adler has argued that Spinoza is 'known to have read *Elim*; indeed, we can be reasonably certain that he read p. 56 of Part I' (Adler 2008, p. 181). While it is plausible that Spinoza came up with these ideas on his own, Adler has offered evidence to suggest that 'it would strain credulity to suppose that Spinoza did not learn the identity of intellect and will from Delmedigo's *Sefer Elim*' (Adler, 2008, p. 181).

BIBLIOGRAPHY
Primary Sources
Crescas, H., '*Or' Adonai [The Light of the Lord]*, Part I.2.11 and I.1.15 in

H. A. Wolfson, *The Philosophy of Crescas* (Cambridge, MA: Harvard University Press, 1929).

Delmedigo, J., *Sefer Elim* (Amsterdam, 1629; repr. Odessa, 1864–7).

Israel, M. ben, *Nishmat Chayim* (Jerusalem: Yedid ha-Sefarim, 1995).

Leone Ebreo, *The Philosophy of Love (Dialoghi d'Amore),* trans. F. Friedenberg-Seeley and J.H. Barnes (London: The Soncino Press, 1937).

Maimonides, M., *The Guide of the Perplexed,* ed. and trans. Shlomo Pines (Chicago: University of Chicago Press, 1963).

Pico della Mirandola, G., *Examen vanitatis doctrina gentium,* in *Opera omnia* (Basel, 1573).

Secondary Literature

Adler, J., 'J.S. Delmedigo as Teacher of Spinoza; The Case of Noncomplex Propositions', *Studia Spinozana,* no. 16 (2008), pp 177–83.

Barzilay I., *Yoseph Shlomo Delmedigo (Yashar of Candia): His Life, Works, and Times* (Leiden: E.J. Brill, 1974).

Brann, H.W., 'Spinoza and the Kabbalah', *Hartwick Review,* no. 3.1 (1967); reprinted in G. Lloyd (ed.), *Spinoza: Critical Assessments,* vol. 1 (London: Routledge, 2001), pp. 185–95.

Bunge, W. van, *From Stevin to Spinoza. An Essay on Philosophy in the Seventeenth Century Dutch Republic* (Leiden: Brill, 2001).

Chalier, C., *Spinoza Lecteur de Maimonide: La question théologico-politique* (Paris: Cerf, 2006).

Curley, E., 'Introduction' and footnotes in *The Collected Works of Spinoza,* trans. Edwin Curley (Princeton: Princeton University Press, 1985).

D'Ancona, J., 'Delmedigo, Menasseh ben Israel en Spinoza', *Genootschap voor de Joodsche wetenschap in Nederland, Bijdragen en mededeelingen,* no. 6 (1940), pp. 105–52.

Dienstag, J.I., 'The Relationship of Spinoza to the Philosophy of Maimonides: an Annotated Bibliography', *Studia Spinozana,* no. 2 (1986), pp. 375–416.

Fraenkel, C., 'Maimonides' God and Spinoza's Deus sive Natura', *Journal of the History of Philosophy,* no. 44 (2006), pp. 169–215.

Freudenthal, J., *Die Lebensgeschichte Spinozas in Quellenschriften, Urkunden und Nichtamtlichen Nachrichten* (Leipzig: Verlag Von Veit, 1899).

———, *Spinoza. Sein Leben und Seine Lehre* (Stuttgart: Fr. Frommanns Verlag, 1904).

Gebhardt, C., *Supplementa [to Spinoza: Opera].* (Heidelberg: Winter, 1987).

Gueroult, M., *Spinoza I-II,* 2 vols (Paris: Aubier, 1968–74).

Harvey, W.Z., 'Spinoza as a Maimonidean', *Journal of the History of Philosophy,* no. 19 (1981), pp. 151–72.

Israel, J., *European Jewry in the Age of Mercantilism 1550–1750* (Oxford: Oxford University Press, 1985).

Kaplan Y., H. Mechoulan and R. Popkin, *Menasseh ben Israel and his World* (Leiden: Brill, 1989).

Kasher, A. and S. Biderman, 'Why Was Baruch de Spinoza Excommunicated', in David S. Katz and Jonathan I. Israel (eds) *Sceptics, Millenarians and Jews* (Leiden: Brill, 1990).

Levy, Z., 'Sur quelques influences juives dans le développement philosophique du jeune Spinoza', *Revue des sciences philosophiques et théologiques,* no. 71 (1987), pp. 67–75.

—, *Baruch or Benedict: On Some Jewish Aspects of Spinoza's Philosophy* (New York: Lang, 1989).

Mechoulan, Henri, *Être juif à Amsterdam au temps de Spinoza* (Paris: Albin Michel, 1991).

Nadler, S., *Spinoza: A Life* (Cambridge: Cambridge University Press, 1999).

—, *Spinoza's Heresy: Immortality and the Jewish Mind* (Oxford: Clarendon Press, 2001).

—, 'The Jewish Spinoza', *Journal of the History of Ideas*, vol. 70 (2009), pp. 491–510.

Pines, S., 'Spinoza's *Tractatus Theologico-Politicus* and the Jewish Philosophical Tradition', in Isadore Twersky and Bernard Septimus (eds), *Jewish Thought in the Seventeenth Century* (Cambridge: Harvard University Press, 1987), pp. 499–521.

Pollock, F., *Spinoza: His Life and Philosophy* (London: C. Kegan Paul & Co, 1880).

Ravven, H.M., 'Some Thoughts on What Spinoza Learned from Maimonides about the Prophetic Imagination: Part 1. Maimonides on Prophecy and the Imagination', *Journal of the History of Philosophy*, no. 39 (2001), pp. 193–214.

—, 'Some Thoughts on What Spinoza Learned from Maimonides about the Prophetic Imagination: Part 2. Spinoza's Maimonideanism', *Journal of the History of Philosophy* 39 (2001), pp. 385–406.

Ravven, H.M. and L.E. Goodman (eds), *Jewish Themes in Spinoza's Philosophy* (Albany: SUNY Press, 2002).

Roth, L., *Spinoza, Descartes and Maimonides* (Oxford: Clarendon Press, 1924; 1963).

Rudavsky, T.M., *Time Matters: Time, Creation and Cosmology in Medieval Jewish Philosophy* (Albany: SUNY Press, 2000).

—, 'Galileo and Spinoza: Heroes, Heretics, and Hermeneutics,' *Journal of the History of Ideas*, no. 62 (2001), pp. 611–31.

Ruderman, D., *Jewish Thought and Scientific Discovery in Early Modern Europe* (New Haven: Yale University Press, 1995).

Smith, S.B., *Spinoza, Liberalism, and the Question of Jewish Identity* (New Haven: Yale University Press, 1997).

Strauss, L., *Spinoza's Critique of Religion* (New York: Schocken, 1965).

Studia Spinozana, no. 13 (1997), special issue on 'Spinoza and Jewish Identity', ed. S. Nadler, M. Walther and E. Yakira.

Tirosh-Rothschild, H., 'Jewish Philosophy on the Eve of Modernity,' in *History of Jewish Philosophy*, ed. D.H. Frank and O. Leaman (London: Routledge, 1997).

Wolfson, H.A., *Crescas' Critique of Aristotle* (Cambridge, MA: Harvard University Press, 1929).

—, *The Philosophy of Spinoza*, 2 vols (Cambridge, MA: Harvard University Press, 1934).

—, *Philo: Foundations of Religious Philosophy* (Cambridge, MA: Harvard University Press, 1947).

Yovel, Y., *Spinoza and Other Heretics: The Marrano of Reason* (Princeton: Princeton University Press, 1988).

T. Rudavsky

STOA

Spinoza's readers have long commented on the heavily Stoic aspect of his philosophical system. Leibniz called him a leader of a 'sect of new Stoics' which held that 'things act because of [the universe's] power and not due to a rational choice' (Leibniz, 1989, pp. 281–2). Around the same time Bayle said in his *Dictionary*, 'The doctrine of the world-soul, which was…the principal part of the system of the Stoics, is at bottom the same as Spinoza's' (Bayle, 1740, vol. 4, p. 253). This entry will identify the main conceptual affinities between Spinozism and Stoicism as well as an important difference. Before getting to those matters, however, it will note a puzzle surrounding the relationship between the two systems.

It may be supposed that Spinoza was acquainted with Stoicism. One reason for taking this to be the case is that Stoicism was enjoying a major revival in the 1600s. So, simply by virtue of living as an intellectual at that time, Spinoza would have been exposed to the main points of Stoic doctrine. An additional reason is that Spinoza owned several works by ancient Stoics, including Epictetus's *Enchiridion* and Seneca's *Epistolae* (Aler, 1965). At the same time, Spinoza can hardly be called a student of Stoicism. There is no evidence that he studied any area of Stoic thought with anything like the intensity that he studied Descartes or medieval Jewish philosophers. Moreover, he only explicitly refers to the Stoics twice in his writings, once at TIE 74 and a second time in E5praef. If they were more important to his thinking, he would have engaged with them more often, in the way that he does with Descartes. Rather than thinking of Spinoza as influenced by the Stoics, it seems more likely that he independently formulated a philosophical system that is astonishingly Stoical. This puzzling feature of their relationship makes the similarities between them all the more interesting.

Those similarities start with the very structure of the two systems. At the end of *De finibus* III Cicero says of Stoicism, 'Where is

lacking such a close interconnexion of the parts that, if you alter a single letter, you shake the whole structure?' (Cicero, 1931, p. 295). While scholars continue to dispute about the meaning of Spinoza's *mos geometricus*, one common interpretation sees it as an attempt to represent in linguistic terms the conceptual structure of nature. On this reading, if the *Ethics* is successful, it would be as impossible to change any part of the system presented therein as it would be to change nature. The rationalist ambitions of both Stoicism and Spinozism are closely analogous, and they undergird the overlap in the metaphysical and ethical positions held by the two camps.

Much of the overlap in their metaphysical views can be discerned by comparing a passage from Alexander of Aphrodisias to some of Spinoza's texts. According to Alexander, the Stoics hold 'that this world is one and contains all beings within itself; it is organized by nature, living, rational and intelligent, and it possesses the organization of beings, an organization that is eternal and progresses according to a certain sequence and order … Nothing comes to be in the world in such a way that there is not something else that follows it with no alternative and is attached to it as to a cause' (Alexander of Aphrodisias, 1983, p. 70). Like the Stoics, Spinoza was a substance monist, holding that there is only one substance, which is ultimately to be identified with nature itself (E1p14). Like the Stoics, Spinoza held that everything within nature is to be regarded as variations on or (to use Spinoza's word) 'modifications' of the one substance (E1p16). Just as the Stoics did, Spinoza believed in a causal network based on the one substance which includes all things within its domain and strictly binds causes to effect (E1p18, p29, p33). Stoics and Spinoza both stress that humans are just as much a part of and governed by the world-order as all other discrete individuals (E3praef). The close resemblance of the ultimate metaphysical pictures painted by Stoicism and Spinozism – pictures which depict the universe as a unitary system containing all beings and ordered by substance – is reinforced by the way in which both use the words 'God' and 'nature' when referring to the universe as a whole.

Leaving metaphysics for ethics, Stoics and Spinoza both insist that free will, in the sense of choosing between two equally available alternatives, is ruled out by the causal series (compare Alexander, 1983, p. 73, with E1p32). Nonetheless, even though humans are not free in that sense, they are still fully responsible for their own well-being. To maximize well-being, Stoics and Spinoza both thought that humans should accept and conform to the order of nature. As the Stoics put it, 'living in accordance with nature is the goal of life, that is, in accordance with the nature of oneself and that of the universe' (Diogenes Laertius, 1970, p. 195). In Spinoza's parlance, 'we do not have an absolute power to adapt things outside us to our use. Nevertheless, we shall bear calmly those things which happen to us contrary to what the principle of our advantage demands, if we are conscious…that we are a part of the whole of nature, whose order we follow' (E4app32).

While Spinoza's philosophy bears more than a superficial resemblance to that of the Stoics, it would be a mistake to assimilate the two entirely. One key area of disagreement will illustrate the point. Stoicism is thoroughly and profoundly teleological. This is true both of the world as a whole – it is supremely good and designed for the benefit of humans – and of how humans think and act. Scholars may argue about the role accorded by Spinoza to teleology in human lives but there is no question that he rejected cosmic teleology of the sort so prominent in Stoicism. He states flatly, 'Nature has no aim set before it' (E1app).

BIBLIOGRAPHY
Primary Sources
Alexander of Aphrodisias, *On Fate. Text, Translation and Commentary*, ed. and transl. by R.W. Sharples (London: Duckworth, 1983).
Bayle, P., *Dictionaire historique et critique*, 4 vols (Amsterdam, 1740).
Cicero, *De finibus* (Cambridge, MA: Harvard University Press, 1931).
Diogenes Laertius, *Lives of the Philosophers* (Cambridge, MA: Harvard University Press, 1970).
Leibniz, G.W., *Philosophical Essays*, ed. and transl. by R. Ariew and D. Garber (Indianapolis: Hackett Publishing, 1989).

Secondary Literature
Aler, J.M.M. (ed.), *Catalogus van de bibliotheek der Vereniging 'Het Spinozahuis' te Rijnsburg* (Leiden: Brill, 1965).
Long, A.A., 'Stoicism in the Philosophical Tradition: Spinoza, Lipsius, Butler', in J. Miller and B. Inwood (eds), *Hellenistic and Early Modern Philosophy* (Cambridge: Cambridge University Press, 2003), pp. 7–29.

J. Miller

3

EARLY CRITICS

PIERRE BAYLE, Dictionnaire historique et
critique (1697)

Like many of his contemporaries, Pierre
Bayle (1647–1706) was haunted by Baruch
Spinoza: 'a Jew by birth, and afterwards a
deserter from Judaism, and lastly an atheist'.
The article 'Spinoza' is the longest of the *Dictionnaire historique et critique* and the interpretation it offers was to become the most
influential of its time. The corresponding
entry of the *Encyclopédie* – written, or rather
compiled, by Diderot himself – will be nothing but a reworking of Bayle's article, whose
popularity is enormous throughout the whole
eighteenth century, from Hume's *Treatise of
Human Nature* to Condillac's *Traité des sys-
tèmes* and Voltaire's *Le Philosophe ignorant*.
It was Bayle who construed the double portrait of Spinoza as 'the virtuous atheist' and
'the systematic atheist', though he was not
the first to accuse Spinoza of atheism. Spinoza
had already been tagged as an atheist early in
his lifetime, and the publication of the *Tractatus theologico-politicus* had confirmed his
bad reputation in the eyes of most of his contemporaries. Atheism, in early modern culture, did not require an overt rejection of the
existence of a deity: the simple denial of the
moral attributes of God (and especially of
God's 'providence') was enough to be called

an 'atheist', and there is no doubt, from a
contextual point of view, that Spinoza
deserved this epithet. In the age of Bayle,
philosophers and theologians used to discuss
the real existence of the so-called 'speculative
atheists', who denied the existence of God
from a philosophical stance. Atheism was
generally considered to be a state of mind, or
a moral vice, but not a theoretical position:
'the atheist, it was claimed, could *will* himself into being, but could not truly think
atheistically' (Kors, 1991, p. 17). In Bayle's
opinion, the philosophy of Spinoza was a *de
facto* proof of the contrary.

Bayle dealt with Spinoza from the late
1670s, when he was still in France. He mentions the *Tractatus theologico-politicus* for
the first time in 1677 (Bayle, *Correspondance*, vol. 2, p. 457). In May 1679, he finds a
copy of Saint-Glain's French translation, and
some months later he buys the *Opera posthuma* and *Principia philosophiae Renati des
Cartes* (Bayle, *Correspondance*, vol. 3, p. 181,
204). However, Spinoza is not among the
authors quoted in the original edition of
Bayle's first printed work, the *Pensées diverses
sur la comète* (1682), published by Reinier
Leers in Rotterdam, where Bayle had moved
the previous year. Spinoza is mentioned only
in the second edition of the *Pensées* (1683),
first in section 175 and then, more diffusely,

85

in section 181, which bears the following title: 'Men do not live according to their principles'. Here Bayle argues that just as many believers act and live immorally, so might an atheist live a moral life. This could explain Spinoza's commitment to moral principles, which was nonetheless accompanied – in Bayle's opinion – by a great deal of vanity:

'[Spinoza] was the greatest atheist there ever was and who was so infatuated with certain principles of philosophy that, to meditate on them better, he went into retirement, renouncing all that may be called the pleasures and vanities of the world and concerning himself only with abstruse meditations. Sensing that he was near his end, he had his landlady come and begged her to prevent any minister from coming to see him in that condition. His reason was, as is known from one of his friends [Adriaan Paets, according to Vernière, 1954, p. 30], that he wished to die without a dispute and that he feared falling into some weakness of the understanding which would make him say something that could be used against his principles. This is to say that he feared that it would be spread about in the world that, when facing death, his conscience having awoken, it made him give the lie to his bravery and renounce his sentiments. Can a more ridiculous and more extreme vanity be seen than this one, and a crazier passion for the false idea one forms of constancy?' (Bayle, *Various Thoughts*, p. 227)

If one compares this ambiguous and somewhat malevolent portrait of Spinoza with the one which is to be found in the *Dictionnaire historique et critique*, the development of Bayle's thoughts on Spinoza will be evident.

In the *Dictionnaire*, Spinoza is painted as 'sociable, affable, honest, obliging, and of a well-ordered morality', though this still seems 'strange' to Bayle, who does not dare to abandon entirely the prudent viewpoint of the *Pensées diverses*. In his later writings, he will go a step further, suggesting that Spinoza and the atheists are moral persons not *in spite*, but *because* of their atheism. This final evolution is due to many factors, philosophical and rhetorical. Bayle has discovered that religion is not only independent from morals, which is an obvious consequence of the position taken in the *Pensées diverses*, but also dangerous for man's moral behaviour. Religion is the realm of 'conscience', which Bayle regards, following Malebranche, as the opposite of reason. For Bayle, religious conscience may suggest the cruellest acts in order to serve its God, leaving no remorse in men's souls. On the other hand, a speculative atheist (such as Spinoza) does not have to fight for a supernatural divinity, and cannot appeal to God's unquestionable will to cover his deeds. This train of thought will get more and more consistent in the *Continuation des pensées diverses* (1705, §§ 114 and 149) and in the last two parts of the *Réponse aux questions d'un provincial* (1706–7, part 3, chaps 17 and 20). In these late works, Bayle develops a full anthropology of atheism: atheists are no angels, but they care about their lives, about their children, about their estates. An atheist subject has no reason to reject his king for professing this or that religion, and, conversely, an atheist king will never persecute his subjects because their religion is different from his. Spinoza and Spinozists are explicitly quoted, in both these works, to support this theory.

Bayle's official position on Spinoza could be outlined as follows: Spinoza was a virtuous atheist, yet his philosophical system is absurd and incomprehensible. For Bayle, the absurdity of Spinozism lies essentially in the doctrine of the unity of substance. This is Spinoza's original sin, and the basis of most of his contradictions. However, from Bayle's standpoint, Spinozism is not an original position: monism is a recurrent temptation of philosophical thought, from ancient Greece to China (see also Budde, 1701). The philosophy of Spinoza is only the most recent, and the most elaborated expression of a meta-historical position, which is as ancient as the world. The history of Spinozism is thus incorporated into a larger (and vaguer) history, which comprehends also the Stoics' *anima mundi*, the Averroist dogma of the universal intellect, the Scotists' position on the universals, and several doctrines from Eastern philosophies. This is the reason why Bayle finds so many objections ready to use: he only has to translate the ancient arguments against the *anima mundi*, or against Averroism, and to point them against the new enemy. And this is why Spinoza and Spinozists are mentioned in many other articles of the *Dictionnaire historique et critique*: 'Abélard', C, 'Abumuslimus', A, 'Agésipolis', A, 'Andlo', *in textu*, 'Aristote', *in textu*, 'Averroès', E, 'Brunus', D, 'Buridan', C, 'Caïnites', D, 'Césalpin', C, 'Chrysippe', S, 'Critias', H, 'Démocrite', R, 'Diogène', B, 'Epicure', notes, 'Euclide', *in textu*, 'Ezéchiel', D, 'Hénault', *in textu*, 'Japon', D, 'Jupiter', G, 'Leucippe', G, 'Lucrèce', Q, 'Origène', K, 'Pauliciens', I, 'Plotin', D, 'Soranus', F, 'Stilpon', H, 'Synergistes', C, 'Weidnerus', *in textu*, 'Xénophanes', B, L, and 'Zénon d'Elée', I.

Like other readers, from the first adversaries of Spinoza to present-day critics such as Curley (1969, pp.4–77), Bayle discusses several possible conceptions of the relationship between the infinite substance and its modes, which he holds to be the weakest side of Spinozism. For Bayle, Spinoza's God is either identified with Nature, or is a collection of finite material beings, which is equally blasphemous. Though Bayle's objections are various and multiple, his different approaches to the question of the relationship between God and the world in Spinoza's system may be reduced to three main models: (1) the distinction of finite parts within an infinite (or indefinite) space, like that of Cartesian physics; (2) the relationship of inherence which subsists between a substance and its accidents (or properties) in Aristotle's metaphysics; (3) the logical inclusion of lower species into a supreme genus in a Porphyrian tree. In all these cases, many absurdities arise from Spinoza's metaphysics, which Bayle colours in various ways, using his rhetorical talent and his irony.

(1) In Spinoza's system, extension is an attribute of God; it follows, according to Bayle, that God must be divisible in actual parts, which is pointless and inconceivable. Bayle offers this argument in the first part of Remark N, where he temporarily abandons his Cartesianism for a more traditional position, founded on the scholastic doctrine of distinction between substances (a full-blooded Cartesian, for whom matter and space are one and the same thing, could not easily distinguish two extended substances 'with regard to space', as Bayle does here – he himself proposes this objection to the Cartesians in another article: see *Dictionnaire*, 'Zenon d'Elée', I). One could add that the same objection had already been proposed in the 1680s by two other critics of Spinoza, Pierre Poiret and the Socinian Noël Aubert de Versé – who are, as will soon appear, among the most important sources of Bayle's article.

(2) The second part of Remark N is dedicated to the analysis of the relationship

between the infinite substance and its modes in terms of 'inherence'. If the finite modes, that is to say – in Spinoza's system – the various beings of this world with their accidental characters, are to be conceived as properties of one single infinite substance, it will follow that God is at the same time sad and happy, good and bad, German and Turkish. Bayle is even less original here: the same argument had already been exploited by the first adversaries of Spinozism, among whom one might include the collegiant Frans Kuyper (Cuperus), *Arcana atheismi revelata*, p. 213, and the aforementioned Pierre Poiret, *Cogitationes rationales*, bk III, chap. 13, note 1 and bk III, chap. 20, note 4, and Noël Aubert de Versé, *L'Impie convainvu*, p. 49; but also Nicolas Malebranche raises a similar objection in his *Entretiens sur la métaphysique*, in *Œuvres complètes*, vol. 12–13, p. 199. Bayle adds that Spinoza's God would be the author of all of man's sins, which contradicts his goodness: this is the first allusion, in this article, to the question of theodicy, which will be the crucial point of Remark O.

(3) The third approach to the question of the relationship between God and the world in Spinoza's system is analysed in Remark P (not included here). For Bayle, Spinoza's unique substance might be considered a sort of 'supreme genus' – a genus which is not a relative species, since there is no concept above it (a similar approach in Wolfson, 1934, vol. 1, pp. 61–77) – but even in this case a plurality of beings would still be thinkable: Peter and Paul belong to the same genus and share the same attributes (they are both 'rational animals'), but this does not mean that they are one single entity. The same objection had already been sketched by Bayle in his Sedan *Theses* of 1680 (see *Œuvres diverses*, vol. 4, p. 134) and is the exact application to Spinozism of an old argument used

in medieval discussions on the universals, and especially against the position of the followers of Duns Scotus (see also Bayle, *Dictionnaire*, 'Abélard', C).

As clearly appears from Remark N, Bayle is able to propose a cluster of objections for every possible interpretation of the relationship between God and the world in Spinoza's system. But did he really understand Spinoza's metaphysical views? And did his objections reach the heart of Spinozism? Some of his contemporaries thought that this was not the case. Bayle's broad apology is contained in Remark DD, added to the second edition of the *Dictionnaire* (1702), where he repeats many times that he takes the words 'substance' and 'modification' in the same way as the Cartesians (and presumably Spinoza) did. But this was not sufficient to change the opinion of all his readers: Herder wrote in *Gott* (1787, p. 3) that Bayle 'is not the best authority' to understand Spinoza, and, more recently, Peter Gay stated that he 'misled a whole century' (1973, vol. 1, p. 293). One thing is certain: if Bayle did not understand Spinoza, the same should be said of Malebranche and Leibniz – whose interpretations of Spinozism are not different from his – and of most early-modern philosophers and theologians. Hence, it is not because of his limited philosophical genius that Bayle did not explain Spinoza's system as well as modern critics claim that they do. There was a well-established interpretation of Spinozism which had circulated since the 1680s, and Bayle's article reflects exactly this vulgate, which had easily found its way into early modern European philosophical culture.

But Bayle did not limit himself to repeating this common interpretation: he added something of his own, even though still following the path of the first adversaries of Spinoza. The key to Bayle's reading lies probably in Remark O, where he proposes a theoretical reconstruction of the genesis of Spinozism. According to Bayle – who is again very close to Aubert de Versé and Poiret (see Mori, 1999, pp. 166–73) – Spinoza had to deal with two major difficulties of orthodox theology: the problem of creation and the problem of free will. But Spinoza was led by reason, and reason alone; he did not want to accept the absurd doctrine of creation from nothing (which contradicts, as Bayle remarks, a universal axiom such as *ex nihilo nihil fit*) and he did not think that human freedom of choice and subjection to original sin could be compatible with the existence of a good and omnipotent God (Bayle will take the same position in his late works such as the *Réponse aux questions d'un provincial*, part 2, chaps 138–42). Only one way was open to Spinoza and could allow the eradication of all difficulties: the inclusion of all creatures in God, which eliminated the metaphysical myths of creation and free will and dissolved the problem of theodicy. When seen from this perspective, Spinozism becomes the most consistent theology; therefore, its patent absurdity – which Bayle still maintains in Remark O – becomes the absurdity of every rational conception of God.

Like many other writings of Bayle, the article on Spinoza in the *Dictionnaire historique et critique* admits of many possible readings. Prima facie Bayle is only the last and the harshest of Spinoza's orthodox adversaries. But a deeper analysis is possible and required: by criticizing Spinoza, Bayle rejects the project of a philosophical theology as such. As Bayle does not fail to observe at the end of Remark DD, orthodox theology faces the same difficulties as Spinozism when it tries to justify the dogmas of Transubstantiation (this concerns mainly the Roman Catholics) and the Trinity (this holds true for every Christian theologian, with the possible exception of Socinians and other heretics). So, just as Spinoza is absurd when he postulates a being that is at the same time sad and happy, Christian theologians are equally illogical when they proclaim that God is one and three. From this point of view, the final quotation from Averroes sounds like a sort of theoretical imperative: never try to translate your theology into philosophical terms. For this might give rise to self-contradiction, that is to say, the most unwanted occurrence in a philosophical discourse.

The following texts are taken from P. Bayle, *Historical and Critical Dictionary. Selections*, ed. R. Popkin, art. 'Spinoza', pp. 288 ff. Bayle's original footnotes have either been deleted or incorporated into the text.

HISTORICAL AND CRITICAL DICTIONARY, ART. 'SPINOZA'

1. Spinoza, Benedictus de, a Jew by birth, and afterwards a deserter from Judaism, and lastly an atheist, was from Amsterdam. He was a systematic atheist who employed a totally new method, though the basis of his theory was the same as that of several other ancient and modern philosophers, both European and Oriental....

I have not been able to learn anything special about Spinoza's family, but there are grounds for believing that they were poor and not very important. He studied Latin under a physician (Franciscus van den Enden) who taught it at Amsterdam, and he applied himself at an early age to the study of theology, to which he devoted several years. After this he devoted himself completely to the study of philosophy. Since he had a mathematical mind and wanted to find a reason for everything, he soon realized that rabbinical doctrine was not for him. As a result, it was easily seen that he disapproved of Judaism in several respects; for he was a man who was averse to any constraint of conscience and a great enemy of dissimulation. This is why he freely set forth his doubts and his beliefs. It is said that the Jews offered to tolerate him, provided that he would conform outwardly to their ceremonial practices, and that they even promised him an annual pension, but that he could not submit to such hypocrisy. However, he estranged himself little by little from their synagogue; and perhaps he would have kept up some degree of contact with them for a longer time had he not been treacherously attacked by a Jew who struck him with a knife when he was leaving the theatre. The wound was minor but he believed that the assassin's intention was to kill him. After this event he broke off from the Jewish community, and this was the cause of his excommunication. I have looked into the circumstances of it without having been able to dig them out. He wrote an apology in Spanish for his quitting the synagogue. This work has never been published. However, it is known that he put many things in it that later appeared in his *Tractatus theologico-politicus*, published in Amsterdam in 1670, a pernicious and detestable book in which he slips in all the seeds of atheism that were plainly revealed in his *Opera posthuma*....

When Spinoza turned to philosophical studies, he quickly became disgusted with the usual theories and was wonderfully pleased with that of Descartes. He felt such a strong passion to search for truth that to some extent he renounced the world to be better able to carry on that search. He was not content with having removed himself from all sorts of affairs; he also left Amsterdam because his friends' visits interrupted his speculations too much. He retired to the country, he meditated there at his leisure, and he worked on microscopes and telescopes there. He kept up this kind of life after he settled in The Hague; and he gained so much pleasure from meditating, from putting his meditations in order, and from communicating them to his friends, that he allowed very little time for mental recreation; and sometimes he let three whole months go by without setting foot outside his lodgings. This retired life did not hinder the spreading of his name and reputation. Freethinkers came to him from all over. The court of the Palatinate wanted him and offered him a chair as professor of philosophy at Heidelberg. He turned it down as a post that would be little compatible with his desire to search after truth without any interruption. When he was a little more than forty-four years old, he sank into a long illness that ended his life on February 21, 1677. I have heard it said that when the Prince de Condé was at Utrecht, he asked him to come and see him. Those who were acquainted with him, and the peasants of the villages where he had lived in retirement for some time, all agree in saying that he was sociable, affable, honest, obliging, and of a well-ordered morality. This is strange; but, after all, we should not be more surprised by this than to see people who live very bad lives even though they are completely convinced of the Gospel. Some people claim that he followed the maxim, 'Nobody grows very bad suddenly', and that he only fell into atheism gradually and that he was far from it when he published the geometrical demonstration of Descartes' principles. He is as orthodox in this work about the nature of God as Descartes himself; but it must be said that he did not speak thus on account of his own convictions. It is not wrong to think that the ill use he made of some of this philosopher's maxims led him to the precipice....

It is not as easy to deal with all the difficulties contained in [the *Tractatus theologico-politicus*] as to demolish completely the system that appeared in his *Opera posthuma;* for this is the most monstrous hypothesis that could be imagined, the most absurd, and the most diametrically opposed to the most evident notions of our mind [see below, Remark N]. It might be said that Providence has punished the audacity of this author in a peculiar way by blinding him in such manner that, in order to avoid some difficulties that can cause trouble to a philosopher, he threw himself into other perplexities infinitely more inexplicable and so obvious that no balanced mind could ever be unaware of them. Those who complain that the authors who have undertaken to refute him have not succeeded confound things. They would like to have the difficulties he succumbed to completely removed [see below, Remark O], but it ought to suffice for them that his hypothesis has been completely overthrown as has been done by even the weakest of his adversaries. ...

His friends claim that for modesty's sake he wished not to give his name to a sect. It is not true that his followers have been very numerous. Very few persons are suspected of adhering to his theory; and among those who are suspected of it, there are few who have studied it; and among the latter group, there are few who have understood it and have not been discouraged by the perplexities and the impenetrable abstractions that are found in it. But here is what happens. At first sight, all those are called Spinozists who have hardly any religion and who do not do much to hide this. It is in this way that in France all those are called Socinians who are thought to be incredulous about the mysteries of the Gospel although most of these people have never read either Socinus or any of his disciples. Besides, the same thing happened to Spinoza

that is inevitable for those who construct systems of impiety. They defend themselves from certain objections, but they expose themselves to other more perplexing difficulties. If they cannot submit to orthodoxy, if they are so fond of disputing, it would be much more comfortable for them not to become dogmatists. But of all the hypotheses of atheism, Spinoza's is the least capable of misleading anybody; for, as I have already said, it opposes the most distinct notions in the human mind. Objections arise in crowds against him, and he can only make answers that are more obscure than even the thesis itself that he is obliged to maintain. Thus his poison carries with it its own antidote. ...

[This section added in 1702:] Let us say something about the objections I have proposed against Spinoza's theory. I could add a very ample supplement to them if I did not think that they were already too long, in view of the nature of my work. Here is not the place to engage in a regular dispute. It will suffice for me to set forth some general observations that attack the foundations of Spinozism, and that show that it is a system that is based on so strange a supposition that it overthrows most of the common notions that serve to regulate philosophical discussions. To attack this system by its opposition to the most evident and most universal axioms we have had up to now is no doubt a very good way of combating it, although it is perhaps less fit for curing the old Spinozists than if it were made known to them that the propositions of Spinoza contradict one another. They would feel the weight of prejudice much less if they were forced to agree that he is not always in agreement with himself, that he proves poorly what he ought to establish, that he leaves items unproven that need to be established, that his conclusions do not follow logically, and so on. But let us speak of the supplement that I am going to give. It consists of a clarification ... of the question whether it is true, as I have been told that several people claim, that I have not understood Spinoza's theory at all [see below, Remark DD]. This would be very strange since I have only endeavoured to refute the proposition which is the foundation of his system and which he expresses with the greatest clarity. I have confined myself to opposing what he clearly and precisely sets forth as his first principle, namely, that God is the only substance that there is in the universe and that all other beings are only modifications of that substance. If one does not understand what he means by this, it is no doubt because he has given to the words a completely new signification without warning the reader. This is a capital way of becoming unintelligible by one's own doing....

2. Remark N (The most monstrous hypothesis ... the most diametrically opposed to the most evident notions of our mind).

He supposes that there is only one substance in nature, and that this unique substance is endowed with an infinity of attributes – thought and extension among others. In consequence of this, he asserts that all the bodies that exist in the universe are modifications of this substance in so far as it is extended, and that, for example, the souls of men are modifications of this same substance in so far as it thinks; so that God, the necessary and infinitely perfect being, is indeed the cause of all things that exist, but he does not differ from them. There is only one being, and only one nature; and this nature produces in itself by an immanent action all that we call creatures. It is at the same time both agent and patient, efficient cause, and subject. It produces nothing that is not its own modification. There is

a hypothesis that surpasses all the heap of all the extravagances that can be said. The most infamous things the pagan poets have dared to sing against Venus and Jupiter do not approach the horrible idea that Spinoza gives us of God, for at least the poets did not attribute to the gods all the crimes that are committed and all the infirmities of the world. But according to Spinoza there is no other agent and no other recipient than God, with respect to everything we call evil of punishment and evil of guilt, physical evil and moral evil. Let us touch on some of the absurdities of his system.

That according to Spinoza God and extension are the same thing.

I. It is impossible that the universe be one single substance; for everything that is extended necessarily has parts, and everything that has parts is composite; and since the parts of extension do not subsist in one another, it must be the case either that extension in general is not one substance, or that each part of extension is a particular substance distinct from all the others. Now, according to Spinoza extension in general is the attribute of one substance. He admits, along with all other philosophers, that the attribute of a substance does not differ actually from that substance. Therefore he must acknowledge that extension in general is a substance. From which it necessarily follows that each part of extension is a particular substance, which destroys the foundations of the entire system of this author. He cannot say that extension in general is distinct from the substance of God; for if he said that, he would teach that this substance in itself is not extended. Then, it could never be able to acquire the three dimensions except by creating them, for it is obvious that extension can never arise or emanate from an unextended subject except by way of creation. Now Spinoza did not believe that nothing could be made from nothing [see below, Remark O]. It is even more obvious that an unextended substance by its nature can never become the subject of three dimensions, for how would it be possible to place them on a mathematical point? They would therefore subsist without a subject; they would then be a substance; so that, if this author admitted a real distinction between the substance of God and extension in general, he would be obliged to say that God would be composed of two substances distinct from one another, namely his unextended being and extension. We see him thus obliged to recognize that extension and God are only the same thing; and since, in addition, he maintains that there is only one substance in the universe, he has to teach that extension is a simple being, as exempt from composition as the mathematical points. But is it not a joke to maintain thus? Is this not to fight against the most distinct ideas we have in our minds? Is it not more evident that the thousandth number is composed of a thousand unities than even that a body of a hundred inches is composed of a hundred parts actually distinct from one another, each having one inch of extension?

That extension is composed of parts which are each a particular substance.

Let no one come and urge objections to us against the imagination and the prejudices of the senses; for the most intellectual notions, and the most immaterial ones, make us see with complete evidence that there is a very real distinction between things, one of which possesses a quality and the other of which does not. The Scholastics have perfectly well succeeded in showing us the characteristics and the infallible signs of distinction. When one can affirm of a thing, they tell us, what one cannot affirm of another, they are distinct; things that can be separated from one another with regard to time or place are distinct. Applying these characteristics to the twelve inches of a foot of extension, we will find a real distinction between them. I can affirm of the fifth that it is contiguous to the sixth, and I deny this of the first, the second, and so on. I can transpose the sixth to the place of the twelfth. It can then be separated from the fifth. Observe that Spinoza cannot deny that the characteristics of distinction employed by the Scholastics are very just; for it is by these marks that he recognizes that stones and animals are not the same modality of infinite being. He admits then, I will be told, that there is some difference between things. It is most necessary that he admit it since he was not enough of a madman to believe there was no difference between himself and the Jew who struck him with a knife, or to dare to say that in all respects his bed and his room were the same being as the emperor of China. What then did he say? You are about to see. He taught not that two trees were two parts of extension, but two modifications. You will be surprised that he worked so many years constructing a new system, since one of its principal pillars was the alleged difference between the word 'part' and the word 'modification'. Could he promise himself any advantage from this change of words? Let him avoid as much as he wants the word 'part'; let him substitute as much as he wants the word 'modality' or 'modification'; what does this accomplish? Will the ideas attached to the word 'part' vanish? Will they not be applied to the word 'modification'? Are the signs and characteristics of difference less real or less evident when matter is divided into modifications than when it is divided into parts? Poppycock! The idea of matter still continues to be that of a composite being, that of a collection of several substances. Here follows what will prove this.

Incompatible modalities require distinct subjects

Modalities are beings that cannot exist without the substance they modify. It is therefore necessary that there be substance everywhere for modalities to exist. It is also necessary that it multiply itself in proportion as incompatible modifications are multiplied among themselves, so that wherever there are five or six of these modifications, there are also five or six substances. It is evident, and no Spinozist can deny it, that a square shape and a round one are incompatible in the same piece of wax. It must necessarily then be the case that the substance modified by a square shape is not the same substance as that modified by a round one. Thus, when I see a round table and a square one in a room, I can assert that the extension that is the subject of the round table is a substance distinct from the extension that is the subject of the other table; for otherwise it would be certain that a square shape and a round one would be at the same time in one and the same subject. Now this is impossible. Iron and water, wine and wood, are incompatible. Therefore they require subjects distinct in number. ...

The immutability of God is incompatible with the nature of extension. Matter actually allows for the division of its parts.

II. If it is absurd to make God extended because this would divest him of his simplicity and make him consist of an infinite number of parts, what will we say when we consider that this is reducing him to the condition of matter, the lowest of all beings, and the one that almost all the ancient philosophers placed immediately above nonbeing? He who speaks of matter speaks of the theatre of all sons of changes, the battlefield of contrary causes, the subject of all corruptions and all generations, in a word, the being whose nature is the most incompatible with the immutability of God. The Spinozists, however, maintain that it allows for no division, but they support this claim by the most frivolous and lowest chicanery that can be imagined. They contend that for matter to be divided it is necessary that one of its portions be separated from the others by empty spaces, which never happens. It is most certain that this is a very bad way of defining division. We are as actually separated from our friends when the interval that separates us is occupied by other men ranged in a file as if it were full of earth. One overthrows, then, both our ideas and our language when one asserts to us that matter reduced to cinders and smoke is not divided. But what will they [the Spinozists] gain if we give up the advantage that their false way of defining the divisible gives us? Would we still not have enough proofs of the mutability and corruptibility of Spinoza's God? All men have a very clear idea of the immutable. They understand by this term a being that never acquires anything new, that never loses anything that it once had, that is always the same, both in its substance and in its ways of being. The clarity of this idea shows that we comprehend very distinctly what mutable being consists in. It is not only a nature whose existence can begin and end, but a nature that, always subsisting in terms of its substance, can acquire successive modifications and lose accidents or forms that it has sometimes had. All the ancient philosophers have recognized that this continual series of generations and corruptions that is seen in the world neither produces nor destroys any portion of matter, and it is from this that they say that matter is 'ingenerable' and 'incorruptible' in terms of its substance while it is the subject of all the generations and corruptions. It is the most obvious and most suitable example, however, that can be given of a mutable being, subject actually to all sons of variations and interior changes.... The forms produced in matter are united to it internally and penetratively. It is their subject of inherence; and according to sound philosophy, there is no other distinction between them and matter than that which there is between modes and the thing modified; from which it follows that the God of the Spinozists is a nature actually changing, and which continually passes through different states that differ from one another internally and actually. It is therefore not at all the supremely perfect being, 'with whom is no variableness, neither shadow of turning' (James 1:17)....

God cannot be the subject of inherence of man's thoughts since these thoughts are contrary to one another
III. We are going to see still more monstrous absurdities by considering the God of Spinoza as the subject of all the modifications of thought. The combining of extension and thought in a single substance is already a great problem; for it is not a question here of an alloy like that of metals, or a mixture like that of water and wine. That requires only *juxtaposition;* but the alloy of thought and extension ought to be an *identity;* thinking and being extended are two attributes *identified* with the substance. They are therefore *identified with* each other by the fundamental and essential rule of human reasoning, *quae sunt idem uni tertio, sunt idem inter se* [things equal to the same thing are equal to each other]. I am sure that if Spinoza had found such a perplexity in another sect, he would have judged it unworthy of his attention; but he did not regard this to be so in his own cause, so true is it that those who most

contemptuously criticize the droughts of others are most indulgent to themselves. He no doubt ridiculed the mystery of the Trinity; and he marvelled that an infinity of people dared to speak of a Being terminated by three hypostases, he, who properly speaking, gives to the divine nature as many persons as there are persons on the earth. He regards as fools those who, admitting transubstantiation, say that a man can be at the same time in several places, alive in Paris, dead in Rome, and so on; he who maintains that the extended, unique, and indivisible substance is everywhere at the same time, cold here, hot elsewhere, sad here, elsewhere gay, and so on [see below, Remark DD, *in fine*]. This should be said in passing, but consider attentively what I am about to say. If there is anything certain and incontestable in human knowledge, it is this proposition, *Opposita sunt quae neque de se invicem, neque de eodem tertio secundum idem, ad idem, eodem modo atque tempore vere affirmari possunt* ('two opposite terms cannot be truly affirmed of the same subject, in the same respect, and at the same time'). For example, it cannot be said without lying, 'Peter is well, Peter is very sick: he denies this, and he affirms it', assuming that the terms always have the same relation and the same meaning. The Spinozists destroy this idea and falsify it in such a way that one can no longer know where they will be able to find the mark of truth; for if such propositions were false, there would be none that one could guarantee as true. One could then hope for nothing in a dispute with them; for if they are capable of denying this, they will deny any other argument that is offered them. Let us show that this axiom is completely false in their system, and let us assume at the outset as an incontestable maxim that all the names that are given to a subject to signify either what it does or what it suffers apply properly and physically to its substance and not to its accidents. When we say that iron is hard, iron is heavy, it sinks in water, it splits wood, we do not intend to say that its hardness is hard, that its heaviness is heavy, and so on. That language would be very extravagant. We intend to say that the extended substance of which it is composed resists, is heavy, sinks in water, divides wood. In the same way, when we say that a man denies, affirms, gets angry, caresses, praises, and the like, we ascribe all these attributes to the substance of his soul itself, and not to his thoughts as they are either accidents or modifications. If it were true then, as Spinoza claims, that men are modalities of God, one would speak falsely when one said, 'Peter denies this, he wants that, he affirms such and such a thing'; for actually, according to this theory, it is God who denies, wants, affirms; and consequently all the denominations that result from the thoughts of all men are properly and physically to be ascribed to God. From which it follows that God hates and loves, denies and affirms the same things at the same time; and this according to all the conditions required to make false the rule mentioned above concerning opposite terms; for it cannot be denied that, taking all these terms with all possible rigour, some men love and affirm what other men hate and deny. Let us proceed further. The contradictory terms of willing and not willing belong at the same time to different men. It must be the case in Spinoza's system that they belong to that single and indivisible substance called God. It is God then who, at the same time, forms an act of will and does not form an act of will with regard to the same object. Two contradictory terms are then true of him, which is the overthrow of the first principles of metaphysics. I know indeed that in the disputes about transubstantiation, a

cavil is employed that may here be of help to the Spinozists. It is said that if Peter wills something at Rome that he does not will at Paris, the contradictory terms 'willing' and 'not willing' would not be true with regard to him; for since it is supposed that he wills at Rome, one would lie in saying that he does not will. Let us allow them this vain subtlety. Let us say only that just as a square circle is a contradiction, so also is a substance when it loves and hates the same object at the same time....

Another proof of what is said above, drawn from the wickedness of man's thoughts
IV. But if it be, physically speaking, a prodigious absurdity that a simple and single subject be modified at the same time by the thoughts of all mankind, it is an execrable abomination when this is considered from the point of view of morality. What then? The infinite being, the necessary being, the supremely perfect being would not be steady, constant, and immutable! Why did I say immutable? He will not be the same for a moment. His thoughts will succeed one another ceaselessly and without end. The same medley of passions and feelings will not recur twice. This is hard to digest, but here is something much worse. This continual mobility will retain much uniformity in this sense, that for one good thought the infinite being will always have a thousand foolish, extravagant, impure, and abominable ones. It will produce in itself all the follies, all the dreams, all the filthiness, all the iniquities of the human race. It will not only be the efficient cause of them, but also the passive subject, the subject of inhesion....

Several great philosophers, not being able to comprehend how it is consistent with the nature of the supremely perfect being to allow man to be so wicked and miserable, have supposed two principles, one good, and the other bad; and here is a philosopher who finds it good that God be both the agent and the victim of all the crimes and miseries of man. Let men hate one another, let them murder one another in a forest, let them meet in armies to kill one another, let the conquerors sometimes eat the vanquished; this may be understood, because it is supposed that they are distinct from one another and that the *mine* and *thine* produce contrary passions in them. But that there should be wars and battles when men are only the modifications of the same being, when, consequently, only God acts, and when the God who modifies himself into a Turk is the same God in number as the God who modifies himself into a Hungarian; this is what surpasses all the monstrosities and chimerical disorders of the craziest people who were ever put away in lunatic asylums. Observe carefully, as I have already said, that modes do nothing; and it is the substances alone that act and are acted upon. This phrase, 'the sweetness of honey pleases the palate,' is only true in so far as it signifies that the extended substance of which the honey is composed pleases the tongue. Thus, in Spinoza's system all those who say, 'The Germans have killed ten thousand Turks', speak incorrectly and falsely unless they mean, 'God modified into Germans has killed God modified into ten thousand Turks', and the same with all the phrases by which what men do to one another are expressed. These have no other true sense than this, 'God hates himself, he asks favours of himself and refuses them, he persecutes himself, he kills himself, he eats himself (the fable of Saturn devouring his own children is infinitely less unreasonable than what Spinoza asserts), he slanders himself, he executes himself; and so on.' This would be less inconceivable if Spinoza had presented God

as an assemblage of distinct parts; but he has reduced him to the most perfect simplicity, to unity of substance, to indivisibility. He asserts therefore the most infamous and most monstrous extravagances that can be conceived, and much more ridiculous than those of the poets concerning the gods of paganism. I am surprised either that he did not see them, or if he did, that he was so opinionated as to hold on to his principle. A man of good sense would prefer to break the ground with his teeth and his nails than to cultivate as shocking and absurd a hypothesis as this.

Another proof of what is said above, drawn from the misery of man.
V. Two more objections. There have been some philosophers impious enough to deny that there is a God. But they have not pushed their extravagances as far as to say that if he existed, he would not be of a perfectly happy nature. The greatest sceptics of antiquity have said that all men have an idea of God according to which he is a living being, happy, incorruptible, perfect in felicity, and not susceptible of any evil [Bayle here refers to Sextus Empiricus, *Adversus mathematicos* IX, 33]. Happiness was the most inseparable property contained in the idea of him. Those who deny him the authority over, and the direction of, the world at least leave him felicity and immortal beatitude. Those who made him subject to death at least say that he was happy all his life. It was no doubt an extravagance bordering on madness not to unite immortality and happiness in the divine nature. Plutarch refutes this absurdity of the Stoics very well [Bayle here refers to Plutarch, *Moralia*, 'De Stoicorum repugnantiis']. But no matter how foolish this dream of the Stoics was, it did not deprive the gods of their happiness during their lifetime. The Spinozists are perhaps the only ones who have

reduced the divinity to misery. Now what misery? Sometimes so great that it is thrown into despair, and it would annihilate itself if it could; it tries; it deprives itself of anything it can; it hangs itself; it jumps over precipices, not being able to bear the frightful grief any longer that devours it. These are not just declamations. This is an exact and philosophical language; for if man is only a modification, he does nothing. It would be an impertinent, comical, jocular way of expressing things to say, 'Joy is merry, sadness is sad'. In Spinoza's system, to say, 'Man thinks, man afflicts himself, man hangs himself, and so on', would be expressing oneself in the same way. All these propositions ought to be said of the substance of which man is only a mode. How can it be imagined that an independent being who exists by himself and who possesses infinite perfections might be subject to all the miseries of mankind? If some other being forced it to vex itself, to feel pain, we would not find it so strange that it turned its own activity to making itself unhappy; we should say, 'It must be obeying a *force majeure;* obviously it is giving itself the stone, colic, high fever, and madness in order to avoid a greater ill.' But it is the only being in the universe. Nothing orders it, exhorts it, begs it. It is its own nature, Spinoza will say, that leads it to give itself in certain circumstances great vexation and very severe pain. But, I will reply to him, did you not find something monstrous and inconceivable in such a fatality? ...

The hypothesis of Spinoza would make all his conduct and his discourse appear ridiculous.
VI. If I did not remember that I am not writing a book against this man, but merely a few brief remarks in passing, I would show many other absurdities in his system. Let us finish with this one. He has embarked on a hypothesis that would make all his work ridiculous, and I am very sure that on each page of his *Ethics* one could find some pitiful nonsense. First, I would like to know what he means when he rejects certain doctrines and sets forth others. Does he intend to teach truths? Does he wish to refute errors? But has he any right to say that there are errors? The thoughts of ordinary philosophers, those of Jews, and those of Christians, are they not modes of the infinite being, as much as those of his *Ethics*? Are they not realities that are as necessary to the perfection of the universe as all his speculations? Do they not emanate from the necessary cause? How then can he dare to claim that there is something to rectify? In the second place, does he not claim that the being of which they are modalities acts necessarily, that it always goes on its course, that it cannot turn aside, cannot stop, nor, since it is the sole entity in the universe, can any external cause ever stop it or correct it? Then, there is nothing more useless than the lectures of this philosopher. Is it right for him, being only a modification of substance, to prescribe to the infinite being what he must do? Will this being hear him? And if he hears, could he profit from this? Does he not always act according to the entire extent of his powers, without knowing either where he is going or what he is doing? A man like Spinoza would sit absolutely still if he reasoned logically. 'If it is possible,' he would say, 'that such a doctrine might be established, the necessity of nature would establish it without my book. If it is not possible, all of my writings would accomplish nothing.'

3. Remark O (They would like to have the difficulties Spinoza succumbed to completely removed).

We will not be mistaken, it seems to me, if we suppose that he only threw himself over this precipice by not having been able to comprehend either that matter is eternal and different from God, or that it has been produced from nothing, or that an infinite and supremely free mind, creator of all things, could produce a work such as the world. A matter that necessarily exists, and that nevertheless is destitute of activity and subject to the power of another principle, is not something that agrees with reason. We see no harmony between these three qualities. The idea of order opposes such a combination. A matter created from nothing is inconceivable, whatever efforts we make to form an idea of an act of will that might convert into a real substance that which was formerly nothing. This principle of the ancients, *ex nihilo nihil fit*, 'from nothing, nothing comes', continuously presents itself to our imagination and shines there in so brilliant a manner that it stops us short in case we have begun to form any notion about the creation. Finally, that an infinitely good, infinitely holy, infinitely free God, being able to make creatures always holy and happy, should have preferred that they should be eternally criminal and miserable is something that troubles reason, and all the more so since reason cannot reconcile the free will of man [i.e. liberty of indifference] with the quality of a being produced from nothing. Now it would be incomprehensible that man could deserve any punishment under a free, good, holy, and just Providence, without reconciling these two items. These are three difficulties that obliged Spinoza to look for a new system in which God would not be distinguished from matter and in which he acts necessarily and in accordance with the full extent of his powers, not outside of himself, but in himself. It follows from this supposition, that this necessary cause, setting no limits to its power and having as a rule of its actions neither goodness, nor justice, nor knowledge, but only the infinite force of his nature had to modify itself according to all possible realities; so that errors and crimes, pain and vexation, being modalities as real as truths, and virtues, and pleasures, must be contained by the universe. Spinoza thought that by this means he could satisfy the objections of the Manicheans against one principle. They are forceful only against the supposition that a unique principle acts by choice, that it can act or not act, and that it limits its power in accordance with the rules of its goodness and equity, or in accordance with malicious instinct. Supposing this, one asks, 'Where does evil come from if this unique principle is good?' Spinoza would reply, 'Since my unique principle has the power to do evil and good and does all that it can do, it is completely necessary that there be good and evil in the universe.' Weigh, I beg you, on an impartial balance the three difficulties that he wished to avoid and the extravagant and abominable consequences of the hypothesis that he adopted. You will find that his choice is not that of a good man or of a man of judgment. He gave up some things, of which the worst that can be said is that the weakness of our reason does not allow us to know clearly if they are possible, and he embraces others the impossibility of which is manifest. There is a great deal of difference between not understanding the possibility of a thing and understanding the impossibility of it. Now see the injustice of readers. They claim that those who write against Spinoza are obliged to show them with the utmost clarity the truths which he [Spinoza] could not understand, the difficulties of which forced him into another theory. And because they do not find this in the anti-Spinoza writings, they announce that these works are unsuccessful. Is it not enough that the edifice of this atheist has been overthrown? Good sense tells us that custom ought to be maintained against the undertakings of innovators unless the latter produce better laws. Their views ought to be rejected from the fact alone that they are not better than the established opinions even though they be not worse than the abuses they fight against. Submit to custom, these people ought to be told, or offer us something better. With much greater reason it is just to reject the system of the Spinozist since it only gets us away from some difficulties in order to get us into much more inexplicable perplexities. If the difficulties were equal on both sides, the common system ought to be maintained since, in addition to the privilege of possession, it would also have the advantage of promising us great benefits for the future and giving us a thousand consolations for the miseries of this life. Is it not some consolation in misfortune to flatter oneself that the prayers that are addressed to God will be answered and that in any case he will reward us for our patience and will furnish us with a magnificent compensation? It is a great consolation to be able to flatter ourselves that other men will have some regard for the dictates of their conscience and the fear of God. This means that the ordinary theory is at the same time truer and more convenient than the theory of impiety. [Bayle's note: I have already said in the article 'Socinus, Faustus', remark I, that it is in the interest of each individual person that all the others be conscientious and God-fearing.] To have good grounds for rejecting Spinoza's hypothesis, it would suffice then to be able to say, 'It is open to no fewer objections than the Christian hypothesis.' Thus, every writer who shows that Spinozism is obscure and false in its first principles and perplexed with impenetrable and contradictory absurdities in its consequences ought to be considered as having well refuted it, even though he does not answer all the objections clearly. Let us reduce the whole matter to a few words. The ordinary hypothesis, compared with that of the Spinozists in those matters that are clear, has more evidence of truth. And when it is compared with the other with regard to the obscure matters, it seems less opposed to the natural light; and besides, it promises us an infinite happiness after this life and brings us a thousand consolations in this one, whereas the other promises us nothing beyond this world and deprives us of confidence in our prayers, and in the remorse of our neighbours. The ordinary hypothesis is then preferable to the other.

4. Remark DD (Whether it is true, as I have been told that several people claim, that I have not understood Spinoza's theory at all.)

I have heard this from several quarters, but nobody has been able to tell me what those who make this judgment base it on. Thus, I cannot answer them precisely, or examine if I ought to give in to their arguments since they are unknown to me. I can only justify myself in a general way; and I think that I can say that, if I did not understand the proposition I undertook to refute, it is not my fault. I would speak with less confidence had I written a book against Spinoza's entire system, following it page by page. No doubt, it would have happened more than once that I did not understand what he intended; and it is improbable that he completely understood himself and could make all the consequences of his hypothesis intelligible in great detail. But, since I stopped at one single proposition which is stated in very few words, which seems to be clear and precise, and which is the foundation of the entire structure, it must be the case either that I have understood it or that it contains some ambiguities entirely unworthy of a system-builder. In any case, I can console myself that I have given the same sense to Spinoza's proposition that his other adversaries have given it and that his followers can give no better answer than to say that he has not been understood. This reproach did not hinder the last person who wrote against him from understanding the proposition in question just as I did, an evident sign that their accusation is groundless.

But, to say something less general, here is what I suppose in my objections. I attribute these teachings to Spinoza: (1) that there is only one substance in the world; (2) that this substance is God; and (3) that all particular beings with corporeal extension – the sun, the moon, plants, animals, men, their motions, their ideas, their imaginings, their desires – are modifications of God. I now ask the Spinozists, has your master taught this, or has he not? If he did teach this, it cannot be said that my objections suffer from the defect called *ignoratio elenchi* (ignorance of the state of the question); for they suppose that such was his doctrine and attack it only on these grounds. I am then safe, and one would be wrong every time it was claimed that I refuted what I did not understand. If you say that Spinoza did not teach the three doctrines stated above, I ask you why, then, did he express himself exactly as would men who had the greatest passion in the world to convince the reader that they taught these three things? Is it fair or commendable to employ the common language, without attaching the same ideas to words that other men do and without announcing the new sense in which they are to be taken? But, to discuss this a little, let us see where the misunderstanding may be. I have not been

mistaken with regard to the word 'substance', for I have not opposed Spinoza's view on this point but I have admitted what he supposes, that for something to deserve the name of substance, it must be independent of all causes, or exist by itself eternally and necessarily. I do not believe that I could have been mistaken in imputing to him the view that God alone has the nature of a substance. I believe, then, that if there were any mistake in my objections, it would consist only in that I have understood by 'modalities', 'modifications', and 'modes' something different from what Spinoza intended by these words. But, once again, if I were mistaken on this point, it would be his fault. I took these terms in the sense that they have always been understood, or at least in the sense that all the new philosophers understand them [Bayle's note: I employ this restriction because of the difference that exists between the theory of the modern Aristotelians and that of the Cartesians, Gassendists, etc., concerning the nature of accidents. This difference is significant, but it amounts to the same thing with respect to the objections against Spinoza.]; and I had the right to assume that he took them in this same sense since he had not warned the world that he took them in some other sense. The general doctrine of the philosophers is that the idea of being contains, immediately under it, two species – substance and accident – and that substance subsists by itself (*ens per se subsistens*), and an accident subsists in some other being (*ens in alio*). They add that 'to subsist by itself' signifies only 'not being dependent on any subject of inhesion'; and since this agrees, according to them, with matter, angels, man's soul, they admit two kinds of substance, one uncreated, the other created; and they subdivide created substance into two species. One of these two is matter, the other is our soul. With regard to accidents, they all agreed, before the wretched disputes that divided Christendom, that they depend so essentially on their subjects of inhesion that they cannot exist without them. This was their specific characteristic, which differentiated them from substances. The doctrine of transubstantiation overthrew this whole idea and forced philosophers to say that an accident can subsist without its subject. They had to say this since they believed, on the one hand, that after consecration the substance of the bread of the Eucharist no longer subsisted, and they saw, on the other hand, that all the accidents of the bread subsisted as before. They therefore admitted a real distinction between a substance and its accidents, and a reciprocal separability between those species of beings, which would result in the fact that each of them could exist without the other. But some of them continued to say that there were accidents whose distinction from their subject was not real, and which could not subsist outside of it. They called these accidents 'modes', such as union, duration, and ubiquity. Descartes, Gassendi, and, in general, all those who have abandoned Scholastic philosophy, have denied that an accident is separable from its subject in such a way that it could subsist after its separation, and have ascribed to all accidents the nature of those that are called 'modes' and have employed the term 'mode', 'modality', or 'modification', rather than that of 'accident'. Now, since Spinoza had been a great Cartesian, it is reasonable to suppose that he ascribed to these terms the same sense that Descartes did. If this is the case, by 'modification of a substance' he only understood a way of being that has the same relation to substance as shape, motion, rest, and location have to matter, and as pain, affirmation, love, and the like, have to man's soul. For these are what the Cartesians call 'modes'. They acknowledge no others than these, from which it appears that they have kept the old idea of Aristotle according to which accidents are of such a nature that they are no part of their subject, that they cannot exist without it, and that the subject can lose them without prejudicing its existence. All this agrees with roundness, motion, rest, with relation to a stone, and does not agree any less with respect to pain and affirmation with regard to man's soul. If our Spinoza has joined the same idea to what he calls 'modification of substance', it is certain that my objections are just. I have attacked him directly according to the true sense of his words. I have rightly understood his theory, and I have refuted it in its actual sense. In short, I am safe from the accusation I am examining. But if he had the same conception as Descartes of matter (or extension) and the human soul, and if, however, he did not want to ascribe the status of substance either to extension or to our souls, because he believed that a substance is a being that does not depend on any cause, I admit that I have attacked him without grounds, have attributed to him a view that he does not hold. This is what remains for me to examine.

Having once set forth that substance is that which exists by itself, as independently of every efficient cause as of every material one or every subject of inhesion, he could not say that either matter or men's souls were substances. And since, according to the usual view, he divided being into only two species, namely substance and modification of substance, he had to say that matter and men's souls were only modifications of substance. No orthodox person will disagree with him that, according to this definition of substance, there is only one single substance in the universe, and that substance is God. It will only be a question of knowing whether he subdivides the modification of substance into two species. In case he makes use of this subdivision and means that one of those two species is what the Cartesians and other Christian philosophers call 'created substance,' and the other species what they call 'accident' or 'mode', there will be only a dispute about words between him and them; and it will be very easy to bring his whole system back to orthodoxy and to make his sect vanish; for a person is only inclined to be a Spinozist because he believes that Spinoza has completely overturned the Christian philosophers' system of the existence of an immaterial God governing all things with a perfect liberty. From which we can conclude in passing that the Spinozists and their adversaries agree completely about the meaning of the phrase 'modification of substance'. They both believe that Spinoza employed this term only to designate a being that has the same nature as what the Cartesian philosophers call 'modes', and that he never understood by this term a being that had the properties or nature of what we call 'created substance'.

Those who should insist strongly that I have been mistaken might suppose that Spinoza only rejected the designation, 'substance,' given to beings dependent on another cause with respect to their production, their conservation, and their operation *in fieri, in esse et in operari*, as is said in the Schools. They could say that, while retaining the entire reality of the thing, he avoided using the word, because he thought that a being so dependent on its cause could not be called *ens per se subsistens*, 'a being subsisting by itself', which is the definition of substance. I reply to them, as I did above, that there will then be only a pure logomachy, or dispute about words, between him and the other philosophers, and that I will admit my mistake with the greatest pleasure in the world if it is the case that Spinoza actually was a Cartesian but had been more careful than Descartes in employing the word 'substance', and that all of the impiety attributed to him consists only in a misunderstanding. He meant to say nothing else, it will be added, than what is found in the books of the theologians, namely that the immensity of God fills heaven and earth and all the imaginary spaces to infinity [Bayle's note: Note that the Cartesian theologians explain the immensity of God in another way.], that consequently his essence penetrates and locally surrounds all other beings, so that it is in him that 'we live and move' (Acts 17:28), and that nothing has been produced outside of him. For, since he fills all spaces, he can place a body in himself only, in view of the fact that outside of him there is nothing. Besides, we know that all beings are incapable of existing without him. It is then true that the properties of Cartesian modes agree with what are called 'created substances'. These substances are in God and cannot subsist outside of him and without him. It must not then be found strange that Spinoza called them 'modifications'; but on the other hand, he did not deny that there was a real distinction, and that each of them constituted a particular principle of either actions or passions in such a manner that one does what the other does not do, and that when it is denied of one what is affirmed of the other, this is done in accordance with the rules of logic, without anyone being able to object to Spinoza that it follows from his principles that two contradictory principles are true of one and the same subject at the same time.

All this discourse has no purpose, and if one wants to get to the point, one ought to answer this precise question: does the true and proper characteristic of a modification belong to matter with respect to God, or does it not? Before answering me, wait until I explain to you, by examples, what a characteristic of a modification is. It is to be in a subject in the way in which motion is in a body, and thought is in man's soul, and the form of a bowl is in a vase that we call a bowl. It is not sufficient to be a modification of the divine substance to subsist in the immensity of God, to be penetrated with it, to be surrounded by it on all sides, to exist by virtue of God, and not to be able to exist without him or outside him. It would also be necessary that the divine substance be the subject of inherence of a thing, just as in the ordinary view, the human soul is the subject of inherence of feeling and desire, pewter is the subject of inherence of the form of the bowl, and the body is the subject of inherence of motion, rest, and shape. Answer me now; and if you say that according to Spinoza the substance of God is not in that way the subject of inherence of that extension, or motion, or human thoughts, I will admit to you that you make him an orthodox philosopher who did not deserve to have the objections made against him that have been offered, and who only deserved to have been reproached for having gone through so much trouble to embrace a view that everyone knows and for having constructed a new system that is only built on the ambiguity of a word. If you say that he claimed that divine substance is the subject of inherence of matter and of all the varieties of extension and thought, in the same sense that according to Descartes extension is the subject of inherence of motion and man's soul is the subject of inherence of sensations and passions, then I have all that I ask for. That is exactly how I understood Spinoza, and it is on this that I based all my objections....

The Spinozists could take advantage of the doctrine of transubstantiation; for if they will consult the writings of the Spanish Scholastics,

they will find an infinite number of subtleties there to give some answer to the arguments of those who say that the same man cannot be a Mohammedan in Turkey and a Christian in France, sick in Rome and healthy at Vienna. But I cannot tell, after all, if they will not find themselves obliged to compare their theory with the mystery of the Trinity in order to extricate themselves from the contradictions with which they are overwhelmed. If they do not say that the modifications of God, Plato, Aristotle, this horse, this monkey, this tree, this stone, are so many personalities, which, although *identified* with the same substance, can each be a particular and determinate principle, and distinct from the other modifications, they can never parry the blow that can be struck against them concerning the principle that 'two contradictory terms cannot belong to the same subject at the same time'. Some day perhaps the Spinozists will say that just as the three persons of the Trinity, without being distinct from the divine substance, according to the theologians, and without having any absolute attribute that is not numerically the same in all of them, do not fail to have, each one of them, properties that can be denied of the others, so nothing stops Spinoza from admitting an infinite number of modalities or personalities in the divine substance, one of which does something that the others do not do. This will not be a real contradiction, since the theologians acknowledge a virtual distinction *in ordine ad suscipicienda duo praedicata contradictoria* (with respect to the susceptibility of the two terms that are contradictory). But as the subtle Arriaga judiciously remarks, on the subject of the metaphysical degrees [Bayle's note: This is what they call the attributes that constitute the nature of man: being, substance, body, living, animal, rational. It is agreed that they are not distinct one from the other, but really one and the same entity.], which some men would maintain are capable of receiving two contradictory propositions: to undertake to transfer to natural things what Revelation teaches us about the nature of God would be to ruin philosophy completely; for this would open the door to proving that there is no real difference between creatures [Bayle here refers to Arriaga, *Disput. V Logica*, Sec. II, no. 29].

Here is the great debt we owe to Spinoza: he takes away from us, with all the force he commands, the most necessary of all principles. For if it were not certain that at the same time the same thing cannot be such and such and not such and such, it would be useless to meditate or to reason....

BIBLIOGRAPHY
Primary Sources
Aubert de Versé, N., *L'Impie convaincu, ou dissertation contre Spinoza* (Amsterdam, 1684).
Bayle, P., *Pensées diverses sur la comète* (Rotterdam, 1682). English translation: *Various Thoughts on the Occasion of a Comet*, transl. by Robert C. Bartlett (New York: State University of New York Press, 2000).
———, *Commentaire philosophique* (Rotterdam, 1686). English translation: *A Philosophical commentary*, edited, with an Introduction, by J. Kilcullen and C. Kukathas (Indianapolis: Liberty Fund, 2005).
———, *Continuation des pensées diverses* (Rotterdam, 1705).
———, *Réponse aux questions d'un provincial* (Rotterdam, 1704–7).
———, *Œuvres diverses*, 4 vols (The Hague, 1727–31; repr. Hildesheim: Olms, 1984–90).
———, *Dictionnaire historique et critique*, 5th edn (Amsterdam, 1740).
———, *Historical and Critical Dictionary. Selections*, ed. R. Popkin (Indianapolis: Hackett, 1965).
———, *Écrits sur Spinoza*, ed. P.-F. Moreau and F. Charles-Daubert (Paris: Berg Int., 1983).
———, *Correspondance*, ed. É. Labrousse and A. McKenna, 10 vols (Oxford: The Voltaire Foundation, 1999–).
Budde, J.F., *De spinozismo ante Spinozam* (Halle and Magdeburg, 1701).
Herder, J.G., *Gott* (Gotha, 1787).
Kuyper, F., *Arcana atheismi revelata* (Rotterdam, 1676).
Malebranche, N., *Œuvres complètes*, 20 vols (Paris: Vrin, 1958–70).
Poiret, P., *Cogitationum rationalium de Deo, anima et malo libri quatuor*, 2nd edn (Amsterdam, 1685).

Secondary Literature
Curley, E.M., *Spinoza's Metaphysics* (Cambridge, MA: Harvard University Press, 1969).
Gay, P., *The Enlightenment. An Interpretation*, 2 vols (London: Wildwood House, 1973).
Israel, J.I., *Radical Enlightenment. Philosophy and the Making of Modernity, 1650–1750* (Oxford: Oxford University Press, 2001).
Kors, A.C., *Atheism in France (1650–1729): The Orthodox Sources of Disbelief* (Princeton: Princeton University Press, 1991).
Mori, G., *Bayle philosophe* (Paris: Champion, 1999).
Nadler, S., *Spinoza: A Life* (Cambridge: Cambridge University Press, 1999).

Vernière, P., *Spinoza et la pensée française avant la Révolution* (Paris: Presses Universitaires de France, 1954).

Wolfson, H.A., *The Philosophy of Spinoza*, 2 vols (Cambridge, MA: Harvard University Press, 1934).

G. Mori

SAMUEL CLARKE, A Demonstration of the Being and Attributes of God (1705)

In the early eighteenth century, Newton's physics came to be transformed into a school of thought called 'Newtonianism'. The Cambridge-educated philosopher and theologian Samuel Clarke (1675–1729) soon developed into one of its most influential protagonists by the way in which he turned Newtonian physics into the cornerstone of a comprehensive natural theology. It would seem that to many of his early eighteenth-century readers one of the major benefits of Clarke's Newtonianism was its ability to counter the threat of Spinozism. Indeed, to Clarke's mind, the defence of Newtonian natural philosophy and the destruction of Spinozism were closely related endeavours: before his thirtieth birthday, he had composed not only several theological treatises but also a heavily annotated Latin translation of Jacques Rouhault's Cartesian physics (1697), designed to demonstrate the superiority of Newton's physics over Descartes's, as well as *A Demonstration of the Being and Attributes of God: More Particularly in Answer to Mr. Hobbs, Spinoza, And their Followers*. This book was based on the eight Boyle Lectures Clarke had held in 1704.

One of Clarke's main targets in *A Demonstration of the Being and Attributes of God* was, incidentally, John Toland's view that motion was essential to matter (pp. 45–59), while his chief affirmation concerned the possibility of a vacuum, that is the possibility for matter *not* to exist. Matter, according to Clarke, exists *in* space, which is a *property* of the necessary substance that is God. Clarke's attempts to lay a metaphysical foundation for Newton's physics was bolstered by the second edition of the latter's *Principia*, and more in particular by the inclusion of its famous 'General Scholium' (1713). Newton much appreciated Clarke's efforts, including his well-known correspondence with Leibniz.

Recently, interest in Samuel Clarke's legacy has revived. The real impact Newtonianism made on the French Enlightenment in particular has been the subject of several critical studies, in which the foundational myth propagated by the Encyclopedists, turning Newton into their scientific point of departure, has been re-examined in considerable detail (Israel, 2001, pp. 519–27 and 599–609; 2006, pp. 201–22; Force and Hutton (eds), 2004; Mandelbrote (ed.), 2004; Shank, 2008). It has recently also been argued that Clarke's rationalist natural theology was among the chief targets of Hume's *Treatise* (Russell, 2008).

The following pages are taken from *A Demonstration of the Being and Attributes of God*, pp. 50–7 and 93–129. Clarke's footnotes, mostly referring to Spinoza's works, have been deleted.

A DEMONSTRATION OF THE BEING AND ATTRIBUTES OF GOD

Spinoza, the most celebrated Patron of Atheism in our Time, who taught that there is no Difference of Substances; but that the Whole and every Part of *the Material World* is a Necessarily-existing Being; and that there is no other God, but the Universe: That he might seemingly avoid the manifold Absurdities of that Opinion; endeavours by an Ambiguity of Expression in the Progress of his Discourse, to elude the Arguments by which he foresaw his Assertion would be confuted: For, having at first plainly asserted, that All Substance is Necessarily-existing; he would afterward seem to explain it away, by asserting, that the Reason why every thing exists necessarily, and could not possibly have been in any respect different from what it Now is, is because every thing flows from the *Necessity of the Divine Nature.* By which if the unwary Reader understands, that he means things are therefore Necessarily such as they are, because Infinite Wisdom and Goodness could not possibly make Things but in that Order which is Fittest and Wisest in the Whole; he is very much mistaken: For such a Necessity, is not a Natural, but only a Moral and Consequential Necessity; and directly contrary to the Author's true Intention. Further, if the Reader hereby understands, that God was determined, not by a Necessity of Wisdom and Goodness, but by a mere Natural Necessity, exclusive of Will and Choice, to make all Things just as they now are; neither is this the whole of *Spinoza*'s meaning: For this, as absurd as it is, is still supposing God, as a Substance distinct from the Material World; which He expressly denies. Nay further, if any one thinks his meaning to be, that all Substances in the World, are only Modifications of the Divine Essence; neither is This *All*: For thus God may still be supposed as an Agent, acting upon *himself* at least, and manifesting *himself* in different manners, according to his own Will: Which *Spinoza* expressly denies. But his true meaning therefore, however darkly and ambiguously he sometimes speaks, must be this; and if he means any thing at all consistent with himself, can be no other than this: That, since it is absolutely impossible for any thing to be created or produced by another; and also absolutely impossible for God to have caused any thing to be in any respect different from what it now is; every thing that exists, must needs be *so* a Part of the Divine Substance, not as a Modification caused in it by any Will or Good-Pleasure or Wisdom in the whole, but as of Absolute Necessity in it self, with respect to the *manner* of the Existence of each Part, no less than with respect to the Self-Existence of the whole. Thus the Opinion of *Spinoza*, when expressed plainly and consistently, comes evidently to this: That the *Material World,* and every Part of it, with the order and manner of Being of each Part, is the only Self-Existent, or Necessarily-Existing Being. And now Consequently, he must of Necessity affirm all the Conclusions, which I have before shown to follow demonstrably from that Opinion. He cannot possibly avoid affirming that 'tis a Contradiction, (not *to the Perfections of God;* For that is mere senseless Cant and Amusement in Him who maintains that there is but One Substance in the Universe; But he must affirm that it is *in it self and in Terms* a Contradiction,) for any thing to be, or to be imagined, in any respect otherwise than it Now is. He must say 'tis a Contradiction, to suppose the *Number,* or *Figure,* or *Order* of the Principal Parts of the World, could possibly have been different from what they Now are. He must say Motion is necessary *of it self*; and consequently that 'tis a Contradiction in Terms, to suppose any Matter to be at Rest: Or else He must affirm, (which is rather the more absurd of the two; as may appear from what has been already said in proof of the *Second*

General Head of the foregoing Discourse: And yet he has chosen to affirm it;) that Motion, as a Dependent Being, has been eternally communicated from one piece of Matter to another; without having at all any Original Cause of its Being, either within it self or from without: Which, with other the like Consequences, touching the Necessity of the Existence of Things; the very mention of which, is a sufficient Confutation of any Opinion they follow from; do, as I have said, unavoidably follow from the foremention'd Opinion of *Spinoza*: And consequently that Opinion, *viz. That the Universe or Whole World is the Self-existent or Necessarily-existing Being,* is demonstrated to be false....

VII. *The Self-Existent Being, must of Necessity be but One.* This evidently follows from his being *Necessarily-Existent.* For Necessity Absolute in it self, is Simple and Uniform, without any possible Difference or Variety: And all Variety or Difference of Existence, must needs arise from some External Cause, and be *dependent* upon it. For to suppose *two* (or more) *different* Natures existing of *themselves,* necessarily, and *independent* from each other; implies this plain *Contradiction*; that each of them being independent from the other, they may either of them be supposed to exist alone, so that it will be no contradiction to imagine the other not to exist, and consequently neither of them will be Necessarily-Existing. Whatsoever therefore exists necessarily, is the One Simple Essence of the Self-Existent Being: and whatsoever differs from that, is not Necessarily-Existing: Because in absolute Necessity there can be no Difference or Diversity of Existence. Other Beings there may be innumerable, besides the One Infinite Self-Existent: But no Other Nature can be Self-Existent, because so it would be individually the same, at the same time that it is supposed to be different.

From hence it follows,

1st. That the *Unity* of God, is an *Unity of Nature* or *Essence*: For of *This* it is that we must be understood, if we would argue Intelligibly, when we speak of Necessity or Self-Existence. As to the *Diversity of Persons* in that One and the same Nature: That is; whether in the Unity of the Divine Nature, there may not co-exist with the First Supreme Cause, such Emanations from it, as may themselves be equally Eternal, Infinite, and Perfect, by an absolute and complete Communication of all the Divine Attributes in an infinite and perfect degree, excepting only that of Self-Origination: Of this, I say; as there is nothing in bare Reason, by which it can be demonstrated that there is actually any such thing; so neither is there any Argument, by which it can be proved impossible or unreasonable to be supposed; and therefore when declared and made known to us by clear Revelation, it ought to be believed.

2dly. From hence it follows, That *it is impossible there should be two different Self-existent Independent Principles, as some Philosophers have imagined; such as God and Matter.* For since Self-Existence is Necessary Existence; and since it is an express Contradiction (as has already been shown) that two different Natures should each be Necessarily-existing; it evidently follows, that 'tis absolutely impossible there should be Two Independent Self-existent Principles, such as *God and Matter.*

3dly. From hence we may observe the Vanity, Folly and Weakness of *Spinoza*: who because Self-existent Nature must necessarily be but One, concludes from thence, that *the whole World, and every thing contained therein, is One Uniform Substance, Eternal, Uncreated and Necessary*: Whereas just on the contrary he ought to have concluded, that because all things in the World are very different one from another, and have all manner of Variety and all the Marks of Will and Arbitrariness and Changeableness, (and none of Necessity) in them, being plainly fitted with very different Powers to very different Ends, and distinguished one from another by a diversity, not only of Modes, but also of essential Attributes, and consequently (if we have any Knowledge at all of them) of their Substances themselves also; therefore *none of these things are necessary or Self-existent, but must needs depend all upon some External Cause, that is, on the One Supreme, Unchangeable, Self-existent Being.* That which led *Spinoza* into his foolish and destructive Opinion, and on which alone all his *Argumentation* is entirely built, is that *absurd* Definition of Substance; that *it is Something, the Idea of which does not depend on, or presuppose, the Idea of any other thing, from which it might proceed; but includes in it self Necessary-existence.* Which Definition is either false and signifies nothing; and then his whole Doctrine built upon it, falls at once to the Ground: Or if it be true; then neither Matter, nor Spirit, nor any *Finite* Being whatsoever, (as has been before shown), is in that Sense properly a Substance, but (*the* ἀών) the Self-existent Being alone; and so it will prove Nothing (notwithstanding all his *Show* and *Form* of Demonstration,) to his main Purpose; which was, to make us believe that there is no such Thing as Power or Liberty in the Universe, but that every particular thing in the World is by an Absolute Necessity just what it is, and could not possibly have been in any respect otherwise: Supposing, I say, his Definition of Substance to be true; yet even *That* would really conclude nothing to his main Purpose concerning the Necessity of all Things: For since, according to that

Definition, neither Matter nor Spirit nor any Finite Beings whatsoever, are Substances, but only Modes; how will it follow, that because Substance is Self-existent, therefore all these Modes are so too? Why, because *from an Infinite Cause, Infinite Effects must needs follow.* Very true; supposing That Infinite Self-existent Cause, not to be a Voluntary, but a mere Necessary Agent, that is, no Agent at all; Which Supposition (*in the present Argument*) is the Question begged; And what he *afterwards* attempts to allege in proof of it, shall *afterwards* be considered in its proper place.

VIII. *The Self-Existent and Original Cause of all things, must be an Intelligent Being.* In this Proposition lies the main Question between us and the Atheists. For that Something must be Self-Existent; and that That which is Self-Existent, must necessarily be Eternal and Infinite and the Original Cause of all things; will not bear much dispute. But all Atheists, whether they hold the World to be *of it self* Eternal both as to the Matter and Form, or whether they hold the Matter only to be Necessary and the Form Contingent, or whatever Hypothesis they frame; have always asserted and must maintain, either directly or indirectly, that the Self-Existent Being is not an Intelligent Being, but either pure unactive Matter, or (which in other Words is the very same thing) a mere Necessary Agent. For a Mere Necessary Agent must of necessity either be plainly and directly in the grossest Sense Unintelligent; which was the antient Atheists Notion of the Self-Existent Being: or else its Intelligence (which is the assertion of *Spinoza* and some Moderns,) must be wholly separate from any Power of Will and Choice; which in Respect of any Excellence and Perfection, or indeed to any common Sense at all, is the very same thing.

109

Now that the Self-Existent Being, is not such a Blind and Unintelligent Necessity, but in the most proper Sense an Understanding and really Active Being; cannot indeed be Demonstrated strictly and properly *a priori*; because we know not wherein Intelligence consists, nor can see the immediate and necessary Connection of it with Self-Existence, as we can that of Eternity, Infinity, Unity, &c. But *a posteriori,* almost every thing in the World Demonstrates to us this Great Truth, and affords undeniable Arguments to prove that the World, and all things therein, are the Effects of an Intelligent and Knowing Cause.

And *1st*, Since in general there are manifestly in Things, various kinds of Powers and very different Excellencies and Degrees of Perfection; it must needs be, that in the Order of Causes and Effects, the Cause must always be more Excellent than the Effect; and consequently the Self-Existent Being, whatever That be Supposed to be, must of necessity (being the Original of all things) contain in it self the Sum and highest Degree of all the Perfections of all things. Not because that which is Self-Existent, must *therefore* have all possible Perfections: (For This, though most certainly true in it self, yet cannot be so clearly demonstrated a priori:) But because it is impossible that any effect should have any Perfection, which was not in the Cause: For if it had, then that Perfection would be caused by Nothing; which is a flat Contradiction. Now an Unintelligent Being, 'tis evident, cannot be indued with all the Perfections of all things in the World. All things therefore cannot arise from an Unintelligent Original: and consequently the Self-Existent Being, must of Necessity be Intelligent.

There is no Possibility for an Atheist to avoid the Force of this Argument any other way, than by asserting one of these two things: Either that there is no Intelligent Being at all in the Universe; or that Intelligence is no distinct Perfection, but merely a Composition of Figure and Motion, as Colour and Sounds are supposed to be. Of the former of which, every Mans own Consciousness is an abundant Confutation: And that the latter, (in which the main strength of Atheism lies,) is most absurd and impossible, shall be shown immediately: Which nevertheless if it could be supposed to be True, yet that even upon That Supposition it would still follow that the Self-Existing Being must needs be Intelligent; shall be proved in my 4th Argument upon this present Head. In the mean time, that it is most absurd and impossible to suppose Intelligence not to be any distinct Perfection, properly speaking, but merely a Composition of Unintelligent Figure and Motion; will appear from what shall be said in the ensuing Argument, which is

2ly. Since *in Man in particular* there is undeniably that Power, which we call Thought, Intelligence, Consciousness, Perception or Knowledge; there must of Necessity either have been from Eternity *without any Original Cause at all,* an infinite Succession of Men, whereof *no one* has had a *Necessary,* but *every one* a *Dependent and Communicated* Being; or else these Beings, indued with Perception and Consciousness, must at some time or other have arisen purely out of that which had no such Quality as Sense, Perception or Consciousness; or else they must have been produced by some *Intelligent* Superiour Being. There never was nor can be any Atheist whatsoever, that can deny but that One of these three Suppositions must be the Truth: If therefore the two former can be proved to be false and impossible, the latter must be owned to be Demonstrably true. Now that the first is impossible, is evident from what has been already said in proof of the *Second* General Head of this

Discourse. And that the second is likewise impossible; may be thus Demonstrated. If Perception or Intelligence, be a *distinct Quality* or Perfection; and not a mere Effect or Composition of Unintelligent Figure and Motion; then Beings indued with Perception and Consciousness, can never have arisen purely out of that which had no such Quality as Perception or Consciousness; because nothing can ever give to another any Perfection, that it hath not either actually in it self, or at least in a higher degree: *But* Perception or Intelligence, is a distinct Quality or Perfection; and not a meer Effect or Composition of Unintelligent Figure and Motion. *First, if Perception or Intelligence, be any real, distinct Quality or Perfection; and not a mere Effect or Composition of Unintelligent Figure and Motion; then Beings indued with Perception or Consciousness, can never possibly have arisen purely out of that which it self had no such Quality as Perception or Consciousness; because nothing can ever give to another any Perfection, that it hath not either actually in it self, or at least in a higher degree.* This is very evident; because if any thing could give another any Perfection which it has not it self, that Perfection would be caused absolutely by *Nothing*; which is a flat Contradiction. If any one here replies, (as Mr. *Gildon* has done in a Letter to Mr. *Blount* [*Oracles of Reason,* p. 186.]) that Colours, Sounds, Taste, and the like, arise from Figure and Motion, which have no such Qualities in themselves; or that Figure, Divisibility, and other Qualities of Matter are confessed to be given it by God, who yet cannot without extreme Blasphemy be said to have any such Qualities himself; and that therefore in like manner Perception or Intelligence may arise out of that which has no Intelligence it self: The Answer is very easie: first, That Colours, Sounds, Taste, and the like, are by no means

Effects arising from mere Figure and Motion, there being nothing in the Bodies themselves, the Objects of the Senses, that has any manner of Similitude to any of these Qualities; but they are plainly *Thoughts* or Modifications of the Mind it self, which is an Intelligent Being; and are not properly *Caused,* but only *Occasioned,* by the Impressions of Figure and Motion: Nor will it at all help an Atheist (as to the present Question,) thought we make for his sake (that we may allow him the greatest possible Advantage) even That most absurd Supposition, that the Mind it self is nothing but mere Matter, and not at all an Immaterial Substance; For even supposing it to be mere Matter, yet he must needs confess it to be such Matter, as is indued not only with bare Figure and Motion, but also with the Quality of Intelligence and Perception; and then, as to the present Question, it will still come to the same thing; that Colours, Sounds, and the like, which are not Qualities of Unintelligent Bodies, but Perceptions of Mind, can no more be caused by, or arise from, mere Unintelligent Figure and Motion, than Colour can be a Triangle, or Sound a Square, or Something be caused by Nothing. And then, as to the Second Part of the Objection; that Figure, Divisibility, and other Qualities of Matter are (as we our selves acknowledge) given it by God, who yet cannot without extreme Blasphemy be said to have any such Qualities himself; and that therefore in like manner Perception or Intelligence may arise out of that which has no Intelligence it self; The Answer is still easier; That Figure, Divisibility, and other such like Qualities of Matter, are not real, proper, distinct and Positive Powers, but only Negative Qualities, Deficiencies or Imperfections; and tho' no Cause can communicate to its Effect any real Perfection which it has not it self, yet the Effect may easily have many Imperfections or Negative Qualities which are not in the Cause. Though therefore Figure, Divisibility and the like, (which are mere Negations, as all Limitations are,) may be in the Effect, and not in the Cause; yet Intelligence, (which we now suppose, and shall prove immediately, to be a distinct Quality; and which no Man can say is a mere Negation;) cannot possibly be so. And now, having thus demonstrated, that if Perception or Intelligence be supposed to be a *distinct Quality* or Perfection, (though even but of *Matter* only, if the Atheist pleases,) and not a mere Effect or Composition of Unintelligent Figure and Motion; then Beings indued with Perception or Consciousness, can never have risen purely out of that which had no such Quality as Perception or Consciousness; because nothing can ever give to another any Perfection, which it has not it self: It will easily appear, *secondly,* That *Perception or Intelligence is really such a distinct Quality or Perception; and not possibly a mere Effect or Composition of Unintelligent Figure and Motion:* And that for this plain Reason; because Intelligence *is not* Figure, and Consciousness *is not* Motion. For whatever can arise from, or be compounded of any Things; is still only those very Things, of which it was compounded: And if infinite Compositions or Divisions be made eternally, the Things will still be but eternally the same: And all their possible Effects, can never be any thing but Repetitions of the same. For instance: All possible Changes, Compositions or Divisions of *Figure,* are still nothing but *Figure*: And all possible Compositions or Effects of *Motion,* can eternally be nothing but mere *Motion.* If therefore there ever was a Time, when there was nothing in the Universe but Matter and Motion; there never could have been any thing else therein, but Matter and Motion: And it would have been as impossible, there should have existed any

such thing as Intelligence or Consciousness; or even any such thing as Light, or Heat, or Sound, or Colour, or any of those we call Secondary Qualities of Matter; as it is now impossible for Motion to be Blue or Red, or for a Triangle to be transformed into a Sound. That which has been apt to deceive Men in this matter, is this; that they imagine Compounds to be somewhat really different from that of which they are compounded: Which is a very great Mistake. For all the Things, of which Men so judge; either, if they be really different, are not Compounds nor Effects of what Men judge them to be, but are something totally distinct; as when the Vulgar thinks Colours and Sounds to be Properties Inherent in Bodies, when indeed they are purely Thoughts of the Mind: Or else, if they be really Compounds and Effects, then they are not different, but exactly the same that ever they were; as when two Triangles put together make a Square, that Square is still nothing but two Triangles; or when a Square cut in halves makes two Triangles, those two Triangles are still only the two halves of a Square; or when the mixture of Blew and Yellow Powder makes a Green, that Green is still nothing but Blew and Yellow intermixed, as is plainly visible by the help of Microscopes: And, in short, every thing by Composition, Division, or Motion; is nothing else but the very same it was before, taken either in whole or by Parts, or in different Place or Order. Mr. *Hobbs* seems to have been aware of this: And therefore, though he is very sparing, and as it were ashamed to speak out; yet finding himself pressed in his own Mind with the Difficulty arising from the Impossibility of Sense or Consciousness being merely the Effect of Figure and Motion; and it not serving *his* Purpose at all, (were the thing never so possible,) to suppose that God by an immediate and voluntary Act of his *Almighty*

Power indues certain Systems of Matter with Consciousness and Thought, (of which Opinion I shall have occasion to speak somewhat more hereafter;) he is forced to recur to that prodigiously absurd Supposition, that All Matter, as Matter, is indued not only with Figure and a Capacity of Motion, but also with an actual Sense or Perception; and wants only the Organs and Memory of Animals, to express its Sensation.

3dly, That the Self-existent and Original Cause of all things, is an Intelligent Being; appears abundantly from the excellent *Variety, Order, Beauty* and *Wonderful Contrivance* and *Fitness of all things in the World, to their proper and respective Ends.* This Argument has been so Learnedly and Fully handled, both by Ancient and Modern Writers; that I do but just mention it, without inlarging at all upon it. I shall only at this Time make this One Observation: That whereas *Des Cartes* and others have indeavoured to give a Possible Account, how the World might be formed by the Necessary Laws of Motion alone; they have by so seemingly Vast an Undertaking, really meant no more, than to explain Philosophically how the inanimate part, that is, infinitely the least considerable part of the World, might possibly have been framed: For as to Plants and Animals, in which the Wisdom of the Creator principally appears; they have never in any tolerable manner, or with any the least appearance of Success, pretended to give an Account, how *They* were originally Formed. In these Things, Matter and the Laws of Motion, are able to do nothing at all: And how ridiculous the Epicurean Hypothesis is, of the Earth producing them all at first by chance; (besides that I think it is now given up, even by all Atheists;) appears from the late Discovery made in Philosophy, that there is no such thing as equivocal Generation of any the meanest Animal or Plant; the Sun and Earth and Water, and all the Powers of Nature in Conjunction, being able to do nothing at all towards the producing any thing indued with so much as even a Vegetable Life: (From which most excellent Discovery, we may *by the by* observe the Usefulness of Natural and Experimental Philosophy, sometimes even in Matters of Religion.) Since therefore things are thus, it must unavoidably be granted (even by the most Obstinate Atheist,) either that all Plants and Animals are originally the Work of an Intelligent Being, and Created by him in Time; or that having been from Eternity in the same Order and Method they now are in, they are an Eternal Effect of an Eternal Intelligent Cause continually exerting his Infinite Power and Wisdom; or else that without any Self-existent Original at all, they have been derived one from another in an Eternal Succession, by an infinite Progress of Dependent Causes: The first of these three ways, is the Conclusion we assert: The second, (so far as the Cause of Atheism is concerned,) comes to the very same thing: And the third I have already shown, (in the Proof of the Second General Head of this Discourse,) to be absolutely Impossible and a Contradiction.

4thly, Supposing it was possible that the Form of the World and all the Visible things contained therein, with the Order, Beauty, and exquisite Fitness of their Parts; any supposing that even Intelligence it self, with Consciousness and Thought, in all the Beings we know, could possible be the Result or Effect of mere Unintelligent Matter, Figure and Motion: (which is the most unreasonable and impossible Supposition in the World:) Yet even still there would remain an undeniable Demonstration, that the Self-existent Being, (whatever it be supposed to be,) must be Intelligent. For even these Principles themselves [*Unintelligent Figure* and *Motion*] could never have possibly existed without there having been before them an Intelligent Cause. I instance in *Motion*. 'Tis evident there is Now such a thing as Motion in the World: Which either began at some Time or other, or was Eternal: If it began at any Time, then the Question is granted, that the First Cause is an Intelligent Being; For mere Unintelligent Matter, and that at Rest, 'tis manifest could never of it self begin to Move: On the contrary, if Motion was Eternal; either it was eternally caused by some Eternal Intelligent Being; or it must of it self be Necessary and Self-existent; or else, without any Necessity in its own Nature, and without any External Necessary Cause, it must have existed from Eternity by an Endless Successive Communication: If Motion was eternally Caused by some Eternal Intelligent Being; this also is granting the Question, as to the present Dispute: If it was of it self Necessary and Self-existent; then it follows, that it must be a Contradiction in Terms, to suppose any Matter to be at Rest; And it must also imply a Contradiction, to suppose that there might *possibly* have been originally more or less Motion in the Universe than there *actually* was; which is so very absurd a Consequence, that *Spinoza* himself, though he expressly asserts all Things to be *Necessary*, yet seems ashamed to speak out his Opinion, or rather plainly contradicts himself in the Question about the Original of Motion: But if it be said that Motion, without any Necessity in its own Nature, and without any External Necessary Cause, has existed from Eternity, merely be an Endless Successive Communication; as *Spinoza*, inconsistently enough, seems to assert; This I have before shown, (in the Proof of the Second General Proposition of this Discourse,) to be a flat Contradiction. It remains therefore,

that Motion must of Necessity be Originally Caused by Something that is Intelligent; or else there never could have been any such Thing as Motion in the World: And consequently the Self-existent Being, the Original Cause of all Things, (whatever it be supposed to be,) must of Necessity be *an Intelligent Being.*

From hence it follows again, that the material World, cannot possible be the Original Self-Existent Being. For since the Self-Existent Being, is demonstrated to be Intelligent; and the Material World plainly is not so; it follows that the Material World cannot possibly be Self-Existent. What some have fondly imagined concerning *a Soul of the World;* if thereby they mean a Created, Dependent Being; signifies nothing in the present argument: But if they Understand thereby Something Necessary and Self-Existent; then it is nothing else, but a false, corrupt, and imperfect Notion of *God.*

BIBLIOGRAPHY
Primary Sources
Clarke, S., *A Demonstration of the Being and Attributes of God: More Particularly in Answer to Mr. Hobbs, Spinoza, and their Followers* (London, 1705).
Newton, I., *Philosophiae naturalis principia mathematica* (Cambridge, 1713).
Rouhault J., *Physica. Latine reddidit, et annotationculis quibusdam illustravit S. Clarke* (London, 1697).

Secondary Literature
Dobbs, B.J.T. and M. Jacob, *Newton and the Culture of Newtonianism* (Amherst: Humanity Books, 1995).
Force, J. and S. Hutton (eds.), *Newton and Newtonianism. New Studies* (Dordrecht, Boston and London: Kluwer, 2004).

Israel, J.I., *Radical Enlightenment. Philosophy and the Making of Modernity, 1650–1750* (Oxford: Oxford University Press, 2001).

———, *Enlightenment Contested. Philosophy, Modernity, and the Emancipation of Man, 1670–1752* (Oxford: Oxford University Press, 2006).

Mandelbrote, S. (ed.), Newton and Newtonianism, *Studies in the History and Philosophy of Science*, no. 35 (2004), issue 3.

Russell, P., *The Riddle of Hume's Treatise. Skepticism, Naturalism, and Irreligion* (Oxford: Oxford University Press, 2008).

Shank, J.B., *The Newton Wars and the Beginning of the French Enlightenment* (Chicago: Chicago University Press, 2008).

Stewart, L., 'Samuel Clarke, Newtonianism and the Factions of Post-Revolutionary England,' *Journal of the History of Ideas*, no. 42 (1981), pp. 53–71.

W. van Bunge

HENRY MORE, Confutatio (1679)

To the Cambridge Platonist Henry More (1614–87) Spinoza was only one of several contemporary philosophers bent on promoting materialism as well as atheism (Popkin, 1990). To More's mind Descartes had paved the way for the proliferation of materialism by turning matter into an autonomous substance, and although More initially felt attracted to the apologetic possibilities implied by Cartesian dualism, he soon felt Descartes's mechanistic philosophy of nature would yield atheist results (Gabbey, 1982).

More's opposition to Hobbes's materialism in *The Immortality of the Soul* (1986) is also well known. His reaction to Spinoza, however, has so far received little attention, despite the recent growing interest in Cambridge Platonism (Colie, 1957, pp. 66–116; Hutton, 1984). Throughout his life More expounded an explicitly Christian Neo-Platonism, fused with Hermetic elements, which he felt could provide an alternative to the materialism and mechanicism of his day.

More's *Confutatio* first appeared in his *Opera Omnia* of 1679, turning it into one of the earliest refutations of the *Ethics*, which was not published until the end of 1677. It was translated into Dutch by Frans Kuyper or Cuperus (1629–91) in 1687, who at the time was locked in battle with Johannes Bredenburg (1643–91) over the latter's alleged Spinozism (Israel, 2001, pp. 342–58). Kuyper shared with More in particular his insistence on the gratuity of Spinoza's geometrical method (Petry, 1981). More, for his part, in his *Ad V.C. Epistola altera, quae brevem Tractatus theologico-politici confutationem complectitur* was abhorred by Kuyper's own refutation of Spinoza's *Tractatus theologico-politicus* (1676), since it was based on the assumption that reason has no role to play in the assessment of revelation. According to More, reason and revelation are inseparable, but Spinoza's rationalist analysis of miracles in particular was even more misguided and dangerous than Kuyper's denial of what Locke was to dub 'the reasonableness of Christianity'. To More's mind, Spinoza's rationalism smacked of pure 'Enthusiasm'.

The following selection contains the opening pages of More's *Confutatio*, translated and annotated by Alexander Jacob (pp. 55–9), in which More attempts to deconstruct Spinoza's proof of the existence of a single substance, called God. Some of the footnotes have been left out.

A BRIEF AND FIRM CONFUTATION OF THE DEMONSTRATION OF THE TWO PROPOSITIONS IN SPINOZA WHICH ARE THE CHIEF COLUMNS OF ATHEISM, NAMELY THAT NECESSARY EXISTENCE PERTAINS TO SUBSTANCE AS SUBSTANCE, AND THAT THERE IS BUT A SINGLE SUBSTANCE IN THE UNIVERSE.

The first principle which he posits in order to establish this matter is to be found in Epistle 29 [Ep 12], and in this manner: *That existence pertains to the essence of substance, that is, that its existence follows from its mere essence and definition*. This is what Spinoza plainly acknowledges in Epistle 39 [Ep 34]. *Of each existing thing*, he says, *there must necessarily be a positive cause through which it exists. This cause must be placed either in the nature and definition of the thing itself (since it obviously pertains to its nature of existence or necessarily includes it), or outside the thing*. To which sense philosophizes Prop. 11 of Part I of the *Ethics*: *For the existence or non-existence of everything there must be a reason or cause. For example, if a triangle exists there must be a reason or cause why it exists; and if it does not exist there must be a reason or cause which hinders its existence or which negates it. But this reason or cause must either be contained in the nature of a thing or lie outside it. For example, the nature of the thing itself shows the reason why a square circle involves a contradiction. And the reason, on the other hand, why substance exists follows from its nature alone, which involves existence*. And this refers the reader then to Prop. 7 of Part I of the *Ethics*, which is this: *It pertains to the nature of substance to exist*. Which is the same as that famous principle above, namely, that existence pertains to the essence of a substance.

Before we judge the truth of this, it is necessary to determine its clear and definite sense, indeed whether this proposition is to be understood universally or particularly, or whether it is to be understood altogether differently. If it is a universal affirmation, that is, that it pertains to the nature of all substance to exist, I say that it is plainly false. For, I contend that it pertains neither to the nature of matter, which is indeed of such a quality that it perishes, neither to the nature or spirits, angels, or human souls which I clearly consider as substances. If the latter proposition, which supports a secret purpose, were indeed passed over, it would overturn things from within. Not only the existence of spirits, angels, and human souls, but also the existence of the infinite and eternal, omnipotent and omniscient spirit, that is, of what is properly called the true God, or even of Spinoza, is unwillingly destroyed at the same time. If the affirmation is particular, that existence pertains to the nature of some particular substance, I admit the proposition is certainly true, but nevertheless that that precept of science that it must be true as whole, that is, κατὰ παντὸς, καθ' αὐτὸ, καθ' ὅλου πρῶτον [(predicated) 'of all, by itself, and of a primary universal', Aristotle, *Posterior Analytics*, 73a–74a] is at least legitimate.

This precept is not even true κατὰ παντὸσ. Although I admit it to be true particularly understood, I plainly see that it does not contribute anything clearly to his goal. Nothing makes us conclude of the necessary existence of his beloved matter (which he so greatly desires) but the eternal and infinite spirit, that is of the true God, which is alone a substance to whose nature it pertains to exist, or whose intellectual Idea clearly involves necessary existence in it.

Indeed, you say that Spinoza has demonstrated that seventh proposition of his in a definite, and, as it were, mathematical method. Certainly, it is to be admitted that he has affected a certain mimo-mathematical disposition of his precepts, and proclaimed the grand title of geometric order and demonstration to his proofs be they of whatever kind (in order to impress the unlearned and the common people). Indeed, that geometric order does not have any more worth among the learned since its precepts are false, that right figure and mode in a syllogism, as long as either both or one of the two premises are false. I shall proceed, therefore, and by backwards steps, from that same seventh proposition to all the remaining antecedent ones in which the truth of it is resolved. I proceed even to the first of all principles and finally reveal whether the individual precepts are, on examination, sound or not.

In fact, he demonstrates this seventh proposition from the corollary of the sixth proposition, *That a substance cannot be produced from another*. The sixth proposition is, *One substance cannot be produced by another substance*. Which, if it be true, I concede that a substance by no means can be produced by another. Nothing else is relinquished apart from the modes which produce it, which are not found unless in some substances, nor can they properly be said to act apart from that substance itself of which they are modes.

That another judgement, quite different, can be made of the sixth proposition is established by the determinate mark of either universal or particular affirmation, that it, it is said, *That no substance can be produced by another, or, that some substance by another substance*. If the proposition is understood in the first sense, I say that it is completely false. For it implies no contradiction that a substance exist as infinitely perfect as possible. As, indeed, that that a substance is which was not before implies no contradiction. Therefore, an infinitely perfect substance can easily effect it, and, indeed, anyone who has acquired logic in earliest childhood has learnt that it does not imply a contradiction for a substance to exist which did not exist earlier, though it implies existence and non-existence simultaneously. That, however, perfect substance exists so absolutely and infinitely that no perfection is wanting to it that is not entirely contradictory to what is contained in it, is manifest from the common principle which is agreed upon by us: *From the essence, certainly, or from the definition of a thing, its existence can be concluded*. Therefore, that the existence of *an absolutely perfect Being* can be deduced from the true essence of its Idea is evident from what has been said above. Since, therefore, a sufficient cause exists by which a substance can be produced, it is manifestly false that no substance can be produced by another. And, certainly, if the *absolutely perfect Being*, or infinitely perfect substance, of whose perfections one is *omnipotence* (indeed the power of creating), by virtue of the perfection of its nature is, as it were, the cause *of itself*, that is, of a *Being infinitely perfect*, it is surprising that it can be cause of beings inferior to it by infinite degrees, namely worldly matter, the spirit of nature, the spirits of men and angels? Which indeed arrives at the particular affirmation of the sixth proposition, *That a substance cannot be produced by another substance*, which I concede to be true, but it is true of no substance except of the absolutely and consummately perfect, of which kind only the true God is, that infinite, omniscient, and omnipotent spirit which I have described

above, and hence the proposition so understood does not grant anything to Spinoza's
aim. From this it does not in the least follow
that material substance indeed cannot be
produced by another substance. Which he so
much wishes....

More then completes his analysis of the first
eleven proposition of *Ethics* 1, which as far
as he is concerned leads to the view that the
universe consists of nothing but extended
matter. More is particularly concerned to
uphold the spiritual nature of a free God and
the existence of final causes in nature. He
lashes out against Spinoza's letter to Albert
Burgh (Jacob, 1991, pp. 102ff.; Ep. 76) on
the merits of Roman Catholicism, and finally
he briefly discusses Spinoza's view of the
human mind as a mode of thought. In the
final paragraph, More asks to be pardoned
for the 'rather rough and somewhat hurried
manner' in which he has dealt with the
Ethics: 'all good men will forgive me this just
indignation of mine. The present age, foremost in all excess and perverseness, has con-
sumed enough poison' (Jacob, 1991, p. 119).

BIBLIOGRAPHY
Primary Sources
Kuyper, F., *Arcana atheismi revelata,
philosophice et paradoxe refutata,
examine Tractatus theologico-politici*
(Rotterdam, 1676).
More, H., *Ad V.C. Epistola altera, quae
brevem Tractatus theologico-politici
confutationem complectitur, paucaque
sub finem annexa habet de libri Franscici
Cuperi scopo, cui titulus est, Arcana
atheismi revelata*, in *Opera omnia. Tum
quae latine, tum quae anglicae scripta
sunt*, 2 vols (London, 1679), I,
pp. 563–614.

————, *Demonstrationis duarum
praepositionum, viz. Ad substantiam
quatenus substantia est, necessarium
existentiam pertinere, &, unicam in
mundo substantiam esse quae praecipue
apud Spinozium atheismi sunt columnae,
brevis solidaque confutatio* in *Opera
omnia. Tum quae latine, tum quae
anglicae scripta sunt*, 2 vols (London,
1679), I, pp. 615–35.
————, *Korte en bondige weederlegging van
het wiskunstige bewijs van B.D. Spinoza,
met welk hij zijn atheistise gronden, heeft
gepoogd te bekrachtigen* (n.p., 1687).
————, *The Immortality of the Soul*, ed.
A. Jacob (Dordrecht, Boston and
Lancaster: Kluwer, 1986).

Secondary Literature
Colie, R., *Light and Enlightenment.
A Study of the Cambridge Platonists and
the Dutch Arminians* (Cambridge:
Cambridge University Press, 1957).
Gabbey, A., '*Philosophia Cartesiana
Triumphata*: Henry More (1646–1671)',
in N. Davis and T. Lennon (eds),
Problems of Cartesianism (Toronto:
McGill-Queens University Press, 1982),
pp. 171–250.
Hutton, S., 'Reason and Revelation in the
Cambridge Platonists, and their
Reception of Spinoza', in K. Gründer
and W. Schmidt-Biggemann (eds),
*Spinoza in der Frühzeit seiner religiösen
Wirkung* (Heidelberg: Schneider, 1984),
pp. 181–200.
Israel, J.I., *Radical Enlightenment.
Philosophy and the Making of Modernity,
1650–1750* (Oxford: Oxford University
Press, 2001).
Jacob, A., *Henry More's Refutation of
Spinoza* (Hildesheim, Zürich and New
York: Olms, 1991).

Petry, M.J., 'Kuyper's Analysis of Spinoza's Axiomatic Method', in K. Cramer, W.G. Jacobs, W. Schmidt-Biggemann (eds), *Spinozas Ethik und ihre frühe Wirkung* (Wolfenbüttel: Herzog August Bibliothek, 1981), pp. 231–41.

Popkin, R.H., 'The Spiritual Cosmologies of Henri More and Anne Conway', in S. Hutton (ed.), *Henry More (1614–1687). Tercentenary Studies* (Dordrecht: Kluwer, 1990), pp. 97–114.

W. van Bunge

BERNARD NIEUWENTIJT, Het regt gebruik der werelt beschouwingen [The Religious Philosopher] (1718)

Today, Bernard Nieuwentijt (1654–1718) is probably one of the more obscure early critics of Spinoza. He was a medical doctor, trained at Leiden and Utrecht, who also served as mayor of Purmerend. By the end of his life, he enjoyed considerable success as the author of a book largely directed against Spinoza, entitled *Het regt gebruik der werelt beschouwingen, ter overtuiginge van ongodisten en ongelovigen* (1715). This book went through eight editions until 1759 and was translated into English (*The Religious Philosopher*, 1718) as well as French (*De l'existence de Dieu démontrée par les merveilles de la nature*, 1725) and German (*Die Erkänntnüsz der Weisheit, Macht und Gütte des göttlichen Wesens*, 1732). These translations also went into several editions. Posthumously, Nieuwentijt's more detailed analysis of Spinoza's use of mathematics was published under the title *Gronden van zekerheid*

(1720). Nieuwentijt's earliest publications were also devoted to mathematics, including a textbook (1695) on infinitesimal methods. His criticism of Leibniz's views provoked a debate with several of Leibniz's admirers as well as with the great philosopher himself (Vermij, 1991).

The main thrust of *The Religious Philosopher* is directed against the view, attributed to atheism in general and Spinoza in particular, that nature is the result of blind chance. Following the ancient metaphor according to which man is able to read the book of nature, Nieuwentijt presented many hundreds of examples which he felt demonstrated the presence of Providence. The book of nature showed manifest signs of having been composed by God. To many eighteenth-century readers, Nieuwentijt's physico-theology prevented a clash between science and religion. Instead, it turned the natural sciences into a natural ally of Reformed orthodoxy. Although Nieuwentijt died a champion of the moderate Enlightenment, he admitted that as a young student he had been a radical, a 'Spinozist' himself. To many contemporaries Nieuwentijt's analysis of the 'geometric order' in which the *Ethics* had been written was the more effective in view of the rapidly increasing prestige of the mathematics employed by Newton, whose physics by the early eighteenth century was transformed into an essentially providential natural theology fundamentally at odds with Spinoza's atheism.

The following sections are taken from W. Boucher (ed.), *Spinoza. Eighteenth and Nineteenth-Century Discussions*, 6 vols (Bristol: Thoemmes Press, 1999), I, pp. 128–30, quoting the fourth edition of *The Religious Philosopher* (1730) which was translated by J. Chamberlayne.

BERNARD NIEUWENTIJT

THE RELIGIOUS PHILOSOPHER

Sect. X. *The fourth cause is too great a Conceit of one's own Wisdom.*

The Fourth Cause of *Atheism*, as far as my Observations and Experience reach, proceeds from *a too great Conceit of our own Wisdom, and from an implicit admitting that to be Truth which we are wont to deduce from our own Ideas or Notions.* And some Men are apt to advance such their Notions with great Arrogancy, as well concerning the divine Attributes and Properties, as about the smallest Appearances in the Creatures: In short, they except nothing, and pretend to reduce every thing to an infallible Rule of Possibility and Impossibility, Truth and Falshood, Good and Evil.

This is the most dangerous Kind of all: *First,* Because they deny every thing that they do not conceive; and therefore all divine Revelation (which is above their Understanding) is not only rejected by them, but ridiculed also. *Secondly,* Because they have the greatest Opportunity to support their Errors with specious and plausible Arguments, and to evade the Force of those Objections that are brought against them, which they immediately make use of as soon as their Adversary commits the least Oversight or Blunder. *Thirdly,* Because many of them, in their Conversation, do assume an external Appearance of Morality, and other social Virtues, whereby they sometimes acquire a certain Esteem with the Ignorant, which may be of dangerous Consequence; the rather, because divers of them having learned the Elements of *Euclid, Algebra,* and other speculative Parts of the *Mathematicks,* pass amongst the Unknowing for great *Mathematicians*; which Title does really no more belong to them, than that of a great Philosopher to one that understands nothing but a little *Logick*; since People may be very well experienced in these Ideal or Notional Sciences, and yet be Masters of very little, or no Knowledge at all, in Things that actually exist and come to pass.

But we must not from hence conclude, that such noble Studies do of themselves lead those miserable Men into such erroneous Opinions; for these, in many Cases, open the *Way to the Discovery of the Wisdom of God in the Works of the Creation,* to which we could not otherwise attain: On the contrary, they are exceeding useful, unless when misapplied by these half-learned Men, who being puffed up with a little Knowledge, fancy they know every thing, and despise all those who do not just understand as much as they themselves, about *Lines* and *Quantities,* though they be much wiser, and more judicious in other Kinds of Learning.

Sect. XI. *Spinosa briefly confuted.*

Thus we find at present, that in order to make even *Atheistical* Writings to pass for uncontroverted Truths, the Authors thereof have endeavoured to give them the Form of Mathematical Demonstrations. A remarkable Instance of which may be seen in the Book of *Spinosa,* which has for that Reason gained so much Credit with many of these unhappy Persons; because those who do not rightly understand the *Mathematicks,* judge from the external Appearances, that what is laid down therein is deduced from just *Mathematical* Principles.

Perhaps we may hereafter find an Opportunity more fully to shew the Mistakes that are there advanced under the Name of *Demonstrations,* when we shall compare them with such as are truly *Mathematical.* To say a Word or two thereof *en passant:*

1. There are two Kinds of Objects, about which the *Mathematicians* do treat or employ themselves, *viz.* Ideas simply considered as such, and Ideas of Things really existing; that is, to speak more clearly, *Mathematicians* discourse either only about their Ideas, or else about Things that are really existing out of their Ideas.

2. The first Manner is seen in the *Speculative Geometry,* such as the Elements of *Euclid, Algebra, &c.* where they conceive a Point as something that has no Parts, a line without Breadth, *&c.* So likewise they here consider Magnitudes, which have more than three Dimensions, *&c.* which every body knows are only certain Ways of our Conceptions, having no real Existence out of them.

3. The second Kind of Object occurs in *Astronomy, Opticks, &c.* where Things are considered, which, besides our Ideas of them, have a real Existence in themselves.

4. The Foundation of the first, besides *Axioms,* are *Definitions,* in which they describe their Ideas, without troubling themselves whether there is any thing really existing that agrees therewith: Instances of which we have just now given. Accordingly it is with them a Truth, that *the three Angles of a Triangle are equal to two right ones,* and would still be so although every thing in the World were circular, and that there were not really such a Thing as a Triangle.

5. The other Way is founded upon Experiments and Discoveries, which either they themselves, or other credible Persons make of Things which are out of their Ideas, and something more than meer Conceptions. Thus a good *Astronomer* lays down for the Foundation for his Science, that which he, or those whom he can believe, have experimentally discovered, namely, that there is really such a Thing as a *Globe* of the *Earth,* a *Sun,* a visible *Moon,* five *Planets,* some of which have their *Satellites,* or Bodies circulating about them, and a great Number of fixed *Stars*; but does by no means extend his Imagination or Fancy to the Supposition of other Worlds, and other Sorts of Bodies; as for Instance, that there are ten Suns, a hundred Moons, a thousand Planets, and a very few fixed Stars; of which imaginary Worlds he might nevertheless bring a great many Proofs, which according to the first Way of arguing, we may allow to be Mathematical enough, but when adapted to the Things themselves, would appear to be entirely false.

6. Now those that have read and understood *Spinosa,* are sensible that he only lays down his own Ideas and Notions for the Foundation of every thing, which therefore needs not to be farther proved here: From whence it may appear to every one, that he applies this Manner of discovering Truths preposterously to Things really existing, of which true *Mathematicians* never make use, but only about their own Ideas: Wherefore the whole Series of so many Hypotheses and pretended Demonstrations in *Spinosa's* Book (though he should argue rightly upon those Principles of which, however, the contrary may be proved in many Cases) do represent nothing else to us than only the Properties of those Imaginations or Conceptions which that unhappy Author had formed in himself; nor can any Man thereby conclude any thing more from the Things themselves than an Astronomer can do, who advances his own Fancies for the true Structure of the Heavens.

7. So that from this Mistake alone the Weakness of all *Spinosa's* Arguments appear at one view, and how little his Way of demonstrating agrees with that of true *Mathematicians.*

Sect. XII. *The Remedies against this Fourth Cause.*

But to return from this Digression. Since these unhappy Philosophers ascribe so much to their own Understanding, and do exert their whole Strength to oppose the Weight of all *Metaphysical* Arguments, though they are supported by strong Reason; the only Way that I have ever seen used with Success to overthrow their proud Fancies, that they can conceive every thing, and to shew them the Narrowness of their Understandings (which is particularly necessary to their Conversion) is this: Let them be brought into a *Chymical Laboratory,* or other Places where People are wont to make Physical Experiments, such as are not commonly known to every body, and let them be asked what will be the Result of such, or such an Operation, pursuant to their own Notions and Conceptions? In which, if they mistake, and Things appear quite contrary to what they expected, they can have no Subterfuge or Evasion, but will be compelled to acknowledge, that their Understandings have been very little conversant upon Objects really existing: And in case they themselves are versed in natural Experiments, let them be desired to contemplate, without Prejudice, the Manner how every thing they see comes to pass, and to think whether the Power and Wisdom of the Great Creator and Ruler of all Things does not appear as incontestably in them, as the Judgement and Skill of any Artificer in the Machines that he has invented.

BIBLIOGRAPHY
Primary Sources

Nieuwentijt, B., *Het regt gebruik der wereltbeschouwingen ter overtuiginge van ongodisten en ongelovigen* (Amsterdam, 1715). English transl. as *The Religious Philosopher: Or the Right Use of Contemplating the Works of the Creator* (London, 1718). French transl. as *De l'existence de Dieu démontrée par les merveilles de la nature, ou traité téléologique dirigé contre la doctrine de Spinoza par un médecin hollandais* (Paris, 1725). German transl. as *Die Erkänntnüsz der Weisheit, Macht und Gütte des göttlichen Wesens, aus dem rechten Gebrauch aller irrdischen Dinge dieser Welt* (Amsterdam and Frankfurt, 1732).

———, *Gronden van zekerheid, of de regte betoogwyse der wiskundigen, so in het denkbeeldige, als in het zakelyke: Ter wederlegging van Spinosaas denkbeeldig samenstel: en ter aanleiding van eene sekere sakelyke wysbegeerte* (Amsterdam, 1720).

Secondary Literature

Bots, J., *Tussen Descartes en Darwin. Geloof en natuurwetenschap in de achttiende eeuw* (Assen: Van Gorcum, 1972).

Israel, J.I., *Enlightenment Contested. Philosophy, Modernity, and the Emancipation of Man, 1670–1752* (Oxford: Oxford University Press, 2006).

Jorink, E., *Het Boeck der Natuere. Nederlandse geleerden en de wonderen van Gods schepping, 1575–1715* (Leiden: Primavera Pers, 2006).

Petry, M.J., 'Nieuwentijt's Criticism of Spinoza', *Mededelingen vanwege Het Spinozahuis* 40 (Leiden: Brill, 1979).

Vermij, R.H., *Secularisering en natuurwetenschap in de zeventiende eeuw: Bernard Nieuwentijt* (Amsterdam: Rodopi, 1991).

———, 'The Formation of the Newtonian Philosophy: the Case of the Amsterdam

Mathematical Amateurs', *British Journal for the History of Science*, no. 36 (2003), pp. 186–200.

Wall, E.G.E. van der, 'Newtonianism and Religion in the Netherlands', *Studies in the History and Philosophy of Science*, no. 35 (2004), pp. 493–514.

W. van Bunge

JOHN TOLAND, Letters to Serena (1704)

The dependence of John Toland (1670–1722), the English deist and self-proclaimed 'pantheist', upon Spinoza is a subject of debate. Many of his contemporaries saw no problem in labelling Toland a Spinozist. Modern historians, on the other hand, have most often put him in the context of an indigenous British tradition, drawing its origin from the radicalism of the English civil war. More recently, however, Jonathan Israel has vigorously argued that Spinoza's philosophy was actually one of the main sources of Toland's ideas (Israel, 2001, pp. 609–14).

Toland did not refer to Spinoza's work very often, but there is a fairly extensive discussion of Spinoza's philosophy in his *Letters to Serena*, first published in 1704. This book contains five letters on various philosophical subjects, of which only the last two interest us here. These are not directed to 'Serena', by the way. The fourth letter was purportedly directed to 'a gentleman in Holland', whom Toland in his preface called 'an excessive admiror of SPINOSA' (C2v); and the fifth letter was to yet another Spinozist from the Netherlands, who had questioned him about the earlier letter. It is probably safest to regard these persons as literary fictions.

In the fourth letter, Toland discussed Spinoza's philosophy at length, claiming that it was 'without any Principle or Foundation'. His main objection was that Spinoza had failed to give a proper definition of motion. Even when specifically asked (by Tschirnhaus, Ep. 59) to give his ideas on motion, he had given only vague and evasive answers. This not only left his system without a secure base but, far worse, it also disqualified Spinoza as a philosopher. The attack here is directed at Spinoza's character rather than at his ideas. It does not appear that by exposing the defects of Spinoza's system Toland aimed to refute it. Rather, he used the occasion to strengthen Spinoza's system by repairing its perceived deficiency. In his fifth letter, Toland argued that the problems could be solved by assuming that motion is essential to matter.

Toland's support for Spinoza's basic tenets was quite open. His disparaging remarks about Spinoza as a philosopher therefore cannot be regarded as a disguise to defend Spinozism more safely, as it has sometimes been assumed. His critical remarks must have served another purpose. Partly they may have been inspired by ambition or envy. But apparently he felt that he really was making a positive contribution and his philosophical objections appear to be genuine. It would seem, however, that he was addressing general implications of mechanical philosophy, rather than anything that Spinoza specifically did or did not say.

As is well known, motion had always been a key concept in natural philosophy. Traditionally, in Aristotelian philosophy, the concept of motion coincided largely with the concept of change in general. Moreover, all motion needed a mover. Any change in the universe was ultimately effected by the prime mover, who later came to be identified with the Christian Creator God. In the 'mechanical philosophy' of the seventeenth century, motion was not less important, as all nature was reduced to matter in motion. All phenomena could be explained from small particles in all kinds of changing configurations. However, motion now was reduced to 'local motion': a body's change of position with respect to another body. Thereby it had become a purely mathematical concept. Moreover, such change of place did not need a mover. Any body, once set in motion, would move on eternally if it was not stopped by an outside force; just as a body at rest would stay at rest until moved by an outside force. In fact, motion and rest had the same ontological status. Building upon this new understanding of motion, natural philosophy became 'mathematized' in a revolutionary way in the works of Galileo, Descartes, Huygens, Newton and others.

However, it took quite some time before a fully developed science of mechanics could take account of all the implications of the new idea of motion. Concepts like momentum or energy were developed only much later. This lack of clarity left room for much philosophical speculation. Descartes stated as one of his laws of nature that the total quantity of motion in the universe was constant. But if 'motion' was just a relative change of place, what was 'quantity of motion'? How can quantity of motion be preserved if motion itself has no ontological significance? To many, motion was still felt to be in need of some cause or metaphysical justification.

Toland agreed with the mechanical philosophers that all sensible qualities of bodies, as well as their forms, generation, corruption etc., followed from 'the numberless Mixtures, Transpositions, and other Arrangements of their parts, all which are the natural and undoubted Effects of Motion, or rather motion it self under these several names and Determinations' (pp. 168–9). Still, he felt hesitant towards regarding this as a real cause, exactly because such motion was not something real. As he wrote in the eighth section of the fourth letter, local motion was just a change of position with respect to other bodies, and therefore not 'any real Being in Nature'. And although the 'Mathematicians … treat of local Motion as they find it, without giving themselves much trouble about its Original', philosophers could not do so. Reality should be explained from philosophical principles. Toland felt he could ignore mathematics and mechanics in this respect. (For instance, he completely ignored Newton's demonstration that force is not needed to explain motion, but only change of motion.)

As Toland could not accept an external Prime Mover, which could be equated with the Christian God, the first cause should be in matter itself, which therefore was not merely passive, as was assumed in mechanical thinking. Underlying all change we perceive in objects, be it of place or otherwise, there is a principle which he called Force, Action, or Energy. Of course, this 'energy' has nothing to do with the mathematical concept of energy as it would arise in the nineteenth century. It is an essential quality of matter which manifests itself among other things as local motion, divisibility, but also as motionlessness.

Toland's problem, then, was his inability to accept the full implications of mechanical thinking. He might accept mechanistic explanations of the phenomena, but he rejected its basic tenet: that reality as such is mathematical. Spinoza felt much more at home in the new mechanical universe. Having adopted Descartes's ideal of reducing physics to mathematics, he was perfectly happy to have explained nature from mathematical concepts. He did not feel that these were in need of a physical foundation, even if he failed to say so openly.

LETTER IV. TO A GENTLEMAN IN HOLLAND, SHOWING **SPINOSA'S** SYSTEM OF PHILOSOPHY TO BE WITHOUT ANY PRINCIPLE OR FOUNDATION.

3. For my part, I shall always be far from saying that SPINOSA did nothing well, because in so many things he succeeded so ill. On the contrary, he has had several lucky Thoughts, and appears to have bin a Man of admirable natural Endowments, tho his share in Learning (except in some parts of the Mathematicks, and in the understanding of the Rabbins) seems to have bin very moderate. ...
5. Let him have bin never so honest a man, yet I suppose you'l not exempt him from many human Frailtys to which the best are subject: and I am inclin'd to suspect that his chiefest Weakness was an immoderate Passion to become Head of a Sect, to have Disciples and a new System of Philosophy honor'd with his Name, the example being fresh and inviting from the good Fortune of his Master CARTESIUS. I do not make this Conclusion from his frequent use of such Expressions as "my Philosophy", or "our System", and the like: nor wou'd I have every man accus'd of this Affectation who makes some particular Discoverys, or who even changes the whole Face of Philosophy, and introduces a method absolutely new; for such Persons may without all question be acted by no other Motives besides the love of truth and the benefit of the Society, nor will they reject any thing but what they really conceive to be hurtful, erroneous, or unprofitable. ...

6. But when a man builds a whole System of Philosophy either without any first Principles, or on a precarious Foundation; and afterwards when he's told of his Fault, and put in mind of the Difficultys that attend it, yet neither supplies that Defect, nor accounts for those Difficultys by any thing he has already establish'd, nor yet acknowledges his mistake; we may reasonable suspect that he's too much in love with his new World (for such is a System of Philosophy) ever to admit of a better Creator: whereas a person that proposes no other view but the manifesting and propagating of Truth, and that cannot rest satisfy'd with Fancys or Conjectures, wou'd in such Circumstances be nothing ashame'd to confess and amend his Error.
7. Now let's examine whether SPINOSA be guilty of the Charge I have drawn up against him. ... I need not prove to his greatest Admirer that he acknowledges but one Substance in the Universe, or that the Matter of all the things in the Universe is but one continu'd Being, every where of the same nature, however differently modify'd, and endu'd with unchangeable, essential, and inseparable Attributes. Of these Attributes (which he supposes eternal as well as the Substance to which they belong) he reckons Extension and Cogitation to be the most principal; tho he supposes innumerable others which he has not bin at the pains to name. He has no where so much as insinuated that motion was one of them; or if he had, we shou'd not have believ'd it on his word, nor without more convincing Arguments than he has given that every Portion and Particle of matter always thinks: for this is contrary to Reason and Experience, both which demonstrate the Extension of Matter. Whatever be the Principle of Thinking in Animals, yet it cannot be perform'd but by the means of the Brain. ...

8. We agree on every side that the perpetual Changes in Matter are the effects of Motion, which produces an infinity of different Figures, Mixtures, and sensible Qualitys. But we must distinguish between local Motion and the moving Force or Action: for local Motion is only a Change of Situation, or the successive Application of the same Body to the respective Parts of several other Bodys; so that this motion is nothing different from the Body it self, nor any real Being in Nature, but a mere mode or Consideration of its Situation, and the Effects of some Force or Action without or within the Body. Tho the ordinary Rules of motion are but the Observations learnt from the Experience of what commonly passes in local Motion, or probable Calculations deduc'd from such Observations; yet the Action or moving Force is likewise often call'd by the name of motion, and thus the Effect is confounded with the Cause, which has occasion'd a world of Perplexitys, and Absurditys. But all those who have treated of the Diversitys that happen in Matter, must have meant this Action as their Cause, or labor'd to no purpose: for this being once explain'd, we can easily account for local Motion as its Effect, and not otherwise. The Mathematicians generally take the moving Force for granted, and treat of local Motion as they find it, without giving themselves much trouble about its Original: but the Practice of the philosophers is otherwise, or rather ought to be so.

9. Whoever then goes about to explain by their first Causes the Origin of the World, its present Mechanism, or the Affections of Matter, must begin with the first Cause of Motion: for no manner of Variety is included in the bare Idea of Extension, nor any Cause of Alteration; and seeing it is Action alone that can possibly produce any Change in Extension, this Action or Principle of

Motion must be well clear'd and establish'd, or the System must quickly be found defective. If it be only taken for granted, the System will be but a Hypothesis; but if prov'd and explain'd, than we may expect to find some greater Certitude than hitherto in natural Philosophy. It is not enough then to build on local motion, which, as we said before, is but an Effect of this Action, as well as all the other Varietys in nature: so is Rest, which is now generally acknowledg'd to be no Privation nor a State of absolute inactivity, as much Force being necessary to keep Bodys at rest as to move them; wherefore local Motion and rest are only relative Terms, perishable modes, and no positive or real Beings.

11. SPINOSA has no where in his System attempted to define Motion or Rest, which is unpardonable in a Philosopher, whether done with or without design. And yet according to himself in his *Ethicks*, "Motion and Rest are the Causes of all the Diversitys among Bodies", thence "proceeds the distinction of particular Bodys", and "an infinity of things proceed from Motion and Rest." ... [E2lem1, E2lem3dem, E1p32c2] ... there's no need of showing by Inferences that he did not hold Motion to be an eternal Attribute to matter; which if he had done, we cou'd not have believ'd it without good proof: I say, we are spar'd these pains, since he expresly asserts the contrary, and he was surely best able to acquaint us with his own Opinion. In his first letter to OLDENBURG, whereby he communicates to him some part of his *Ethicks*, thus he writes. "You must take heed that by Attribute I understand every thing that is conceive'd by it self and in it self, in such a manner as that the Conception of it does not involve *or suppose* the Conception of any other thing: as Extension, for example, is conceiv'd by it self and

in it self, but Motion not so; for the Conception of it involves Extension." [Ep 2, G IV, 7:26–8:1] This is extremely plain and peremptory; nor shall we examine at present how true or false it may be of extension, which is but an abstracted idea, and no more conceivable without a Subject than Motion is.

12. SPINOSA then, who values himself in his *Ethicks* on deducing things from their first Causes (which the Schoolmen term *a priori*) SPINOSA, I say, having given no account how Matter came to be mov'd or Motion comes to be continu'd, not allowing God as first Mover, neither proving nor supposing Motion to be an Attribute (but the contrary) nor indeed explaining what Motion is, he cou'd not possibly show how the Diversity of particular bodys is reconcilable to the Unity of Substance, or to the Sameness of Matter in the whole Universe: wherefore I may safely conclude that his System is intirely precarious and without any sort of ground, indigested and unphilosophical. But lest your Affection shou'd biass you to think, that such a great man cou'd not stumble so at the Threshold, and he has somewhere supply'd this enormous defect tho it might escape my Observation, I hope you'll believe his own Words to a Person who wou'd not implicitly swear to his Philosophy, but whose Difference of Opinions did probably make as little Difference in their Affections as in yours and mine. 'T is a very remarkable thing by what Delays, Shifts, and Excuses he wou'd avoid solving the Objections that were made to him on this Head, which keeps me still in the Belief that he cou'd not bear to part with his System, nor to lose the hopes of heading a new Sect.

[Follows, in section 13, a summary of the exchange in Ep 63, 64, 69, 71, 72.]

LETTER V. MOTION ESSENTIAL TO MATTER; IN ANSWER TO SOME REMARKS BY A NOBLE FRIEND ON THE *CONFUTATION OF SPINOSA*.

7. On this occasion, to avoid all Ambiguity, 'tis convenient to inform you, that by Bodys I understand certain Modifications of Matter, conceiv'd by the Mind as so many limited Systems, or particular Quantitys mentally abstracted, but not actually separated from the Extension of the Universe. We therefore say that one body is bigger or less than another, is broken or dissolv'd, from the multifarious Change of Modifications: But we cannot properly say that matters are bigger one than another, because there's but one sort of Matter in the Universe; and if it be infinitely extended, it can have no absolute Parts independent of one another, Parts and Particles being conceiv'd as I told you just now that Bodys were. A world of other words are invented to help our Imagination, like Scaffolds for the Convenience of the Workmen; but which must be laid aside when the building is finish'd, and not be mistaken for the Pillars or Foundation. Of this sort are Great and Small, for example, which are but mere Comparisons of the Mind, and the Names of any positive Subjects; as you are Big in respect of your little Sister, but Little in respect of an Elephant, and she is Big when compar'd to her Parrot, but very Little when she stands by her Mother. These and such words are very serviceable when rightly apply'd; yet they are often abus'd, and from relative or modal, are made real, absolute, and positive: such are bodys, Parts, Particles, Somthing, a certain being, and the like, which may be well allow'd in the Practice of Life, but never in the Speculations of Philosophy. ...

12. But no Word has bin more misapply'd, nor consequently has given occasion to more Disputes than Space, which is only an

abstracted notion (as you shall percieve here-after.) or the Relation that any thing has to other Beings at a distance from it, without any Consideration of what lies between them, tho they have at the same time a real Existence. Thus Place is either the relative position of a thing with respect to the circum-ambient bodys, or the Room it fills with its own Bulk, and from which it is conceiv'd to exclude all other Bodys, which are but mere Abstractions, the Capacity nothing differing from the Body contain'd: and so Distance is the Measure between any two Bodys, without regard to the things whose Extension is so measur'd. Yet because the Mathematicians had occasion to suppose Space without Matter, as they did Duration without Things, Points without Quantity, and the like; the Philosophers, who cou'd not otherwise account for the Generation of Motion in Matter which they held to be inactive, imagin'd a real Space distinct from matter, which they held to be extended, incorporeal, immovable, homogeneal, and infinite. But this whole Dispute depends on the Action and Infinity of Matter. In the first place, if Matter it self be essentially active, there's no need to help it to Motion by this Invention, nor is there any Generation of Motion. Secondly, if it be infinite, it can have no separate Parts that move independently of one another in crooked or streight Lines, notwithstanding those modifications which we call particular divisible Bodys. Thirdly, Matter must be like-wise homogeneal, if it has Action of it self as well as Solidity or Extension, without being divided into Parts. And fourthly, if it be infinite, the Universe must be without all local motion, there being no fix'd Points without it, to which it might be successively apply'd, nor any place into which it cou'd possible remove. ...

17. ...But you must always distinguish between the internal Energy, Autokinesy, or essential Action of all matter, without which it cou'd be capable of no particular Altera-tion or Division; and the external local motion or Changes of Place, which are but the various modifications of the essential Action as their Subject; the particular motions being determin'd by other more prevalent Motions, to be direct of circular, fast or slow, continu'd or interrupted, accord-ing to the occurrent, subsequent, or circum-ambient Motions of other Bodys; no part of matter being without its own internal Energy, however thus determin'd by the neighboring Parts according as their particu-lar Determination is stronger or weaker, yields or resists; and these again continue to be vary'd after some other manner by the next; and so every thing proceeds in endless Changes, that is (as I maintain) in perpetual Motion. Now all the local Motions imagin-able being acknowledg'd Accidents, increas-ing, altering, diminishing, and perishing, without the Destruction of the Subject which they modify, or in which they exist, this Sub-ject cannot be wholly imaginary, a mere abstracted Notion, but something real and positive. Extension cannot be this Subject, since the Idea of Extension does not neces-sarily infer any Variety, Alteration, or Motion; and therefore (as I said just now) it must be Action, since all those motions are but the different Modifications of Action, as all par-ticular Bodys or Quantitys are but the differ-ent modifications of Extension.

18. ... Nor is Iron, Stone, Gold, or Lead, more void of this internal Motion, than those they call fluid Bodys: for otherwise they cou'd never undergo those Alterations which Air, or Fire, or Water, or any thing else produces in them. (19) Nevertheless the very remaining

of such Bodys in one place is a real Action, the Efforts and Resistance of this Parcel being equal for some time to the determining Motions of the neighboring Bodys that act upon it, and that will not suffer it to pass certain Bounds; which is easily understood from what I have already no less copiously than plainly said of the numberless successive Determinations of Motion, of which this is one kind, and call'd by the people Rest, to distinguish that State of body from the local motions that are visible.

BIBLIOGRAPHY
Secondary Literature
Champion, J., *Republican Learning. John Toland and the Crisis of Christian Culture, 1696–1722* (Manchester: Manchester University Press, 2003).
Colie, R.L., 'Spinoza and the Early English Deists', *Journal of the History of Ideas*, no. 20 (1959), pp. 23–46.
Daniel, S.H., *John Toland. His Methods, Manners, and Mind* (Kingston and Montreal: McGill-Queen's University Press, 1984).
Israel, J.I., *Radical Enlightenment. Philosophy and the Making of Modernity, 1650–1750* (Oxford: Oxford University Press, 2001).
Lurbe, P., 'Le spinozisme de John Toland', in O. Bloch (ed.), *Spinoza au XVIII siècle* (Paris: Méridiens Klincksieck, 1990), pp. 33–47.
Sullivan, R.E., *John Toland and the Deist Controversy. A Study in Adaptations* (Cambridge, MA: Harvard University Press, 1982).
Vermij, R.H., 'Matter and motion: Toland and Serena', in W. van Bunge and W. Klever (eds), *Disguised and Overt*

Spinozism around 1700. Papers Presented at the International Colloquium Held at Rotterdam, 5–8 October 1994 (Leiden: Brill, 1996), pp. 275–88.

R.H. Vermij

CHRISTOPH WITTICH, Anti-Spinoza (1690)

The publication of Spinoza's *Opera posthuma* in 1677 caused outrage among anti-Cartesians and Cartesians alike. Spinoza was already notorious for being the writer of the *Tractatus theologico-politicus* (1670), a fact that was widely known, even though the *Tractatus* had been published anonymously. It testifies to the stir provoked by Spinoza's philosophy among Cartesians that one of the foremost Cartesians in the Low Countries, Christoph Wittich (1625–87), wrote a thorough refutation of the *Ethics* within a decade of its publication. This refutation appeared posthumously, in 1690, under the title *Anti-Spinoza*, but from two letters printed at the end of the *Anti-Spinoza* it is clear that he wrote parts of it as early as 1681, or even earlier. In any case, it is one of the earliest refutations of Spinoza's *Ethics*.

At the time when Wittich wrote the *Anti-Spinoza*, he was professor of theology at Leiden University. Together with theologians such as Abraham Heidanus (1597–1678) and Franciscus Burman (1628–79), as well as philosophers including Johannes de Raey (1622–1702) and Johannes Clauberg (1622–65), Wittich belonged to an influential circle of Dutch Cartesians. He was already exposed and won over to Cartesian philosophy during his study in Leiden. After having studied theology at Groningen and Leiden, Wittich became a professor of mathematics at Herborn, in the German principality of Nassau, in 1651. In the same year, however, Cartesianism was banned at Herborn, and for that reason Wittich, along with Johannes Clauberg, moved to Duisburg to teach mathematics and theology (from 1652). After that he taught theology in Nijmegen (from 1655), and finally in Leiden (from 1671). In his private courses he most likely taught philosophy as well, since we owe to one of his students, Salomon van Til (1643–1713), a commentary by Wittich on Descartes's *Meditationes*, which clearly appears to be a result of private courses on this topic.

Most of his writings, besides his works on biblical theology, deal with the relation between Cartesian philosophy and theology. In these writings he insists that philosophy and theology have to be strictly separated, while also maintaining that they do not contradict one another. In other publications of a more strictly philosophical nature, Wittich deals with natural theology, which is thus excluded from theology in a narrow sense, since theology is based on revelation rather than reason. This interest in natural theology is also apparent in his criticism of Spinoza.

The *Anti-Spinoza* contains a thorough discussion and assessment of nearly every definition, axiom and proposition of Spinoza's *Ethics*. The text shows us how someone who was steeped in Cartesian philosophy interpreted Spinoza's *Ethics*. This may shed some further light on the relation between Descartes and Spinoza. Wittich does not only clarify some passages in the *Ethics* that are difficult to understand but he also points out where he considers Spinoza to be dishonest in his arguments or his use of traditional philosophical terminology, generally from a Cartesian point of view.

Preceding Wittich's examination of the *Ethics* in the *Anti-Spinoza* is a discourse entitled *On the method of demonstrating*. In it, he makes a distinction between the analytical and synthetic method. By the latter he understands the geometrical order of demonstration, that is, a method starting with definitions, axioms and postulates, from which propositions are deduced. His assessment of this method agrees with that of Descartes: the synthetic method does not require as much attention for someone to become convinced of the proofs as does the analytical method, but it forces one to accept the propositions or conclusions as true (see Descartes, *Second Replies*, AT VII, 155–9). In fact, the synthetic method is largely a method of persuasion or a rhetorical device. Moreover, Wittich's critique of this method corresponds in part with Descartes's remarks. On the one hand, he objects that the synthetic method does not show how something is found, and on the other he holds that there is a danger that the definitions may prove incorrect because they do not concern things existing outside the mind – a danger that does not occur when the analytical method is used, since that method aims at starting with or finding the correct definitions of real things. For unlike the synthetic method, the analytical method starts with particular things themselves, such as God or the mind, in order to consider them closely and attentively, in a manner that is free from all prejudices.

According to Wittich, Spinoza's main error is that he does not commence with particular things, but with definitions of 'second notions', like that of substance. Then he defines the things themselves, like God, on the basis of these second notions. Hence, Spinoza's definitions do not correspond to things as they are in themselves, but concern merely second notions, though he supposes that they are true definitions of real objects. Besides this, his definitions differ from the common use of the terms. Second notions or intentions (*secundae notiones* or *intentiones*) are, according to Wittich, fashioned by philosophers when they compare things with each other (see Wittich, 1690, on E1def1, pp. 7–9; see Verbeek, 2005, pp. 118–20, for the historical background of the terms primary and second notion).

In such a way, notions like substance, essence, genus, species, subject, property, accident and mode are formed. These are traditional philosophical concepts with which logic in particular is concerned, and which are used to clarify our knowledge of things. They are, in fact, ways in which we can consider a thing, and hence are always relative to our understanding. Moreover, they only acquire a precise meaning when linked to knowledge of a particular thing. In consequence, they should not be regarded as real aspects of things outside the mind. In the above-mentioned text, Wittich discusses for example the notion of substance – palpably the most interesting second notion in Spinoza's philosophy. On the one hand, extension can be considered a substance, particular bodies of which, such as stones, can be regarded as modes. On the other hand, a stone too can be considered a substance to which we assign particular properties or modes, like the property of being grey. Consequently, one and the same thing – a stone – can be said to be a substance in one respect and an accident in another. So the precise meaning of the notion of substance is relative to our understanding of a thing.

As a result, one is not allowed to just start with the notion of substance without having prior knowledge of a particular thing or, in other words, without considering a primary notion (*prima notio*) which is a concept of a particular thing outside the mind. Moreover, the idea of substance, used generally and abstractly, does not concern any real thing but only our way of apprehending a thing. Since Spinoza proceeds by defining real things in terms of our ways of apprehending them, so by employing second notions, his definitions are wrong. Showing this is one of the aims of Wittich's commentary on Spinoza's *Ethics*.

Wittich's main point is, then, that second notions, such as substance and accident or mode, as well as *causa sui*, only have a fixed meaning when they are tied to primary notions, which concern the things themselves. In other words, Wittich's criticism of Spinoza boils down to the claim that Spinoza confounds knowing a real thing, existing outside the mind, with knowing abstract concepts which, although they can be used to clarify our knowledge of a thing, acquire a fixed meaning only when they are based on knowledge of particular things. This implies that the analytical instead of the synthetic method has to be followed. In the case of God, for instance, we first have to acquire a clear and distinct idea of him, that is a primary notion. This is done by using the analytical method, as with Descartes's procedure in the *Meditationes*, that is, by setting aside all prejudices and starting with the knowledge of oneself as a thinking thing, from which, in the order of thought, the knowledge of God follows. Wittich follows this procedure himself in an appendix to the *Examen ethices*, the *Commentary on God and his Attributes*, which amounts to a fairly complete natural theology. From this text it is clear that he thought of this treatise as a Cartesian alternative to Spinoza's philosophy.

The following text is a translation from the Latin of the first eight propositions of the

CHRISTOPH WITTICH

first part of the *Anti-Spinoza* (Wittich, 1690, pp. 40–57). As far as possible the original sentence structure has been preserved. The same English word is generally used for every occurrence of the same Latin word, particularly the more technical terms, some of which have also been given explanations within square brackets. The translation by Samuel Shirley has been used for Wittich's quotations from the *Ethics*, all of which have further been checked with the Gebhardt-edition of Spinoza's writings.

EXAMINATION OF THE PROPOSITIONS.

PROPOSITION 1.

Substance is by nature prior to its affections.
Examination.
The author seems here to understand by affections modes, since he refers for proof of the proposition to definition 5, which is concerned with mode. The term *affection*, however, has a much broader meaning, including also essential attributes (*attributa essentialia*). [Wittich refers to Descartes's notion of an essential attribute. In Descartes's view, every substance has one and only one unique attribute or principal property, which constitutes its essence. Contrary to Spinoza, he also uses the term attribute in a broader meaning, including every possible property of a thing. See Descartes, *Principia* I, §53, AT VIIIa, 25; *Principia* I, §56, AT VIIIa, 26.] But even apart from this, the proposition is completely ambiguous. For either substance and affections are taken in the abstract and as second notions (*notiones secundae*) or they are considered in the concrete particulars (*in particularibus*). [The term second notion is explained in the commentary. Wittich contrasts here two uses of the notion of substance. On the one hand, it can be used

abstractly or generally, that is, without having a particular thing in mind to which it is applied. In this sense, it is used by Spinoza both in his definition of substance and in the propositions here under consideration. On the other hand, substance may have a more specific meaning when it is applied to a particular thing. His main point is that one cannot draw valid inferences as to real beings on the basis of abstract or second notions, and that thus Spinoza's deduction in the first part of the *Ethics* is unwarranted and erroneous.]

If concrete particulars are taken in the latter meaning, the sense will be: when we have considered the concrete particulars of a thing existing external to the intellect, and discover what are real entities (*realia*) in them, then prior in nature is what constitutes their nature and posterior what modifies that nature. If it is taken in the first meaning, the sense will be: when we have marked the concrete particulars with second notions, regarding one as a substance and the other as a mode, then a substance is prior in nature to the affections. We admit the proposition in both meanings, although we reject Spinoza's demonstration, because it depends on definition 3 and 5, which are not sufficiently true, as we have seen before.

PROPOSITION 2.

Two substances having different attributes have nothing in common.
Examination.
This proposition, proposed at the outset of a philosophy, is very obscure and difficult to understand, since the human mind seeks rather to be guided by things that are clear and easy to understand. The term substance is abstract, and designates nothing but a singular thing existing external to the intellect in such a way that it is in itself and not in

132

another, and so does not depend on something else as a subject. Therefore, whenever we hear of a substance, we hear nothing but a certain general concept (*conceptum communem*) or second notion; and when we learn that they are counted and called two substances, we cannot form a concept of the twofold number of substances, at least unless we think in a confused way of the singular substances, and so suppose that there can be two, or can be two particular or singular things, to each of which belongs the name and the notion of substance. But this is completely contrary to the intention of the author, who wants that there is but one single and singular substance, which is God, and that all other things are merely certain modes of that single substance, as we shall see in what follows. Meanwhile, if this proposition is regarded as applying to particular substances, as should be done, then its truth is certain. Indeed, the extended and thinking substance have nothing in common in concrete particulars, since the attributes of extension and thought are completely different. There is only one real attribute of each thing, which constitutes their nature. So therefore two substances having different attributes, by which they differ from one another, cannot have any real attribute in common. For each of them has only one real attribute, by which the whole nature of that substance is completed; and since this attribute differs from that of the other substance, no real attribute common to both can remain. Nonetheless, these two substances may have many notional attributes (*attributa notionalia*) in common, including also that each of them is called substance, and more of that sort. ['Notional attributes' are attributes that things in themselves do not have, but are concepts under which we bring or consider things.] We rightly reject Spinoza's

demonstration, for it relies on definition 3, which, taken in Spinoza's sense, we have rightly rejected above.

PROPOSITION 3.

When things have nothing in common,
one cannot be the cause of the other.
Examination.
If this proposition is taken in the sense that the words *nothing in common* designate a real attribute common to several things, like Spinoza undoubtedly wants to have it understood, it is entirely false. In fact, he intends to make it absolutely clear, as will appear from what follows, that God cannot be the cause of bodies unless he was extended, which we have proved above to be very false when we demonstrated that God has made all things from nothing.

It could seem that this proposition is equivalent to this axiom: *A cause can give nothing to an effect, which it does not have itself*. But if this axiom is rightly understood, it is easily perceived that this proposition is not equivalent to this axiom. Indeed, the sense is: *A cause can give nothing to an effect except that which the cause has either formally or eminently (formaliter vel eminenter)*. [The scholastic distinction between having something formally or eminently is used by Descartes in the third meditation (AT VII, 41–6) for his a posteriori proof of the existence of God. As is clear from Wittich's usage, it functions also to explain how God is able to create extension or matter without being himself material, namely, by possessing extension eminently.] What *having something formally* means is clear in itself. But what *having eminently* means is not so obvious. A king has formally money, an estate, a house, and so forth, which he gives to me. But he does not have formally a doctorate, the office of secretary or professor, which he confers on me, but one says rather that he has them eminently, that is, he has the right to give it to me. Likewise God contains extension eminently, which he nevertheless produces from nothing, as we have shown in its appropriate place.

Spinoza's demonstration depends on axiom 5 and 7, and therefore proves only that *if things having nothing in common* is taken broadly, taking *having* whether as real or as notional (*sive reale sive notionale*), *one cannot be the cause of the other*. In this sense we admit this proposition willingly, but in this sense the proposition will not contribute to Spinoza's intention.

PROPOSITION 4.

Two or more distinct things are distinguished from one another either by the difference of the attributes of the substances or by the difference of the affections of the substances.
Examination.
This proposition is sufficiently obscure because of its generality and abstractness, so that we will compare it with the demonstration, in order to understand it. *All things that are, are either in themselves or in something else (by axiom 1); that is (by definition 3 and 5), nothing exists external to the intellect except substances and their affections. Therefore, there can be nothing external to the intellect through which several things can be distinguished from one another except substances or (which is the same thing) (by definition 4) the attributes and the affections of substances.* One might think, when comparing this demonstration with the proposition itself, that the meaning of this proposition is that there is a twofold distinction among things, namely thus, that things are distinguished from one another either as different

substances or as different modes of one and the same substance. And if the proposition is taken in this sense, we can admit it, as well as its demonstration. But actually it appears from the use of this proposition in what follows that he means something very different. Spinoza establishes that there can only be one substance on the basis of the term substance, which is too narrowly defined in definition 3, namely, that it eventually denotes that thing which is by itself, as we have seen when discussing that proposition. Therefore, the meaning of the proposition can only be this: Things are distinguished either by attributes, so that there could be several attributes of one substance which are really distinct from one another (*realiter inter se invicem distincta*), none of which is contained in the concept of the other, or by modes; in this sense we rightly reject this proposition. For we have established that there are as many substances as there are really distinct attributes, so that the concept of the one is not contained in that of the other. We also observe that one and the same thing can be considered in different respects (*pro diverso respectu*) either as a mode of a thing or as an attribute constituting a substance. In such a way, the essential attributes of a diamond and a sapphire, by which one gem is distinguished from the other, are only certain modes of extension or of an extended thing. Accordingly, the numerical distinction between this or that sapphire, by which one individual is distinguished from another, is taken from the different modes of each, which, nonetheless, taken all together constitute the substance of this or that sapphire.

PROPOSITION 5.

In the universe there cannot be two or more substances of the same nature or attribute.

Examination.

This proposition is false when *the same nature or attribute* is understood of a specific identity (*de identitate specifica*) rather than a numerical identity (*de identitate numerica*). [Wittich refers to the traditional distinction between specific and numerical identity so as to clarify his notion of substance. Specific identity means an identity in kind. For example, the essence of the mind of both Peter and Paul consists in thought, so that they are of the same kind or have a specific identity. Both can be regarded as substances having the same essential attribute, namely thought, while differing from one another numerically by their individual attributes, which, in that case, are considered to be modes.]

The demonstration is similarly ambiguous on account of the ambiguity of proposition 4 on which it depends. For he says the following: *If there were several such distinct substances, they would have to be distinguished from one another either by a difference of attributes or by a difference of affections (by the previous proposition). If they are distinguished only by a difference of attributes, then it will be granted that there cannot be more than one substance of the same attribute*. To which I respond that two substances can be distinguished by the difference in individual attributes, which can be considered as affections or modes of a substance insofar as it is conceived abstractly (*generatim*). In such a way, the minds of Peter and Paul are distinguished. Likewise, two bodies. That is why Descartes has long since observed in *Principia* I, §63: *Thought and extension can be regarded as constituting the natures of intelligent substance and corporeal substance; they must then be considered as nothing else but thinking substance itself and extended substance itself* [AT IXb, 30–1; CSM I, 215], and so on. In §64: *Thought and extension may also be taken as modes of a substance, insofar as one and the same mind is capable of having many different thoughts; and one and the same body, with its quantity unchanged, may be extended in many different ways.* [AT IXb, 31; CSM I, 215] Having observed this, it will follow: if there are several distinct substances in virtue of the difference in individual attributes, though they may have a specific attribute (*attributum specificum*) in common, there is but one substance of the same individual attribute; which is not inconsistent with the fact that there can be several individual substances distinct by individual attributes, and at the same time having a specific attribute in common. Spinoza continues his demonstration as follows: *But if the substances are distinguished by a difference of affections, then, since substance is by nature prior to its affections (by Prop. 1), disregarding therefore its affections and considering substance in itself, that is, (by Definition 3 and Axiom 6), considering it truly, it cannot be conceived as distinguishable from another substance. That is, (by the preceding proposition) there cannot be several such substances but only one. Q.E.D.* As to which I observe that those affections, insofar as they distinguish substances, are considered their essential attributes, although insofar as those two substances agree in kind (*in genere*), and so can said to be a substance of one species or kind, they can be regarded as affections of that substance generally considered. As such, figure, movement, rest and place are affections of the extended substance, but they are also attributes of this or that substance, insofar as its particles have a certain rest or motion, a certain figure and place relative to one another, by which they differ from another extended substance. There also seems to be a mystery hidden in these words: *A substance considered in itself,*

CHRISTOPH WITTICH

that is, (by Definition 3 and Axiom 6), con-sidering it truly. Definition 3 is as follows: *By substance I mean that which is in itself and is conceived through itself; that is, that the con-ception of which does not require the con-ception of another thing from which it has to be formed.* And definition 6 is as follows: *By God I mean an absolutely infinite being, that is, substance consisting of infinite attributes, each of which expresses eternal and infinite essence.* He must prove, namely, that *a sub-stance considered in itself is a substance rightly considered*, which he proves on the basis of these two definitions. But I do not see how this follows, unless the first defin-ition expresses that which *in itself is a sub-stance*, and the other definition *that which is truly a substance*, and that, consequently, these two definitions are of the same thing, so that a substance and God are completely one and the same. Which we have already observed above on definition 3. But still this way of proving is not evident, is not math-ematical, because what mathematicians prove from definitions in such a way is expressly said in those definitions: but in neither of these definitions it is expressly said that what *is a substance in itself* is the same as what *is truly a substance*: therefore, that must not be inferred except as a conjecture.

PROPOSITION 6.

One substance cannot be produced by another substance.
Explanation.
The demonstration of this proposition depends on two false propositions, namely, on the preceding proposition, *that in the uni-verse there cannot be two or more substances of the same nature or attribute*, while we have shown to the contrary that there are in the universe several substances, which have

common, that is either the same specific or generic attributes (*communia sive eadem attributa specifica & generica*), and on prop-osition 2, *that two substances having differ-ent attributes have nothing in common*, of which we have also shown that it is false. Therefore, these supports being taken away, the proposition necessarily collapses, and so we reject it as false. Likewise, also the corol-lary is false, *that substance cannot be pro-duced by anything else*, which is completely contrary to creation, that it is, as we have shown above, not only not absurd what this man wants but also completely necessary. He adds, however, another demonstration of this corollary: *If substance could be produced by something else, the knowledge of substance would have to depend on the knowledge of its cause (by Axiom 4), and so (by Definition 3) it would not be substance.* From this we learn the tricks of Spinoza, which we already suspected when discussing definition 3, for evidently the concept of a dependent sub-stance needs the concept of God, insofar as he is considered as a cause and that sub-stance as dependent, but not insofar as it is considered as a substance. Thus, I deny that it follows that if a dependent substance has to depend on the knowledge of its cause inso-far as it is dependent, it therefore cannot be a substance, because that is not required for the concept of a substance as such....

PROPOSITION 8.

Every substance is necessarily infinite.
Examination.
The demonstration of this proposition depends, among others, on the false propos-ition 5 and proposition 7, which is also false. However, he only infers from these propositions: *It must therefore exist either as finite or as infinite*, which conclusion can be

136

admitted as a certain proposition, but does not mean the same as the proposition that he should have proved here: *Every substance is necessarily infinite.* Now he further tries to show that *existence does not come from a finite nature,* which is indeed true, but the added proof does not proceed in a linear fashion. He says the following: *For (by Definition 2) it would have to be limited by another substance of the same nature, and that substance also would have to exist (by Proposition 7).* For when he speaks in definition 2 of a thing finite in its own kind, everyone understands by that a substance finite in its own kind, of which he says that *it can be limited by another of the same nature,* and of which he gives the example of a body that is *finite, because we can always conceive of another body greater than it,* and so he seems to suppose that there exists a finite substance, a finite body, of which we can always conceive another greater than it. And indeed a finite body cannot be conceived unless it is called a finite extended substance, of which another body with a greater extension can be conceived. But then he does not prove what he intended to prove, *that there does not exist a finite substance,* which would be much easier to prove in the following way: because a finite substance is not of itself, but its essence and existence depend on something else. But also in scholium 1 he tries to demonstrate with another argument that *every substance is necessarily infinite,* in the following way: *Since in fact to be finite is in part a negation and to be finite is the unqualified affirmation of the existence of some nature, it follows from Proposition 7 alone that every substance must be infinite.* But he here confounds the negation with the thing to which it adheres. That which is finite has some reality, to which the negation is attached, which prevents the thing from

extending itself further. Which he himself, however, seems to concede when he says: *to be finite is in part a negation*; from which it certainly does not follow what he was intending. For if that which is finite (*finitum*) is nothing but a negation, if it does not contain anything real, then it will ultimately follow that every substance must be infinite; but that does not follow when that which is finite contains some reality.

We now approach the scholium, in which he attempts to illustrate proposition 7. *I do not doubt,* he says, *that for those who judge things confusedly and are not accustomed to know things through their primary causes it is difficult to grasp the proof of proposition 7; surely, this is because they neither distinguish between the modifications of substances and substances themselves, nor do they know how things are produced. And so it comes about that they ascribe to substances a beginning which they see natural things as having.* But this is the question, whether a finite extension and a finite thought (*cogitatio finita*) are merely modifications of a substance and are not themselves substances as well? This is also to be questioned, and is not proved by him, that one and the same substance can have different infinite attributes, only two of which we know, extension and thought. And I do not know whether he better understands how the things are produced than those which understand it in the ordinary way (*illi more vulgari concipiunt*); and we have seen above when discussing definition 6, to which Spinoza clings, where he should have explained how the things flow from God's nature, which he understands as a way of producing. But hereafter there will be a new occasion to discuss this issue. He also distinguishes natural things from natural substances, and thus, like it ought to be, he understands by natural things only modes, more about which soon.

Later he gives examples of confused thoughts, which we admit.

But we have to look further into what he adds. On page 6 [G II, 50] he says the following: *But if men were to attend to the nature of substance, they would not doubt at all the truth of Proposition 7; indeed, this Proposition would be an axiom to all and would be ranked among universally accepted truisms. For by substance they would understand that which is in itself and is conceived through itself; that is, that the knowledge of which does not require the knowledge of another thing. By modifications they would understand that which is in another thing, and whose conception is formed from the thing in which they are. Therefore, in the case of nonexistent modifications we can have true ideas of them since their essence is included in something else, with the result that they can be conceived through that something else, although they do not exist in actuality externally to the intellect.* Which are truly strange words if we pay attention to the distinction between kinds of definitions that we have already observed before at the outset of *On the method of demonstrating.* Since those definitions of substance and mode, to which he here appeals, are merely *such that are proposed for examination, and do not serve to explicate a thing whose essence is sought and the subject of doubt* [on page 461, Spinoza, Ep 9 (G IV, 42), Shirley, 2002, p. 781], as we have heard him say above. Now here is added, as it were, that which serves to explicate the very essence of the thing that is sought. However, I do not see yet how it follows from that definition *that existence pertains to the nature of a substance,* unless he understands being in itself and conceived by itself in such a way that it denotes being (*esse*) thus that it is in itself sufficient for existing and the cause of itself, in other

words, that being in itself is identical with being by itself, which we have refuted when discussing definition 6. Thus, he understands by substance something which is completely different from what is commonly and usually understood by it. In such a way, then, only God would exist, which is wholly absurd. And if God alone would be a substance, then it will have to be said that all other things are modifications of God, of which I reasonably do not know how it can be conceived: for if all other things would be parts of God, how can they be said to be modifications? For it cannot be understood how a part is a modification of a substance, and not rather the substance itself with a determinate modification, by which it is distinguished from another part and thus also from another substance.

Spinoza continues: *However, in the case of substances, because they are conceived only through themselves, their truth external to the intellect is only in themselves. So if someone were to say that he has a clear and distinct – that is, a true – idea of substance and that he nevertheless doubts whether such a substance exists, this would surely be just the same as if he were to declare that he has a true idea but nevertheless suspects that it may be false (as is obvious to anyone who gives his mind to it). Or if anyone asserts that substance is created, he at the same time asserts that a false idea has become true, than which nothing more absurd can be conceived. So it must necessarily be admitted that the existence of substance is as much an eternal truth as is its essence.* This whole inference depends on the ambiguity of the phrases *being in itself,* and *to be conceived through itself....* Thus, when a substance is said to be *in itself* or *by itself,* this is to be understood in such a way that it is in thought, in the intellect, that is to say that we understand by substance a thing of which we cannot determine from our concept whether it does or does not exist, just as one is not permitted to infer that there exists a whole when someone says that 'a whole is that which is composed of all its parts', because when we attribute *being* (*esse*) in this way to a whole, this is only to be understood of our intellect, namely that it is a whole in our intellect. We have such a true, that is a clear and distinct, idea of substance, yet we cannot say therefore that such a substance exists. So we have a clear and distinct idea of an angel, that he is a mind separated from a body, but one is not allowed to infer from that idea that an angel exists. Therefore, we can only infer from the definition of substance that a substance formally, or in its formal reason (*in sua ratione*), does not need another thing for existing, or which goes into it or constitutes its being, although it may be the case that a substance needs another thing which produces it in its being and preserves it. All substances have a certain self-sufficiency, by which they have some essence (*essentiam*), through which they are constituted intrinsically, and by which they are distinguished from every other thing, an issue I have discussed more fully when discussing Definition 3. But they all have only being in thought. If, however, a substance is conceived whose essence contains existence in our thought, then we can rightly infer therefrom that the existence of that substance is necessary; but we cannot know its existence a priori if the substance is not of such a kind, but that can only be known a posteriori.

As a result, saying that a certain substance is created is not the same as saying that *a false idea is true*. For that which is not created is not yet a substance, but when it is created it becomes a substance, and when there is a substance, it does not need in its form and intrinsically another thing for existing,

although it may need it extrinsically. Everything seems to hinge on that common definition of substance, which is accepted by everyone, *substance is that which exists by itself*. Hitherto nobody has taken these words in the sense used by Spinoza (words, however, are like money) [Wittich refers to the Latin proverb *verba valent ut nummi*], but all have taken it in this sense: Whenever a certain thing exists, if it exists in such a way that it is not in another, it is called a substance. Thus it does not follow that when I conceive a thing as a substance, it has to exist. For what if someone conceives a centaur, what if he conceives an omnipotent angel, does it follow therefrom that such things exist? What if someone conceives a substantial form, does it follow that it exists? Therefore, nothing must be inferred from that definition other than that if a thing exists which you conceive in such a way that it is not in another, it is a substance. It is the nature of every substance that it possesses some being or reality or essence proper to it, by which it is constituted intrinsically, and by which power it is not something of a being (*aliquid entis*) but truly a being by itself, in which respect it is opposite to modes and accidents, which are conceived to have their being and reality, by which they are constituted intrinsically, in another. It is true that there is a particular substance that does not merely possess its reality by itself and in itself, but which is also by itself and exists by the power of its own nature, so that it does not depend on another either as to its origin or insofar as it perseveres, which is a unique substance and is completely sufficient for the existence of itself and all other things external to it. But apart from this substance there are also certain other substances, which do not exist by the power of their own nature, nor from an intrinsic necessity and self-sufficiency of their

CHRISTOPH WITTICH

nature, but solely by the power of him, by which they are and are preserved, or are made in order to continue to be. And indeed those do not come to exist only because there exists a substance by which they can be produced, but for that reason they should only be considered as possible, whereas they are only to be conceived as existent when it is conceived that that substance wills that they exist at that time. When, however, that substance wills that they exist, their reality follows from that very will, a reality, though limited, by which they are constituted intrinsically, as well as limited from every other substance, so that they indeed have to differ really (*realiter*) and be really (*realiter*) distinguished from that substance from which they continually receive that reality. Nor should they be confounded with the modes, which do not possess any reality, but whose being and reality is conceived to be completely in another thing or substance. And certainly while these dependent substances admit various modes, undoubtedly they must necessarily be distinguished from those same modes. But that man has invented definitions to his own liking, and has only assigned to the term 'substance' the infinite and independent substance, from which definitions he nonetheless later wanted to form demonstrations by which the essences of things are explained, so that he acts contrary to his own rule, which we have considered at the outset of *On the method of demonstrating*. And he certainly is unable to deny that it differs a lot. Thus, the concept of the human mind differs from the concept of a mode of imagining, of perceiving (*sentiendi*), of purely understanding, of willing, all of which are modes of the human mind, and likewise the concept of a body from a triangle, square, circle, which are modes of the body. These minds and bodies will therefore be an intermediary between God and the

modes of thinking, as well as the modes of the body; we call that intermediary substance, whereas he calls them modes. We agree in substance, but from what is said it is clear that our term is better and more suitable....

BIBLIOGRAPHY
Primary Sources
Wittich, C., *Anti-Spinoza sive Examen Ethices Benedicti de Spinoza, et commentarius de Deo et ejus attributis* (Amsterdam, 1690).
———, *Ondersoek van de Zede-konst van Benedictus de Spinoza en een verhandeling van God en desselfs eigenschappen*, trans. A. van Poot (Amsterdam, 1695).

Secondary Literature
Bordoli, R., 'Wittichius, Christopher', in W. van Bunge et al. (eds), *The Dictionary of Seventeenth and Eighteenth-Century Dutch Philosophers* (Bristol: Thoemmes Press, 2003), pp. 1083–6.
Hubert, C., *Les premières réfutations de Spinoza. Aubert de Versé, Wittich, Lamy* (Paris: Presses Universitaires de France, 1994).
Pape, G., *Christoph Wittichs Anti-Spinoza* (Berlin: n.p., 1910).
Savini, M., 'Notes au sujet de la publication de l'Anti-Spinoza de Christoph Wittich', *Nouvelles de la République des Lettres*, no. 2 (2000), pp. 79–96.
Verbeek, Th., 'Wittich's Critique of Spinoza', in T. M. Schmaltz (ed.), *Receptions of Descartes. Cartesianism and Anti-Cartesianism in Early Modern Europe* (London and New York: Routledge, 2005), pp. 113–27.

M. Aalderink

4

GLOSSARY

Accidens

The Latin noun *accidens* – and its Dutch counterpart *toeval* – is used only in Spinoza's early works; in the *Ethics* it occurs only once and in the fixed expression *per accidens*. In the *Tractatus de intellectus emendatione* Spinoza refers to the logical priority of the essence regarding the accidents, 'which are never clearly understood, unless the essence of the things in question be known first'. The ontological posteriority of the accidents with respect to the SUBSTANCE and the partition of being into substances and accidents is mentioned in letter 4. The ontological and logical dependence are basic scholastic notions, but the direct source of Spinoza was Descartes.

From the priority of substance Descartes deduces both that the body is the immediate subject of the accidents, such as figure, place, local motion, which presuppose extension and that substance possesses a greater REALITAS than the accidents. Moreover in a Cartesian manner Spinoza observed that the objective reality of substance is greater than the objective reality of the accidents. He also adopted Descartes's refutation of the scholastic doctrine of real accidents in the *Responsiones* VI. According to scholastic doctrine such accidents had to be called 'real', for they would be able to exist without their corresponding substance. Such real accidents were

the red of the wine and the white of the bread transformed during the Eucharist. However, according to Descartes all things, which might exist independently (*separatim*) are substances and never accidents. Spinoza adopted the Cartesian identification of accident and MODUS as well. Only in *Cogitata metaphysica* does he explicitly distinguish between both concepts. By describing the traditional division of being in terms of 'substance' and 'mode' and not in terms of 'substance' and 'accident' and observing that an accident merely denotes a 'mode of thing', he reshuffled the conceptual order of scholasticism.

TEXTS
Dan waren de toevallen door haar natuur eer als de zelfstandigheid (KVap). *Substantia est subjectum immediatum extensionis et accidentium quae extensionem praesupponunt, ut figurae, situs, motus localis* (PPC1def7). *Substantia plus realitatis habet quam accidens vel modus* (PPC1ax4). *Expresse dicimus ens dividi in substantiam et modum, non vero in substantiam et accidens, nam accidens nihil est praeter modum cogitandi* (CM1.1). *Aliquid de formis substantialibus et realibus accidentibus dicamus, sunt enim haec et hujus farinae alia plane inepte* (CM2.1). *Accidentium et modorum nullam dari creationem,*

praesupponunt enim praeter Deum substantiam creatam (CM2.12). *Per modificationem sive per accidens.... Substantia sit prior natura suis accidentibus* (Ep 4). *Non ex accidenti, sed ex ipsa natura rationis oriri* (E5p36s).

BIBLIOGRAPHY
Primary Sources
Burgersdijk, F., *Institutiones metaphysicae* (Leiden, 1642).
Descartes, R., *Principia Philosophiae, Responsiones Sextae.*
Heereboord, A., *Hermeneia logica, sive synopseos logicae Burgersdicianae explicatio* (Leiden, 1640).
Maccovius, J., *Metaphysica ad usum questionum in philosophia ac theologia adornata et applicata per A. Heereboord* (Leiden, 1658).

Secondary Literature
Richter, G.T., *Spinozas philosophische Terminologie. I: Grundbegriffe der Metaphysik* (Leipzig: Barth, 1913).

Acquiescentia in se ipso

The phrase *acquiescentia in se ipso* occurs thirteen times in parts three and four of the *Ethics*. Related expressions (*mentis acquiescentia, animi acquiescentia*) occur in a variety of passages in parts four and five, as well as in the *Tractatus theologico-politicus*. The noun *acquiescentia* is a neologism, which is found in neither classical nor medieval Latin. Spinoza adopts it from the 1650 Latin edition of Descartes's *Les passions de l'âme*, where it renders the French expression 'satisfaction de soi-même' (art. 190). Like Descartes, Spinoza associates acquiescence with a feeling of contentment or satisfaction; thus, *acquiescentia in se ipso* can be glossed as a 'self-contentment'.

Formally, Spinoza defines the affect as a species of *laetitia*: 'a joy born of the fact that a man considers himself and his own power of acting' (E3aff25). He equates this with self-love (E3aff28exp). Love, in general, is joy accompanied by the idea of an external cause (E3aff3). *Acquiescentia in se ipso* is the same affect accompanied by the idea of an internal cause (E3p30s). The full import of this definition is revealed through the links Spinoza establishes between it and those of related affects. *Acquiescentia in se ipso* is contrasted most directly with humility, which is 'a sadness born of the fact that a man considers his own lack of power or weakness' (E3aff26). But the same contentment is associated with awareness of the effects of our power, in which case it is opposed to repentance: 'a sadness accompanied by the idea of some deed we believe ourselves to have done from a free decision of the mind' (E3aff27; E3p51s). *Acquiescentia in se ipso* that is based on others' recognition of our power is distinguished as 'glory'; and from excessive self-love, there follows 'pride': 'thinking more highly of oneself than is just, out of love of oneself' (E3aff28).

With respect to each of these definitions, Spinoza acknowledges that the idea one forms of one's power, either directly or through the testimony of others, is almost always only an inadequate idea of the imagination. Accordingly, the satisfaction one takes in this power may be exaggerated or even baseless (E3p51s, p55s). *Acquiescentia in se ipso* that is encouraged only by the opinion of the multitude, he says, is 'empty' (E4p58s). Because man's 'true power of acting', or virtue, is reason itself, only that contentment that arises from awareness of our power of understanding is well founded, and 'the greatest there can be' (E4p52).

Such self-contentment, Spinoza says, is the 'highest thing we can hope for' (E4p52s). This claim is most plausibly associated with the affect he distinguishes as 'contentment of mind', identifying it with the joy arising from the mind's awareness of itself as possessing the third kind of knowledge (E5p27). Like blessedness, 'true contentment of mind' is the sole preserve of the wise man, who 'by a certain necessity is conscious of himself, and of God and of things' (E5p42s).

TEXTS

Laetitiam concomitante idea causae externae (E3p30s); E3p51s. *Philautia vel Acquiescentia in se ipso* (E3p55s); *Acquiescentia in se ipso est Laetitia, orta ex eo, quod homo se ipsum, suamque agendi potentiam contemplatur* (E3aff25). *Acquiescentia in se ipso Humilitati opponitur* (E3aff26ex). *Amor sui, sive Acquiescentia in se ipso* (E3aff28ex). *Acquiescentia in se ipso ex ratione potest oriri...summum quod sperari possumus* (E4p52 and s). *Acquiescentia in se ipso, quae sola vulgi opinione fovetur* (E4p58s).

BIBLIOGRAPHY
Primary Sources
Descartes, R., *Passiones animi.*

Secondary Literature
Rutherford, D., 'Salvation as a State of Mind: The Place of *Acquiescentia* in Spinoza's Ethics', *British Journal of the History of Philosophy*, no. 7 (1999), pp. 447–73.
Totaro, G., '*Acquiescentia* dans la cinquième partie de l'Ethique de Spinoza', *Revue philosophique de la France et de L'étranger*, no. 130 (1994), pp. 65–79.

Voss, S., 'How Spinoza Enumerated the Affects', *Archiv für Geschichte der Philosophie*, no. 63 (1981), pp. 167–79.

D. Rutherford

Actio

In Spinoza's works the word *actio* – and its Dutch counterparts *doening*, *werk* and *werking* – is mostly related to man as a whole or to his mind. However, man being part of nature, human actions are to be studied as all natural phenomena, 'as if it were a question of lines, planes and bodies' (E3praef). Action in Spinoza has two meanings. In a general sense, imitating Descartes, it refers to the activity of a power, which contrary to the Aristotelian tradition is not considered to be connected to an act of an agent on a passsive matter (cf. Goclenius's definition: 'action is the impact of an agent on a *patiens*, causing a change in this passive principle'; hence 'action is a perfection of the agent as such'). Chauvin defined the Cartesian notion as follows: 'an action is a manifestation of the vigour of substances'. What is more, Descartes – with Hobbes in *De Corpore* – meant action and passion to be relative terms, which does not form a strict opposition. In the world of corporeal substance action is identified with local motion, or at least the power to move. Taken in relation to the moving body such motion is called action, Descartes in a letter to Regius (nr. 255, AT III, pp. 454–5) observed, with respect to the body moved, passion. By analogy these terms are used with respect to the immaterial world. In the mind we call willing, being a moving force, an action, whereas in the same mind mental perception is a passion. The same interrelatedness of action and passion is stated in the

ACTIO

Passions de l'âme art. 1–2, where Descartes observed that one and the same event may be called an action with respect to one subject, which makes it happen (the body) and a passion with respect to the subject in which it happens (the mind). The cause of action seems to be substance itself. However, in the *Discours de métaphysique* § 8 Leibniz observed that 'some philosophers think that God causes all things'. So creatures in a proper sense may not be called actors. In this general sense of action Spinoza just like Descartes does not strictly oppose passions to actions. For men's actions are often caused by passive affects. Moreover, all actions according to Spinoza are a kind of perfection or virtue (PPC 1p15s and E5p4s)

In a particular sense, peculiar to Spinoza, action is distinguished from passion. It is a technical concept, which is defined in definition 3 of *Ethics* 3 and elaborated in its proposition 59 scholium. Action is a kind of affect which results from an adequate or total cause, that is to say a cause we can explain by referring to our nature only, while passion is a kind of affect which results from an inadequate or partial cause, that is to say a cause the effects of which we cannot explain by referring only to our nature but to the nature of other things as well. Affects which are called 'actions' imply an affection by which the human body increases its power of acting and, at the same time, an IDEA of this affection. Actions are joyful affects. Spinoza includes all actions under the term FORTI-TUDO and divides it into animosity, which refers to all the actions we do in order to preserve our being, and generosity, which includes all the actions we do in order to preserve others and to be friends with them.

General and particular meanings are not opposed, for passion is not the opposite of action but a lesser form of action. When we feel a passion, we are partly active because we are partly the cause of what occurs. Passion can be turned into action when the mind stops thinking in a confused manner and starts forming adequate ideas.

TEXTS

De werkingen die de ziel heeft in het lighaam (KV 2.19). Voor zoo veel te meer als een zaake wezen heeft, voor zoo veel te meer heeft zij ook van de doening en te min van de lijding (KV 2.26). *Vis vel actio quae transfert* (PPC 2def8ex). *Finis omnium humanarum actionum est amor Dei* (TTP 4, G III, 62). *Conceptus actionem mentis exprimit* (E2def-3ex). *Quo unius corporis actiones magis ab ipso solo pendent eo ejus mens aptior est ad distincte intelligendum* (E2p13s). *Humanas actiones considerabo ac si questio de lineis, planis, aut de corporibus esset* (E3praef). *Si alicujus affectionum adaequata possimus esse causa, tum per affectum actionem intelligo* (E3def3). *Ordo actionum et passionum corporis nostri simul sit natura cum ordine actionum et passionum mentis* (E3p2s). *Mentis actiones ex solis ideis adaequatis oriuntur* (E3p3). *Omnes actiones, quae sequuntur ex affectibus, qui ad mentem referuntur, quatenus intelligit, ad fortitudinem refero* (E3p59s). *Ad omnes actiones, ad quas ex affectu, qui passio est determinamur, possumus absque eo a ratione determinari ... nulla actio in se sola considerata bona aut mala* (E4p59). *Actio seu virtus* (E5p4s). *Quae cupiditates non tam actiones, quam passiones sint* (TP 2.18).

BIBLIOGRAPHY
Primary Sources
Descartes, R., *Epistolae, Dioptrique, Passions de l'âme.*

144

Hobbes, Th., *De Corpore.*
Leibniz, G.W., *Discours de métaphysique.*

Secondary Literature

Daniel, S.H., 'The Nature of Light in Descartes's Physics', in G.J.D. Moyal (ed.), *René Descartes, Critical Assessments* 4 (London: Routledge, 1991), pp. 175–93 (previously in *The Philosophical Forum*, no. 7 (1976), pp. 325–44).

James, S., *Passion and Action. The Emotions in 17th-century philosophy* (Oxford: Clarendon Press, 1997).

Macherey, P., *Introduction à l'Éthique de Spinoza. La troisième partie: la vie affective* (Paris: Presses Universitaires de France, 1995).

Prendergast, Th.L., 'Motion, Action and Tendency', in G.J.D. Moyal (ed.), *René Descartes, Critical Assessments* 4 (London: Routledge, 1991), pp. 89–100 (previously in *Journal of the History of Philosophy*, no. 13 (1979), pp. 453–62).

Ch. Jaquet

Adaequatus

In Spinoza's works the noun 'adequacy' never occurs but only the adjective which he opposes to 'inadequate'. Spinoza uses the term not only to characterize an idea and knowledge but also to characterize a proportionality, an essence (resp. TIE 24 and 29) and a cause (E3def1; E4p4 and E5p31dem). In scholastic discourse *adaequatum* basically indicated the 'equality' between two things in the sense that they are reciprocal in a certain sense or correspond with one another in quantity or structure (Chauvin). Thus, an extramental entity may correspond with a concept in our mind, or an object corresponds

with its science, for example being in metaphysics or the syllogism in logic. Moreover, a cause is adequate or precise if by its powers and species it produces the effect in such a manner that they are reciprocal, such as rationality and the ability to laugh (cf. Micraelius). However, the combination of adaequate and idea seems to be rare before Spinoza and apperently only occasionally occurs in Descartes, for example in the *Quartae Responsiones* (AT VII, 200) and is introduced in order to be able to distinguish between a clear and distinct idea which a man may acquire of God, and an adequate idea of God, which only an infinite intellect possesses. The phrase is popularized by Spinoza.

The author of the *Ethics* defines an adequate idea in E2def4: 'By an adequate idea I mean an idea which, insofar as it is considered in itself without relation to its object, has all the properties, that is, intrinsic characteristics, of a true idea.' He explains the – minor – difference between an adequate idea and a true idea also in letter 60.

All knowledge of the human body (E2p19), the human mind (E2p23) and the external bodies (E2p26) begins with affections of the body. Simultaneously with these affections there are ideas of these affections. These ideas are inadequate because they are confused and fragmentary (E2p29c). They are confused because they represent rather the human body than the external bodies affecting it (E2p16c2) and fragmentary because an affection of the human body only involves the essence of an external body in so far as the human body is affected by this external body (E2p35s). Spinoza calls these ideas knowledge of the first kind, which is necessarily inadequate and the only source of falsehood (E2p41). The mind perceives this type of ideas when it is externally determined 'by the fortuitous run of circumstance'. On the other hand, when it is determined internally 'through its regarding several things at the same time, to understand their agreement; their difference, and their opposition', then it sees things clearly and distinctly (E2p29s).

Adequate ideas are deduced from common notions or from already existing adequate ideas (E2p40s2) because whatever ideas (E2p40) follow in the mind from adequate ideas are also adequate, just as inadequate ideas follow necessarily from already existing inadequate ideas (E2p36).

A cause is adequate if the effect can be clearly and distinctly understood through that cause only and inadequate or partial when this is not the case (E3def1). We only really act when we are the adequate cause of what occurs inside or outside us and we are passive when we are only partially the cause of it (E3def2). Consequently, the mind is necessarily active in so far as it has adequate ideas and necessarily passive (*passiones*) in so far as it has inadequate ideas (E3p3).

The introduction of 'adequate' should be understood within the philosophy of Spinoza where there is no causality between the mind and the body and vice versa (E3p2). The mind and the body are two distinct modes belonging to two different attributes that should be understood through themselves (E1p10). The introduction is an original attempt to understand objectivity without referring to the world of objects.

TEXTS

Naturae Dei adaequata cognitio (CM 1.2). *Inter ideam veram et adaequatam nullam aliam differentiam agnosco, quam quod nomen veri respeciat tantummodo conventiam ideae cum suo ideato; nomen adaequati autem naturam ideae in se ipsa* (Ep 60). *Per ideam adaequatam intelligo ideam, quae,*

quatenus in se sine relatione ad objectum consideratur, omnes verae ideae proprietates, sive denominationes intrinsecas habet (E2def4). *Causam adaequatam appello eam, cujus effectus potest clare et distincte per eandam percipi* (E3def1). *Homo se ipsum clare et distincte sive adaequate percipit* (E3p52).

BIBLIOGRAPHY

Primary Sources
Descartes, R., *Responsiones quartae.*

Secondary Literature
Gueroult, M., *Spinoza II – L' âme.* (Paris: Aubier-Montaigne, 1974).
Marion, J.L., 'Aporias and the Origins of Spinoza's Theory of Adequate Ideas', in Yirmiyahu Yovel (ed.), *Spinoza on Knowledge and the Human Mind. Papers presented at the Second Jerusalem Conference (Ethica II)* (Leiden: Brill, 1994), pp. 129–58.
Parkinson, G.H.R., *Spinoza's Theory of Knowledge.* (Oxford: Clarendon Press, 1954).

F. Buyse

Aequalitas

Equality, though a term rarely appearing in the indexes of commentaries on Spinoza's thought and not especially stressed anywhere in his work as a social or political ideal is nevertheless fundamental to the structure of his philosophy. This is because in his system men are determined beings that all function in the same way, obey the same psychological laws, and are all strictly equal in their desire to conserve their own beings, to be happy in their own way, and in striving for what seems good or bad to them. Generally speaking, men and women do not view or treat each other as equals but this is because of their prejudices and irrationality. The more rational they become the more they will conceive of each other as equal. Consequently, according to proposition 36 of *Ethics* 3, 'the highest good of those who follow virtue is common to all, and all can enjoy it equally'.

When Spinoza states, in proposition 37 of *Ethics* 4 that 'the good which each person who follows virtue seeks for himself he also desires for all other men, and the more so, the more he has a greater knowledge of God', he is arguing that what is best in human life can be shared equally and would be so shared in the best form of society or community. This is stated as a moral principle and is certainly basic to Spinoza's ethics but it is also clearly the strand of his moral philosophy that most obviously connects with his political philosophy and theory of freedom of expression. Thus, in *Tractatus theologico-politicus* 16 one of the chief reasons Spinoza alleges why the democratic form of government is preferable to monarchy or aristocracy is that under the laws of a democracy 'all remain equal, as they had been previously in the state of nature'.

In the same way, moreover, the moral principle underpins freedom of thought and expression. Hence, in E4p37s2 Spinoza adds that 'it is by the highest right of Nature that each person judges what is good and bad, considers in accordance with his own way of thinking what is useful to him, revenges himself, and endeavours to preserve what he loves and to destroy what he hates'. Reason in Spinoza is the guide that leads to a moral life but it is also reason that leads to citizenship and obedience to the law on an equal basis, eliminating servile subjection and tyranny. Thus in the final proposition of *Ethics* 4 he concludes that the man led by reason does not obey the laws of society through fear but precisely insofar as he desires to live freely 'he desires to have regard for a common life and a common advantage. Consequently, he desires to live in accordance with the common decree of the Commonwealth'.

TEXTS

In imperio democratico omnes manent ut antea in statu naturali aequales (TTP 16, G III, 196). *Certum est quod aequalitas qua semel exuta communis libertas necessario perit* (TP 10.8)

BIBLIOGRAPHY
Primary Sources
Enden, F. van den, *Vrye politijke stellingen, en consideratien van staat, gedaen na der ware christenens even gelijke vryheits gronden; strekkende tot een rechtschape, en ware verbeeteringh van staat, en kerk. ... door een liefhebber van alle der welbevoeghde borgeren even gelijke vryheit, en die, ten gemeene-beste, meest van zaken houdt* (n.p., 1665)
Hobbes, T., *Leviathan*.

Secondary Literature
Israel, J.I., *Radical Enlightenment. Philosophy and the Making of Modernity* (Oxford: Oxford University Press, 2001).
Israel, J.I., *Enlightenment Contested. Philosophy, Modernity and the Emancipation of Man* (Oxford: Oxford University Press, 2001).

J.I. Israel

Aeternitas

In Spinoza's works 'eternity' and its Dutch counterpart *eeuwigheid* are primarily related to God. Eternity is discussed in letter 12, the *Cogitata metaphysica* 1.4 and 2.1 and the first part of the *Ethics*. The concept is used to qualify the substance and its attributes. Definition 8 of *Ethics* 1 runs: 'by eternity I understand existence itself, insofar as it is conceived to follow necessarily from the definition alone of the eternal thing'. This definition is rather enigmatic, since on the one hand it seems to identify eternity with existence, which appears to be too general, but on the other hand by referring to 'an eternal thing' the definition tends to become circular. Hence, the definition should be read in combination with the following explanation which specifies that eternity 'on that account cannot be explained by duration or time, even if the duration is conceived to be without beginning or end'. Implictly here in the *Ethics* and even more explicitly in the *Cogitata metaphysica* 1.3 Spinoza denounces the main traditional definitions: first the identification of eternity with unlimited or infinite duration (which Hobbes for example adhered to, or all those such as Descartes who shared the Boethian notion of eternity as the total and at the same time perfect possession of endless life). Secondly eternity was defined negatively as the exclusion of all time and duration. Unlike eternity a distinct feature of time is its measurability. The distinction with duration is more complicated. Often commentators yield to the temptation to set the stable and necessary world against the transient and contingent world, which tends to platonize Spinozism. However, Spinoza acknowledges only one universe and when he speaks of duration, it is always the duration of particular things. As a matter of fact, conceiving all things as necessary, Spinoza often tends to identify necessity and eternity (E1p11s, for example), but more often, acknowledging a necessity according to the laws of nature, eternity is a kind of necessity by an internal reason or cause, which for the rest implies a kind of perpetuity.

Secondly, eternity is related to man. Of course man is not eternal, but his view of things might be marked by eternity. This is a feature of reason, which may perceive things under a certain species of eternity (E2p44c2; cf. SUB SPECIE AETERNITATIS). Some commentators read *species* as the logical species, which would imply the existence of more kinds of eternity: an eternity in a proper and absolute sense, and a less perfect, human eternity, being its fragile emanation. Apparently, this interpretation results from a Christian reading of Spinoza. Other commentators tend to read *species* as meaning 'view', or a form known by the mind. But such an eternity is not relative to man's mind or limited by man's capacity to perceive the necessary relations between things. It is eternity itself which transforms man or a part of him in as far as he is capable of assuming this necessity (E5p22ff.). 'We', therefore, 'feel and know that we are eternal'. We mistake this eternity for immortality if we apply it to the duration of the mind.

Thirdly the adjective 'eternal' occurs in the *Tractatus politicus*, denoting the eternity of the state and its power and the measure to be taken to ensure its perseverance. Although the phrase is adopted from Quintus Curtius in an address he attributes to Alexander, the notion is not incompatible with Spinoza's system. An eternal state is one that does not succumb by internal necessity, while the existence of most states is threatened more by their own citizens than by foreign nations.

TEXTS
In alle eeuwigheid onveranderlijk blijven (KV 1.1). God...en dat deze voorbepaald-heid van hem van eeuwigheid moet zijn in welke eeuwigheid geen voor of na is (KV 1.4). *Cum in aeternitate non detur quando, nec ante, nec post, neque ulla affectio tempo-ris* (CM 1.3). *Ex eo quod divisimus ens in ens, cujus essentia involvit existentiam et in ens cujus essentiam non involvit nisi pos-sibilem existentiam, oritur distinctio inter aeternitatem et durationem. De aeternitate ... hic dicimus eam esse 'attributum sub quo infinitam Dei existentiam concipimus'* (CM 1.4). *Authores errarunt...aeternitas sine essentia divina non potest concipi ... Hanc infinitam existentiam aeternitam voco* (CM 2.1). *Falsissimum Deum suam aeternitatem creaturis communicare posse* (CM 2.10). *Oritur differentia inter aeternitatem et dura-tionem ... substantiae vero per aeternitatem hoc est infinitam existendi, sive invita latinate essendi fruitionem ... solo intellectu assequi possumus* (Ep 12). *Vulgus superstitioni addictum temporis reliquias supra aeterni-tatem amat* (TTP praef, G III, p. 10). *Per aeternitatem intelligo ipsam existentiam quatenus ex sola rei aeternae definitione necessario sequi concipitur. Talis existentia ... sicut rei essentia concipitur* (E1def8). *Neces-sitatem sive aeternitatem* (E1p11s). *Ad natu-ram substantiae pertinet aeternitas* (E1p19). *Aeternitas est ipsa Dei essentia, quatenus haec necessariam involvit existentiam* (E5p30). *Civitatis potentia aeterna* (TP 7.25). *Quale imperium aeternum esse possit* (TP 10.1).

BIBLIOGRAPHY
Secondary Literature
Hallet, H.F., *Aeternitas, a Spinozistic Study* (Oxford: Clarendon Press, 1930).
Gueroult, M., *Spinoza I. Dieu (Éthique I)* (Hildesheim: Olms, 1968).
Moreau, P.-F., *Spinoza, l'expérience et l'éternité* (Paris: Presses Universitaires de France, 1994).
Prélorentzos, I., *Temps durée et éternité dans les Principes de la philosophie de Descartes de Spinoza* (Paris: Presses de l'Université Paris-Sorbonne, 1996).
Robinson, L., *Kommentar zu Spinozas Ethik* (Leipzig: Meiner, 1928).

P.-F. Moreau

Affectio

The Latin noun *affectio* – and the corre-sponding verb *affici* – is a term originating in scholasticism, and is used by Spinoza rather frequently. The Dutch counterpart *aandoe-ning*, however, occurs only once. Three differ-ent meanings may be discerned.

Spinoza uses 'affection' firstly as a syno-nym of MODUS, primarily of substance. He identifies both concepts in the definitions of modes in the first part of the *Ethics* and letter 12: 'The affections of substance I call modes'. Elsewhere mode and affection are linked by SIVE, or *seu*. In proposition 1 of *Ethics* 1 the ontological priority of substance over modes is expressed by using the word *affectio* instead of modes and in proposition 4 the traditional division of being is stated by means of affection: 'nothing is granted in addition to the understanding, except sub-stance and its modifications' (the word used by most English translators in rendering *affectio*). Secondly, like the word 'mode', 'affection' is used to designate the ontological constitution of the particular things: 'Indi-vidual things are nothing but modifications of the attributes of God, or modes by which the attributes of God are expressed'. Finally, according to Spinoza an affection like a mode is only indirectly caused by substance. In E1p14c2 he writes: 'that extension and thought are either attributes of God or accidents [*affectiones*] of the attributes of God'. It is effected by means of the divine attributes and it is the result of the power of God's essence expressing his nature. Hence the essence of man is 'constituted by certain modifications of the attributes of God'. Such essence is 'something which is in God, and which without God can neither be nor be conceived, whether it be a modification or a mode which expresses God's nature in a certain conditioned manner'.

Affection in this sense may also denote modes of specific entities, such as the qualities of bodies. In letter 6 Spinoza observed that 'all tactile qualities depend only on motion, shape and the remaining mechanical' affections. In the PPC Spinoza stated that he used 'affection' in the way Descartes used 'attribute' in order to refer to the modes of things, time, existence, extension and essence. However, although 'affection' and 'mode' are equivalent, since contrary to affection mode is carefully defined, affection is much less than mode a basic concept in Spinoza's philosophy.

Affectio in Spinoza's works also refers to changes suffered by man and his faculties. In the first definition of the affects Spinoza states: 'by a modification of man's essence, we understand every disposition of the said essence, whether it be conceived solely under the attribute of thought, or solely under the attribute of extension, or whether, lastly, it be referred simultaneously to both these attributes'. However, with regard to the mind the word *affectio* is rarely used and the cognate noun AFFECTUS is preferred. The affections of the human body are the images

of external things which refer to the properties of the bodies. They dispose the human body to act in a certain manner and enlarge or diminish its acting power. Spinoza also speaks of an affection of thinking or the imagination. In this third sense affection denotes the transcendental terms.

Affectio is the Latin word translating Aristotle's *pathos*, one of the three terms the Greek philosopher used to denote a quality, which may be predicated of a substance; the other ones being *sumbebèkos* (accident) and *tropos* (mode). The generality of its meaning appears from the fact that an affection might refer to the transcendental terms, the intrinsic attributes of an essence or the changing accidents. According to Burgersdijk this generality is due to the fact that 'in Being there are many things which are not [independent] beings, yet they are not nothing at all' (*Institutiones metaphysicae* 1.9). Simple affections of being' such as true, one and good 'add' something to an ESSENTIA, while others are duration, place and time, which add something to EXISTENTIA. In Burgersdijk's general metaphysics mode and affection are dealt with, but accident primarily denotes a 'certain kind of being', in particular metaphysics.

The same applies to the lexica. According to Micraelius an affection needs: (1) to be formally different from the subject it is predicated of; (2) to denote the same thing; and (3) that its concept follows from the concept of its subject. Goclenius derives the concept from the notion of enduring (Greek: *paschein*) in its most general sense, that is being informed, being disposed, being moved, receiving an impression. Hence, its equivalents are the accident, the affect and the passion. Chauvin explains the term by deriving affection from the influence of the predicate on the subject. Due to this modifying influence all affections are particular and are

150

owned by its proper subjects. Hence, the affections of the mind possess a specific nature and are more properly called *affectus*. This notion Chauvin elucidates by starting from the Stoic tradition. In this manner he links the ontological tradition deriving from Aristotle with the use in moral discourse. Both traditions are present in Spinoza's *Ethics*.

TEXTS

Aandoeningen van de ziele (KV 1.9). *Praeter extensionem et ejus affectiones* (PPC 2def7). *Per modem cogitandi ... cogitationis affectiones* (CM 1.1). *Per affectiones id quod per attributa denotavit Cartesius ... sub quibus essentiam vel existentiam ... impossibilitas inter affectiones entis numerari non potest* (CM 1.3). *Terminus transcendentalis sive affectio entis* (CM 1.6). *Per modum intelligo substantiae affectiones* (E1def5). *Substantia prior est natura suis affectionibus* (E1p1). *Extra intellectum nihil datur praeter substantias earumque affectiones* (E1p5). *Rem extensam et rem cogitantem vel Dei attributa esse vel affectiones attributorum Dei* (E1p14c2). *Res particulares nihil sunt, nisi Dei attributorum affectiones, sive modi* (E1p25c). *Imaginationis affectiones* (E1app). *Ut verba usitata retineamus, corporis humani affectionibus* (E2p17s). *Corporis affectiones quibus ipsius corporis agendi potentia augetur* (E3p3). *Rerum imagines sunt ipsius humani corporis affectiones sive modi* (E3p32s). *Mentis affectio* (E3p52s). *Affectio, qua agendi hominis potentia, seu conatus coërcetur* (E3p59s). *Per affectionem humanae essentiae quamcumque essentiae constitutionem intelligimus* (E3def-aff1). *Prout cogitationes, rerumque ideae ordinantur et concatenantur in mente, ita corporis affectiones seu rerum imagines ad amussim ordinantur et concatenantur in corpore* (E5p1).

BIBLIOGRAPHY
Primary Sources
Burgersdijk, F., *Institutiones metaphysicae* (Leiden, 1642).

Secondary Literature
Richter, G.T., *Spinozas philosophische Terminologie I: Grundbegriffe der Metaphysik* (Leipzig: Barth, 1913).
Robinson, L., *Kommentar zu Spinozas Ethik* (Leipzig: Meiner, 1928).

H. Krop

Affectus

It is significant that the first word of the *Tractatus politicus* is 'affects'. Spinoza says effective political theory must be based on an understanding of how people actually are, not on our wish for how they might be, in other words, it depends on an understanding of the human affects (TP 1.1 and 7.2). Spinoza's theory of the affects describes their common properties, their origin, distinguishes between active and passive affects, and describes how passive affects harm both individuals and society. Most importantly, he provides methods for moderating and restraining the passive affects, both in the individual and in the state. These are, in essence, his ethical and political projects. It is therefore not surprising that affect is a basic notion. Both AFFECTIO and *affectus* are derived from the verb *afficio* and both translate the Greek *pathos* (Chauvin). However *affectio* is a broad concept with many diverse connotations, whereas affect in seventeenth-century Latin tended to denote only the 'perturbations, the passions and the motions of the soul' (Micraelius). Notably, *affectus* (as opposed to *affectio*) occurs over three hundred times in Spinoza's

151

mature writings. The *Korte verhandeling* used *passie* to denote the psycho-physiological phenomena of love, desire, hatred etc. In Latin *passio* in this sense is rare and Henri Desmarets, the editor of the Latin version of the *Passions de l'âme*, wrote justifying himself for using the word that it would more clearly express 'Descartes's principles' (*Ad lectorem*). According to Descartes the bodily process is the cause, that is the action, of the event, which by its perception in the mind, the subject, which endures is turned into a passion. However, action and passion are one and the same thing (PA 1–2). It is tempting to assume that the basic doctrinal differences between Descartes and Spinoza stimulated Spinoza to return to traditional Latin usage. However, it should be noted that the project of the *Passiones animi* remained Spinoza's point of reference. Both philosophers firmly wanted to deal with the affects in a scientific manner and denounced a purely moral or rhetorical attitude towards the subject (E3praef, PA praef; Jaquet, 2004).

Spinoza defines affects as affections of the body, which increase or diminish the power of the body (affects of body) and the ideas of such affections (affects of mind) (E3def3). Spinoza does not say much about the affects of the body, but devotes *Ethics* 3 and 4 to the affects of mind. As Beyssade points out, this emphasis on mental affects should not be surprising given Spinoza's focus on attaining freedom from the mind's bondage to passive affects (Beyssade, 1999, p. 122).

According to Spinoza, affects can be either active or passive (E3p58). Passive affects are called passions and are by their nature confused and partial ideas (E3affgen). Since human suffering is caused by the passive affects and power and joy come through activity, an understanding of the affects and how to mitigate them is the basis for Spinoza's

ethics. It is noteworthy that his ethical theory does not treat the affects as human vices, but rather as properties pertaining to human nature (E3praef and TP 1.4). The affects are natural and universal and therefore subject to study through the geometrical method (E3praef). He considers this approach to ethics his greatest innovation.

Spinoza defines all affects in terms of three primary ones from which they arise: joy, sadness and desire (E3aff58exp). He reduces in this manner the Cartesian six primary passions: 'admiration, love, hatred, desire, joy and sadness, and that all the other[s] are compounded of some of these six, or are sorts of them' (PA 66). Joy occurs when the mind passes to a greater perfection and sadness when it passes to a lesser perfection (E3p11s). Desire, the very essence of humans, is appetite together with a consciousness of that appetite (E39s and E4p19dem). Desire and joy can be either active or passive, sadness is always passive (E4p34dem).

Bondage is a lack of power to moderate the affects, that is, being at the mercy of circumstance (E4praef). Since circumstances are various and ever-changing, people ruled by the passions differ from one another and contain contrary passions within themselves (E3p17s, E3p57, E4p33, E4p34). Such contrary affects cause vacillation of mind, doubt, and endless suffering in individuals and disunity in the state (E3p17s).

Affects cannot be overcome except by stronger, opposite affects and affects from things we imagine as necessary are stronger than affects from things we take to be contingent (E4p7, E4p11 and E4p11dem). Passive affects of mind indicate the constitution and circumstance of one's particular body and things viewed from this perspective appear contingent (E4p9dem). However, passive affects can become active if we form clear and distinct ideas of them, that is, if we move to the second form of knowledge, i.e. reason, and understand them as necessary (E5p2c). The mind, then, gains power over the affects by understanding them as necessary through the second and finally third type of knowledge, which relates the ideas of all of the bodies' affections to the idea of God (E5p6 and E5p14). Such is human blessedness, the goal of Spinoza's ethics. Unfortunately, few humans will achieve such blessedness. Therefore, government must have an effective way of ruling people living according to the first type of knowledge.

Government is needed to provide unity, stability and peace in human interaction precisely because most individuals act from passive affects, which are necessarily at variance with one another (TP 1.6, 2.14, 8.6, 10.9, TTP 5). If it were the case that all people acted out of reason alone, they would agree in all things and government would not be needed (E4p35dem). Unfortunately, this is not the case (E3p37s2, TP 1.5, TTP 5). Therefore, an effective sovereign skilfully unites the affects of its people by overpowering divisive affects through some common affect of hope or fear (TP 6.1, 7.10, 10.10. Since superstition follows from the most powerful affects, it is particularly dangerous to the well-being of the state (TTP praef). For this reason, the sovereign must have the final say on matters of religion and, if necessary, use superstition to support the unity of the state (TTP 16).

TEXTS

Ex hac itaque superstitionis causa clare sequitur, omnes homines natura superstitioni esse ... nimirum, quia non ex ratione, sed ex solo affectu, eoque efficacissimo oritur (TTP praef, G III, 6). *Quoniam Scriptura Deo ... animi affectus tribure solet* (TTP 1, G III,

26). *Sed perplurimum ex sola libidine, & animi affectibus abrepti* (TTP 5, G III, 73). *Multitudo non ratione sed solis affectibus gubernatur* (TTP 17, G III, 203). *Deo affectus humanos tribure* (E1p8Is2). *Plerique, qui de Affectibus, & hominem vivendi ratione scripserunt videntur non de rebus naturalibus agere ... Affectus itaque odii, irae, invidiae &c. in se considerati ex eadem naturae necessitate, & virtute consequuntur, ac reliqua singularia ... eadem methodo agam ... ac si quaestio de lineis, planis aut de corporibus esset* (E3praef). *Per Affectum intelligo Corporis affectiones, quibus ipsius Corporis agendi potentia augetur, vel minuitur, juvatur, vel coercetur, & simul harum affectionum ideas* (E3def3). *Unusquisque ex suo affectu omnia moderatur* (E3p2s). *Porro affectum laetitiae ad mentem et corpus simul relatum titillationem vel hilaritatem voco; tristitiae autem dolorem vel melancholiam. ... deinde cupidatas ... praeter hos tres nullum alium agnosco affectum primarium* (E3p11s). *Unum idemque objectum posse esse causam multorum contrariumque affectuum* (E3p17s). *Quilibet uniuscujusque individui affectus ab affectu alterius tantum discrepant, quantum essentia unius ab essentia alterius differt* (E3p57). *Praeter Laetitiam, & Cupiditatem, quae passiones sunt, alii Laetitiae, & Cupiditatis affectus dantur, qui ad nos, quatenus agimus, referuntur* (E3p58). *Affectus, qui animi Pathema dicitur, est confusa idea ... Dico primo Affectum, seu passionem animi esse confusam ideam* (E3affgen). *Homo enim affectibus obnoxius sui iuris non est* (E4praef). *Affectus nec coerceri, nec tolli potest, nisi per affectum contrarium & fortiorem affectu coercendo* (E4p7) *Est igitur affectus ... imaginatio, quatenus corporis constitutionem indicat* (E4p9). *Affectus erga rem, quam ut necessariam imaginamur, ceteris paribus intensior est, quam erga possibilem vel contingentem, sive non necessariam* (E4p11). *Homines natura discrepare possunt, quatenus affectibus, qui passiones sunt, conflictantur, et eatenus etiam unus idemque homo varius est et inconstans* (E4p33). *At affectus tristitiae semper passio est; ergo homines, quatenus conflictantur affectibus, qui passiones sunt, possunt invicem esse contrarii.* (E4p34). *Affectus igitur eo magis in nostra potestate est et mens ab eo minus patitur* (E5p3c). *Quatenus mens res omnes ut necessarias intelligit, eatenus maiorem in affectus potentiam habet, seu minus ab iisdem patitur* (E5p6). *Affectus, quibus conflictamur, concipiunt Philosophi veluti vitia, in quae homines sua culpa labuntur; quos propterea ridere, flere, carpere, vel (qui sanctiores videri volunt) detestari solent* (TP 1.1). *Homines necessario affectibus esse obnoxios ... hanc tamen persuasionem in affectus parum posse ostendimus ... quando scilicet morbus ipsos affectus vicit ... rationem multum quidem posse affectus coercere* (TP 1.5). *Quia homines, uti diximus, magis affectu, quam ratione ducuntur, sequitur multitudinem non ex rationis ductu, sed ex communi aliquo affectu naturaliter convenire, & una veluti mente duci velle* (TP 6.1). *Quod in iaciendis fundamentis maxime humanos affectus observare necesse est* (TP 7.2).

BIBLIOGRAPHY

Primary Sources
Descartes, R., *Passiones animi.*

Secondary Literature
Beyssade, J.-M., 'Can an Affect in Spinoza be "of the Body"?', in Y. Yovel (ed.), *Desire and Affect: Spinoza as Psychologist* (New York: Little Room Press, 1999), pp. 113–28.

Jaquet, Ch., *L'unité du corps et de l'esprit. Affects, actions et passions chez Spinoza* (Paris: Presses Universitaires de France, 2004).

T. Nyden

Amicitia

In Spinoza's correspondence the addressee in the salutation and in the complimentary close is often called 'friend' – in the Dutch letters *waarde vrient*. Spinoza and Bouwmeester, Jelles, Meyer, Ostens, De Vries, Balling, Van Blijenberg and Schuller in his last letter address each other as friends. However, in the letters to Jelles only the Dutch original uses this form of address, since in the *Opera posthuma* the editors changed the *waarde vrient* of the original to 'most courteous Sir' (*humanissime vir*). Writing to Hudde, Leibniz, Burgh and Stensen, Spinoza never used this clause and Oldenburg is only once addressed in this manner (letter 26), whereas Oldenburg in the first part of their correspondence, i.e. till 1665, used this form of address without exception. In the second part beginning in 1675 he only once refers to the duty of friendship in the opening sentence of letter 62. How this use of the word 'friend' is to be interpreted is not quite clear. A comparison with other scholars in the seventeenth century who exchanged letters shows that intimacy does not explain this form of address completely, since it is for example found in scholars who never met in person, or in letters between an aged civil servant and his much younger protégé. Blijenberg began his first letter to Spinoza with 'unknown friend' as well.

However, the moral nature of friendship between correspondents is beyond doubt. In the letters 2, 13 and 19 Spinoza deals with such friendship. Referring to a maxim summing up the Greek *Freundschaftsethik*, Spinoza observes that friends ought to have all things in common, especially spiritual things. This spiritual community requires honesty, love of truth, openness, sincerity and a refraining from sheer flattery. These ideas are not particular to Spinoza. Chauvin in his dictionary observes that a 'friend' might refer to 'a good man linked to another similar to him by the continuous interchange of his will, study and opinions. This link is not the result of profit, but of moral integrity, equality and virtue'. Besides 'natural friendship', i.e. sympathy, according to Micraelius three other kinds of friendship are to be distinguished according to their different goals: utility, honesty and joy.

In the political writing the notions of friend and friendship are rarely used. In the *Tractatus politicus* Spinoza sometimes writes about political friendship: 'the patricians will always think those are the best men who are wealthy, or near akin to themselves, or close friends' (11.2) and 'a king looks about him for generals or counsellors or friends to whom he entrusts his own security and the security of all citizens (6.5). The 'affect' of friendship, however, is detrimental to aristocracy and monarchy, because it hampers the following of the common good and the conduct of the magistrate in accordance with the law, as 'experience itself teaches us only too well'.

The difference between common friendship of the ignorant men and true friendship of men living according to the guidance of reason is basic to Spinoza's philosophy of friendship. Both can be perceived as love, relationship, bond, connection – all words that appear in the context of *amicitia*. Both types of persons want and strive to make the others think and do the same as they think and do. But the first kind of friendship is a passion that makes dependent and leads to disagreement and conflicts with other men and is connected with other passions like hate, envy and sadness. The other is active, free, virtuous and constitutes an agreement among people, giving them greater power of action and enjoyment. Spinoza observed that only free men are useful to one another. Hence, only they are joined by friendship and equally eager for love. Although friendship is not listed in the *Ethics* as an affect, in E3p59s Spinoza uses the notion of nobility (the Cartesian *génerosité*) and honesty as equivalents.

Spinoza's view of friendship is traditional. It is the classical idea of friendship, important in Stoic philosophy in particular. The notion of equality and mutuality that distinguishes friendship from love is also conventional.

TEXTS
Waarde vrient (Ep 39, 40, 50). *Amice colende* (Ep 1, 9, 10, 31). *Praesertim amicorum omnia communia, nempe spiritualia, habere debuere. ... quod a me jure amicitiae peteris* (Ep 2). *Vir amicissime* (Ep 3, 25). *Amice plurimum colende* (Ep 5, 14, 33). *Amice charissime* (Ep 6, 20). *Amice colendissime* (Ep 6). *Amice integerrime* (Ep 8, 26). *Nolim officio amici deesse* (Ep 62). *Amice singularis* (Ep 12, 37). *Dilecte amice* (Ep 17). *Amice ignote* (Ep 18, 19). *Amice* (Ep 21, 23, 24, 27). *Chare amice* (Ep 22). *Amicos in re indifferenti salva amicitia dissentire posse* (Ep 54). *Rem amatam eodem, vel arctiore vinculo amicitiae* (E3p35). *Per generositatem cupiditatem intelligo, qua unusquisque ex solo rationis dictamine conatur reliquos homines juvare et sibi amicitia jungere* (E3p59s).

Cupiditatem, qua homo qui ex ductu rationis vivit, tenetur, ut reliquos sibi amicitia jungat honestatem voco (E4p37s1). E4p70; E4p71. *Homines apprime utile est ea agere quae firmandis amicitiis inserviunt* (E4app12, 14, 17, 26). *Rationem boni, quod ex mutua amicitia et communi societate sequitur* (E5p10s).

BIBLIOGRAPHY
Secondary Literature
Laufhütte, H., 'Freundschafte. Ihre Spuren im Briefarchiv Sigmund Birkens', in *Ars et Amicitia, Chloe,* Beiheft zum Daphnis, no. 28 (Amsterdam, 1998), pp. 309–30.

M. van Reijen

Amor intellectualis Dei

The notion of love of God occurs as an expression of human VIRTUS and BEATITUDO in almost all of Spinoza's works. In a technically more developed sense, however, the idea of *amor Dei, amor erga Deum, amor intellectualis Dei, liefde* or *lievde Gods* and *lievde tot God* features first in the *Korte verhandeling* and later in the *Ethics*. It is in the *Ethics* that more than half of all of Spinoza's references to *amor Dei* are made. The *Korte verhandeling* explains the love of God and towards God as forms of love that result from a true knowledge of man's total dependence on God, since God is 'that without which neither the body nor the idea itself could exist nor be conceived' (cf. KV 2.19). It is here that references are made to 'him' (God) and 'we' and that Spinoza's view of *amor Dei* is formulated in spiritual terms as a 'rebirth', a 'second', or 'spiritual' birth – as against the 'carnal' delivery that marks the initial start of

our lives. In rather ecstatic terms, God is said to be 'magnificent' and a 'perfect good'. He is therefore the only object in which our love must 'rest'. According to the *Korte verhandeling*, we are even more closely connected to God than to our own body.

The idea that human felicity is dependent on God because God is the highest object of human love has been presented as an argument in favour of the view that Spinoza's notion of love of God resembles the Platonic notion of love found in the *Dialoghi d'amore* of the fifteenth-century Portuguese Jewish syncretist writer Jehuda Abravanel, or Abarbanel (1465–after 1521), better known as Leo Hebraeus or Leo Ebreo (Calvetti). According to the catalogue of his library Spinoza possessed a copy of Ebreo's book and the way in which the *Korte verhandeling* deals with the topic of *amor Dei* suggests that the young Spinoza was inspired by this Renaissance type of Platonic spiritualism. If so, this would be true not only of the young Spinoza, since it is hard to distinguish between earlier and later notions of ecstatic love in his works. In fact, the text of the *Ethics* closely follows the earlier line of thinking in the *Korte verhandeling*. In the *Ethics*, Spinoza argues that all ideas known *sub specie aeternitatis* involve 'the eternal and infinite essence of God' (E2p45, E5p29s); that the intellectual love of God that arises from the third type of knowledge involves an understanding of God as eternal (E5p32c); that God's infinity and infinite perfection define the way he loves himself (E5p35); and that, finally, the intellectual love in which God and the mind may share (and which constitutes our blessedness) is accompanied by the idea of God as cause and thus by a knowledge of 'how our mind ... follows from the divine nature, and continually depends on God' (E5p36s). The mature Spinoza, in other words, not only continues to give prominence to the concept of 'love' in the definition of human felicity, but also, in accordance with Ebreo's *Dialoghi*, continues to emphasize that this love has its basis in an awareness of our dependence on God. Moreover, although Spinoza now accentuates the epistemological aspects of his notion of love of God by his frequent use of the adjective 'intellectual', his concept of love continues to give expression to the idea of a unification with the divine.

There is, on the other hand, much more to Spinoza's conception of intellectual love of God than may be found in Ebreo. First, the notion of *Amor intellectualis Dei* in Spinoza links up with a far broader tendency within early-modern humanism to link the philosophical concept of happiness to a Judeo-Christian notion of salvation. Resorting to a medieval viewpoint already present in St Bernard of Clairvaux and others, Desiderius Erasmus had long before associated the mental pleasures of the pious Christian with the delights that accompany a person on the road to virtue. The idea of an earthly beatitude is thus linked to practical forms of piety through which the soul may be liberated from its enslavement to the passions. In the New Testament, the psychological effect of this mental development had been explained as a spiritual two-way traffic. According to St Paul, God prepared 'comforts' for 'those that love him' (1 Corinthians 2.9). Acknowledging the fundamental likeness between philosophy and religion on this point, Spinoza explains in E5p36s that the kind of 'salvation, or blessedness, or freedom' which is found in a 'constant and eternal love of God, or in God's love for men', is a form of spiritual blessedness identical to what 'is called glory in the Sacred Scriptures'.

Secondly, if Spinoza shared with many of his contemporaries the view that conversions to moral piety went hand in hand with the kind of joy, felicity or love of God that the Stoics had presented in terms of a cheerfulnes (*gaudium*) or mental tranquillity and the Epicureans in terms of a mental pleasure (*voluptas*) or ataraxy, it is his emphasis on the *intellectual* aspects of love of God that links his position more particularly to the archetypical expression of contemplative happiness found in book 10 of Aristotle's *Nicomachean Ethics*. Indeed, Spinoza's distinctive 'virtue of the mind' in *Ethics* 4 and 5 combines all intellectualist elements crucial to the Aristotelian view, such as that it is only through man's most excellent part, viz. the intellect, that supreme happiness is achieved; that, in contemplation, man does what is most akin to the activity of God; that through a contemplative life one receives delights that are uniquely characteristic of the divine faculty; that the objects of contemplation are themselves divine; that the highest goal of human striving is what marks the activity of the divine itself, namely, the contemplation of the divine essence; and, finally, that the exercise of this activity will make us share in immortality. All such notions may have come to Spinoza through a vast number of Christian and Judaic neo-Aristotelian sources as well as directly from the *Metaphysics*, the *De Anima*, or the *Nichomachean Ethics* of Aristotle himself.

Thirdly, although the notion of intellectual love of God (which also occurs in Aquinas; Wolfson, 1934, pp. 304–5) originally reflected the Aristotelian division between the vegetative, sensitive and intellectual functions of the soul, Spinoza's way of contrasting intellect and imagination points more particularly to Descartes rather than to Aristotle or Maimonides (as has been claimed by Harvey). Descartes adapted Aristotle's tripartite anthropology in such a way that he transformed it into an epistemological dichotomy between the imaginative/sensitive kinds of knowledge on the one hand and intellectual knowledge on the other. Further Cartesian elements in the development of Spinoza's notion of intellectual love of God include Descartes's definition of love, which Spinoza literally copied in the *Korte verhandeling* (Wolfson, 1934, p. 303); the idea of an intellectual joy (which occurs in Descartes's *Principia philosophiae* IV, art. 190 as the '*gaudium intellectuale* ... without any bodily disturbance and which, for that reason, the Stoics allowed that the man of wisdom could experience'; the idea that a 'frequent reflection' upon the fact 'that nothing can possibly happen other than as Providence has determined from all eternity' is morally relevant since it is one of the main remedies against destabilizing kinds of desire (ibid. art. 155); and, finally, the notion of self-contentedness.

If we are to establish how Spinoza's notion of intellectual love of God relates to this spectrum of earlier philosophical ideas, it is important to note that Spinoza did not in any significant way appreciate the neo-Platonic notion of a cycle of divine love emerging from, and eventually returning to, the One – an idea that had indeed inspired Ebreo (Dethier, 2006, pp. 375ff.). We should, on the other hand, be equally cautious not to deny the importance of earlier systems altogether. On account of Spinoza's identification of God with Nature and his rejection of a creationist view of the world and a personal notion of the deity, it has been argued that, with respect to the idea of *amor intellectualis Dei*, it is the differences rather than the similarities between Spinoza and his possible medieval and Renaissance sources that should be appreciated (Wolfson, Rice). Such an emphasis on his 'naturalism', however, tends to invite an anachronistic reading of Spinoza.

In his second letter to Willem van Blijenbergh of 28 January 1665 (Ep 21), Spinoza argues that 'our supreme blessedness' is to be found 'in love towards God', and that such love necessarily results from a 'knowledge of God'. He emphasizes that this should be interpreted along the lines of what he had written concerning the 'divine decree' in the *Cogitata metaphysica* (presumably 1.3 and 2.9), and not according to the view of those who 'confuse divine with human nature'. If one sees God as a 'judge' who arbitrarily bestows sanctity, one will fail to see the necessary connection between the intellectual insight of the righteous and their subsequent bliss. A sharp dividing line is thus drawn between the views of his Protestant correspondent, who clung to the idea of a personal deity, and Spinoza's own, necessitarian, viewpoint. This disparity, however, does not alter the fact that Spinoza and Van Blijenbergh shared a similar standpoint on man's incapacity to contribute to his own spiritual bliss (*Sociniaensche Ziel*). Indeed, since Spinoza's metaphysics leaves no room for any human involvement in the attainment of blessedness, his notion of salvation is just as much characterized by a notion of inevitability as was the Reformed view on grace. In order to explain the preferential treatment of those who are able to reach the level of intuitive knowledge, Steven Nadler has even spoken of a necessitarian form of 'special providence' (Nadler, 2005, pp. 19–21). In Spinoza, as in Calvinism, beatitude was only for the chosen.

Besides this, the naturalist standpoint tends to blur not only what inspired Spinoza, but also what precisely he contributed. If, with respect to the evolution of the notion of *amor Dei*, there is a new development in Spinoza vis-à-vis earlier formulations, Spinoza's account is characterized by a new attentiveness to mechanical causality and a concomitant commitment to necessitarianism, rather than by the naturalistic context in which he places the idea of moral ecstasy. This enabled him to interpret traditional notions of divine love in new metaphysical terms. As far as naturalism is concerned, Cartesians could equally well consider it an unvarying gift of God that happiness is given to those who accept the natural course of things on reasonable grounds. Happiness, as Arnold Geulincx argued, will befall those who see calamity and catastrophe for the natural necessities that they are and who are therefore able to check their mental 'unwillingness and resistance' to such phenomena (*Ethics* 5.2, p. 131). Cartesian mental freedom, in other words, went together well with Stoic resignation. Since for theological reasons a state of epistemological bliss could not simply be seen as the causal effect of man's love for God, but only as an essential and intrinsic counterpart to it, Geulincx could also maintain, much like Spinoza, that God's reciprocal love was not a form of sanctity bestowed at random, but one that was intrinsic to the development of a rational attitude.

In Spinoza, however, such Cartesio-Aristotelian and Cartesio-Stoic views are marked by a distinctly neo-Platonic belief in their metaphysical significance. Spinoza's view obviously agrees with neo-Platonic readings of Aristotelian psychology according to which the human intellect in its highest state arrives at a unification with God – a notion that any reader of Ebreo's text would be likely to pick up besides the idea of the intellectual love that accompanies it. Arguing that God's mind is the 'idea' of the universe in which all intellection takes place (and in which all intellection partakes), Spinoza provided his epistemological explanations with a metaphysical surcharge in which the individual mind may come to see itself as forming part of the divine essence in exceptional instances

of intuitive knowledge. Moreover, since, according to Spinoza, a natural causality governs the sphere of human experience as much as it governs parallel processes within the material world, such intuitive insights bring with them an overpowering simultaneous awareness of their inescapability.

The mind, according to Spinoza, will be extraordinarily affected by these cases of intuitive knowledge in which God as well as the mind's essence are simultaneously involved. On a theoretical level, this may be explained by the assumption that the individual mind's intellectual love of God forms part of God's eternal love for himself. In this sense, the notion of the mind's unification with God was implied all along in the metaphysics of Ethics 1. As Spinoza himself argues in E5p36s, however, it is not by way of a sober explanation of the metaphysics involved, but only through an intuitive grasp of its own essence, that the mind actually comes to experience the epistemological bliss called *amor intellectualis Dei*.

TEXTS
Ende lievde komt altijd uijt de kennisse voort van dat de zaak heerlijk is. Nu wie isser heerlijker als God ergo (KV 2.5). Indien wij eens God komen te kenen ... wij als dan ook nauwer met hem als met ons lichaam moeten verenigt worden ... want dat wij zonder hem noch bestaan noch verstaan konnen worden (KV 2.19). Zo worden dan alle door de Natuur verenigt en tot een verenigt, namelyk God ... zoo word zij dan ook dan met dat na voorgaande kennisse door liefde terstond vereenigt ... En dit mag daarom te meer met recht en waarheid de Wedergeboorte werde genoemt, om dat uijt deze Liefde en Vereenige eerst komt te volgen een Eeuwige en onveranderlijke

bestandigheid (KV 2.22). *Ex tertio cognitionis genere oritur necessario Amor Dei intellectualis ... Amor Dei quatenus Deum ut aeternum intelligimus et hoc est quod amorem Dei intellectualem voco ... nullum amorem praeter amorem intellectualem esse aeternum* (E5p32c–34c). *Deus se ipsum amore intellectuali infinito amat* (E5p35). *Mentis amor intellectualis erga Deum est ipse Dei amor ... Ex his clare intelligimus, qua re in nostra salus, seu beatitudo, seu libertas consistit nempe in constanti et aeterno erga Deum amore, sive in amore Dei erga homines. Atque hic amor seu beatitudo in sacris codicibus gloria appellatur* (E5p36). *Hic intellectualis amor ex mentis natura necessario sequitur* (E5p37).

BIBLIOGRAPHY
Primary Sources
Blijenbergh, W. van, *Sociniaensche Ziel Onder een Mennonitisch Kleedt* (Utrecht, 1666).
Geulincx, A., *Ethics: With Samuel Beckett's Notes*, eds H. van Ruler, A. Uhlmann and M. Wilson (Leiden and Boston: Brill, 2006).

Secondary Literature
Calvetti, C.G., *Benedetto Spinoza di fronte a Leone Ebreo (Jehudah Abarbanel): Problemi etico-religiosi e 'amor Dei intellectualis'* (Milano: CUSL, 1982).
Dethier, H., 'Love and Intellect in Leone Ebreo: The Joys and Pains of Human Passion', in L.E. Goodman, (ed.), *Neoplatonism and Jewish Thought*, vol. 7 (Albany: State University of New York Press, 1992), pp. 353–86.
Harvey, W.Z., 'A Portrait of Spinoza as a Maimonidean', *Journal of the History of Philosophy*, no. 19 (1981), pp. 151–72.

Nadler, S., *Spinoza's Theory of Divine Providence. Rationalist solutions, Jewish Sources*, Mededelingen vanwege het Spinozahuis, vol. 87 (Budel: Damon, 2005).
Rice, Lee C., 'Love of God in Spinoza', in H.M. Ravven and L.E. Goodman (eds), *Jewish Themes in Spinoza's Philosophy* (Albany: State University of New York Press, 2002), pp. 93–106.
Wolfson, H.A., *The Philosophy of Spinoza: Unfolding the Latent Processes of His Reasoning* (Cambridge, MA and London: Harvard University Press, 1934).

H. van Ruler

Apostolus

According to the *Tractatus theologico-politicus* 11 an apostle differs from a prophet in that he proceeds by rational argument rather than by writing and teaching through revelation supported by signs. The prophet uses his imagination and by means of a revelation enunciates dogmas. In contrast, the apostles – except when, as prophets, they support what they say with signs – argue and preach in defence of their faith and use their natural light to do so: they are teachers (2 Timothy 1.11). Also Hobbes in *Leviathan* chapter 42 considers the apostles to be teachers and preachers due to the Holy Gost given to them by Christ himself. They are no chiefs of the Christian communities, since Christ does not reign in majesty till the day of Judgement.

According to Spinoza, 1 Corinthians 7.6 proves the human nature of the apostolic messages. They speak hesitatingly and without authority. Their arguments are based on the natural light of reason (Acts 15.36-40) and therefore each of them chose the words and images he thought the most suitable to their listeners (Romans 15.20). The apostles addressed everyone; the prophets only one people, which is why they acted on a special mandate from God. The apostles gave up the ceremonies of the Jews because they were tied to the existence of the Hebrew state; the end of this state (Jeremiah 9.23) cancelled all rites and ceremonies and turned religion into a universal morality. Neither Christ nor the apostles introduced any ceremonies: baptism, supper, feasts, prayers (chapter 5). The apostles professed the same religion but were in disagreement over speculative matters: for example Paul (Romans 3.27-8) differed from James (2.24) over justification. The history of the Christian Church is full of schisms because doctrine rested on conflicting foundations: one, philosophical, current aimed at the pagans (Paul), the other (aimed at the Jews) by contrast despised philosophy (Peter).

Spinoza's view of the apostles followed the ideas current in latitudinarian and reasonable Protestantism. The theological school of Saumur, in particular Amyraut in *Six livres de la vocation des pasteurs*, pp. 152–3 maintained that, unlike the prophets who relied on imagination, the apostles made use of reasoning and argument. The New Testament is in fact clear and rational since it reveals the kernel of truth hidden in the Old Testament. This conviction is grounded in the distinction between prophetic inspiration (ecstatic and based on the senses) and non-prophetic inspiration (non-ecstatic and rational). However, Voetius unconditionally rejected the distinction between prophets and apostles. In the *Disputationes Selectae* I, disp. 3, p. 44–7 and IV, disp. 3, p. 36–7 he defended the *verbatim ac syllabatim* inspiration of the apostles. The Old Testament was written in the same way

as the New Testament: the spirit acted directly on the authors. All the words and ideas derive directly from God, leaving the prophets and apostles no freedom of ideas or literary style. Arminius, however, in *Disputationes de religionis christianae* (pp. 167 ff.), is more cautious and, referring to Calvin, points out that the divine nature of the apostles is sufficient, though he too asserts that supernatural inspiration is at an end.

TEXTS

Deus per mentem Christi sese Apostolis manifestavit (TTP 1, G III, 21). *Verum si ad stylum attendere volemus, eum a stylo prophetiae alienissimum inveniemus ... Apostoli ubique ratiocinantur* (TTP 11, G III, 151); Ep 75.

BIBLIOGRAPHY

Primary Sources

Amyraut, M., *Six livres de la vocation des pasteurs* (Saumur, 1648).

Arminius, J., *Opera theologica* (Frankfurt, 1635).

Calvin, J., *Institutio christianae religionis* (Geneva, 1559).

Hobbes, Th., *Leviathan*.

Voetius, G., *Selectarum disputationum theologicarum pars prima-quinta*, 5 vols (Utrecht, 1648–69).

Secondary Literature

Tosel, A., *Spinoza ou le crépuscule de la servitude. Essai sur le Traité Théologico-Politique* (Paris: Aubier Montaigne, 1984), pp. 233–45.

Verbeek, Th., *Spinoza's Theologico-Political Treatise. Exploring the Will of God* (Aldershot: Ashgate, 2003).

R. Bordoli

Appetitus

The Latin noun *appetitus* and the corresponding verb *appetere* are commonly used in the non-technical meaning of '(to) want' or '(to) desire'. Spinoza uses these words in this way dozens of times in the *Ethics* and (less often) in the *Tractatus theologico-politicus*. In the last work the term arises most often when he is contrasting RATIO with appetite – for example 'sound reason' versus 'immoderate appetite' or the 'laws of reason' versus the 'laws of appetite'. He speaks of the Psalmist as imploring God's help against the 'appetites of the flesh'. There is an obvious evaluative distinction being drawn (in favour of reason over appetite), but Spinoza is careful, too, to give the appetites their due; emphasizing that in the absence of reason or a virtuous disposition, one would live under 'the laws of appetite with supreme right'.

But in E3p9s he assigns to the noun a more technical meaning. From that point on, it serves to remind the reader that human will and desire are never merely mental, but always involve the body and reflect the individual's essential conatic striving. Each individual thing strives to persevere in its being, and that striving (CONATUS) is the actual essence of the thing (E3p6–7). This striving manifests itself as desire for continued being and for that which is conducive to one's perseverance in being. If the conatus is referred to the mind alone, it is called will. If it is related to the mind and body together, it is called appetite. To the extent that the individual is conscious of the appetite, it is called desire (E3p9s). These are not three different things, but three different ways in which the individual's fundamental striving for perseverance in being can be manifest and classified.

Wolfson provides a number of quotations to remind us that the use of the term *appetitus* in connection with an organism's desire for self-preservation has a long history. He cites passages from Cicero, Aquinas, Duns Scotus, Dante and Telesio, all of which explicitly say that every natural being desires its own self-preservation. Wolfson notes that this usage can be traced to the Greek term *horme* – a word that is often also translated by *conatus*: 'Cicero himself uses *conatus* and *appetitio* as synonymous terms, and considers both of them as Latin equivalents of the Greek *horme*)' (vol. 2, p. 196). The scholastic tradition of Spinoza's time distinguished between the Stoic *appetitus naturalis*, an innate instinct for self-preservation, and the Peripatetic notion of an *appetitus*, defined as the soul's power which desires a thing perceived as an apparent good or joyful object (Micraelius). Chauvin adds that according to 'recent' philosophers animals lacking a soul are incapable of possessing an appetite in the proper sense.

Spinoza sees all human desires as manifestations of the fundamental *conatus*, and develops his systematic psychology accordingly. *Appetitus*, then, can be used to explain human action undertaken to achieve an end. Spinoza avoids the problems of teleological explanations by focusing not on the end (as final cause), but on the desire (*appetitus*) for the end (which can serve as efficient cause). E4def7 states the point straightforwardly: 'By the end for which we do something I understand appetite.'

TEXTS

Appetitus non confundendus est cum voluntate (CM 2.12). *Experientia satis superque doceat quod homines nihil minus posse, quam appetitus moderari suos* (Ep 58). *Cor purum in me crea Deus, et Spiritum (id est appetitum) decentem (sive moderatum)* (TTP 1, G III, 25). *Omnes suum utile quaerunt, at minime ex sanae rationis dictamine, sed plurimum ex sola libidine et animi affectionibus abrepti res appetunt* (TTP 5, G III, 73). *Ex legibus rationis vivendi, ex legibus appetitus* (TTP 16, G III, 190). *Humanas actiones atque appetitus considerabo perinde ac si questio de lineis, planis, aut de corporibus esset* (E3praef). *Hic conatus cum ad mentem solam refertur, voluntas appellatur; sed cum ad mentem et corpus simul refertur, vocatur appetitus, qui proinde nihil aliud est, quam ipsa hominis essentia, ex cuius natura ea, quae ipsius conservationi inserviunt, necessario sequuntur; atque adeo homo ad eadem agendum determinatus est* (E3p9s). *Per finem, cuius causa aliquid facimus, appetitum intelligo* (E4def7). *Unum et eundemque esse appetitum per quem homo tam agere quam pati dicitur* (E5p4s). *Hominum naturalis potentia, sive jus, non ratione sed quocunque appetitu definiri debet* (TP 2.5). *Humana libertas eo major est, quo homo appetitus moderari potest* (TP 2.20).

BIBLIOGRAPHY
Secondary Literature
Wolfson, H. A., *The Philosophy of Spinoza: Unfolding the Latent Processes of His Reasoning* (Cambridge: Harvard University Press, 1934; reprinted in 2 vols, New York: Schocken, 1969).

T. Cook

Aristocratia

The *Tractatus politicus* (2.17) defines an aristocracy or nobilary regime as a political order in which society is governed by a council of men selected by this council itself, e.g. a political elite of regents (*patricii*). Those excluded from election are considered 'foreigners'. Aristocracy comes close to an absolute and perfect dominion (IMPERIUM), which combines an unchanging will and unanimity (TP 8.3). An aristocracy should exclude all others from government. This regime should represent the community as one body and one mind. In order to avoid any serious opposition, the regime should rule by reason.

According to Spinoza, it is always better to involve more people in governing a state. About two percent of the male citizens older than thirty should be elected in the supreme council (TP 8.13). The general principle is that a reduction of the number of regents leads to instability (MONARCHIA), because the number of possible opponents grows. The human mind on its own is not fit to see all problems and solutions in political matters. On the contrary, deliberation is the best method (TP 9.14). Hence, the basic rule for establishing a stable regime is to increase the number of regents. Other reasons are that there is a greater chance that among them there will be clever people who know how to rule a city or a state (TP 8.2), that deliberation tends to be reasonable (8.6), that equality among the members is preserved (8.11), and finally that it has a basis in the community (8.13 and 39). The members of the aristocracy should distinguish themselves from ordinary people by religion, clothing, and so on (8.46-7).

Spinoza elaborates on the constitution of the regime. Political power should not be in the hands of a few people, or families, but must be divided. Also for practical reasons, it makes sense to let the supreme council choose representatives who rule effectively. So, from the supreme council a senate is selected; the senate leaves the preparation of political decisions to a select committee of rulers. Differentiated from these councils and statesmen are a court and a council of older aristocrats who supervise the regents.

Spinoza prefers an aristocratic regime extended to more than one city (TP 9.1). In such a federation of cities citizens can be treated as equal, but the cities cannot. The status of the cities should be differentiated according to their power, which is determined by their magnitude. The unity of the cities is guaranteed by the senate and the court. The regents have full power in their own cities, but political matters concerning the federation of cities should be handled by the senate.

A major advantage of a large number of regents is that most citizens, entitled to perform political functions, have a chance to fulfill their ambitions, their striving for honour (TP 10.7). Political order has to become a system in which people act freely without damaging the system (10.8).

TEXTS

Si haec cura reipublicae ad concilium pertineat, quod ex quibusdam tantum selectis componitur, tum imperium aristocratia appellatur (TP 2.17). *Aristocraticum imperium illud esse diximus, quod non unus, sed quidam ex multitudine selecti tenent, quos imposterum patricios appellabimus* (TP 8.1). *In [aristocratico imperio] a sola supremi concilii voluntate et electione pendeat, ut hic aut ille patricius creetur* (TP 11.1).

BIBLIOGRAPHY

Secondary Literature
Haitsma Mulier, E., *The Myth of Venice and Dutch Republican Thought in the*
Seventeenth Century (Assen: Van Gorcum, 1980).
Matheron, A., *Individu et communauté chez Spinoza* (Paris: Éditions de Minuit, 1969).

M. Terpstra

Atheismus

In letter 30 to Oldenburg and letter 43 to Ostens, Spinoza, who had been charged with atheism, vented his indignation and tried to rebut that accusation by emphasizing his morality. To some scholars Spinoza's reply is unconvincing and a sign of his 'Marrano' mind (Misrahi). In the view of others it did not necessarily reflect his inner convictions (Caillois). However, in the *Tractatus theologico-politicus* the philosopher himself denounces the atheism of those who acknowledge miracles and deny the order of nature created by God's eternal laws. Apparently both parties just used the term 'atheism' to slander their opponents. As Voetius in the disputation on atheism observed, atheism is often used in a very broad and 'calumnious sense' (1648, p. 116).

More particularly Van Velthuijsen identified 'atheists' with 'deists', a group dealt with by Mersenne in his *L'impieté des déistes, athées et libertins* (1624), which was one of the first tracts on the subject. According to Van Velthuijsen Spinoza was an atheist, although he acknowledged the existence of a Creator-God, because he subjected the world to a fatuous necessity. Such a fatalism made moral language metaphorical and pointless. Atheism moreover implied the complete subjection of religion to the state. Van Velthuijsen was the first of many contemporaries who tended to denounce the atheism of the philosopher. Well before the turn of the century he was followed by two Huguenot scholars: Bayle, calling Spinoza an 'atheist with a system', and Jaquelot, denouncing him as an 'Epicurean'. According to Lagrée both designations are more or less equivalent because, as Leclerc observed, Epicurus was the first philosopher who on the basis of his atomism developed an atheist philosophical system, which was revived by Hobbes and Spinoza. They, like the Hellenistic philosopher, denied creation, and consequently contingency, and human freedom.

In the second half of the seventeenth century the term 'atheism' had a very vague meaning denoting all kinds of deviant religious behaviour. Some of its many equivalents were superstition, idolatry, irreligion, libertinage, deism, Machiavellianism, indifferentism, neutralism, Socinianism and heterodoxy in general. The denial of the existence of God therefore was by no means a necessary condition for calling a philosophy atheistic. Voetius even took for granted that no 'speculative atheists' existed, while the Arminian scholar Vossius in De theologia gentili 1.3 stated that only in a frenzy will a man be able to deny the existence of God. Besides theoretical atheists the other main category of atheists were the 'practical' atheists, who negated God by their actions. Other kinds of atheism listed by Vossius were the Epicurean denial of the providence of God, who consequently did not inspire any love in man, and the Sadducean belief in a God who merely rewarded human virtue in this world. Voetius even listed no less than twelve kinds of atheism.

The common measure, however, of all types of atheism is that according to Voetius they are 'directly or indirectly' at variance with 'the proper knowledge of God, a real Faith and a just worship of God, which may be accompanied with attempts to remove

religion and morality from themselves or from others'. The last clause refers in particular to a magistrate who did not properly promote the cause of true religion and wrongfully tolerated false ones. The first clause denounces the atheism of sceptics and all false philosophers. In particular it must be noted that in this definition the knowledge of God is intrinsically linked with morality. This link is also assumed in the correspondence of Van Velthuijsen and Spinoza with Ostens as intermediary. Till Bayle's 'virtuous atheist' scholars took this link for granted. Therefore in the context of seventeenth-century discourse Spinoza's answer to Van Velthuijsen was obviously appropriate.

TEXTS

Vulgus me atheismi insimulare non cessat (Ep 30). *Primo ait ... me atheismum docere. Solent enim athei honores et divitias supra modum quaerere, quas ego semper contempsi* (Ep 43). *Res eo jam pervenit, ut qui aperte fatentur se ideam Dei non habere et Deum non nisi per res creates (quarum causas ignorent) cognoscere, non erubescant Philosophos atheismi accusare* (TTP 2, G III, 30). *Si quid ... ordini, quem Deus in natura statuit, repugnaret, adeoque contra naturam ejusque leges esset et consequenter ejus fides nos de omnibus dubitare faceret et ad atheismum duceret* (TTP 6, G III, 86–7).

BIBLIOGRAPHY
Primary Sources
Voetius, G., 'De atheismo' and 'An sint athei', in *Disputationum selectarum pars prima* (Amsterdam, 1648), pp. 116–226.
Vossius, G.J., *De theologia gentili* (Amsterdam, 1641).

Secondary Literature

Barth, H.M., *Atheismus und Orthodoxie, Analysen und Modelle christlicher Apologetik im 17. Jahrhundert* (Göttingen: Moltmann, 1971).

Caillois, R., 'Spinoza et l'athéisme', in E. Giancotti (ed.), *Spinoza nel 350° anniversario della nascita. Proceedings of the First Italian Congress on Spinoza,* (Naples: Bibliopolis, 1985), pp. 3–33.

Lagrée, J., 'Spinoza, athée et épicurien', *Archives de Philosophie*, no. 57 (1994), pp. 541–58.

Misrahi, R., 'L'athéisme et la liberté chez Spinoza', *Revue internationale de philosophie*, no. 31 (1977), pp. 217–30.

Mori, G., 'L'athée spéculatif selon Bayle, permanence et développements d'une idée', in M. Magdelaine (ed.), *De l'humanisme aux lumières. Bayle et le protestantisme* (Paris and Oxford: Universitas and Voltaire Foundation, 1996), pp. 595–609.

Schöder, W., *Urprünge des Atheismus. Untersuchungen zur Metaphysik- und Religionskritik des 17. und 18. Jahrhunderts* (Stuttgart: Frommann-Holzboog, 1999).

H. Krop

Attributum

Although the concept of 'attribute' plays a crucial role in both the *Korte verhandeling* (*eigenschap*) and the *Principles of Cartesian Philosophy*, it would appear that only the way in which Spinoza deals with attributes in the *Ethics* conveys his mature assessment, since he there finally supersedes the Cartesian conception which identified a substance with its unique attribute. However, Spinoza continued to use 'attribute' in the traditional scholastic sense as well, denoting the perfections of God which are not really distinct, but only appear so to the human intellect (cf. Descartes, *Secundae Responsiones*, AT VII, 138).

'By attribute', Spinoza writes in *Ethics* 1 definition 4, 'I understand what the intellect perceives of a substance, as constituting its essence.' This definition has given rise to subjective (Wolfson, 1934, vol. I, pp. 142ff.) as well as objective or realist interpretations (Curley, Donagan; Gueroult, 1968, pp. 428–61). According to the former, 'attribute' stands for the way in which man, being a modification of substance, perceives substance. According to the latter, attributes are part of what makes a substance what it is, for *Ethics* 2 definition 2 states: 'I say that to the essence of any thing belongs that which, being given, the thing is necessarily posited and which, being taken away, the thing is necessarily taken away; or that without which the thing can neither be nor be conceived, and which can neither be nor be conceived without the thing.'

Regardless of the question whether attributes are part of reality as such, it is clear that they belong to substances, and more in particular to the one substance that Spinoza calls 'God': 'By God I understand a being absolutely infinite in its own kind, i.e. a substance consisting of an infinity of attributes, of which each one expresses an eternal and infinite essence.' (E1def6) In *Ethics* 1 Spinoza uses the concept of attributes in order to deduce the impossibility of there being other substances besides God. A realist reading is strongly suggested by proposition 9, according to which '(t)he more reality or being each thing has, the more attributes belong to it.' What is more, the scholium following proposition 10 adds that each attribute 'expresses a certain eternal and infinite essence' after which proposition 11, in which the necessary existence of God is demonstrated, refers to 'God or a substance consisting of infinite attributes, each of which expresses eternal and infinite essence'.

The identification of God with all existing attributes is further corroborated by proposition 19, in which God's eternity is identified with the eternity of God's attributes, and by corollary 2 of proposition 20, according to which 'God, *or* all of God's attributes, are immutable'. The same holds for the famous digression on NATURA NATURANS and NATURA NATURATA: 'by *natura naturans* we must understand what is in itself and is conceived through itself, *or* such attributes of substance as express an eternal and infinite essence', and 'by *natura naturata* I understand whatever follows from the necessity of God's nature, *or* from any of God's attributes' (E1p29s).

Having demonstrated the necessary existence of God, Spinoza continues to argue that this being, constituted by infinitely many attributes, each of which is infinite in its own kind, cannot be divided (E1p12–13), and must be deemed the only existing substance (E1p14–15), producing 'infinitely many things in infinitely many modes' (E1p16), precisely because God consists of infinite attributes, each of which expresses an essence infinite in its own kind (E1p16dem). Thus, modes are always produced by some attribute of God, and it is only in the second part of the *Ethics*, in which Spinoza focuses his attention on the mind as a finite mode of the attribute of thought, that it becomes evident that man, consisting of mind and body, has access to two of the infinitely many attributes which exist: besides the attribute of thought, the attribute of extension (E2p1–2).

The relationship between the attributes is dealt with by Spinoza in proposition 7: 'The order and connection of ideas is the same as the order and connection of things', which is generally supposed to refer to the modes produced by God's attributes. While each attribute produces its own modes (E2p6) they do so in the same causal order. This has often been identified as constituting Spinoza's 'parallelism', although the preferred view of some scholars is that for instance Spinoza conceives of the human organism not as a composite of two separate modes, but rather as a single mode, which can be perceived from the point of view of two different attributes (Della Rocca, 2008, pp. 99–104). This much is clear, however, that Spinoza's metaphysics precludes any causal interaction between modes produced by separate attributes. Thus, he is able to deliver an alternative to Cartesian dualism.

From the letters Spinoza exchanged with his friend Simon Joosten de Vries (Ep 8–10), however, it becomes evident that the members of the Amsterdam circle studying an early version of the *Ethics* had considerable difficulty in grasping the concept of a single substance constituted by really different attributes. Apparently, they failed to comprehend how Spinoza's treatment of Descartes's comments in his *Principles* I art. 53 on the necessity of each substance having a single 'really distinct' attribute could result in the conception of an indivisible, unitary substance made up of infinitely many attributes. In fact, this question came to dominate many early Cartesian 'refutations' of Spinozism, and it has continued to haunt the experts, including for instance Pierre Macherey, who recently suggested that we should conceive of the unity of substance as proposed by Spinoza as the unity of reality, which being absolutely infinite holds no number. As a consequence, Spinoza's alternative to Cartesian dualism should no longer be regarded as a variety of metaphysical 'monism'.

167

TEXTS

Na voorgaande overweginge van de Natuur zoo vinden wij alleen twee eigenschappen die aan dit alvolmaakte wezen toebehooren (KV 1.1). Oneijndelijke eigenschappen (KV 1.2). Aangaande de eigenschappen van de welke God bestaat, die zijn niet als oneijndige zelfstandigheden, van de welke een iederdes zelfs oneindig volmaakt moet zijn ... dat tot nog toe maar twee door haar zelfs wezen ons bekend zijn ... de denking en de uitgebreidheid (KV 1.7). Wezen van oneijndelijke eigenschappen, waar van ieder des zelfs oneijndelijk en volmaakt is ... God (KV 1.19). *Proprietas, sive qualitas, sive attributum* (PPC 1def5). *Per affectiones hic intelligimus id, quod alias per attributa denotavit Cartesius* (CM 1.3). *Omnes distinctiones quas inter Dei attributa facimus, non alias esse quam rationis* (CM 2.6). *De Deo ... Ens constans infinitis attributis* (Ep 2). *Multa attributa quae ab iis deo tribuuntur, ego tamquam creatura considero* (Ep 6). *Per attributum intelligo nisi quod attributum dicatur respectu intellectus substantiae certam talem naturam tribuentis* (Ep 9). *Deo humana attributa ... non adsigno* (Ep 56). *De divinis attributis* (TTP 2, G III, 37). *Per attributum intelligo id, quod intellectus de substantia percipit, tanquam ejusdem essentia constituens* (E1def4). *Per Deum intelligo ens absolute infinitum, hoc est substantiam constantem infinitis attributis, quorum unumquodque aeternam et infinitam essentiam exprimit* (E1def6). *Quo plus realitatis aut esse unaquaeque res habet eo plura attributa ipsi competunt* (E1p9). *Quamvis duo attributa realiter distincta concipiantur ... non possumus tamen inde concludere ipsa duo entia sive duas substantias constituere* (E1p10s). *Natura divina infinita absolute attributa habet* (E1p16). *Deum sive omnia Dei attributa* (E1p20c2). *Substantia quae jam sub hoc jam sub illo attributo comprehenditur* (E2p7s).

BIBLIOGRAPHY

Primary Sources

Descartes, R., *Principia philosophiae, Secundae responsiones*.

Secondary Literature

Curley, E., 'On Bennett's Interpretation of Spinoza's Metaphysics', in Y. Yovel (ed.), *God and Nature. Spinoza's Metaphysics* (Leiden: Brill, 1991), pp. 35–51.

Della Rocca, M., *Spinoza* (London and New York: Routledge, 2008).

Donagan, A., 'Essence and the Distinction of the Attributes in Spinoza's Metaphysics', in M.G. Grene (ed.), *Spinoza. A Collection of Critical Essays* (New York: Doubleday Anchor, 1973), pp. 164–81.

Gueroult, M., *Spinoza I. Dieu (Éthique I)* (Hildesheim: Olms, 1968).

Macherey, P., 'Spinoza est-il moniste?', in M. Revault D'Allones and H. Rizk (eds), *Spinoza: puissance et ontologie* (Paris: Éditions Kimé, 1994), pp. 39–53.

Wolfson, H.A., *The Philosophy of Spinoza. Unfolding the Latent Processes of His Reasoning*, 2 vols. (Cambridge, MA and London: Harvard University Press, 1934).

W. van Bunge

Axioma, *see* **Ordo Geometricus**

Beatitudo

The term *beatitudo*, usually rendered as 'blessedness' or 'beatitude' in English, occurs more frequently in the *Tractatus theologico-politicus* than in the *Ethics*. Its Dutch counterpart *zaligheid* is only used once. According to TTP 5, beatitude is not acquired through ceremonies. Although Psalms 15 and 24 mention 'God's mountain, his tent and their inhabitants', these, according to Spinoza, do not refer to the mount in Jerusalem, nor to the Tabernacle, but rather *parabolice* to 'beatitude and tranquillity of mind'. Hence, beatitude and 'man's true happiness' are defined as something to be found 'in wisdom alone, and in true knowledge', and man's highest good (SUMMUM BONUM) and ultimate end (*finis ultimus*) are said to be found in the knowledge and the love of God, just as Spinoza would later claim in books 2, 4 and 5 of the *Ethics* (AMOR INTELLECTUALIS DEI).

Spinoza's notion of salvation, blessedness, or liberty, although it consists in a 'constant and eternal love of God, or in God's love for men' (E5p36s), shares with the mainstream tradition in pre-modern Western moral philosophy the Aristotelian idea that the highest happiness is to be found in contemplation. As Aristotle himself had expressed it in *Nicomachean Ethics*, book 10: 'philosophy is thought to offer pleasures marvellous for their purity and their enduringness'. In the seventeenth century, this widely accepted link between contemplative happiness and the highest good was reflected in elaborate handbook discussions on the relation of virtue to pleasure (e.g. in Walaeus's *Compendium Ethicae*, and De Courcelles's *Synopsis Ethices*). Contemporaries could accordingly find references to the contemplative essence of an enduring 'mental tranquility', 'inward joy', 'mental pleasure', or *beatitudo*, and to the notions of moral types of happiness LAETITIA and felicity in any number of works.

Spinoza, however, would rather have found his examples in Cartesian sources. As early as Rule 1 of the *Regulae*, Descartes had argued that 'the pleasure to be gained from contemplating the truth...is practically the only happiness in this life that is complete and untroubled by any pain'. In the *Principia*

IV, art. 190 Descartes again referred to the idea of an undisturbed *gaudium intellectuale*, now linking the notion to Stoic philosophy. Spinoza's first published reference to human beatitude occurs in his positive discussion of Descartes's ontological argument for the existence of God in PPC 1p5s, where he also mentions Descartes's fifth *Meditation* and *First Replies* as sources for a notion of God that may serve as 'the first foundation of human blessedness'.

A Cartesian background for Spinoza's way of defining beatitude is also evident from his use of the uncharacteristic term *acquiescentia* (satisfaction) (E5p27). Though it has been argued that this notion reveals a Jewish background on account of its Ladino grammatical form (Agamben, 1999, pp. 137–8), it actually occurs in the 1650 Latin translation of the *Passions de l'âme*, art. 190 which was reprinted in the editions of Descartes's collected works (Van Ruler, 2004, p. 25 and 35, n. 12). Following Descartes, Spinoza argues that self-contentedness may also occur in untruthful and negative ways, for instance when people have too high an esteem for themselves, or when such contentedness is fed only by a quest for popularity (E3def-aff28e, E4p58s). In its positive form, however, satisfaction is the pinnacle of blessedness and philosophy's highest goal.

Parallel to Spinoza's elaboration of human freedom on the basis of the Cartesian idea of an *émotion intérieure* (Beyssade; Wilson), other self-taught students of Descartes also adopted the notion of satisfaction. Cornelis Bontekoe (c. 1644–85), for instance, defined intellectual joy as a satisfaction in what is good, in so far as this pertains to the mind considered in itself (Bontekoe, *Tractatus Ethico-Physicus*, p. 14). Confining beatitude to a special form of understanding by the separate mind, Bontekoe developed the idea of satisfaction in a similar way to Spinoza, mirroring the latter's notion of a special 'virtue of the mind' (E4p28) and his explanation of beatitude 'without reference to the body' (E5p20s). Finally, Spinoza's interpretation of beatitude as a state of freedom and blessedness that finds its basis in an intuitive knowledge of God, has its Cartesian precedent in Descartes's view that mental satisfaction is increased by a 'frequent reflection upon divine Providence', whereby a mental disposition may be formed in which 'our soul always has the means of happiness within itself' (*Passions de l'âme*, art. 155). Again, we find a Cartesian theme developed by both Bontekoe and Spinoza. 'To always be happy,' Bontekoe argues, one should first acquire 'a good knowledge of God' and 'be convinced of God's predestination and direction (*bestel*) of all things'. On this basis 'a good philosopher' and 'enlightened Christian' may, by the use of reason, 'forge happiness and pleasure' from whatever occurs (Bontekoe, *Alle de Werken* 3.2, p. 231). Whereas Bontekoe thought that to find such enduring happiness was 'easier than most people believe, and without...much difficulty' (ibid.), Spinoza was to repeat the Platonic dictum that 'all things excellent are as difficult as they are rare' (E5p42s).

Identifying beatitude with a 'love of God' that arises out of the third kind of knowledge (COGNITIO), Spinoza restricted blessedness to a specific kind of intellectual grasp with which he could explain the knowing mind's intellectual power, or VIRTUS, as a preliminary to restraining the affects. Hence Spinoza argued (E5p42d) that beatitude was not 'the reward of virtue', but rather 'virtue itself'. Thereby giving a new interpretation to an old Stoic doctrine, the *Ethics* stayed true to the classical idea of a morally-induced type of felicity that functions as an emotional

shell. This position contrasts sharply with that of Hobbes, who had argued in *Leviathan* I, chap. 12 that 'there is no such *Finis ultimus*, (utmost ayme,) nor *Summum Bonum*, (greatest Good,) as is spoken of in the Books of the old Morall Philosophers'. Spinoza, by contrast, linked blessedness not only to psychological, but also to social wellbeing (E2p29s). He thereby supplemented the Hobbesian idea of egoism with a broader account of self-preservation – a strategy that was already apparent in the works of Lambert van Velthuijsen and Johan and Pieter de la Court (Nyden-Bullock). Nevertheless, Spinoza continued to focus more particularly on mental and spiritual effects in his account of the *summum bonum*. Ignoring Descartes's dualistic attempts to arrive at a psychology of behavioural change, Spinoza even reverted more unambiguously than Descartes himself to the classical belief that true happiness is found in an intellectual redirection of the mind. His theory of beatitude thus saved what could be saved of classical morality and religious grace in spite of the naturalistic standards set by Hobbesian politics and Cartesian biology.

TEXTS

Als wij op deze manier God komen te kennen, wij dan noodzakelijk ... met hem moeten vereenigen. In het welk alleen ... onze zaligheid bestaat (KV 2.22). *Per cognitionem Dei, in illius amorem, sive summam beatitudinem ducimur* (PPC 1p5s); Ep 21, Ep 73. *In vita itaque apprime utile est intellectum seu rationem ... perficere et in hoc solo summa hominis felicitas seu beatitudo consistit* (E4c4). *Mentis libertas seu beatitudo* (E5praef). *Beatitudo sane in eo consistere debet, quod mens ipsa perfectione sit praedita* (E5p33s). *Nostra salus, seu beatitudo, seu*

*libertas consistit, nempe in constanti et
aeterno erga Dei amore* (E5p36). *Beatitudo
non est virtutis praemium, sed ipsa virtus*
(E5p42). *Vera foelicitas, et beatitudo uniuscujusque in sola boni fruitione consistit ...
vera beatitudo in sola sapientia et veri cognitione consistit* (TTP 3, G III, 44). *Amor Dei
summa hominis foelicitatis est et beatitudo et
finis ultimus* (TTP 4, G III, 60), TTP 5, G III,
69–72.

BIBLIOGRAPHY
Primary Sources
Bontekoe, C., *Tractatus Ethico-Physicus
de Animi & Corporis Passionibus,
Earundemque Certissimis Remediis,*
ed. Johannes Flenderus (Amsterdam,
1696).
——, *Alle de Philosophische, Medicinale
en Chymische Werken* (Amsterdam,
1689).
Curcellaeus, S. [= Étienne de Courcelles],
Synopsis Ethices, in *Opera Theologica,*
ed. P. van Limborch (Amsterdam, 1675).
Descartes, R., *Passiones animae* (1650), in
Opera philosophica III (Amsterdam,
1656).
Walaeus, Ant., *Compendium Ethicae
Aristotelicae ad normam veritatis
Christianae revocatum* (Leiden, 1620).

Secondary Literature
Agamben, G., *Potentialities: Collected
Essays in Philosophy* (Stanford, CA.:
Stanford University Press, 1999).
Beyssade, J.-M., 'De l'émotion intérieure
chez Descartes à l'affect actif spinoziste',
in Edwin Curley and Pierre-François
Moreau (eds), *Spinoza: Issues and
Directions. The Proceedings of the
Chicago Spinoza Conference* (Leiden:
Brill, 1990), pp. 176–90.

Nyden-Bullock, T., *Spinoza's Radical
Cartesian Mind,* (London and New York:
Continuum, 2007).
Ruler, H. van, 'Calvinisme, cartesianisme,
spinozisme', in Gunther Coppens (ed.),
Spinoza en het Nederlands cartesianisme
(Louvain and Voorburg: Acco, 2004),
pp. 23–37.
Wilson, M.D., 'Comments on
J.-M. Beyssade, "De l'émotion intérieure
chez Descartes à l'affect actif spinoziste"',
in E. Curley and P.-F. Moreau (eds),
*Spinoza: Issues and Directions. The
Proceedings of the Chicago Spinoza
Conference* (Leiden: Brill, 1990),
pp. 191–5.

H. van Ruler

Bonum

Spinoza employs the term 'good' in various
contexts. As part of the phrases 'highest
good' and 'true good' it is found in the
narrative of Spinoza's search for the highest
good in the opening paragraphs of the
Tractatus de intellectus emendatione, in the
discussion of the knowledge and love of God
in the *Tractatus theologico-politicus* (chap.
4), and in the account of 'the greatest good of
those who seek virtue' in *Ethics* 4. More
often, though, when Spinoza discusses the
good (in its nominal and adjectival form) it is
in order to explain where the notion comes
from and to argue that nothing is good in
itself, but only in relation to some entity
whose well-being is presumed to be furthered
or thwarted. This discussion is found in *Cogitata metaphysica* 1.6, in the appendix to
Ethics 1, in the preface to *Ethics* 4 and is
alluded to in the first sentence and twelfth
paragraph of the TIE. Finally, there are

171

repeated references to the true knowledge of good and evil in *Ethics* 4.

The reflections on the true good and the highest good that open the TIE bring to mind similar meditations in Plato, Aristotle, the Stoics, Boethius and others in the reflective wisdom tradition. Spinoza identifies the highest good as arriving (with others, if possible) at 'the knowledge of the union that the mind has with the whole of Nature'. But even as he identifies this as the *summum bonum* he makes it clear that this judgement is based on his projection of what would be conducive to his enjoying a stronger and more enduring nature than his own. This is in keeping with his general analysis of the origins of notions such as good and evil.

In the *Cogitata metaphysica* Spinoza argues that there is no intrinsic or 'metaphysical good' – that is to say a *bonum in se* according to Chauvin – and that things can be said to be good only with respect to other things. In the appendix to *Ethics* 1 we learn that 'good' is only a mode of imagining in us that is often mistaken for an objective property of things. In fact, Spinoza says, people call *good* 'whatever is conducive to health and the worship of God'. The preface to *Ethics* 4 provides Spinoza's clearest formulation of his understanding of what is meant by saying that something is good. Though the terms 'good' and 'evil' refer to no intrinsic property in things but are modes of thinking only, nonetheless we must retain these words. We form an idea of man as a model of human nature, and we can then call 'good' whatever we certainly know to be a means by which we can approach this model of human nature. Spinoza's model of human nature is of course a model of maximal understanding. Thus the true good is that which can lead to understanding. It is the

true good because we desire the strength, stability, power and activity found in understanding (having adequate ideas of God or Nature). This exemplifies Spinoza's earlier claim (E3p39s) that we do not want something because it is good, but rather we call it good because we want it. This understanding of the good is shared by Hobbes, cf. *De homine* 11, 4, but diverges from that of Descartes.

TEXTS

Goet en kwaat, of zonden, en zijn niets anders als wyzen van denken (KV 1.6). Dat Goet en kwaad niets anders is als betrekkinge … onder de entia rationis moeten geplaatst worden (KV 1.10). *Nam quae … apud homines bonum aestimantur ad haec tria rediguntur, divitias, scilicet, honorem, atque libidinem* (TIE 4, G I, 5–6). *Per verum bonum intelligam et simul quod sit summum bonum. Notandum est quod bonum et malum non nisi respective dicantur … perfectionem et omne quod potest medium vocatur verum bonum, summum bonum est eo pervenire, ut ille cum aliis individuis, si fieri potest, tali natura fruatur. Esse cognitionem unionis quam mens cum tota natura habet* (TIE 13, G I, 8). *Res bona dicitur, tantum respective ad aliam, cui conducit ad id, quod amat. Salus bona hominibus, sed vero neque bona neque mala brutis aut plantis. Qui autem bonum aliquod metaphysicum quaeritant, quod omni careat respectu, falso aliquo praejudicio laborant* (CM 1.6). *Per bonum hic intelligo omne genus laetitiae et praecipue id quod desiderio satisfacit* (E3p39s). *Unusquisque ex ingenio suo affectu judicat, quid bonum sit* (E3p51s). *Bonum et malum nihil positivum in rebus indicant* (E4praef). *Per bonum id intelligam, quod certo scimus nobis esse utile* (E4def1). *Summum bonum est cognitio Dei* (E5p28).

BIBLIOGRAPHY
Primary Sources
Hobbes, Th., *De homine*; *Leviathan*, chap. 6.

T. Cook

Caeremonia

According to chapter 5 of the *Tractatus theologico-politicus* natural divine law does not prescribe ceremonies, since 'they were instituted for the Hebrews alone' and 'were closely accommodated to their state'. They were only relevant to the Hebrews, and after the downfall of their state they lost all significance. Rites are morally indifferent and only valid by institution: they are not something good in itself but only the representation of something good, as the Socinian theologian Crellius observed: 'the Truth is chiefly opposed to ceremonies, which are like shadows' (*Opera exegetica* I, p. 434). Just like God's election of the Jews the practice of certain ceremonies is a matter of political opportunity: rites and ceremonies are used by the Jews (and other peoples) to preserve their state. When political circumstances change, the ceremonies lose their relevance. The prophets deal with them in order to reach the people, who confuse spiritual meaning and material images. Salvation is ensured only through observance of universal divine law, as Isaiah and the New Testament teach us. The same is true of Christian ceremonies (baptism, supper,

feasts, prayers), which were introduced neither by Christ nor by the apostles and are called 'external signs' of the universal Church. Ceremonies are merely social practices. Hence, the first French version of the *Tractatus* was entitled *Traitté des cérémonies superstitieuses des juifs tants anciens que modernes.*

In this respect Spinoza agrees with the view of both orthodox and liberal Protestantism. The Arminian theologian Episcopius, for example, observed: 'According to us the rites [or ceremonies or sacraments] are nothing else than symbols, signs or markings' (*Disputationes* in *Opera* II, p. 437). Hebrew ceremonies are laws of the state, whereas Christian ones are social norms. Apparently the Roman Catholic view of ceremonies was opposed to the Protestant view. The famous Roman Catholic controversialist Bellarmine, for example, in his *Disputationes* III 1, p. 335, observed that ceremonies distinguish Christians from heretics and are an *actus religionis*. The orthodox Reformed theologian Maresius, however, in his *Systema theologicum* 7.63ff. equates the Old Testament ceremonies with civil laws: 'Thus they possess a natural equity, but they are specified according to the circumstances of the persons, time and place' and maintains that they were abrogated in practice by Christ. Equally in favour of the total abrogation of ceremonies is Episcopius, stating: 'Scripture ... contains all things that are for ever and ever necessary to know, believe, hope and do for salvation. For it is beyond doubt that Scripture contains many things, that ... are not absolutely necessary ... Some are of a speculative nature ... others practical, dealing with rites, ceremonies and habits' (*Institutiones theologicae* I, p. 243). The Leiden theologian Coccejus

CAUSA

observed: '[the cultivation of the law of ceremonies] is not the practice of true religion' (*Ad ultima Mosis* 30, I, p. 227). The indifferent nature of ceremonies in comparison with true religion is also asserted by Grotius in *Meletius* § 67, Hobbes in *Leviathan* 12.57, which section explains the origin of the religious ceremonies in the same manner as Spinoza and Herbert of Cherbury in *De Veritate*, pp. 222, 286–7.

TEXTS

Videamus hanc legem divinam naturalem non exigere caeremonias, hoc est actiones in se indifferentes (TTP 4, G III, 62). *Caeremoniae ... quae habentur in Vetero Testamento, Hebraeis tantum institutae et eorum imperio accommodatae fuerint ... certum eas ad legem divinum non pertinere, adeoque nec etiam ad beatitudinem et virtutem aliquid facere ... imo qui in imperio ubi Christiana religio interdicta est, vivit, is ab his caeremonias abstinere tenetur et nihilominus poterit beate vivere* (TTP 5, G III, 69 and 76).

BIBLIOGRAPHY
Primary Sources
Bellarminus, R., *Disputationes de controversiis christianae fidei adversus hujus temporis haereticos*, 4 vols (Ingolstadt, 1605).
Coccejus, J., *Ad ultima Mosis* in *Opera omnia I* (Amsterdam, 1675).
Crellius, J., *Opera omnia exegetica*, 3 vols ([Amsterdam], 1656 [1665]).
Episcopius, S., *Opera theologica* (Amsterdam, 1650).
———, *Operum theologicorum pars altera* (Amsterdam, 1665).
Grotius, H., *Meletius* [1611], ed. G. H. M. Posthumus Meyes (Leiden: Brill, 1988).
Herbert of Cherbury, *De veritate* [1645], facsimile ed. G. Gawlick (Stuttgart-Bad Cannstatt: Frommann, 1966).
Hobbes, Th., *Leviathan*.
Maresius, S., *Systema theologicum* (Groningen, 1673).

Secondary Literature
Lagrée, J., *La raison ardente. Religion naturelle et raison au XVIIe siècle* (Paris: Vrin, 1991), pp. 247–53.

R. Bordoli

Causa

Although 'cause' and its Dutch counterparts *oorzaak* and *reden* abundantly occur in all Spinoza's works, the philosopher only dealt with this concept in his commentary on Descartes's *Principia* and in the first part of the *Ethics*. In the axioms of part one of the PPC he adopted without comment some Cartesian notions, such as the causal dependence of all things including God (7 and 11) and the ontological dependence of an effect on its cause. An effect, therefore, derives all its reality from its cause (8) and the cause in order to do so has to be ontologically superior to the effect. Moreover, he stated a parallelism between causal generation and preservation (10). Goclenius and Micraelius recapitulated these traditional notions by observing that a cause is 'the generating principle of being' and 'its *conditio sine qua non*'. Thus, in seventeenth-century philosophical discourse, causal relation implied far more than just temporal succession.

In the first part of the *Ethics*, Spinoza has two axioms concerning the causal relation. In axiom 3, he lays down that effects necessarily follow from their causes. This definition is conventional and in conformity with how causation was defined in scholastic philosophy from Ockham onwards.

Axiom 4, however, Spinoza's famous causal axiom, is new and much more interesting. This axiom states that the knowledge of an effect depends on and involves the knowledge of its cause. In letter 72 it took the form of 'the knowledge or the idea of an effect depends on the knowledge of the cause or the idea of the cause'. A cautious reading of this would say that once we know about the causes of things we know more about those things themselves. If I know what causes the pain in my shoulder, I know more about the pain itself. However, what seems to be packed into this axiom 4 is Spinoza's belief in the basic intelligibility of nature. Things can be *understood* through their causes. Even though this sounds trivial, it is far from that. Suppose a causes b. Knowing both that b exists and that it is caused by a in the sense of the regularity theory of causation does not by itself make the causal relation intelligible, because we are still in complete darkness as to *how* a causes b. For Spinoza, the paradigmatic case of causation seems to be geometrical. We understand, for example, a sphere when we think of it as being produced through a semicircle rotating around its axis. Thinking of the sphere in this way first gives us a complete understanding of how the effect originates from the cause and second also helps us to deduce the properties of the sphere, thus providing us with knowledge of the effect. In this geometrical case, the production of the sphere is in accordance with the order of the intellect. Thus, if Spinoza can somehow prove that the world conforms to the model provided by the geometrical theory of causation, there is place for an infinite thinking thing for which the world is completely intelligible. In the

Tractatus de intellectus emendatione 72 Spinoza goes so far as to claim that ideas that do not involve their causal history are not even true. This may sound odd but the point behind this is that ideas without causal history are devoid of meaning in one sense of meaning. The idea of the motion of the semicircle, if not related to bringing something about, is just a fragmentary pointless thought. However, when its motion is tied to the bringing about of the sphere the sequence makes sense – not so that the motion happens *in order to* produce the sphere but so that the relation becomes intelligible. So while Spinoza wants to abandon all explanation through final causes his substitute for that is not a universe of blind causes. For Spinoza, causation as the cement of the universe also makes the world follow the order of the intellect.

A full understanding of causality in nature requires the knowledge of God's causal working. Spinoza claims that God is the efficient and first cause of everything there is (E1p16). Moreover, in the propositions 16–18 he applied the scholastic classification of the causes, quoting almost literally from Burgersdijk's manual of logic. God is an immanent cause, that is to say the cause and the effect – the universe – do not exist as two really distinct beings, because all things stay within God. He cannot be a transient cause of anything because besides God no substance can be or be conceived. Moreover, God has to be cause through himself and not an accidental cause because nothing except God's essence can prompt him to action. Hence by definition 7 he is the only really free cause. God's causal working by his nature implies that we should not conceive his acting by analogy with man, assuming the (Aristotelian) distinction between a deliberating intellect and a choosing will. Will and intellect are no principles to be distinguished from his essence (E1p17s). Spinoza's emphasis on God's being the first and efficient cause of everything underlines his position that there are no final causes.

Spinoza seems to use 'e follows from God' as equivalent to 'God is the cause of e', which suggest that effects of God somehow flow or emanate from God's nature (E1p17s). This picture of God's causation quickly leads to attributing a necessitarian position to Spinoza. God exists by necessity and all things necessarily flow from his essence. In this scholium Spinoza compares the essence of God to the essence of a triangle from which all its properties, such as having the sum of its internal angles as equal to two right angles, necessarily follow.

The geometrical model of the universe and causation described above is threatened by what could be called the *fact of change*. There are finite things which come into existence and then pass away. However, if such things followed from God's eternal and unchanging essence, they would have to be eternal. Thus, in proposition 28 Spinoza denies that finite things follow from the absolute nature of God by geometrical necessity and claims that they must be determined by other finite things. There is, then, an obvious problem. How is the geometrical model of God's causation reconcilable with finite causation? There are several ways to deal with this problem. One possibility that stems from Curley is to suggest that God participates in finite causation through laws of nature which follow from God's eternal essence. This solution is praiseworthy but one might grumble that it is insensitive to Spinoza's basic idea that all things flow from God's essence. Another possibility is to place emphasis on Spinoza's view that any finite thing can also be conceived from the viewpoint of eternity.

Thus, even though finite things as such do not flow from the eternal and infinite essence of God, they, as conceived from the viewpoint of eternity, follow from that essence. There is, as it were, an eternal four-dimensional static universe which is in accordance with the geometrical model and which acquires its durational realization through the activity of finite things.

Spinoza's causal axiom has interesting consequences. For him thought and extension are the basic ways in which human beings think of the universe and thought and extension are also attributes or infinite essences of the universe. Attributes are conceived through themselves and particular things are seen either as modes of thought or modes of extension. So there is a conceptual barrier between bodies and mental items. Because of this conceptual barrier the cognition of an idea cannot involve the cognition of any body and, also, the cognition of a body cannot involve the cognition of any idea. Thus, in accordance with the causal axiom it can be concluded that there can be no causal interaction between mental and bodily items; Descartes's problem of interaction vanishes simply because there is no such interaction. It might seem, then, that for Spinoza mental items and physical items form two causally independent but parallel series. This would mean that Spinoza anticipated Leibniz's theory of pre-established harmony. But it should be noted that Spinoza, maybe more than any of his contemporaries, emphasized the close relation human beings have to their bodies. In fact, he included it as an axiom (E2a4) that we feel a certain body to be affected in many ways. But how can this be once there is no room for mind-body interaction? It has been suggested that in his apparent denial of mind-body interaction, Spinoza only claimed that mentality cannot be explained through physicality and vice versa. This means that for Spinoza causation is causal explanation. There are good general philosophical reasons for drawing a distinction between causation and causal explanation but it seems that there is not enough textual evidence for attributing such a distinction to Spinoza. Maybe a more plausible solution to this problem can be found from Spinoza's ingenious theory of the human mind. The human mind for him is an idea of the existing human body. So what happens in the body is perceived by the mind not through a causal process but through the nature of the human mind.

TEXTS

Oorzaak sijns zelfs ... van zig zelfs ... Eerste oorzaak (KV 1.1). Inblijvende ... uijtvloejende, daarstellende oorzaak (KV 1.2). Oorzaak door een toeval ... algemeene oorzaak (KV 1.3) Datter in de natuur geen zaak en is van de welke men niet kan vraagen, waarom datze is ... door welke oorzaak iets wezentlijk is ... Deze oorzaak dan moeten wij of in of buijten de zaak zoeken (KV 1.6). Onverbrekelijke ordre en gevolg van oorzaaken (KV 2.9). *Ab aliquo effectu causam colligere* (TIE f, G II, 10). *Res per primas suas causas cognoscere ... cogitatio vera quod causam non habet et per se et in se cognoscitur* (TIE 70, G II, 26). *Causa sui* (TIE 92, G II, 34). *Causa perfectiones effectus exellentius continere* (PPC 1ax7). *Formaliter vel eminenter in causa esse* (PPC 1ax8). *Non minor causa requiritur ad rem conservandum quam ad ipsum primum producendam* (PPC 1ax10). *Causam positivam sive rationem cur existat assignare debemus, eamque externam vel internam hoc est quam in natura et de definitione rei ipsius*

existentis comprehenditur (PPC 1ax11). *Causa primaria sive generalis ... particularis* (PPC 2p11s). *Causa immanens ... transiens* (Ep 73). *Naturae cujusque rei nihil aliud competit, quam id quod ex data ipsius causa necessario sequitur* (Ep 78). *Causa sui ... cujus essentia involvit existentiam* (E1def1). *Ex data causa determinata necessario sequitur effectus* (E1ax3). *Effectus cognitio a cognitione causae dependet* (E1ax4). *Quae res nihil inter se commune habent, earum una alterius causa esse non potest* (E1p3). *Qui veras rerum causas ignorant omnia confundunt* (E1p8s2). *Causa per se ... per accidens* (E1p16c2). *Causa prima* (E1p16c3). *Causa libera ... Causatum differt a sua causa praecise in eo quod a causa habet* (E1p17c2 and s). *Causa immanens ... transiens* (E1p18). *Causa proxima ... remota* (E1p28s). *Dei potentia omnium rerum causa* (E1p36). *Causas finales humana figmenta* (E1app). *Connexio et ordo causarum* (E2p7). *Causam adaequatam* (E3def1). *Causa finalis ... humanum appetitum* (E4praef). *Effectus potentia definitur potentia ipsius causae* (E5ax2).

BIBLIOGRAPHY
Primary Sources
Descartes, R., *Principia philosophiae, Meditationes.*
Burgersdijk, F., *Institutiones logicae.*

Secondary Literature
Bennett, J., *A Study of Spinoza's Ethics* (Cambridge: Cambridge University Press, 1984).
Curley, E., *Spinoza's Metaphysics, an Essay in Interpretation* (Cambridge, MA: Harvard University Press, 1969).
Gueroult, M., *Spinoza I. Dieu (Éthique I)* (Hildesheim: Olms, 1968).

Koistinen, O., *On the Metaphysics of Spinoza's Ethics* (Turku: Turku University Press, 1991).

Robinson, L., *Kommentar zu Spinozas Ethik* (Leipzig: Meiner, 1928).

O. Koistinen

Christus

In the *Tractatus theologico-politicus* Spinoza deals with the figure of Christ in chapters 1 ('on prophecy') and 4 ('on the divine law'). Besides, we find some disconnected remarks about Christ scattered across chapters 5, 7, 9, 12, 14 and 19. Moreover, Christology is commentated on in Spinoza's last letters to Henry Oldenburg. In the *Ethics* the name of Christ is mentioned once.

In the *Tractatus* Christ is set apart from the human figures of the prophets. In chapter 1 Spinoza argues that God's ordinances leading men to salvation were not indirectly revealed to Christ by words and visions, but directly. Therefore Christ's mind surpasses all other human minds, since it knows God directly and in an incorporeal manner. Unlike MOSES who as Scripture says communicated with God 'face to face as a man with his fellow', Christ knew God's mind directly with his own intellect and without the help of the senses. Hence, Spinoza observed that it may be said – in a figurative manner – that the wisdom of God acquired human nature in Christ. Here and in letter 73 Spinoza advances a spiritualistic and rationalistic reading of the dogma of incarnation and dissociates himself from the views of Christ professed by the orthodox churches, claiming that his conception of Christ is gathered from Scripture itself.

In chapter 4 Christ is distinguished from the prophets as well. 'And surely this fact, that God revealed himself to Christ, or to Christ's mind, directly and not through words and images as in the case of the prophets, can have only this meaning, that Christ perceived truly, or understood, what was revealed.' So Christ was not a prophet but should be 'called the mouthpiece of God'. The consequence is that unlike the prophets and Moses in particular Christ is a philosopher and no politician. If it is said that Christ like the prophets proclaimed the revealed truths as laws, Scripture did so because of the people's ignorance. But to Christ the knowledge of the mysteries of Heaven was granted. Hence his teaching took the form of eternal truths, not of laws. Moreover, Christ was sent to teach the whole human race, not only the Jews. So his doctrine had to be adapted to the beliefs and notions held in common by all mankind, and consists of adequate knowledge, its axioms being universally true.

In the *Tractatus* Christ is often set against Moses as a universal teacher; Moses being merely a prophet. Moses is a statesman and lawgiver; Christ is not a political figure or a lawgiver, but a moral teacher (TTP 7). Moses promises a material reward, Christ a spiritual reward (TTP 5). The former is sent to teach the Hebrew people, the latter the whole of mankind.

Spinoza's opposition of Christ to the prophets seems to be linked to a spiritualistic and rationalistic view of Christ as a uniquely inspired individual and was based on an allegorical reading of the biblical texts with respect to Christ. Such views of Christ, according to which he was just an exceptional man, were quite common in Socinian and Collegiant circles, and Spinoza commented favourably on Jelles's profession of faith written in 1673 which was sent to Spinoza (Ep 30). However, Jelles seems to have accepted the doctrine of Christ's resurrection in a literal sense (Spruit, 2004, pp. xlv–xlvi). Hence Jonathan Israel argues that Spinoza's favourable view of Christ might be explained by the need Spinoza felt to form a tactical alliance with these fringe Christians (Israel, 2006, pp. 121–2 and 2007, pp. xvii–xx).

In the last letters written to Oldenburg Spinoza defended a view of Christ totally devoid of dogma and 'mysteries'. He denied Christ's incarnation and resurrection taken in a literal sense and urged Oldenburg to conceive these dogmas in a symbolic sense. Moreover, he makes a distinction between knowing Christ according to the flesh and knowing Christ according to the spirit. The latter is required for salvation, the former is not. Knowing Christ according to the spirit is tantamount to the possession of divine wisdom. In this way Spinoza interprets the well-known verse from the Gospel of John: 'The Word has become flesh.' In the *Ethics* he reads the story of the Fall in a spiritual sense as well. Adam came to believe that he was equal to the animals, imitating their passions. Guarded by the spirit of Christ man regained his initial freedom. Hence, the notion of the spirit of Christ is associated with the notion of a free man and the spirit of Christ is identified with the idea of God.

TEXTS

Ad salutem non esse omnino necesse Christum secundum carnem noscere, sed de aeterno illo Dei filio, hoc est aeterna sapientia, qui se in omnibus et maxime in Christo Jesu manifestavit (Ep 73). Itaque Christi a mortuis resurrectionem revera spiritualem, et solis fidelibus ad eorum captum revelatam fuisse (Ep 75). Resurrectionem allegorice (Ep 78). Quare, si Moses cum Deo de facie *ad faciem, ut vir cum socio solet (hoc est mediantibus duobus corporibus) loquebatur, Christus quidem de mente ad mentem cum Deo communicavit (TTP 1, G III, 21). Et sane ex hoc, quod Deus Christo, sive ejus menti sese immediate revelaverit, & non ut Prophetis, per verba, & imagines, nihil aliud intelligere possumus, quam quod Christus res revelatas vere percepit, sive intellexit (TTP 4, G III, 64–5). Ut Christus fecit, qui tantum documenta universalia docuit et hac de causa Christus praemium spirituale non autem ut Moses corporeum promittit (TTP 5, G III, 70). Christus non tam actiones externas, quam animum corrigere voluit (TTP 7, G III, 103). Libertatem suam amittere, quam Patriarchae postea recuperaverunt, ducti Spiritu Christi, hoc est, Dei idea, a qua sola pendet, ut homo liber sit (E4p68s).*

BIBLIOGRAPHY

Primary Sources

Jelles, J., *Belydenisse des algemeenen en christelyken geloofs, vervattet in een brief aan N. N.* (Amsterdam, 1684; modern edn with Italian translation by L. Spruit, Macerata: Quodlibet, 2004).

Secondary Literature

Israel, J. (ed.), *Spinoza. Theological-Political Treatise* (Cambridge: Cambridge University Press, 2007).

Israel, J., *Enlightenment Contested* (Oxford: Oxford University Press, 2006).

Mason, A., *The God of Spinoza, a Philosophical Study* (Cambridge: Cambridge University Press, 1997).

Matheron, A., *Le Christ et le salut des ignorants chez Spinoza* (Paris: Aubier Montaigne, 1971).

P.C. Juffermans

Civis

In the third chapter of the *Tractatus politicus* the concept of citizen is defined. Spinoza called 'citizen' 'a man as far as he enjoys by the civil law all the advantages of a state'. In E4p37s2 Spinoza says that a society maintained by laws and having the power to defend itself is called a state (*civitas*) and those defended by its laws are termed citizens, who by obeying its laws are 'judged worthy of enjoying the advantages of the state'. Such definitions were common in the seventeenth century. Chauvin for example observed that a citizen is 'a free man living under a supreme authority in order to enjoy rights and safety', while Micraelius uses the phrase 'rights and advantages'. However, the author of this lexicon draws the attention of the reader to the particular meaning of the word 'citizen' in the Aristotelian tradition. For Aristotle defined a citizen as a 'free man partaking in elections and in political power'. Micraelius partly retained this notion by distinguishing between citizens who are 'subjects' and citizens who 'possess authority and are called magistrate'. However, Spinoza fully identified a citizen with a 'subject', being a man 'as far as he is bound to obey the ordinances or laws of the commonwealth', equating those concepts by means of *seu*. Moreover he observed that a citizen lives after his own mind only 'by the ordinances of the state'. He is not allowed to interpret these laws by himself. The 'supreme authorities' have rights which oblige the citizens always and without exception. In this identification of the citizen with the subject Spinoza follows Hobbes who called a citizen a person 'subjected to the laws ordained by the supreme authority' (*De cive* 5). However, according to Spinoza a blind subjection would transform a citizen into a mere slave. Although citizens have lost the freedom of the natural state, they are no slaves if the laws are designed with a view to obtaining the common good and their own benefit (TTP 16).

In his definitions Spinoza presupposes a well-ordered state giving citizens rights and freedom to optimize their life. This is why a government should take human nature seriously (E2p49s). Political order has its foundation in laws which protect the citizens and determine their rights. The rights of the citizen are the same as the natural rights of man, but this time guaranteed and determined by political power, on condition that the citizen subjects himself to this power. These laws are enacted by general consent. As far as possible, citizens should be treated as equals (TP 7.20). They have to be informed about politics. By keeping politics a secret affair a government gives citizens the impression that they are not free (7.29)

The connection between the rights of citizens and their duty to obey as subjects is most clear in the biblical Hebrew state, as described by Spinoza in chapter 17 of the *Tractatus theologico-politicus*. Citizens may be punished when they have broken the law, but punishment should be motivated by piety, not by indignation (E4p51s). A citizen or subject, who arrogates to himself political rights against the will of the political power can be put to death (TTP 16). Only if there are decisions made by political power to protect the citizen can a violation of his right by another citizen (not by political power!) be called unjust. Citizens cannot be granted the right to be judged in their own case without destroying political order (TP 3.3). Political power, not the citizen, is the source of what is just and unjust (3.5).

Nevertheless, despite this absolute right of political power, the citizen enjoys a kind of pseudo-rights. Political power always fears its citizens more than its foreign enemies, which makes their subjection less absolute (TTP 17; TP 6.6). As more people doubt the legitimacy of political power, the latter cannot enforce its will: the right of the state is determined by the power of the multitude (TP 3.9). Therefore, experience teaches that political power cannot exercise its absolute 'right' without jeopardizing itself. Expedience requires that the rulers restrict themselves and refrain from impairing the 'rights' of the citizen (TTP 20). However, the individual citizen as such is without rights when confronted with the power of the state, being the power of the multitude (TP 3.2).

Citizenship can take different active forms. Citizens can make a valuable contribution to political order by giving their opinion in a reasonable way (TTP 20). Citizenship may demand taking part in the army (TP 6.9–11; 7.17), which guarantees the freedom of the people (TP 7.22). Rulers cannot suppress citizens unless they have their own army of foreigners who are paid and do not fight for the freedom of their own country. The citizen has an affectionate relationship (piety, which is more than love) with his fatherland, and hence with its rulers; he hates to be subjected to foreign powers. His loyalty shapes his sense of freedom (TTP 17). Hence, an army of citizens is more in line with a preference for peace, than an army of mercenaries. Such an army is not compatible with aristocracy (TP 8.9).

However, when dealing with the status of the citizen in the different regimes Spinoza returns to the classical concept of a 'restricted citizenship'. In a well-ordered monarchy there should be a council composed of citizens (TP 6.15). In an aristocracy the citizenry is composed of an upper class of the population, often the descendants of the original inhabitants; those excluded are as a rule a large number of 'foreigners' who came into a city or territory later than its original inhabitants (TP 8.12). In a democracy, the law determines who is a citizen and who is eligible for election in the supreme council (TP 11.2). Citizenship is limited to specific people, selected by criteria of age, sex, property, descent, social position, religion, and so on.

TEXTS

Injuria est, cum civis vel subditus ab alio aliquod damnum contra jus civile sive edictum summae potestatis pati cogitur ... in subditis sive civibus (TTP 16, G III, 196–7). *In hoc imperio singulare fuit, quo cives maxime retineri debuerunt, ne de defectione cogitarent et ne unquam desiderio tenerentur deferendae patriae nimirum ratio utilitatis ... cives nullibi majore jure sua possidebant, quam hujus imperii subditi* (TTP 17, G III, 215–16). *Cives levissimis de causis ad necem ducere, at omnes negabunt haec salvo sanae rationis judicio fieri posse* (TTP 20, G III, 240). *Qui ipsius juris defenduntur cives appellantur ... contra obedientia civi meritum ducitur* (E4p37s2). *Homines, quatenus ex jure civili omnibus civitatis commodis gaudeant, cives appellamus et subditos, quatenus civitatis institutis seu legibus parere tenentur* (TP 3.1). *Unusquisque civis, seu subditus tanto minus juris habet, quanto ipsa civitas ipso potentior est* (TP 3.2). *Nulla ratione posse concipi, quod unicuique civi ex civitatis instituto liceat ex suo ingenio vivere et consequenter hoc jus naturae cessat* (TP 3.3). *Unumquemque civem non sui, sed civitatis juris esse* (TP 3.5).

BIBLIOGRAPHY
Primary Sources
Hobbes, Th., *De cive, Leviathan.*

M. Terpstra

Cogitatio

Spinoza defines *cogitatio* ('thought' or 'the process of thinking') as 'whatever is in ourselves of which we are immediately conscious' (PPC 1def1). For Spinoza, as for Descartes (*Secundae responsiones*, AT VII, p. 160), 'thought' and 'thinking' are the most general terms for whatever is going on in the mind, as distinct from the body. Accordingly, 'thinking' figures as one of two attributes that characterize substance. 'Thought' and 'thinking' can be qualified in various ways. 'Intellect, joy and imagination' are 'affections of thought' (CM 1.1). *Entia rationis* are 'modifications of thought' (CM 1.5; cf. 2.7; Ep 12). Passions are *modi* of thinking (E2ax 3). However, there is a twofold ambiguity. First, the word 'thought' (*cogitatio*) is not only the act of thinking, but also its contents (the act of conceiving a circle as well as the circle itself in so far as it is thought). Thus 'there should be a fundament for directing our thoughts' (TIE 105), where 'thought' signifies the process of thinking; but 'the right method of invention is to form thoughts on the basis of some given definition' (TIE 94), where 'thought' means a particular idea. Second, in his early works especially Spinoza sees 'thinking' as a specific activity of the intellect forming true thoughts: 'what constitutes the form of a true thought, must be sought in the very act of thinking and be deduced from the nature of the intellect' (TIE 71). It belongs 'to the nature of a thinking being to form true, that is, adequate, thoughts' (TIE 73; cf. 106). The idea behind this is that thinking is an act of the divine intellect (E2p5), whose object is God himself (E1p30; E2p3) and which cannot think something without causing it to be (E1p32c2).

TEXTS

Oneijndige uijtgebreidheid en denking (KV 1.2). *Quare forma verae cogitationis in eadem ipsa cogitatione sine relatione ad alias debet esse sita; nec objectum tanquam causam agnoscit, sed ab ipsa intellectus potentia et natura pendere debet* (TIE 71, G II, 26–7). *Quod si de natura entis cogitantis sit, ut prima fronte videtur, cogitationes veras sive adaequatas formare* (TIE 73, G II, 28). *Quare recta inveniendi via est ex data aliqua definitione cogitationes formare* (TIE 94, G II, 34). *Methodus est ipsa cognitio reflexiva, hoc fundamentum quod nostras cogitationes dirigere debet* (TIE 105, G II, 38). *Cogitationis nomine complector omne id, quod in nobis est et cujus immediate sunt conscii sumus. Ita omnes voluntatis, intellectus, imaginationis, et sensuum operationes sunt cogitationes. Sed addidi immediate ad excludendam ea, quae ex iis consequuntur ut motus voluntarius* (PPC 1def1). *Cogitationis affectationes videlicet intellectus, laetitia, imaginatio* (CM 1.1). *Cogitationes vel determinantur a rebus extra mentem, vel a sola mente* (CM 2.12). *Cogitatio ... in suo genere, hoc est in certo genere entis perfectae esse possunt* (Ep 36). *Cogitatio alia cogitatione terminatur. At corpus non terminatur cogitatione* (E1def2). *Cogitatio attributum Dei est sive Deus est res cogitans* (E2p1). *Cogitationis conceptus ... ne in picturas incidat* (E2p48s). *Qui ad naturam cogitationis attendit, quae extensionis conceptus minime involvit atque in re alicujus imagine, neque in verbis consistere* (E2p49s).

BIBLIOGRAPHY
Primary Sources
Descartes, R. *Secundae Responsiones,*
  Principia philosophiae.

Secondary Literature
Verbeek, Th., *Spinoza's Theologico-Political Treatise. Exploring 'the Will of God'* (Aldershot: Ashgate, 2002).

Th. Verbeek

Cognitio

Although Spinoza like Descartes never directly defined knowledge, he provides an indication as to its meaning by his famous classification to be found from his earliest works onwards. However, he did not adopt the Cartesian approach which tended to ascertain absolutely certain principles by means of systematic doubt. Moreover, Spinoza does not classify ideas according to their origin, whether in the mind itself or in the external world, and in his works there is no equivalent of the Cartesian doctrine of innate ideas.

Both in the *Tractatus de intellectus emendatione* and in the *Korte verhandeling*, Spinoza distinguishes four (respectively three) types of knowledge: indirect perception (from hearsay), vague experience (*waan*), inadequate knowledge of the essence of a thing (*geloof*), and adequate knowledge of an object through its essence only (*klaare kennisse*). In the *Ethics* Spinoza's analysis of human cognition was set in the context of the relations between the finite modes of the unique substance. The mind's knowledge is inadequate or of the first kind (empirical knowledge) when God has an idea not only insofar as he constitutes the essence of the mind, but when he simultaneously also has ideas of other things. It is adequate cognition or knowledge of the second and third kind

(rational cognition and intuitive science) when God has an idea insofar as he constitutes the essence of mind (E2p1cor1; E5p29 and E5p40cor).

In these three texts Spinoza's terminology and partition varies. However, apparently the notion of 'vague experience' is adopted from Francis Bacon's *Novum Organum* 1, aphorisms 70 and 82. In aphorism 70 Bacon deals with men who experience the world without method. Such men are 'wandering (*vagantur*) and straying'. In aphorism 82 he observed: 'There remains simple experience (*mera experientia*) which, if taken as it comes, is called accident; if sought for, experiment. But this kind of experience is no better than a broom without its band'. A likely candidate for the origin of the terms RATIO and *scientia intuitiva* is Descartes's distinction between *deductio* and *intuitus* in his *Regulae ad directionem ingenii* 3, a text Spinoza might have known in the 1659 Dutch Glazemaker version. Intuition Descartes definied as 'neither the fluctuating testimony of the senses ... but the conceptual act of the pure and attentive mind...which is simpler and more certain than deduction'. The older literature (Robinson for example) tended to trace Spinoza's typology of knowledge back to Plato.

Spinoza agreed with Peripatetic psychology that man's empirical knowledge of the world depends on material bodies stirring sense organs. Perceptual knowledge characterizes man as the finite mind of a finite body, involved in an infinite network of things continuously affecting one another. This knowledge is confused and inadequate, however, because in the ideas we thus form of the bodies no distinction can be made between the true nature of the bodies and that of the sense organs. The idea of any mode in which the human body is affected by external bodies must involve the nature of the human body and at the same time the nature of the external body (E2p16; for a discussion of the neuro-physiological presuppositions of this view, see Gueroult, 1974, pp. 204–7). Empirical knowledge is principally mediated, in the sense that the mind perceives external things only insofar as they affect our body. All perceptual knowledge is based on the ideas which the mind forms of these affections (E2p22 and 26). These ideas make external bodies known to us, for the affections are caused by external bodies, and therefore they also involve the nature of these bodies. Spinoza subscribed to the principle that there is nothing in the effect that was not first in the cause. Hence, the knowledge of an effect involves the knowledge of the cause (E1ax4).

In inadequate or perceptual knowledge the mind may be seen as a sort of monitoring device, such that mental processes are just the reflection of physical processes, governed by the laws of nature as expressed in the attributes. The ideas of affections thus generated provide only inadequate knowledge of the material world surrounding us. Sensation is a bodily phenomenon; it is a prerogative of animal and human bodies, and results from the superior organization of these bodies. Perception, on the other hand, is a mental fact: simultaneously as the body is affected by an excitation the mind creates an image or idea of this excitation. The simultaneity of these two states is explained by the identity of the mental and bodily substance. The mind is always what the body is, and a well-formed soul necessarily corresponds to a well-organized brain (E3p2s). Bodily sensations are at first confused and uncertain; to these confused modifications of the imperfect organism correspond confused and inadequate ideas of the imagination, the source of prejudice, illusion and error. This makes us believe in general ideas existing independently of individuals, in final causes presiding over the creation of things, in incorporeal spirits, in a divinity with human form and human passions, in a free will and other idols (E2p36; E2p40s; E2p48; E3p2s).

Although the issue of the isomorphism between functionally described mental states and physiologically described states of the body finds no solution (Cook, 1990, pp. 81–97), Spinoza's metaphysical approach to empirical knowledge circumvented some of the classical puzzles of mind and body that had tantalized Peripatetics and Descartes alike. The mental and the physical are properties of the same underlying reality, the substance, which in itself is neither mental nor physical. Perceptual ideas do not originate from the interaction between mind and sensory representations, nor are they generated on the basis of innate dispositions. Rather, they are modes of cogitation giving a partial, fragmentary or personal representation of events occurring in the attribute of extension.

The mind starts to generate knowledge of the second kind when it recognizes common notions, which arise when we are affected by a feature that we share with an external body (E2p39). Sensation or imagination represents things as they are in relation to us (E2p18: the hoofprints in the sand are interpreted differently by a soldier and a farmer). Reason conceives them from the standpoint of the whole in which they are produced and in their relation to the universe. The imagination makes man the centre of the world, and what is human the measure of all things. By contrast, reason rises beyond the self; it contemplates the universal and eternal, and refers all things to God (E2p32: all ideas are true in so far as they are referred to God). Furthermore, reason rejects the notion of contingency, and conceives the concatenation of things as necessary. The idea of contingency, like so many other inadequate ideas, is a product of the imagination, and is entertained by such as are ignorant of the real causes and the necessary connection of facts. The imagination loses itself in the details of phenomena, while reason grasps their unity. Finally, reason rejects, as products of the imagination, final causes and universals considered as realities.

Common notions arise when the mind subsumes individual entities under general principles (E2p44c2dem; cf. TTP 14, *in fine*). Reason organizes the world in a system of common notions and properties of things, but it does not grasp what each individual and nature essentially are. A next stage is reached when the mind is able to discover that the common notions are due to the attribute. In intuitive science or knowledge of the third kind, the mind explains things through the attribute, not through 'perceived' characteristics. Now, human knowledge is founded upon the knowledge of the eternal and infinite essence of God (E2p40s2). Man may arrive at intuitive knowledge because God generates in the attribute of cogitation essences which include his idea as well as the capabilities to express this idea on its own. Insofar as it is an eternal essence, that is, insofar as it is the idea of the eternal essence of the body, the human mind is part of the infinite intellect of God. To the extent that God constitutes the essence of the mind, the mind perceives or knows whenever God has an idea. Intuitive ideas constitute the mind's immortality (E5p33) and ground the intellectual love of God (E5p36).

TEXTS

Waan, geloof en klaare kennisse. ... Waan dan noemen wij die omdat ze de dooling onderwurpen is en nooijt plaats heeft in iets daar wij zeker van sijn, maar daar van gissen en meijnen gesprooken word. Geloof dan noemen wij de tweede, om dat die dingen die wij alleen door de rede vatten, van ons niet en worden gezien, maar <sijn> alleen aan ons bekend door overtuijginge in 't verstand dat het soo en niet anders moet zijn. Maar klaare kennisse noemen wij dat 't welk niet en is door overtuijginge van reden maar door een gevoelen en genieten van de zaak zelve, en gaat de andere verre te boven (KV 2.2). *Possunt omnes ad quatuor reduci. I. Est perceptio, quam ex auditu, aut ex aliquo signo quod vocant ad placitum habemus. II. Est perceptio, quam habemus ex experientia vaga, hoc est ab experientia, quae non determinatur ab intellectu, sed tantum ita dicitur, quia casu sic occurrit ... III. Est perceptio ubi essentia rei ex aliqua re concluditur, sed non adaequate; quod fit cum vel ab aliquo effectu causam colligimus, vel cum concluditur ab aliquo universali quod semper aliqua proprietas concomitatur. IV. Denique perceptio est ubi res percipitur per solam suam essentiam vel per cognitionem suae proximae causae* (TIE 19, G II, 10). *Nos multa percipere et notiones universales formare 1. ex singularibus, nobis per sensus mutilate, confuse et sine ordine ad intellectum repraesentatis et ideo talem perceptionem cognitionem ab experientia vaga vocare consuevi. II. Ex signis ex. gr. ex eo quod auditis, aut lectis quibusdam verbis rerum recordemur et earum quasdam ideas formemus similes iis, per quas res imaginamur. Utrumque hunc res contemplandi modum cognitionem primi generis vocabo. III. Denique ex eo, quod notiones communes, rerumque proprietatum ideas, adaequatas habemus atque hanc rationem et secundi generis cognitionem vocabo. Praeter haec duo cognitionis genera datur aliud tertium quod scientiam intituitivam vocabimus.*

Atque hoc cognoscendi genus procedit ab adequata idea essentiae formalis quorumdam Dei attributorum ad adaequatam cognitionem essentiae rerum (E2p40s2).

BIBLIOGRAPHY
Primary Sources
Descartes, R., *Regulae ad directionem ingenii.*
Bacon, F., *Novum Organum.*

Secondary Literature
Cook, J.Th., 'Spinoza's Science of the *Idea of the Body*', in J.-C. Smith (ed.), *Historical Foundations of Cognitive Science* (Dordrecht: Kluwer, 1990), pp. 81–97.
Ellsipen, Ch., 'Die Erkenntnisarten', in M. Hampe and R. Schnepf (eds), *Baruch de Spinoza. Ethik* (Berlin: Akademie-Verlag, 2006), pp. 133–50.
Giancotti-Boscherini, E., 'Sul concetto spinoziano di *mens*', in G. Crapulli et al. (eds), *Ricerche lessicali su opere di Descartes e Spinoza* (Rome: Ateneo, 1969), pp. 119–84.
Gueroult, M., *Spinoza. II. L'âme (Éthique II)* (Hildesheim: Olms, 1974).
Robinson, L., *Kommentar zu Spinozas Ethik* (Leipzig: Meiner, 1928).
Steinberg, D., 'Knowledge in Spinoza's *Ethics*', in O. Koistinen (ed.), *The Cambridge Companion to Spinoza's Ethics* (Cambridge: Cambridge University Press, 2009), pp. 140–66.
Wilson, M.D., 'Spinoza's Theory of Knowledge', in Don Garrett (ed.), *The Cambridge Companion to Spinoza* (Cambridge: Cambridge University Press, 1996), pp. 89–141.

L. Spruit

Conatus

Conatus is not a new theoretical concept that suddenly appears for the first time in *Ethics* part 3. The notion – originally used, along with APPETITUS, to translate the Stoic *ormè* – had also been used in a specifically war-related context to describe the conflict between forces (Caesar, Livy, Cicero). Machiavelli (*virtù*), and later Spinoza (FORTITUDO) belong to this polemological heritage. Spinoza actually introduces the notion sometime between 1671 and 1675, after his reading of Hobbes's (physical) writings. But it is only on the basis of an ontology of power that Spinoza's *conatus* will assume, in the *Ethics* and the *Tractatus politicus*, its original signification. 'Each thing as far as it can by its own power strives to persevere in its own being' (E3p6). And there is no real distinction between a thing and its tendency to preserve itself (*conatus*). The 'thing' is the complex and determined singularity, constituted by a number of individual things that, as they 'concur in one action…are all simultaneously the *cause* of one effect' (E2def7). Through *conatus*, it is possible to consider the *duration* of the process of *determination* from an ontological perspective. In this sense, each thing contains, *quantum in se est*, the cause or the immanent reason of its effort or striving. As a precise and determined expression of divine power (POTENTIA), *conatus* is a mode of being that is also 'a' being's mode of being or its tendency to persevere 'in its being'.

In the theory of *conatus* we find once again the notions of perseverance and of *quantum in se est* that one could already find in Descartes's *Principia philosophia* II, art. 37. In the *Cogitata metaphysica* 1.6 it was in fact the principle of inertia that served as its model. Thus, the theory of *conatus* of *Ethics* 3 is the point where the physics of individual bodies from *Ethics* 2 and the metaphysics of power from *Ethics* 1 meet. The striving of perseverance should therefore be conceived as a consistent, insistent and resistant dynamic affirmation. The *existent* thing is the power in act of a cause. It is first and foremost the cause that prevents two contrary things from coinciding, since such a coincidence would destroy it. Everything is held, by 'natural right' (another name for *conatus*), 'not to be its own enemy and not to kill itself' (TP 4.4). This is the 'prudence' (*sane cautio*) proper to each thing, inherent in its own 'striving' which is, in itself and as a continuous determination, without object or end.

While aiming at or intending no end and without using any means, this striving is, in act, in and through its effects, the actively strategic power of affirmation and resistance of a thing to everything that might hinder its indefinite perseverance. It is its *mathematical* (and, for this reason, non-teleological) and *effective* truth. This second aspect (with reference to Machiavelli's *verità effettuale*) is justified by and through the practice of *appetitus*, of affirmation and resistance immanent in relations of force. In this way, the striving of perseverance (a thing's *conatus*, its regime of existence, of causality and/or its strategy) is always as perfect as it can be with regard to the affections it is capable of, in and through the affirmation of the determination that constitutes it. The problem, both ethical and political, is thus to arrive at the affirmation *omnino absolutum* of the singular right-power (*potentia*) that is the individual *conatus*.

TEXTS
Per conatum ad motum non intelligimus aliquam cogitationem, sed tantum, quod pars materiae ita est sita, et ad motum incitata, ut

revera esset aliquo itura, si a nulla causa impeditur (PPC 3def3). *Illi conatum rei a re ipsa distinguunt* (CM 1.6). *Conatus, quo unaquaeque res in suo esse perseverare conatur, nihil est praeter ipsius rei actualem essentiam* (E3p7). *Hic conatus cum ad mentem solam refertur, voluntas appellatur; sed cum ad mentem et corpus simul refertur, vocatur appetitus, qui proinde nihil aliud est, quam ipsa hominis essentia, ex cuius natura ea, quae ipsius conservationi inserviunt, necessario sequuntur; atque adeo homo ad eadem agendum determinatus est* (E3p9s). *Mentis conatus seu potentia ad agendum* (E3p28). *Hominis agendi potentia vel conatus, quo homo in suo esse perseverare conatur* (E3p37). *Conatus sese conservandi primum et unicum virtutis est fundamentum* (E4p22c). *Omnes nostri conatus, seu cupiditates ex necessitate nostrae naturae ita sequuntur, ut vel per ipsam naturam, tanquam per proximam suam causam possint intelligi* (E4app1). *Summus mentis conatus, summaque virtus est res intelligere tertio cognitionis genere* (E5p25). *Conatus omnibus hominibus inest, sive ignari sive sapientes sint* (TP 3.18).

BIBLIOGRAPHY
Primary Sources
Descartes, R., *Principia philosophiae.*
Hobbes, Th., *De motu, De corpore, Leviathan* (Latinus).

Secondary Literature
Bove, L., 'De la prudence des corps. Du physique au politique', in Spinoza, *Traité politique* (Paris: Le Livre de Poche, 2002), pp. 9–101.
———, 'Éthique III', in P. Moreau and Ch. Ramond (eds), *Lectures de Spinoza* (Paris: Ellipses, 2007), pp. 109–31.

Matheron, A., *Individu et communauté chez Spinoza* (Paris: Éditions de Minuit, 1969).

Macherey, P., *Introduction à l'Éthique de Spinoza. La troisième partie. La vie affective* (Paris: Presses Universitaires de France, 1995).

Rousset, B., 'Éléments et hypothèses pour une analyse des rédactions successives de *Éthique IV*', *Cahiers Spinoza* no. 5, (1985) pp. 129–45.

———, 'Histoire d'un météore. Le *conatus* selon ses diverses dimensions', in *Geulincx, entre Descartes et Spinoza* (Paris: Vrin, 1999), pp. 189–99.

L. Bove

Conceptus

Although Spinoza never defines the term *conceptus* and the corresponding verb *concipi*, he provides various indications as to its meaning. Thus an idea is a 'concept of the mind' (E2def3; cf. E2p48s2; E2p49s) – 'concept' instead of 'perception' (the term used by Descartes, *Passions de l'âme*, art. 17) because 'perception' suggests passivity whereas 'concept' presupposes an act of the mind. A true concept of a thing allows us to deduce 'all its properties in so far as it is considered in itself, apart from its relations to other things' (TIE 96; cf. Ep 9). A concept is 'the coherence between a subject and a predicate in the mind' and so contains the reason why something is predicated of something (TIE 62). No concept must ever be abstract or general (TIE, note h; 55; note x; 75; cf. E2p49s). It is an 'objective essence' (TIE 36), that is, a real and particular thing represented in thought. Any concept must be based on, or deduced from, that of 'the origin of being' (TIE 76), so is part of a conceptual network, which ideally represents the whole of reality. However, there are also numerous cases in which Spinoza uses concept unspecifically, like, for example, when he claims that the adequate concept of a finite thing does not imply an existential judgement (TP 2.2; cf. E2p24; E4p37s2; TTP 16, G III, 189–91), where given Spinoza's own premises *concept* can only mean 'class concept'. Indeed, a truly adequate concept of a finite thing would imply its very existence (TIE 55; 69).

TEXTS

Ut nullus detur conceptus, id est idea, sive cohaerentia subjecti et praedicati in mente (TIE 62, G II, 24). *Deceptio ex eo oritur, quod res nimis abstracte concipiunt* (TIE 75, G III, 28). *Talis requiritur conceptus rei, sive definitio, ut omnes proprietates rei, dum sola, non autem cum aliis conjuncta, spectatur* (TIE 96, G II, 35). *Quod petis an ex solo extensionis conceptu rerum varietas a priori possit demonstrari ... id impossibile esse* (Ep 83). *Certum est, omnia in natura sunt, Dei conceptum pro ratione suae essentiae suaeque perfectionis involvere et exprimere* (TTP 4, G III, 60). *Philosophi ex claris conceptibus res conantur intelligere* (TTP 6, G III, 88). *Per ideam intelligo mentis conceptus ... Dico potis conceptum quam perceptionem, quia perceptionis nomen indicare videtur Mentem ab objecto pati. At conceptus actionem mentis exprimere videtur* (E2def3). *Distinguant inter ideam, sive Mentis conceptum et inter rerum imaginationes* (E2p49s).

BIBLIOGRAPHY

Primary Sources
Descartes, R., *Passions de l'âme*.

Th. Verbeek

Conscientia

Conscientia occurs fifteen times in Spinoza's Latin writings. The Dutch equivalents are *conscientie* and *medegeweten*, used in respectively *Korte verhandeling* 2.6 and 2.1. Two appear in the Cartesian phrase *conscientia morsus*, meaning 'remorse' (E3p18s2 and E4p47s, cf. PA 3.177). The rest of the occurrences can be divided into two categories (as can uses of the related verb *conscire* and adjective *conscius*): (1) awareness of the mind itself (TIE 47, TTP 1, and Ep 58); and (2) awareness of particular ideas *within* the mind and their affects (E3p9s, E3p30, and E3p59aff). In this second category, consciousness of internal ideas of actions or appetites is often contrasted to ignorance of their external causes (E1app, E2p35s, E3p2s2, andE3P59aff).

In letter 58 Spinoza equates consciousness with reason and experience and the consciousness of a particular mind will mirror its body's functional complexity (E5p39s). Nadler (2008) is right to say that the differences between consciousness that Spinoza attributes to humans and for example stones is accounted for in terms of a high level of such complexity and that this theory is less problematic than those that explain Spinoza's theory of consciousness in terms of reflexive ideas alone. Apparently Descartes introduced the second meaning of *conscientia*, not recorded in seventeenth-century dictionaries, into philosophical discourse, identifying it with cogitation and perception in *Responsiones tertiae*: 'cognitive acts, such as understanding, willing, imagining, sensing, and so on. All these are united by having in common the essential principle of thought, that is perception, or consciousness'. Moreover, he observed: 'the word 'cogitation' includes all that is in us in such a way that we are immediately conscious

of it' (*Responsiones secundae*). However, in Descartes a clear notion of the reflexivity of consciousness is still absent. Is is a basic feature of several Cartesian epistemologies. Van Velthuijsen, for example, in *De initiis primae philosophiae* 1, called it a requirement of all cognition and sensing.

TEXTS

Medegeweten van de kennisse onzes zelfs (KV 2.1). Van onse goede conscientia zelve gestadig geleerd en vermaand worden (KV 2.6). *Ille profecto aut contra conscientiam loquetur* (TIE 47, G II 18). *Quis enim, ait, nisi propriae contradicendo conscientiae, negaret ... Ego sane, ne meae conscientiae, hoc est, ne rationi, & experientiae contradicam, & ne praejudicia, & ignorantiam foveam, nego, me ulla absoluta cogitandi potentia cogitare posse, quod vellem, & quod non vellem scribere. Sed ipsius conscientiam appello, qui sine dubio expertus est, se in somnis non habere potestatem cogitandi, quod vellet & quod non vellet scribere; nec cum somniat se velle scribere* (Ep 58). *Nisi forte aliquis intelligere, vel potius somniare velit, Prophetas corpus ... adeoque eorum sensationes, & conscientiam alterius prorsus naturae, quam nostrae sunt, fuisse* (TTP 1, G III, 16). *Cupiditas ad homines plerumque referatur, quatenus sui appetitus sunt conscii, & propterea sic definiri potest, nempe, Cupiditas est appetitus cum eiusdem conscientia* (E3p9s). *Ex modo dictis intelligimus, quid sit spes, metus, securitas, desperatio, gaudium, & conscientiae morsus* (E3p18s2). *Cum autem homo sui sit conscius per affectiones ... Laetitia cum conscientia sui* (E3p30dem); E3p59aff. *Conscientiae morsus est Tristitia, concomitante idea rei praeteritae, quae praeter Spem evenit* (E3aff17). *Conscientiae morsus animi impotentis sunt signa* (E4p47s).

BIBLIOGRAPHY
Primary Sources
Descartes, R., *Responsiones secundae et tertiae.*
Velthuijsen, L. van, *De initiis primae philosophiae*, in *Opera omnia* (Rotterdam, 1680), pp. 851–954.

Secondary Literature
Nadler, S., 'Spinoza and Consciousness', *Mind*, no. 117 (2008), pp. 575–92.

T. Nyden

Corpus

Both in his commentary on the Cartesian *Principia* and in the *Ethics* Spinoza dealt with the concept of body. The latter presentation, the so-called 'Physical Interlude' which follows E2p13, in all less than five pages in the version of the *Opera posthuma*, contains Spinoza's most extended and detailed discussion of views on the nature of bodies and their principles of distinction and individuation, but is in fact only an introduction to his treatment of the human body.

However, although Spinoza started his incomplete career as a physical theorist by expounding the basics of Cartesian physics, it is obvious that he did not simply accept the Cartesian view of the body as a mere extended thing. In letter 81 he categorically rejects the Cartesian concept of extension as inert mass. Furthermore, in the Physical Interlude he neither defines a body or physical individual as an extended thing (as he had done in PPC 1def7) nor as a piece of matter which is transferred (PPC 2def8). According to the Dutch philosopher, a body is an extremely dynamic, complex individual, the parts of which can be separated and replaced and become greater or smaller, the direction and speed of their motions may vary and the body may be at rest or move in any direction. Nonetheless, the body preserves its nature as long as the ratio of motion and rest among its parts is preserved.

In the Physical Interlude Spinoza divides bodies according to their increasing complexity, starting with the simplest bodies. These corpuscles, however, are not real indivisible bodies or atoms. On the contrary, they are double abstractions (E1p15s and Ep 12), abstractions from external bodies which necessarily surround them, since there is no vacuum, and abstractions from the internal bodies by which they are necessarily composed since all bodies are complex.

According to Spinoza the human body is not an exception amongst bodies. In opposition to the Aristotelian tradition, he does not divide bodies into lifeless and living bodies with a soul, life being the mere force of things to persevere in their existence (CM 2.6). In fact, Spinoza writes that the human body is a model for all bodies, 'which are all animate albeit in different degrees' (E2p13s). Contrary to many seventeenth-century 'mechanical philosophers', he does not conceive the human body through the analogy of a machine since 'the very structure of the human body far surpasses in ingenuity all the constructions of human skill' (E3p2s). Hence, body and mind are only modally distinct and are basically one and the same thing (E2p21s). They are, however, distinct modes belonging to different attributes of Nature each of which should be understood through itself (E1p10). Nonetheless, the self-declared aim of the Physical Interlude is to explain how minds differ and to that end Spinoza will deal with the body because the body is the object of the mind.

Like all knowledge, knowledge of bodies starts with the human body affected by other bodies. Simultaneously with these affections, the mind acquires ideas of these bodies, which, however, represent the human body much more than external bodies. Based on ideas of common aspects of bodies, Spinoza comes to the adequate knowledge of a body in itself. However, in order to understand more completely what a body is, Spinoza explains in letter 12 that this mode should be defined in terms of an eternal essence. Accordingly, Spinoza defines the body as 'a mode which expresses in a definite and determinate way God's essence insofar as he is considered an extended thing' (E2def1). As a consequence, nature as a whole is not a body since it is the absolutely infinite totality.

TEXTS

In spatio imaginario sive ubi nulla dantur corpora (TIE 57, G II, 21). *Substantia quae est subjectum immediatum extensionis et accidentium quae extensionem praesupponunt, ut figurae, situs, motus localis etc. vocatur corpus* (PPC 1def7). *Ultra sensiles qualitates nihil remanet in corpore praeter extensionem et ejus affectiones* (PPC 2ax7). *Quamvis durities, pondus et reliquae sensiles qualitates a corpore aliquo separantur integra remanebut nihilominus natura corporis* (PPC 2p2). *Corpora quae aequale spatium occupant, puta aurum et aer, aeque multum materiae sive substantiae corporeae habent* (PPC 2p4c). *Corpora in fluida et consistentia, ac in visibilia et invisibilia ... ratione et calculo corpora in infinitum dividimus* (Ep 6). *Insaniunt qui substantiam extensam ex partibus sive corporibus ab invicem realiter distinctis*

conflatam esse putant (Ep 12). *Ex extensione ut eam Cartesius concipit molem sc. quiescentem corporum existentiam demonstrare omnino impossibile est* (Ep 81). *Corpus dicitur finitum, quia aliud semper majus concipimus* (E1def2). *Per corpus intelligimus quamcumque quantitam, longam, latam et profundam certa aliqua figura terminatam* (E1p15s). *Per corpus intelligo modum qui Dei essentiam quatenus ut res extensa consideratur certo et determinato modo exprimit* (E2def1). *Omnia corpora vel moventur vel queiescunt* (E2ax1 after p13). *Corpore ratione motus et quietatis, celeritatis et tarditatis et non ratione substantiae ab invicem distinguuntur* (E2lem1 after p13). *Corpora simplicissima* (E2lem6 after p13).

BIBLIOGRAPHY
Primary Sources
Descartes, R., *Principia philosophiae.*

Secondary Literature
Deleuze, G., *Spinoza, philosophie pratique* (Paris: Éditions de Minuit, 2003).
Della Rocca, M., *Representation and the Mind-Body Problem in Spinoza* (Oxford: Oxford University Press, 1996).
Gueroult, M., *Spinoza II. L'âme* (Paris: Aubier, 1974).
Jonas, H., 'Spinoza and the Theory of Organism', *Journal of the History of Philosophy*, no. 3 (1965), pp. 43–57.
Klever, W., 'Moles in Motu', *Studia Spinozana*, no. 4 (1988), pp. 165–93.

F. Buyse

Definitio, *see* Ordo geometricus

Democratia

The *Tractatus politicus* (2.17) defines democracy or a democratic regime (*democraticum*, sometimes *populare imperium*) as a political order in which society is governed by a council of men gathered from the populace as a whole. Spinoza believes democracy to be the most original regime, but it often degenerates into an aristocracy, and into a monarchy later on (TP 8.12), a view shared by the brothers De la Court and Pufendorf in his influential natural law treatise *De jure naturae et gentium* (1673). Government by the multitude is an absolute and perfect regime, which combines rule and unanimity (TP 8.3). Hence, Spinoza did not share the verdict of tradition. In 1653 Micraelius for example could still define a democracy as 'a form of a state which deviates from the pure polity'. Those adult males, who were born in the homeland from parents who are citizens, are eligible. The constitution may restrict those eligible for election, but this selection cannot be done by the supreme council as happens in an aristocratic regime (TP 8.1). In a democracy, the election of those who will take political responsibility is not based on arbitrary will but on the law (TP 11.2). As the case may be, democracy can take different forms. The form Spinoza had in mind excludes from election those who are loyal to another country, dependent on others (women, employees, children), indecent, or who have violated the law (TP 11.3). Spinoza wrote a special paragraph to refute the opinion that women can take part in political life on the same footing as men (11.4).

Whereas Spinoza was unable to complete the sections on democracy in the *Tractatus Politicus*, the political part of the *Tractatus theologico-politicus* is devoted exclusively to democracy. Chapter 16 presents a definition by referring to the fact that men hand over their power to society as a whole. Every man will be subjected completely to the rule of society as a whole, which becomes the supreme power, acquiring the unrestricted right to do what it is capable of. This subjection, however, does not mean slavery. In democracy, the supreme power will only continue to exist if it promotes the common interest and thus prevents revolt or overthrow. Similar thoughts are expressed in chapter 5 of the *Tractatus politicus*. It is unlikely that in a gathering of many people unreasonable decisions will be taken. The goal of a democracy is to secure a harmonious and peaceful social life. Although Spinoza does not enter into details concerning this regime, the political order he has in mind is a free one. Citizens have to conform to the decisions of the supreme council, because they are part of its deliberations. In this sense, this regime stays close to the natural condition of man, i.e. freedom. Because the general foundation of political order is the transfer of power to government, and therefore is synonymous with obedience, it makes a difference whether one obeys one person or a small group, or the people as a whole.

In chapter 20 of the TTP, democracy, in which all citizens or a majority of the people rule, is called a free republic. What may be possible in a theocracy or monarchy is not likely any more in democracy: preventing people speaking what they think. Freedom means that political power is accepted because it only interferes with men's deeds, not with their words. Democracy is a regime in which it is very unlikely that political power is challenged. People decide in majority and keep their right to criticize or even change decisions taken.

Following Machiavelli (*Discorsi*, 1.4.5), Spinoza admits that freedom implies conflict, but that this is not necessarily in contradiction to living in unanimity and harmony. If one wants to avoid discord, one has to give up freedom and give power to one man (TP 6.4). Nevertheless, Spinoza concedes that conflicts can get out of hand. If the people cannot handle their internal conflict, or are involved in an external conflict (war), it might be imperative that a king is chosen. Democracy fares well in peace (TP 7.5). In chapter 18 of the TTP, Spinoza notes that during the time Israel was a democracy, there were hardly any civil wars.

TEXTS

Talis vero societatis jus democratia vocatur, quae proinde definitur coetus universus hominum qui collegialiter summum jus ad omnia, quae potest, habet. Ex quo sequitur summum potestatem nulla lege teneri, sed omnes ad omnia ei parere debere (TTP 16, G III, 193). *Si haec cura ad concilium pertineat, quod ex communi multitudine componitur, tum imperium democratia appellatur* (TP 2.17).

BIBLIOGRAPHY

Primary Sources
V.H. [i.e. Jan de la Court], *Consideratien en exempelen van Staat* (Amsterdam, 1660).
Machiavelli, N., *Discorsi sopra la prima deca di Tito Livio* (Florence, 1519).
Pufendorf, S., *De lege naturae et gentium* (Amsterdam, 1672).

Secondary Literature
Matheron, A., 'La fonction théoretique de la démocratie chez Spinoza', *Studia Spinozana*, no. 1 (1985), pp. 259–73.

M. Terpstra

Denominatio

Denomination and its Dutch counterpart *benaming* is a scholastic term denoting the semantic relationship between a word, be it spoken, written or thought, and the object signified. Spinoza infrequently used the term in all his non-political writings and in accordance with medieval tradition he distinguished between an intrinsic and an extrinsic denomination, which is also called 'absolute' and 'relative' denomination. The latter kind is, Spinoza observed, used 'rhetorically' (CM 1.6), disqualifying the arguments based on it (CM 2.2), and denotes the circumstances of things or their relations, while the first kind is related to the 'inmost essence of things' (TIE 101). Being modes of thought, referring to an observer, 'good', 'perfect' and 'beautiful' are external denominations of things (Ep 54).

Although Spinoza never defined denomination, he is in line with tradition in presupposing an ontological difference between an intrinsic form and an external form attributed to a thing (*forma adjacens*). On this difference of forms the semantic distinction is based. To the intrinsic form belong a thing's essence and the intrinsic, that is inherent, accidents, for example if we call snow white, a man black, and a fire hot or if we denominate Spinoza 'learned' on account of his learning, and to the external form belong the circumstances, the activities and passions, for example calling a table 'seen', food 'tasted', a jingling bell 'heard', a hand 'left', and Spinoza 'honoured' (Micraelius). Both by 'seen', 'heard', 'tasted' and 'honoured' a thing is named on account of something external: the seeing, hearing, tasting, honouring people (Chauvin). Scholastic authors dealt with the ontological nature of this external form. According to some this external form was a real entity, according to others, however, it was a mere conceptual being. Like Descartes, who in *Meditationes* 6 underlined the fact that an extrinsic denomination is created by thought, Spinoza belonged to this last group.

TEXTS

Al wat de menschen aan God buijten deze twee eijgenschappen meer toeschrijven dat zal moeten zijn oft' een uijtwendige benaming (KV 1.2). *Cognitionem veram a falsa non tantum per denominationem extrinsecam, sed maxime per intrinsecam distingui* (TIE 69, G II, 26). *Nihil aliud praeter denominationes extrinsecas, relationes, aut ad summum circumstantias, quae omnia longe absunt ab intime essentia rerum* (TIE 101, G II, 36). *De his [affectionibus] quasdam hic explicare, et a denominationibus quae nullius entis sunt affectionibus separare conabur* (CM 1.3). *Verum et falsum ... non nisi rerum denominationes extrinsecas esse* (CM 1.6). *Argumenta a relationibus aut denominationibus extrinsecis petita* (CM 2.2). *Perfectio atque imperfectio sunt denominationes, quae non multum a denominationibus pulchritudinis et deformitatis differunt* (Ep 54). *Per ideam adaequatam intelligo ideam, quae quatenus in se sine relatione ad objectum consideratur, omnes verae ideae proprietates sive denominationes intrinsecas habet* (E2def4). *Idea ... quandoquidem per solam denominationem extrinsecam distinguuntur* (E2p48s). *Affectuum unusquisque variis nominibus appellari solet propter varias eorum relationes et denominationes extrinsecas* (E3aff48exp).

BIBLIOGRAPHY
Primary Sources
Descartes, R., *Meditationes*.

H. Krop

Determinatio

In Spinoza's works the verb 'determine' – its Dutch equivalents *noodzaken* (necessitate), *bepalen* (qualify) and *veroorzaken* (cause) reflect its divergent meanings – and the adjective 'determinate' occur much more frequently than the noun, 'determination', which in the correspondence and the *Ethics* is rare (used only four times). In accordance with seventeenth-century usage Spinoza made use of 'determination' and its Dutch counterpart *bepaling* in several interconnected ways.

In logic and semantics 'determination' meant the restriction or qualification of a concept indicating in what sense a sentence is true or false, for example 'Rome was not the seat of the emperor, that is the Byzantine' (Chauvin). Hence, 'determine' might mean to specify, for example general concepts, which in themselves are indeterminate with respect to time and place, are transformed into more particular notions referring to individual beings (Goclenius). The process of determination means a limitation by acquiring a more specific form but is also a kind of privation or negation (cf. Ep 50). Due to such determination by nature and thought a thing – or a concept and definition – is well established and concrete (cf. Spinoza's 'in a certain determinate manner' and Descartes's 'determinate nature' in his definition of motion in *Principia* 2.25 or the determination of a body's space in PP 2.20).

In physics determination denotes the action which causes an indeterminate cause to act in a certain specific way. The cause that effects such determination may be of an efficient, formal, material or final kind. Such causal determination compels a thing to act. God, being the First Cause of nature – in a physical sense at least – determines the acts of all natural things. However, 'the Jesuits' – and the Arminians – 'tended to exclude from this universal determination of God the secondary causes, which their own nature would determine to act', Chauvin says. The third kind of determination acknowledged by Chauvin is the moral determination of a free and intelligent being, whose will is determined to act by the ordering, persuading and advising intellect. Apart from this last kind of determination, Spinoza adopted the logical and causal meanings of 'determination'.

If infinite quantity is determined either in duration or extension, this kind of determinate quantity is a being of reason, which is useful in practical matters but lacks a solid metaphysical basis. For Spinoza, both duration and extension are infinite quantities, which generates paradoxes if determinations of these are seen as giving information about the intrinsic nature of things (E1p15s). So when a determinate quantity is assigned to something, this gives nothing but relational information. Spinoza uses determination also as a causal concept: for example, when he speaks of things being determined to exist and to act by other things (E1p28) and when he denies that the mind can determine the body to motion or rest (E3p2). Determination as a causal concept is also at work when Spinoza considers the nature of geometrical entities. For example, the idea of a sphere can be determined by seeing it as evolving from the motion of a semicircle around its axis. Thus, there is room for several ways in which a geometrical object can be determined to exist. In Spinoza's doctrine of nature, individual things are actualizations of their essences and in accordance with the nature of the geometrical model these essences can prima facie be seen to be determined in

several ways. What lies at the core of Spinoza's necessitarianism is that there is a unique way in which this determination occurs. Spinoza speaks also of an intellect determining another intellect (E5p40s). This kind of talk makes sense in Spinoza's substance monism where all intellects are parts of the infinite intellect of God so that all intellects are embedded in this one intellect.

TEXTS
Isser noodzakelijk bepaling (KV 1.2). De bepaling van beweging (KV 2.19). *Determinatio motus corporis* (PPC 1p16). *Motus in se spectatus differt a sua determinatione* (PPC 1p19). *Determinatio unius corporis aequalem vim requirat ut mutetur, quam motus* (PPC 1p26c). *Determinatio ad rem juxta suum esse non pertinet ... Quia ergo figura non aliud quam determinatio et determinatio negatio est* (Ep 50). *Appetitum et corporis determinationem simul esse natura* (E3p2s). *Determinatio voluntatis secundum Cartesius* (E5praef).

BIBLIOGRAPHY
Primary Sources
Descartes, R., *Principia philosophiae.*

Secondary Literature
Bennett, J., *A Study of Spinoza's Ethics* (Cambridge: Cambridge University Press, 1984).
Gueroult, M., *Spinoza I. Dieu (Éthique I)* (Hildesheim: Olms, 1968).
Robinson, L., *Kommentar zu Spinozas Ethik* (Leipzig: Meiner, 1928).

O. Koistinen

Deus, Intellectus and Voluntas Dei

The God of Spinoza is the unique substance, the nature of which is constituted by an infinity of attributes each perfect in its own kind (E1def6). Spinoza's God shares with tradition only the notion of perfection. Chauvin for example defined God as 'a Being of the highest and infinite perfection'. As *causa sui* God is a NATURA NATURANS producing necessarily a NATURA NATURATA, i.e. 'all the modes of God's attributes', or infinitely many things in infinitely many ways (E1p29s; E1p16). Accordingly, there is what one could call a radical 'ontological difference' between God, the substance, and the universe as a whole ('all the modes of God's attributes'). This means that, although God cannot not produce the universe (*natura naturata*), neither the universe nor its parts belong to God's absolute nature (*natura naturans*); only attributes belong to it. The opposite is true as well, both with respect to the whole of the modes, and with respect to particular modes. Although human beings are necessarily produced by God, although they are *in* God, and although they depend on God with respect to their essence as well as their existence (E1p25), yet God 'does not pertain to their essence', because he is the substance, different in nature and existence from his modes (E2p10s).

From each attribute of God a modification follows which is eternal and infinite (E1p21); and from this follows a second one, which also exists necessarily and is infinite (E1p22). Scholars call these the infinite immediate and the infinite mediate modification respectively. In the *Ethica* Spinoza gives as an example of the first one, under the attribute COGITATIO: the idea of God (E1p21dem; E2p2). Asked by a correspondent for 'examples of those things immediately produced by God, and of those

things produced by the mediation of some immediate modification' (Ep 63), Spinoza answers 'the examples you ask for of the first kind are: in the case of thought, absolutely infinite intellect; in the case of extension, motion and rest. An example of the second kind is the face of the whole [physical] universe, which, although varying in infinite ways, yet remains always the same' (Ep 64). (For a discussion of what could be the infinite mediate mode of cogitation, see Gueroult I, 1968, pp. 316–19, and Beyssade.)

An IDEA (*adequata*) and intellect stand for the same thing (E2p48 and s). Consequently, it is clear that an idea of God or an infinite intellect constitute the infinite immediate mode under the attribute of cogitation. This means that the infinite intellect (of God) or the idea of God do not belong to *natura naturans* but to *natura naturata*. The infinite intellect, which is of course an *active* intellect (E1p31s), is a product, an infinite mode of substance as having some attribute, in this case cogitation. The *Korte verhandeling* expresses the same idea thus: the infinite intellect is not God, but only 'the Son of God' and 'an immediate creature of God' (KV 1.9 and 2.22 n.1). Since intellect and will cannot be really distinguished (E2p48), the infinite will is the same as the infinite intellect, and thus it too is only an infinite mode which does not properly speaking belong to God's absolute nature. This is why Spinoza says explicitly that '[t]he actual intellect, whether infinite or finite, like will...must be referred to *Natura naturata*, not to *Natura naturans*' (E1p31). As an (infinite) effect of God, the (infinite) will cannot be called free (E1p32 and c1). Intellect and will are related to God's nature in the same way as 'motion and rest', i.e., as an infinite immediate mode completely dependent on the divine substance as *causa sui* (E1p31c2).

Some commentators keep ascribing intellect and will to God's proper nature on the basis of E1p17s. An attentive reading of this scholium shows however that here Spinoza is discussing the common view on God's intellect and (free) will, a view he considers false, and with the absurd consequence that divine understanding and human understanding differ *toto coelo*. If this were the case, humans could never arrive at any adequate understanding. (For a proper interpretation of E1p17s, see Koyré; Gueroult, 1968, pp. 272–94 and 562–3; De Dijn, 1996, p. 209.)

The infinite intellect is the infinite mode or whole which contains as parts all the eternal essences of the finite modes of cogitation, including the eternal modes of all human intellects (E2p8c; E5p40c and s). That the infinite intellect does not belong to God's essence (*natura naturans*), but is an effect of the *causa sui*, and that our intellect is part of the whole formed by the infinite intellect – these are the metaphysical conditions of the possibility of adequate understanding in human beings (E2p11c). This means that the doctrine of the relation between God as cogitation and the infinite intellect is crucial for Spinoza's theory of knowledge.

Since self-consciousness (*idea ideae*) and affect presuppose thinking (an idea) (E2p21s; E2ax2), neither self-consciousness nor any emotion like love or glory can be ascribed to God's essence properly speaking. However, this is precisely what Spinoza seems to be doing in proposition 35 and 36 of *Ethics* 5, in violation of its proposition 17 corollary, where he says that 'God is...not affected with any affect of joy or sadness'. It should be observed that even where Spinoza speaks of God loving himself and man (as in E5p35 and 36 with c and s), there is always a reference to the idea of God. God's love for men and men's love of God are one and the same

(E5p36c and s), just as God's intellect and man's intellect are one and the same. This does not mean that the ontological difference between *natura naturans* and *natura naturata* is suddenly eliminated. Both self-consciousness and affect presuppose the production of the idea of God, the infinite mode. God loves himself and men only insofar as he produces first his 'Son'. The proper interpretation of passages seemingly denying the ontological difference should be consistent with the passages of *Ethics* 1 affirming this difference, and with the interpretation of those passages where God as cogitation is said 'to have ideas', e.g. in E1p21dem. This cannot be interpreted as meaning that idea belongs to God's nature properly speaking, because these passages are precisely intended to prove the existence of an infinite *mode* essentially different from the divine attribute. When I have ideas, it can be said that 'God has ideas' (E2p11c), because God is the ultimate cause of everything. But this cannot possibly mean that my mind, or I as having an idea, belong to *natura naturans* (E2p10s). God's cogitation having or forming ideas, finite or infinite, always implies the 'prior' production of an infinite modification, the idea of God or infinite intellect, which as *natura naturata* is ontologically different from *natura naturans* (cogitation).

The expression 'God's having [or forming] an idea' cannot then have the same meaning as 'the human mind has an idea' or 'God's intellect contains or has an idea'. In the case of God, to have an idea means to produce an 'ontologically different' effect in which some object can be (re)presented, i.e. a mode of thought, in which of course God expresses himself. In the case of my mind or of the infinite intellect, to have an idea refers to the relation of part-whole, a relation between modes of cogitation.

God as *natura naturans* (cogitation) is characterized neither by intellect nor by will. According to common (Jewish-Christian) thinking, these characteristics define God's proper nature, and constitute the ground for calling God a person. There is no doubt that Spinoza rejects this notion of a personal God completely (E1p17s and E1app).

There is a certain discrepancy between the infinite immediate mode of thought and the infinite immediate modes of the other attributes. Whereas an infinite immediate mode like 'motion and rest' simply contains the principles of the whole of all existing bodies (according to letter 64 this whole is called the *facies totius universi*), the infinite immediate mode of thought contains the whole of *all* eternal modes of thought, not only the ideas of bodies, but also the ideas of any modes of any attribute. Whereas the *potentia agendi* of the divine substance works itself out via all attributes, the *potentia cogitandi*, through which God thinks everything or infinitely many things in infinitely many ways, works itself out via only one attribute, i.e. cogitation (E2p7c; see also E1p16 and dem). This discrepancy is not a breach of the 'parallelism'; rather, it is a requirement of the special nature of thought in combination with the intelligibility of everything (Gueroult, 1974, pp. 72–84).

TEXTS

God is een wezen van de welke alles ofte oneijndelijke eigenschappen gezeijd worden, van welke eijgenschappen een ijder des zelfs in sijn geslagte oneijndelijk volmaakt is ... eijgenschap van God denking en uijtgebreidheid (KV 1.2). *Deniqe exempla, quae petis, primi generis sunt in cogitatione, intellectus absolute infinitus; in extensione autem motus et quies; secundi autem. Facies totius universi,* *quae quamvis infinitis modis variet, manet semper eadem* (Ep 64). *Per Deum intelligo ens absolute infinitum, hoc est substantiam constantem infinitis attributis, quorum unumquodque aeternum, et infinitam essentiam exprimit* (E1def6). *Quicquid est, in Deo est, et nihil sine Deo esse, neque concipi potest* (E1p15). *Ad Dei naturam neque intellectum neque voluntatem pertinere* (E1p17c2); E1p29s. *His Dei naturam, ejusque proprietates explicui, ut quod necessario existit, quod sit aeternus, quod ex sola naturae necessitate sit et agat, quod sit omnium rerum causa libera et quomodo; quod omnia in Deo sint, ab ipso ita pendeant ut sine ipso nec esse, nec concipi possint et denique quod omnia a Deo fuerint praedeterminata non quidem ex libertate voluntatis, sed ex absoluta Dei natura, sive infinita potentia* (E1app). *Mentem humanam partem esse infiniti intellectus Dei* (E2p11c). *Deum seu naturam* (E4praef). *Deus proprie loquendo neminem amat neque odio habet* (E5p17c). *Deus se ipsum Amore intellectuali infinito amat* (E5p35). E5p36.

BIBLIOGRAPHY
Secondary Literature

Beyssade, J.-M., 'Sur le mode infini médiat dans l'attribut de la Pensée. Du problème (lettre 64) à une solution (*Ethique* V, 36)', *Revue Philosophique de la France et de l'Etranger,* no. 130 (1994), pp. 23–6.

De Dijn, H., *Spinoza. The Way to Wisdom* (West Lafayette, IN: Purdue University Press, 1996).

Gueroult, M., *Spinoza I. Dieu (Ethique, I)* (Paris: Aubier-Montaigne, 1968).

Gueroult, M., *Spinoza II. L'Âme (Ethique, II)* (Paris: Aubier-Montaigne, 1974).

Koyré, A., 'Le Chien, constellation céleste, et le chien, animal aboyant', *Revue de métaphysique et de morale,* no. 55 (1950), pp. 50–9.

H. de Dijn

Distinctio

The traditional doctrine of the kinds of (metaphysical) distinction is mentioned by Spinoza only in the *Korte verhandeling* and the *Ethics.* He deals with it in *Cogitata metaphysica* 2.5. Like Descartes in the *Regulae,* he contemptuously dismissed 'scholasticism's craving for shallow distinctions'. In rule 14 the French philosopher had observed already that 'scholars often use too far-fetched distinctions, which extinguish the natural light of the intellect'. In the *Cogitata metaphysica* Spinoza closely reproduced the Cartesian partition of the distinction, developed in the *Principia philosophiae* I, art. 60–2, into a real, modal and rational kind. Such a classification clearly simplified the elaborate scholastic theories. A real distinction, both Descartes and Spinoza felt, distinguishes 'two substances from one another, whether of different or of the same attribute; as, for example, thought and extension or the parts of matter'. (Spinoza added the phrase about attribute to the Cartesian text, since according to Descartes a substance basically possesses only one attribute). A real distinction can be identified if of two things one 'can be conceived without the help of the other' and 'consequently may so exist' (cf. *Responsiones secundae* ax. 10). Spinoza, however, omits the conventional reference to the power of God, which according to Descartes made the two clauses of the definition 'may be conceived apart from each other' and 'exist separately' not equivalent. He observed that although mind and body are to be conceived distinctly, in man the substances of mind and body are by God's power so narrowly linked that in this universe they never exist apart. Yet they are *realiter* distinct, because by God's absolute power they might have existed separately. (Caterus in the *Responsiones primae* argued that Descartes here approches the Scotistic formal distinction between really distinct quiddities together constituting a single being, cf. Schmidt). In Spinoza the traditional distinction between God's absolute and ordained (*ordinata*) power, based on the difference between God's intellect and will and implying the notion of power which he *previously* had and another afterwards, makes of course no sense at all. Spinoza therefore added 'consequently'. However, according to Descartes a real distinction only applies to 'complete things' such as bodies, for although by abstraction motion and figure can be conceived separately, a body cannot exist without both motion and figure (*Responsiones primae,* AT VII, 121).

Secondly, the modal distinction, as Spinoza and Descartes observed, is of two kinds, 'that between a mode of substance and the substance itself, and that between two modes of one and the same substance. The latter we recognize from the fact that although either mode can be conceived without the help of the other' – Spinoza omits the Cartesian 'clearly' – 'neither can be conceived without the help of the substance of which they are modes'. The first distinction we recognize from the fact that 'although substance can be conceived without its modes, the mode cannot be conceived without the substance'. In his answer to Caterus in the passage of the *Responsiones* just referred to, Descartes identified the modal distinction with the Scotistic formal distinction, which assumed a firm basis of the distinction in reality, that is a *fundamentum in re.*

Finally, a rational distinction according to Spinoza denotes the 'distinction between a substance and its attribute, for example, as duration is distinguished from extension. And this distinction is also recognized from the fact that such a substance cannot be understood' (Descartes: we are unable to form a clear and distinct idea) 'without that attribute'. This rational distinction Descartes, in a letter to an unknown Jesuit, identified with the distinction of reasoned reason developed by Suarez. Its counterpart, the distinction of resoning reason, Descartes dismissed as worthless, since it lacked a basis in reality (*Epistolae* 116, AT IV, 349). Such a rational distinction is only of a verbal nature. Hence in axiom 2 of the *Korte verhandeling*'s appendix Spinoza merely listed two kinds of distinction: the real and the modal one.

With some small changes Spinoza merely reproduced the Cartesian doctrine of the kinds of distinction and consequently in the *Cogita metaphysica* he adopted the theory of Maimonides that the attributes of the one and unique God are only 'conceptually' distinct. However, Descartes's doctrine of distinction is closely related to his ontology. Hence, in the *Ethics* Spinoza had to adapt the application of his definitions. On the one hand a real distinction between the attributes of the substance – God – is granted, for the 'one is conceivable without the help of the other', but a real distinction, Spinoza now adds, does not necessarily imply a plurality of real beings or a diversity of substances. On the other hand a real distinction between the parts of matter is in opposition to Descartes denied (E1p10s and 15s, cf. Ep 8). As a result Spinoza no longer adhered to the classical principle of God's utmost 'simplicity' (E1app).

The difficulty of reconciling both a real distinction between the attributes with a non-Cartesian monism is dealt with by several scholars. According to Deleuze a real distinction in the *Ethics* does not imply a numerical distinction, because the plurality of really distinct attributes coincides with the numerically one substance. Apparently there is a parallel with the Scotistic formal distinction. On the other hand the definition of modal distinction is weakened and its difference from the real distinction is somewhat blurred by calling a mode a *res* (E1p29s), or a real being (E5p30). Here Spinoza is in opposition to scholastic tradition, which maintained that 'a mode taken as such is not in a proper sense a being or a thing' (Di Vona, 1988, p. 159). Hence in his mature works Spinoza adapted the Cartesio-scholastic doctrine of the kinds of difference to his new ontology.

TEXTS

Een wettige beschrijvinge bestaan moet van geslacht en onderscheid (KV 1.7). De dingen welke verscheiden zijn worden onderscheiden of dadelijk of toevallig (KV appax2). Van welke andere zaak men dit wezen niet en zal konnen dadelijk, maar alleen wijzenlijk (modaliter) onderscheiden (KV appp4). *Realis distinctio inter animam et corpus* (PPC 1prol). *Distinctionem rationis cum distinctione modali vel modali confundant* (CM 1.6). *In rerum natura nihil praeter substantias, et earum modos dari, unde triplex rerum distinctio deducitur, Art. 60. 61. et 62. realis scilicet, modalis et rationis. Realis vocatur illa, quae duae substantiae inter se distinguuntur, sive divers, sive ejusdem attributi ut ex. gr. cogitatio et extensio sive partes materiae. Haeque ex eo cognoscitur, quod utraque sine op alterius concipi et per consequens existere possit. Modalis duplex ostenditur, nimirum quae est inter modum substantiae et ipsam substantiam ac quae est inter duos modos unius ejusdemque substantiae. Atque hanc ex eo cognoscimus, quod quamvis uterque modus absque alterius concipitur, neuter tamen absque ope substantiae cujus sunt modi. Rationis denique ea esse dicitur, quae oritur inter substantiam et suum attributum, ut cum duratione ab extensione distinguitur .. omnes distinctiones qua inter Dei attributa facimus, non alias esse, quam rationis ... . Peripateticorum distinctionum farraginem non curamus* (CM 2.5). *Distinctiones in rebus non fingo* (CM 2.9). *Duae aut plures res distinctae vel ex diversitate earundem affectionum* (E1p4). *Duo attributa realiter distincta concipere, hoc est unum sine ope alterius ... ex signo diversitatem substantiarum diagnoscere* (E1p10s). *Rerum quae realiter ab invicem distinctae sunt una sine alia esse et in suo statu remanere potest* (E1p15s).

BIBLIOGRAPHY

Primary Sources
Descartes, R., *Regulae, Principia philosophiae, Meditationes.*

Secondary Literature
Deleuze, G., *Expressionism in Philosophy: Spinoza* (New York: Zone Books, 1990; original French edn 1968).
Di Vona, P., 'Il problema delle distinzioni nella filosofia di Spinoza', *Studia Spinoza,* no. 4 (1988), pp.147–64.
Donagan, A., 'Essence and the Distinction of Attributes in Spinoza's Metaphysics', in M. Greene (ed.), *Spinoza. A Collection of Critical Essays* (Notre Dame: Notre Dame University Press, 1979), pp. 164–81.
Schmidt, A., 'Substance, Monism and Identity-Theory in Spinoza', in O. Koistinen (ed.), *The Cambridge Companion to Spinoza's Ethics* (Cambridge: Cambridge University Press, 2010), pp. 79–97.

H. Krop

Duratio

With the exception of the political writings, 'duration' and its Dutch equivalent *during* are used in all Spinoza's works. The Latin word occurs, in particular, in the *Cogitata metaphysica,* letter 12 and the first parts of the *Ethics.* Spinoza usually contrasted duration with eternity and linked it with time, change, quantity, modes, existence and imaginary being.

In the earliest works Spinoza merely followed Descartes's deviation from (late) scholastic notions and clarified some of his ambiguities. In scholasticism, from Aquinas to Burgersdijk, duration had served as an overall notion that included eternity, endless time (*aevum,* which Descartes stopped using) and time. In the *Institutiones metaphysicae* 1.21 Burgersdijk for example defined the concept as 'a contuinity of existence' which as such is indivisible. Duration is either infinite or finite. If it is infinite it may be called eternal, if finite it is either permanently enduring and to be named endless – for example the heavens, which according to Aristotle are eternally moving – or temporal if the duration of a thing has both a beginning and an end.

In the first part of the *Principia philosophiae* Descartes implicitly made duration an attribute of finite substance by linking it to time ('the nature of time, that is of the duration of things', art. 21), divisibility (duration may be attributed to God, since even

God's duration can be divided into infinite parts. However, the nature of both God and thought is in itself indivisible: see *Entretien avec Burman*, AT 5, 148. Apparently 'duration' with respect to God and thought is in a certain sense metaphorically used.) and succession, for 'obviously we perceive succession in our thoughts' (letter 68, AT 5, 193). Duration, number and order denote only the modes by which we consider the enduring, numbered and ordered things. Since duration is only conceivable as the continuation of a thing's existence, it is only conceptually distinct from the thing itself. However, contrary to time and number both duration and existence remain unmodified in the existing and enduring things. Hence according to Descartes we have to call them attributes (*Principia philosophiae* 1.55–7). But Descartes's attempts to attribute duration to God and thought also tended to restrict the realist nature of duration.

In the *Cogitata metaphysica* Spinoza adopted these Cartesian notions by opposing being whose essence includes existence and which is therefore eternal, to being that has no such essence. In this manner Spinoza applied the Cartesian definition of God to eternity. Like Descartes he called duration an attribute of the last kind of being, denoting the perseverance of actual existence, its distinction from existence being merely a conceptual one. In CM 2.1, however, he erased the distinction between duration and time and called duration 'an affect of being', or (*sive*) a mode. This prepared the way for identifying eternity with substance and duration with created being. In letter 12 Spinoza also observed that the existence of modes is explained only by duration. Not attending to the 'order of nature' we are able to conceive the modes of things in abstraction from substance and attribute to them divisibility and

duration. So, duration tended to be only a being of reason, or rather a being of the imagination. However, at the end of the letter Spinoza sets duration once more apart from time, denying that duration is a series of instants – for that is 'as if to make number simply by adding up noughts' – and extension a series of distinct bodies. Unlike Descartes Spinoza stated that to God no duration is to be attributed (CM 2.10).

In the *Ethics* Spinoza continues to oppose duration to eternity, but like Burgersdijk he acknowledges the possiblity of duration without beginning and end. This change of mind is reflected in his definition of duration in *Ethics* 2: 'an indefinite continuation of existing', which is practically the same as Burgersdijk's. Duration is indefinite, Spinoza explained, for neither the nature nor the efficient cause of the thing determines it. Only God determines all duration (E1p24c). As such its nature possesses neither an internal limitation nor a defect (Jaquet, 1997) and hence the duration of being is substantially CONATUS. Along these lines Chauvin wrote: 'duration is the continuation of existence, or rather the perseverance of a thing's existence'.

TEXTS

Wat de ziele is en waar uijt hare verandering en geduuringe ontstaan ... na de duuringe en verandering van de zaake is, daar na dan ook de duringe en veranderinge van de ziele moet zijn (KV 2.23). Onse liefde tot God is ... onse eeuwigduurentheid (KV 2.24). *Assueti sumus durationem determinare ope alicujus mensurae motus* (TIE d, G II, 31). *Res non tam sub duratione, quam sub quadam specie aeternitatis percipit* (TIE 108, G II, 39). *Tempus inservit durationi explicandae* (CM 1.1). *Ex eo quod divisimus ens in ens, cujus essentia involvit existentiam et in ens cujus essentia non involvit nisi possibilem existentiam, oritur distinctio inter aeternitatem et durationem. ... Duratio vero est attributum sub quo rerum creatarum existentiam prout in sua actualitate perseverant concipimus. Ex quibus clare sequitur durationem a tota alicujus rei existentia non nisi ratione distingui (CM 1.4). Ante creationem nullum nos posse imaginari tempus neque durationem, sed haec cum rebus incepisse. ... Talis est natura durationis, ut semper major et minor data possit concipi (CM 2.10). Per durationem modorum existentiam explicare possumus ...clare constat nos modorum existentiam et durationem ... ad libitum concipere et in partes dividere posse; aeternitam et substantiam; quandoquidem non nisi infinitae concipi possunt, nihil eorum pati possunt, nisi simul eorum conceptum destruamus (Ep 12). Enti aeterno determinata duratio attribui nequit (Ep 35). Talis existentia, ut aeterna veritas, sicut rei essentia, concipitur, proptereaque per durationem aut tempus explicari non potest tametsi duratio principio et fine carere concipiatur (E1def8exp) Existentia sive duratio (E1p21). Duratio est indefinita existendi continuatio (E2def5). Nos de duratione rerum singularium nullum nisi admodum indaequatum cognitionem habere possumus (E2p31). Durationem hoc est existentiam quatenus abstracte concipitur et tanquam quaedam quantitatis species (E2p45s). In suo esse perseverare indefinita quaedam duratione (E3p9).*

BIBLIOGRAPHY
Primary Sources
Burgersdijk, F., *Institutiones metaphysicae*.
Descartes, R., *Principia philosophiae*.

Secondary Literature
Gueroult, M., *Spinoza I: Dieu* (Hildesheim: Olms, 1968). An English

version of appendix 9 in M. Greene (ed.), *Spinoza. A Collection of Critical Essays* (Notre Dame: University of Notre Dame Press, 1973), pp. 182–212.

Jaquet, Ch., 'La perfection de la durée', in *Durée, temps, éternité chez Spinoza, Études philosophiques*, no. 2 (1997), pp. 147–56.

Kopper, J., 'Einige Bemerkungen zur Ewigkeit und Dauer in Spinoza's Ethik', *Zeitschrift für philosophische Forschung*, no. 43 (1989), pp. 432–48.

Prelorentzos, Y., 'Le temps chez Descartes et chez Spinoza, du *Discours* aux *Pensées métaphysiques*' and 'Bibliographie', in *Durée, temps, éternité chez Spinoza, Études philosophiques* no. 2 (1997), pp. 157–70 and 249–61.

Robinson, L., *Kommentar zu Spinozas Ethik* (Leipzig: Meiner, 1928).

H. Krop

Electio

This term has both a theological and a political meaning. In the *Tractatus politicus* the word is used in its political sense and denotes the choice of public or law officers and members of the royal council made by the monarch, the multitude or any kind of assembly. In the *Tractatus theologico-politicus* election is used in the theological sense of the calling of the Jews or the gentiles and is a synonym of *vocatio* (calling); see for example Voetius's disputation on the calling of the gentiles in *Disputationes selectae* II, pp. 621–43 and Episcopius's *In primam epistolam ad Joannis* (*Opera theologica altera* I, pp. 193–4). (Spinoza uses *vocatio* as well when he deals with the calling of the apostles and prophets and as an equivalent of grace, referring to Romans 9.10ff. Here Paul according to Spinoza adapted himself to the limited understanding of the multitude.)

Spinoza primarily uses 'election' with respect to the divine election of the Hebrews in the Old Testament. According to Spinoza God's election is a political and not a religious fact. He did not elect the Jews for their virtue and truth but on account of their social order which for many years guaranteed safety and stability. The revelation of truth and good is a matter for all peoples (referring to Romans 3.9; 3.29; 4.15). Hence, divine election denotes the temporary phenomenon of political prosperity and was destined to cease when this came to an end. Hobbes in *Leviathan* 35 and 44 shared such a view and held that the kingdom of God exerted civil rule over the Jews, of whom God is absolute sovereign; with the election of Saul as their monarch, this state of affairs came to a close. According to La Peyrère in his *Systema* 2.1, however, God chose the Jews first out of his own goodness and not on account of their virtue. Their election did not last for some brief time, but was to last eternally. After the Israelites, and on their account, the other gentile nations were elected. Both elections are mystical rather than political. Mortera in his *Tratado*, p. XII maintains that the election of the Hebrews is eternal ('em todos os tempos'). According to Episcopius in *Apologia* II, pp. 205–6, however, the Scriptures consider their election to be *in tempore* and not *ab aeterno*.

TEXTS

Quaesivi propter quod Hebraei Dei electi fuerint (TTP praef, G III, 9). *Cum igitur Scriptura, ut Hebraeos ad obedientiam legis*

hortetur, dicit Deos eos pro caeteris nationibus sibi elegisse ... ad captum eorum tantum loquitur ... nam sane ipsi non minus beati fuissent, si Deus omnes aeque ad salutem vocavisset ... Pauli sententia de Judaeorum electione refertur (TTP 3, G III, 44–5 and 54); TTP 4, G III, 65. *Differentiam inter vocationis Apostolorum et Prophetarum* (TTP 11, G III, 154). *Electio consiliariorum* (TP 6.15–16). *Regis electio* (TP 7.25); TP 8.1; TP 11.1

BIBLIOGRAPHY

Primary Sources

Ben-Israel, Menasseh, *De resurrectione mortuorum libri III* (Amsterdam, 1636).

Episcopius, S., *Apologia* and *Lectiones sacrae in I Epistolam catholica Joannis*, in *Opera theologica altera* I (Amsterdam, 1665).

Hobbes, Th., *Leviathan*.

Mortera, S. L., *Tratado da verdade da lei de Moisés[...]* ed. H. P. Salomon (Coimbra: Por ordem da universidade, 1988).

[Peyrère, I. La], *Systema theologicum, ex praeadamitarum hypothesi*, in *Praeadamitae [...]* ([Amsterdam], 1655).

Voetius, G., *Selectarum Disputationum theologicarum pars prima-quinta*, 5 vols (Utrecht 1648–69).

Secondary Literature

Geller, J., 'Spinoza's Election of the Jews: The Problem of the Jewish Persistence', *Jewish Social and Studies*, no 12 (2005), pp. 39–63.

Verbeek, Th., *Spinoza's Theologico-Political Treatise. Exploring the 'Will of God'* (Aldershot: Ashgate, 2003).

R. Bordoli

Ens

Although in the *Cogitata metaphysica* Spinoza introduces his metaphysics by defining 'a being', it is obvious that he in no way continued the tradition of Duns Scotus, Suarez and finally Wolff, which took for granted the univocity of being and transformed the Aristotelian-Thomistic metaphysics of analogy into an ontology. In the mature works of Spinoza the concept *ens* plays only a very minor part.

The definition of the *Cogitata* 1.1, by calling being 'all that exists necessarily, or at least is able to exist', limited *ens* to the scholastic 'real being'. Here Spinoza followed Descartes, who in the *Epistola ad Voetium* (AT VIII2a, 60) had done the same by deriving *ens* from the verb 'to be' or 'to exist' and hence identified being with a being in the world outside the mind. Both philosophers ignored the distinction Heereboord, for example, made between on the one hand 'a being' as a noun meaning a 'being in its broader sense' and denoting all things which are not completely nothing, for example the objects of thought or imagination, and on the other hand 'being' as a participle of *esse* which has a more restricted sense and denotes the things which existed, exist or will exist.

Spinoza introduced a Cartesian vein into the definition of being by making 'being' dependent on its 'clear' and 'distinct' perception. Moreover, by identifying 'a being' with 'being as such' Spinoza turned the 'beings of reason' into mere modes of thought, nonbeings, since they are without any reality in the outside world. Consequently he rejected the doctrine of the transcendentals as well. A second consequence of the definition in CM 1.1 is the division of being into 'substantial and modal beings'. The first kind of beings is necessary, because their essence includes their existence, the second kind is only possible. In the *Ethics* 'being' is nearly always identified with the perfect being of substance that is the infinite being of God. Tradition called this meaning 'being in a strict sense' (Chauvin). 'Being' in the sense of modal being is rare in the *Ethics*, occurring only four times (E1p10s, E2p43s, 48s, 49s). By number alone 'being' primarily refers to 'infinite Being'. Apparently Spinoza returned to a metaphysics of analogy, in which the substance is a real being and the other things are only beings in an analogous sense.

TEXTS

Aan de natuur van een wezen dat oneijndige eigenschappen heeft, behoort een eigenschap, de welke is zijn...alvolmaakt wezen (KV 1.1). Wezen uijt of van zich zelfs bestaande...door zig zelfs zijnde (KV 1.7). Wezen van reeden...waar of dadelijk wezen (KV 2.1). *Cum existentia generaliter ac ens concipitur, tum facile applicatur omnibus quae simul in memoria occurrunt* (TIE x, G II, 21). *A rebus physicis, sive ab entibus realibus omnes nostra ideas deducamus* (TIE G II, 36). *Deus sive ens summe perfectum* (PPC 1ax6). *Incipiamus igitur ab ente per quod intelligo 'id omne quod cum clare et distincte percipitur, necessario existere, vel ad minimum posse existere reperimus'. Ex hoc definitione...sequitur quod 'chimaera', 'ens fictum', vel 'ens rationis' nullo modo ad entia revocari possint.... Ex entis definitione facile videre est, quod ens dividendum sit in ens, quod sua natura necessario existit, sive cujus essentia involvit existentia et in ens cujus essentia non involvit existentiam nisi possibilem. Hoc ultimum dividitur in substantiam et modum* (CM 1.1). *Ens verbale* (CM 1.3). *Hi termini ab omne fere metaphysicis pro generalissimis entis affectionibus habentur; dicunt enim omne ens esse unum, verum et bonum, quamvis nemo de iis cogitet* (CM 1.6). *Ens constans infinitis attributis* (Ep 2). *Quo plura attributa alicui enti tribuo, eo magis cogor, ipsi existentiam tribuere, hoc est magis sub ratione veri ipsum concipio* (Ep 9). *Ens rationis seu imaginationis* (Ep 12) *Breviter ostendam, quas proprietates ens necessariam includens existentiam habere debet* (Ep 35). *In suo genere, hoc est in certo genere entis* (Ep 36). *Ens quod semper extitit, existit et semper existet* (TTP 2, G III, 38). *Ens absolute infinitum* (E1def6). *Termini 'transcendentales' dicti suam duxerunt originem, ut ens, res, aliquid* (E2p40s1). *Entia metaphysica* (E2p48s). *Individua ad unum genus, quod generalisimum appellatur revocare, nempe ad notionem entis* (E4praef).

BIBLIOGRAPHY

Primary Sources
Descartes, R., *Epistola ad Voetium.*
Heereboord, A., *Meletemata.*

Secondary Literature
Di Vona, P., *Studi sull'ontologia di Spinoza parte 1* (Florence: La nuova Italia editrice, 1960).
Gueroult, M., *Spinoza II. L'Ame (Éthique II)* (Hildesheim: Georg Olms, 1974).
Rivaud, A., *Les notions d'essence et d'existence dans la philosophie de Spinoza* (Paris: Félix Alcan, 1906).
Robinson, L., *Kommentar zu Spinozas Ethik* (Leipzig: Meiner, 1928).
Schnepf, R., *Metaphysik im ersten Teil der Ethik Spinozas* (Würzburg: Königshausen and Neumann, 1996).

H. Krop

Ens rationis

Spinoza rejects the traditional ('Aristotelian') division of being into 'real being' (sticks and stones) and 'beings of reason' (that is, privations, relations, fictitious beings, possible worlds, etc). According to him – and other 'famous *philosophi*' (Chauvin) – all *beings of reason* 'cannot be counted among beings at all' (CM 1.1). They are not ideas, have no *ideatum* and cannot be true or false (CM 1.1; cf. 1.6; KV 2.16). As a result, they are not even conceived by God, except in so far as he conceives the human mind that constructs them (CM 2.7). So an *ens rationis* is 'nothing but a modification of thinking' (*modus cogitandi*), designed to facilitate reasoning and discourse. Typical examples are *time* (CM 1.4; cf. 1.10; E1p 21dem; Ep 12), *genus* and *species* (CM 1.1), *part* and *whole* (KV 1.2). Universals and class concepts are probably also amongst them. Accordingly, one would say that in scientific thinking they are indispensable. However, the particular class of *entia rationis* we call normative concepts, like good and evil, order and disorder, etc. (KV 1.6; 1.10), are so little scientific that Spinoza calls them *entia imaginationis* – beings of the imagination (E1app; cf. E4p37s2; Ep 12).

TEXTS

Dat hij de dadelijke wezens niet genoeg van de wezens van reden en onderscheid...een wijze van denken...zo en kan dan van haar niets veroorzaakt worden (KV 2.16). *Ens fictum et ens rationis nullo modo ad entia revocari possint. Ens denique rationis nihil est praeter modum cogitandi, qui inservit ad res intellectas facilius retinendas, explicandas atque imaginandas. Multi confundunt ens rationis cum ente ficto. Ens rationis nec a sola voluntate dependet* (CM 1.1). *Modus cogitandi sive ens rationis* (CM 1.4); CM 2.6. *Ens rationis seu imaginationis* (Ep 12). *Entibus rationis at non in realibus* (Ep 73). E1app; E2p49s.

BIBLIOGRAPHY
Secondary Literature
Verbeek, Th., *Spinoza's Theologico-Political Treatise. Exploring 'the Will of God'* (Aldershot: Ashgate, 2002).

Th. Verbeek

Error

The term 'error' is closely related to the terms 'falsity' and 'false'. In this entry, error is discussed insofar as it concerns the theory of the cause or origin of error. In this sense, it occurs several times in Spinoza's writings, while he dealt with his theory of error only in the second part of the *Ethics*. Philosophers have faced the problem of error ever since Plato. Roughly, erring was traditionally problematic because an erroneous judgement refers to a state of affairs that does not obtain, which is thus nothing and about which nothing can be said or thought. As a result, error seems to be impossible. Hence Spinoza had no systematic interest in the problem stated in this manner. It is more likely that he was forced to deal with it both because Descartes's explanation of error runs counter to his philosophy, so that he needed an alternative explanation, and because his naturalistic philosophy itself gives rise to the problem of error in a different way.

Spinoza's account of error starts in proposition 17 of *Ethics* 2. In this proposition, Spinoza deals with IMAGINATIO. The mind imagines when it regards bodies by means of ideas of corporeal images. As long as the mind has those imaginings, it considers the external bodies as present, and therefore also as existent, even though those objects need not actually exist. Only if another idea excludes the existence of those things, the judgement that those objects exist will be removed. Error is thus closely related to the imagination, which is the source of inadequate ideas (E2p41). Since Spinoza ascribes language to the imagination, the possible range of errors is endless (TIE 88, E2p47s). Spinoza insists, however, that the imagination as such does not amount to error, but only the imagination without concomitant adequate ideas excluding the existence of objects. Error consists, then, in a lack of (adequate) ideas, and is not something positive, that is to say some sort of being, but a privation of being. Hence in proposition 35 he relates error to the privation of knowledge and inadequate ideas, that is, fragmentary and confused ideas. Consequently, there is no real cause of error, and thus God is prevented from being its possible cause. The only way to correct error is by forming adequate ideas through reason.

Spinoza's theory of error is largely a response to Descartes. This is clear from the earliest letter of Spinoza as well as the introduction of Meyer to the PPC. Descartes states in the fourth meditation that error only arises when the will affirms or denies an idea that is not clear and distinct. Judgement is thereby attributed to the will, while Descartes says at the same time that the will is essentially free, and that that feature makes man responsible for his errors – simply because he could, and should, have refrained from making a judgement in the case of obscure ideas. This goes against the grain of Spinoza's metaphysics, in which there is no room for this type of freedom. The human will cannot be free, but is as determined as a stone to act or not to act (E2p48–9). But that also implies that Spinoza had to conceive a different theory of error.

TEXTS

Het eerste [geloof] is gemeenlyk dooling onderworpen (KV 2.1). *Nos licet ad libitum sine ullo erroris scrupulo ideas simplices formare* (TIE 72, G I, 31), TIE 88. *Si error quid positivum esset, solum Deum pro causa haberet* (PPC 1p15). *Veram causam erroris numquam assecuti sunt, Baco et Cartesius* (Ep 2). *Ostendisse id, quod formam mali, erroris, sceleris ponit, non in aliquo, quod essentiam exprimit, consistere, ideoque non dici posse, Deum ejus esse causam* (Ep 23). *Quid sit error indicare incipiam ... mentis imaginationes in se spectatas nihil erroris continere* (E2p17s). *Error in cognitionis privatione consistit* (E2p35s). *Errores in hoc solo consistunt, quod nomina rebus non recte applicamus* (E2p47s).

BIBLIOGRAPHY

Primary Sources
Descartes, R., *Meditationes* IV; *Principia* I, art. 29–44.

Secondary Literature
Bennett, J., 'Spinoza sur l'erreur', *Studia Spinozana*, no. 2 (1986), pp. 197–217.
Brochard, V., *De l'erreur* (Paris: Vrin, 1926).

M. Aalderink

Esse

Although Spinoza never dealt with the concept of being, he 'probably' would have accepted the traditional definition as 'the act of existing' (Di Vona, 1960, p. 178). The identification of both notions is of scholastic origin and dominated seventeenth-century dictionaries. Chauvin and Goclenius for example define: 'being is the same as an essence which is actual, or exists in act' and quote the Suarezian definition: 'being is commonly called the last, or rather the first actuality of a thing'. Heereboord observed that 'a being' (ENS) is a broader concept than that of 'being' (*esse*), because 'a being' as a noun does not imply the 'being' or the 'existing' of a thing. This noun denotes also a thing which might exist, or which is an object of fiction etc. and excludes only things which are completely nothing, for example 'a squared circle', due to the self-contradiction in their definition. On the other hand 'being' (*esse*) denotes a real being, i.e. a being existing in the reality outside the mind. Being is the act proper to it. This notion occurs in Spinoza and he frequently pointed to the identity between 'being' or 'entity' on the one hand, and 'reality' or 'perfection' on the other. Moreover, like Descartes Spinoza adopted the traditional notion of different degrees of being, reality and perfection, God being their ultimate source and cause.

Heereboord continues by observing that being is to be divided into 'being of esence' and 'being of existence'. The first kind of being is the act of being proper to a real being, since a real being may be conceived apart from existential being but not from being of essence. The Greek poet Homer for example is a real being, although he does not exist at this moment and so lacks being of existence. The same applies to a rose during wintertime. Heereboord concludes that real beings have to include things that were and that will be (*Meletemata* 1.48–9). Such 'hypothetical beings' are real beings, because as ideas in the divine mind they eternally exist. Therefore, 'the essences of things in God have both virtual, possible, ideal and willed being'. They are the objects of God's intellect, power and will. To these essences in God must be attributed an 'objective being' (*Meletemata* 2.37). Also in our senses or mind, the things by being sensed or known acquire 'an intentional or objective being' (Chauvin).

These scholastic notions Spinoza merely reproduced in *Cogitata metaphysica* 1.2. In the first part of *Ethics* 2 he applies these distinctions to the ideas of God, linking them with the Cartesian notion of the formal being of ideas developed in *Meditationes* 3 (cf. *Praefatio ad lectorem*). According to Descartes in the *Responsiones quartae* we may consider an idea both formally, that is produced by an operation of the intellect, and materially, that is as representing a thing in the outside world. In the propositions 5–8 of *Ethics* 2 Spinoza attempted to solve the metaphysical problem that vexed Heereboord earlier: how the factual non-existence of real being is possible. New in the *Ethics* is how Spinoza linked the concepts of *conatus* and being, and tranformed his ontology into a dynamic one.

TEXTS

Zo moet God formelijk zijn ... (on)eindelijk zijn ... uijtstekentlijk zijn (KV 1.1). Voorwerpelijk zijn ... voorwerpelijk, formelijk wezen (KV app). *Infinitum, hoc est, est omne esse praeter quod nullum datur esse* (TIE 76, G II, 29). *Eadem dicuntur esse formaliter in idearum objectis quando talia sunt in ipsis qualia percipimus. Et eminenter quando non quidem talia sunt, sed tanta, ut talium vicem supplere possint* (PPC 1def4). *Nempe dantur diversi gradus realitatis sive entitatis: nam substantia*

plus habet realitatis, quam accidens vel modus (PPC 1ax4). *Idea, quae objective continet esse* (PPC 1p4s). *Per perfectionem intelligo tantum realitem sive esse* (PPC 1p7lem). *Primum esse essentiae nihil aliud est quam modus ille quo res creatae in attributis Dei comprehenduntur: esse deinde ideae dicitur prout omnia objective in idea Dei continentur; esse porro potentiae dicitur tantum repectu potentiae Dei qua omnia nondum adhuc existentiae ex absoluta libertate voluntatis creare potuerat: esse denique existentiae est ipsa rerum essentia extra Deum et in se considerata tribuiturque rebus postquam a Deo creatae sunt. Ex quibus dare apparet haec quattuor non distingui inter se, nisi in rebus creatis* (CM 1.2). *Infinita perfectio, hoc est infinita essentia, seu infinitum esse* (CM 1.6). *Vis, per quam res in suo esse perseverat* (CM 2.6). *Quomodo res coeperint esse et quo nexu a prima causa dependeant* (Ep 6). *Perfectionem in toi esse et imperfectionem in privatione tou esse consistit* (Ep 36). *Quo plus realitatis aut esse unaquaeque res habet* (E1p9). *Quicquid est, in Deo est et nihil sine Deo esse neque concipi potest* (E1p15). *Causa essendi rerum* (E1p24c). *Esse formale idearum Deum quatenus tantum ut res cogitans consideratur pro causa agnoscit* (E2p5). *Esse formale rerum* (E2p6c). *Esse objective rerum sive ideae* (E2p8c). *Deum non tantum est causa rerum secundum fieri, ut ajunt, sed etiam secundum esse* (E2p10cs). *Unaquaeque res, quantum in se est, in suo esse perseverare conatur* (E3p6). *Alia plus realitatis, sive entitatis, quam alia habere comperimus* (E4praef).

BIBLIOGRAPHY

Primary Sources
Descartes, R., *Meditationes, Responsiones quartae*.
Heereboord, A., *Meletemata*.

Secondary Literature

Di Vona, P., *Studi sull'ontologia di Spinoza
 parte 1* (Florence: La nuova Italia editrice,
 1960).
Rivaud, A., *Les notions d'essence et
 d'existence dans la philosophie de
 Spinoza* (Paris: Alcan, 1906).
Robinson, L., *Kommentar zu Spinozas Ethik*
 (Leipzig: Meiner, 1928).
Rousset, B., *Spinoza, lecteur des objections
 faites aux Méditations de Descartes
 et ses réponses* (Paris: Éditions Kimé,
 1996).

H. Krop

Essentia

Spinoza's definition of essence in *Ethics* 2 is
complicated, running over more than three
lines. It says: 'to the essence of any thing
belongs that which, being given, the thing is
necessarily posited and which, being taken
away, the thing is necessarily taken away; or
that without which the thing can neither be
nor be conceived, and which can neither be
nor be conceived without the thing'. According to Gueroult (1974, pp. 27–8) its length
and deviations from tradition and Descartes
(cf. PPC 2ax2) are due to the fact that only in
part two, dealing with finite things, did it
become necessary to distinguish between
cause and essence, which by the Cartesian
phrase 'that without which the thing can neither be nor be conceived' are identified and
coincide in God. Moreover, God, being the
cause of both the existence and essence of
all things, would pertain to their essence
(E2p10s). Spinoza's definition also announces
the crucial notion of an individual
essence, which is made explicit in *Ethics* 2,
proposition 37.

According to scholasticism 'essence' consisted of two basic notions: the ontological
difference by which a thing is distinguished
from all other things, and the identity or
rather quiddity of a thing. 'An essence is all
that makes a thing be and is what it is' (Chauvin), or 'an essence constitutes a thing with
forbearence of all its accidents' (Goclenius).
An essence, Chauvin observed in a Cartesian
vein, is 'the attribute' of a thing, which
'always and exclusively belongs to all things
identical with it'. For, according to tradition,
an essence is common to all individuals
belonging to one and the same species. Moreover, as such an essence is not real and does
not actually exist. So, we call nature 'the
internal principle, which perfects the essence
and makes it a complete thing' (Goclenius).
Spinoza obviously adopted the notion that
an essence constitutes a thing, but qualified
the scholastic notions by completely identifying essence and nature. By depriving the species of its ontological nature he created the
concept of an individual essence. The possibility of such an individual essence was
acknowledged earlier by Duns Scotus who
called it the *haeceitas* (thisness), but in
doing so he was an exception in scholastic
thought.

Spinoza also introduced an epistemological feature in the definition of essence.
According to Descartes 'being', 'substance',
'duration' 'truth' and 'essence' are primitive
notions. Difficult to define, they belong to all
we can perceive (letters to Elisabeth and
Clerselier, AT III, 665, 691 and V, 355). In the
Principia 1.53 Descartes stated that a substance's principal property, i.e. its attribute,
constitutes its nature or essence. However, he
gave these notions a logical twist by creating
a conceptual order conceived analogously to
the ontological order. 'Shape is unintelligible
except in an extended thing...and imagination

sensation and will are intelligible only in a thinking thing'. Hence, as implied in the story of the wax, the object of clear and distinct knowledge is only the nature or essence of things (*Meditationes* 2, see also PP 1.46).

In his early works Spinoza adopted these Cartesian hints and developed 'a logically organized system of essences forming knowledge' (Balz, 1918, p. 35). In the *Tractatus de intellectus emendatione* he introduces the Cartesian distinction between a formal and an objective essence. The last essence is an idea, as far as it is clearly and distinctly conceived. Having such an essence in the mind we are certain and in the possession of truth (TIE 35). Perfect knowledge requires the perfect perception of the 'adequate essence of a thing' – in the case of God (TIE 92) – or their proximate cause, and in the perfect definition of a thing we account for its 'intimate essence'. The essences determine the intellect and their knowledge checks the imagination. If the imagination is checked error will be impossible (TIE 58). However, perfect knowledge of the finite things requires that we know the essences in relation to other essences. The better we know the particular essences of the individual things, the more perfect is our knowledge (TIE 98, cf. Hegel's notion of concrete versus abstract knowledge). These essences exist in a fixed and eternal sequence (TIE 100).

The formal essence is an essence in itself, but it exists independently of the things. It is uncreated, although unlike God, it does not exist of itself (CM 1.2) and exists objectively – and eternally – in God's intellect (E1p17s). The sequence of formal essences corresponds with the eternal sequence of essences in God.

Apparently, in the *Ethics* Spinoza returned to a more ontological conception of essence. A thing's active or actual essence is the same

as its power. This applies to both God's essence (E2p3s) and man's (E3p7). God's nature produces all things (E1p17s) and man's essence is identified with his *conatus*. The essence of a thing is the cause of all its activity. The last meaning of essence confirms the dynamic nature of Spinoza's ontology.

TEXTS

Andere ideas wel mogelijk maar niet noodzakelijk datze zijn ... nogtans haar wezen altijd noodzaakelijk is (KV 1.1). Daar is geen zaak in de nature, of daar is een idea van in de denkende zaak voortkomende uijt haar wezen ... idea's die ontstaan uijt de wezentlijkheid der dingen met het wezen zamen in God (KV 2.20). Het waare wezen van een voorwerp is iets het welk dadelijk onderscheiden is van de idea des zelven voorwerps (KV app). *Perceptio, ubi essentia rei ex alia re concluditur, sed non adequate* (TIE 19, G II, 10). *Singularis essentia* (TIE 26, G II, 12). *Certitudo nihil sit praeter ipsam essentiam objectivam, id est modus quo sentimus essentiam formalem* (TIE 35, G II, 15). *Definitio ut dicatur perfecta debebit intimam essentiam rei explicare* (TIE 95, G II, 34). *Rerum singularium mutabilium essentiae non sunt depromendae ab earum serie sive ordine existendi* (TIE 101, G II, 36). *De omni re cujus essentia non involvit necessariam existentiam* (PPC 1ax10). *Vis sive essentia, qua in meo esse conservo* (PPC 1p7s). *Id quod si auferatur rem tollit ejus essentiam constituit* (PPC 2ax2). *Quaestiones de essentia* (CM 1.2). *Res necessaria respectu suae essentiae, vel respectu causae* (CM 1.3). *Formam mali, erroris, sceleris non in aliquo quod essentiam exprimit consistere ... [entia] non solum gradibus, sed et essentia ab invicem differunt* (Ep 23). *Cujuscunque rei potentia sola ejus essentia definitur* (Ep 64).

Id cujus essentia involvit existentiam
(E1def1). *Veritas et formalis rerum essentia*
talis est, quia in Dei intellectu existit object-
ive (E1p17s). *Ad essentiam alicujus rei id*
pertinere dico, quo dato res necessario
ponitur et quo sublato res necessario tollitur,
vel id sine quo res et vice verso quod sine re
nec esse nec concipi potest (E2def2). *Res sin-*
gulares non possunt sine Deo esse nec con-
cipi ... tamen Deus ad earum essentiam non
pertinet (E2p10s). *Definitio cujuscunque rei*
ipius rei essentiam affirmat sed non negat,
sive ponit (E3p4). *Conatus rei actualis essen-*
tia (E3p7).

BIBLIOGRAPHY
Primary Sources
Descartes, R., *Meditationes, Epistolae.*

Secondary Literature
Balz, A.G., *Idea and Essence in the*
    Philosophies of Hobbes and Spinoza
    (New York: Columbia University Press,
    1918).
Gueroult, M., *Spinoza II. L'Ame (Éthique*
    II) (Hildesheim: Olms, 1974).
Rivaud, A., *Les notions d'essence et*
    d'existence dans la philosophie de
    Spinoza (Paris: Alcan, 1906).
Richter, G.T., *Spinozas philosophische*
    Terminologie, I: Grundbegriffe der
    Metaphysik (Leipzig: Barth, 1913).
Robinson, L., *Kommentar zu Spinozas Ethik*
    (Leipzig: Meiner, 1928).
Rousset, B., *Spinoza, lecteur des objections*
    faites aux Méditations de Descartes
    et ses réponses (Paris: Éditions Kimé,
    1996).

H. Krop

Existentia

Spinoza never dealt with the concept of
existence, or with its Dutch counterpart
wezentlijkheid, but apparently he rejected
the univocity attributed to it by the scholastic definitions ('to be in act in the natural
world', Goclenius). The basic division of
existence, Spinoza acknowledged, is into
necessary and possible. The first kind of
existence is the eternal and necessary existence of perfect being. Here existence 'pertains to the essence', or is included in it. In
God, therefore, both concepts do not refer to
distinct realities, since in Him existence cannot be conceived without essence and vice
versa (CM 1.2). Necessary existence is infinite and therefore eternal. The second kind of
existence is that of possible beings whose
existence is not included in their essence. It is
limited and has duration. Spinoza also
assumed a division of existence according to
a hierarchy which corresponds to the order
of the essences (TIE 55). Existence, he
observed, is primarily the existence of the
individual things and is therefore distinct
according to their differences. The more we
conceive existence in abstract and general
terms, the less we consider it clearly and distinctly. Taken abstractly existence is duration
with a measurable quantity. Moreover, the
existence of things which is due to their being
in God's nature, differs from the existence
they acquire by being caused by other individual things (E2p45s).

Although 'existence' denotes concepts
with only a family resemblance, Spinoza
probably would have accepted the scholastic
identification of existence and the actual
being of an essence as a nominal definition.
Hence, the *actuosa essentia* of God means
his necessary existence (CM 2.11, E2p3s).

Spinoza's dynamic metaphysics exploits to the full the scholastic identification of existence and the actuality of being. In the definition of the conatus he equates 'being' with 'persevere in existing'. The perseverance in existing of the things is due to their power, or force (E3p7, E4p26, TP 2.2).

TEXTS

Niet noodzaakelijke wezentlijkheid (KV 1.1). Wezentlijkheid niet aan wezentheid behorende (KV 2.16). *Singularis existentia alicujus rei non noscitur nisi cognita essentia* (TIE, G II, 12). *Notandum est, quod illa differentia, quae est inter essentiam unius rei et essentiam alterius, ea ipsa sit inter actualitatem et existentiam ejusdem rei* (TIE 55, G II, 20). *In omni rei idea sive conceptu continetur existentia vel possibilis vel necessaria* (PPC 1ax6). *Quo res sua natura perfectior est eo majorem existentiam et magis necessariam involvit* (PPC 1p7lem1). *Ens dividendum est in ens quod sua natura necessario existit, sive cujus essentia involvit essentiam et in ens cujus essentia non involvit existentiam* (CM 1.1) *Necessitas in rebus creatis dicitur vel respectu essentiae vel respectu essentiae* (CM 1.3). *Duratio tantum est attributum existentiae ... non nisi ratione distingui* (CM 1.4). *Non ex definitione cujuscunque rei sequitur existentia rei definitae* (E1def7ex). *Perfectio rei existentiam non tollit, sed contra ponit* (E1p11s). *Infinitam et necessariam existentiam* (E1p23). *Per res singulares intelligo res, quae finitae sunt et determinatam habent existentiam* (E2def7). *Hic per existentiam non intelligo durationem hoc est existentiam quatenus abstracte concipitur* (E2p44s). *Rerum in existendo perseverantia* (TP 2.2).

BIBLIOGRAPHY
Secondary Literature
Balz, A.G., *Idea and Essence in the Philosophies of Hobbes and Spinoza* (New York: Columbia University Press, 1918).
Rivaud, A., *Les notions d'essence et d'existence dans la philosophie de Spinoza* (Paris: Alcan, 1906).
Robinson, L., *Kommentar zu Spinozas Ethik* (Leipzig: Meiner, 1928).

H. Krop

Experientia

The word 'experience' and its three Dutch counterparts *ondervinding, ervarentheid* and *bevinding* frequently occur in Spinoza's works. Its abundance obviously suggests its significance. Moreover, in the famous first line of the *Tractatus de intellectus emendatione* Spinoza wrote that experience taught him the real values in life and according to the *Ethics* (E5p23s) we feel and know by experience the partial eternity of our mind. Experience shows us the facts – 'all too plainly', for example our inability to restrain our tongue (E3p2s) – demonstrates, confirms ideas and corroborates premises. With reason experience readily convenes. It is also the 'master of the politicians'.

Spinoza uses 'experience' both in an informal sense and in a technical sense borrowed from Bacon. Random or vagrant experience is the first of the three or four kinds of knowledge he distinguishes at the beginning of the TIE and in E2p40s2. Although Spinoza never really elaborated the notion and meditated on its distinction with experiment, this does not necessarily imply a lack of interest or even a repudiation of experience. Such a conclusion would reproduce the polemical view of Spinoza as a sterile 'rationalist philosopher' and obstinate foe of sound philosophy, a view created in the first decades of the eighteenth century (Moreau, 1994, pp. 227–45). Although according to Spinoza imagination is the source of error, he, unlike Descartes who in the second *Meditation* wrote a famous 'critique of experience', never repudiated it.

In seventeenth-century discourse two views on experience were current. The Aristotelian-scholastic view still enjoyed support. In 1627 Richter for example underscored the distinction between experience and art due to the fortuitous acquirement – hence experience could not be learned – and contingent use of the former. Besides, in *Leviathan* 1.2 Hobbes called it 'much memory, or memory of many things'. Hence experience was basically knowledge of particulars, created by memory, a notion that Wolff in the eighteenth century still adhered to. Micraelius qualified this Aristotelian element by observing: 'experience consists of a universal science derived from a great number of individual observations'.

Bacon, however, transformed seventeenth-century thinking on experience by advancing two new notions: experience is a necessary condition of (natural) philosophy – 'a principle of physics' (Chauvin) – and it consists of a hierarchy of kinds. In the *Novum Organum* 1.82 Bacon distinguished between random or vagrant experience (*experientia vaga*) which occurs if man 'strays with no settled course' taking counsel 'only from things as they fall out'. Hence, this kind of experience is called 'accident'. The second kind is experience 'sought for' (*ordinata*) which is identified with experiment and requires written records (aph. 100). Here a method is applied which begins with experience 'duly ordered and digested',

inferring from it axioms, and from 'established axioms again new experiments'. Such a method 'leads by an unbroken route through the woods of experience to the open ground of axioms'. According to Chauvin there are even three kinds of experience, ranging from the simple use of the external senses, to experiments used in order to refute or confirm a certain theory. In the last case experience is linked with reason.

It is obvious that Spinoza adopted the Baconian model of experience. He distinguished (1) random experience, a term directly adopted from Bacon. Such knowledge is 'without order' (E2p40s2), since 'it is not determined by the intellect' and 'comes by chance' (TIE 19) and is therefore confused. (2) Knowledge from report, or from heard or read words. In the *Ethics* these kinds of experience are identified with imagination, which is a necessary condition of the other kinds of knowledge. Reason, for example, consisting of common notions and adequate ideas of the properties of things, is based, Spinoza observed, on our perception of the singular things. (3) Knowledge from experiments, that is observation done in an orderly manner, according to fixed rules and by means of instruments. This knowledge, which corresponds with the Baconian 'experience sought for', effects an accurate definition and an intimate insight into the nature of the phenomena perceived (TIE 103, cf. Ep 6). This kind of experience may be 'clearly and distinctly understood', but contrary to the intellect it is unable to dissipate all doubt completely (TTP 5). These kinds of experience together form a Baconian history (Ep 37), which may serve as a means to interpret nature (TTP 7). Experience is therefore, according to Spinoza, a necessary condition of philosophical knowledge as well, but only in a chronological, not in a logical sense.

Intellectual knowledge once acquired needs no further justification.

However, it is obvious that a life without empirical knowledge is impossible. This we might infer from the examples given in the *Tractatus*: 'I know only from report my date of birth and who my parents were'. Moreover by experience I know my death and 'that oil is capable of feeding fire and that water is capable of putting it out'. Thus, by it 'I know almost all the things that are useful in life'. However, such 'moral certainty' is to be excluded from the sciences (TIE 26). According to letter 10 experience is only required to know the existence of the modes, which cannot be inferred from the definition or essence of a thing. They are beyond the range of experience, although observation can pave the way for the intellect.

In political philosophy, however, experience reigns supreme, as the first chapter of the *Tractatus politicus* shows us. In political life men have to substantiate their points by experience, since only the small group of the learned advances to higher kinds of knowledge and will be convinced by reason alone (TTP 5). Consequently Spinoza opposed the politicians to the philosophers and theologians, who deal with society arguing from a purely theoretical model constructed by reason or religion, and disregard practical reality. In a Tacitean vein he adopts experience as the master of the statesmen. Although he pretends to be able to prove their experimental knowledge with certain and incontestable arguments, in political science he refrained from applying the geometrical method.

TEXTS
Geloof door ondervinding, of door hooren zeggen ... hoe kan hij doch zeeker zijn dat de ondervinding van eenige bijzondere hem een regul kan zijn van alle [gevallen] (KV 2.1). Begeerte komt ook uijt bevindinge (KV 2.3). Het begrip hebben wij in vierdelijk verdeeld, als in horen zeggen alleen, in ervarentheid, in geloov, en klare kenisse (KV 2.4). *Experientia vaga, hoc est experientia quae non determinatur ab intellectu ... scio me moriturum ... quod oleum sit aptum alimentum ad nutriendam flammam ... et sic fere omnia novi quae ad usum vitae faciunt ... alii ab experientia simplicium faciunt axioma universale ... agam de experientia et empiricorum et recentium philosophorum procedendi methodum* (TIE 19–23, i, G II, 10–13). *Nos non egere experientia nisi ad illa quae rei definitione non possunt concludi ut ex gr. existentia modorum ... nam experientia nullas rerum essentias docet* (Ep 10). *Cum experientia et ratio convenire* (TTP1, G III, 29). *Nisi experientia talis sit, ut clare et distincte intelligatur* (TTP 5, G III, 77). *Quandoquidem omnia postulata vix quicquam continent, quod non constat experientia, de qua nobis non licet dubitare* (E2p17s). *Tales perceptiones cognitionem ab experientia vaga vocare consuevi* (E2p40s2). *Quae modo ostendimus, ipsa etiam experientia quotidie tot, tamque luculentis testimoniis testatur* (E4p35s). *Artes quas experientia longo usu docuit ... Quoniam politici experientiam magistram habuerunt* (TP 1.2). *Experientia omnia genera civitatum, quae concipi possunt ... ostendisse* (TP 1.3).

BIBLIOGRAPHY
Primary Sources
Bacon, F., *Novum Organum*.
Descartes, R., *Meditationes*.

Secondary Literature
Curley, E.M., 'Experience in Spinoza's Theory of Knowledge', in M. Grene (ed.), *Spinoza, a Collection of Critical Essays*

(Garden City, NY: Anchor Books, 1973), pp. 25–59.

Ellsipen, Chr., 'Die Erkenntnisarten', in M. Hampe and R. Schnepf (eds), *Baruch de Spinoza. Ethik* (Berlin: Akademie Verlag, 2006), pp. 133–50.

Gueroult, M., *Spinoza II: L'âme* (Hildesheim: Olms, 1974).

Moreau, P.-F., *Spinoza, l'expérience et l'éternité* (Paris: Presses Universitaires de France, 1994).

Robinson, L., *Kommentar zu Spinozas Ethik* (Leipzig: Meiner, 1928).

H. Krop

Femina / Mulier

Although Spinoza rarely uses the word 'woman' – in Latin *femina* or its equivalent *mulier* – and its meaning is uncontroversial, the place of women in his political theory and his perception of women in general is a topic dealt with in recent (feminist) literature. These words occur in sentences about women in the context of historical or political customs or rules. In the second chapter of the *Tractatus theologico-politicus*, for example, it is observed that no wise men became prophets, but only coarse men and women, and in chapter 13 it is said that women and men are alike able to obey but unequal in wisdom. However, in the last chapter Spinoza is apparently talking about human beings in general, and not differentiating between men and women.

Moreover, admonitions in chapters 6–8 of the *Tractatus politicus* encouraging kings and patricians not to take foreign wives, should not be read as a disparagement of women. On the contrary, Spinoza's reference to women's inconstancy in E5p10s is an example of the impotence of the human mind in general and in E3p35s he merely explains the origin of jealousy. In chapter 20 at the end of *Ethica* 4 Spinoza not only warns against the sensual love produced by bodily appearances, but acknowledges the possibility of mental freedom in a woman as well.

However, in chapters 2 and 13 of the *Tractatus theologico-politicus* and once in *Ethics* 2 Spinoza uses *womanish* as a negative adjective, which combined with references to pity or tears denotes an effeminate sentimentality opposed to manly rationalism. This is the attitude of a man in the grip of fear and credulity and driven to insanity. The use of this adjective, however, might be merely a reflection of conventional wisdom without having deeper roots in Spinoza's philosophy.

Only in the last section of the unfinished chapter 11 of the *Tractatus politicus* is the nature of women dealt with in a philosophical manner. This chapter deals with the democratic state, treating in detail its constitution, institutions and councils, as Spinoza also did for monarchy and aristocracy. A regime is a democracy if no one has a *hereditary* right to vote and to participate in the offices of the state. Participation in politics is granted to all citizens. But Spinoza restricts this political right to those who are independent (*sui iuris*). That restriction excludes from political society – besides children, criminals and foreigners – women and servants, 'who are under control of their husbands and masters'. For experience shows that their weak nature makes women dependent on men and hence unfit for participation in a democratic regime. The Amazons are no argument for the contrary, as Hobbes thought, since their domination was only possible because they killed the males whom they had borne. Without such 'cruelty' resulting from their power female rule is impossible. Apparently the exclusion of women from power rests on the naturalistic argument that is the premise of Spinoza's political philosophy in general. For the political rights of citizens are coextensive with their powers. Because of the radical unity of body and mind, a less powerful body (in a more complex and sophisticated way than just fewer muscles) means a less powerful mind. Moreover, due to the affective laws of sexuality, equal participation of men and women in politics would cause jealousy and disturb social peace.

Even women philosophers in the seventeenth century such as Anne Conway (1631–79) and Anna Maria van Schurman (1607–78) shared Spinoza's conviction of the natural inequality of men and women.

TEXTS
Votis et lacrimis muliebribus divina auxilia implorare (TTP praef). *Contra homines rustici et extra omnem disciplinam, imo mulierculae etiam dono prophetico fuerunt praeditae* (TTP 2, G III, 29). *Viri, mulieres, pueri et omnes ex mandato obtemperare quidem aeque possunt, non autem sapere* (TTP 13, G III, 146). *Muliebri misericorda* (E2p49s), E3p35s, E4p37s, E4p68s. *Viri et foeminae amor non solam formam sed animi libertatem pro causa habeat* (E4app20), E5p10s. TP6.5; TP 7.24; TP 8.10; TP 11.4.

BIBLIOGRAPHY
Primary Sources
Conway, A., *The Principles of the Most Ancient and Modern Philosophy* (London, 1692; Latin original Amsterdam, 1690).
Schurman, A.M. van, *Dissertatio de ingenii muliebris ad doctrinam* (Leiden, 1641).

Secondary Literature
Gullan-Whur, M., 'Spinoza and the Equality of Women', *Theoria,* no. 68 (2002), pp. 91–111.
Gatens, M., *Feminist Interpretations of Spinoza* (Pennsylvania: State University Press, 2009).
Klever, W., 'Een zwarte bladzijde? Spinoza over de vrouw', *Algemeen Nederlands tijdschrift voor wijsbegeerte,* no. 84 (1982), pp. 38–51.
Matheron, A., 'Femmes et serviteurs dan la démocratie spinoziste', in S. Hessing (ed.), *Speculum Spinozanum (1677-1977)* (London: Routledge, 1978), pp. 91–111.

H. Krop

Fides

In the *Korte verhandeling* the Dutch word *geloof* (faith or belief) denotes a form of knowledge in between opinion (*waan*), deriving from experience, and reason (*weeten, klare kennis*). According to the KV faith tells us what must be, not what is. For, although we possess a firm conviction based on strong reasons, we merely know a 'thing ... outside my understanding. I say, a strong proof based on reasons, in order thereby to distinguish it both from opinion, which is always doubtful and liable to error, and from knowledge which does not consist in being convinced by reasons, but in an immediate union with the thing itself'. In its political sense, the term indicates the reliability of rulers (TP 1.6) or states (TP 3.14) in which trust can be put, or the act by which the social pact is established (TTP 16; TP 2.2).

In its theological sense, faith is knowledge resulting in obedience towards God and love for one's neighbour (TTP 14). Thus, faith is never true in itself but only inasmuch as it leads to obedience. The *fides catholica sive universalis* (TTP 14 and Ep 76) does not prescribe contentious dogmas but merely states that there exists one God who is good and that obedience is due to him and love to one's neighbour (see FUNDAMENTA FIDEI).

The basically practical nature of religious faith is acknowledged by philosophers and theologians alike. For Hobbes in *De cive* 18 and *Leviathan* 43, obedience to civil and divine law (repentance and justice) and faith in Christ are the *necessaria ad salutem*. Episcopius in *Confessio* II, pp. 83–4 believes that those who obey Christ and do *bona opera* possess true faith. The same applies to Coccejus, who in *Disputationes selectae* 1.1 defined faith as *amor Dei*, and to Socinus in *Opera exegetica* II, pp. 238–9. Maresius in his *Systema theologicum* 11.18–21) distinguished between faith in a philosophical meaning (a certain conviction, which implies the possibility of doubt) and a theological sense, which is generated by the *vocatio Dei*. The first is a *fides historica* and the second a *fides salvifica*: the second is distinct from the first in respect of origin and nature and not only, as Grotius in his commentary on the New Testament would have it, by constancy and duration.

Finally, in Spinoza faith occurs also in a polemical and negative sense, being an equivalent of credulity (as in TTP praef.) or superstition (Ep 73) and taking as its object miracles (TTP 6). In TTP 4 and 11 he refers to the Protestant doctrine of the *sola fide*.

TEXTS

Deze begrippen dan verkrijgen wij of enkelijk door geloof (welk geloof hervoort komt of door ondervinding, of door hooren zeggen) (KV 2.1); KV 2.2. Het ware geloof (KV 2.4). *Historiae fide dignus* (Ep 54). *Fidem catholicam* (Ep 76). *Fides jam nihil aliud est ... quam credulitas et praejudicia* (TTP praef, G III, 8). *Ex sola fide* (TTP 4, G III, 65). *Fides miraculorum* (TTP 6, G III, 96). *Hominem justificari non ex fide* (TTP 11, G III, 157). *Ad fidem cognitionem* (TTP 14). *Fidem pacti* (TTP 16). *Fides in Republica apprime necessaria est* (TTP 19, G III, 243); TP 1.6; TP 2.12. *Fides quam sana ratio et religio servandam docet* (TP 3.14).

BIBLIOGRAPHY

Primary Sources
Coccejus, J., *Disputationes selectae*, in *Opera omnia* VI (Amsterdam, 1675).
Episcopius, S., *Confessio*, in *Opera theologica* II (Amsterdam, 1665).
[Grotius, H.], *Explicatio ... N. Testamenti ... In quibus agitur de fide et operibus* (Amsterdam, 1640).
Hobbes, Th., *De cive, Leviathan*.
Maresius, S., *Systema theologicum* (Groningen, 1673).
Socinus, F., *Opera omnia* ([Amsterdam], 1656).

Secondary Literature
Lagrée, J., *La raison ardente. Religion naturelle et raison au XVIIe siècle* (Paris: Vrin, 1991).
Matheron, A., *Le Christ et le salut des ignorants chez Spinoza* (Paris: Aubier Montaigne, 1971).
Rosenthal, M.A., 'Spinoza's Dogmas of the Universal Faith and the Problem of Religion', *Philosophy and Theology*, no. 13 (2001), pp. 53–72.
Verbeek, Th., *Spinoza's Theologico-Political Treatise. Exploring 'the Will of God'* (Aldershot: Ashgate, 2003).

R. Bordoli

Finis

In Spinoza's works the Latin word *finis* and its Dutch counterparts *eijnd* and *oogmerk* cover two distinct but related notions. In English the first is translated by 'limit', while 'end', 'aim' and 'purpose' render the second one. In the first meaning its cognates are *finitum*, *terminus*, *extremum* and *definitum*. Its opposite is the infinite, which is eternal by its nature and lacks all limits (Ep 12). As such *finis* apparently denotes a deficiency and is at least in part a negation (E1p8s1). In a polemical way limit is associated with blindness and darkness (CM 1.1). In the second meaning *finis* is equivalent to goodness. Traditionally *finis* in this sense referred to a thing's perfection by which it is an object of desire causing the action of lesser perfect beings. As such a thing, by being an end, is a final cause. The link between both notions is dealt with by Chauvin, who observed that *finis* 'as to the meaning of the word is equivalent to goal (*meta*) and boundary, limit (*terminus*)'. Hence the good, which induces the will, is called 'an end, since some goods calm down the appetite and the motion of the agent. A well-known saying therefore runs: 'after attaining its end motion ceases'. In scholasticism the traditional definitions of an end, ultimately going back to Aristotle, gave rise to many distinctions, which left some traces in Spinoza. In definition 7 of *Ethics* 4 for example he uses the term *finis cujus* in the phrase 'an end, for which the means are applied', and in the appendix of *Ethics* 1 is found the pair of concepts 'an end of need' and 'an end of assimilation' (that is in order to assimilate other things with himself). The direct source here is Heereboord's *Meletemata* 2.24, reproduced almost literally.

It is only in the first chapter of *Cogitata metaphysica* 1 and the famous passage in the appendix of *Ethics* 1 that we encounter two notions of *finis* peculiar to Spinoza. In both texts he assumed as a premise that *we* consider something to be an end. In accordance with his parsimonious ontology an end is taken to be only a 'being of reason', or even 'a being of fiction', and consequently in the preface of *Ethics* 4 both perfection and good are also unmasked as modes of thinking, which does not denote an intrinsic property of the things. Moreover, calling a thing 'finite' or 'limited' is also merely an act of thought, or rather of imagination. This applies to the supposed finite quantity of the extended substance as well. Hence, its parts are only modally and not really distinct. (E1p15s2).

The second notion is the famous critique of finalism in nature, this 'common and persistent' prejudice (Gueroult, 1968, p. 393). Against this fiction he advances physical, epistemological and theological arguments and he attempts to give a genealogical explanation. In nature all phenomena happen in accordance with the divine laws of mechanics. Being the effect of an efficient cause, a lawlike explanation of all things, man included, is possible. If we attribute purposes to actors, this is merely out of ignorance. Even God does not act purposively, since that would imply an imperfection in him. Genetically the doctrine of finalism is caused by the human passion of pride, and originates in the fiction that man is the centre of the universe.

Though radical, Spinoza's anti-finalism is not exceptional among 'new' philosophers. Telesio and Bacon already called finalism in physics sterile and in *De corpore* II.10.7 Hobbes wrote that the phrase 'a final cause' is only intelligible if referring to beings with senses and will who in fact are the efficient causes of their actions. Moreover, in the *Meditationes* 4 Descartes stated that 'this consideration alone is sufficient to convince me, that the whole class of final causes is of no avail in physical or natural things'. Like Spinoza he argued that we should not conceive God in the image of man: a willing and purposefully acting person. This rejection of the final cause by modern philosophy is reflected in Chauvin's dictionary. He wrote that this notion is useful only in ethics, in physics however it is barren.

TEXTS
Dat dat werkstuk met het oogmerk van den maker wel overeenkomt, zo zegt men goet te wezen (KV 1.6). Eijnd des menschen ... eens Ens rationis is (KV 2.4). Het laatste eynde van een slaaf en van een werktuijg is dit datze haar opgeleiden dienst behoorlijk volvoeren ... alzoo ook de mensch, zoo moet hij de wetten van de natuur volgen, het welk de Gods dienst is (KV 2.18). De goddelijke wetten zijn het laatste eijnde om het welke wij zijn (KV 2.24). *Indefinitum id cujus fines investigari nequeunt* (PPC 2def4). *Omnes modos, quibus mens utitur ad negandum, quales sunt caecitas, extremitas sive finis, terminus, tenebrae etc. Tanquam entia imaginamur* (CM 1.1). *Bonum esse per se et tanquam finis ultimus ad quem omnia diriguntur* (TIE 5, G II, 6). *Finis in scientiis est unicus* (TIE e, G II, 9). *Finis universae societatis et imperii* (TTP 3, G III, 48). *Finis humanarum actionum* (TTP G III, 61). *Finis ultimus reipublicae* (TTP 20, G III, 240). *Omnia praejudicia pendent ab hoc uno, quod communiter supponunt homines omnes res naturales ut ipsos propter finem agere ... omnes causas finales nihil nisi humana figmenta ... si Deus propter finem agit, aliquid necessario appetit, quo caret. Et quamvis Theologi et metaphysici distinguant inter finem indigentiae et finem assimilationis* (E1app). *Causa quae finalis dicitur, nihil est praeter ipsum*

humanum appetitum (E4praef). *Per finem cujus causa aliquid facimus appetitum intelligo* (E4def7). *Nemo suum esse alcujus finis causa conservare conatur* (E4p52s). *Finis status civilis* (TP 5.2). *Finis optimi imperii* (TP 5.7).

BIBLIOGRAPHY
Primary Sources
Descartes, R., *Meditationes.*
Hobbes, Th., *De Corpore.*

Secondary Literature
Vurley, M., 'On Bennett's Spinoza, the Issue of Teleology', in E. Curley and P.-F. Moreau (eds), *Spinoza. Issues and Directions* (Leiden: Brill, 1990), pp. 39–53.
Garret, D., 'Teleology in Spinoza and Early Modern Rationalism', in R.J. Gennaro and Ch. Huenemann (eds), *New Essays on the Rationalists* (Oxford: Oxford University Press, 1999), pp. 310–35.
Gueroult, M., *Spinoza I: Dieu* (Hildesheim: Olms, 1968).
Robinson, L., *Kommentar zu Spinozas Ethik* (Leipzig: Meiner, 1928).

H. Krop

Fortitudo

Fortitude (strength of character) and its Dutch counterparts *kloekheid* and *dapperheid* are rarely used by Spinoza. Only in his last works does the Latin word occur five times, in the *Ethics* and the *Tractatus politicus*. However, transformed and adopted to the system the cardinal virtue of the Stoic tradition in particular retained a basic role in Spinoza's philosophy.

After having dealt with the passions in *Ethics* 3 Spinoza continues in proposition 59 with the active affects. They originate, he argues, in merely two of the three primitive affects: joy and desire. Opposing Descartes who refrained from excluding sadness and its derived forms from the list of the affects caused by an activity of the mind (*Passiones animi* art. 91–2), Spinoza definitely ruled out such a possibility, for active affects presuppose clear and distinct knowledge. It is, moreover, impossible that by adequate ideas our power to exist will be diminished or that our CONATUS will be restrained, as in the case of sorrow happens to the mind. Although Spinoza, imitating Descartes, who in the French text of the *Passions de l'âme* art. 171 uses 'courage' and in the Latin version *animositas* and *audacia*, considers fortitude to be an affect, he does not supply a real definition. According to the definitions 1 and 3 of the third part all affects of which the mind is the adequate cause are active. This implies that the resulting human actions are in accordance with the dictates of reason, as is apparent from the common phrase in the definition of both tenacity (*animositas*) and generosity: 'the desire by which each one strives solely from the dictate of reason'. Afterwards Spinoza lists three individual active affects – moderation, sobriety, presence of mind in danger – and two social affects – courtesy, mercy (E3p59s). The 'dictates of reason' are dealt with in *Ethics* 4 from proposition 24 onwards. Their adoption makes man free (E4p69–72). Being related to all rational acting, fortitude does not specify certain affects. Hence, fortitude of the mind may be taken as the necessary condition of all active affects.

However, both in *Ethics* 4 and 5 and the *Tractatus politicus* Spinoza calls fortitude not an affect, but a virtue, identifying it with the virtue of magnanimity (E4p69). As such it is related to the basic virtues of piety and religion (E5p41s) and fortitude is even identified with human liberty. Hence a 'free man' is equivalent to a 'vigourous man' (E4p73s and TP 1.6). Encompassing piety (morality with respect to oneself), honesty (morality with respect to others) and religion (morality with respect to God), fortitude is the most general of all virtues. Its intellectual nature implies that fortitude is a private virtue and as such not required in politics (TP 1.6).

In the *Korte verhandeling* Spinoza alludes to the Greek origin of the concept – *andreia* manliness, which Plato included in the list of four cardinal virtues. The Stoa gave the initially martial virtue a definitely intellectualistic character. Seneca for example defined fortitude as the moral science of distinguishing between good and evil, which prepares the mind to despise dangers. The Stoic sage is the *vigorous* man who possesses a steady, *persevering* and magnanimous mind. However, in the Aristotelian tradition the virtue of fortitude was of a basic nature as well. According to Aquinas fortitude is a general virtue or its necessary condition, providing the mind with the firmness and the perseverance required in order to act virtuously and so enabling man to live in accordance with reason (*Summa theologiae* II-II, q. 123). Like Spinoza Aquinas observed that fortitude keeps the middle ground between fear and audacity. As often Spinoza elegantly used the full resources of tradition.

TEXTS

Als de ziel tot het voortbrengen van de zaake mannelijk besluit…en die zaake beswarlijk om voort te brengen zijnde, zo word het kloekmoedigheid genoemd of dapperheid

(KV 2.9). *Spiritus ... fortitudinis sumitur ad significandum animum fortem vel virtutem fortitudinis* (TTP 1, G III, 22). *Omnes actiones quae sequuntur ex affectibus qui ad mentem referuntur quatenus intelligit ad fortitudinem, quam in animositatem et generositam refero* (E3p59s). *Magna animi virtus, seu fortitudo requiritur ad audaciam quam ad metum coërcendum* (E4p69). *Haec et similia quae de vera hominis libertate ostendimus ad fortitudinem referuntur* (E4p73). *Communia vitae pericula et quomomodo animi praesentia et fortitudine optime vitari et superari possunt* (E5p10s). *Pietatem igitur et religionem et absolute omnia quae ad animi fortitudinem significandum referuntur* (E5p41s). *Animi libertas seu fortitudo privata virtus est* (TP 1.6). *Humana potentia non tam ex corporis robore, quam ex mentis fortitudine aestimanda est* (TP 2.11). *Pax virtus est quae ex animi fortitudine oritur* (TP 5.4); TP 6.3. *Si ex natura foeminae viris aequales essent, et animi fortitudine et ingenio in quo maxime humana potentia et consequenter jus consistit, aeque pollerent* (TP 11.4).

BIBLIOGRAPHY
Primary Sources
Aquinas, *Summa theologiae.*
Descartes, R., *Passions de l'âme, Passiones animi.*

Secondary Literature
Jaquet, Ch., 'La fortitude cachée', in Ch. Jaquet, P. Sévérac and A. Suhamy (eds), *Fortitude et Servitude, lectures de l'Éthique IV de Spinoza* (Paris: Éditions Kimé, 2003), pp. 15–25.

H. Krop

Fundamenta fidei

In the seventeenth century, phrases in the *Tractatus theologico-politicus* such as 'biblical dogmas and principles', 'foundations of religion', or 'the fundamentals of faith' were akin to other expressions such as the articles of faith, doctrine, catechism, profession, confession or rule of faith, *symbolum* and *credo* (FIDES). All these phrases express the conviction, shared by almost all confessions that faith basically consists of a limited set of coherent propositions and precepts, which a Christian had to believe and observe. Micraelius, for example, defined an article of faith as follows: 'a tenet of a doctrine contained in the Word of God which is put before the Christians to believe in order to acquire salvation'. Al least sometimes Spinoza seems to share this conviction, for example when attempting in TTP 14 to define faith by listing the 'dogmas of universal faith'. Roman Catholic authors tended to underline the role the Church had to play in formulating these articles, while Protestant authors focused on Scripture, which seemed perfectly to contain all the propositions needed to formulate a salutary faith. The Leiden theologian Coccejus, for example, observed that 'in the Law and by the prophets no superfluous doctrine is taught' (*Demonstratio potentiae Sacrae Scripturae* 31.123, where he rejects the distinction made by the brothers Walenburg, Roman Catholic controversialists, between the principles taught by the Church and the principles of Scripture, which no one happens to know in full). In his dispute with Protestants, the famous Roman Catholic apologist Bellarmine (*Disputationes* II, controversia 1, p. 295) claimed that Scripture and the Fathers did not write down catechisms, and rejected the 'pernicious' Protestant principle that the Bible contains all the articles of faith. In the same book he stated: 'if this was the real view of Calvin, the greater part of the tenets of faith would become doubtful and many tenets of faith are not absolutely necessary for salvation' (p. 260). Although the Reformed theologian Voetius in the *Selectae disputationes* II, p. 530 observed that it is a 'false hypothesis of the Papists that all tenets which the Church proclaims to be necessary belong to the articles of faith', he had to agree to the notion that some biblical tenets are less necessary to salvation than others. Some tenets, for example, are like axioms, others are to be inferred from these premises. Apparently, by using the phrase 'principles of Scripture', Spinoza shared the Protestant belief in the self-sufficiency of the Bible. However, he never employed the term 'article', which apparently had a too ecclesiastical and confessional connotation. But some correspondents use this term; for example Oldenburg (Ep 79) talks of *resurrectionis articulus* as a basis of Scripture, when he learns that Spinoza understands the resurrection of Christ only in a metaphorical sense (see also Ep 61: 'the traditional forms of the confessions').

However, more basic to Spinoza's argument is the distinction between absolutely necessary principles and non-necessary tenets of faith. From the sixteenth century onwards 'irenic'-minded theologians tended to formulate a universal confession of faith, which would be acceptable to all Christians (Ep 48a). To that end they attempted to restrict the number of articles to a minimum. Van Velthuijsen in his *De articulis fidei*, first published in his 1680 *Opera omnia*, restricted the number of the articles of faith in fact to one (vol. I, p. 744): every Christian must believe in the universal damnation of man due to sin and the salvation of mankind by

Christ. According to Hobbes in *De cive* 18.6 and *Leviathan* 43, the sole article of faith required by Scripture for salvation is that which declares Jesus to be Christ, the Messiah.

TEXTS

Fundamenta fidei (TTP praef, G III, 11). *Fundamenta et dogmata Scripturae* (TTP 6, G III, 95); TTP 7. *Nos ex Scripturae jussu nihil aliud teneri credere, quam id, quod ad hoc mandatum exequendum absolute necessarium sit ... Ad fidem catholicam sive universalem nulla dogmata pertinere, de quibus inter honestos potest dari controversia* (TTP 14).

BIBLIOGRAPHY
Primary Sources
Bellarminus, R., *Disputationes de controversiis christianae fidei adversus hujus temporis haereticos*, 4 vols (Ingolstadt, 1605).
Coccejus, J., *Demonstratio potentiae Sacrae Scripturae*, in *Opera omnia* VII (Amsterdam, 1675).
Hobbes, Th., *De cive, Leviathan*.
Velthuijsen, L. van, *De articulis fidei,* in *Opera omnia* I (Rotterdam, 1680).
Voetius, G., *Selectae disputationes theologicae*, 5 vols (Utrecht, 1648–69).

Secondary Literature
Matheron, A., *Le Christ et le salut des ignorants chez Spinoza* (Paris: Aubier, 1971).
Verbeek, Th., *Spinoza's Theologico-Political Treatise. Exploring 'the Will of God'* (Aldershot: Ashgate, 2003).

R. Bordoli

Generositas

Despite a single occurrence in the *Tractatus politicus*, Spinoza's use of the term 'generosity', or 'nobility of mind', is typical of the *Ethics*, in which the term and its derivatives occur 15 times in total. In E3p59s, *generositas* is defined as 'the desire by which each man strives, solely from the dictate of reason, to aid other men and join them to him in friendship'. Generosity, like its counterpart 'mental vigour' or 'tenacity' (*animositas*), forms a species of FORTITUDO or 'strength of character', tenacity being directed at the preservation of oneself, generosity at that of others. In E4p46, generosity is also identified with 'love'.

In spite of its relatively rare occurrence, the concept is of crucial importance to Spinoza's idea of man as a social and political being, as presented in the fourth part of the *Ethics*. Since generosity conquers hate and thereby aids social well-being through an increase of joy in others, this altruistic side to fortitude will enhance political peace. Not only will the acceptance of all that is due to 'true life and religion' (E4p73s) be improved in a social environment – the man of reason is also bound to improve the lives of others, not least because generosity and love will be appreciated by them as an enhancement of their own powers (E4p46). Thus, minds 'are conquered not by arms, but by love and nobility' (E4app9).

A link is also made between the notion of generosity and the idea of the free human being as it occurs in the fifth part of the *Ethics*, in so far as Spinoza links the avoidance of evil affects to the fact that 'a man strong in character considers ... most of all, that all things follow from the divine nature' (E4p73s; cf. E4p50s). In the end, however, the beatifying spiritual insights of part 5 are not deemed necessary in order for the moral and political advantages of tenacity and nobility to have an effect within the sphere of political friendship. Generosity, in other words, may be accepted on the reasonable grounds of its moral and political effectiveness alone (E5p41).

With his concept of generosity, Spinoza gave a more restricted interpretation to a notion that had become the central focus of Descartes's moral psychology in the *Passions de l'âme*: *la générosité*. Though Spinoza follows Descartes in the idea that generosity is what prevents us from holding others in contempt (PA 3.153–4; E4p73s), the affect of generosity is interpreted in rather different ways in the works of both philosophers. As the ultimate measure of our self-esteem, generosity, according to Descartes, amounts to (1) a knowledge 'that nothing truly belongs to [oneself] but [the] freedom to dispose of [one's] volitions', combined with (2) 'a firm and constant resolution to use [this freedom] well' (PA 3.153). When applied to our esteem of others, this Cartesian type of generosity amounts to a conscious form of benevolence on account of our shared – and all too human – nature. In Spinoza, by contrast, not only is no such well-willing excluded on metaphysical grounds, it is also supplanted by a rigorously intellectualistic notion of generosity that substitutes Descartes's idea of a mental determination with a notion of nobility that, in its purest form, is a mere side-effect of knowledge.

In the absence of perfect knowledge, we may train our imagination in such a way as to have the attitude of nobility always at hand as a steady medicine against the evils that prevent the mind from understanding (E5p10 and s). Yet whether as the result of imaginative training, or as a result of reasonable insight, nobility adds a social aspect to our emotional life. Indeed, since generosity occurs next to mental vigour and is included together with the latter as an equally important part of our strength of character, Spinoza's concept of human emotional life contrasts sharply with Hobbes's more pessimistic view. Besides allowing for the idea of an enlightened self-interest that includes the interests of others, Spinoza's generosity is what inspires us 'to act well and rejoice' (E4p73s; cf. E4p50s).

TEXTS

Omnes actiones, quae sequuntur ex affecti-bus, qui ad mentem referuntur, quatenus intelligit, ad fortitudinem refero, quam in animositaten et generositatem distingui. Per generositatem autem cupiditam intelligo, qua unusquisque ex solo rationis dictamine conatur reliquos homines juvare et sibi amici-tia jungere ... Modestia autem, clementia etc. species generositatis sunt (E3p59s). *In ipsum odium, iram, contemptum etc. amore contra sive generositate compensare* (E4p46); E4p73s; E4app11; E5p10s. *Illa tamen quae ad animositatem et generositatem prima hab-eremus* (E5p41). *Rex ... animi generositate ductus. ut scilicet utilitati publicae consulat* (TP 7.11).

BIBLIOGRAPHY

Primary Sources
Descartes, R., *Passions de l'âme.*

Secondary Literature
Deregibus, A., 'Il sentimento morale della *generosità* nelle dottrine di Descartes e di Spinoza', in Emilia Giancotti (ed.), *Spinoza nel 350° anniversario della nascita. Atti del congresso* (Urbino, 4–8 Ottobre 1982) (Naples: Bibliopolis, 1985), pp. 221–35.

Matheron, A., *Individu et communauté chez Spinoza* (Paris: Éditions de Minuit, 1969).
Rosenthal, M.A., 'Tolerance as a Virtue in Spinoza's Ethics', *Journal of the History of Philosophy*, no. 39 (2001), pp. 535–57.

H. van Ruler

Historia

With the notable exception of the *Tractatus theologico-politicus,* where the Latin word *historia* apparently occurs no less then 147 times (Akkerman, 1997, p. 10), the word is rather infrequently used by Spinoza. In both the *Cogitata metaphysica* and the *Ethics* it occurs only once and in the *Tratatus politicus* merely four times. The different ways in which Spinoza uses the word more or less reflect seventeenth-century usage.

A clear overview of this usage is given in Goclenius's entry. In a general sense 'history', Goclenius observes, refers to an investigation or 'our knowledge of the particular things or the description or exposition of a thing's existence'. In this sense we call anatomy the 'history of the parts of the human body'. Characteristic of these descriptions of nature is that they are put together without making use of arguments. The use of reason will transform such a history into scientific knowledge, i.e. philosophy. We meet the same notion in Bacon's definition of (natural) his-tory in *De dignitate et augmentis scientiarum* 2.1: 'history in its proper sense is about indi-vidual things, i.e. those determined in place and time'. In philosophical discourse, Gocle-nius continues, history denotes observation, i.e. knowledge based on the experience of one or more individuals. This observation may be acquired by hearing, seeing, or reading. Finally history may refer to the accounts of man's former deeds, which causes them to be remembered by posterity. Such a history may be called 'sacred' if it pertains to the church or 'profane' if it is relative to a particular state, people or human institution. Only history in the last sense corresponds more or less to contemporary usage.

In CM 1.6 for example 'history' occurs in the general sense of a description of nature. Spinoza defines an idea as a report, i.e. a 'history' of a natural phenomenon which is recorded in the mind. The same general sense occurs in adnotatio 8 of the TTP (G III, 253) where it is stated that the 'accounts of things relating to the past and future ... are also intelligible and clear, although they cannot be mathematically demonstrated'. All particular histories put together form a 'universal history of nature', which 'is the sole ground of philosophy'. In letter 37 'a little history' has a technical sense as well. Apparently like in Bacon the borderline between natural history and philosophy is not so clear-cut.

Spinoza generally used 'history' in the contemporary sense of 'civil, or ecclesiastical history' (Bacon) or of history with respect to man. This meaning ranges from a strictly objective connotation denoting the deeds of a man or the vicissitudes of a nation (TTP 17) and a structured record (TTP 9), to the utterly subjective view of past events (TTP 6). Also a book dealing with history is called a 'history' (TP 7). However, contrary to modern usage 'civil' history has an aim and a moral quality.

In chapters 7–9 of the TTP Spinoza used 'history' in the technical sense borrowed from Bacon, denoting a systematic record of observations dealing with natural phenomena, which may be used as the basis for nature's interpretation in natural philosophy.

Such interpretation must be distinguished from rash and premature judgement (*Novum Organum* 1.26). According to the British philosopher history consists of three parts: a philological one, which clarifies the words and concepts; a descriptive phase, which consists in making an accurate image of the phenomena; and lastly the methodical performing of real experiments. All observations are recorded in tables (*Parasceve ad historiam naturalem et experimentalem*). Apparently Spinoza was familiar with Bacon's ideas (Ep 37) and he transformed his scientific model into a hermeneutics. The historical phase is to collect facts about the biblical texts and this should provide us with information about the author(s) and their idiom. This was common practice in humanistic biblical scholarship. However, peculiar to Spinoza is the use of the Baconian name 'history'. Among other things it listed the biblical doctrines and in this manner prepared the way for inferring the universal truths of the Bible by means of induction. The second part of Spinoza's hermeneutic method is the interpretation, that is the inference of laws. However, since our histories of Scripture are intrinsically defective, a philosophy or a science based on the Bible is hardly possible (TTP 8).

TEXTS

Ideae nihil aliud sunt quam narrationes sive historiae naturae mentales (CM 1.6). *Ad haec intelligendum ... non est opus naturam mentis per primam ejus causam cognoscere, sed sufficit mentis sive perceptionum historiolam concinnere modo illo, quo Verulamius docet* (Ep 37). *Historiae ... narrationes in Vetere et Novo Testamento contentae, reliquis profanis praestatiores sunt pro ratione salutarium opinionum quae ex iis sequuntur* (TTP 5, G III, 79). *Homines in suis chronicis et historiis magis suas opiniones, quam res ipsas actas narrent ... Multa philosophorum qui historiam naturae scripserunt ... Historiam prophetiae concinnare et ex ea dogmata formare* (TTP 6, G III, 92, 95). *Ut mentem a praejudiciis theologicis liberemus, de vera methodo Scripturam interpretandi agendem est ... Sicuti methodus interpretandi scripturam haud differre a methodo interpretandi naturam in hoc potissimum consistit, in concinnandis sc. historia naturae, ex qua, utpote ex certis datis, rerum naturalium definitiones concludimus ... Denique enarrare debet haec historia casus omnium librorum prophetarum ... Mens prophetarum ex historia Scripturae eruenda, nempe a maxime universalibus incipiendum ... Linguae Hebraicae perfectam historiam non possumus habere ... Consimilem historiam in Ovidio de Perseo legeram ... hae omnes hujus methodi interpretandi Scripturam ex ipsius historia difficultates* (TTP 7, G III, 98, 101, 104, 106, 110–11). *Ut Scripturae historia non tantum imperfecta ... hoc est ut fundamenta cognitionis Scripturam non tantum pauciora ... sed etiam vitiosa sint* (TTP 8, G III, 118). *Historia Hiskiae ... Nathanis ... In hisce quinque libris praecepta et historiae promiscue sine ordine narrentur ... Scriptura historias multorum annorum comprehenderit* (TTP 9, G III, 131, 133). *Historia diversis modis repetitur ... De Libro Jobi quidam putant Mosen scripsisse et totam historiam non nisi parabolicam esse ... Ea quae circa historiam librorum Veteris Testamentis notare volueram* (TTP 10, G III, 142, 144, 149). *Quod ad totam Scripturam in genere attinet ... ejus sensum ex sola ejus historia, et non ex universali historia naturae quae solius philosophiae fundamentum est, determinandum esse* (TTP 15, G III, 185). *Hebraeorum historias et successus perpendemus* (TTP 17, G III, 203). *In illa primi hominis historia* (E4p68s). *Nemo qui historias legit* (TP 7.14).

Historias tam sacras quam profanas legerunt (TP 7.17).

BIBLIOGRAPHY

Primary Sources
Bacon, F., *Sylva sylvarum, Novum organum, De dignitate et augmentis scientiarum.*

Secondary Literature
Akkerman, F., 'Mots techniques, Mots classiques', in P. Totaro (ed.), *Spinoziana* (Florence: Olschki, 1997), pp. 1–22.
Jacobs, W.G., 'Spinozas Theologisch-politischer Traktat und das Problem der Geschichte', in W. Kluxen (ed.), *Tradition und Innovation* (Hamburg: Meiner, 1988), pp. 82–9.
Rooden, P. van, 'Spinoza's bijbeluitleg', *Studia Rosenthaliana*, no. 18 (1984), pp. 120–33.
Verbeek, Th., *Spinoza's Theologico-Political Treatise. Exploring 'the Will of God'* (Aldershot: Ashgate, 2003).
Zac, S., *Spinoza et l'interprétation de l'Écriture* (Paris: Presses Universitaires de France, 1965).

H. Krop

Homo

In the first two axioms of part two of the *Ethics* it is stated that human essence does not include its existence and that man thinks. Spinoza's account of COGITATIO as a capacity of man as a whole and not of the mind only – not the Cartesian *cogito*, but the Spinozistic *homo cogitat* – can be read as his reaction to Descartes's conception of man as being at the same time a thinking ego and an essentially different body. However, he did not bother to discuss scholastic definitions of man, such as those mentioned in *Cogitata metaphysica* 1.1.

Spinoza's theory of man contains four major elements: (1) nature, (2) desire, (3) psycho-physical parallelism and (4) the activity of understanding as the ultimate end of life for free men.

1. Nature. According to E4p4 man is a part of nature, that is to say he undergoes only changes 'which can be understood through his own nature alone, and of which he is the adequate cause'. This naturalism as regards the *content* of Spinoza's anthropology is matched by a *methodological* naturalism which he formulates most concisely in the preface of the third part of the *Ethics*, where he says that he will 'consider human actions and appetites just as if it were a question of lines, planes, and bodies'.

2. Although Spinoza states axiomatically that man thinks, man is not essentially a thinking entity, but a desiring thing. According to the definition of the affects at the end of part three of the *Ethics* man is not the only being with such a striving essence, for as E3p7 observes the striving (CONATUS) for self-preservation is the actual essence of all things. Essence, striving, appetite, desire and will are only nominally distinct and differentiated on the basis of external relations (E3p9s).

3. That Spinoza can consider the striving of man as either something purely mental (VOLUNTAS) or as something that relates also to the body (APPETITUS) is a manifestation of his psycho-physical parallelism, which applies to everything, including man. The application of this parallelism to man means that all events in the human body – the object of the idea constituting the human mind – must be perceived by the mind (E2p12). This perception need not be clear and distinct,

so that there may well be unconscious perceptions in the human mind of what goes on in the body.

4. Since understanding is for Spinoza an activity, and being active leads to joy, the striving for happiness is a striving for understanding. The greatest striving of the mind that leads to the most satisfying happiness is the intuitive understanding of God (E5p25). 'So the ultimate end of the man who is led by reason, i.e. his highest desire ... is that by which he is led to conceive adequately both himself and all things that can fall under his understanding' (E4app4).

TEXTS

Hominis essentia non involvit necessariam existentiam (E2ax1). *Homo cogitat* (E2ax2). *Essentiam hominis constitui a certis Dei attributorum modificationibus* (E2p10c). *Hominem in natura velut imperium in imperio concipere videntur* (E3praef). *Hominem mente et corpore constare* (E2p13c). *Hic conatus cum ad mentem solam refertur, voluntas appellatur; sed cum ad mentem et corpus simul refertur vocatur appetitus, qui proinde nihil aliud est quam ipsa hominis essentia* (E3p9s). *Fieri non postest, ut homo non sit naturae pars et ut nullas possit pati mutationes, nisi, quae per solam naturam possint intelligi, quarumque adaequata sit causa* (E4p4). *Cupiditas est ipsa hominis essentia, hoc est conatus* (E4p18). *Homini nihil homine utilius* (E4p18s). *Longe majus homines in bruta, quam haec in homines jus habent* (E4p37s1).

BIBLIOGRAPHY
Secondary Literature
Bartuschat, W., *Spinozas Theorie des Menschen* (Hamburg: Meiner, 1995).

Machery, P., *Introduction à l'Éthique de Spinoza. La quatrième partie. La condition humaine* (Paris: Presses Universitaires de France, 1998).

Matheron, A., *Anthropologie et politique au XVII siècle. Études sur Spinoza* (Paris: Éditions de Minuit, 1986).

Nadler, S., *Spinoza's Ethics. An Introduction* (Cambridge: Cambridge University Press, 2006). In particular chapter 5.

M. Hampe

Idea

Spinoza defines 'idea' as 'a concept of the mind, which the mind forms because it is a thinking thing' (E2def3). This suggests that Spinoza simply takes over Descartes's use of the term, who in opposition to the schools identified an idea with everything that is immediately perceived by the mind (*Responsiones* III, AT VII, p. 181) or the first COGITATIO of the human mind (Chauvin). According to the schoolmen an idea denoted the forms of perception by the *divine* mind. However, there are numerous complications with this suggestion. To start with, in the explication Spinoza highlights the term concept: 'I prefer to speak of *concept* rather than *perception* because the word *perception* seems to indicate that the mind is passive with regard to its object, whereas *concept* seems to express an act of the mind.' By claiming that an idea is not a passive perception Spinoza distances himself from Descartes (*Passions de l'âme* §19), probably because he also rejects the latter's theory of judgement, according to which a judgement combines a basically passive idea with a volition, that is, the act by which the will affirms that perception to be true

(E2p49). According to Spinoza, however, it is impossible to isolate the contents of an idea from the act by which it is affirmed to be true: all we need to deduce true judgements about triangles is to have the concept of a triangle. So 'in so far as they are ideas' (ibid.) all ideas already involve a judgement: By forming the idea of A we legitimately claim that A is part of the actual world (TIE 55, 69). To a certain extent that is true even of ideas of the imagination, albeit that in this case the judgement often is not true: to imagine a flying horse is to believe in the existence of a flying horse (E2p17s; cf. E2p49s). This belief is shaken, or suspended, not by an act of the will (as in Cartesian doubt), but by the presence of other ideas that are incompatible with the existence of the thing we imagine: the belief that the stick in the water is broken is shaken by feeling with our hand that it is straight; the belief that we see a ghost, by the knowledge that ghosts do not exist. Accordingly, doubt and uncertainty arise only if we have more than one idea and if these ideas are inconsistent (TIE 77–80). However, the notion that all ideas are 'active' seems to be contrary to the fact that the imagination is essentially passive: 'with respect to the imagination the soul is passive only' (TIE 86; cf. 84, 90). Moreover, 'to eliminate all doubt it is enough to have objective essences, or, what is actually the same, ideas' (TIE 35). So only true ideas, that is, ideas formed by the intellect, would be truly ideas. Chimeras, fictions and *entia rationis* are not ideas but modes of thought (CM 2.1; cf. 1.6; KV 2.16). So some contents of the mind at least are not ideas. In the *Ethics*, too, Spinoza urges his readers 'to make a careful distinction between an idea, that is, a concept of the mind, and the images of the things we imagine' (E2p49s). So images are not ideas. Moreover, it is impossible to form a false idea given the fact that the idea of something impossible is itself impossible: 'an idea contains nothing positive which would constitute the form of falsehood' (E2p35). So if an idea is false that can only be to the extent that it is not an idea but an image. And, finally, 'modes of thought like love, desire...cannot exist unless the same individual has an idea of the thing loved, desired, etc.' (E2ax 3). So any content of the mind (the affective element connected to an idea) is not an idea. But it is easy to find counter-examples (quite apart from the fact that 'idea' is often used in a non-specific sense). Thus, in the general definition of affective states, a passion is called 'a confused idea by which the mind affirms a greater or smaller capacity to exist of its body or any part of that body' (E2aff) – so not only would a passion be an *idea* (albeit a confused idea); it could also be expressed as a judgement (something is *affirmed* to be the case). In sum, Spinoza seems to use 'idea' in two rather different ways: (1) Neoplatonic (the true concept of a particular thing as it is formed in God's intellect), which excludes ideas of the imagination, *entia rationis*, etc.; (2) Cartesian (any content of the mind), which includes them. Presumably, this ambiguity arises from the fact that all thinking is an activity of God, who cannot think something (have an idea of something) without causing it to be – which would mean that any idea is true – whereas actually we often find that our ideas are false. In principle, there are two ways of solving this problem. One could say that, in so far as it is a function of the brain, all human thinking is part of nature, so must be conceived by God somehow. Accordingly, a false idea must be conceived by God in so far as God conceives the brain of the individual having that idea. This is what Spinoza has in mind when he claims that *entia rationis* are conceived by God *only* in so far as he conceives the human

mind (CM 2.7). Conversely, one could hold that any idea (in the Cartesian sense) is true *only* in so far as it is truly an idea, that is, in so far as it incorporates an act of thinking on the level of God's intellect. This road is explored in part 2 of the *Ethics* (prop. 32–5).

TEXTS

Daar is geen zaak in de Natuur, of daar is een idea van in de denkende zaak (KV 2.20). *Cum itaque veritas nullo egeat signo, sed sufficiat habere essentias rerum objectivas, aut quod idem est, ideas, ut omne tollatur dubium* (TIE 55, G II, 20). *Hucusque de idea falsa. Superest, ut de idea dubia inquiramus* (TIE 77, G II, 28). *Distinximus inter ideam veram et caeteras perceptiones, ostendimusque quod ideae fictae, falsae et caeterae habent suam originem ab imaginatione* (TIE 86, G III, 32). *Per ideam intelligo Mentis conceptum, per quem Mens format, propterea quod est res cogitans. Expl.: dico potius conceptum quam perceptionem, quia perceptionis nomen indicare videtur, Mentem ab objecto pati.... Per ideam adaequatam* (E3def3 and 4). *At idea dari potest, quamvis nullus alius detur cogitandi modus* (E2ax3). *Esse formale idearum Deum pro causa agnoscit* (E2p5). *Nihil in ideis positivum est, propter quod falsae dicuntur* (E2p33). *Non enim per ideas imagines, quales in fundo oculi, sed cogitationis conceptus intelligo* (E2p48s). *Lectores moneo, ut accurate distinguant inter ideam et inter imagines ... ideam (quandoquidem modus cogitandi est) neque in rei alicujus imagine, neque in verbis consistere* (E2p49s).

BIBLIOGRAPHY
Primary Sources
Descartes, R., *Passions de l'âme,*
  Meditationes, Tertiae Responsiones.

Secondary Literature
Gueroult, M., *Spinoza II De l'Âme*
  (Hildesheim: Olms, 1974).
Verbeek, Th., *Spinoza's Theologico-Political
  Treatise. Exploring 'the Will of God'*,
  (Aldershot: Ashgate, 2002).

Th. Verbeek

Imaginatio

In the *Ethics*, Spinoza frequently uses the nouns *imaginatio* and *imago* and the corresponding verb *imaginari*, notably in the elaboration of his theory of knowledge in part 2 and of the affects in parts 3 and 4. As in Descartes (and in contrast with scholastic tradition), the imagination is related to the mind and is identified with the first – lowest – kind of knowledge. In E2p17s the imagination is treated in connection with 'images', which are those affections of the body whose ideas represent external bodies as though they are present to us. In his early works, imagination merely contrasts negatively with (pure) intellect, as it does in Descartes's *Meditationes* 6, but in his mature thought it has developed into a powerful tool for understanding human psychology and behaviour. The turning point appears to be the TTP, where he analyses prophecy in terms of the imagination (influenced, it seems, by Maimonides; see Ravven, 2001). Spinoza thus brings the notion of the imagination into play in order to account for the way religion works in society.

Spinoza's treatment of the imagination is original in that it is based on the complex and composite character of the mind in relation to the body: what the body perceives directly is not the external thing itself, but the way the human body is affected by it; hence the perception is indicative of the body's own constitution rather than of the nature of the external thing. Thus, the imagination can also account for the mental function of memory (E2p18s). In the common order of nature (E2p29c), the imagination is the default position in the interaction of human beings with their environment. Spinoza distinguishes three kinds of cognition: the imagination (here also called opinion), reason and intuitive knowledge (E2p40s2). To the extent that ideas are inadequate, they must necessarily belong to the first kind of cognition. Spinoza speaks of 'random experience', because it results from fortuitous encounters with external things (E2p29s). The imagination is the sole origin of inadequate ideas and of error, whereas reason and intuitive knowledge yield adequate ideas. Yet the imagination is also a power (and hence a virtue) in itself, since it is an expression of God's power. Without the imagination, the mind would be deprived of all knowledge of its body and of external things. Though inadequate, this knowledge is essential for interacting with the world around us and thus forms part of our CONATUS, our essential striving to maintain our existence. It allows us to use words and images and thus enables us to do geometry and science (Gueroult 1974, pp. 217–8). The power to imagine is proportional to the degree of complexity of the individual body. The superiority of human minds in general (and, within the human species, of specific individuals in particular) is determined by a greater physical complexity and a correspondingly greater power of imagining. One of the precepts for a rational life, therefore, is to render the body capable of being affected by more external bodies (E4p38).

The emphasis on inadequate ideas in the formation of the passions accounts for the pivotal part played by the imagination in Spinoza's theory of affective life. Affects always operate through the medium of the imagination. Since this is an active process that flows necessarily from nature's laws and cannot simply be dispelled by insight into the true state of affairs, it is pointless to ignore or deny it. The power of the mind over the passions is defined solely by knowledge (E5p20s). But though knowledge as such does away with error, it does not cancel the physical phenomenon of the imagination, which follows with necessity from its natural causes (E4p1s). The imaginations the mind is subject to are not at odds with the truth, nor are they dispelled by the appearance of the truth. Those that make us suffer cannot be cured simply by confronting the real state of affairs: they require something that excludes their presence in the mind. This may well be another imagination. The *conatus* operates in such a way that the mind strives to imagine those things which posit its power of acting (E3p54). Spinoza therefore concentrates on the dynamics of the affects, on the interaction between them, on their relative strengths. Good affects are to be strengthened by combining them, bad affects are to be expelled by good ones. This can be achieved only through training, and here the imagination has an important part to play.

One of Spinoza's strategies to undermine anthropomorphic notions of God is to show that they are nothing but 'modes of the imagination', different ways in which our imagination is affected. Since these modes will vary according to the constitution or disposition of individual brains, they give rise to endless confusion and disagreement. Once such notions have emerged, however, people label them with names and henceforth treat them as real entities. Spinoza calls such reified or hypostasized imaginary notions 'beings of the imagination'.

Imagination and memory are firmly rooted in physical experience, and they can express affects of the body as actual only as long as the body exists. They will come to an end when the body ceases to be. The imagination has no role to play in Spinoza's final discussion of the part of the mind that will remain (E5p20s–40s).

TEXTS

Hic per imaginationem, quicquid velis, cape, modo sit quid diversum ab intellectu, et unde anima habeat rationem patientis (TIE 84, G II, 32). *Ad prophetizandum non esse opus perfectiore mente, sed vividiore imaginatione* (TTP 1, G III, 21). *Prophetas non fuisse perfectiore mente praeditos, sed quidem potentia vividius imaginandi* (TTP 2, G III, 29). *Quantitatem attendimus, prout in imaginatione est,...prout in intellectu est* (E1p15s). *Porro, ut verba usitata retineamus, corporis humani affectiones, quarum ideae corpora externa, velut nobis praesentia repraesentant, rerum imagines vocabimus, tametsi rerum figuras non referunt. Et cum mens hac ratione contemplatur corpora, eandem imaginari dicemus...Mentis imaginationes in se spectatas nihil erroris continere* (E2p17s). *[Memoria] est enim nihil aliud, quam quaedam concatenatio idearum, naturam rerum, quae extra corpus humanum sunt, involventium, quae in Mente fit secundum ordinem et concatenationem affectionum corporis humani* (E2p18s). *Utrumque hunc res contemplandi modum cognitionem primi generis, opinionem, vel imaginationem in posterum vocabo* (E2p40s2). *Hinc sequitur, a sola imaginatione pendere, quod res tam respectu praeteriti, quam futuri, ut contingentes contemplemur* (E2p44c1). *Mentis imaginationes magis nostri Corporis affectus, quam corporum externorum naturam indicant* (E3p14). *Nam imaginatio idea est, quae magis Corporis humani praesentem constitutionem, quam corporis externi naturam indicat ... sic reliquae imaginationes, quibus Mens fallitur, sive eae naturalem Corporis constitutionem sive quod ejusdem agendi potentiam augeri vel minui indicant, vero non sunt contrariae, nec ejusdem praesentia evanescunt* (E4p1s). *Mens nihil imaginari potest, neque rerum praeteritarum recordari, nisi durante Corpore* (E5p21). *Illa [pars mentis], quam perire ostendimus, est ipsa imaginatio* (E5p40c).

BIBLIOGRAPHY
Primary Sources
Descartes, R., *Meditationes.*

Secondary Literature
Bostrenghi, D., *Forme e virtù della immaginazione in Spinoza* (Naples: Bibliopolis, 1996).
Deugd, C. de, *The Significance of Spinoza's First Kind of Knowledge* (Assen: Van Gorcum, 1966).
Gueroult, M., *Spinoza, II: l'âme: Éthique, II* (Paris: Aubier-Montaigne, 1974), chapters VI–VIII, appendix 10.
Mignini, F., *Ars imaginandi: apparenza e rappresentazione in Spinoza* (Naples: Edizioni Scientifiche Italiane, 1981).
Moreau, P.-F., *Spinoza: l'expérience et l'éternité* (Paris: Presses Universitaires de France, 1994).
Ravven, H. M., 'Some Thoughts on What Spinoza Learned from Maimonides about the Prophetic Imagination: Part 1. Maimonides on Prophecy and the Imagination', *Journal of the History of Philosophy*, no. 39 (2001), pp. 193–214.

Steenbakkers, P. 'Spinoza on the Imagination', in L. Nauta and D. Pätzold (eds), *The Scope of the Imagination: 'Imaginatio' Between Medieval and Modern Times* (Leuven: Peeters, 2004; Groningen Studies in Cultural Change, vol. xii), pp. 175–93.
Zac, S., 'Le Spinoza de Martial Gueroult: le théorie de l'imagination dans le livre II de l'Ethique', *Revue de synthèse* no 96 (1975), pp. 245–82.

P. Steenbakkers

Imperium

'Dominion' or 'supreme authority' is according to the *Tractatus politicus* (2.17 and 3.1–2) 'usually defined' as the 'right determined by the power of the multitude' to take care of the affairs of the state, that is, in particular, the right to lay down laws, to establish cities and to make decisions on war and peace. Here Spinoza basically reproduces the traditional view of *imperium* as substantially the authority to rule, which is intimated by Micraelius's definition: 'the right and authority of someone to rule someone else and direct his actions'. Hence Spinoza could identify the neo-classical term to denote the sovereign – SUMMA POTESTAS – with *imperium*: 'the right of the Highest Authority *seu* the Sovereigns' – the plural in this phrase refers to the plurality of the body which held sovereignty in the Dutch Republic: the States. However, contrary to tradition this authority denoted by *imperium* is equated with the right of nature. In the first chapter of his political treatise Spinoza refers to the common nature of man, on which the state and its natural principles are grounded, instead of on a rational doctrine. Moreover, in the

233

Tractatus politicus and the *Tractatus theologico-politicus* chapter 16 Spinoza implicitly dismisses the conventional distinction between 'despotic' on the one hand and 'paternal' or 'civil' dominion on the other, which from Aristotle onwards were defined with respect to their different goals, the good of the ruler (*dominus*), for example in the case of the owner of slaves, or the good of the children of the citizens. Sometimes *imperium* is equated with the state as such (TP 2.2, 3.3, 4.1). According to Akkerman, Spinoza substantially imitated the use of this term in classical Latin, its equivalents being state, power and authority of the state, taken as a group of men with military power and juridical authority. He refers to Ulrik Huber, the Frisian lawyer, who defined *imperium* as the will to form a *civitas*, a political body (Akkerman, 12–13). In another sense, rare in Spinoza's writings, *imperium* denotes the power that either the will or reason exercises on the motions of the limbs or the human body as a whole or on the affects.

Without *imperium* there is no civil state. The civil state or an imperium may adopt three forms. In chapter 3 of the *Tractatus politicus* Spinoza refers to the classical division of regimes: MONARCHIA (rule by one), ARISTOCRATIA (rule by some), and DEMOCRATIA (rule by all), sometimes supplemented by THEOCRATIA. This division is as old as political philosophy and was dealt with by Hobbes in chapter 7 of *De cive* using the phrase *species civitatium*. Spinoza diverges on four points from the traditional doctrine.

Firstly, he does not explicitly treat the opposites of the three regimes. It is common to distinguish between regimes led by the public interest and regimes led by their own interests (tyranny, plutocracy, rule by the mob). Spinoza starts with the observation

that man will always be led by his own interests. Hence, it is important that the constitution of a state is such that despite this human inclination the final result is public interest. Secondly, following Flavius Josephus in *Contra Apion* 2.17, he adds theocracy as a fourth regime to the ancient three forms. Thirdly, Spinoza drops the ancient doctrine of the cyclical order of the regimes, according to which each regime will expire and be followed by the next one. In the introduction to his *Discorsi*, Machiavelli proposes a way to escape this fatal cycle of regimes by establishing a mixed regime. Spinoza, however, explains for each regime how it can be made stable. Nevertheless, he is aware of the possibility of regime changes as a danger threatening each regime (TP 7.25). Also some evolution of regimes is possible (TP 8.12). Part of this doctrine is the idea that a people should stick to their regime. From time to time, it is necessary to return to the original constitution (TP 10.1). It is a general principle of all regimes in Spinoza's political thought that their constitution should be such that it remains intact forever. The laws, then, should be in harmony with both reason and the human passions (TP 10.9). Fourthly, the difference between aristocracy and democracy is not whether some rule or many rule but lies in the different ways of electing members to the supreme council: co-optation by the council itself or the legal right to be eligible (TP 8.1, 11.1). This agrees with Hobbes's distinction in his definition of social contract that one man or a council can be authorized to rule the commonwealth (*Leviathan* 17.13). Spinoza also follows Hobbes in the idea that any regime is based on a transfer of power from the people to the highest power, whether this is one person, a council of elected persons, the people as a whole, or God (TTP 16, 19).

TEXTS

Ostendo eos qui summum imperium tenent, jus ad omnia, quae possunt habere ... non tantum juris civilis, sed etiam sacri vindices, et interpres esse (TTP praef, G III, 6–7). *Hinc fit, quod societas non potest subsistere absque imperio et vi et consequenter legibus ... Tota societas collegialiter imperium tenere debet, vel si pauci, aut unus solus* (TTP 5, G III, 74). *Sub imperio naturae ... imperii democratici fundamenta ... Ut subditus imperium civitatis agnoscit* (TTP 16, G III, 190, 195, 197). *Imperium ita administrandum successoribus reliquit ... imperii domus regia templum erat* (TTP 17, G III, 208, 211). *Jura imperii* (TTP 19, G III, 231). *Hominem in natura, veluti imperium in imperio concipere videntur ... in affectus imperium* (E3praef). *Imperium mentis in corpore* (E3p2s). *Ex rationis imperio vivere* (E4app9). *Quantum et quale imperium in affectus* (E5praef). *Quia omnes homines ... statum aliquem civilem formant, ideo imperii causas et fundamenta naturalia, non ex rationis documentis petenda, sed ex hominum communi natura* (TP 1.7). *Hoc jus, quod multitudinis potentia definitur, imperium appellari solet. Atque hoc is absolute tenet, qui curam reipublicae ex communi consensu habet, nempe jura* (TP 2.17). *Peccatum non nisi in imperio concipi potest ... ex communi totius imperii jure decernitur* (TP 2.19). *Imperii cujuscunque status dicitur civilis; imperium autem integrum corpus civitas appellatur, et communia imperii negotia. Denique status civilis tria dari genera ... imperii seu summarum potestatum jus ... imperii corpus et mens tantum juris habet quantum potentia valet* (TP 3.1–2). *Jus summarum potestatum ... imperii veluti mens sit* (TP 4.1). *De optimo cujusque imperii statu* (TP 5.1). *Mediis princeps uti debet ut imperium stabilire et conservare possit* (TP 5.7). *Imperium indivisibile*

esse debet (TP 6.37). *Officium ejus, qui imperium tenet* (TP 7.3). *Ne paulatim ad pauciores deveniat imperium, sed contra ut pro ratione incrementi ipsius imperii eorum augeat numerus* (TP 8.11).

BIBLIOGRAPHY

Primary Sources
Machiavelli, N., *Discorsi sopra la prima deca di Tito Livio* (Florence, 1519).
Hobbes, Th., *Leviathan*.

Secondary Literature
Akkerman, F., 'Mots techniques, Mots classiques', in P. Totaro (ed.), *Spinoziana* (Florence: Olschki, 1997), pp. 1–22.
Curley, E., 'Troublesome Terms for Translators in the TTP', in P. Totaro (ed.), *Spinoziana* (Florence: Olschki, 1997), pp. 39–62.
Moreau, P.F., 'La notion d'imperium dans le Traité politique', in E. Grancotti (ed.), *Spinoza nel 350 anniversario della nascita, Atti del congresso/Proceedings of the First Italian International Congress on Spinoza* (Naples: Bibliopolis, 1985), pp. 355–66.

M. Terpstra

In se esse

In Spinoza's works the phrase 'to be in itself' denotes on the one hand a thing, conceived and thought, without considering its relations to other beings or without comparing it to other things (Ep 8 and E4praef). This denotation was quite conventional and used by scholastics and modern philosophers alike as may be gathered from Descartes's *Meditationes* 3: 'ideas, if these are considered only in themselves, and are not referred to any object beyond them'. In this traditional sense an equivalent is 'to conceive absolutely'. A thing *in se* is the thing as it really is and hence 'in itself' tends to indicate the essence of a thing and the object of real knowledge (Ep 34, CM 1.6). With this connotation the expresssion also figures in the definition of the conatus (E3p6, TP 2.6).

On the other hand 'in itself' traditionally denoted one of the basic features of substance, indicating its existing not in something else. As such Spinoza used the expression in his definition of substance in *Ethics* I definition 3. However, in letter 4 'in itself' is not linked with 'being' but with 'conceiving'. In the second sense 'in itself' is not opposed to 'relatively', but to 'being in another thing' or 'inherence'. In scholastic discourse the notion of non-inherence was often also denoted by *per se*. In the *Ethics*, however, apart from *per se bonus* Spinoza only uses *per se* in combination with 'conceive' or 'understand', which refers to substance's logical priority over the modes. The direct link between 'being in itself' and the notion of 'causal independence' (*causa sui*) made in the *Tractatus de intellectus emendatione* 34 is rare both in tradition and in Spinoza's works, and hence did not return in the *Ethics*.

In the first axiom of *Ethics* 1 Spinoza says that everything that there is is either in itself or in something else. There has been much debate about the meaning of these expressions. It has been suggested that what Spinoza means by 'being in itself' is the traditional Aristotelian conception of substance as the ultimate subject of predication. While properties can be predicated of substance, substances cannot be predicated of anything else. In Aristotle's view snubness can be predicated of the nose while the nose cannot be predicated of anything else. To think that by 'being in itself' Spinoza understood the Aristotelian criterion of substancehood is problematic, because in Spinoza's monism noses and other finite things are in God and thus they should be capable of being predicated of him. Because of this problem Curley suggests that by the *in se esse* condition of substancehood Spinoza means nothing but causal independence. Spinoza's only substance is its own cause and the efficient cause of everything there is and thus it is the only thing that is in itself while all other things as its effects are in it. This alternative interpretation is very interesting but faces an obvious problem. 'Being in itself' is included in the definition of substance (E1def3) but in spite of that Spinoza gives in proposition 6 an elaborate proof that any substance has to be causally independent. This proof would have been superfluous if the distinction between 'being in itself' and 'being in something else' were the distinction between self-caused and other caused entities. In Bennett's field-metaphysical interpretation, the problem receives a solution that is in line with the traditional conception of substance. Closely related to the *in se/in alio* distinction is the distinction between being conceived through itself and being conceived through another. It seems that these distinctions pick up the same entities, but Spinoza does not present any argument for that.

TEXTS

Si res sit in se sive ut vulgo dicitur causa sui, tum per solam suam essentiam debebit intelligi; si vero res non sit in se, sed requirat causam ut existat, tum per proximam suam causam debebit intelligi (TIE 92, G II, 34). *Idea vera dicitur illa, quae nobis ostendit rem ut in se est* (CM 1.6). *Notiones quae naturam explicant non ut in se est, sed prout ad sensum humanum refertur* (Ep 6). *Res duobus potest considerari: vel prout in se est, vel prout respectum habet ad aliud* (Ep 8). *In se esse et per se concipi* (Ep 9). *Res ut in se est, percipere difficillime est* (Ep 12). *Definitio rei naturam, prout in se est involvit et exprimit* (Ep 34). *Intellectualis cognitio ejus naturam, prout in se est considerat* (TTP 13, G III, 171). *In se esse et per se concipi* (E1def3). *Omnia quae sunt, vel in se vel in alio sunt* (E1ax1). *Id quod in se est et per se concipitur, sive talia substantiae attributa ... hoc est Deus quatenus ut causa libera consideratur* (E1p19s). *Rerum ut in se sunt Deus revera est causa, quatenus infinitis constat attributis* (E2p7s). *De natura rationis est res vere pericipere, nempe ut in se sunt* (E2p44). *Unaquaeque res quantum in se est in suo esse perseverare conatur* (E3p6). *Bonum et malum ... in se consideratis ... ex eo quod res ad invicem comparamus* (E4praef).

BIBLIOGRAPHY
Primary Sources
Descartes, R., *Meditationes.*

Secondary Literature
Bennett, J., *A Study of Spinoza's Ethics* (Cambridge: Cambridge University Press, 1984).
Curley, E., 'On Bennett's Interpretation of Spinoza's Metaphysics', in Y. Yovel (ed.), *God and Nature. Spinoza's Metaphysics* (Leiden: Brill, 1991), pp. 35–51.
Gueroult, M., *Spinoza I. Dieu (Éthique I)* (Hildesheim: Olms, 1968).
Koistinen, O., *On the Metaphysics of Spinoza's Ethics* (Turku: Turku University Press, 1991).
Richter, G.Th., *Spinozas philosophische Terminologie. I. Grundbegriffe der Metaphysik* (Leipzig: Barth, 1913).
Robinson, L., *Kommentar zu Spinozas Ethik* (Leipzig: Meiner, 1928).

O. Koistinen

Infinitum

Although Spinoza adopted the classic distinction between the finite and the infinite from his early works onwards, only in the first part of the *Ethics* and letter 12 did he define these concepts in a way stipulated by his system.

Spinoza defines the finite by its limited or negative nature. The second definition of *Ethics* 1 reads: 'a thing is said to be finite in its kind, which can be limited by another thing of the same kind', and in the first scholium of proposition 8 it says: 'as finite being is in reality a partial denial'. According to Chauvin the first notion is conventional and the second notion of Cartesian origin. He observed: 'a thing is finite, which does not contain all reality or perfection. Hence, although the Cartesians assume that the world is infinite by extension, it is finite by its essence or perfection'.

This negative notion of the finite seems to support all readings of Spinozism as a kind of pantheism, which tends to contemplate the finite things as mere epiphenomena destined to be reabsorbed into the unique substance. However, other texts oppose such a reading and state that the finite is also an equivalent of the singular (E1p28). The real universe in which we live consists of singular things, each having their own power, and the negation marking their limitations is at the same time a determination which guarantees their individuality. The natural individuals possess their own power which is only a transformation of God's eternal power, as Spinoza states in *Tractatus politicus* 2.2. Hence, instead of conceiving the finite as a depreciation of the infinite, one may well interpret it as the particular form of existence acquired by the infinite within the universe consisting of concrete beings.

Accordingly in the same scholium (E1p8s1) Spinoza defines the infinite as 'the absolute affirmation of a nature', which he depicts as a consequence of the infinity of substance. Here the absolute infinity of God is defined, which essence excludes all negation (E1def6). This is the 'absolute' infinite of tradition, opposed to infinite 'in a certain respect' (Micraelius). However, the term 'infinite' may be applied to several things. There is first the infinite that the mathematicians deal with and in this case, as Spinoza suggests to Meyer, we should prefer the term 'indefinite'. He specifies that we cannot consider number, measure and time infinite in a proper sense, since they are only devices of the imagination. The infinite in a proper sense is a term which we are able to attribute only to substance, the attributes and certain modes. Substance is absolutely infinite, that is to say not only that no things limit it, but it also consists of infinities (the attributes). The attributes are only infinite in their kind, that is to say their nature (extension, thinking, or whatever other attribute unknown to us) does not tolerate any limitation, unlike the particular modes – a thought limits another thought and a body another body – but of each them the specific property of the other modes may be denied. However, the modes which directly or indirectly depend on the nature of the attribute are infinite as well. Unfortunately Spinoza deals with these infinite modes only briefly, both in E1p21-3 and in his answer to Schuller (letter 64). He mentions the infinite intellect as the infinite mode of thinking,

motion and rest as the immediate infinite mode of extension, and as the mediate infinite mode the so-called *facies totius universi*. However, he leaves undecided whether such a mode only follows from extension, or from the other attributes as well.

Commentators often raise the question of how the finite may be deduced from the infinite. However, it is uncertain if such a question is really a Spinozistic one. It seems to imply the notion of emanation. A truly Spinozistic outlook tends to trace the development of the infinite by means of the causality of the finite.

TEXTS

God oneijndige eigenschappen heeft (KV 1.1). Door haar natuur zijn alle deelen eijndelijk (KV 1.2). Oneijndig in haar geslagt (KV 2.9). *Dei infinitas invito vocabulo, sit quid maxime positivum, nam eatenus ipsum infinitum esse dicimus, quatenus ad ejus essentiam sive summam perfectionem attendimus* (CM 2.3). *Ens constans infinitis attributis, quorum unumquodque est infinitum sive summe perfectum in suo genere* (Ep 2). *Non distinxerunt inter id quod sua natura, sive vi suae definitionibus sequiter esse infinitum et id quod nullos fines habet non quidem vi suae essentiae, sed vi suae causae* (Ep 12). *Ea res dicitur in suo genere finita, quae alia ejusdem naturae terminari potest. Ex. gr. Corpus dicitur finitum, quia semper majus concipimus* (E1def2). *Ens absolute infinitum ... absolute infinitum, non autem in suo genere ... negationem nullam involvit* (E1def6). *Omnis substantia necessario infinitum ... finitum esse revera ex parte negatione* (E1p8s1). *Omnis quae ex absoluta natura alicujus attributi Dei sequuntur, semper et infinita existere debuerunt, sive per idem attributum aeterna et infinita sunt* (E1p21). *Quodcunque singulare,*

sive quaevis res, quae finita est et determina-
tam habet existentiam (E1p28).

BIBLIOGRAPHY
Secondary Literature
Gueroult, M., *Spinoza I. Dieu (Éthique I)*
  (Hildesheim: Olms, 1968).
Robinson, L., *Kommentar zu Spinozas Ethik*
  (Leipzig: Meiner, 1928).
Saverio, A., *Spinoza et le baroque. Infini,*
  désir, multitude (Paris: Éditions Kimé,
  2001).

P.-F. Moreau

In suo genere

The expression *in suo genere* occurs six times
in Spinoza's Latin works (four times in combination with its opposite *absolute*). Its
Dutch counterpart *in syn/haar geslagt* is
used no fewer than twelve times. The Latin
word *genus*, or the Dutch expression *geslagt* –
literally genus or gender – belongs to the language of scholastic logic. In this context it is
not opposed to *species*: it refers rather to a
summum genus, that is to say a category of
being. In CM 2.1 Spinoza refers to the two
supreme genera of being in Cartesian philosophy, that is to say extension and thought,
and in letter 36 Spinoza uses the phrase *'in
certo genere entis'* as an equivalent of *in suo
genere*. For genus in the sense of category see
Chauvin, s.v.: 'There are two kinds of genus:
a highest and a subaltern one. The highest
genus occupies the highest rank in its class
and category.'
  In the *Ethics* Spinoza identifies these 'categories of being' with the attributes of God,
nature or substance. In E1p16 he observes,
'the divine nature has absolutely infinite

attributes, each of which also expresses an
essence infinite *in suo genere'*. As such the
phrase is of vital importance to his definition
of God in that it distinguishes the finite infinity of the attributes from the absolute infinity
of the substance. Hence the phrase is only to
be found in the first part of the *Ethics*. Moreover, the scant use of the phrase in comparison with the *Korte verhandeling* seems
to indicate a changing focus in Spinoza's
thought.
  In suo genere is derived from contemporary Dutch neo-scholastic manuals of
logic. Burgersdijck, for example, uses the
phrase when dealing with the concept of 'first
cause'. In *Institutiones logicae* I, chap. 17,
sect 29, he observes that the phrase 'a first
cause' is used in two ways. On the one hand
there is 'the cause on which all things depend
in their origin, being and working, cf. Acts
17;28'. Such a cause is 'absolutely first and
unique, that is to say God'. On the other hand
there is 'a first cause *in suo genere'*. On such
a cause only the other causes of the same category (*ejusdem generis*) depend. Burgersdijk
illustrates the latter with the examples of the
first man Adam, who is the cause of all further human generation, and the soul, which
is the base and origin of all vital operations. Heereboord's discussion in *Hermeneia*
I, chap. 17, q. 26 is parallel to Burgersdijk's.
He opposes an absolutely first cause – 'with
nothing prior to it in the universe' – to a cause
first *in suo genere*, that is to say in creation.
This is the context to which Spinoza refers in
E1p28s, when he states that 'God is absolutely the proximate cause of all things produced immediately and not *in suo genere'*.

TEXTS
In sijn geslagte oneijndelijk volmaakt (KV
1.2). Beweginge…oneijndig in haar geslagt

(KV 1.9). Uijtgebreijdheid een eigenschap is die wij oneijndelijk in haar geslagt betoond hebben te sijn (KV 2,19). Oneijndige eigenschappen .. volmaakt in sijn geslagt (KVapp p4). *Attributa...summe perfecta in suo genere* (Ep 2). *Extensio non absolute infinita sed in suo genere* (Ep 4). *Extensio et cogitatio in suo genere, hoc est in certo genere entis perfectae esse queunt* (Ep 36). *Res in suo genere finita* (E1def2). *Absolute infinitum, non autem in suo genere* (E1def6ex). *Natura divina infinita absolute attributa habeat, quorum etiam unumquodque infinitam essentiam in suo genere exprimit* (E1p16). *Deus sit rerum immediate ab ipso productarum causa absolute proxima, non vero in suo genere* (E1p28s).

BIBLIOGRAPHY
Primsary Sources
Burgersdijk, F., *Institutiones metaphysicae* (Leiden, 1642).
Heereboord, A., *Hermeneia logica, sive synopseos logicae Burgerdicianae explicatio* (Leiden, 1640).

Secondary Literature
Gueroult, M., *Spinoza I: Dieu* (Hildesheim: Olms, 1968).

Intellectus

Expressed in his typical metaphysical terminology, Spinoza's doctrine of the intellect was unprecedented in his day. Neither the divine infinite nor the human finite intellect are part of an essence, but they belong to 'natured nature' (E1p31). According to Spinoza they are modifications of the attribute of Thought. Constituted by specific and individual acts the intellect is always actual. Spinoza, therefore, rejects the Aristotelian theory of the intellect which distinguished between a potential and an actual intellect, which is active (E1p31s). Moreover, Spinoza rejects as fictitious the Aristotelian notion of the intellect as a faculty, for the intellect is merely a metaphysical entity, like the universal. The intellect is a rational entity, with no reality beyond the particular acts of knowing and the ideas contained in the human mind at a specific moment (E2p48s). Hence the intellect can only be defined by virtue of its properties (TIE 107). Typical of Spinoza is, thirdly, the notion that the will is not essentially different from the understanding (E2p49c). Time and again Spinoza denounces the notion that the will might 'extend' itself further than the intellect and could enforce man to action although the mind lacks clear and distinct knowledge (Ep 2, Ep 21, E2p49). The tendency to identify will and intellect was apparently inherent in modern philosophy. Chauvin s.v. *voluntas* observed that 'since according to modern philosophers the intellect is the same as the knowing soul the will is identical with the willing soul as well. Hence intellect and will are no more differentiated than by a modal distinction'. In this respect Descartes, who assumed two distinct faculties and two corresponding categories of acts of the mind seems to be an exception (PP 1.33).

The intellect is not a part of the mind but is the mind as far as it knows adequately and is opposed to the imagination (TIE 66). Hence, it is only the intellect which knows substance and eternity. When the mind *knows* it is called intellect. However, when it imagines the mind is passive (TIE 64). The mind is active if it forms ideas which are clear and distinct (TIE 108). By virtue of this activity, that is by obtaining knowledge of God and his attributes, the mind becomes more perfect and we acquire our beatitude. Hence the intellect is the part of the mind which is eternal (E5p40c).

intelligere (E4app4). *Pars mentis aeterna est intellectus per quem solum nos agere dicimur* (E5p40c). *Humana potentia ad coërcendos affectus in solo intellectu consistit* (E5p42)

TEXTS

Gelijk als daar is het verstand, het welke zoo ook de Philosoophen zeggen een oorzaak is van sijn begrippen, maar aangezien het een inblijvende oorzaak is (KV 1.2). *Voluntatem distinctam ab intellectu, multo minus tali praeditam esse libertate* (PPC praef). *Intellectus vi sua nativa facit sibi instrumenta intellectualia* (TIE 32, G II, 14). *Definitio intellectus per se innotescet, si ad ejus proprietates, quas clare et distincte intelligimus, attendamus* (TIE 107, G II, 38). *Intellectum, quamvis infinitum ad Naturam naturatam pertinere* (Ep 9). *Multa nequaquam imaginatione, sed solo intellectu assequi possumus, talia sunt substantia et aeternitas et alia* (Ep 12). *Intellectus, actu finitus aut actu infinitus Dei attributa, Deique affectiones comprehendere debet* (E1p30). *Intellectus actu sive is finitus sive infinitus ad naturam naturatem referri debent* (E1p31). *Non concedo ullum dari intellectum potentia* (E1p31c). *Concetenatio idearum quae fit secumdum ordinem intellectus quo res per primas causas mens pericpit et qui in omnibus hominibus idem est* (E2p18s). *Eodem hoc modo demonstratur in mente nullam dari facultatem absolutam intelligendi, cupiendi, amandi, etc. Unde sequitur, has, et similes facultates, vel prorsus fictitias, vel nihil esse praeter entia metaphysica, sive universalia* (E2p48s). *Voluntas et intellectus unum et idem sunt* (E2p49c). *In vita itaque apprime utile est intellectum seu rationem quantum possumus perfice et in hoc uno summa hominis felicitas seu beatitudo consistit ... intellectum perficere nihil etiam, est quam Deum, Deique attributa*

BIBLIOGRAPHY

Primary Sources
Descartes, R., *Principia philosophiae, Meditationes.*

Secondary Literature
Gueroult, M., *Spinoza I. Dieu (Éthique I)*, (Hildesheim: Olms, 1968).
————, *Spinoza II – L'âme* (Hildesheim: Olms, 1974).
Verbeek, Th., *Spinoza's Theologico-Political Treatise. Exploring 'the Will of God'.* (Aldershot: Ashgate, 2003).

L. Spruit

Interpretatio

In chapters 16–18 of the *Tractatus theologico-politicus* the term 'interpretation' has a juridical-political meaning, denoting a correct understanding of a lawgiver's will. Justice in daily practice, Spinoza observed, is the result of a correct interpretation of the law, while wrongdoing is facilitated by the possession of the power to interpret the laws at one's own discretion. Therefore, in the former Hebrew state the princes were deprived of the authority to intepret the laws, which power was granted to the Levites. Religious practice is based on correct interpretation of the law as well. According to chapter 18 the decadence of the Mosaic laws and the perversion of their true sense and correct interpretation resulted in the degeneration of true religion.

The philological sense of interpretation is defined by Micraelius as 'the explanation of an obscure text in clearer terms'. Such an explanation may be given in an infallible manner by God himself or by man. A method to interpret the texts of the Bible, which according to Spinoza are often obscure, is developed in TTP 7, the initial kernel of the treatise. According to letter 30 this chapter dates back to the autumn of 1665. Spinoza borrowed his view of method from Bacon's hermeneutical model. The interpretation of the Bible had to imitate the method of natural science (*Novum organum* 26 ff.). The method consists in a careful reading of the text and a review of all relevant non-textual facts, such as the date of composition, the type of language, who the author was and what he intended, and so on. This method aims to produce a so-called 'history' and to gauge the author's beliefs from the text. Knowledge of Scripture could only be drawn from such histories, which consider text and context, practical teachings as well as speculative opinions. The interpreter must use the natural light shared by all people in order to avoid disputes that fuel superstition. Implicitly Spinoza rejects both the 'orthodox' Reformed thesis that identifies the word of God with Scripture and the Roman Catholic view according to which the interpreter is tradition, by dealing with the view of Jehudah Alpakhar (d. 1235) that the interpreter of the Bible has at his disposal a supernatural light granted by God, and with Maimonides's thesis which says that philosophers and theologians are the interpreters. For Spinoza that which is against nature is against reason, and that which is against reason is absurd (TTP 6). In letter 75 a spiritual and allegorical interpretation of some New Testament texts is put forward.

Any method of biblical interpretation requires a clear principle, and every confession in the seventeenth century put forward its own principle. According to the Socinians in *Bibliotheca* II, p. 240 the interpreter is the *recta ratio*, in Meyer's view in the *Interpres* 5 it is the *nova philosophia*, while according to Wolzogen in the *Orthodoxa fides* II the intention of the author (*mens auctoris*) is the paramount factor. The Remonstrant Episcopius in *Vedelius rhapsodus* pp. 331–5 observed that the supposed mysteries of Scripture foment disputes and schisms (see TTP 6). Voetius in the *Disputationes selectae* V, p. 423–35 declares the Holy Spirit speaking through Scripture to be its infallible interpreter. According to Bellarmine in *Disputationes* I, 1, p. 212 and II, 1, p. 421 Scripture is abstruse and only the Church can interpret it. Hobbes's view therefore in *De cive* 17.18 and 27 and *Leviathan* 33 and 42 is that the true interpreter is he who holds legislative power (if the prince is a Christian).

TEXTS

Ep 30; Ep 75. *Quod ex ipsa Scriptura, qua minime humanis figmentis indiget, longe melius edoceremur, in primo limine pro regula ipsius interpretationis statuunt* (TTP praef, G III, 9). *Pauca de interpretatione miraculorum notare* (TTP 6, G III, 91). *Ut mentem a theologicis praejudiciis liberemus ... nobis de vera methodo interpretandi Scripturam agendum est* (TTP 7, G III, 98). *Injustitia est sub specie juris alicui detrahere quod ei ex vera interpretatione legis competit* (TTP 16, G III, 196). *Ex quo manifestum fit, quod magnam Hebraeorum principibus causam facinorum sublatam fuisse, eo quod omne jus interpretandi legum Levitis datam fuerit* (TTP 17, G III, 212). *Ut religio in exitiabilem superstitionem declinaret et legum verus sensus et interpetatio corrumperetur* (TTP 18, G III, 222).

BIBLIOGRAPHY
Primary Sources
Bacon, F., *Novum organum* (London, 1620).
Bellarminus, R., *Disputationes de controversiis christianae fidei adversus hujus temporis haereticos*, 4 vols (Ingolstadt, 1605).
Bibliotheca Fratrum Polonorum ([Amsterdam], 1656).
Episcopius, S., *Vedelius rhapsodus*, in *Opera theologica* II (Amsterdam, 1665).
Hobbes, Th., *De cive, Leviathan.*
[Meyer, L.], *Philosophia S. Scripturae interpres* ([Amsterdam], 1666).
Voetius, G., *Selectae disputationes theologicae*, 5 vols (Utrecht, 1648–69).
Wolzogen, L., *Orthodoxa fides* (Utrecht, 1668).

Secondary Literature
Adler, J., 'Letters of Judah Alfakhar and David Kimhi', *Studia Spinozana*, no. 12 (1996), pp. 141–67.
Bordoli, R., *Ragione e Scrittura tra Descartes e Spinoza* (Milano: Franco Angeli, 1997).
Verbeek, Th., *Spinoza's Theologico-Political Treatise. Exploring 'the Will of God'* (Aldershot: Ashgate, 2003).

R. Bordoli

Involvere

The idea of A involves the idea of B – or A cannot be conceived without B (E2p49d) just in case the idea of A has to be formed from the idea of B (E1def3). This relation comes close to logical entailment, i.e. to the notion that the truth of an idea of A is sufficient for the truth of an idea of B, but is not quite the same. One reason for this non-identity is that in Spinoza's necessitarianism all ideas entail each other but they do not involve each other.

A good grasp of 'involvement' helps to explain, among other things, Spinoza's ontological argument, i.e. his proof that any possible substance exists by necessity (E1p7) as well his theory of adequate ideas. The attributes of thought and extension are for Spinoza such expressions of God's or nature's force which we conceive in themselves and through which we conceive everything else. For example, we cannot conceive motion without a moving body. Thus the idea of motion involves the idea of a body. However, bodies cannot be conceived without the attribute of extension and thus the idea of a body involves the idea of extension. Finally, extension is something that we conceive in itself and so it does not involve the idea of any other thing. This is to say that anyone has an adequate idea of extension from which idea the intellect may infer new adequate ideas. The ideas of attributes are what the mind needs to have any ideas at all. So to say that the idea of A involves the idea of B means, at least in part, that nobody can have the idea of A without having the idea of B. When an idea does not involve any other idea, it cannot of course involve a separate idea of existence; however, such an idea involves existence. We can conceive existing things as non-existing while we think of something in which their possibility is not realized. We can conceive space without the sun once we think of space as not containing the sun but we cannot conceive space as non-existing. Thus, a conceptually independent idea of a thing involves the existence of the thing thought about.

TEXTS

Dei conceptum pro ratione suae essentiae suaeque perfectionis involvere (TTP 4, G III, 69). *Per causam sui intelligo id, cujus essentia involvit existentiam* (E1def1). *Effectus cognitio a cognitione causae dependet et eandem involvit* (E1ax4). *Quicquid ut non existens potest concipi, ejus essentia non involvit existentiam* (E1ax7). *Id cujus definitio necessariam existentiam involvit* (E1p8s). *Contradictionem involvere* (E1p11al). *Absolutam perfectionem involvere* (E1p11s). *Id quoad substantiam pertinet attributa involvunt* (E1p19dem). *Ejusdem attributi conceptum involvere* (E2lem2 after p13). *Haec affirmatio conceptum sive ideam trianguli involvit, hoc est sine idea trianguli non potest concipi* (E2p49).

BIBLIOGRAPHY

Secondary Literature

Richter, G.Th., *Spinozas philosophische Terminologie. I. Grundbegriffe der Metaphysik* (Leipzig: Barth, 1913).

Wilson, M.D., 'Spinoza's Causal Axiom (Ethics I, axiom 4)', in Y. Yovel (ed.), *God and Nature. Spinoza's Metaphysics* (Leiden: Brill, 1991), pp. 133–60.

O. Koistinen

Iudicium

In the preface to the PPC, Lodewijk Meyer observed that the theory of judgement is one of the basic differences between Descartes's and Spinoza's philosophy. According to Descartes's *Principia philosophiae* I art. 32 in the mind two general classes of modes of thinking may be distinguished. To the first class belong all perceptions or operations of the understanding and to the second one all volitions or operations of the will. Passive *cogitationes* such as to sense, to imagine and to conceive things purely intelligible, are to be attributed to the intellect; but active *cogitationes* such as to desire, to be averse from, to affirm, to deny, to doubt, are different modes of willing. In *cogitationes* such as perceiving, imagining, the mind is passive, since the mind is passively formed by the ideas, according to Chauvin who expounds the Cartesian theory. A judgement, however, is an action of the mind, since 'the mind is moving and determining itself ... by combining or separating ideas'. Therefore a judgement is a free act of affirmation or negation by the mind, whereas the forming of an idea is a passive cogitation. The ideas are the raw material supplied by the intellect, but they are removed from another or conjoined by a mind determining itself, i.e. the will. Moreover, according to Descartes a judgement is an act of the will, for the mind is judging whenever it assents to the truth or the plausibility of something. Basic to Descartes's theory of judgement is the distinction in the mind between a free and active will and a passive intellect.

By denouncing the Cartesian doctrine of free will and a real distinction between the will and the intellect Spinoza denounced his theory of judgement as well. Spinoza defines the will as the faculty of affirming or denying ideas, and not a desire (E2p48s), because there is no absolute will that is distinct from the intellect (E2p49c) and each idea is necessarily determined by a cause, which is likewise determined by another cause, and so on *ad infinitum* (E2p48). Doubt or uncertainty is untruth (E2p49s). Hence not only is the will really identical with the intellect (E2p49c), but also is there no difference between an act of willing, i.e. affirming and the act of having an idea (E2p49). To think is to judge, he observed in *Cogitata metaphysica* 2.12. Spinoza's theory of judgement follows from his definition of having an idea. Unlike Descartes he observes that an idea is a concept of the mind, which term expresses an activity of the mind (E2def3). The Cartesian account of judgement is for Spinoza an important cause of prejudices which he discusses in the appendix of *Ethics* 1.

TEXTS
Ad secundam objectionem respondeo negando nos liberam habere potestatem judicium suspendendi. Nam cum dicimus aliquem judicium suspendere, nihil aliud dicimus quam quod videt se rem non adæquate percipere. Est igitur judicii suspensio revera perceptio et non libera voluntas (E2p49s).

BIBLIOGRAPHY
Primary Sources
Descartes, R., *Meditationes de prima philosophia, Principia philosophiae.*

Secondary Literature
Gueroult, M., *Spinoza II – L'âme* (Paris: Éditions Aubier-Montaigne, 1974).
Parkinson, G.H.R., *Spinoza's Theory of Knowledge* (Oxford: Clarendon Press, 1954).
Verbeek, Th., *Spinoza's Theologico-Political Treatise. Exploring 'the Will of God'* (Aldershot: Ashgate, 2003).
Wilson, M.D., 'Spinoza's theory of knowledge', in Don Garret (ed.), *The Cambridge Companion to Spinoza* (Cambridge: Cambridge University Press, 1996), pp. 89–141.

F. Buyse

Lex

The word *lex* and its Dutch synonym *wet* occur in all of Spinoza's works. These words are primarily combined with 'God' or 'nature', but also with 'human', 'Hebrew', 'human reason' or 'pure intellect'. The complex nature of the concept appears from its main discussion in the *Tractatus theologico-politicus* chapter 4, which starts with an overall definition: 'the word *lex* taken in its absolute sense [as such], means that according to which each individual thing – either in general or those of the same kind – act in one and the same fixed and determinate manner'. Further, a law may depend either on nature's necessity or on a decision of the human will.

As to the first category, these laws follow from the nature or definition of a particular thing. The universal laws of nature, those according to which all things happen and are determined, are the eternal decrees of God, which always involve eternal truth and necessity (TTP 3). Only in this respect is natural law to be called divine law. Although these expressions frequently occur in scholastic and pre-modern discourse as well, the Spinozistic notion of a natural law without a divine lawgiver who promulgates these rules is relatively new. In this respect Spinoza's view is intimately linked to that of Descartes who in the *Principia philosophiae* 2.37 defined the laws of nature as 'rules which may be known by means of God's immutability' and like Newton later on identifies these rules with the laws of mechanical motion.

Spinoza stated that commonly the word 'law' is applied to natural phenomena only by analogy. It seems that in a proper sense we call 'laws' only those rules which depend on human will, i.e. the second category of laws. For as Spinoza clarifies: ordinarily 'law' is used to mean simply a command which men can either obey or disobey, in as much as it restricts the total range of human power within set limits and demands nothing that is beyond human power. 'Thus it is expedient to define law more particularly as a plan of life laid down by man for himself or others with a certain object'. The legislator may establish law with respect to an end to be achieved. This end should not be understood as a goal which should be in conformity with higher, God-decreed law.

Such notions in part sum up the gist of scholastic discourse as is apparent from the contemporary dictionaries. Chauvin for example observed that 'a law is a rule of a moral action' and Goclenius stated 'a law taken as such is a rule and measure of human actions'. Morever, this linking of law with an end was an intrinsic part of Thomistic tradition. Aquinas in his famous question 90 on 'the essence of the law' in the *Summa theologiae* part 1 stated that 'law is nothing else than an ordinance of reason for the common good'. Spinoza links this notion elegantly to the voluntaristic tradition originating in Duns Scotus and Ockham, by focusing on the will of the legislator, observing: 'However, as the true object of legislation is only perceived by a few, and most men are almost incapable of grasping it, though they live under its conditions, legislators promise' rewards and punishments. 'Thus endeavouring to restrain the masses, as far as may be, like a horse with a curb'. Hence a law is a mode of life 'enjoined on men by the sway of others' and 'those who obey the law are said

to live under it and to be under compulsion' (TTP 4). This conception of law takes human nature as its starting point. Moreover, Spinoza continues his survey of the notion of law by disconnecting the traditionally linked notions of law and morals: 'sin is action that cannot lawfully be done, i.e. is prohibited by law' (TP 2.19). Sin cannot be conceived except in a state with its civil law.

A distinct feature of Spinoza's political thought is that in the first instance he does not argue from the first (quasi-mechanical) conception of law. By observing that 'laws prescribe or prohibit behaviour ordained to achieve a goal', he infers that a 'law which depends on human will is one which men ordain for themselves and for others in view of making life more secure and more convenient, or for other reasons'; such a law is more properly called *ius* (ordinance). Generally Spinoza follows the common usage of law and right, which imply different perspectives on behaviour. Human laws are imperative general rules regulating human or institutional behaviour. They forbid, prescribe, or enable certain behaviour; in this way they establish a normative order. These civil laws are the basis of rights, for these general rules address persons and institutions which derive the right (or competence) or obligation to act. *Ius* (right) generally expresses the liberty to act in the sense of that part of a citizen's natural right which is allowed and left by the civil laws, as Hobbes writes in *De Cive* 13.5. It is the liberty left to the subject addressed by this general rule to behave in a certain way, be this subject a citizen, society at large, or (an organ of) the state. In case of a prescriptive rule, for example, an individual may be obliged to behave in a certain way and the state has the right to enforce obedience. In the end, however, for Spinoza one's right is always determined by one's natural right; a man's right extends as far as his power does (TP 2.3–4).

As for ordained law, this is to be divided into human law and divine law (TTP 4.3). Human law is a rule of conduct whose sole aim is to safeguard life and the commonwealth, whereas divine law aims at the supreme good, the true knowledge and love of God. This law is a divine law for it is a way of life ordained by us in as far as we know God. These divine laws consist of divine commands, which are ordained as it were by God, that is by our notion of him in our minds. Thus, the philosophical life may well be called a 'divine law' and is dealt with in general ethics. The aim of this divine law, the true knowledge and love of God, can be achieved through the knowledge of natural phenomena; the greater our knowledge of natural phenomena, the more perfect our knowledge of God's essence. Consequently, in this way, these so-called divine laws are connected to natural law or divine law in the first (proper) sense. Spinoza calls the divine law which is deduced from human nature, the natural divine law. Such laws are universal and exclude the belief in historical narrations, presumably about their promulgation.

As for the other kind of ordained law, human law, Spinoza regards it as an agency to safeguard life and the commonwealth. Civil law, therefore, is an important means by which the state can achieve its end, i.e. the peace and security of the citizens. The law preserves their liberty by coercing citizens to act in a particular way. Law as a means to create security for people by ensuring their peaceful co-operation reflects in a way Machiavelli's statement in the *Discorsi* 1.3 that it is the laws that make them good. Citizens of a state are not in a position to decide what is just or unjust, right or wrong; they must

submit their will to that of the commonwealth. For citizens, the state is a co-operative enterprise for their mutual advantage, so they have to obey its commands and the ordinances, which must be taken to be the will of all. Thus, the citizen acts in his own interest by obeying the civil laws. Therefore, he is one who recognizes the true plan of the civil laws and their necessity and acts accordingly in a steadfast spirit and 'on the basis of his own decree, not, in truth, some alien one' (here, the idea of self-legislation – Rousseau, Kant – is dimly visible). Furthermore, the right of 'being one's own judge ceases in the civil state' (TP 3.3). This right rests only with the ruler of the state; the commonwealth has the (civil) right to enact laws and to interpret and enforce these laws (TP 4.5–6).

The commonwealth or the state is the sole author of the laws and, therefore, is not bound by them. However, there are limitations to its power, for the commonwealth is bound by natural law. Civil laws which conflict with nature's necessity go beyond the limits of human power and will not be obeyed. Civil laws should not demand the impossible, be it actual behaviour or a particular attitude towards the law, such as respect for a law which actually moves people to disgust. Otherwise, the subject (citizens) will not be willing to act in one and the same fixed and determinate manner, and the law might not be called a proper law anymore. Civil laws, therefore, should inspire obedience, rather than rely on force.

Thus, civil laws are posited, established by the state, and laws are not determined by moral essences like good or evil. By contrast, traditional natural law theory offers arguments for the existence of a 'higher law.' In the natural law theory of the Middle Ages God lays down express commands for all mankind, which served as the higher standards for positive law. According to Thomas Aquinas human (positive) law, which deflects from the higher law, the law of nature, is not law. Spinoza denies this teleological essence of law, nor does he advocate a voluntaristic conception of law. Unlike Hobbes he views law as not simply *voluntas* or will (cf. *Leviathan* 26). Therefore, the power of the legislator is not unlimited, his commands have to take into account the power of the subjects. This power is determined by the laws of nature, for 'man, whether guided by reason or mere desire, does nothing save in accordance with the laws and rules of nature, that is, by natural right' (TP 2.5). Good laws enhance the citizens' power which in turn increases the power of the commonwealth and the sovereign. Spinoza, therefore, views the relationship between state and citizens *ex parte populi*, as Bobbio rightly remarks (1989, p. 144).

TEXTS

Als de wetten van de natuur machtiger zijn, worden de wetten van de menschen vernietigt. De goddelijke wetten zijn het laatste eijnde om het welke zij zijn (KV 2.26). *Anima secundum certas leges agens* (TIE 88, G II, 35). *Leges naturae extensae* (PPC praef). *Leges naturae sunt decreta Dei lumine naturali revelata* (CM 2.12). *Leges mechanicae* (Ep 13). *Leges naturae universales secundam quas omnia fiunt et determinantur nihil esse nisi Dei aeterna decreta quae semper aeternam veritatem et necessitatem involvunt* (TTP 3, G III, 46). *Legis nomen absolute sumptum significat id, secundum quod unumquodque individuum, vel omnia vel aliquot ejusdem speciei una eademque certa ac determinata ratione agunt ... communiter per legem nihil aliud intelligitur quam mandatum ... per [lex] humanam intelligo rationem vivendi, quae ad* *tutandam vitam et rempublicam tantum inservit ... at is qui unicuique suum tribuit, ex eo quod veram legum rationem et earum necessitatem novit, is animo constanti agit et ex proprio, non vero alieno decreto, adeoque justus merito, vocatur* (TTP 4, G III, 59). *Qui omnia legibus determinare vult, vitia irritabit potius, quam corrigibit* (TTP 20, G III, 243). *Leges motus et quietis* (E2p2s). *Communes leges naturae sequuntur affectus* (E3praef). *Naturae leges et regulae secundum quas omnia fiunt* (E3p2s). *Peccatum est, quod jure fieri nequit, sive quod jure prohibetur* (TP 2.19). *Optimi imperii jura ex rationis dictamine institui debent* (TP 2.21). *Nam si civitas nullis legibus seu regulis, sine quibus civitas non esset civitas, adstricta esset, tum civitas non ut res naturalis sed ut chimaera esset contemplenda* (TP 4.4).

BIBLIOGRAPHY
Primary Sources
Aquinas, *Summa theologiae*.
Descartes, R., *Principia philosophiae*.
Hobbes, Th., *De Cive, Leviathan*.
Machiavelli, N., *Disputationum de republica, quas discursus nuncapavit libri III, ex Italico Latini facti* (Leiden, 1649).

Secondary Literature
Belaief, G., *Spinoza's Philosophy of Law* (The Hague: Mouton, 1971).
Bobbio, N., *Democracy and Dictatorship* (Cambridge: Polity Press, 1989; original Italian edn 1980).
Grawert, R., 'Gesetz', in O. Brunner, W. Conze and R. Koselleck (eds), *Geschichtliche Grundbegriffe*, vol. 2 (Stuttgart: Klett Cotta, 1975), pp. 863–922.
Gribnau, H., 'La Force du Droit: La contribution de Spinoza à la théorie du

droit', *Revue interdisciplinaire d'études juridiques,* no. 35 (1995), pp. 19–39.

Skinner, Q., 'The Republican Ideal of Political Liberty', in G. Bock, Q. Skinner and M. Viroli (eds.), *Machiavelli and Republicanism* (Cambridge: University Press, 1990), pp. 293–309.

Steffen, V.H., *Recht und Staat im System Spinozas* (Bonn: Bourvier, 1968).

Walther, M., 'Spinoza und der Rechtspositivismus', in E. Giancotti (ed.), *Spinoza nel 350 anniversario della nascità* (Naples: Bibliopolis, 1985), pp. 401–18.

———, 'Die Transformation des Naturrechts in der Rechtsphilosophie Spinozas', *Studia Spinozana,* no. 1 (1985), pp. 73–104.

Uyl, D. den and S.D. Warner, 'Liberalism and Hobbes and Spinoza', *Studia Spinozana,* no. 3 (1987), pp. 261–318.

Zac, S., 'L'idée de loi', in idem, *Philosophie, théologie, politique dans l'oeuvre de Spinoza* (Paris: Vrin, 1979), pp. 191–214.

J.L.M. Gribnau

Liber

Applied to 'cause', 'imagination', 'man', 'multitude', 'Republic', the adjective *liber* is not the opposite of 'necessary' but of 'compelled' (cf. Ep 56). 'That thing is called free which exists from the necessity of its own nature alone, and is determined to action by itself alone. That thing, on the other hand, is necessary or rather compelled which by another is determined to existence and to action in a fixed and prescribed manner' (E1def7). In this respect only God is a free cause and his will a necessary cause (E1p17c2, E1p32). With this definition Spinoza imitated

tradition. Chauvin, for example, observed that 'free' in its most general sense means a thing liberated from its restraining ties or impediments. In this sense it can be attributed to inanimate things, such as stars, as he argues by referring to Cicero's *De natura deorum*. Hence, to be free is not to be undetermined or to act without cause, and Spinoza rejects the doctrine of a free, that is an indeterminate, will (E2p48, E3p2s). Men have the illusory belief that they are free because they are aware of their appetites while not knowing the causes which determine them. There is no free will, such as Descartes believed in; all actions are determined by causes and obey the law of necessity (E2p49s). Even in God the infinite will cannot be called 'free cause' but only 'necessary', because it is determined by the attribute of thought. It does not follow that freedom is an illusion, for one must distinguish the internal necessity of one's nature from external necessities. To be free is not to do as one pleases, it is to live under the guidance of reason.

In *Ethics* 4, propositions 67–73, Spinoza draws the portrait of the free, reasonable man and shows that he does not live alone but amongst the others and obeys the laws of the state. To obey is not the opposite of being free. It depends on the nature of the order, whether it is useful or harmful to the agent who must carry it out (cf. TTP 16). In a free republic, submitting to orders has nothing to do with slavery; it means obeying the law of reason, and thus being free.

TEXTS

Dat de wille geen zaak is in de natuur, maar een verzieringe, men niet en behoeft te vraagen of de wil vrij of niet vrij is (KV 2.16). De waare kennis maakt ons vrij van die passien

(KV 2.19). *Rem libere agamus, ejusque causa simus, non obstante, quod eam necessario et ex Dei decreto agamus* (Ep 21). *Definitionem libertatis. Vides igitur me libertatem non in libero decreto ponere. Ex. gr. Lapis* (Ep 58). *Ex libero animo societati parere ... solus ille liber, qui integro animo ex solo ductu rationis vivit* (TTP 16, G III, 181–2). *Ea res libera dicetur, quae ex sola suae naturae existit, et a se sola ad agendum determinatur* (E1def7). *Solum Deum est causam liberam* (E1p17c2). *Voluntas non est causa libera, sed necessaria* (E1p32). *In mente nulla est absoluta, sive libera voluntas* (E2p48); E2p49s. *Qui igitur credunt, se ex libero mentis decreto loqui, vel tacere, vel quicquam agere oculis apertis somniant* (E3p2s). *Homo liber ex solo rationis dictamine vivit ... nihil minus quam de morte cogitat ... adaequatas habet ideas ... reliquos homines amicitia jungere studet ... semper cum fide agit* (E4p67–73). *Sed quo homo a nobis magis liber conciperetur, eo magis cogeremur statuere, ipsum sese necessario debere conservare et mentis compotem esse* (TP 2.7–8). *Homo magis ratione ducitur, hoc est, quo magis liber est* (TP 3.6).

BIBLIOGRAPHY
Secondary Literature
Gueroult, M., *Spinoza I. Dieu* (Hildesheim: Olms, 1968), pp.75–7.

Ch. Jaquet

Libertas

Unlike the adjective LIBER, the substantive *libertas* is not found among the series of definitions in Spinoza's *Ethics*, but it is both the most important notion of Spinoza's philosophy and the most widely misunderstood.

The *Ethics*, indeed, aims to lead the human mind to freedom, identified with salvation and blessedness (E5p36s). Freedom has nothing to do with a power of acting without any causes. This human prejudice is due to an ignorance of the causes which determine actions.

Freedom is the power of acting which is determined by the necessity of the nature of a thing alone (Ep 58). This definition imitates tradition, since liberty according to Chauvin requires the power over its own acts and the absence of coercion. A man is free if he acts at his own discretion, provided with certain reasons. Chauvin's article continues by advancing three arguments against the Aristotelian identification of liberty with the indifference of the will. Apparently, Spinoza's rejection of the doctrine of indifference was largely shared by his contemporaries. However, his critique was based on his peculiar metaphysics.

To understand Spinoza's rude dismissal of this prejudice, it is necessary to distinguish what he calls true freedom from what men usually imagine by the word. In the *Korte verhandeling* 1.4 Spinoza criticizes those who wrongly believe that God could abstain from doing what he does because he is free. In *Ethics* 1 he refuses to identify freedom with God's pleasure or indifferent will. God does not operate by free or absolute will, and he cannot change his decrees. If this were the case, God would be inconsistent and thus imperfect. Freedom has nothing to do with Descartes's free will. True freedom for God consists only in producing every perfection without being compelled or determined by anything but his own nature or perfection.

Human freedom must not be confused with license, satisfaction of all the appetites, or the power of doing or not doing something bad or good. In the *Korte verhandeling*

2.26 true freedom for men consists in being bound by the knowledge and the love of God and it is defined as a solid reality obtained by the intellect which is immediately united with God and produces ideas and effects which agree with its nature, free from external causes. In the *Ethics*, while man is conceived of as being more active, freedom does not change its nature; it is synonymous with 'power of intellect' as shown by the title of *Ethics* 5, and is nothing but salvation or blessedness. This freedom consists in a constant and eternal love for God, and it is always connected with life by the guidance of reason and the third kind of knowledge. True freedom depends on FORTITUDO, that is to say, actions born from adequate knowledge.

In the *Tractatus theologico-politicus*, however, Spinoza posits a notion of freedom of thought which does not necessarily rest upon adequate ideas but may rely upon mere opinions. He shows that freedom of thought is not a threat to theological and political authorities, it is on the contrary necessary for their survival. Theology has no speculative purview; it only requires obedience to the law of justice and charity, and lets everybody be free to think whatever they want, provided that they love their neighbour. The state, however tyrannical it may be, cannot prevent men thinking what they want, because when they assemble to form a republic they desist from acting according to their own decrees but they still retain their liberty of judgement. The aim of the republic is freedom (TTP 20) so that the state is compelled to allow freedom of thought and speech – which is not the freedom to act against the law, however just or unjust it may be. Men can fight against the laws by using their reason to convince the lawmaker to change the laws, but they are not allowed to rebel against it and abolish it. Freedom of thought excludes seditious opinions which lead to actions against the right of the sovereign and jeopardize peace. True freedom, nevertheless, does not rely upon mere opinions even when they are harmless; in *Tractatus politicus* 2.20 it is identified with rational life and it increases with the power of thinking adequately and governing the affects.

TEXTS

Om dat niet regt begreepen wort, waarin de Ware Vryheid bestaat ... de ware vryheid is alleen of niets anders als de eerste oorzaak, de welke geenszins van iets anders gepranght of genoodzaakt word, en alleen door zijne volmaaktheid oorzaak is van alle volmaaktheid (KV 1.4). De menschelijke vryheid ... is een vaste wezentlykheid, de welke ons verstand door de onmiddelijke vereeninginge met God verkrijgt (KV 2.26). *Nostra libertas nec in contingentia nec in indifferentia sita est, sed in modo affirmandi et negandi* (Ep 21). *Vides, igitur me libertatem non in libero decreto; sed in libera necessitate ponere* (Ep 58). *In Republica vivamus, ubi unicuique judicandi libertas* (TTP praef). *Nihil difficilius quam libertatem hominibus semel concessam iterum adimere* (TTP 5, G III, 74). *Libertas sentiendi ... Deus res dirigit ex libertate vel necessitate naturae ... Fides summum unicuique libertatem ad philosophandum concedit* (TTP 14, G III, 173, 178 and 180). *Libertas philosophandi ... libertas sentiendi* (TTP 16, G III, 189). *Imperium violentissimum erit, ubi unicuique libertas docendi et docendi, quae sentit negatur ... Finis reipublicae revera est libertas ... hujus libertatis fructus in Amstelodami* (TTP 20, G III, 240, 241 and 246). *Deum non operari ex libertate voluntatis* (E1p32c1). *Deo aliam libertatem attribuere longe diversam ab illa quae a nobis* (E1p33s2). *Eorum idea voluntatis* (E2p35s).

Ipsa virtus Deique servitus ... felicitas et summa libertas (E2p49s). *Quae de vera hominis libertate ostendimus, ad fortitudinem referuntur* (E4p73s). *Omnis amor, qui aliam causam praeter animi libertatem agnoscit* (E4app19). *Mentis libertas, seu beatitudo* (E5praef). *Appetitus ex solo libertatis amore moderari studet* (E5p10s). *Salus, seu beatitudo seu libertas* (E5p36s). *Mentis in affectus potentia ... de Mentis libertate* (E5p42s). *Animi libertas seu fortitudo* (TP 1.6). *Libertatem non cum contingentia confundit* (TP 2.7). *Humana libertas eo major est, quo homo magis ratione duci* (TP 2.20).

BIBLIOGRAPHY
Secondary Literature
Macherey, P., *Introduction à l'Éthique de Spinoza. V: La cinquième partie, les voies de la libération* (Paris: Presses Universitaires de France, 1994), chap. 2.

Ch. Jaquet

Libertas philosophandi

In the seventeenth century 'freedom to philosophize' usually refers to the professional freedom of philosophers, that is, the freedom they should enjoy to pursue their own programme, without interference of the 'higher faculties' (medicine, law and especially theology). Accordingly, it is close to what we call 'academic' freedom. That in any case is meant when, being offered a chair at the University of Heidelberg (1673), Spinoza is promised 'the most ample freedom to philosophize' (Ep 47) – a promise Spinoza deeply distrusts (Ep 48). In a letter to Oldenburg of 1665, on the other hand, in which Spinoza announces the project of the *Tractatus theologico-politicus*,

he connects this freedom with a more inclusive notion of freedom, telling his correspondent that he will discuss 'the freedom to philosophize and to speak our mind'. From a seventeenth-century point of view these two freedoms or rights would presumably overlap but yet be distinct. In modern terms: one is a *professional* right (comparable to that of lawyers and physicians) to be granted only to philosophers and academics, whereas the other is a *civil right* which belongs to all adult citizens. Of these the first only is retained in the TTP's definitive title, which announces 'several dissertations, showing not only that the freedom to philosophize can be granted without any risk for peace and piety but also that it cannot be suppressed without also suppressing peace and piety.' In the preface on the other hand Spinoza presents this professional right as one that follows from the more general 'freedom to exercise one's own judgment and to adore God according to one's own fantasy' – a right which Spinoza says is already granted to all citizens of Holland. The primary object of the book therefore would be to show that, far from undermining the public order, the extension of this fundamental right to philosophers is essential to the preservation of peace and piety. As a result, the argument would be that to do what he must do a sovereign must know the things demonstrated by true philosophy (that is, Spinoza's own philosophy), like that there is no God-Lawgiver who has revealed his will in a written document; that all religions are equally based on false ideas of the imagination; that any religion should be subordinate to civil law; that no citizen can take pretext from religion to disobey the law. As far as the title goes, therefore, the TTP would not so much contain a theory as an illustration of such a theory; not so much provide an argument for the general freedom to speak (which is taken for granted) as apply philosophy to theological and political problems; not so much present a particular philosophy as show that no true philosophy can be a threat to the public order. That being said, it is clear that the more inclusive notion of freedom (the freedom to speak one's mind) is not forgotten; indeed, it is discussed in chapters 19 and 20.

TEXTS
Pro libertate philosophandi cuivis concessa (Ep 13). *Libertas philosophandi dicendique quae sentimus; quam asserere omnibus modis cupio* (Ep 30). *Ut in Republica vivamus, ubi unicuique judicandi libertas integra et Deum ex suo ingenio colere conceditur* (TTP praef, G III, 7). *Hucusque ... curavimus et libertatem philosophandi ostendere, quam haec unicuique concedit. Quare tempus est, ut inquiramus, quo usque hae libertas sentiendi et quae unusquisque sentit, dicendi* (TTP 16, G III, 189). *Imperium violentissimum erit, ubi unicuique libertas dicendi et docendi, quae sentit, negatur ... optima respublica unicuique eadem libertatem philosophandi concedit* (TTP 20, G III, 240).

BIBLIOGRAPHY
Primary Sources
Bornius, H., *Oratio de vera philosophandi libertate* (Leiden, 1654).

Secondary Literature
Mowbray, M. de, '*Libertas philosophandi, wijsbegeerte in Groningen rond 1650*', in H.A. Krop, J.A. van Ruler and A.J. Vanderjagt (eds), *Zeer kundige geleerden, beoefening van de filosofie in Groningen van 1614 tot 1996* (Hilversum: Verloren, 1997), pp. 33–46.

Sutton, R.B., 'The Phrase Libertas Philosophandi', *Journal of the History of Ideas,* no. 14 (1953), pp. 310–16.
Verbeek, Th., *De vrijheid van de filosofie, reflecties over een cartesiaans thema* (Utrecht: Universitaire Pers, 1994).

Th. Verbeek

Mens

In the Cartesian tradition the word 'mind' which denoted a distinct and consciously thinking substance tended to replace the Aristotelian notion of a tripartite soul, which is the principle of all life. According to Descartes in the *Responsiones quintae* (AT VII, 355–6) the word *anima* is equivocally used, since it denoted both the bodily 'principle of nutrition' common to all animals and the 'immaterial principle of thinking' unique to man. Hence he prefers 'mind', Descartes observed, using the word in the sense of the human mind taken as a whole, not merely a part of it. Due to its ambiguity and its corporeal connotations Spinoza denounces the use of the word *anima* as well (PPC 1def6 and TIE note z). Hence the term *mens* occurs 553 times in the *Ethics* and substitutes almost completely the traditional term *anima* (only six times in the *Ethics*), which was still frequently used in his earlier writings. However in the *Korte verhandeling* and in the Dutch version of the *Ethics* in the *Nagelate schriften* the Dutch counterpart of *anima* is used: *ziel*.

Although by preferring 'mind' to 'soul' Spinoza is part of the Cartesian tradition, he interpreted the term in accordance with his own philosophy. Mind principally denotes the human mind as the idea of an actually existing body (E2p13–15). Man is a complex unity of two modes of the attributes

253

cogitation and extension, that is, he consists of a body and the idea of that body (E2p1–13). Spinoza developed this unitary concept of man as an alternative to earlier psychologies, such as Descartes's doctrine of the independent existence of human mind as a substance (a difference highlighted by Lodewijk Meyer in the preface of the PPC) or the Peripatetic view of mind as a faculty of soul (CM 2,6). The human mind is a mode and thus not defined as 'a thinking thing', but as 'a mode of thinking', a particular COGITATIO, and 'a power to think'.

On the basis of the laws that govern the relations between the attributes (E2p3–8) and the physics of the human body (E2p13s) the structure of the human mind is defined as a very complex idea made up of many individual ideas (E2p15). The relation between mind and body is not causal, for modes of one attribute cannot cause or affect modes of another attribute. Mind and body are the same thing seen from two different points of view. Thus, mind neither passively suffers the affections of the body nor does mind reign over the body. Mind actively elaborates, produces and combines ideas.

As idea of the eternal essence of the body, that is, as being an eternal essence itself, mind is an eternal mode and thus a part of God's infinite intellect (E2p11cor; E5p40cor). Thus, 'a mind knows', is equivalent with the proposition that 'God as far as he constitutes the essence of the human mind, possesses an idea'.

As idea of an active, existing body, a mind is composed of adequate and inadequate ideas, but as idea of the eternal essence of the body, its essence is constituted of knowledge the principle and foundation of which is God (E5p36s). The human mind does not survive the body and yet something remains, that is, the part which expresses the essence of the body SUB SPECIE AETERNITATIS. It is eternal as far as it expresses the divine essence (E5p23).

The ontological-psychological definition of mind in the *Ethics* is reflected in the *Tractatus theologico-politicus* on a theological and political level. Biblical passages referring to the human soul or spirit are interpreted by Spinoza in terms of his psychology (chapter 1). Through his mind man participates in God (chapter 12), this mind is defined as divine light and spark of divinity, and as supreme gift of God to men it stands for the (rational) capability to fathom God's order and the laws of nature (chapter 15). In the end, the harmony of mind and body, argued for in the *Ethics*, is revealed to contain a political value: the body of the state may reflect the rationality of its members as a whole (chapter 20).

TEXTS

Author noster substantiam cogitantem negat illam constituere substantiam mentis humanae; sed statuat, eodem modo, quo extensio nullis limitibus determinari cogitationem etiam nullis limitibus determinari ... sic etiam mentem sive animam humanum non absolute, sed tantum secundum leges naturae cogitantis per ideas certo modo determinatam cogitationem (PPC praef). *Loquor autem hic de mente potius quam de anima quoniam animae nomen est aequivocum et saepe pro re corporea usurpatur* (PPC 1def6). *Nos de tempore creationis mentis humanae nihil dixisse* (CM 2.12). *Clamant Dei aeternum verbum et pactum, veramque religionem hominum cordibus hoc est humanae menti divinitus inscriptam esse* (TTP 12, G III, 158). *Primum quod actuale mentis humanae esse constituit, nihil aliud est, quam idea rei alicujus singularis actu existentis* (E2p11). *Hinc sequitur humanam mentem partem esse infiniti intellectus Dei* (E2p11cor). *Ad determinandum quid mens humana reliquis intersit ... necesse nobis est, ejus objecti, hoc est Corporis humani naturam cognoscere* (E2p13s). *Ideae, quae esse formale humanae mentis constituit ex plurimis ideis composita* (E2p15). *Mentem humanam ... sui ipsius sed confusam tantum habere cognitionem* (E2p29cor). *Cartesium licet etiam crediderit, mentem in suas actiones potentiam absolutam habere* (E3praef). *Decreta mentis nihil aliud sunt praeter ipsos appetitus* (E3p2s). *Mens humana non potest cum Corpore absolute destrui, sed ejus aliquid remanet, quod aeternum est* (E5p23). *Quia nostrae mentis essentia in sola cognitione constituit, cujus principium et fundamentum Deus est* (E5p36s).

BIBLIOGRAPHY

Primary Sources
Descartes, R., *Meditationes de prima philosophia, Responsiones quintae.*

Secondary Literature
Della Rocca, M., *Representation and the Mind-Body Problem in Spinoza* (Oxford: Oxford University Press, 1996).
Gueroult, M., *Spinoza. II. L'âme (Éthique II)* (Hildesheim: Olms, 1974).
Renz, U., *Die Erklärbarkeit von Erfahrung: Realismus und Subjektivität in Spinozas Theorie des menschlichen Geistes* (Frankfurt am Main: Klostermann, 2010).
Robinson, L., *Kommentar zu Spinozas Ethik* (Leipig: Meiner, 1928).

L. Spruit

Metaphysica

In Spinoza's works the terms *metaphysica* and 'metaphysician' are rarely used. The Dutch counterpart *overnatuurkunde*, which is found in the title of the Dutch version of the *Cogitata metaphysica*, Spinoza never used. One of the reputed godfathers of Western metaphysics, Spinoza showed no apparent interest in dealing with its definition and object. In the *Cogitata metaphysica* 1.1 he merely hints at his views on the subject. In CM 1.6 he seems to be prepared to call metaphysics a universal science of being, which in opposition to the particular sciences deals with its general affects or modes: unity, truth, goodness and other transcendental terms. Metaphysics uses natural reason as a vehicle of knowing, that is why angels are not to be considered. He always speaks in the third person about metaphysicians, a group of scholars that apparently did not include himself. His attitude towards metaphysics conceived as an ontology or an *ontosophia* is negative. In his rejection of metaphysics Spinoza followed in Hobbes's footsteps, who in the dedicatory letters of *De corpore* explicitly denounced metaphysics, and expressed his desire to exorcise its evil spirit that threatens church and state. First philosophy, no longer equivalent to metaphysics, is left the task of elucidating the general notions of physics (*Leviathan* 46). Aristotelian metaphysics, by contrast, due to its vain distinctions and its dealing with purely abstract entities, is a 'supernatural philosophy', as the literal translation of the Latin *metaphysica* runs, and hence utterly pointless.

The second view of metaphysics that Spinoza hinted at is the Cartesian one, which is developed in the Préface to the French version of the *Principia philosophiae*. In letter 27 Spinoza refers to metaphysics as the first philosophy, dealing with the principles basic to physics and consequently to all the other sciences such as medicine, mechanics and ethics. Although it may be said that *Ethics* 1 and 2 like part 1 of the *Principia* deal with the fundamentals of philosophy, it comes as no surprise that after June 1665 Spinoza did not use the notion of metaphysics any more. The mature Spinoza found it obviously inappropriate to call the science of the general principles of ethics by the name of 'metaphysics'.

TEXTS

Ab authoribus metaphysicis (CM 1.1). *Ab omnibus fere metaphysicis pro generalissimis entis affectionibus habentur* (CM 1.6). *Et quamvis angeli etiam creati sint, quia tamen lumine naturali non cognoscuntur ad metaphysicam non spectant* (CM 2.12). *Magnam ethices partem, quae ut cuivis notum, metaphysica et physica fundari debet* (Ep 27). *Quamvis theologi et metaphysici distinguant inter finem indigentiae et finem assimilationis* (E1app).

BIBLIOGRAPHY

Primary Sources
Descartes, R., *Principes de la Philosophie.*
Hobbes, Th., *De Corpore, Leviathan.*

Secondary Literature
De Dijn, H., 'Metaphysics as Ethics', in Y. Yovel (ed.), *God and Nature in Spinoza's Metaphysics* (Leiden: Brill, 1991), pp. 119–31.

H. Krop

Miraculum

Spinoza deals with miracles mainly in chapter 6 of the *Tractatus theologico-politicus*, although he makes several comments on miracles elsewhere in the treatise (preface and the chapters 1- 3, 7, 12–13, 15 and 17–19). Moreover, we find remarks about miracles in the letters 73, 75, 76 and 78, and in the appendix of *Ethics* 1. Spinoza does not adopt the traditional definition as reproduced by Goclenius and Micraelius, for example, who basically observed that a miracle is an event 'which cannot be produced by natural agents', 'exceeds nature' and hence requires a 'supernatural extraordinary force'. Such a supernatural force could only be God, which supersedes all natural causality. However, Spinoza's definitions of a miracle as an astonishing, unusual or unexpected work of nature, transcending the understanding of ordinary man, reproduce Hobbes's definition in *Leviathan* chapter 37: 'By miracles are signified the admirable works of God: and therefore they are also called wonders'. In itself they may well be 'wrought by ordinary means'. Like Spinoza Hobbes ignored the supernatural character a miracle had to possess according to tradition. But Protestant theologians seem to favour a tendency to downplay miracles, which to a certain extent was received in Christianity since Augustine who wrote in *De civitate Dei* 21.8 that a miracle is 'not contrary to nature, but contrary to our understanding of nature'.

In letter 75 the belief in miracles is presented as an effect of human ignorance. 'Those who endeavour to establish the existence of God and religion from miracles are seeking to prove the obscure through the more obscure, of which they are quite ignorant.' It is better to explain miracles as far as possible through natural causes (Spinoza gives such an explanation of miracles, described in Scripture, in several places in the *Tractatus*) and, if we cannot explain them by natural causes, to suspend judgement.

In chapter 6 of the *Tractatus* it is argued that nothing in nature happens which contravenes its universal laws, nor anything that is not in agreement with these laws or does not follow from them. So any apparent miracle must be a natural event. A miracle is the result of men's beliefs and means simply 'an event whose natural cause we – or at any rate the writer or narrator of the miracle – cannot explain by comparison with any other normal event'. In biblical times people were quite ignorant of the principles of science. They regarded as a miracle whatever they could not explain in the way the common people are accustomed to explaining natural phenomena. Therefore, there are many alleged miracles in Scripture which we nowadays can explain by means of scientific principles. Hence, in order to understand why some natural phenomena in the Bible are described as miracles, it is necessary to know the beliefs of those who originally related them and left us written records of them in order to distinguish between these beliefs and what really happened. For many things were believed to be real, but were nevertheless merely symbolical and imaginary, adapted to the beliefs of those who transmitted them to us as they were represented to them, that is, as actual happenings. Moreover, the circumstances surrounding these miraculous events were often not reported in Scripture. Besides, for a proper understanding of the reality of miracles it is important to be acquainted with the diction and metaphors of the biblical writers. Otherwise we will ascribe to Scripture many miracles which its authors never conceived as such.

The general conclusion of the discussion of miracles in chapter 6 is that miracles cannot be considered events contravening the fixed and immutable order or laws of nature and that neither God's essence nor his existence can be known from miracles. On the contrary, if miracles are conceived as events contravening the laws of nature, they cast

doubt on God's existence, since but for them we can be absolutely certain of this. So belief in miracles is an obstacle to a true knowledge of God and keeps men from a scientific investigation of the causes of natural events (E1app). It is only human ignorance, connected with passions like astonishment and surprise, which generates faith in miracles (E3aff4, E3p52s1).

TEXTS
Miracula, & ignorantiam pro aequipollentibus sumpsi, quia ii, qui Dei existentiam, & Religionem miraculis adstruere conantur, rem obscuram per aliam magis obscuram, & quam maxime ignorant, ostendere volunt (Ep 75). *Miracula opera Dei vocantur, hoc est opera stupenda* (TTP praef). *Vulgus opera naturae insolita vocat miracula ... Nos ex miraculis, nec essentiam, nec existentiam, nec providentiam Dei posse cognoscere ... nomen miraculi non nisi respective ad hominum opiniones posse intelligi et nihil aliud significare quam opus, cujus causam naturalem exemplo alterius rei solitae explicare non possumus, vel saltem ipse non potest, qui miraculum scribit aut narrat ... miracula ad captum vulgi facta fuerunt* (TTP 6, G III, 83–4). *Ut qui miraculorum causas veras quaerit, quique res naturales ut doctus intelligere, non autem, ut stultus, admirari studet, passim pro haeretico, et impio habeatur* (E1app).

BIBLIOGRAPHY
Primary Sources
Augustine, *De civitate Dei.*
Hobbes, Th., *Leviathan.*

Secondary Literature
Curley, E., 'Spinoza on Miracles', in
    E. Giancotti Boscherini (ed.), *Spinoza*

350° *anniversario della nascità. Atti/ Proceedings of the First Italian International Congress on Spinoza* (Naples: Bibliopolis, 1985), pp. 421–38.

Parkinson, G., 'Spinoza on Miracles and Natural Law', *Revue internationale de philosophie,* no. 31 (1977), pp. 145–57.

Tosel, A., *Spinoza ou le crepuscule de la servitude. Essai sur le Traité Théologico-Politique* (Paris: Aubier Montaigne, 1984).

P.C. Juffermans

Modificatio

The Latin noun *modificatio* and its Dutch equivalent *wijzing* (once *toeval)* are occasionally used by Spinoza. Only in *Ethics* 1 and the appendix to the *Korte verhandeling* do both nouns derived, respectively, from the verbs *modificare* and *wijzigen,* occur more frequently. Apparently modification is a synonym for MODUS.

The first argument for this is its definition. In Ep 4 Spinoza identifies modification with ACCIDENS in defining the concept in more or less the same manner as mode in E1def3: 'by modification or accident I mean that, which is in something else, and is conceived through that wherein it is'. The definition of E1p8s2 combines the wording of the definitions of substance and mode in the beginning of this part by calling a modification: 'that which is in something else, and whose conception is formed from the conception of whatever it is in'.

Moreover, just like the modes the modifications are directly linked in a Cartesian manner to the ATTRIBUTUM or *eigenschap*. In the *Korte verhandeling* Spinoza calls the soul a modification of the attribute 'thinking': 'I call that modification the most immediate modification, which, in order to exist, requires no other modification.' Such an immediate modification includes other modifications such as 'Love, Desire, and Joy', which originate in the first 'utmost immediate' modification of the attribute: the idea. Spinoza here notes a certain hierarchy within the modifications. In the appendix Spinoza also calls the human body a 'modification of the attribute extension, which can be destroyed although the attribute remains unchanging'. However, since 'extension contains no other modifications than motion and rest' a 'particular corporeal thing is nothing else than a certain proportion of motion and rest'.

The same view on the relation between modifications and attribute is adopted in E1. In propositions 22 and 23 Spinoza states that the modifications of an attribute by a necessary and infinite modification will result in an equally necessary mode. According to E2p10c the human essence is constituted by certain modifications of the divine attributes and is therefore a mode itself, expressing God's nature.

The third argument which favours the identification of mode and modification is the traditional division of being which Spinoza formulates in axiom 1 of the appendix by means of the Dutch word *toevallen,* to which the Latin *modificatio* between brackets is added.

However, a slight distinction of meaning between both concepts may be discerned. Although modification in contemporary philosophical dictionaries is only rarely dealt with and then sometimes under the heading *modificatum* (both Goclenius and Micraelius in fact derive the noun from a verb stating a thing is modified because it is 'affected by a mode'), in the eighteenth century the distinction between both concepts was well entrenched, probably due to Spinoza. Wolff, for example, in his *Ontologia* § 703–4 observed that 'the change of a temporary thing consists of the variety of modes'. This 'variety of modes, that is to say a succession or substitution of one mode by another, we call modification'. In the last sections of his *Theologia naturalis* Wolff uses the concept in order to deal with Spinoza's idea of the development of the souls and the bodies *per modificationem* from the divine attributes. Apparently modification primarily expresses the process and result of change and variation. Such associations are found already in scholastic predecessors of Spinoza such as Burgersdijk and Heereboord – Descartes hardly ever used the word 'modification'. In defining a mode, Burgersdijk observed that by a mode things are modified with respect to their being and their becoming (*Institutiones metaphysicae* I, chap. 7), while the accidents modify the substances and cause them to act (II, chap. 17), and Heereboord stated that 'the matter of all natural bodies is the same, their diversity is caused by their different modification caused by diverse motion' (*Philosophia naturalis*, chap. 5). Here the concept of modification is nuanced by the reference to a condition of a thing being modified in one way or the other. This shade of meaning might explain why Spinoza sometimes prefers to use the term 'modification' in the second part of E1 which deals with the production of the finite things from the divine substance.

TEXTS

De zelftandigheid staat wegens sijn natuur voor alle sijn toevallen (modificationes). ... Ziel zulks zij een wijzing van die eigenschap, die wij denking noemen ... Alle de overige wijzingen gelijk als Lievde, Begeerte, Blijdschap ... alleronmiddelijkste wijzing van de eigenschap, die wijzing de welke, om wezentlijk te zijn niet van noden heeft eenige ander wijzing in de zelfde eigenschap ... dat in de uijtgebreidheid geen andere wijzinge is als beweging en stilte (KV app). *Modificationes in materia realiter existentes* (PPC 3, post 1). *Per modificationem sive per accidens ... id quod in alio est et per id in quo est concipitur* (Ep 4). *Non dubito quin omnibus qui de rebus confuse judicant ... non distinguunt inter modificationes substantiarum et ipsas substantias ... Si autem ad naturam substantiae attenderent ... intelligerent per modificationes id quo in alio est et quarum conceptus a conceptu in qua sunt formatur, quodcirca modificationum non existentium veras ideas possumus habere, quandoquidem quamvis non existant actu extra intellectum earum tamen essentia ita in alio comprehenditur, ut per idem concipi possint* (E1p8s2). *Quicquid ex aliquo Dei attributo, quatenus modificatum est tali modificatione, quae et necessario et infinita per idem existit, sequitur, debet quoque et necessario et infinitum per idem existere* (E1p22); E1p23; E1p28. *Essentiam hominis constitui a certis Dei attributorum modificationibus* (E2p10c).

BIBLIOGRAPHY
Primary Sources
Burgersdijk, F., *Institutiones metaphysicae* (Leiden, 1642).
Heereboord, A., *Philosophia naturalis* (Leiden, 1658).
Wolff, Chr., *Philosophia prima, sive ontologia modo scientifica pertractata* (Frankfurt and Leipzig, 1730).
———, *Theologia naturalis, modo scientifica pertractata* (Frankfurt and Leipzig, 1737).

Secondary Literature

Melamed, Y., 'Spinoza's Metaphysics of Substance: the Substance-Mode Relation as a Relation of Inheritance and Predication', *Philosophy and Phenomenological Research,* no. 78 (2009), pp. 17–82.

Robinson, L., *Kommentar zu Spinozas Ethik* (Leipzig: Meiner, 1928).

Richter, G.T., *Spinozas philosophische Terminologie I: Grundbegriffe der Metaphysik* (Leipzig: Barth, 1913).

H. Krop

Modus

The Latin noun *modus*, and its Dutch counterpart *wijse*, acquired its full Spinozistic meaning only in Spinoza's mature work, the *Ethics,* by replacing the traditional *accidens* as the opposite of SUBSTANTIA. However, this process of substitution was already well underway in the earlier works. In definition 5 of the first part of the *Ethics* Spinoza identified 'mode' with an *affectio* of a substance, something which 'is in something else through which it may be conceived'. According to this definition a mode is ontologically and logically dependent on the substance. The interrelation of both concepts appears from the fact that just like substance mode disappears from the scene after *Ethics* 2. However, contrary to substance mode does not resurface in *Ethics* 5. Due to the focus on God, in the first part of the *Korte verhandeling wijse* plays only a minor part as well. In the PPC Spinoza occasionally identifies accident with mode, but in the first chapter of the *Cogitata metaphysica* he clearly distinguishes between both concepts. For 'mode' refers to a real being, while 'accident' merely

denotes a mode of thought and 'exists only in regard to this'. In the correspondence Spinoza presents in letter 12 a second definition of mode: 'The affections of substance I call modes'. Hence, 'their definition ... cannot involve any existence, whence it is abundantly clear, that we conceive the existence of substance as entirely different from the existence of modes. From this difference arises the distinction between eternity and duration. Duration is only applicable to the existence of modes; eternity is applicable to the existence of substance'. So, we need experience to know whether modes exist (Ep 10).

Modus is a technical philosophical term, but Spinoza also frequently used the Latin word in a non-technical sense in which case it might well be rendered by way or manner. Sometimes it is unclear whether the technical or the non-technical sense is intended, e.g. at E1p16; see the divergences in the translations.

In his definitions of mode Spinoza presents an ontological 'mark of mode', namely a distinguishing feature – a phrase coined by Heereboord with respect to substance – which is denoted by 'being in something else', as well as a logical one, which is described by the phrases 'being conceived through something else' and 'having a definition which does not involve its existence'. This ontological mark of mode refers to the traditional theory of the inherence of an accident in the substance, which Aristotle formulated in his *Categories* chap. 2. 'By being present in a subject (*in aliquo*) I do not mean present as parts are present in a whole, but being incapable of existence apart from the said subject' (translated from Burgersdijk's version in *Institutiones metaphysicae* II, chap. 17). This notion of inherence Spinoza used in construing the traditional 'division of being', which in axiom 1 he formulated in the following words: 'all things which exist, exist either in itself or in something else' (cf. CM 1.1). This division is absolute, since according to Heereboord the inherence of an accident in substance excludes the possibility that an accident in a strict sense (the so-called *accidens praedicamentale* of scholastic tradition) will ever be a substance (*Hermeneneia logica* I, chap. 13). In letter 12 Spinoza argues that substance exists in an eternal way and is therefore radically opposite to the mode's way of being: with duration, which is either infinite or finite.

From the notion of inherence Spinoza infers in E1p15 a second ontological 'mark of mode': the dependence of modes on substance. 'But modes (by E1d5) cannot be ... without substance'. However, since God is the only substance, all things apparently inhere in God. E1p15: 'Whatsoever is, is in God, and without God nothing can be' (see also E1p2). According to Chauvin this dependence of the modes is to be distinguished in an ontological and a causal sense: *in esse, in fieri* and *in agendo* (s.v. *accidens*). However, of these elements the determining power of substance in the acting of the modes is only mentioned in proposition 29 of *Ethics* 1.

In the second part of *Ethics* 1 Spinoza focuses on the causal relation between substance and modes. For every mode is causally dependent on the one and only substance, namely God, being its absolutely primary efficient cause (E1p16). Hence he is their cause of being (E1p24c), effecting the modes in a necessary way. E1p29: 'But God cannot be called a contingent thing. For (by p11) he exists necessarily, not contingently. Next, the modes of the divine nature have also followed from it necessarily, and not contingently (by p16)'.

It should be noted that according to Spinoza a mode is only indirectly caused by substance. It is caused by means of the divine attributes and it is the result of the power of God's essence expressing his nature. E2def1: 'By body I understand a mode that in a certain and determinate way expresses the essence of God, in so far he is conceived as an extended thing'. The same applies to the modes of thought, the ideas. Bodies, ideas and affects are the only modes we perceive.

The third mark of mode is its particularity. According to E1p25c all modes are individual things such as ideas or stimuli on parts of the body (cf. E2p8 and E2p28). Taken together the modes constitute *natura naturata*. E1p29s: 'By *natura naturata* I understand whatever follows from the necessity of the nature of God, or from any of the attributes of God, that is, all the modes of the attributes of God, in so far as they are considered as things which are in God, and can neither be, nor be conceived without God'. Arguing in this manner Spinoza adopted Aristotle's anti-Platonism in its nominalist form and transformed the individual things, which were substances in a primary sense into their opposite: modes.

The last mark of mode is a logical one. In letter 10 Spinoza observes that experience is needed to ascertain the existence of a mode, since this does not follow from the definition of substance. According to the scholastic tradition this notion of a mode being not included in the definition of its substance was linked to the etymology of the word accident. 'By this word generally are denoted all things which may be attributed to substances, but are not contained in their essence or definition'. Hence an accident may be predicated or negated of a substance without causing a contradiction. (Burgersdijk, *Institutiones metaphysicae* II, chap. 17). In the *Ethics* Spinoza, following Descartes, transformed the ontological notion of modal dependence into a conceptual one, stating that the knowledge of an effect depends on the knowledge of its cause (ax. 4). In E1p8s2 he observed: 'For, by substance, they would understand what is in itself and is conceived through itself – that is, the knowledge of which does not require the knowledge of any other thing. But by modifications ... those things whose concept is formed from the concept of the thing in which they are'.

As such *modus* is part of the traditional scholastic discourse, which, as often happened, reached Spinoza by means of Descartes in a radically changed form. Seventeenth-century scholasticism dealt with modes in the first part of metaphysics, discussing being in general and its 'principles' and 'affects'. However, the analysis of accident and substance belongs to the *metaphysica specialis*, dealing with particular beings. Hence, according to Burgersdijk a mode, in opposition to an accident, denotes not a real being, but 'an appendicle of a thing by which the thing is modified either with respect to being or with respect to becoming'. For example, although 'to subsist by itself' is a mode-constituting substance distinguishing it from the accidents, it is not a real being, which is to be conceived somehow 'between substance and accident', since it modified substance (*Institutiones metaphysicae* I, chap. 7). According to Maccovius's manual of metaphysics (re-edited in the 1650s by Heereboord with an extensive commentary) modes may be real: 'they are to be conceived as an accident, but not being the same', such as the transcendental terms unity, truth and goodness; modes may be notional – in Latin *modi considerandi*, i.e. the different ways by which we know and conceive a thing; or they are of a verbal nature – *modi praedicandi*, modes by which a known thing is spoken of. Like Burgersdijk,

Maccovius underlines the fact that a mode in itself is not a being, since a mode possesses no 'entity besides the being of which it is a mode'. 'A mode', he defines, 'is an internal disposition of being, a relation or a negation of a relation'. In his commentary on this definition Heereboord adds that this definition proves that a mode is not an accident, because an accident, besides the being of the substance, possesses a being of its own. Hence the theory of modes proves its use in dealing with the theological doctrine of the Trinity (*Metaphysica* I, chap. 4).

Descartes paved the way for Spinoza in three ways: (1) by eliminating the scholastic distinction between mode and accident and preferring the first notion; (2) by linking the modes to the attributes; and (3) by tending to relegate the finite substances to the rank of mere modes. Some basic Cartesian texts will be quoted to argue for the first two observations. Firstly, in *Meditationes* III Descartes explicitly identified mode with accident. Moreover, in the *Principles of Philosophy* I, § 56 he states: 'Indeed we are understanding by modes exactly the same thing as we understood elsewhere by attribute or quality. But when we consider that the substance is affected or altered by these things we call them modes'. Thus, according to Descartes the admittance of variation or change is a basic feature of the modes. Apparently this feature was acknowledged in scholasticism as well. Goclenius, for example, wrote: 'in a universal, since it is a perfection, different degrees or modes of things, attributed to them by God'. Hence: 'a mode is a particular determination of a thing'. Secondly, in the *Principles of Philosophy* I, § 53 he underlined the secondary character of the modes with respect to the attribute: 'Since everything else which can be attributed to the body presupposes extension, and is only a certain mode of an extended thing, and similarly all the things, which we find in mind are only diverse modes of thinking. Thus, for example, figure cannot be understood except in an extended thing, nor can motion except in an extended space ... But on the contrary, extension can be understood without figure or motion.'

TEXTS

Ik zegge van eenige wijzen, omdat ik geenszins versta dat de mensch, voor zo veel hij uit geest, ziel of lichaam bestaat een selfstandigheid is (KV 2.1). *Ex. gr. existentia modorum: haec enim a rei definitione non potest concludi* (Ep 10). *Substantiae vero affectiones modos voco, quorum definitio, quatenus non est ipsa substantiae definitio, nullam existentiam involvere potest ... ubi ad solam modorum essentiam; non vero ad ordinem totius naturae attendimus, non posse concludere ex eo, quod iam existent, ipsos postea exstituros, vel antea exstitisse* (Ep 12). *Substantia plus realitatis habet quam accidens vel modus* (PPC 1ax4). *In substantia plus realitatis contineri percipio, quam in modis, sive accendentibus* (PPC 2ax19). *Ens, cujus essentia non involvit existentiam, nisi possibilem ... divitur in substantiam et modum ... expresse dicimus ens dividi in substantiam et modum, non vero in substantiam et accidens, nam accidens nihil est praeter modum cogitandi* (CM 1.1); CM 2.1. *Accidentium et modorum nullam dari creationem, praesupponunt enim praeter Deum substantiam creatam* (CM 2.12). *Per modum intelligo substantiae affectiones, sive id quod in alio est, per quod etiam concipitur* (E1def5). *Modi sine substantia nec esse, nec concipi possunt, quare hi in sola divina natura esse et per ipsam solam concipi possunt. Atqui praeter substantias et modos nil datur* (E1p15); E1p23; E1p25c. *Modi*

nihil sunt nisi Dei attributorum affectiones (E1p28). *Horum modorum Deus non tantum est causa quatenus existunt ... sed etiam quatenus ad aliquid operandum determinati considerantur* (E1p29). *Corpus ... modum, qui Dei essentiam, quatenus ut res extensa consideratur, certo et determinato modo exprimit* (E2def1). *Ideae rerum singularium sive modorum* (E2p8). *Affectiones, namque modi sunt, quibus partes corporis humani et consequenter totum corpus afficitur* (E2p32).

BIBLIOGRAPHY
Primary Sources
Burgersdijk, F., *Institutiones metaphysicae* (Leiden, 1642).
Heereboord, A., *Hermeneia logica, sive synopseos logicae Burgersdicianae explicatio* (Leiden, 1640).
Maccovius, J., *Metaphysica ad usum questionum in philosophia ac theologia adornata et applicata per A. Heereboord* (Leiden, 1658).

Secondary Literature
Curley, E., *Behind the Geometrical Method* (Princeton: Princeton University Press, 1984).
Hartbecke, K., 'Zur Geschichte des Modusbegriffes. Suárez – Descartes – Spinoza – Holbacht', *Studia Spinozana*, no. 16 (2008), pp. 19–40.
Koistinen, O.V., *On the Metaphysics of Spinoza's Ethics* (Turku: Turku University Press, 1991).
Gueroult, M., *Spinoza I: Dieu* (Hildesheim: Olms, 1968).
Robinson, L., *Kommentar zu Spinozas Ethik* (Leipzig: Meiner, 1928).
Rocca, M. della, *Spinoza* (London and New York: Routledge, 2008).

Richter, G.T., *Spinozas philosophische Terminologie. I: Grundbegriffe der Metaphysik* (Leipzig: Barth, 1913).

H. Krop

Monarchia

According to the definition in the second and third chapters of the *Tractatus politicus* a monarchy or a royal regime is a political order in which a society is governed by one person. A monarchical government in the sense of the definition is never real, because it is impossible for one person to govern a society.

Spinoza is very critical about monarchy, although he thinks a stable monarchy is feasible under certain conditions, and that a monarchy is still better than a decomposing state (TP 7.1–2). In fact, he is mainly interested in a specific kind of monarchy, i.e. one that is established by a free people (TP 7.26). For kings tend to be oppressive, enslave the people, and prefer a state of war above a state of security and peace. The monarchical regime is rooted in a persistent image of the political order from which it is difficult to free oneself. A very critical evaluation of monarchy can be found in the preface of the *Tractatus theologico-politicus* as well. Monarchy is incompatible with a free society, since its power, based on deception, necessarily restricts the freedom of thought. By means of SUPERSTITIO people are made to believe that their well-being depends on the rule of one person. The relation between monarchy and religion is made more clear in chapter 17 of the TTP, where Moses as a king is depicted as a mediator between God and the people. His power is even greater than that of a 'normal' king, because people believe they obey God if they comply with the monarch. In chapter 18 Spinoza says that monarchy is an imaginary scheme from which it is hard to escape. When the English people disposed of their king, they found themselves governed by another tyrant, who in turn was succeeded by yet another king. Only the name changed, the power structure remained the same. Moreover, if a king is chosen as a military leader, the danger of monarchy is that the people will remain in a perpetual state of war (TP 7.22).

Because of the false character of monarchy, it needs a strong foundation in order to be stable. Its stability results from its power to guarantee the well-being of the multitude. Hence, the monarch has to be supported by a council of citizens (TP 6.15ff), which mediates between the king, who is the soul of the state, and the multitude, and even between the king and foreign rulers. In this constitutional monarchy, all obey the king, but the council takes care of the promulgation of his decisions. Here Spinoza shares the position of the monarchomachs such as Althusius.

Spinoza rejects Hobbes's view of (monarchical) sovereignty as well on grounds of inconstancy of will. He favours the rule of law, binding the king as well as citizens, over the rule of one man (TP 7.1). The king becomes a symbol of political and legal power. In fact, a monarch always remains dependent on the will of the multitude or that part that is superior. Nevertheless, there are particular circumstances, i.e. when people are divided or when there are urgent tasks, in which the people are inclined to overcome their aversion to monarchy. Monarchy being intrinsically unstable, it can be made more stable by countermeasures, e.g. courtiers and the rule of hereditary succession.

Hence Spinoza is inclined to support a monarchy under specific conditions. The monarchy he has in mind is the choice of a free people, is bound to a constitution, and in it the king has to share power with a council of citizens. This is the best form of a monarchical regime. This can hardly be proven from historical examples, because such a state never existed, but experience demonstrates these conditions indirectly. Only one example seems to sustain Spinoza's position: the kingdom of Aragon (TP 7.30). A monarchy can only be allowed if it is strongly based on a more fundamental democratic order.

TEXTS

Regiminis monarchici summum sit arcanum, ejusque omnino intersit, homines deceptos habere, et metum, quo retineri debent, specioso religionis nomine adumbrare, ut pro servitio, tanquam pro salute pugnent (TTP praef, G III, 7). *Si succcesorem Moses eligisset, qui ut ipse totam imperii administrationem haberet ... imperium mere monarchicum fuisset* (TTP 17, G III, 207). *Donec imperium iterum in monarcham, mutato etiam tantum, ut in Anglia nomine cessit. Quoad autem ad Hollandiae ordines attinet, hi numquam reges habuerunt* (TTP 18, G III, 227). *Si denique reipublicae cura et consequenter imperium penes unum sit, tum monarchia appellatur* (TP 2.17). *Denique status civilis tria dari genera, nempe...monarchicum* (TP 3.1).

BIBLIOGRAPHY
Primary Sources
Althusius, Johannes, *Politica methodice digesta* (Herborn, 1604).
Hobbes, Thomas, *Leviathan*.

Secondary Literature
Matheron, A., *Individu et communauté chez Spinoza* (Paris: Éditions de Minuit, 1969).

M. Terpstra

Moses

In chapter 8 of the *Tractatus theologico-politicus*, 'it is shown that the Pentateuch and the Books of Joshua, Judges, Ruth, Samuel and Kings were not written by themselves'. According to Spinoza, Ibn Ezra in his commentary on Deuteronomy was the first to point out that Moses could not possibly have been the author of the Pentateuch, since it recounts events that took place after his death. Just as Hobbes had done in the *Leviathan* (chapter 33), Spinoza completely agrees with this, and adds many instances of post-Mosaic historiography in the Pentateuch. Moses' responsibility for the Pentateuch is, however, only one detail of his general perception of Moses, which is mainly concerned with a consideration of Moses as a 'teacher or prophet' and as a 'lawgiver or ruler' (TTP 5).

Spinoza acknowledges the pre-eminence of Moses among the prophets of the Old Testament, by emphasizing that he was the only one to whom God 'with a real voice revealed ... the laws which he willed to be enjoined by the Hebrews' (Exodus 25.22; Deuteronomy 5.4; Numbers 12.6–7) (TTP 1). This was an exceptional event, since revelations usually occur by means of signs. Elsewhere he simply calls Moses 'the greatest of the prophets' (TTP 11). Spinoza is not concerned with what actually happened on Mount Sinaï, but rather with what Scripture tells us about Moses' encounter with God. For interpreting Scripture, according to Spinoza, is an attempt not to reconstruct the truth about the actual history of a number of real *events*, but to understand the moral meaning of the biblical text relating these events. Thus, Moses' warning in Deuteronomy 31.27 that the Hebrews will surely rebel against the Lord after he has passed away 'are merely a moral exhortation where, in a rhetorical expression, he predicts the future backsliding of the people as his lively imagination enabled him to picture it' (ibid.).

This does not diminish Moses' biblical pre-eminence, although being a prophet Moses was only able to provide moral certainty. This Spinoza infers from Moses' own words in Deuteronomy 13, where it is said that the Lord also tries his people by false revelations, so that prophetic revelation is by its very nature open to doubt and at best highly probable (TTP 2). Moses' prophecies, like those of any other prophet, were adapted to his beliefs, since the contents of any revelation by necessity are determined by the nature of the imagination receiving it (TTP 2 in fine). It was revealed to Moses, for instance, that Israel would be taken care of by angels (Exodus 33.2–3). Moses' affirmation (Deuteronomy 10.15) that God had chosen the Israelites for himself above all other nations should also be understood as an example of God accommodating himself to the understanding of the Hebrews.

Next, Spinoza moves on to a treatment of Moses as legislator and politician. Significantly, he compares Moses to Christ: 'since Christ was sent to teach not only the Jews but the entire human race', he had to have a mind 'adapted to the beliefs and doctrines held in common by all mankind, that is, to those axioms that are universally true' (TTP 4). Accordingly, Spinoza continues, 'this fact that God revealed himself through Christ, or to Christ's mind, directly, and not through words and images as in the case of the prophets, can have only this meaning, that Christ perceived truly, or understood, what was revealed'. Moses on the other hand was exclusively the saviour of Israel. His revelations *were* adapted to his own understanding, his law 'was not of

universal application but specially adapted to the character and preservation of one particular people'. In a sense, Moses' legislation must be said to have resulted from a – very fortunate – misunderstanding on his part:

as a result of revelation or basic principles revealed to him, he perceived a way by which the people of Israel could well be united in a particular territory to form a political union or state, and also a way by which that people could well be constrained to obedience. But he did not perceive, nor was it revealed to him, that this way was the best of all ways, nor that the end for which they were striving would be a consequence necessarily entailed by the general obedience of the people in such a territory. Therefore he perceived these things not as eternal truths, but as instructions and precepts, and he ordained them as laws of God. Hence it came he imagined God as a ruler, lawgiver, king, merciful, just, and so forth; whereas these are all merely attributes of human nature, and not at all applicable to the divine nature.

This is why the ceremonial observances laid down by Moses no longer hold. They pertained to the Hebrew commonwealth alone and bore no moral sanction. Their lack of universality is evident from the fact that they were enforced by means of material penalties, whereas the law of Christ is universal and promises only spiritual rewards.

This is not to say that according to Spinoza a universal morality based on a clear understanding of eternal truths would suffice, and that Christ 'abrogated' the law of Moses. Without Moses, Israel would surely have perished. The poor state of Israel, however, after so many years of captivity, did force him to take three extraordinary measures in order to secure the survival of the Hebrews. First he introduced a state religion in order to replace fear as his people's strongest source of inspiration by devotion. Next, 'he bound them by consideration of gifts received, while promising many more benefits from God in the future'. Thus he turned the Hebrews into a grateful and hopeful people. Finally, he made sure that even the most intimate details of the private lives of his people were constantly associated with ceremonial observances to the effect that each and every member of his nation 'should be utterly subservient to its ruler' (TTP 5): 'their life was one long schooling in obedience' (TTP 19). They were never to forget who had saved them from slavery and he succeeded by creating a covenant, specifically designed to promote obedience (TTP 14).

Next, Spinoza stresses that the people of Israel, after their flight from Egypt, were free to establish new laws of their own, but decided to transfer all their natural rights to God alone, whom they held responsible for their liberation. And since the Hebrews recognized that Moses was a genuine prophet, their obedience to his prophetic revelations was unconditional. It was, however, God who held sovereignty over Israel, which was called the kingdom not of Moses but of God, and all its enemies were enemies of God. As far as the internal constitution of this state was concerned, there was no difference between civil law and religion, so that Israel was in fact a theocracy (TTP 17). However, the first covenant, according to which all Israelites were equal since they had all equally transferred their rights to God alone, took on a completely new dimension once they decided that they did not *want* to hear God speaking to them. As is shown in Exodus 19.16 and 20.18-20, they became so frightened of 'God speaking in the midst of fire', that they asked Moses to speak to them on God's behalf. This created the opportunity for Moses to establish a monarchy, but from the fact that Moses ordered his successors as prophets – his brother Aaron and the Levites – to have hardly any civil rights, and made them dependent for their livelihood on the other tribes, we must infer that he actually avoided the institution of hereditary kingship. Jewish priests on the other hand were not to control the army. Moses therefore made sure that he was succeeded by ministers, by *servants* of the state, that is (ibid.).

From the history of the commonwealth of the Hebrews Spinoza deduces several political principles. First, Moses' example goes to show that 'it is not inconsistent with God's kingship to elect a supreme ruler who would have complete command over the state' (TTP 18). But the fact that the gradual emergence of a monarchy among the Hebrews after Moses' instructions had fallen into neglect, reveals that popular sovereignty was far more beneficial to the peace within the commonwealth than investing sovereignty in hereditary kings. According to Spinoza, the history of Moses and his successors proved:

1. How disastrous it is for both religion and state to grant to religious functionaries any right to issue decrees or to concern themselves with state business.... 2. How dangerous it is to refer to religious jurisdiction matters that are purely philosophical, and to legislate concerning beliefs that are frequently subject to dispute, or can so be.... 3. How essential it is for both commonwealth and religion that the sovereign power should be given the right to decide what is right and what

267

is wrong.... 4. Finally, we see how fatal it is for a people unaccustomed to the rule of kings, and already possessing established laws, to set up a monarchy (ibid.).

TEXTS

Voce enim vera revelavit Deus Mosi leges, quas Hebraeis praescribi volebat ... Cogimur distinguere inter Prophetiam Mosis et reliquarum Prophetarum (TTP 1, G III, 17). *Deut. Cap. 13. monet Moses, quod si quis Propheta novos Deos docere velit, quamvis suam confirmet doctrinam signis, et miraculis, mortis tamen damnetur: nam, ut ipse Moses pergit Deus signa etiam et miracula facit ad tentandam populam... Moses non satis percipit, Deum esse omniscium, humanasque actiones omnes ex solo decreto dirigi... Si jam ad Mosis revelationes attendamus, eas hisce opinionibus accomodatas fuisse reperiemus ... Moses nullam Dei imaginem in cerebro formaverat* (TTP 2, G III, 31, 38–40). *De ipso Mose etiam dicendum est eum ex revelatione vel ex fundamentis ei revelatis percepisse modum, quo populus Israëliticus in certa mundi plaga optime uniri posset et integram societatem formare, sive imperium erigere; deinde etiam modum, quo ille populus optime posset cogi ad obediendum, sed non percepisse modum illum optimum esse ... Quapropter haec omnia mon ut aeternas veritates, sed ut praecepta et instituta percepit et tanquam Dei leges praescripsit; et hinc factum est, ut Deum rectorem, legislatorem, regem, misericordem, justum etc. imaginaretur; cum tamen haec omnia solius humanae naturae sint attrributa et a natura divina prorsus removenda* (TTP 4, G III, 64); TTP 5, G III, 70; TTP 8, G III, 118. *Cum Moses Deuter. Cap. 31. vers. 27 Israëlitis dixit ... Quare*

verba illa Mosis moralis locutio tantum sunt, qua rethorice et prout futurum populi defectionem vividius imaginari potuerat (TTP 11, G III, 152). *Deus Mosi ad singularem gratiam ipsi largitam indicandum ait .. nomine meo Jehova non sum cognitus ipsis* (TTP 13, G III, 169). *Moses non suduit Israëlitas ratione convincere, sed pacto, juramentis et beneficiis obligare* (TTP 14, G III, 174). *Moses nullum talem succesorem eligit, sed imperium ... theocraticam appellari potuerit* (TTP 17, G III, 207–8). *Hebraei... imperii jus in Mosen transtulerunt, qui deinceps rex absolute mansit* (TTP 18, G III, 230).

BIBLIOGRAPHY
Primary Sources
Hobbes, Th., *Leviathan.*

Secondary Literature
Bunge, W. van, 'Spinoza and the Idea of Religious Imposture', in T. van Houdt, J.L. de Jonge, Z. Kwak, M. Spies, M. van Vaeck (eds), *On the Edge of Truth and Honesty. Principles and Strategies of Fraud and Deceit in the Early Modern Period* (Leiden and Boston: Brill, 2002), pp. 105–26.
Terpstra, M., 'De betekenis van de oudtestamentische theocratie voor de politieke filosofie van Spinoza. Een hoofdstuk uit de geschiedenis van de politieke theologie', *Tijdschrift voor filosofie,* no. 60 (1998), pp. 292–320.
Zac, S., 'Spinoza et l'état des Hébreux', in S. Hessing (ed.), *Speculum Spinozanum, 1677–1977* (London, Henley and Boston: Routledge and Kegan Paul, 1977), pp. 543–71.

W. van Bunge

Motus

The concept of motion (Dutch, *beweging*) plays an important role in Spinoza's philosophical system. In place of the scholastic definition of motion, from Aristotle's *Physics*, as 'the act of a being in potency, insofar as it is in potency', Spinoza offered in his summary of Descartes's *Principia philosophiae* the alternative definition of motion as the transfer of one part of matter from the vicinity of other parts contiguous to it. But though Spinoza followed Descartes in restricting motion in the material world to local motion, and though he held that such motion is a mode of the principal attribute of corporeal substance, namely, extension, his mature account of motion, as found in the *Ethics* but also in his correspondence, has features that go beyond what can be found in Descartes.

For instance, in a sketch of his physics that follows proposition 13 of *Ethics* 2, Spinoza derived as a lemma the claim that bodies are distinguished from each other 'by reason of motion' and not 'by reason of substance'. In support of this claim he offered the result in E1p15s that corporeal substance is indivisible as substance, in contrast to Descartes's own official position that corporeal substance is by its nature divisible into really distinct parts. For Spinoza, the division of matter into parts can occur only at the modal level, with the distinction deriving from differences in motion and rest.

Spinoza held not only that motion and rest serve to distinguish different bodies as modes, but also that particular instances of motion and rest are themselves modifications of *motus* and *quies* as the 'immediate infinite mode' of extension. Though some have insisted that the laws governing motion and rest constitute this infinite mode, there is also the suggestion in Spinoza that the mode is a concrete quantity, namely, the total quantity of motion and rest in nature. Such a suggestion helps to make sense of the fact that in letter 64 Spinoza offered as an example of an infinite modification of the immediate infinite mode of extension, that is, the 'mediate infinite mode' of that attribute, the 'whole of nature' as an 'individual' that has its own 'ratio of motion and rest' among all of the finite bodies in nature that constitute it.

Towards the end of his life, Spinoza indicated in correspondence with Tschirnhaus that he differed from Descartes in his conception of motion and its relation to extension. When Tschirnhaus noted that in Descartes's view motion cannot derive internally from extension, but must be imposed on it by God, Spinoza responded in letter 83 that Descartes is mistaken and that he should instead have defined motion 'through an attribute that expresses eternal and infinite essence'. The suggestion here is that insofar as extension is an attribute that expresses eternal and infinite essence, it involves an internal dynamic feature that explains the immediate derivation from it of motion and rest as an infinite mode. Moreover, particular bodies in motion and at rest possess not merely the presence or absence of *translatio*, but also, as proposition six of *Ethics* 3 makes clear, an internal CONATUS that serves to explain the existence of their states.

TEXTS

KV 2.9; Uijt deze proportie dan van beweginge en stilte komt ook wezentlijk te zijn dit ons licham (KV 2voorr). Zoo wanneer wij dan aanschouwen de uijtgebreidheid alleen, zoo is 't dat wij in de zelve niets anders gewaarworden als beweging en ruste, uijt de welke wij alle de uijtwerkingen, die daar af herkomen, vinden (KV 2.19); KV 2. 20.

Corpus humanum non absolute, sed tantum secundum leges naturae extensae per modum motum et quietatem determinata extensio (PPC 1praef). '*Motus localis*' *est translatio unius partis materiae, sive unius corporis, ex vicinia eorum corporum, quae illud immediate contingunt, et tanquam quiescentia spectantur, in viciniam aliorum* (PPC 2def8); PPC 2p6s; PPC 2p8c; PPC 2p11s. *Extensio per se, et in se concipitur; ac motus non item. Nam concipitur in alio, et ipsius conceptus involvit extensionem* (Ep 2). *Exempla, quae petis, primi generis [eorum, quae immediate a Deo producta sunt] sunt in cogitatione, intellectus absolute infinitus; in extensione autem motus et quies* (Ep 64). Ep 81; Ep 83. *Mens corpus ad motum, neque ad quietum determinare potest* (E3p2). *Corpora ratione motus et quietis, celeritatis et tarditatis, et non ratione substantiae ab invicem distinguuntur* (E2lem1); E5praef.

BIBLIOGRAPHY
Primary Sources
Descartes, R., *Principia philosophiae.*

Secondary Literature
Gabbey, A., 'Spinoza's Natural Science and Methodology', in S. Nadler (ed.), *The Cambridge Companion to Spinoza* (Cambridge: Cambridge University Press, 1996), pp. 142–91.
Garrett, D., 'Spinoza's Theory of Metaphysical Individuation', in K. Barber and J. Gracia (eds), *Individuation in Early Modern Philosophy* (Albany: State University Press, 1994), pp. 73–101.
Gueroult, M., *Spinoza* II: *De l'âme* (Hildesheim: Olms, 1974), app. 5, 8.
Lachterman, D.R., 'The Physics of Spinoza's *Ethics*', in R. Shahan and J. Biro (eds), *Spinoza: New Perspectives* (Norman: University of Oklahoma, 1978), pp. 77–111.
Matheron, A., *Individu et Communauté chez Spinoza* (Paris: Éditions de Minuit, 1969).

T.M. Schmaltz

Mulier, *see* **Femina/Mulier**

Natura

Although in Spinoza's writings 'nature' and its Dutch counterparts *natuur* and *aard* are often used, the concept is never defined by the philosopher. Apart from the scholastic pair of concepts NATURA NATURANS and *natura naturata*, which he deals with both in the *Korte verhandeling* and *Ethics* 1, he apparently took the traditional meanings for granted. The first meaning of 'nature' is very classical and denotes the essence of a thing in contrast with its properties. Examples are the nature of God, man, a triangle etc. Denoting a thing's essence and fabric, an avantage of the term 'nature' in comparison with essence is that it has fewer logical connotations. Since it is used in a more definite way, it refers to a scientific approach to reality; the geometricians study the nature of a triangle and its properties, that is to say how certain properties follow from the nature of the triangle, or formulated in a negative way, how certain properties are impossible to attribute to a thing given the fact that a certain figure is a triangle. Such research implies both a dispassionate attitude towards the object, which is not to be 'mocked, lamented, or execrated', and the denial of final causes. An examination of nature and its properties is opposed to a contemplation of its end or ideal essence, in the name of which something is denounced for not satisfying its own purpose, which makes it a vice or sin. In this sense the *Ethics* and Spinoza's letters often use 'Nature' with a capital letter.

The second meaning, just as classical as the first, denotes the whole of all existing things (in this sense also *natura rerum* is used). This whole is ruled by internal laws. We should not imagine that an external authority ('the rulers of nature') is required to direct nature in accordance with the needs of man. The whole of these laws may have a principle, traditionally called God (which justifies the appearance of the phrase 'God or Nature') but not to be identified with any part of Nature any more than the triangle may be identified with any of its properties. Spinoza marks the difference by using to his own end the scholastic distinction between *natura naturans* (God – substance and attribute) and *natura naturata* (the things).

The originality of Spinoza's thought does not reside in its reduction of God to nature, but in its contention that the laws of nature are universal and unchanging. It is this constancy that renders out of the question the existence of miracles violating the order of nature. It is this universality which makes man 'a part of nature' unable to escape from its laws. Specific laws of human nature are merely the general laws of extension and thinking applied to a particular area. Hence, they too are marked by their permanence and their unity. As to the psychological level, the passions are not vices but only the necessary application of the natural laws to human nature; who ignores them is even more seriously their victim. On a political level the social contract does not abolish these necessary laws of human nature. That is why institutions must be created which reckon with them. In the end there are no basic differences between men, neither between nations ('nature does not create peoples') nor between individuals (the patricians possess the same emotional life as the multitude despised by them).

In this situation, it is impossible to use the word 'supernatural' and acknowledge the existence of a category of knowledge different from our natural knowledge. Nature does not exclude anything, but either we understand the order of nature or we do not. The supernatural is merely nature not grasped in its due order (*debito ordine*). Prophetic knowledge is, therefore, supernatural in the sense that it is produced by the phenomena we perceive but do not (yet) understand (for instance effects caused by the body and the imagination). Consequently we are convinced that these phenomena exist outside nature.

If all things obey the laws of nature, how is a morality to be grounded? Reason does not demand anything against nature, but allows for a choice between possible human actions – all equally natural – which bring about a better equilibrium of the body, better relationships with other men and more versatile relations with the external world. In order to reach that end, we have to construe a model of human nature not based on imaginary ends but on the best knowledge of the natural powers of man and his laws that we are capable of attaining.

TEXTS

In de natuur geen scheppen, maar alleen genereeren ... door haar natuur oneijndelijk (KV 1.2). In de natuur geen zaak en is, van de welke men niet kan vragen waarom datze is (KV 1.3). Dingen door eigen aard en natuur vergankelijk (KV 2.14). De natuur word gekend door zig zelfs en niet door eenig

ander ding. Zy bestaat van oneyndige eigenschappen, een ieder van de zelve oneyndig
(KV aanhp4c). *Bonum sua natura incertum*
(TIE 6, G II, 7). *Cognitio unionis, quam mens
cum tota natura habet ... Nihil enim in sua
natura spectatum perfectum dicetur* (TIE 12,
G II, 8). *In natura nihil possit dari quod ejus
leges oppugnet* (TIE a, G II, 23). *Si ad analo-
giam totius naturae attendimus, ipsam ut
unum ens considerare possumus* (CM 2.7). *Si
homines clare totum ordinem naturae intelligerent omnia aeque necessaria reperirent,
ac omnia illa quae in Mathesi tractantur* (CM
2.9). *Deum a natura non ita separem, ut
omnes quorum apud me est notitia, fecerunt*
(Ep 6). *Sua natura, sive vi suae definitionis
infinitum ... unica substantia ejusdem natura
existit* (Ep 12). *Partem naturae cum suo toto
convenire* (Ep 32). *Vulgus ad rara et a sua
natura aliena anhelans* (TTP 1, G III, 15).
*Certum est omnia, quae in natura sunt, Dei
conceptum ... exprimere* (TTP 4, G III, 60).
Vulgi de natura et miraculis opiniones (TTP
6, G III, 82). *Universalis historia naturae
solius philosophiae fundamentum est* (TTP
15, G III, 185). *Ex sola sua natura existere*
(E1def7). *Id cujus natura involvit existentiam*
(E1p25). *Ostendam naturam finem nullum
sibi praefixum habere ... rectores naturae*
(E1app). *Naturam sub attributo extensionis
sive sub attributo cognitionis concipiamus
unum eundumque ordinem reperiamus*
(E2p7s). *Totam naturam unum esse individuum* (E2lem7s). *Nihil in natura evenit, quod
ipsius vitio possit tribuit* (E3praef). *Leges
naturae corporis* (E3p2s). *Ex natura aliquid
appetere* (E3p31s). *Ipsam naturam tum defi-
cisse vel peccavisse credunt ... Deum seu
naturam appellamus ... Deus seu natura agit*
(E4praef). *Dei seu naturae potentia* (E4p2s).
Ratio nihil contra naturam (E4p18s). *Homines in natura veluti imperium in imperio
concipiunt* (TP 2.6).

BIBLIOGRAPHY
Secondary Literature
Collins, J., *Spinoza on Nature* (Carbondale
and Edwardsville: Southern Illinois
University Press, 1984).
Espinosa Rubio, L., *Spinoza, Naturaleza y
Ecosistema* (Salamanca: Publicaciones
Universidad Pontificia de Salamanca,
1995).
Yovel, Y. (ed.), *God and Nature. Spinoza's
Metaphysics. Papers Presented at the First
Jerusalem Conference (Ethica I)* (Leiden:
Brill, 1991).

P.-F. Moreau

Natura naturans

Although in Spinoza's writings the scholastic
pair of concepts *natura naturans* and *natura
naturata* rarely occurs, the philosopher – at
least between 1660 and 1663 (Steenbakkers,
2003) – effectively adopted these concepts to
express the basic distinction in his system
between substance and attributes on the one
hand and the subordinate modes on the other.

In the *Korte verhandeling* Spinoza identifies naturing nature with substances – this
early work still acknowledged a plurality of
'selfstandigheden' – and the attributes, which
are all conceived 'clearly and distinctly
through themselves', and God. He denounces
late scholastic doctrine – 'the Thomists' – on
account of its refusal to call God a substance.
Natured nature includes the modes or creatures and is divided into two more kinds: a
universal and a particular. The universal
natured nature consists of the modes immediately depending on God: motion in the
attribute matter and intellect in the attribute
thinking. They are eternal and immutable, 'a
work truly as great as the greatness of the

workman', and Spinoza gives them Christ's predicate 'Son', but they 'neither exist nor are understood through themselves' (KV 1.9). The notion of a universal natured nature recurs in the *Cogitata metaphysica* – 'we may consider nature as one being and consequently based on one idea or decree of God'. However, in the *Korte verhandeling* the particular natured nature is not dealt with. In the *Ethics* the definitions of naturing nature and natured nature are only adapted to the new definitions of substance, attribute and mode by observing that an attribute 'expresses God's eternal essence' and that a mode is 'whatever follows from the necessity of God's nature'.

In the seventeenth century the scholastic origin of these twin concepts was obvious. The two participles in these expressions are both derived from a Latin verb – *naturare* – which apparently is not classical but of scholastic origin. The verb means to generate, to bring forth, or to produce and seems to have been introduced into thirteen-century Latin in the process of translating Averroes's commentaries. Notwithstanding the humanist ban on medieval barbarism, the terms remained in use not only in late scholastic writings – the school of Coimbra's commentaries on Aristotle's *Physics*, Heereboord – but also in the works of 'modern' philosophers such as Bruno, Bacon and Clauberg. Moreover they occur in the dictionaries (Goclenius, Micraelius, Chauvin). Their occurrence is rather infrequent (and they are apparently absent in the writings of luminaries such as Suarez and Burgersdijk), but on the other hand tenacious. Clauberg stated that there is no real need for such 'barbaric terms', because the relation between God and creature may be described in other words (*Paraphrasis in R. Des Cartes Meditationes*, p. 327). According to most commentators nature itself primarily constitutes an activity, the activity of

generating – accounted for by the etymological link between *natura* and *nasci*. Such an activity seems to imply both a generating principle and its effects. According to Chauvin 'nature' is a very broad and ambiguous concept and he lists no less than seven senses. The term may be used, he observed, to denote the generating principle of all things, the Divine mind, which Seneca called the 'workman of all things'. Both Cicero and Augustine stated that nature in this sense is God. However, nature is also the whole of all created things, that is all things immediately dependent on the first principle. More specifically 'nature' may be used to denote all causes in nature acting according to the laws of the Creator. Finally, nature is the essence of a thing. However, the nature of a thing is not the principle of the thing's being, that is essence, but the principle of its acting. More than other pairs of concepts, *natura naturans* and *natura naturata* make explicit the dynamic fabric of the universe. Apparently this part of scholastic heritage appealed to Spinoza.

TEXTS

Kortelijk geheel de natuur te schiften – te weten in 'Natura naturans' en 'Natura naturata'; door de 'natura naturans' verstaan wij een wezen dat wij (door zig zelfs ...) klaar ende onderscheidelijk begrijpen het welk God is. Gelijk ook de Thomisten ... De 'natura naturata' zullen wij in twee verdelen, in een algemene en in een bezondere. De algemene bestaat in alle die wijzen die van God onmiddelijk afhangen. De bezondere bestaat in alle die besondere dingen, de welke van de algemene wijze veroorsaakt werden. Soo dat de naturata naturata om wel begrepen te worden eenige selfstandigheden van noden heeft (KV 1.8); KV1.9. *Dei idea sive decretum de natura naturata* (CM 2.7). *Tota natura naturata non sit nisi unicum ens* (CM 2.9). *Intellectum quamvis infinitum ad naturam naturatam pertinere* (Ep 9). *Per naturam naturantem nobis intelligandum est id quod in se est et per se concipitur sive talia substantiae attributa ... hoc est Deus quatenus ut causa libera consideratur. Per naturatam id omne quod ex necessitate Dei naturae sive uniuscujusque attributorum sequitur, hoc est omnes Dei attributorum modos* (E1p29s); E1p31).

BIBLIOGRAPHY

Primary Sources

Clauberg, J., *Paraphrasis in R. Des Cartes Meditationes* (Duisburg, 1658).

Heereboord, A., *Collegium physicum*, in *Meletemata*.

Secondary Literature

Giancotti, E., 'On the Problem of Infinite Modes', in Yovel, Y. (ed.), *God and Nature, Spinoza's Metaphysics, Papers Presented at the First Jerusalem Conference (Ethica I)* (Leiden: Brill, 1991), pp. 97–118.

Gueroult, M., *Spinoza I. Dieu (Éthique I)* (Hildesheim: Olms, 1968).

Robinson, L., *Kommentar zu Spinozas Ethik* (Leipzig: Meiner, 1928).

Steenbakkers, P., 'Spinoza over *natura naturans* en *natura naturata*', in G. Coppens (ed.), *Spinoza en de scholastiek* (Leuven: Acco, 2003), pp. 35–52.

Weijers, O., 'Contribution à l'histoire des termes *natura naturans* et *natura naturata* jusqu'à Spinoza', *Vivarium*, no. 16 (1978), pp. 70–80.

Yovel, Y., 'The Infinite Modes and Natural Laws in Spinoza', in Y. Yovel, (ed.), *God and Nature, Spinoza's Metaphysics, Papers Presented at the First Jerusalem Conference (Ethica I)* (Leiden: Brill, 1991), pp. 79–96.

H. Krop

Nihil

In Spinoza's Latin works there are several references to *nihil*, and occasionally to its Dutch counterpart *niet*. There are two main contexts in which Spinoza used this term. The first is in discussing the axiom that nothing has no properties. In his *Principia philosophiae* I, art. 11 Descartes initially appealed to a similar axiom to argue that perception shows more evidently the existence of mind than the existence of body, and later in this text (II, art. 16) he derived the impossibility of a VACUUM from the fact that any particular extension must belong to some substance. In the summary of Descartes's *Principia*, Spinoza used the axiom to derive these same results, though only the result concerning the vacuum finds its way into the *Ethics*.

The second context concerns the causal axiom that nothing is produced from nothing (PP 1.18). In his summary of the *Principia* Spinoza followed Descartes in taking this axiom: 'no existing thing can have nothing as the cause of its existence', to show that an effect cannot have more reality or perfection than its cause. However, Spinoza's own writings reveal that he accepted a stronger form of this axiom than can be found in Descartes. For the particularly important axiom 4 of *Ethics* 1 requires that the effect conceptually 'involves' or 'depends on' its cause. Since Spinoza followed Descartes in thinking that mind and body involve attributes that are conceptually independent, he concluded that they cannot causally interact. Descartes's occasional claim that his causal axiom provides no barrier to mind-body interaction can be explained by the fact that he does not require that the reality common to the cause and its effect be conceived in terms of the same attribute. But as Spinoza indicated in letter 4, he thought that if the cause and the effect had no attribute in common, then what the effect does not have in common with its cause would have to come from nothing.

TEXTS

Want van de Niet kan geen Iet voortkomen ... De reden is, omdat de Niet geen eigenschappen konnende hebben, de Al dan alle eigenschappen moet hebben (KV 1.2). *Nulla res, neque ulla rei perfectio actu existens, potest habere nihil, sive rem non existentem pro causa suae existentiae* (PPC 1ax7). *Nihili nullae sunt proprietates* (PPC 2ax1). *Extensio sive spatium non potest esse purum nihil* (PPC 2lem1dem). *Inepta sit illa divisio qua dividitur ens in ens reale et ens rationis; dividunt ens in ens et non-ens ... ens rationis esse mere nihil* (CM 1.1). *Finitum, et imperfectum, id est, de nihilo participans* (CM 1.3); Ep 4. *A nihilo nihil fit* (Ep 10). *Nihili nullae sunt proprietates* (Ep 13).

BIBLIOGRAPHY
Primary Sources
Descartes, R., *Principia philosophiae.*

Secondary Literature
Gueroult, M., *Spinoza* I: *Dieu* (Hildesheim: Olms, 1968).
Wilson, M.D., 'Spinoza's Causal Axiom (Ethics I, Axiom 4)', in Y. Yovel (ed.), *God and Nature: Spinoza's Metaphysics* (Leiden: Brill, 1991), pp. 133–60.

T.M. Schmaltz

Nomen / Verbum

Both in his philosophical and linguistic works Spinoza deals with the concept of the noun. As a philosopher Spinoza subscribes without hesitation to the traditional (Aristotelian) view of the conventionality of language. Chauvin, for example, observes that 'a noun is a diction installed by man in order to signify an idea'. And he refers to Aristotle's famous definition in *De interpretatione* of the noun being 'a sound significant by convention, which has no reference to time, and of which no part is significant apart from the rest without time, being finite and in the nominative case'. However, whereas Aristotle differentiates between the noun and the verb, Spinoza refrains from making such a distinction. The conventional nature of language warrants Spinoza's premise that a philosopher should not bother about the meaning of words, but has to be merely interested in the nature of things. What is more, Spinoza's philosophical theory of language has a definite nominalistic bias, as can be seen in E2p40s. He may well have derived such a nominalism from Hobbes.

Theories of the parts of speech varied widely in the seventeenth century. In general, the parts of speech were divided into eight classes, of which the noun and the verb counted as the principal ones. In traditional Hebrew grammar the parts of speech were divided into three major classes: noun, verb and particle. A conspicuous feature of Spinoza's unfinished Hebrew grammar, *Compendium grammatices linguae Hebraeae*, is that the author considers nearly every part of speech to be a noun. Consequently, Spinoza refers to all parts of speech, with the exceptions just mentioned, as nouns (chap. 5).

However, verbs do exist in his grammatical system. Spinoza arrives at six nominal categories; the infinitive noun is number five in his enumeration of the 'genders of the noun' (ibid.). The infinitive has among other things traits of a proper name, it cannot be pluralized. Now Spinoza regards this *nomen infinitivum*, which expresses an action (chap. 12), as the noun from which the verb is derived by means of conjugation. When the infinitive accepts personal affixes, then it is conjugated and infinitive nouns with affixes are called verbs (chap. 13). A verb, then, is a word predicating something of a subject with relationship to time and it is derived from a *nomen actionis*, which as such has no relation to time (chap. 5).

In stressing the nominal origin of the verb, Spinoza endorses a genetic explanation, which was not uncommon among Hebrew grammarians, that nouns were the very first words to be created in Hebrew. This view, which can be found in the writings of, for example, Abraham de Balmes (c. 1440–1523), has to do with ideas about the origin of the Hebrew language: Adam was made to give *names* to the things, not attributes and (inflected) verbs (cf. Genesis 2.19). From these names – or nouns – the other parts of speech were derived.

It has been suggested that Spinoza's one-part-of-speech theory is a result of his philosophical system in which everything is to be reduced to one substance. Note, however, that Spinoza is not of the opinion that there exists only one part of speech: he explicitly mentions the fact that some categories cannot be counted among the nouns. Among the contemporary grammarians, it is George Dalgarno (1626–87) who is unique in positing only one part of speech, viz. the noun; the particles, i.e. the secondary parts of speech, are all in origin nouns.

TEXTS

Deinde cum verba sunt pars imaginationis, hoc est quod prout vage ex aliqua dispositione corporis componuntur ... possint esse causa multorum errorum (TIE 89, G II 33). *Philosophos verbales ... res enim ex nominibus judicant, non autem nomina ex rebus* (CM 1,1). *Chimaeram, quia neque in intellectu est, neque in imaginatione, a nobis ens verbale commode vocari posse* (CM 1,3). *Nullius momenti iis, qui de rebus, non vero de nominibus sunt solliciti* (CM 1,6). *Si forte (ut soleo propter verborum penuriam) aliquid obscure posui* (Ep 6). *Dividitur apud Latinos oratio in octo partes ... Nam omnes Hebraeae voces, exceptis tantum interjectionibus et conjunctionibus et una et altera particulara vim et proprietates nominis habent* (CG 5). *Nomina infinitiva exprimunt actionem vel ad agentem relatam, vel ad patientem* (CG 12). *Nomina infinitiva quatenus sic conjungata verba appellabimus* (CG 13).

BIBLIOGRAPHY
Secondary Literature
Klijnsmit, A.J., *Balmesian Linguistics. A Chapter in the History of Pre-Rationalist Thought* (Amsterdam: Neerlandistiek, VU, 1992).
———, 'More Notes on Spinoza's *Compendium*', unpubl. ms.
Michael, I., *English Grammatical Categories and the Tradition to 1800* (Cambridge: Cambridge University Press, 1970).
Pettit, Ph., *Made with Words. Hobbes and Language* (Princeton: Princeton University Press, 2009).

J. Noordegraaf

Notio communis

Usually 'common notion' means exactly the same as *axiom*: a self-evident claim that does not have to be proved or demonstrated. It is in that way that the term is used by Spinoza in the preface to the PPC, the *Tractatus theologico-politicus* and at least one passage of the *Ethics* (E1p8s2) (cf. also Descartes's *Principia philosophiae* I, art. 49–50). Traditional notions, such as 'innate', 'self-evident' and 'planted by God into the human mind', however, are not discussed by Spinoza. Whether that is also the meaning we should attach to that word in part two of the *Ethics* is controversial. This part of the text seems to be concerned with scientific reasoning, more particularly notions of time and space, fundamental physical laws, etc., which Spinoza describes as 'what is common to everything and is in both the whole and its parts, without constituting the essence of anything' (E2p37). In the concluding *scholium*, however, Spinoza presents this analysis as an explanation of 'those notions which are called common and which are the foundations of our reasoning' (E2p40s1). This suggests that a 'common notion' is something like a natural law or a shared property. But apart from the fact that that is not a fitting description of 'axioms,' the axioms used by Spinoza himself either are logical or grammatical ('whatever is is either in itself or in something else') or else relate to facts ('a man thinks', 'we feel that our body is affected in many ways'). Spinoza could also mean that we *acquire* common notions in the same way as we do natural laws, that is, by coming to understand that certain principles (causality, intelligibility) uniformly and universally apply (E2p38c). In other words, principles and axioms would be the result of experience – which is not very satisfactory either. In

the same first *scholium* of proposition 40 Spinoza claims that he has a better explanation of common notions, which would show 'what notions are more useful than others and which ones are hardly of any use ... which common and which clear and distinct for those only who are not prejudiced and finally which ones are badly founded'. So the number of common notions would not be fixed – what is a common notion for some would not be one for others. Nor is it clear how this alternative explanation looks. If we assume that 'common notions' refers to general axioms and principles (causality, for example), Spinoza could mean that we can deduce these from the idea of God. For if we prove that 'whatever is is in God' (E1p15) and that God 'acts in virtue of the laws of his own nature' (E1p17), all particular things are parts of God and must be subject to the same necessity. A sketch of such an argument is found in the *Tractatus de intellectus emendatione*, §78–80, the prolegomena to the PPC and chapter 6 of the *Tractatus theologico-politicus*.

TEXTS

Axiomata seu communes animi notiones clarae atque perspicuae sunt enunciationes, ut iis omnes...assensum negare nequaquam possint (PPC praef). *Cognitio ex notionibus per se certis et notis hauriri debet* (TTP 4, G III, 61). *Ex notionibus universalibus et communibus* (TTP 6, G III 88). *Ut Dei natura clare et distincte a nobis possit concipi, necesse est, ut ad quasdam notiones simplicissimas, quas communes vocant* (TTP adn 6). *Omnibus axioma esset et inter notiones communes numeraretur* (E1p8s2). *Dari quasdam ideas, sive notiones omnibus hominibus communes; nam omnia corpora in quibusdam conveniunt, quae omnibus debent adaequate percipi* (E2p38c). *His causam notionum, quae communes vocatur, quaeque ratiocinii nostri fundamenta sunt* (E2p40s1). *Quod homines non aeque claram Dei ac notionum communium habeant cognitionem* (E2p47s).

BIBLIOGRAPHY
Primary Sources
Descartes, R., *Principia philosophiae.*

Th. Verbeek

Ordo et connexio

The phrase *ordo et connexio* occurs for the first time in the *Tractatus theologico-politicus* and is used essentially in the *Ethics,* especially in proposition 7 of *Ethics* 2, where Spinoza assumes that the order and connection of ideas is the same as the order and connection of things. The notion of a corresponding order between ideas and things is a basic one, since Spinoza refers to this proposition 19 times. This thesis called 'parallelism' – which is better termed 'equality' to use Spinoza's own word – is a consequence of the unity of the substance which expresses itself in infinite attributes. According to Spinoza, the Cartesian thinking and extended substances are one and the same substance, which is comprehended now through this attribute and now through that. Thus, also, a mode of extension and the idea of this mode are the same thing expressed in two different ways (E2p7s). Since attributes and modes of attributes are only expressions of one and the same thing, they define mutual and co-ordinate series, which do not interact with each other. In other words, there is a correspondence and an identity between the way of producing ideas and the way of producing things.

Sometimes, Spinoza uses the word *concatenatio* instead of *connexio* but both phrases *ordo et connexio* and *ordo et concatenatio* have the same meaning: they refer to the causal link between things or between ideas and the necessary way the effect depends upon its cause. In fact, the order is nothing but connection, for Spinoza identifies the two in E2p7s where he says *ordo sive connexio.* The word *connexio* determines the nature of the order, which is a real and necessary one that must be distinguished from the confused, imaginary order that men presuppose among things.

TEXTS

Ipsas historias examinemus, nempe earum ordinem et connexionem (TTP 9, G III, 130). *Ordo, et connexio idearum est, ac ordo et connexio rerum ... sive naturam sub attributo extensionis, sive sub attributo cognitionis sive sub alio quocunque concipiamus, unum eundemque ordinem sive unam eandemque causarum connexionem hoc est easdem res invicem sequi reperiemus* (E2p7).

BIBLIOGRAPHY
Secondary Literature
Gueroult, M., *Spinoza II. L'Âme* (Hildesheim: Olms, 1972), chap. 4.
Jaquet, Ch., *L'unité du corps et de l'esprit, affects, actions et passions chez Spinoza* (Paris, Presses Universitaires de France, 2004), pp. 9–16.

Ch. Jaquet

Ordo geometricus. Definitio. Axioma.

Spinoza was familiar with a diversity of contexts: the new philosophy of Hobbes and Descartes (and Bacon), the Dutch *philosophia novantiqua* (particularly Burgersdijk and Heereboord), and Jewish philosophers such as Maimonides and Gersonides. It is very hard to determine with certainty which influences were decisive with respect to his ideas on method (Garrett, 2003, pp. 97–9). But it is clear that he was familiar with Bacon's *Novum Organon* which influenced his conception of *logica* (to be found in his unfinished *Tractatus de intellectus emendatione*, analysed in De Dijn, 1996), and with the widespread 'Aristotelian' conception of a 'Euclidian' geometrical method (De Dijn, 1986). Spinoza's notion of *mos* or *ordo geometricus* seems most close to – even though not perfectly identical with – Hobbes's (Gueroult I, 1968, p. 13; De Dijn, 1986, pp. 68–9; Garrett, 2003, pp. 103–15).

Spinoza scholarship has been divided over the question whether the geometrical method in Spinoza is a rhetorical device or way of exposition (a merely pedagogical instrument), or a real method of proof, or both. Even those who think it is a real method of proof differ as to its precise character (De Dijn, 1986, pp. 67–9; Garrett, 2003, pp. 99–103). Is it a syllogistic method, a formal axiomatic method, or something else altogether? If only in view of the time, effort and care invested in the writing of the *Ethica* in a geometrical way, it is extremely unlikely that this was merely an exercise in style. In E4p18s Spinoza says: 'before I begin to demonstrate these things in our cumbersome [*prolixus*] geometric order, I should like first to show briefly here the dictates of reason themselves, so that everyone may more easily perceive what I think'. Although things can be expressed differently, clearly Spinoza thinks the geometrical deduction is necessary in order to arrive at real knowledge.

A standard distinction within the geometrical method is the distinction between analysis and synthesis (De Dijn, 1986, pp. 69–71). Analysis is said to go from effects to causes, from consequences to principles, from whole to parts; synthesis is the inverse movement of thought. It is clear that causes and parts referred to here are not concrete causes and parts, but the necessary and sufficient elements of intelligibility (principles). Whereas Descartes thought that the proper way to demonstrate *and* discover truths in metaphysics is only the analytic method (used in the *Meditationes*), in his *Ethics* Spinoza clearly seems to think the opposite. It is synthesis that is considered the right way to prove *and* to discover not only metaphysical but also ethical truths (Gueroult I, 1968, p. 35).

In the preface of *Ethics* 3, Spinoza explicitly states that he is going to use the same geometrical method with which he treated God and the mind, in the study of the nature and powers of human affects. This method will allow – as he says a few sentences earlier – an understanding of the *causes* through which the nature and the properties of these affects can be understood. The fundamental aim of the geometrical method is then, in 'Aristotelian' terms, an understanding *propter quid* of things, a 'causal' understanding of the essence such that from it all the properties of the thing can be deduced, and also an explanation of the lawlike relations between things thus defined and understood.

As is said in the same preface, understanding the nature, properties and necessary relations between things is nothing more than understanding them 'through the universal rules or laws of nature', i.e. the laws governing all things as effects or modes of God-Nature. It is indeed precisely on the basis of the universal rules of nature, deduced in *Ethics* 1 from an insight into the nature and properties of the divine substance (the *res* studied in *Ethics* 1, *De Deo*), that Spinoza developed an insight into the specific laws characterizing the human being (the *res* studied in *Ethics* 2, *De natura et origine mentis*). On the basis of the insights into these two parts, general definitions or NOTIONES COMMUNES of the affects will be obtained in part three. The affects or emotions are modifications of a specific, human mode of the divine substance, the ultimate cause of everything. The geometrical method is then intrinsically related to an understanding of the nature and properties of things, substance or modes, via the universal and specific laws that govern them, and using the universal and specific common notions (E2p38 and 39) that constitute an understanding SUB SPECIE AETERNITATIS (E2p44c2). All these really mean the same thing.

It is crucial for the geometrical method to yield *real* definitions explaining fully the nature and properties of real things. The *Tractatus de intellectus emendatione* gives invaluable information concerning Spinoza's views on definition, and these views square with the practice in the *Ethics*, even though there are some differences (Gueroult I, 1968, pp. 25–31; De Dijn, 1996, pp. 150–60). The kernel of the geometrical method is the 'causal' understanding which allows one to obtain definitions that can be shown to apply to real things. Like Hobbes, Spinoza sees 'real' definitions as *genetic* definitions, i.e. definitions giving an insight into how necessary and sufficient elements are combined in such a way that the internal structure of the thing is understood.

Understanding the precise relation between the geometrical or axiomatic deduction and the formation of real definitions is one of the difficulties here. In general, real definitions are the result of a derivation of propositions that combine concepts out of a list of concepts defined in advance, and use axioms also selected in advance. This derivation or deduction leads, in the margin (the *scholia*), to the formulation of the real definition(s). Once the definition is formed, new propositions can be put forward, linking the insight into the essence with the insight into properties of the thing. This clearly is the case with the definition of God, the construction of which is prepared in the propositions 9 and 10 of *Ethics* 1, leading in the scholium of the last proposition to the formulation of the conceivability/constructability of God's essence (as provisionally defined in E1def6). Then, from propositon 11 onwards, Spinoza begins the deduction of God's essential properties, in the first place of God's necessary existence, a deduction which at the same time proves the thing conceived to be a *real* thing (De Dijn, 1996, chap. 9). A similar procedure is to be found in *Ethics* 3 concerning the origin and nature of the affects. These insights are derived from an explanation of the 'origin' of the affects as conceivable modifications of the really existing human mind-body mode, which as *conatus* necessarily expresses God's power.

Not surprisingly, axioms are not as central to the method as definitions. That is why it is not as important for Spinoza to list *all* the axioms, or to enumerate in advance *all* the concepts required for the deduction. That is why in different versions of his philosophy axioms become propositions and vice versa. This also means that Spinoza's method is not the formalized axiomatic method of today (De Dijn, 1986, pp. 67–9).

TEXTS

More geometrico ... geometrico ordine demonstrata ... disposita (PPC praef); *Methodus mathematicis disciplinis peculiaris ... ordo mathematicus* (PPC praef); Ep 2. *More mathematico scire* (Ep 21). *Geometricae demonstrationes* (Ep 56). *Mathematice demonstrare* (TTP 15, G III, 187). *Mos geometricus tractandi* (E3praef). *Prolixus geometricus ordo demonstrandi* (E4p18s).

Optima conclusio erit depromenda ab essentia aliqua particulari affirmativa, sive a vera et legitima definitione ... recta inveniendi via est ex data aliqua definitione cogitationes formare ... Quare cardo totius hujus secundae Methodi partis in hoc solo versatur, nempe in conditionibus bonae definitionis cognoscendis ... Definitio perfecta debebit intimam essentiam rei explicare ... comprehendere causam proximam ... omnes proprietates rei, dum sola spectatur (TIE 94–6, G III, 34–6). *Omnis definitio, sive clara et distincta idea vera* (Ep 4). *Definitio vel explicat rem, prout est extra intellectum et tum vera debet esse et a propositione vel axiomata non differre* (Ep 9). *Veram rei definitionem nihil involvere, neque exprimere praeter rei definitae naturam plus realitatis rei definitio exprimit ... Ex ipsius definitione vel essentia sequitur* (E1p16). *Rei alicujus existentia vel ex ipsius essentia seu definitione ... sequitur* (E1p33s1). *Veram uniusquisque rei definitionem nihil involvere neque exprimere praeter rei definitae naturam* (E1p8s2).

Ab experientia simplicium faciunt axioma universale (TIE 23, G II, 12). *Axiomata intellectualia per se nota* (TTP 5, G III, 76). *Si homines ad naturam substantiae attenderent, minime de veritate 7 prop. dubitarent; imo haec prop. omnibus axioma esset et inter notiones communes numeraretur* (E1p8s2). *Aliae quorundam axiomatum sive notionum*

causae dantur (E2p40s1). *Postulatum seu axioma* (E3post1).

BIBLIOGRAPHY
Secondary Literature
De Dijn, H., 'Conceptions of Philosophical Method in Spinoza: *Logica* and *Mos Geometricus*', *Review of Metaphysics*, no. 3 (1986), pp. 55–78.

De Dijn, H., *Spinoza. The Way to Wisdom* (West Lafayette, IN: Purdue University Press, 1996).

Garrett, A.V., *Meaning in Spinoza's Method* (Cambridge: Cambridge University Press, 2003).

Gueroult, M., *Spinoza I. Dieu (Ethique, I)* (Paris: Aubier-Montaigne, 1968).

H. de Dijn

Passio

The word *passio* occurs several times in *Ethics* 3–5 as a technical term with a specific meaning peculiar to Spinoza's philosophy. Unfortunately, nearly all translations confuse this notion with 'emotion', 'affect' and 'affection', which are clearly distinguished by Spinoza in his main work. However, in the earlier works, the *Korte verhandeling*, for example, Spinoza uses the words *lydinge* or *passien* but these are synonymous with *tochten*, i.e. *hartstochten* or passions (cf. the remark in the margin of KV 2.9). A passion is caused by *waan* (delusion), that is, the first kind of knowledge. According to Spinoza the liberation of the passions is possible by making good use of our intellect. Also in the *Tractatus theologico-politicus* Spinoza once or twice uses *passio* in the sense of *affectus*.

In the *Ethics* – and once in the *Tractatus politicus* – Spinoza as a rule discriminates between affects as such and passions, a subclass of the mental affects, defined as an inadequate or confused idea. In the body a passion denotes a physical affection of which we are not the adequate cause (E3def3ex, E3p1, E3p58–9, E4p32–5, E5p3). The mental passions are inadequate ideas and suffering... (*pati*) as opposed to the active affects which are caused by adequate ideas and acting. This relation between inadequate cause and suffering is clarified by the definitions of an adequate cause and of acting in *Ethics* 3. Their origin, lying in inadequacy, accounts for the fact that according to Spinoza the passions are a sign of human impotence (E4app2, E5p20s). This fact of the different origins of passions and active affects implies that only two of the primary affects – joy and desire – exist both as a passion and as an action, whereas Spinoza in proposition 59 of *Ethics* 3 demonstrates why sadness and its derivatives are only found as passions.

The number of passions easily surpasses that of active affects. Spinoza describes in *Ethics* 3 more than 48 passive affects and in proposition 59 he only names five active affects: moderation, presence of mind in danger, sobriety, courtesy and mercy. What is more, they are all species of tenacity and nobility, which in their turn are the two manifestations of strength of character, so in the end we have only one active affect. This disproportion may be explained by a medical analogy: a physician needs an encyclopedia recording the infinite number of possible diseases in order to restore health, but health itself being the absence of all disease is merely one.

Hence the clear distinction between passions and actions reappears in *Ethics* 4, where the one who is 'a slave of the passions' is contrasted with the one who lives 'according to the guidance of reason'. In order to control the passions we need another affect that is stronger, as Spinoza states in proposition 7. Such a transformation is possible if we substitute the confused ideas, which by definition are linked to passive affects, with clear and distinct knowledge (E5p3). Hence, reason causes more effectively the same self-preserving actions that the passions may cause. In the preface to part 5 of the *Ethics* Spinoza returns to the Cartesian sense of passion. Commenting on Descartes's *Passions de l'âme*, he writes about the 'motion of the passions' and the possibility of absolute dominance. Assuming the unity of body and mind, Spinoza criticizes the Stoics and Descartes for taking the freedom of the will and its capacity to acquire power over the passions for granted. Spinoza wants to teach us how to change our passions into active affects by a transformation inside, that is within our own bodies and minds.

Spinoza's political philosophy in the *Tractatus politicus* is based upon the fact that, 'as he proved to be true' in the *Ethics*, men are necessarily subject to their affects. Society and the state are inevitably based on the affects, especially fear and 'blind desire', which not originating from reason are passions and not actions. Philosophers might meditate about the transformation of the passions, but the politicians have to deal with them. In ruling the state they will neglect the difference between passions and active affects.

In seventeenth-century scholarly Latin the word *passio* was only occasionally used for the human affects in general. Courcelles in the preface of his Latin version of Descartes's *Passions de l'âme* therefore apologizes for using the word *passio* as being more in line 'with the author's principles' than the better

Latin word *affectus*. In using 'passion' for a subclass of human affects Spinoza ignores Descartes and returns to scholastic discourse by making 'affect' the more general notion, and by distinguishing the affects into two kinds related to the Latin verbs *agere* and *pati*. At the end of the seventeenth century this link was still idomatic. Chauvin for example observed that 'a passion is the reception of a form, in particular a form causing an illness or pain' and Micraelius underscores the general notion of the 'aptitude of receiving an action'.

TEXTS

Alle de lydinge (passien), die daar streydig zyn tegen de goede reden (KV 2.2). Ons aanwyst alle passien die te vernietigen zyn (KV 2.4). Onse werken van ons of met of zonder passien gedaan worden (KV 2.6). Uit deze begrippen dan komen hervoort alle deze tochten* – *Hoe nu alle deze passien uijt de begrippen voortkomen (KV 2.9). Van die passien, die wy kwaad hebben geoordeeld, vry konnen worden (KV 2.19). *Haec vox ruagh servit ad exprimendum omnes animi passiones* (TTP 2, G III, 22) *Passiones dominare* (TTP 3, G III, 46). *Si harum affectionum adaequata possimus esse causa, tum per affectum actionem intelligo, alias passionem* (E3def3ex). *Mentis actiones ex solis ideis adaequatis oriuntur; passiones autem a solis inadaequatis pendent* (E3p3). *Ut ordo actionum et passionum corporis nostri* (E3p2s). *Omnes actiones quae sequuntur ex affectibus, qui ad mentem referuntur, quatenus intelligit, ad fortitudinem refero* (E3p59s). *Homines natura discrepare possunt quatenus affectibus, qui passiones sunt, conflictantur* (E4p32). *Imperium acquiremus absolutum in nostras passiones* (E5praef). *Affectus, qui passio est, desinet esse passio*

(E5p3). *Deus expers est passionum* (E5p17). *Cupiditates, quae ex ratione non oriuntur, non tam actiones quam passiones esse humanas* (TP 2.5).

BIBLIOGRAPHY
Primary Sources
Descartes, R., *Passiones animae in Latina civitate donata ab H.D.M.* [Étienne Courcelles] (Amsterdam, 1650).

Secondary Literature
Steenbakkers, P., *Spinoza's Ethica from Manuscript to Print. Studies on Text, Form and Related Topics* (Assen: Van Gorcum, 1994).
Talon-Hugon, C., *Les passions rêvées par la raison. Essai sur la théorie des passions de Descartes et de quelques-uns de ses contemporains* (Paris: Vrin, 2002).

M. van Reijen

Pathema animi

The phrase *pathema animi* is used by Spinoza only twice as an equivalent of 'passion of the mind'. In chapter 7 of the *Tractatus theologico-politicus* Spinoza writes that Moses teaches that God is jealous and never explicitly denies that he is without passions, i.e. *animi pathemata*. This equivalence of *passio* and *animi pathema* is confirmed by the *Ethics*, where Spinoza sympathizes with the traditional wisdom that God is without passions (E5p17). In the general definition of the affects in *Ethics* 3 this equivalence is confirmed, where the definition itself uses *animi pathema* and the explanation 'passion of the mind'.

Although the phrase is rare in scholastic Latin it is sometimes used as a transcription of the Greek, for example in Latin commentaries on Aristotle's *De anima* I, 403a 10. In medical literature the phrase has an overtone of illness. William Harvey in *De motu cordis* XV for example wrote: '*omne animi pathema* is accompanied with emaciation and decay, or with disordered fluids and crudity, which engender all manner of diseases and consume the body of man'. Spinoza's direct source, however, is Descartes, who in *Principia philosophiae* IV art. 190 observed: 'The other internal sense, which embraces all the emotions (*commotiones*) of the mind or passions (*pathemata*) and affections, such as joy, sadness, love, hate, and the like, depends upon the nerves which extend to the heart and the parts about the heart, and are exceedingly small.' Some lines further on he straightforwardly identifies the *animi pathema* with the *affectus*.

TEXTS

Nec ullibi docet, Deum carere passionibus sive animi pathematis (TTP 7, G III, 101). *Affectus qui animi pathemata dicitur, est confusa idea ... Dico primo affectum, seu passionem animi esse confusam ideam* (E3aff gen.def.)

BIBLIOGRAPHY
Primary Sources
Descartes, R., *Principia philosophiae*.
Harvey, W., *De motus cordis*.

Secondary Literature
Marion, J.L., *Cartesian Questions.*
    Method and Metaphysics (Chicago: Chicago University Press, 1999; French original 1991).

M. van Reijen

Paulus

After Christ, Paul is the most cited New Testament figure in the *Tractatus theologico-politicus*. He is considered to be the most philosophical of the apostles. Unlike the prophets who speak with authority by means of direct revelation and whose message is confirmed by mircales, the apostles speak as doctors and teachers by using arguments. Hence Paul did not use a supernatural light, but only reason (TTP 11). To an extent unrivalled by his predecessors Spinoza parallels Paul with Christ. With regard to the election of the Jews, which with Christ becomes universal, Spinoza for example contends that 'Paul teaches exactly what I say' (TTP 3). The same is true for the thesis that 'all things are in God and move in God' (Ep 73). Even more philosophical is the reference in chapter 2 to Romans 3.5, 6.19 and 9.10ff. According to Spinoza Paul maintained the incomparability of human and divine justice and was aware of his speaking about God in a human fashion. Contrary to Genesis 4.7, which reads that a man by himself 'can overcome his temptations to do wrong', Paul observed that men are able to dominate their passions only through a special election and grace of God. This obvious contradiction in the Scriptures proves that God accommodated his revelations to the understanding of the prophets and the apostles. What is highly appreciated by Spinoza is Paul's opposition between the spirituality of the New Testament and the materiality of the Old. An example is the quotation of 1 Corinthians 15 to support the spiritual interpretation of Christ's resurrection (Ep 75). Also, in TTP 4 it is stated that carnal man (Romans 7.14) cannot understand the idea that religion's highest commandment is to love God as the highest good. Moreover, for Paul, God only acts through natural necessity and Christ adapts his language to the mentality of the populace.

The same notion of adaptation is advanced by Coccejus in his *Commentarius in epistolam ad Philippenses*, in *Opera* V, § 76, p. 52, commenting on Philippians 3.15. A similar parallel between Christ and Paul is found in Episcopius's *Institutiones theologicae* 2.5, who contends that Paul may have had the same revelation as Christ, whereas prophets and apostles usually had a merely indirect prophetic revelation. In TTP 4 Paul is quoted as defending a real understanding of revelation, and for this reason he is put together with Solomon and Christ in also maintaining that ignorance is no excuse. Finally, in TTP 16 the distinction between nature and society of Romans 7.7 is referred to: in nature there is no law and no sin.

TEXTS

Ep 73; Ep 75. *Paulus ... gloriatur quod Christum non secundum carnem, sed secundum spiritum noverit* (Ep 78). *Paulus ... nihil apertius docet, quam quod homines nullum imperium, nisi ex Dei singulari vocatione et gratia in carnis tentationes habent ... humano more sic loquatur et propter carnis imbecillitatem* (TTP 2, G III, 42); TTP 3, G III, 54. *Propter imbecillitatem hominum carnalium sua verba accommodat* (TTP 4, G III, 65). *Paulus duo modi praedicandi indicat, ex revelatione unum, ex cognitione alterum ... eum loqui de libertate monendi, quae ipsi tanquam doctori, et non tamquam prophetae erat ... nemo apostolorum magis philosophatus est, quam Paulus* (TTP 11, G III, 151, 156 and 158). *Per excellentiam Paulum apostolum appellamus* (TTP 13, G III, 169).

BIBLIOGRAPHY
Primary Sources
Coccejus, J., *Commentarius in epistolam ad Philippenses*, in *Opera* V (Amsterdam, 1675).

Episcopius, S., *Institutiones theologicae*, in *Opera theologica* I (Amsterdam, 1650).

Secondary Literature
Verbeek, Th., *Spinoza's Theologico-Political Treatise. Exploring 'the Will of God'* (Aldershot: Ashgate, 2003).

R. Bordoli

Percipio

As in art. 19 of Descartes's *Passions de l'âme*, in Spinoza's work *percipere* and its derivatives (*perceptio*) usually figure as the most general terms for whatever goes on in the mind. In the *Korte verhandeling* they usually correspond to *gewaarworden* en *gewaarwording*, that is, sensation or cognition. To 'perceive' something is to register something in one's mind. Chauvin summed up this Cartesian tradition in calling perception 'the first operation of the human mind, or cogitation'. This operation is threefold: pure intellectual perception, sense perception and imagination. Spinoza speaks also of different *modi percipiendi* used to 'affirm something beyond doubt' – that is, the cognitive material used to arrive at a certain judgement. He also claims that in intellectual intuition 'a thing is perceived through its essence alone' (TIE 19). The intellect 'perceives' something not only as it is in time but 'under an aspect of eternity', whereas the imagination 'perceives' the same thing precisely in so far as it is in time and can be numbered. In the *Ethics* an attribute is 'what the intellect perceives of a substance as constituting its essence' (E1def4). In so far as these quotations refer to the intellect, there is a possible contradiction with the definition of 'idea' (E2def 3), where Spinoza rejects the term 'perception' as an apt description of idea. It suggests that, in so far as we simply 'perceive' an attribute (extension, thought), we have no idea of it; we would have an idea of it only if we understand in what way this attribute is a necessary part of a substance.

TEXTS

Omnes modos percipiendi (TIE 18, G II 9). *Est perceptio, quam ex auditu ... Perceptio est ubi res percipitur per solam essentiam* (TIE 19, G II 10). *Quae perceptiones non inserviunt ad intelligendam, sed tantum ad determinandam quantitatem* (TIE 108, G II, 39). *Per attributum intelligo id, quod intellectus de substantia percipit* (E1def4). *Ut demonstratio facilius perciperetur* (E1p11s). *Dico potius conceptum, quam perceptionem, quia perceptionis nomen indicare videtur, mentem ab objecto pati* (E2def3). *Nullas res singulares praeter corpora, et cogitandi modos, sentimus, nec percipimus* (E2ax5). *Eadem facultate possumus sentire, sive percipere* (E2p49s).

BIBLIOGRAPHY

Primary Sources
Descartes, R., *Passions de l'âme*.

Th. Verbeek

Perfectio

The terms 'perfection' and 'imperfection', as well as the related adjectives and adverbs, occur numerous times in Spinoza's Latin works. Their Dutch counterparts *volmaaktheid* and *onvolmaaktheid*, with varying orthography, are used frequently in the *Korte verhandeling*. The philosophical concept of perfection has, of course, a long history. In general, philosophers make a distinction between perfection in a moral and an ontological sense (*perfectio metaphysica* or *transcendentalis*), although both are often considered to have ontological significance (Chauvin).

Spinoza uses 'perfection' in two meanings (see in particular the preface to *Ethics* 4). First, it is used as an equivalent of REALITAS or ESSE. In E2def6 Spinoza identifies both as referring to the same thing. He holds, moreover, that perfection in this sense comes in degrees. God possesses an absolutely infinite perfection or reality, whereas all things that are caused by him have a lesser degree of perfection. Accordingly, the degree of reality of a thing produced depends on 'the number of intermediary causes' (E1app), that is to say the closer a thing is to the first cause, viz. God, the more perfect it is. Spinoza is quite unspecific about how the amount of perfection of a thing should be measured. What is clear, however, is that he puts this notion of reality to various uses throughout his system. His third proof for the existence of God in E1p11s is based on it. Apart from this, the amount of perfection also accounts for the power of true ideas over false ones (E2p43s), as well as for the origin of the primary emotions pleasure and pain (E3p11s). Most significantly, every thing has precisely the amount of perfection that is proper to it, so that *imperfectio* does not mean that a thing lacks something it should have had. Nonetheless, human beings consider things in such a way.

In the second meaning of perfection it is practically equivalent to good. *Perfectio* in this sense does not concern reality, but is merely the result of a comparison by the human mind of a thing with an exemplary model constructed by the mind itself. The more a thing resembles the model, the more perfect it is judged to be. Finally, it is worthwhile to note that it is not always clear in what sense *perfectio* is used.

It is beyond doubt that Spinoza's idiosyncratic use of *perfectio* as an equivalent of reality or being stems from Descartes. In the third meditation, Descartes specifically uses the notion of the objective perfection or reality of an idea, which comes in degrees, as the basis of an a posteriori proof for the existence of God. Apart from that, this notion of perfection also figures in his theory of error in the fourth meditation. In Descartes's view, a lack of perfection of the human intellect is in part responsible for the possibility of error. That Spinoza adopted this notion of perfection from Descartes becomes patently clear in the PPC. Expressions he later uses in the *Ethics* can already be found in this work, which is based on texts of Descartes. But the extent to which Spinoza's notion of perfection actually agrees with that of Descartes is a matter of debate (Ramond).

TEXTS

Daarom alles wat ons tot die volmaaktheid voorderd, dat zullen wy goet noemen (KV 2.4). Als een Timmerman in het maaken van eenig stuk werk zigh van synen Byl op het beste gediend vind, zoo is dien Byl daar door gekomen tot syn eind en volmaaktheid (KV 2.18). *Modus medendi intellectus, ut res feliciter absque omni errore intelligit* (TIE 16, G III, 9). *Per realitatem objectivam ... perfectio objectiva* (PPC 1def3). *Quantum realitatis, sive perfectionis idea* (PPC 1ax4). *Quo res sua natura perfectior est, eo majorem*

existentiam involvit (PPC 1lem1). *Quicquid est in se consideratum sine respectu ad aliud quid perfectionem includere ... tantum perfectionem includit, quantum realitas exprimit ... res plus perfectionis habet eo magis de Deo participat* (Ep 19). *Perfectionem in* toi *esse et imperfectionem in privatione* tou *esse consistere* (Ep 36). *Quicquid substantia perfectionis habet, nulli causae externae debet* (E1p11s). *Ille effectus perfectissimus est, qui a Deo immediate producitur ... rerum perfectio ex sola earum natura et potentia est aestimanda* (E1app). *Per realitatem et perfectionem idem intelligo* (E2def6). *Laetitiam passionem qua mens ad majorem transit perfectionem* (E3p11s). *Per perfectionem ipsam rei essentiam intelligimus* (E3aff3exp). *Perfectio et imperfectio modi solummodo cogitandi sunt ... individua plus entitatis seu realitatis perfectiora esse dicimus* (E4praef). *Ratio id omne quod ad majorem perfectionem ducit, appetat* (E4p18s). *Is ad summum humanam perfectionem transit* (E5p27). *Unusquisque perfectior et beatior* (E5p31s). *Res plus perfectionis habet, eo magis agit* (E5p40).

BIBLIOGRAPHY

Primary Sources

Descartes, R., *Meditationes* III-IV; *Responsiones secundae*; *Principia* I art. 17–20.

Secondary Literature

Ramond, C., '*Degrés de réalité* et *degrés de perfection* dans les *Principes de la philosophie de Descartes* de Spinoza', *Studia Spinozana*, no. 4 (1988), pp. 121–46.

M. Aalderink

Philosophia

Philosophy and its cognates 'philosopher', 'philosophize' and 'philosophical' are used by Spinoza rather infrequently. 'Philosophy' is even completely absent from the *Ethics* and one of the two occurrences of 'philosopher' in that work is even due to a retranslation by Spinoza from Glazemaker's Dutch version of Seneca's *Letters* in his library (Akkerman, 1980, p. 15). Moreover, Spinoza never used the combinations 'first philosophy', 'natural philosophy' or 'rational philosophy' and only once 'moral philosophy' (TIE 14). Sometimes 'philosopher' even possesses an overtly depreciatory connotation. In the *Cogita metaphysica* Spinoza often identified philosophers with verbose and inane scholastics. In CM 1.1, for example, he wrote: 'I do not wonder that philosophers sometimes fall into these verbal or grammatical errors. For they judge objects from the names and not names from the objects', and he dissociated himself from their verbal practices and distinctions, for example in 2.9: 'while we desire to retain this distinction which philosophers in general lay down, viz., the power of God, we are compelled to explain it differently'. Moreover, Spinoza adopted the same detached tone in the *Tractatus politicus* 1.1, opposing the premise of the 'philosophers' in practical philosophy, that the passions as such are vices. Hence in political philosophy, he continues, the tracts of statesmen are to be preferred to the writings of the philosophers.

This neglect does not imply that philosophy is an insignificant notion for Spinoza. Apparently he took philosophy first and foremost as an academic discipline, with its own principles (Ep 13: 'the mechanical principles of philosophy', cf. PPC 1p4s) and its own method and order (Ep 6 and E2p10cs).

Its aim is knowledge equally certain as mathematics (TTP 14: 'the philosophical, that is mathematical certainty of God's existence'). As an academic discipline philosophy is basically different from theology in spite of their common subject-matter (God) since, contrary to the Bible and theology, which teaches elementary truths, its body of knowledge is only accessible to professionals. However, philosophy's fundamentals are the common notions, readily accessible to all who use the natural intellect.

'Philosophy' possesses a subjective connotation as well and may refer to the whole of someone's philosophical notions, for example those of Descartes or Bacon (Ep 2), or, like Descartes (in *Letters* 290, 293, 297 for example), to one's own philosophical writings, using phrases as 'my', or 'our philosophy'. However, this does not imply modern subjectivism. According to Spinoza philosophy is either true or not philosophy at all.

Like all seventeenth-century writers Spinoza assumed that philosophy is a more or less perfect knowledge focusing on the causes of things. Hobbes for example defined philosophy as 'the knowledge of the effects or phenomena by virtue of the insight into their causes or into their generation' (*Computatio* 1). Seventeenth-century authors liked to extol the pursuit of such philosophical knowledge by quoting Virgil's famous saying 'Happy is he who is able to know the causes of things', a sentiment ultimately stemming from Aristotle's definition of science in *Analytica Posteriora* 1.2 (cf. Burgersdijk's preface of the *Idea philosophiae moralis* and TIE 70) Such perfect knowledge may be called both philosophy and 'science'. Moreover philosophy is all-embracing, its object being 'all the things divine and human'. Such a knowledge, Chauvin says, enables man to live in the best possible way

(Hobbes, who in the *Computatio* did not mention the moral aim of philosophy, is a notable exception to this line of thought.) The traditional link between theory and practice hinted at by Chauvin is obviously of a basic concern to Spinoza since he called his philosophy 'ethics'. In the TIE 14–16 he stated as its ultimate aim the acquirement of a real and highest good. In order to obtain that final good we need the following theoretical sciences: physics, medicine and mechanics, the same disciplines Descartes listed in the preface of the French translation of the *Principia*.

In order to reinforce this link Spinoza apparently radicalized the Cartesian conception of philosophy developed in this text by underlining the universal applicability of the geometrical method. By comparing philosophy to a tree – the roots of which represent metaphysics, the trunk physics, while the three principal branches emerging from the trunk are medicine, mechanics and morals – Descartes clearly hinted at the rejection of the Aristotelian division between theoretical and practical philosophy. Neglecting all attempts of some Dutch Cartesians to reintroduce this distinction, Spinoza underscored philosophy's full competence to solve all practical concerns of man, including those traditionally associated with religion. This radicalism made theology as a science superfluous (Verbeek, 2003, pp. 151–4).

Scripturam nihil cum philosophia commune habere (TTP praef, G III, 10). *Separandam philosophia a theologia* (TTP 2, G III, 44). *Arcana philosophiae* (TTP 13, G III, 167). *Theologiam et philosophiam nullum commercium* (TTP 14, G III, 179). *Qui philosophia a theologia separare nesciunt* (TTP 15, G III, 180). *Cartesii et Baconis philosophia* (Ep 2). *Ordinariam philosophiae professionem* (Ep 48). *Non praesumo me optimam invenisse philosophiam; sed veram me intelligere scio* (Ep 76).

BIBLIOGRAPHY

Primary Sources
Descartes, R., *Epistolae*, *Principia philosophiae*.
Hobbes, Th., *Computatio sive logica*, in *Elementorum philosophiae sectio prima De Corpore* (London, 1655).

Secondary Literature
Akkerman, F., *Studies in the Posthumous Works of Spinoza. On Style, Earliest Translation and Reception, Earliest and Modern Edition of Some Texts* (Meppel: Krips Repro, 1980).
Verbeek, Th., *Spinoza's Theologico-Political Treatise. Exploring 'the Will of God'* (Aldershot: Ashgate, 2003).

H. Krop

TEXTS

In mea philosophia explicabimus (TIE k). *Videbimus in philosophia* (TIE 81, G II, 31). *Studium philosophiae* (PPC praef). *'Cogito' fundamentum totius philosophiae* (PPC 1p4s). *Ne philosophia cum theologia confundatur* (PPC 2p13s). *Argumenta quae ex philosophia peti possunt* (CM 2.11).

Pietas

Like the word RELIGIO *pietas* has primarily a moral meaning in Spinoza's works (both words occur seven times in connection with each other): a strictly philosophical one in the *Ethics* and a more traditional religious sense in the *Tractatus theologico-politicus*.

1. Piety occurs eleven times in the *Ethics*. E4p37 contains the following definition: 'The desire to do good which derives from our living by the guidance of reason, I call piety'. *Pietas* in this sense is an active affect or virtue, directed at the reasonable benefit of other persons. Hence piety is related to the cardinal₁ Spinozistic virtue of GENEROSITAS defined in E3p59s. Both concepts refer to an altruistic practice, based on reason and aimed at the benefit of the other person. Piety is also related to religion. They both denote a living under the guidance of reason, but only religion implies knowledge of God. So religion is also piety, but the reverse is not necessarily the case.

The virtue of *pietas* is based on reason and therefore opposed to all affects of sadness (E4app22, 24). Through piety human concord is furthered. See for example E4app15: 'But for winning the love of men the most important factors are those that are concerned with religion and piety'. Both piety and religion are dealt with in the central fourth part of the *Ethics* and are key concepts in Spinoza's philosophical ethics.

2. In the *Tractatus* piety has a more traditional 'religious' meaning than in the *Ethics*. Here Spinoza seems to include conventional religious practices in the notion of piety and in this respect he is in line with contemporary scholastic discourse. Most seventeenth-century scholastic authors underscored the basically moral nature of piety and acknowledged existing religious and social practices as such. Micraelius for example defined piety as: 'the virtue of fulfilling one's obligations towards God, one's homeland and parents'. Burgersdijk in his *Idea philosophiae moralis* chapter 13 observed that 'piety is the first of all virtues requiring the conscientious adoration of God'. The just worship of God we cannot learn from Aristotle, but we have to consult the writings of Pythagoras and Plato.

Spinoza, however, seemed to sever the links between philosophy and conventional religion. The word 'piety' is included in the subtitle of the *Tractatus* and plays a central role in the argumentation in the treatise. The meaning in the treatise, however, is not philosophical but only denotes a line of conduct. Piety is related to faith and obedience, not to truth. See for example chapter 14: 'Finally it follows that faith requires not so much true as pious dogmas, that is, such as move the heart to obedience; and this is so even if many of those beliefs contain not a shadow of truth, provided that he who adheres to them knows not that they are false.' Piety in this religious sense merely belongs to the pseudo-science of theology, not to philosophy (TTP 15).

Although piety on the basis of faith and obedience differs essentially on a cognitive level from piety on the basis of reason, as a moral practice both forms of piety are almost identical. And both forms of piety produce the same political effects: social peace and stability within the commonwealth (TTP 20). Piety in the *Tractatus* is often defined as the practice of justice and charity. It is primarily a matter of works, not of beliefs: 'Thus we should reject the view that anything of piety or impiety attaches to beliefs taken simply in themselves without respect to works. A man's beliefs should be regarded as pious or impious only insofar as he is thereby induced to obey the moral law, or else assumes from them the licence to sin or rebel' (TTP 13). Hence, it is argued that piety must conform to the public good and the decrees of the sovereign (TTP 19).

TEXTS

*Adeoque minime credendum opiniones abso-
lute consideratas, absque respectu ad opera,
aliquid pietatis, aut impietatis habere, sed ea
tantum de causa hominem aliquid pie, aut
impie credere dicendum, quatenus ex suis
opinionibus ad obedientiam movetur, vel ex
iisdem licentiam ad peccandum, aut rebellan-
dum sumit* (TTP 13, G III, 172). *Sequitur
denique fidem non tam requirere vera, quam
pia dogmata, hoc est, talia, quae animum ad
obedientiam movent: Tametsi inter ea plurima
sint, quae nec umbram veritatis habent, dum-
modo tamen is, qui eadem amplectitur, eadem
falsa ignoret* (TTP 14, G III, 176). *Omne pietatis excercitium reipublicae paci et
conservationi debere accomodari* (TTP 19,
G III, 232). *Pietas autem summa est, quae
circa pacem et tranquillitatem reipublicae
excercetur* (TTP 20, G III, 242); E2p49s1.
*Cupiditatem autem bene faciendi, quae ex eo
ingeneratur, quod ex rationis ductu vivimus,
Pietatem voco* (E4p37s1); E4p18s. *Amori
autem conciliando illa apprime necessaria
sunt, quae ad Religionem, & Pietatem spectant* (E4app15); E4app24; E5p41. *Theologi ...
credunt summas potestates debere negotia
publica tractare secundum easdam pietatis
regulas, quibus vir privatus tenetur* (TP 1.2).
Ratio pietatem exercere ... docet (TP 2.21).

BIBLIOGRAPHY

Secondary Literature

Laux, H., *Imagination et religion chez
   Spinoza* (Paris: Vrin, 1993).
Roothaan, A., *Vroomheid, vrede, vrijheid,
   Een interpretatie van Spinoza's Tractatus
   Theologico-Politicus* (Assen: Van
   Gorcum, 1996).
Rice, L., 'Piety and Philosophical Freedom
   in Spinoza', in C. de Deugd (ed.),
*Spinoza's Political and Theological
   Thought* (Amsterdam: North-Holland
   Publishing Co., 1984), pp. 184–204.

P.C. Juffermans

Possibile

There are two key occurrences of *possibile* in
the *Ethics*. In proposition 33 of part 1 Spinoza
says that we call something 'contingent or
possible' when we are ignorant of either its
essence or causes. If we knew its essence and
causes well enough, we would be able to say
with certainty that it is either 'necessary or
impossible'. While Spinoza does not distinguish contingency from possibility in that
passage, he does separate them later in the
Ethics. In definition 3 of part 4 he says that
'singular things' are 'contingent' if and only if
their existence or non-existence is not entailed
by their essence alone. By contrast, according
to definition 4 'the same singular things' are
'possible' just in case we do not know whether
their 'causes are determined to produce them'.
For those wondering why these concepts were
not previously kept apart, Spinoza explains
in a note that 'there was no need to distinguish them accurately'. With these definitions
Spinoza sets himself against the (Aristotelian)
tradition, which opposed the possible both
against the actual being and the impossible,
defining the possible as a being that does not
actually exist but might be, for example a
new star, or another world. Such a being is
called the physically possible. The logically
possible does not contain contradictory predi-
cates (Chauvin). Hobbes, however, in chapter
10 of *De corpore* denies the reality of the
contingent and the possible. The possible is
only apparent, due to our lack of knowledge.

That it will rain tomorrow is necessary, being the effect of necessarily working causes. If we do not know these causes, we will call an event 'contingent' or 'fortuitous'.

There are two distinct exegetical challenges facing readers who wish to make sense of Spinoza's views on the possible. The first involves disentangling his epistemic conception of possibility from his metaphysical one. According to the former, things are regarded as possible just because of the limitations of our knowledge. There are disputes about the proper interpretation of the latter. One reading contends that things are possible just in case they are compatible with the laws of nature; if they are not compatible with those laws, then they are impossible.

The second exegetical challenge can be expressed in the form of a question: did Spinoza think that all possible things are actual? If so, there are no non-actualized possibilities, so that nothing which does not exist could exist. On the other hand, if Spinoza denied that all possible things are also actual, he may have held that there are some things that could exist but do not. In recent decades, scholars have tended to think that Spinoza did take all possibles to be actual, though the issues and texts are difficult enough for the question to be regarded as open.

TEXTS
Possibilem, cujus existentia, ipsa sua natura, non implicat contradictionem, ut existat ... sed cujus existentiae necessitas pendet a causis nobis ignotis (TIE 53, G II, 20). *Contingens, possibile non nisi defectus nostrae perceptionis, nec aliquid reale esse* (CM 1.3). *Res aliqua contingens dicitur, nisi respectu defectus nostrae cognitionis. ... eandem vel contingens, vel possibilem vocamus* (E1p33s1). *Easdem res singulares voco possibiles, quatenus, dum ad causas, ex quibus produci debent, attendimus, nescimus, an ipsae determinatae sint ad easdem producendum ... inter possibile et contingens nullam feci differentiam, quia ibi non erat opus haec accurate distinguere* (E4def4).

BIBLIOGRAPHY
Primary Sources
Hobbes, Th., *De corpore.*

Secondary Literature
Mason, R., 'Spinoza on Modality', *The Philosophical Quarterly,* no. 144 (1986), pp. 313–42.
Miller, J., 'Spinoza's Possibilities', *Review of Metaphysics,* no. 54 (2001), pp. 779–814.

J. Miller

Potentia

Over the years, the concept of *potentia* became increasingly important in Spinoza's writings, though it was never expressly defined. In the *Korte verhandeling* he uses the Dutch counterparts *magt, kragt* and *mogentheid*. He attributes *magt* only to God, but he calls all the modes weak since they have no power to subsist by themselves and must unite with a loved object in order to stay alive and to survive. In the *Ethics*, where the concept of CONATUS plays a major part, this is no longer the case, and one can say that Spinoza's philosophy is an ontology of power.

In Spinoza's later works *potentia* is the active power of the school philosophy and is attributed to all kinds of (human) faculties, such as intellect, mind, reason, body etc. 'Power' lost its passive meaning of potency, which in Aristotelian philosophy was opposed to act. The power of a thing is nothing but its active essence by which it produces the effects included in its nature. In *Leviathan* chapters 10 and 14, Hobbes shared this notion and defined the power of man as 'his means to obtain some future good', that is the power 'to preserve his own nature'. Hence Hobbes identified power with the right of nature. The identity of power and activity applies to God in particular. God as a substance produces everything he can do and which can be conceived by an infinite intellect. There is no difference between his power and his act. Power must not be understood as a potentiality or a possibility but only as a form of activity. God's power is identified with his essence (E1p34) and it expresses his infinite nature, from which there follows by necessity an infinity of things in an infinity of manners. The identity of essence and power also applies to the substance and its modes (E3p7dem). Frequently, Spinoza opposes *potentia* to POTESTAS (E1p33s2; E2p3s, E2p49s, E5praef) when he wants to distinguish the necessary ability to do something from the arbitrary and free will or the absolute power of the soul, which Descartes assumed. However, this opposition is not absolute because the two words are sometimes synonymous (E4def8, E5p42d).

The power of modes is a part of God's infinite power which expresses his essence in a prescribed manner. Therefore everything tries to remain in existence and to assert all the consequences included in its essence proportionately to its power. The power of finite modes takes the form of a strength or an effort (*conatus*) because it has to resist external causes which sometimes run contrary to it and can even destroy it when their power is stronger. External causes may increase or help man's power above all when they have a common nature with him. This is the reason why men are more powerful when they join together and make up a single individual such as the civil state. Real power is to live under the guidance of reason and is identified with virtue (E4def8), and freedom. Human freedom lies in the power of the intellect. It does not mean however that real power is only a mental one. The mind can only do what the body can and its power of thinking is linked with the power of acting.

Unlike the human individual, the power of a state is stronger when it lives under the guidance of reason (TP 5.1). It is more righteous too because the power of a thing defines its natural right. God, indeed, has the right to do everything he can do, and his right is nothing but his power. Since the power of acting of a thing in nature is part of God's power, everything has the right to do what it can do (TTP 16, TP 2.3–4). Thus sovereignty is the law defined by the power of the multitude (TP 2.17) and the right of the state depends on its power. The more reasonable the state is, the more powerful it is.

TEXTS

Kragt om zig te behouden (KV 2.16). Zoo blijkt … welke daar zijn de dingen die in onse magt en geen uytterlyke oorzaaken onderworpen zijn (KV 2.26). *Metus diminutam potentiam supponi* (PPC 1p13). *Potentia ad affirmandum et ad negandum* (CM 1.1). *Cujuscunque rei potentia sola ejus essentia definitur* (Ep 64). *Postquam unusquisque jus suum ex proprio beneplacito vivendi … hoc est suum libertatem et potentiam se defendendi in alium transtulit* (TTP 16, G III, 196). *Nemo unquam suam potentiam neque suum jus ita in alio transferre potuerit ut homo esse desinat* (TTP 17, G III, 201). *Summarum potestatum potentia* (TTP 20, G III, 240). *Posse existere potentia est … rerum perfectio ex sola earum natura et potentia existimanda* (E1p11). *Potentiam Dei* (E1p17s). *Potentia Dei est ipsa ipsius essentia* (E1p34). *Mentem ... absolutam potentiam in actiones ... Virtus et agendi potentia* (E3praef). *Potentia, sive conatus, quo [cujuscunque rei] in suo esse perseverare conatur, nihil est praeter ipsius rei datam, sive actualem essentiam* (E3p7). *Per virtutem et potentiam idem intelligo ... ipsa hominis essentia, quatenus potestatem habet, quaedam efficiendi* (E4def8). *Potentia qua res singulares et consequenter homo suum esse conservat est ipsa Dei sive Naturae potentia* (E4p4). *Hominis potentia, qua existit, et operatur, non determinatur nisi ab alia re singulari* (E4p29). *Uniuscuique jus virtute seu potentia uniuscujusque definitur* (E4p37s1). *Suum essentiam intelligere hoc est suam potentiam* (E4p53). *Dei potentia* (E4p68s). *Actiones nostram potentiam semper indicant* (E4app2). *Humana potentia admodum limitata est* (E4app32). *Potentia rationis* (E5praef). *Mens potestatem habet libidines coërcendi, et quia humana potentia ad coërcendos affectos* (E5p42). *Potentia rerum naturalium* (TP 2.2–5). *Humana potentia magis ex animi fortitudine aestimanda est* (TP 2.11). *Jus hominum naturale et uniuscujusque potentia* (TP 2.15). *Totius imperii corpus et mens tantum iuris habet, quantum potentia valet* (TP 3.2).

BIBLIOGRAPHY
Primary Sources
Hobbes, Th., *Leviathan.*

Secondary Literature
Matheron, A., *Individu et communauté chez Spinoza* (Paris: Éditions de Minuit, 1969), part III–IV.

Ch. Jaquet

Potestas

In Spinoza's works there is a considerable overlap between the meaning of *potestas* and that of related terms such as POTENTIA, *vis*, VIRTUS, *facultas*. Hence, these words may sometimes replace each other, e.g. *potestas affirmandi & negandi* and *potentia ad affirmandum, et ad negandum* (CM 2.12), or both *potestas* and IMPERIUM denote the power of the will and the intellect, for example to suspend its judgement (E2p49s) or to control the passions (E5praef). Such – at least partial – identification of these words was common in seventeenth-century scholastic discourse. Micraelius for example observed: 'often *potentia* is taken as an equivalent of *potestas*. Hence being *in potestate* is the same as being *in potentia*'. Goclenius stated: 'taken as such *potestas* is received as *potentia*. It translates the Greek *dunamis*. ... Potestas is also used in a relative manner. Then it translates the Greek *eksousia*. Such a potestas is active and not passive.' What is more, traditionally (supreme) power is identified with (supreme) authority [*imperium*]. Hobbes for example wrote in *De cive* chapter 5, § 11 that in every state the citizens have 'subjected their will to the supreme power, or [sive] chiefe command (*imperium*), or dominion. Such a *summa potestas* has the right of commanding'.

Potestas is regularly used in all Spinoza's writings with the exception of the *Cogitata metaphysica*, in which *potestas* occurs only once, and the *Tractatus de intellectus emendatione*, which uses the word merely twice. We can distinguish four different meanings.

Firstly, we encounter *potestas* as the capability of our body or mind to do or think something: for example, 'the authority [the capability] to claim the things for themselves' (TP 2.23), to will, deny etc. (CM

2.12). Spinoza also uses this expression with regard to a community: the capability of self-preservation (E4p37s2). This use of the word implies that some things are within our power, other things are not. In the *Korte verhandeling* the difference between 'in' and 'buyten onse macht zyn' (KV 2.5) plays an important role. In letters 57 and 58 to Tschirnhaus and Schuller, dating from 1674, Spinoza insists on this distinction. Something can be within (or outside) my *potestas* actually or essentially. What is within our power essentially depends on what our nature allows (E2p49s).

Secondly, *in potestate esse* has two connotations. Either it signifies force, for example if something is said to be within the power of God (E1p17s and p35) or of the mind (E3p2s). *Sub potestate habere* may also be used in this sense. Or this phrase might signify that man is dependent on circumstances or fortune and it then indicates the limits of his powers for example to use reason or to will independently of the affects (E4praef, TP 2.8). Thus: 'being in the power of something' indicates a certain weakness and impotence.

Thirdly, *potestas* might indicate the power to effect, to exist or to act. According to Spinoza the power (*potentia*) of man – and his virtue – is defined by his *potestas* to effect whatever is in accordance with his nature and therefore to be comprehended by the laws of his own nature alone (E4def8, TP 2.7). Hence, the human condition excludes the acquirement of an absolute power. Spinoza rejects the idea of an absolute power in particular in connection with the idea of free will. A full control over our passions is impossible (E5praef): this control does not depend on our power (here Spinoza uses *imperium* or *potentia*) alone. The circumstances often have more force than we

have to control them (E4app32, cf. TP 2.6). Only God has an absolute power, since everything depends on his power (E1p33s2). Given that a human being can oscillate between strength and weakness, power is the basic element of social hierarchies. This becomes most clear in the distinction between being in the power of another and being rightfully independent (*sui juris*) (TP 2.9). This traditional political distinction is based on the presupposed (natural) ability of some class of human beings to control others (TP 2.10, 11.3). We can think of the relations between master and servant, man and wife, parent and children, teacher and pupil. Hence *potestas* acquires a predominantly juridical connotation. It might mean a legal title to something (to be obeyed, to start a war, or to have the right to use one's property). Grotius distinguishes between being autonomous and being master of something or someone (*De jure belli ac pacis*, 1.1.5).

Fourthly, in Spinoza's social and political philosophy *potestas* means both competence and actual capability to have other people do what you want. Power in the sense of competence can already be found in Roman law. It is attributed to the magistrates (in contrast to the senate, which had authority) or to the father. As an overall competence, Spinoza uses *potestas* to designate the government, the supreme power in the state. This highest power would have been established by transfer of power from the people to a council or a king. This transfer is the transfer of a competence: the natural right to rule one's own life (TP 3.3, 8.17). The highest power is in itself a kind of right (TP 3.8). These rights are described in chapters 3 and 4 of the *Tractatus politicus*. Spinoza also mentions a dictatorial power, a special competence, limited in time, to re-establish the constitution of a state (TP 10.1). Another example of power is the competence handed over to special regents to control those who actually govern the city or the state (TP 8.20).

A main feature of Spinoza's political philosophy is the underpinning of the traditional juridical concept of authority by an economy of power. Power is not simply the unchanging capability and force of the actor, but is also related to the power of the 'patient' (TP 4.4). This becomes evident from Spinoza's earlier remark (TP 2.11), after explaining the ways in which power over other people can be established, that those with mental power may escape this kind of affective manipulation (by the use of passions like fear and hope). The more people are able to use their reason, the less this form of power applies. Since this form of power is a sign of weakness, the multitude will not transfer their power to a king unless they are incapable of solving specific problems themselves (TP 7.5).

According to Spinoza the legal right to rule over people and the real power a government exercises are not the same (TTP 16). This distinction is the premise of Spinoza's argument that people should be free to think what they want and to say what they think, although this freedom has its limits too (TTP 20). In Letter 50 Spinoza claims that this is the main difference between his political philosophy and that of Hobbes.

French and Italian scholars such as Antonio Negri underline the existence of a central distinction between two different concepts of power in Spinoza's philosophy which presumably corresponded to a clear-cut distinction between *potestas* and *potentia*. 'Potentia is power or right that is coextensive with its actual, material realisation (see TTP 16, for example), whereas *potestas* is the mediated articularisation of *potentia* in the form of political authority and institutions. Such a distinction would correspond with the French *puissance* and *pouvoir*, but have no corresponding distinction in English' (Del Lucchese, 2009, p. 186 note 52). However, it might be doubted if the terminological usage warrants such a conclusion, since Negri's position is based on a small selection of texts. What is more, apparently Spinoza does not attempt to convey to the reader the feeling of a tension or even a clear-cut opposition between both concepts (Terpstra, 1990, pp. 4–5). Yet often *potestas* conveys a connotation different from *potentia*. Such a difference between these words in seventeenth-century discourse was noted by the dictionaries as well. Micraelius for example wrote that *potentia* basically 'refers to the capability and force to act' and *potestas* 'to the right and jurisdiction to do something. Hence I may be fully entitled to defend myself, although I lack the power to do so'. In contrast to *potentia* (the internal and ultimately divine force or power of everything that exists), the term *potestas* in Spinoza always refers to a relation. It signifies the power to cause an action, either a thought or a motion, which is inflicted on other things or persons. So *potestas* refers to dependence or subordination on the one hand, and freedom or disposition on the other. As Spinoza explains in the second part of his *Tractatus theologicus-politicus* (chaps 16–20) and in his *Tractatus politicus*, the term especially occurs as designation of the power of the state or the government. Apparently the use of *potestas* marks Spinoza's turn towards politics (Terpstra, ibid.).

TEXTS

Wy zeggen dat eenige dingen in, andere byten onse macht zyn ... in onse macht zyn zulke die wy uytwerken door orde of te zamen met de Natuur waar van wy een deel zyn (KV 2.5). *Homines nullam habere potestatem ferrum cudendi ... instrumenta seu potestatem* (TIE 30, G II, 13–14). *Res in sua potestate* (PPC ax5). *Aequalem potestatem habere affirmandi et negandi* (CM 2.12). *Quisque summam habet potestatem ... ei summum jus, quicquid velit, imperandi, competere ... potestatem se defendendi* (TTP 16). *Summae potestates jus ad omnia habere* (TTP 20, G III, 240). *Omnia a Dei potestate pendent* (E1p33s2). *Per virtutem, & potentiam idem intelligo, hoc est virtus, quatenus ad hominem refertur, est ipsa hominis essentia, seu natura, quatenus potestatem habet, quaedam efficiendi, quae per solas ipsius naturae leges possunt intelligi* (E4def8). *Humana potentia infinite superatur, adeo potestatem absolutam non habemus* (E4app32). *Hac potestate recte ordinandi corporis affectiones* (E5p10s). *Potestas existendi et operandi* (TP 2.7). *Tamdiu alterius juris, quamdiu sub alterius potestate* (TP 2.9). *Is alterum sub potestate habet, cui metum injecit vel quem sibi beneficioita devinxit ut ei potius ex ipsius quam ex sui animi sententia vivere velit* (TP 2.10). *Si civitas alicui concedat jus et consequenter potestas vivendi ex suo ingenio* (TP 3.3). *Summa potestas legibus adstricta sit ... haec potestas non sola agentis potentia, sed etiam ipsius patientis aptitudine definiri debet* (TP 4.4).

BIBLIOGRAPHY

Secondary Literature

Curley, E., 'Troublesome Terms for Translators in the TTP', in P. Totaro (ed), *Spinoziana* (Florence: Olschki, 1997), pp. 39–62.

Lucchese, F. del, *Conflict. Power and Multitude in Machiavelli and Spinoza* (London: Continuum, 2009).

Lübtow, U. von, 'Potestas', in *Paulys Real-Encyclopädie der classischen Altertumswissenschaften* 43, (Stuttgart: Metzler, 1953).

Negri, A., *The Savage Anomaly: the Power of Spinoza's Metaphysics and Politics,* translated [from the Italian] by Michael Hardt (Minneapolis: University Press, 1991; original ed. 1981).

Terpstra, M., *De wending naar de politiek, een studie over de begrippen 'potentia' en potestas' bij Spinoza* (Nijmegen, 1990).

——, 'An Analysis of Power Relations and Class Relations in Spinoza's *Tractatus Politicus*', *Studia Spinozana* no. 9 (1995), pp. 79–105.

M. Terpstra

Propheta

Spinoza deals with prophecy in the first three chapters of the *Tractatus theologico-politicus*. Prophecy is defined in chapter 1 as 'certain knowledge about something revealed to men by God' and is here identified with revelation. On account of this definition the word 'prophecy' may be applied to natural knowledge, he continues, but its practioners cannot be called prophets. Although according to chapter 3 of the TTP prophecy is not exclusive to the Jews, the biblical prophets interpret the divine REVELATIO (TTP 1). Hence, according to Spinoza the Hebrew word for prophet means 'interpreter'. The truth of prophetic interpretation does not rest on arguments but on signs, by which a prophet both acquires authority and becomes convinced of the validity of his revelation. Unlike Maimonides in his *Guide of the Perplexed* 2.36, but in agreement with Hobbes in *Leviathan* 32 and Crellius in his *Opera exegetica* II, p. 70, Spinoza believes that prophets no longer exist. This belief was generally shared by Protestant theologians (Martinech, 1992, p. 229). Revelation takes place either through words or images. Prophets need to have an extremely vivid imagination rather than a perfect intellect; they in fact perceive and teach many things exceeding the limits of the intellect and our understanding and they do so in a parabolical and enigmatic way, giving a material form to spiritual ideas. The prophets were certain about revelation not through revelation itself but through some sign or other; prophetic certainty is not mathematical but rather moral (TTP 2) and depends on the fact that they were predisposed to do good. Only those who made new prophecies needed *signa*, which depended on the prophet's *opiniones* and *capacitas*; the latter varied from prophet to prophet so that revelation also varied. This explains why the prophets held conflicting opinions. Prophecy does not make a prophet wiser but reinforces his prejudices: it has no theoretical value – the opposite view of that of Maimonides (*Guide* 2.36). Men are obliged to believe the prophets only as far as the end and substance of revelation is concerned. Importance is given to what the prophets have seen and heard, not to what meaning it may have (TTP 7; cf. INTERPRETATIO). In addressing the prophets, God adapted himself to their understanding as he also did with the apostles (see Coccejus, *Summa theologiae*, in *Opera* VI, 1.5).

TEXTS

Firmiter credo Prophetas Dei intimos consiliarios et legatos fuisse fidos (Ep 21). *Propheta autem is est, qui Dei revelata iis interpretatur, qui rerum a Dei revelatarum certam cognitationem habere nequeunt ... Propheta apud Hebraeos vocatur nabi, id est orator et interpres, at in Scriptura semper usurpatur pro Dei interprete ... Prophetas extra intellectus limites percipere potuisse. ... Patet cur Prophetae omnia fere parabolice et aenigmatice perceperint* (TTP 1, G III, 15 and 28). *Sequitur prophetas non fuisse perfectiore mente praeditos, sed quidem potentia vividius imaginandi ... Cum certitudo quae ex signis in Prophetis oriebatur, non mathematica, sed tantum moralis erat ... sequitur signa pro opinionibus et capacitate prophetica datur fuisse ... Tota certitudo prophetica his tribus fundabatur: 1. Quod res revelatas vividissime, ut nos vigilando ab objectis affecti solemus, imaginabantur. 2 Signo. 3. Denique, et praecipuo, quod animum ad solum bonum et aequum inclinatum habebant ... Prophetia igitur in ha re naturali cedit cognitione, quae nulla indiget signo* (TTP 2, G III, 29, 31–2). *Donum propheticum Judaeis non peculiare fuerit* (TTP 3, G III, 50). *In rebus speculativis Prophetis inter se dissentiebant ... mens Prophetarum ex historia Scripturae eruenda ... haec methodus tantum investigare docet id, quod revera Prophetae viderint aut audiverint* (TTP 7, G III, 104–5). *Prophaetae non vocati sunt ut omnibus nationibus praedicaverent* (TTP 11, G III, 154); TTP 12; TTP 15. *Rationis dictamina prophetis veluti jura revelata* (TP 2.22).

BIBLIOGRAPHY
Primary Sources
Coccejus, J., *Summa theologiae*, in *Opera omnia* VI (Amsterdam, 1675).
Crellius, J., *Opera omnia exegetica*, 3 vols ([Amsterdam], 1656 [1665]).
Hobbes, Th., *Leviathan*.
Maimonides, M., *The Guide of the Perplexed*, transl. with an introduction and notes by S. Pines (Chicago and London: University of Chicago Press, 1969).

Secondary Literature
Martinech, A.P., *The Two Gods of Leviathan* (Cambridge: Cambridge University Press, 1992).
Verbeek, Th., *Spinoza's Theologico-Political Treatise. Exploring 'the Will of God'* (Aldershot: Ashgate, 2003).

R. Bordoli

Quatenus

With SIVE, *quatenus* is a prominent feature of the syntax of Spinoza's philosophy. Although of scholastic origin and quite often used by Descartes in the *Meditationes* from the third meditation onwards, *quatenus* abounds in all parts of the *Ethics* and the *Tractatus politicus*. In comparison with his mature works the word is rare in the *Correspondence*, *Tractatus theologico-politicus* and the early writings, for example in the *Tractatus de intellectus emendatione* it occurs twice and in two chapters of the *Cogitata metaphysica* (2.1. and 2.3).

The scholastic doctrine of *quatenus* originated in logic. It replaced the medieval *inquantum* of Thomas Aquinas and Duns Scotus and was developed in respect of the formal object of metaphysics: *ens quatenus ens*. *Quatenus* on the one hand specified the ways in which a term is to be understood in order to make a proposition true. 'Fire', for example, 'heats', but only 'if it is near' or 'an Ethiopian is white with respect to his teeth'. On the other hand it could also be used 'reduplicatively', that is indicating the reason why the predicate adheres to the subject. 'Man', for example, 'as far as he is man is capable of learning', but 'as far as he has senses he is an animal'.

According to Chauvin and Goclenius four different connotations are to be distinguished.

We may use *quatenus* in a formal, abstract (mode of consideration), causal or conditional sense. Used in the first sense *quatenus* denotes that in a proposition the predicate is essentially included in the subject. For example 'quantity as substance is indivisible, unique and infinite' (E1p15s). In an abstract sense *quatenus* denotes the quality by which we conceive a thing. 'Man as man is a species', i.e. not as an individual man, for example Peter or Paul. According to Spinoza 'water, in so far as it is water, we conceive to be divided, and its parts to be separated one from the other; – in so far as it is water, but not in so far as it is corporeal substance'. In the third sense *quatenus* denotes the cause or reason why a predicate may be attributed to a subject. According to Spinoza we may call man free in so far as he possesses the power to exist and act according to the laws of human nature (TP 2.7). In the final sense *quatenus* specifies the necessary condition of an effect. 'The fire as far as it is near causes the burning of the wood'. In this case being near as such does not cause the combustion, but is only a necessary precondition. Apparently Spinoza used *quatenus* in all four connotations. It occurs particularly often however in combination with words such as 'consider', 'with respect to', 'conceive' etc.

TEXTS
Neque mali in se habere, nisi quatenus ab iis animus movebatur (TIE 1, G II, 5). *Non autem de sua essentia, quatenus cogitabat* (PPC praef). *Ideas quatenus sunt in phantasia corporea* (PPC 1def2). *Ideis quatenus tantum modi cogitandi considerantur* (PPC 1ax9). *Ens quatenus ens* (CM 1.3). *Trianguli essentiam, quatenus est aeterna veritas* (CM 2.1). *Essentiam, quatenus ex sola rei aeternae definitione concipitur* (E1def8). *Substantia corporea*

quatenus substantia (E1p15s). *Dei essentiam quatenus ut res extensa consideratur* (E2def2). *Deum essentiam quatenus ut res cogitans consideratur* (E2p5). *Mens quatenus adaequatas habet ideas* (E3p1). *Natura quatenus corporea tantum consideratur* (E3p2s). *Quatenus ad hoc exemplar magis ut minus accedunt* (E4praef). *Res singulares voco contingentes quatenus, dum ad causas attendimus* (E4def3). *Quatenus ejus essentia per ipsius causae essentiam explicatur vel definitur* (E5ax2). *Affectu quatenus ad solam Mentem refertur* (E5p3). *Ipsa Dei potentia, quatenus haec absolute libera consideratur* (TP 2.3). *Quatenus haec per naturam hujus, aut illius hominis definiri potest* (TP2.5). *Quatenus potestatem habet existendi* (TP2.7). *Quatenus ejus potentiam, seu minas metuunt* (TP 3.8).

BIBLIOGRAPHY
Secondary Literature
Schnepf, R., *Metaphysik im ersten Teil der Ethik Spinozas* (Würzburg: Königshausen and Neumann, 1996).

H. Krop

Realitas

The word 'reality' occurs only infrequently in Spinoza's Latin works: two times in the correspondence – and *weese* in the Dutch original of letter 19 – eight in the PPC, and about ten times in the *Ethics*. In the political works the word is absent, but notably Spinoza does not use a Dutch counterpart in the *Korte verhandeling*. However, notwithstanding its relative rarity the word 'reality' expresses one of the key notions of Spinoza's philosophy that, like many others, can be read as a radicalization of a Cartesian idea.

This is obvious in Spinoza's commentary on the *Principia* of Descartes. In the second set of axioms presented after proposition 3, which are 'taken from Descartes', he assumes, firstly, that there are degrees of reality just as there are degrees of being. For a 'substance contains more reality than an accident'. This premise is derived from the notion of the different 'objective reality' contained or involved in ideas, which plays such an important part in the argument of *Meditation* III. This Cartesian theory Spinoza applies in his *Ethics*. He observes that the positive affects make the mind more perfect by giving it a greater power of thinking. At the same moment the mind necessarily attributes a greater reality to the body. Hence, at the end of the *Ethics* he concludes that the more reality a thing has – with 'thing' Spinoza refers to the mind in particular – the more active it is and the less passive. Secondly in these axioms of PPC I he identifies 'reality' in these axioms with PERFECTIO and being, a premise some unfortunately deny due to SUPERSTITIO or ignorance.

The third aspect of the notion of reality occurs for the first time in letter 9 written in March 1663 by Spinoza to Simon de Vries in order to clarify some puzzles that have arisen from the definitions and propositions of a proto-*Ethics* sent to Spinoza's circle. Here Spinoza for the first time advances the theory that a thing's degree of reality is related to the number of a thing's attributes, further developed in the *Ethics* as we have it. Every attribute of the substance expresses a reality, or a form of the substantial being. Hence, in marked opposition to Descartes, he observed that the more attributes a substance possesses the more reality it has (E1p10s).

The direct source being Cartesianism, the indirect source of Spinoza's identification of attribute and reality is Scotism. Chauvin notes that 'a reality is a diminutive of a thing.

The Scotists introduced the concept by the distinction between a thing and its realities or formalities. For example the being of a man is constituted by his being a substance, being alive, being an animal and his possession of rationality'. Or in more straightforward language: 'a reality is something in a thing. Hence in a thing many realities might be assumed' (Micraelius).

TEXTS

Per realitatem objectivam ideae intelligo entitatem rei repraesentatis per ideam (PPC 1def3). *Sunt diversi gradus realitatis, sive entitatis ... Quicquid est realitatis sive perfectionis* (PPC 1ax4, ax8). *Quo plus realitatis aut esse unaquaeque res habet eo plura attributa ipsi competunt* (E1p9). *Plus realitatis rei definitio exprimit* (E1p16). *Per realitatem et perfectionem idem intelligo* (E2def6). *Mens ad majorem minoremve perfectionem quando ei aliquid de suo corpore vel aliqua ejus parte affirmare contingit, quod plus, minusve realitatis involvit quam antea* (E3aff. gen.def.). *Quo unaquaeque res perfectior est, eo plus realitatis habet, et consequenter eo magis agit* (E5p40).

BIBLIOGRAPHY

Primary Sources
Descartes, R., *Meditationes de prima philosophia.*

Secondary Literature
Robinson, L., *Kommentar zu Spinozas Ethik* (Leipzig: Meiner, 1928), pp. 255–6.
Totaro, G., '*Perfectio* e *realitas* nell'opera di Spinoza', *Lexicon philosophicum*, no. 3 (1988), pp. 71–113.

H. Krop

Religio

Both in the *Tractatus theologico-politicus* and *Tractatus politicus* the word *religio* is frequently used, though much less in the *Ethics* (nine times) and the correspondence. Its Dutch counterpart *godsdienst* occurs three times in the *Korte verhandeling*. Depending on the context four different meanings may be distinguished.

1. A strictly philosophical meaning, which as such was quite common in scholastic discourse and acknowledged *religio* as a basic moral virtue resulting from the knowledge of God. This is the meaning of *religio* in the *Ethics*, where the word is used six times in a positive sense (E4p37s1, E4p73s, E4app15, E4app24, E5p41 and E5p41s). This meaning is defined in E4p37s1: 'Whatever we desire and do, whereof we are the cause insofar as we have the idea of God, that is, insofar as we know God, I refer to religion.' Several key concepts from different parts of the *Ethics* occur in this definition, namely 'desire', 'doing or acting', and 'idea or knowledge of God'. The concept of religion in this philosophical sense is related to other key concepts of the *Ethics*, namely strength of mind (FORTITUDO) (E3p59s) and PIETAS. We can say that religion is a part of *fortitudo*, because the latter presupposes knowledge both of the second and the third kind, the former only the intuitive knowledge of God (the third kind of knowledge). We find the same difference of meaning between religion and piety: in the definition of the latter 'living by the guidance of reason' is referred to, not the 'knowledge of God'. On account of the place of the word religion in the 'ethical part' of the *Ethics* (parts 4 and 5) and on account of its meaning scholars such as De Dijn, Matheron and Wetlesen have called

Spinoza's philosophy a kind of philosophical religion.

2. A purely practical meaning. In this sense of the word, religion simply denotes a course of action leaving aside any cognitive base. In this sense it occurs numerous times in the *Tractatus theologico-politicus*, often in combination with adjectives like universal, true, natural or catholic. Terms which are closely related to religion in this sense are 'word of God' and 'Divine Law'. See for example TTP chapter 12: 'The phrase "word of God", when used in connection with anything other than God himself, properly means the Divine Law which we discussed in chapter 4; that is, religion universal to the entire human race, or catholic religion.' Religion in this moral religious sense means a moral practice of justice and charity or a true way of life, motivated by religious faith. As far as its moral and political usefulness is concerned the significance of religion in the first and the second sense is the same: 'And this is equally so, I repeat, whether we consider religion revealed by the natural light or by prophecy' (TTP 19). But as far as opinions or ideas are concerned, they are essentially different: 'All this leads to the conclusion that the intellectual love of God which contemplates his nature as it really is in itself has no bearing on faith and on revealed religion.' So the adjective 'true' in *religio vera* has not a cognitive but a moral sense: it means a true way of life, a practice of justice and charity. Such a way of life can be motivated by adequate ideas, but also by what Spinoza calls pious dogmas, which are not true in the cognitive sense. Spinoza describes the catholic or universal religion as a very simple moral practice, which must be dissociated from all philosophic questions and speculations, as far as revealed religion is concerned (TTP 13).

This second conception of religion is peculiar to Spinoza. Although Hobbes in *De homine* chapter 14 imitated Cicero's moral and ritualistic notion of religion, describing religion as the service of those who honestly worship God, he assumed that this worship originated in and required a preceding knowledge of the divinity. Also Burgersdijk observed in chapter 13 of his *Idea philosophiae moralis* that if the accompanying knowledge of God is false, religion degenerates into SUPERSTITIO or idolatry.

3. Religion as superstition or *religio vana, falsa*. This meaning is opposed to the previous meanings having mainly a negative sense: it is a kind of illusionary religion, based on ignorance, idolatry and passions such as pride, hatred and jealousy which generate discord in society and the state. According to the preface of the *Tractatus* such religion consists of 'ridiculous mysteries', a belief in miracles and vain speculations (TTP 19 and Ep 73 and 75). Religion in this negative sense seems to be comparatively rare in Spinoza's works.

4. A conventional meaning of religion, related to revealed, positive and historical religion, especially Judaism and Christianity, for example Christian religion, religion among the Hebrews, antique religion etc. To the extent that positive, historical religions such as Judaism and Christianity are purified from superstition and are solely based on a moral practice of justice and charity, they are part of true or universal religion as described under 2. In that case they are very useful for the strengthening of social peace and political stability in the commonwealth. In this way we can understand Spinoza's exclamation at the end of TTP chapter 11: 'Happy indeed would be our age, if we were to see religion freed again from all superstition.'

TEXTS

Hoc addo, me inter Religionem, & Superstitionem hanc praecipuam agnoscere differentiam, quod haec ignorantiam, illa autem sapientiam pro fundamento habeat (Ep 73). *Jam autem foelix profecto nostra esset aetas, si ipsam etiam ab omni superstitione liberam videremus* (TTP 11, G III, 158). *Nempe, quod Verbum Dei, quando de subjecto aliquando praedicatur, quod non sit ipse Deus, proprie significat legem illam Divinam, de qua in IV. Cap. egimus: hoc est religionem toti humano generi universalem, sive catholicam* (TTP12, G III, 162). *Ex quibus omnibus concludimus, intellectualem Dei cognitionem, quae ejus naturam, prout in se est, considerat ad fidem, & religionem revelatam nullo modo pertineret* (TTP 13, 171). *Perinde, inquam, est, sive Religionem lumine naturali, sive Prophetico revelatam concipiamus* (TTP 19, G III, 230). *Porro quicquid cupimus, & agimus, cujus causa sumus, quatenus Deus habemus ideam, sive quatenus Deum cognoscimus, ad Religionem refero* (E4p37s1).

BIBLIOGRAPHY

Primary Sources

Burgersdijk, F., *Idea philosophiae moralis* (Leiden, 1624).

Hobbes, Th., *De homine.*

Secondary Literature

Dijn, H. de, *The Way to Wisdom* (West Lafayette, IN: Purdue University Press, 1996).

Frankel, S.H., *The Problem of Religion in Spinoza's Tractatus Theologico-Politicus* (Ann Arbor, 1999).

Juffermans, P.C. *Drie perspectieven op religie in het denken van Spinoza: een*

onderzoek naar de verschillende betekenissen van religie in het oeuvre van Spinoza (Budel: Damon, 2003).

Matheron A., 'Philosophie et religion chez Spinoza', *Revue des sciences philosophiques et théoriques*, no. 76 (1992), pp. 56–72.

Wetlesen, J., *The Sage and the Way. Spinoza's Ethics of Freedom* (Assen: Van Gorcum, 1979).

P.C. Juffermans

Respublica Hebraeorum / natio Hebraica

While Machiavelli in his *Discorsi* takes the ancient Roman Republic as *exemplum*, Spinoza chooses the Hebrew state as his point of reference. Many Protestants in the young Republic of the United Netherlands saw themselves as a new Israel, freed from the tyranny of the new Egypt, Spain, chosen by God as his favoured people. The most direct source of inspiration was Grotius's friend Cunaeus, whose *De republica Hebraeorum* went through at least seven editions between 1617 and 1700 and was translated into French, English and Dutch. Although in France and England there had already been written books on this theme, Cunaeus's effort stood apart, for the first time presenting the Israelite state of the First Temple period, and especially the united monarchy under Saul, David and Solomon, as a practical model for the newly independent United Provinces. For Cunaeus, who was the leading expert on Josephus, and a famous Christian Hebraist, the Bible was a legal and juridical model, for Scripture demonstrated that the Hebrew State was of a higher order than the Greek or

Roman states. Its laws corresponded to natural law, and its social spirit flowed directly from the divine imperative of justice. This state was neither a monarchy nor an oligarchy nor a democracy, but a republic, whose senate – the Sanhedrin – and magistrates, including judges and priests, enforced and executed divinely ordained laws in ordinary civic situations. Cunaeus was concerned that the Dutch Republic might fall as Athens and Rome had fallen. The imitation of the Hebrew republic would prevent such a decline.

In the third chapter of the *Tractatus theologico-politicus* Spinoza analyses the reasons why the Jews pretended to be exclusively chosen by God. He interprets this idea as a reflection of the prosperity of their state. After the Jews lost their state and were dispersed over the world, their pretence of being special led people to feel aversion to the Jews.

However, according to Spinoza in chapter 18 of the *Tractatus* the Hebrew state was no model for his own era, since the Israelite nation had a political order which could not be imitated, whatever its merits might have been. Apart from this, much of the materials we need to understand this ancient republic have been lost (TTP 7). And if we are able to grasp the text, the prescriptions found in the Pentateuch, for example, contain no universal morality, but merely a set of laws exclusively made for and adapted to the Hebrew people. Spinoza's aim then is to show that the Hebrew state is only a particular historical phenomenon with no universal significance at all. The particularity of the Hebrew state is brought into play to distinguish between rules (or ceremonies) serving the stability of one state and rules (or eternal laws) which relate to any individual independently of the people or state he is part of. Only these latter, universal rules guarantee true happiness.

Outside the political order, the first rules do not bind (TTP 5).

The political order of the Hebrew state is to be explained by its historical background. It was instituted by a people who were former slaves in Egypt and therefore not well equipped to rule their own state. Because of his 'divine virtue', Moses was the only one able to govern appropriately. However, the Jews were stubborn as well and could not be ruled by force and fear alone; Moses for that reason introduced religion into the commonwealth, so that the people would do their duty more from devotion than from fear. He also thought it better for such an obstinate people to give them laws for every occasion so that they would never do anything at their own discretion, preventing in this manner fatal dissent. Later in the book, Spinoza praises the Hebrew state for not having had sects, at least as long as priests did not seize power (TTP 18).

The story started in TTP 5 is continued in chapter 17, now focusing on the very structure and dynamics of political order. Spinoza distinguishes three phases, the first two being rather short: 40 and 26 years (TTP 9), while the last continues until the fall of Jerusalem. The first period comprises the rule of Moses. His monarchy proved a solution to the intolerable democratic-theocratic order: the people turned to Moses as a ruler because they could not bear the rule of God to which they had submitted. So, Moses ruled in the name of God. In the second period, after his death, this THEOCRATIA returned in a more proper way. Moses did not appoint a successor, and an absolute human power was absent. Moses left a mixed government in which powers were divided between tribal chiefs, priests, the people and the divine laws already revealed. This 'excellent' regime saw only one occasion of civil war and discouraged tyranny or rebellion. Nevertheless, it contained a flaw. The caste of priests was set apart from the others and provoked envy, which led to instability. After the short period of quasi-democratic rule, a struggle for power became the fate of the Hebrew political being, which also made them a prey to other nations. The clue of the story is: never let an elite of priests function as part of political power (TTP 18–19). Although Spinoza rejected Israel as a political model to be followed, he treated the Hebrew state in its second phase as an *exemplum* which taught a great deal about the ways the distinct functions of government should be organized to safeguard peace and prosperity. The theocratic background of the Hebrew state as a form of 'social imaginary' prefigures what democracy will do in practice.

Commenwealth', in M. van Gelderen and Q. Skinner (eds), *Republicanism: A Shared European Heritage* (Cambridge: Cambridge University Press, 2002), pp. 247–62.

Schama, S., *The Embarrassment of Riches: An Interpretation of Dutch Culture in the Golden Age* (New York: Knopf, 1987), chap. 2.

Tuck, R., *Philosophy and Government 1572–1651* (Cambridge: Cambridge University Press, 1993), pp. 167–9.

Zac, S., 'Spinoza et l'État des Hébreux', in *Philosophie, théologie, politique dans l'oeuvre de Spinoza* (Paris: Vrin, 1979), pp. 145–76.

M. Terpstra

TEXTS

His sic universaliter consideratis, ad Hebraeorum rempublicam descendamus (TTP 5, G III, 74). *Hebraea natio omnia ornamenta, omneque decus perdidit (nec mirum postquam tot clades et persecutiones passa est* (TTP 7, G III, 106). *Hebraeorum imperium* (TTP 18, G III, 221). *In theocratia, qualis Hebraeorum civitas olim fuit* (TP 7.25).

BIBLIOGRAPHY

Primary Sources
Cunaeus, P., *De republica Hebraeorum libri III* (Leiden, 1617).

Secondary Literature
Balibar, E., 'L'héritage de la Théocratie', in *Spinoza et la politique* (Paris: Presses universitaires de France, 1985).
Campos Boralevi, L., 'Classical Foundational Myths of European Republicanism. The Jewish

Respublica

The term *respublica* occurs frequently in the *Tractatus theologico-politicus*, where it even features in the subtitle and in the titles of the last political chapters, and in the *Tractatus politicus*. Modern versions predominantly use the term 'state', but 'commonwealth', 'affairs of the state' and 'republic' occur as well. The translation however is problematic, since *respublica* is with *civitas* and *imperium* part of a family of terms which from Antiquity onwards overlapped each other. In the early modern age these three words came to denote the emerging modern state, for which a generic term 'state' was still lacking; at the same time the three terms retained their specific meanings. Apparently the precise connotation depended on the particular context. If seventeenth-century political theorists dealt with these three terms, referring to three different aspects of the state, *respublica* connoted the political life and concrete condition of the state (cf. Spinoza's definition in TP 3.1) whereas *civitas* denoted the multitude of the citizens and *imperium* the authority and power of the state. Akkerman (1997, pp. 12–13) refers to a corresponding definition of the Frisian lawyer Ulrik Huber, who observed that 'a unified multitude is called a *civitas*, the union itself which results in common actions causing concord and the common good a *respublica*, and the unifying will *imperium*'. The notion of a political community in action is confirmed by the dictionaries. Micraelius for example defined a *respublica* as 'an order of citizens providing for mutual needs and assigning tasks and rights', while Goclenius defined it as 'the body of the people and their goods, which by certain laws provides for their happiness'. As such it consists of men, animals and inanimate things. Hence an improperly ruled state, for example a tyranny, 'is not to be called a *respublica*'.

These three notions are to some degree reflected in Spinoza's usage. Sometimes Spinoza uses '*respublica*' to indicate a free and well-ordered state, e.g. when referring to the United Provinces of his day. Here, republic means a state in which the people are sovereign, or more or less a state in which all citizens participate. The end of such a state is freedom (TTP 20).

Elsewhere *respublica* occurs with the connotation of the 'affairs of the state'. This is a more 'active' notion of (political) life where people are living and striving for justice. These affairs of the state are to be managed well. The condition of state, therefore, can be free or corrupt (TTP 7). Skinner points out that Erasmus, for example, contrasted the best and the worst state. Spinoza makes clear that without the power to make political decisions it is not possible to manage the affairs of the state. Therefore, *imperium* is a necessary

condition or feature of any *respublica*: 'to form a state this one thing is necessary, that either everyone, or some people, or one person possessed the whole power of making decrees' (TTP 20). Consequently, Spinoza takes *imperium* to be the power which takes care of the affairs of the state, that is, in particular, the right to lay down laws, to establish cities and to decide on war and peace (TP 2.17, 3.2 and 5.1). The state in the sense of *civitas* seems to have a slightly different meaning, indicating the collective body as such which is able to maintain itself. According to E4p37s2 a *civitas*, meaning 'a society established by laws and the capacity (*potestas*) of preserving itself, is called a state'.

Thus, Spinoza offers some distinctions. However, it should be noted that there are important contexts in which for Spinoza *respublica* is completely equivalent with either *civitas* or *imperium*. For example, in TTP 16 (G III, 197) Spinoza treats *respublica* and *civitas* as synonymous, whereas in the title and the first sentence of chapter 18 he treats *respublica* as equivalent to *imperium*.

The term *respublica* appears as early as the writings of Cicero. Its meaning varies considerably. It may be translated by: commonwealth, government, political community, public affairs, public business, public life. More technically it referred to the constitutional aspect of a state, the way in which power is structured internally. In early modern Europe the institution and the idea of a 'state' or commonwealth made increasing headway. This meant the disconnection between civil society and the order of command and obedience. However, in Spinoza's times the Latin word *status* did not yet replace the traditional terms *respublica* and *civitas*. Of course, *status* was used to distinguish the civil condition from the state of nature. Furthermore, *status* was regularly used to refer to the state or condition of the commonwealth or state (or city), often as an independent political community. This condition can be good, peaceful etc. Spinoza's writings reflect this use (e.g. TP 6.21). A notable exception seems to be TP 8.24 where Spinoza says that no salary has to be paid to syndics or any other minister of state, using *status* in the modern sense of state.

Respublica is a generic term and in the seventeenth century there is not yet a clear-cut conceptual distinction between 'republic' as a specific form of government and other possible forms of government. However, 'state' is slowly becoming the genus, and 'republic' the species. Machiavelli speaks of different states having their own foundations; each state has its own particular laws, customs, and institutions (e.g. *Il principe*, 3.12, cf. TTP 3, G III, 47). Thus in Spinoza's works *respublica* is a term that denotes the 'state' alongside other terms, viz. *civitas* and *imperium*.

TEXTS

Cum nobis haec rara foelicitas contingit, ut in republica vivamus unicuique judicandi libertas integra et Deum ex suo ingenio colere conceditur (TTP praef, G III, 7). *Jussum de non committendo adulterio solius rei publicae et imperii utilitatem respicit* (TTP 5, G III, 72). *Hominibus oppressis, qui vivebant in republica corrupta, et ubi justitia prorsus negligebatur* (TTP 7, G III, 103). *At in republica et imperio, ubi salus totius populi, non imperantis, summa lex est, qui in omnibus summae potestati obtemperat, non sibi inutilis servus, sed subditus dicendus, et ideo illa respublica maxime libera est, cujus leges sana ratione fundata est* (TTP 16, G III, 194–5). *Ex fundamentis reipublicae supra explicatis evidentissime sequitur finem ejus ultimum non esse dominari, nec homines metu retinere*

... Finis ergo respublicae revera libertas est. Porro ad formandam rempublicam hoc unum necesse fuisse vidimus, nempe ut omnis decretandi potestas penes omnes, vel aliquot, vel penes unum esset ... Quod fides uniuscujusque erga rempublicam ex solis operibus cognosci potest ... In libera republica libertatem judicii, quae non potest opprimi (TTP 20, G III, 240–1, 243 and 246). *Hoc imperium is absolute tenet qui curam reipublicae ex communi consensu habet* (TP 2.17). *Imperii cujuscunque status dicitur civilis; imperii autem integrum corpus civitas appellatur & communia imperii negotia, quae ab ejus qui imperium tenet directione pendent, respublica* (TP 3.1). *Rempublicam alicui absolute credere, & simul libertatem obtinere fieri nequaquam potest. Verum eorum, qui sibi imperium absolutum concupiscent ... civitatis omnino interesse, ut ipsius negotia secreto agitentur* (TP 7.29). *Civitas sive respublica* (TP 8.3). *Syndicis, vel cuicunque status ministro stipendium nullum ... Rempublicam administrare ... imperii ministris* (TP 8.24). *Potest non absque magno reipublicae periculo imperium aliquando in monarchicum mutari* (TP 10.1).

BIBLIOGRAPHY
Primary Sources
Hobbes, Th., *Leviathan.*
Machiavelli, N., *Il principe.*

Secondary Literature
Akkerman, F., 'Mots techniques – mots classiques dans le *Tractatus Theologico-Politicus* de Spinoza', in P. Totaro (ed.), *Spinoziana. Ricerche di terminologia filosofica e critica testuale* (Florence: Olschki, 1997), pp. 1–22.
Blom, H., 'Spinoza on *Res Publica*, Republics, and Monarchies', in H. Blom

et al. (eds.), *Monarchisms in the Age of Enlightenment: Liberty, Patriotism, and the Common Good* (Toronto: University of Toronto Press, 2007), pp. 19–44.

Bobbio, N., *Democracy and Dictatorship* (Cambridge: Polity Press 1989; original Italian edn 1980).

Cicero, *On the Commonwealth and On the Laws*, ed. J.E.G. Zetzel (Cambridge: Cambridge University Press, 1999).

Conze, W., 'Staat und Souveränität', in R. Koselleck et al. (eds), *Geschichtliche Grundbegriffe. Historisches Lexikon zur politischen- sozialen Sprache in Deutschland*, vol. 6 (Stuttgart: Klett-Cotta, 1990), pp. 1–25.

Curley, E., 'Troublesome Terms for Translators in the *Tractatus Theologico-Politicus*, in P. Totaro (ed.), *Spinoziana. Ricerche di terminologia filosofica e critica testuale* (Florence: Olschki, 1997), pp. 39–62.

Münkler, H., 'Staat', in J. Ritter and G. Gründer (eds), *Historisches Wörterbuch der Philosophie*, vol. 10 (Darmstadt: Wissenschaftliche Buchgesellschaft, 1998), pp. 1–30.

Skinner, Q., 'From the State of the Princes to the Person of the State', in Q. Skinner, *Visions of Politics. Volume II. Renaissance Virtues* (Cambridge: Cambridge University Press, 2002), pp. 368–412.

J.L.M. Gribnau

Revelatio

In the *Cogitata metaphysica* 2.12 Spinoza contends with regard to angels that what is known only through revelation and not through natural light does not pertain to metaphysics but to theology. Hence, although the first chapter of the *Tractatus theologico-philosophicus* identifies revelation with prophecy and defines it as certain knowledge, almost on the same page he opposes the knowledge produced by revelation to the knowledge resulting from reason. However, in Spinoza revelation as such, resulting from a vivid imagination, is not of a supernatural nature. Spinoza often uses 'revelation' in the plural or sees it as the private experience of a particular prophet. Having a revelation transforms a man into a prophet. Only occasionally does Spinoza use the term in the traditional objective sense of the word of God, which was assumed to be contained in Scripture.

Revelation produces a faith which lays the foundations for obedience, i.e. the core of the creed (FUNDAMENTA FIDEI), and theology deals with these truths on the basis of revelation contained in the Bible (TTP 15). Obeying without understanding is not an expression of mathematical but only of moral certainty, arising out of revelation. The 'Bible, that is revelation' is therefore useful and necessary. The prophets are the interpreters of the divine revelation. Since the mind is a part of divine nature, it is the first cause of revelation. Among the Jews, revelation initially assumed the form of a law due to the inadequacy of reason; then, however, Christ perceived what was revealed in a true light (TTP 4). Rites (cf. CAEREMONIA) do not form part of revelation, contrary to what was envisaged by Jewish law (TTP 5). Also Coccejus in his *Summa theologiae* 46.113 underlines that the divine word is adapted to human intelligence, while Episcopius in his *Notae breves in Matthaeum* p. 96 points out its clarity: 'it is beyond any doubt that revelation is nothing else than a clear and distinct proposition about an intelligible object'.

Hobbes in *De cive* 15.3 considers revelation, alongside reason and prophecy, as one of the ways in which God's word is manifested. The founder of true religion was Abraham, the first to whom God revealed himself in a supernatural form (16.1).

TEXTS

Eorum essentia [Angelorum] et existentia non nisi per revelationem notae sunt (CM 2.12). *Divinas revelationes* (Ep 21). *Divinae revelationis certitudinem sola doctrinae sapientia, non autem miraculis, hoc est ignorantia adstrui posse* (Ep 73) *Apparitiones seu revelationes* (Ep 75). *Prophetia sive revelatio ... prima divinae revelationis causa mens ... revelatio per solas imaginationes continget* (TTP 1, G III, 15–16). *Prophetae non certi erant de Dei revelatione per ipsam revelationem, sed per aliquod signum* (TTP 2, G III, 30). *Prophetae pro vario corpore magis ad has quam ad illas revelationes apti erant* (TTP 2, G III, 32). *Deum revelationes captui et opinionibus prophetarum accommodavisse* (TTP 2, G III, 42). *Leges humanae ex revelatione sancitae* (TTP 4, G III, 61). *Scripturae maximam partem historiae et revelationes componunt* (TTP 7, G III, 98). *Per theologiam praecise intelligo revelationem quatenus indicat scopum quae diximus Scripturam* (TTP 15, G III, 184). *Necessitatem sacrae scripturae sive revelationis* (TTP 15, G III, 188).

BIBLIOGRAPHY
Primary Sources
Coccejus, J., *Summa theologiae*, in *Opera omnia* VI, (Amsterdam, 1675).
Episcopius, S., *Notae breves in Matthaeum*, in *Opera theologica* II (Amsterdam, 1665).
Hobbes, Th., *De cive*.

Secondary Literature
Levene, N. K., *Spinoza's Revelation. Religion, Democracy, and Reason* (Cambridge: Cambridge University Press, 2004).
Martinech, A.P., *The Two Gods of Leviathan* (Cambrige: Cambridge University Press, 1992).
Pacchi, A., '*Leviathan* and Spinoza's *Tractatus* on Revelation: Some Elements for a Comparison', *History of European Ideas*, no. 10 (1989), pp. 577–93.
Verbeek, Th., *Spinoza's Theologico-Political Treatise. Exploring 'the Will of God'* (Aldershot: Ashgate, 2003).

R. Bordoli

Scriptura sacra

Holy Scripture is a main subject of the theological part of the *Tractatus theologico-politicus* and an important topic in Spinoza's final correspondence with Oldenburg and earlier with Van Blijenbergh. According to Spinoza the Old Testament consists of historical narrations written down long ago in an ancient language and prophecies or revelations exceeding the limits of the natural intellect. Even the lessons of the apostles in the New Testament, being essentially teachers and no prophets, sometimes fall outside the scope of reason. The Bible therefore needs interpretation, as Spinoza explains in chapter 7 of the TTP. He denies the Reformed claim that the text of the Bible is essentially clear, a view he attributes to Alpakhar. He nevertheless shares the Reformed principle that we cannot explain the Bible with the aid of reason or philosophy, but only by using Scripture itself. Its basic unclarity, however, causes no great problem to the readers, since the message of the Bible is to a large extent a practical one. By means of stories, Scripture teaches the commandments to the Jews, virtue to Christians and (few) speculative truths to all men: for example, that God exists and rewards the good (TTP 5). Those who deny the stories are impious; those who do not know them but live by reason's light are wise; and those who do not know them but live like beasts are brutes. The stories in the Scriptures are clear for the purpose of making men good; their aim is not to help them know truth (TTP 6). Reformed theologians like Coccejus (*De ecclesia et Babylone disquisitio* in *Opera* VII, § 117, p. 43) shared Spinoza's view that the Bible is basically of a moral nature.

The word of God is inscribed in the hearts and minds of men and was imparted to the Jews in writing due to their immaturity. Scripture is sacred because it leads men to feel devotion towards God, to obedience and hence to salvation; otherwise it would be nothing more than paper and ink (TTP 12). Biblical doctrine – 'ye love one another' (John 13.34) – is clear whereas the text of the Bible is obscure and full of gaps. In contrast, Voetius in his *Disputationes selectae* I, p. 31 defends the orthodox thesis of verbal inspiration while Meyer in the epilogue of his *Interpres* concurs with Spinoza in holding that Scripture is a stimulus to readers in search of truth and gives them the opportunity and basis for thinking about happiness. In order to adapt to the human mind, Scripture represents God as a man (TTP 1). In this sense, Scripture may come across as abstruse. However, it does not conflict with truth since both derive from God. Spinoza contends that the Old Testament and the New Testament canons are the product of decisions made by humans (TTP 8–10). With Hobbes in *Leviathan* 33, he rejects the Mosaic paternity of

the Pentateuch and the autographic nature of other books.

TEXTS

Nam veritas veritati non repugnat, nec Scriptura nugas, quales vulgo fingunt docere potest ... Si enim in ipsa invenerimus aliquod, quod lumini naturali esset contrarium eadem libertate, qua Alcoranum et Thalmud refellimus illam refellere possemus (CM 2.8); Ep 21. *Compono tractatum de meo circa scripturam sensu* (Ep 30). *Scriptura per solam Scripturam debet exponi* (Ep 76); TTP praef. *Scriptura Deum instar hominis depingere, Deoque, mentem, animum, animique affectus ut et etiam corpus et halitum tribuere, propter vulgi imbecillitatem solet* (TTP 1, G III, 25). *Cum itaque tota Scriptura in usum integrae nationis prius et tandem universi humani generis revelata fuerit, necessario ea, quae in ipsa continentur ad captum plebis maxime accommodari debuerunt et sola experientia comprobari* (TTP 5, G III, 69). *Methodus interpretandi Scripturam* (TTP 7). *Perspicuitatem Scripturae plane obscurare* (TTP 10, G III, 147); TTP 12. *Scripturae doctrinam non sublimes speculationes, neque res philosophicas continere, sed res simplicissimas* (TTP 13, G III, 167). *Scripturam solam pietatem docere* (TTP 15, G III, 180).

BIBLIOGRAPHY
Primary Sources
Coccejus, J., *De ecclesia et Babylone disquisitio*, in *Opera omnia* VII (Amsterdam, 1675).
Hobbes, Th., *Leviathan*.
[Meyer, L.], *Philosophia S. Scripturae interpres* ([Amsterdam], 1666).

Voetius, G., *Selectae disputationes theologicae*, 5 vols (Utrecht, 1648–69).

Secondary Literature

Bordoli, R., *Ragione e Scrittura tra Descartes e Spinoza. Saggio sulla* Philosophia S. Scripturae Interpres *di Lodewijk Meyer e sulla sua recezione* (Milan: Franco Angeli, 1997).

Martinech, A.P. *The Two Gods of Leviathan* (Cambridge: Cambridge University Press, 1992).

Verbeek, Th., *Spinoza's Theologico-Political Treatise. Exploring 'the Will of God'* (Aldershot: Ashgate, 2003).

R. Bordoli

Servitudo

According to the *Korte verhandeling* (2.26) *slaverny* consists in being subjected to external causes, and freedom, in emancipating oneself from them. Bondage, however, is not necessarily the opposite of freedom, for we are God's slaves inasmuch as we depend absolutely upon him and we have no real force to subsist without him. True freedom implies being bound up with God and loving him. In the *Ethics* this is no longer the case, because things have a power of acting and the concept of *servitudo* no longer has this meaning and is defined in the preface of part 4 as impotence, namely the impotence of men to govern or restrain their passions. In fact, the word *servitudo* is scarcely used by Spinoza who prefers the other term.

Servitudo also has a political meaning in *Tractatus theologico-politicus* chapter 16 and in the *Tractatus politicus*. In the latter case it refers to subjection to a tyrannical

state where the governors act contrary to the dictates of reason, deceive the people and follow their own interest and passions.

Whatever its meaning, servitude implies that the affects have a force against which reason cannot fight. It is the reason why Spinoza entitles *Ethics* 4 'bondage or the strengths of the affects'. All affects are not a sign of servitude; affects born from reason and called 'actions' express freedom and offset bad and sad passions. Some joyful passions too help us to free ourselves from the impotence due to destructive emotions. Servitude is the impotence connected with sad passions, especially hate, melancholy, lust and superstitious fear.

This servitude or impotence cannot be considered a vice in human nature. It occurs because men are parts of nature and subject to 'fortune', that is to say, external, mutable causes more powerful than themselves, so that they cannot always avoid changes contrary to their nature and their desire. In fact, servitude is mainly due to men's ignorance. Unlike the free man who lives under the guidance of reason, the slave is a man who follows his opinion or his affect, and does willingly or unwillingly things about which he does not know anything (E4p66s). The worst kind of servitude is to follow one's lust like a blind man who does not see where his true interest lies. Men do not know where servitude lies and fight for its sake as if it were their salvation (TTP, preface). For one must distinguish real servitude from what man imagines to be one. Men believe that obedience to moral or political law is a burden and confuse it with bondage (E5p41s). In chapter 16 of the *Tractatus theologico-politicus* Spinoza carefully separates three kinds of obedience and distinguishes between the 'slave', the 'son' and the 'subject'. The slave obeys orders which are useful only to his master. The son obeys his parents whose orders are useful to himself. The subject obeys the sovereign whose orders are useful to the community, therefore to himself.

TEXTS

De slaverny van een zaake bestaat in onderworpen aan uyterlyke oorzaaken ... te zyn (KV 2.26 note 1). *Circa religionis praejudicia, hoc est antiquae servitutis vestigia* (TTP, praef, G III, 7), *Pro virtute et optimis actionibus, tanquam pro summa servitute summis praemiis expectant* (E2p49s). *Humanam impotentiam in moderandis and coërcendis affectibus Servitudinem voco* (E4praef). *Pretium servitutis, nempe Pietatis ac Religionis accipere sperant* (E5p41s). *Si servitus in imperio rationis consisteret* (TP 2.20). *Servos potius quam subditos habere* (TP 5.6). *Servitutis igitur, non pacis, interest, omnem potestatem ad unum transferre* (TP 6.4).

BIBLIOGRAPHY

Secondary Literature
Matheron, A., *Individu et communauté chez Spinoza* (Paris: Éditions de Minuit, 1969), part II.
Macherey, P., *Introduction à l'Éthique. IV. La condition humaine* (Paris: Presses Universitaires de France, 1997).

Ch. Jaquet

Sive

Sive (and its variant form *seu*) is one of the Latin conjunctions that correspond to English 'or'; the other three being *aut*, *vel* and enclitic *-ve*. In Spinoza's usage in the *Ethics*

(and, less systematically, in the *Tractatus de intellectus emendatione* and the *Tractatus politicus*), *sive/seu* typically indicates indifference or even equivalence. This allows Spinoza to expand the scope of definitions and proofs so as to apply them to related terms. Apart from *sive/seu*, he uses other formulas of equivalence as well, such as *hoc est, id est, quod idem est* (Naess, 1974). All this is part of a strategy to express the interconnections of infinitely many modes, comprehended in one substance. An equivalence of this type, however, does not make the notions fully interchangeable. Rather, it specifies the semantic range of the terms in that particular context (Saccaro Del Buffa, 1997, p. 161). Spinoza's most famous equivalence with *seu/sive* is 'God or Nature': though it occurs only four times in the *Ethics*, and relatively late at that (E4præf, E4p4dem; also KV app 2), it conveys one of the central tenets of his system, viz. that there is nothing outside, beyond or against nature. Another important equivalence is that of 'reason or cause' (Carraud, 2002, pp. 295–341): Spinoza thus articulates the Principle of Sufficient Reason, which he employed 'more systematically, perhaps, than has ever been done in the history of philosophy' (Della Rocca, 2008, p. 30). For everything there must be a reason why it exists or does not exist (E1p11).

TEXTS

Cuiuscumque rei assignari debet causa seu ratio, tam cur existit, quam cur non existit. Ex. gr. si triangulus existit, ratio seu causa dari debet, cur existit; si autem non existit, ratio etiam seu causa dari debet, quae impedit quominus existat, sive quae eius existentiam tollat. Haec vero ratio seu causa vel in natura rei contineri debet, vel extra ipsam (E1p11).

Aeternum namque illud & infinitum ens, quod Deum seu naturam appellamus ... Ratio igitur seu causa, cur Deus seu natura agit & cur existit, una eademque est (E4praef). *Ipsa Dei sive naturae potentia ... Potentia itaque hominis ... pars est infinitae Dei seu naturae potentiae* (E4p4dem).

BIBLIOGRAPHY
Secondary Literature
Carraud, V., *Causa sive ratio. La raison de la cause, de Suarez à Leibniz* (Paris: Presses Universitaires de France, 2002).
Della Rocca, M., *Spinoza* (London: Routledge, 2008).
Naess, A., *Equivalent Terms and Notions in Spinoza's Ethics* (Oslo: Inquiry, Filosofisk Institutt, Universitet i Oslo, 1974).
Saccaro Del Buffa, G., 'I connettivi sintattici e le strutture binarie dell'*Ethica* di Spinoza', in Pina Totaro (ed.), *Spinoziana. Ricerche di terminologia filosofica e critica testuale* (Rome: Olschki, 1997), pp. 155–83.

P. Steenbakkers

Societas

In comparison with *civitas* Spinoza only rarely uses the word 'society', in the *Ethics* often in combination with 'common'. Apparently it was a broader concept, which probably due to its basic nature was never defined by Spinoza. In the literature on Spinoza's political terminology it is also hardly dealt with. In the seventeenth century the word as such denoted only a collection of men or things. Micraelius defines: 'a combination or collection of several things, which is opposed to things existing in isolation'. In political

discourse it refers to any human society, which may be 'domestic' (family) or 'civil and public'. Spinoza distinguishes but does not separate the 'common' society from the state (it should be noted that in Spinoza the expression 'civil society', the usual translation of Aristotle's *koinonía politiké*, does not occur). No wonder, a sharp distinction between state and (common) society in political philosophy had yet to be made. Hobbes, for example, in *De cive* 5.9 identified *civitas* (commonwealth or state) with *societas civilis* (civil society).

In its original sense 'society' allowed no distinction between 'state' and 'society' or between political and civil society. Civil society became a distinct concept as the corollary of a depersonalized state authority. It was Hegel who finally demolished the Aristotelian notion. Although Machiavelli already spoke of the state as the greatest power exercised over the inhabitants of a given territory with political institutions to exercise and maintain this power, in Spinoza's time there was still no sharp conceptual distinction between state and society, as a result of which he could define the state as 'a common society confirmed by laws'. Therefore, 'society' was primarily a civil or political society but depending on its context, as in contemporary English, it might refer to any society, either a domestic one, a natural society, or a religious society.

According to Spinoza, men cannot live without a society. Because men are scarcely able to lead a solitary life, they are social animals. Moreover, social organization offers men far more profit than loss (E4p35s). The formation of a society is advantageous, even absolutely essential, not merely for security against enemies but for the efficient organization of an economy and the like.

The order and security afforded by the civil state is also vitally important to the practical aim of individual salvation. The human needs are not only a matter of economy, but also of civilization. Spinoza explicitly points out the advantages of the division of labour in a community. Consequently, a person may specialize and exchange his products for others to satisfy his needs. By this division of labour time becomes available to spend on the arts and sciences, 'which are also indispensable for the perfection of human nature and its blessedness' (TTP 5).

Society may be advantageous, or even essential to men, but how does it come about? For Spinoza, the existence of civil society is a fact of life, and not, as Hobbes argued, the result of a voluntaristic pursuit: 'all men, whether savage or civilized, everywhere enter into relationship with one another and set up some kind of civil state' (TP 1.7). All men naturally put together their respective powers so as to form a more powerful whole. The formation of societies is an empirical fact. 'Since fear of solitude exists in all men, because no one in solitude is strong enough to defend himself, and procure the necessaries of life, it follows that men naturally aspire to the civil state; nor can it happen that men should ever utterly dissolve it' (TP 6.1). Human reason is not the driving force in this formation of society. On the contrary, society springs from the passions and is worked out in them and through them. Spinoza summarizes his view just before the passage just cited, referring to *Tractatus politicus* 3.9. 'Since men are led more by passion than reason, it follows, that a multitude agrees by nature, and wishes to be guided, as it were, by one mind, not at reason's prompting, but through some common passion – that is, common hope, or fear, or the desire of avenging some common hurt.' Thus, society results from the imagination and people come to agree on

appropriate constraints to the exercise of the natural rights they each individually possess, because such a collective life will promote self-preservation. Hence, the social dimension of imagination, itself driven by the *conatus*, is crucial. The interaction of imagination and the passions creates the dialectical relation of collaboration and antagonism, which bind people together in society. It is the inherent social dimension of imagination which accounts for the necessity of all human endeavour to take the form of collective action. However, state and society being indispensable for the self-preservation of men, this form of collective will make people behave as if they were led by reason, which is to a certain degree the product of effective civil laws. This is best done by a state that is based on reason and directed by reason, for such a state 'is most powerful and most in control of itself' (TP 3.7). Therefore, the state is useful for a man who is driven by his passions, for the state compels him to live a life which meets the demands of reason. Moreover, a man who is guided by reason 'is more free in a state, where he lives according to a general law, than in solitude, where he obeys only himself' (E4p73).

A well-ordered society being a state must claim for itself the right that everyone has of avenging himself, and deciding what is good and evil. Moreover, society must possess the power to lay down common rules of conduct, and to pass laws to enforce them. Spinoza immediately moves on to the state, for 'such a society, established by laws and the capacity (*potestas*) of preserving itself, is called a state' (E4p37s2). Apparently, the state is a society supported by a legal structure, which enables it to preserve itself. Thus society is governed by laws which each will obey, because they are enforced by the effective power of the state. The citizen subjects himself to the power of the state. The legal foundation of the state protects the citizens. The laws determine the rights of citizens, who 'enjoy the advantages of political order on a legal base' (TP 3.1). Such a well-structured society will achieve levels of power beyond the anticipation of those who designed the system itself or act within it. In passing, Spinoza notes that nations differ from another precisely in respect of the kind of society and laws under which they live and are governed (TTP 3).

Spinoza's conception of society differs on the one hand from the Aristotelian model. For Aristotle, this society is still a natural society on a level with the family – in the sense that it corresponds perfectly to man's social nature. Spinoza considers man to be a social animal, but this is not a matter of finding his true (moral) destiny in the political society; rather man can hardly survive without society. On the other hand, Spinoza's naturalism which combines sociality and egoism differs from the Hobbesian model, based on egoism devoid of sociality, in which civil society is an instituted or artificial society.

Thus, Spinoza's naturalistic theory of socialization explains society (and the state) as an effect of the laws of nature. He takes human nature as its starting point. Divine teleology, therefore, does not account for the association of men. Spinoza rejects the view that God himself directs all men to certain ends. Unlike scholastic philosophers such as Aquinas, he does not maintain that the formation of society is willed by God, though he agrees with them that man is a social animal.

TEXTS

Hic finis ad quem tendo, talem scilicet naturam acquirere ... hoc est de mea felicitate

operam dare ... necesse est talem societatem formare, ut quamplurimi quam facillime et secure eo perveniant (TIE 14, G II, 8–9). *Ad secure vivendum et injurias aliorum hominum et etiam brutorum evitandum nullum certius medium est et experientia docuit, quam societatem certis legibus formare* (TTP 3, G III, 47). *Societas non tantum ad secure ab hostibus vivendum, sed etiam ad multarum rerum compendium faciendum perutilis est, et maxime etiam necessaria; nam nisi hominis invicem operam mutuam dare velint, ipsis et ars et tempus deficeret ad se, quoad ejus fieri potest, sustentandum et conservandum ... Hinc fit, ut nulla societas possit subsistere absque imperio et vi et consequenter legibus* (TTP 5, G III, 73). *Sine ulla naturalis juris repugnantia societas formari potest ... Talis societatis jus democratia vocatur* (TTP 16, G III, 193). *Denique confert etiam haec doctrina non parum ad communem societatem* (E2p49s). *At nihilominus vitam solitariam vix transigere queunt, ita ut plerisque illa definitio, quod homo sit animal sociale, valde arriserit; et revera res ita habet, ut ex hominum communi societate multo plura commoda oriantur quam damna* (E4p35s). *Hac igitur lege societas firmari poterit, si modo ipsa sibi vendicet jus, quod unusquisque habet, sese vindicandi, et de bono, et malo judicandi; quaeque adeo potestatem habeat communem vivendi rationem praescribendi, legesque ferendi, easque non ratione, quae affectus coercere nequit; sed minis firmandi. Haec societas, legibus, et potestate sese conservandi, civitas appellatur* (E4p37s2). *Quae ad hominum communem societatem conducunt ... utilia sint et illa contra mala, quae discordiam in civitatem inducunt* (E4p40). *Rationem veri utilis, quod ex mutua amicitia et communi societate sequitur* (E5p10s). *Vix credibile est nos aliquid quod communi societati ex usu esse queat posse concipere, quod occasio seu*

315

casus non obtulerit (TP 1.3). *Ex discordiis igitur ... numquam fit ut cives civitatem dissolvant, (ut in reliquis societatibus saepe evenit)* (TP 6.2). *Quia controversiae et dissensiones ex societate praecipue, quae ex matrimonio fit oriuntur ... imperio exitiale esse arctam societatem cum alio inire* (TP 7.24).

BIBLIOGRAPHY
Primary Sources
Hobbes, Th., *De Cive, Leviathan.*
Machiavelli, N., *Il Principe.*

Secondary Literature
Akkerman, F., 'Mots techniques – mots classiques dans le *Tractatus Theologico-Politicus* de Spinoza', in P. Totaro (ed.), *Spinoziana. Ricerche di terminologia filosofica e critica testuale* (Florence: Olschki, 1997), pp. 1–22.
Balibar, E., *Spinoza and Politics* (London: Verso, 1998; original French edn 1985).
Blom, H.W., 'The Moral and Political Philosophy of Spinoza', in G.H.R. Parkinson (ed.), *The Renaissance and 17th Century Rationalism* (London and New York: Routledge, 1993), pp. 313–48.
Curley, E., 'Troublesome Terms for Translators in the *Tractatus Theologico-Politicus*, in P. Totaro (ed.), *Spinoziana. Ricerche di terminologia filosofica e critica testuale* (Florence: Olschki, 1997), pp. 39–62.
Gaetens, M. and G. Lloyd, *Collective Imaginings. Spinoza, Past and Present* (London: Routledge, 1999).
Matheron, A., *Individu et communauté chez Spinoza* (Paris: Editions de Minuit, 1969).
———, 'Ethik und Politik bei Spinoza (Bemerkungen zur Funktion von E4LS37A2)', in K. Hammacher et al. (eds), *Zur Aktualität der Ethik Spinozas*

(Würzburg: Königshausen and Neumann, 2000), pp. 317–27.
McShea, R.J., *The Political Philosophy of Spinoza* (New York and London: Columbia University Press, 1968).
Miller, F.D., 'Naturalism', in C. Rowe and M. Schofeld (eds), *The Cambridge History of Greek and Roman Political Thought* (Cambridge: Cambridge University Press, 2000), pp. 321–43.
Uyl, D. den, 'Sociality and Social Contract: A Spinozistic Perspective', *Studia Spinozana*, no. 1 (1985), pp. 19–52.
Zac, S., 'Société et communion chez Spinoza', in *Philosophie, théologie, politique dans l'oeuvre de Spinoza* (Paris, Vrin, 1979), pp. 97–116.
———, 'État et nature chez Spinoza', in *Philosophie, théologie, politique dans l'oeuvre de Spinoza* (Paris: Vrin, 1979), pp. 117–43.

J.L.M. Gribnau

Status naturae

The concept of the state of nature is introduced in chapter 16 of the *Tractatus theologico-politicus* and dealt with in the famous second scholium of *Ethics* 4 proposition 37 as well. The phrase also frequently occurs in the unfinished *Tractatus politicus*. Spinoza uses the concept in a threefold way. First, the 'state of nature' denotes the condition of men living outside a society, that is leading an insecure and unsafe life without moral notions. The civil state is its opposite. Secondly, in Spinoza this notion denotes the condition of men led by their passions. Thirdly, he uses the state of nature as a measuring-rod for assessing the quality of a state (and its organization).

Spinoza both claims that the state of nature is impossible in the sense of being incompatible with human survival, and that man always lives in the state of nature and never escapes from it. On the one hand, human beings are too weak to live on their own. On the other hand, man in the state of nature is driven by his passions, and this does not change with the establishment of society (TP 3.3; though few men may come to live by reason). Spinoza's naturalism does not stop at the threshold of the civil society. Therefore, no one is ever completely freed from the pre-civil, that is natural state, but everyone always lives within both the natural and civil states.

Spinoza adopted the notion of a natural state from Hobbes, who radically transformed this theological notion of the human condition before the Fall, but he is not interested in showing its historical reality: 'all men, whether savage or civilized, everywhere enter into relationship with one another and set up some kind of civil state' (TP 1.7 and 6.1). Neither does he attempt to argue that in the state of nature the war of all against all prevails. In the anarchical natural state man's power and freedom are limited by his fear of being attacked by others, and by the natural human inability to satisfy all his own needs and wants. Therefore, man living by the laws of his own nature and striving for his advantage is powerless. In the state of nature the concept of a natural right is meaningless, because man is unable to defend himself against the others. Without mutual assistance man is unable to preserve himself. Co-operation of men creates a collective power (TP 2.13) and the more men join forces the more rights they have in common (TP 2.15).

Furthermore, in the natural state morality does not exist and all things are permitted, for there is no common notion of good and evil. Without collective power, no common decree and consent, defining what is prohibited by law, is possible. Everyone is his own judge. Consequently, in the state of nature all things are permitted (TP 2.18). The hallmark of a state, however, is a common decree which restricts the right of individual citizens to live just as they please. If a state grants anyone the right to live just as he pleases, its right and power vanishes. The collective power crumbles, and the state is not *sui iuris* anymore, it disintegrates. Therefore, the disappearance of the common decree and consensus implies the return of a state to the state of nature (TP 3.3).

In the state of nature, man's CONATUS makes him choose the lesser evil, i.e. a smaller loss of power and freedom, by co-operating in a society where he submits to the constraints imposed by the authorities. Here, the social dimension of imagination is at work. The natural formation of society driven by human imagination makes superfluous Hobbes's notion of the transition to a society by means of a social contract which is dictated to man by natural reason in order to escape from the state of permanent insecurity and devastating warfare.

The state of nature is also a point of reference, a measuring-rod for assessing the quality of a state and its regime. For Spinoza, in a democracy man – indirectly – exerts his natural right for he is a member of a greater political body. Thus 'delegating' their natural rights, everyone continues to be as equal as they were in the preceding state of nature (TTP 16). Here, Spinoza anticipates the central idea of Rousseau, which is the idea of a society through which each one, but uniting with all, obeys no one but himself, remaining free as before.

However, Spinoza starts from a different conception of the state of nature, for Rousseau views the state of nature as a primitive self-contained community in which people live harmoniously together based on inalienable freedom and equality of all men. This organic community is lost in modern civilization. For Rousseau, the state is a form of social organization which guarantees those natural rights of freedom and equality. Before Rousseau, Locke conceptualized the state of nature as a state of peace, good will, mutual assistance and preservation. Men have natural rights, they unfortunately lack the organization. Here, the function of the state is to preserve and protect the individual's inalienable rights already existent in the state of nature. Unlike Spinoza, Locke views these inalienable rights as a kind of values which are superior and immutable by positive law in a state. Furthermore, Locke stops short of a democratic theory. As for Hobbes, man can only escape the state of nature by transferring his natural right to a sovereign, thereby establishing an artificial society. Spinoza does not 'advocate' such a complete transfer of natural right to a collective body (letter 50).

Two states necessarily live in a state of nature with each other; they are in the same relation as two men in the state of nature (TP 3.11). They are enemies by nature, each trying to extend its own power as far as it can, and each concluding temporary alliances for the sake of self-preservation. However, a treaty of alliance stays fixed as long as the reason for the alliance, fear of loss or hope of gain, remains operative. If this fear or hope disappears, an alliance loses its cause or motive. Consequently it is rightfully denounced as soon as it is no longer in the interest of one of the partners to maintain it (TP 3.14; TTP 16). The states then revert to a state of nature (TP 3.15).

TEXTS

Nam in eo nemo jus suum naturale ita in alterum transfert, ut nulla sibi imposterum consultatio sit, sed in majorem totius societatis partem, cujus ille unam facit. Atque hac ratione omnes manent, ut antea in statu naturali, aequales ... status naturalis ... absque religione et lege concipiendus (TTP 16, G III, 195). *In statu naturali non plus juris rationi quam appetitui esse* (TTP 19, G III, 229). *Imperium democraticum maxime ad statum naturale accedit* (TTP 20, G III, 245). *Nihil in statu naturali dari, quod ex omnium consensu bonum, aut malum sit; quandoquidem unusquisque, qui in statu est naturali, suae tantummodo utilitati consulit et ex suo ingenio ... quid bonum, quidve malum sit decernit ... atque adeo in statu naturali peccatum concipi nequit. ... In statu naturali nemo ex communi consensu alicujus rei est Dominus* (E4p37s2). *Cum in statu naturali tamdiu unusquisque sui juris sit, ... et unus solus frustra ab omnibus sibi cavere conetur, hinc sequitur quamdiu jus humanum unius potentia determinatur ... nulla ejus obtinendi est securitas* (TP 2.15). *In statu naturali non dari peccatum* (TP 2.18). *In statu naturali nititur unusquisque nihil minus sibi vindicare et sui juris facere potest quam solum* (TP 7.19).

BIBLIOGRAPHY
Primary Sources
Hobbes, Th., *De Cive, Leviathan*.

Secondary Literature
Friedmann, W., *Legal Theory* (New York: Columbia University Press, 1967, first edition 1944), pp. 117–27.
Hampshire, S., *Spinoza* (London: Penguin, 1951).
Hofmann, H., 'Naturzustand', in J. Ritter and K. Gründer (eds), *Historisches*

Wörterbuch der Philosophie, Band 6 (Darmstadt: Wissenschaftliche Buchgesellschaft, 1984), coll. 653–8.

Israel, J.I., *Radical Enlightenment* (Oxford: Oxford University Press, 2001).

Matheron, A., *Individu et communauté chez Spinoza* (Paris: Éditions de Minuit, 1969).

McShea, R.J., *The Political Philosophy of Spinoza*, (New York and London: Columbia University Press, 1968).

Walther, M., 'Die Transformation des Naturrechts in der Rechtsphilosophie Spinozas', *Studia Spinozana,* no. 1 (1985), pp. 73–104.

———, 'Grundzüge politischen Philosophie Spinozas', in M. Hampe and R. Schnepf (eds), *Baruch de Spinoza: Ethik in geometrischer Ordnung dargestellt* (Berlin: Akademie Verlag, 2006).

Uyl, D. den, 'Sociality and Social Contract: A Spinozistic Perspective', *Studia Spinozana*, no. 1 (1985), pp. 19–52.

Zagorin, P., *Hobbes and the Law of Nature* (Princeton and Oxford: Princeton University Press, 2009).

J.L.M. Gribnau

Sub specie aeternitatis

In *Ethics 5 sub specie aeternitatis* occurs no less than 23 times, but only twice in the rest of this book and once both in the *Tractatus de intellectus emendatione* and the *Tractatus theologico-politicus*. Of these four occurrences outside *Ethics 5*, three times 'a certain' is added before eternity. Familiar from German idealism onwards, this particular phrase seems to have originated with Spinoza.

'Species' was of course a basic term in Aristotelian logic. Another source might be Cicero's *Timaeus*, where the Platonic idea is denoted by *speciem aeternitatis*, imitated by the divine Maker in ordering the visible word. A third possible source is the scholastic *sub ratione* (E1p33s2) translated in the *Korte verhandeling* as *onder scheijn van*. Its retranslation from the vulgar into Latin would be *sub specie*.

The phrase is often linked with the verb 'conceive', but 'perceive', 'know', 'contemplate' and 'consider' also occur. The subject of the related verb is nearly always the mind or its faculties – the intellect or reason. Only twice is the subject an idea in God, which expresses the essence of a human body (E5p22, 23s). Its objects are more diverse: the human body, its essence, the essence of the human mind, natural laws and most regularly the things. In this phrase an equivalent of 'eternity' is 'necessity' (E4p62) which confirms the idea of their idenfication by Spinoza. Its opposite is 'under duration'.

The three sources suggested before have resulted in three different interpretations. Robinson for example took the logical connotation of species as his starting point and the phrase should then be translated as 'a kind of eternity'. (By the way, in this meaning *species* figures in the Roman Catholic docrine of communion taken under both kinds (*sub utraque specie*). Moreover, Hallet argued that with rational knowledge we only approach the eternal nature of God, which explains why Spinoza thrice uses 'under a certain kind of eternity', leaving the full understanding of eternity to intuitive knowledge. However, Gueroult observed that Spinoza did not distinguish between different kinds of eternity. There is only God's eternity. Species in this phrase must mean perspective or viewpoint, and we should read *sub specie* as if Spinoza had written *sub ratione*. In this reading the phrase assumes a more subjective connotation than in the first. Finally, Hubbeling and Di

Vona tend to read *species* in the light of the Platonic-Augustinian tradition. They underline the fact that *sub specie aeternitatis* in *Ethics* 5 at first takes 'the human body' and afterwards 'the things' as its object. They are no longer perceived in the light of faith, but in the true light of eternity, i.e. beatific vision. In that light we see the things as they really are, as necessary (E2p44c2).

TEXTS

Res non tam sub duratione, quam sub quadam specie aeternitatis percipit et numero infinito (TIE 108, G III, 39). *Naturae leges ad infinita se extendunt et sub quadam specie aeternitatis a nobis concipiuntur* (TTP 6, G III, 86). *De natura rationis est res sub quadam aeternitatis specie percipere* (E2p44c2). *Quicquid mens ducente ratione concipit, id omne sub eadem aeternitatis seu necessitatis specie concipit* (E4p62). *Corporis humani essentiam sub aeternitatis specie exprimit* (E5p22). *Mens nostra quatenus se et corpus sub aeternitatis specie cognoscit, eatenus Dei cognitionem necessario habet ... Res sub specie aeternitatis concipere est res concipere quatenus per Dei essentiam ut entia realia, concipiuntur, sive quatenus per Dei essentiam involvunt existentiam* (E5p30). *Mens nihil sub aeternitatis specie concipit, nisi quatenus aeterna est* (E5p31). *Mentis amor intellectualis erga Deum et ipse Dei amor. Quo Deus se ipsum amat ... quatenus per essentiam humanae mentis, sub specie aeternitatis consideratam explicari potest* (E5p36).

BIBLIOGRAPHY

Secondary Literature

Di Vona, P., *La conoscenza 'sub specie aeternitatis' nell' opera di Spinoza* (Naples: Loffredo, 1995).

Gueroult, M., *Spinoza I. Dieu (Éthique I)* (Hildesheim: Olms, 1968).

Hallet, H.F., *Aeternitas, a Spinozistic Study* (Oxford: Clarendon Press, 1930).

Hubbeling, H.G., *Spinoza's Methodology* (Assen: Van Gorcum, 1964).

Jaquet, C., *Sub specie aeternitatis, études des concepts de temps, durée et éternité chez Spinoza* (Paris: Éditions Kimé, 1997).

Mignini, F., '*Sub specie aeternitatis*, notes sur *Éthique*', *Revue philosophique de la France et de l'étranger*, no. 1 (1994), pp. 41–54.

Robinson, L., *Kommentar zu Spinozas Ethik* (Leipzig: Meiner, 1928).

H. Krop

Substantia

The Latin noun *substantia* and its Dutch counterpart *zelfstandigheid* acquired their full Spinozistic meaning only in Spinoza's mature work, the *Ethics*. Both in the *Korte verhandeling* and in the PPC his conception of substance still resembled the Cartesian one in important respects. For Descartes linked substance and attribute in so far as substances are identified and really distinct by their uniquely proper attribute. So, Descartes identified a corporeal substance essentially different from the mental substance by having as its attribute extension and not thinking (cf. PPC 1p8). However, from the outset Spinoza adopted the Cartesian rationalism, which ended in a dismantling of the Aristotelian conception emanating from the concrete things in the phenomenal world. It is therefore hardly controversial to say that Spinoza's understanding of substance is 'in many ways a principled transformation and criticism of Descartes' (Della Rocca, p. 33).

Although Spinoza's much debated definition of substance is only given as the third one of the first book, it is not far off the mark to maintain that the first part of *Ethics* 1, the propositions 1 through 15, focuses on the notion of substance, which since Aristotle and during the scholastic period had been basic to all metaphysical speculation. It is interesting to note that the *Korte Verhandeling* hardly deals with 'substance' as such. Contrary to the clear-cut argument of the *Ethics*, in KV 1.2 Spinoza without much ado presents four preliminary theses about substance to clarify his notion of God. However, it should be noted that after a last mention in the lemmas of part 2, the concept of substance in the *Ethics* is relegated to the background and contrary to the concept of 'God' it does not resurface in part 5. An exception to this general negligence might well be his theory of the parallelism between the mental and bodily order that in the scholium of E2p7 is argued for by means of the one substance comprehended through different attributes: 'thinking substance and extended substance are one and the same thing, which is now comprehended through this and now through that attribute'. Although in order to criticize Cartesianism Spinoza used the Cartesian way of expression, the theory of parallelism seems to be a new discovery of the *Ethics* (Nyden-Bullock, 2007, pp. 107–10).

Spinoza's familiar, but in itself rather intricate definition in E1def3 runs as follows: 'by substance I understand what is in itself (a) and is conceived through itself (b), i.e. that whose concept does not require the concept of another thing, from which it must be formed' (c). The same definition, without the last six words (in the original Latin four), is given in letter 9 dating from March 1663, which makes it plausible that Spinoza reached his conception of substance at quite

an early stage of his philosophical development. Two years before, in letter 4 of October 1661, he had even presented to Oldenburg a version of the definition with at least two of the three salient features: (a) [a thing] '*conceived* through and in itself', that is (c) the concept of which 'does not involve the concept of another thing', a definition that by using *concipitur* instead of the *est* of the *Ethics* formulated (a) in a more epistemological way. However, it should be noted that this definition is identical with the definition of the ATTRIBUTUM as given in letter 2. In other letters, the *Cogitata metaphysica*, and the PPC. Spinoza used 'substance' in a more Cartesian way, writing without hesitation about a 'created', 'extended', 'corporeal', or 'thinking' substance. Finally, Spinoza uses substance (though rarely) in a non-philosophical or polemical sense. In the *Tractatus theologico-politicus* 2 for example, Spinoza writes that 'we must believe the prophets only with regard to the purpose and substance of the revelation'. In letter 56 (and CM 2.1) he rejects the substantial forms: 'The authority of Plato, Aristotle, and Socrates, carries little weight with me...It is not surprising that those, who have thought up occult qualities, intentional species, substantial forms, and a thousand more bits of nonsense, should have also devised spectres and ghosts, and given credence to old wives' tales, in order to take away the authority of Democritus'.

The first feature (a) of the definition of substance underscores the traditional notion of 'independence', or 'existence by itself'. This notion is according to Richter conventionally expressed by the phrase '*in se*' or its synonym '*per se*'. This feature of independence included according to Richter and Robinson three notions: aseity, continued existence and non-inherence. This is the reason why Spinoza in the *Tractatus de intellectus emendatione* identifies *in se* with *causa sui*: 'if the thing is in itself or as it is commonly said self-caused, than it will have to be understood solely through its essence', and in CM 2.5: 'because each [substance] can exist through itself, it must exist of itself [*a se*]'. In this respect *substantia* was etymologically derived from *subsistendo* which means 'that a thing by itself subsists' (Chauvin). By opposing a substance to a mode, or an affection, which contrary to a substance is in 'something else' (E1def5) and referring to the traditional division of being in things that are in itself and things that are in something else (E1ax1), Spinoza seemingly also retains in one way or another the second conventional notion of a substance, namely its being the subject of modes. On account of axiom 1 Spinoza more than once observed that substances and modes are the only two categories of real beings in the universe (E1p15 and 29 and letter 3). This notion was etymologically explained by deriving substance from *substando*, meaning 'a thing which supports its perfections'. Both notions mentioned refer to the ontological nature of substance.

The features b and c refer to the epistemological relationship between a self-contained concept of substance and the relative concepts of the modi. Apparently these epistemological features are peculiar to Spinoza. Even Richter did not succeed in tracing real predecessors. However, in the *Notae ad programma quoddam* Descartes argues for the real difference of attributes by observing that 'the attributes which form the nature of things are diverse if neither is contained in the concept of the other' and 'there is a duality or plurality of attributes is one can be understood without the other'. After Spinoza the Cartesian Malebranche mentioned feature b in his *Entretiens métaphysiques* 1.2:

'Whatever exists either can be conceived by itself or çan't be conceived by itself. There's no middle ground, for the two propositions are contradictories. Now, if something can be conceived all on its own as existing without depending on anything else – can be conceived without our idea of it also representing some other thing – then it is certainly a being or a substance'.

From the definition of substance Spinoza deduces the following notions. In scholastic discourse such notions following from the definition were called 'properties' or '*notae*'. (1) A substance is prior to its modes. By invoking definitions 3 and 5 Spinoza proves the first proposition of *Ethics* 1 by means of the conceptual relation of priority between the concepts of substance and modes (cf. letter 4). (2) The same applies to the second notion, the ontological and conceptual uniqueness of substance, by which two substances have nothing in common. According to the definition, if two things are conceptually related, they both cannot be substances (proposition 2, 4, 5, cf. proposition 1 in letter 2). (3) Hence a substance is casually independent (proposition 3, 6, cf. proposition 1 in letter 2 and proposition 4 of letter 4). A substance also (4) necessarily exists, because it is impossible for a substance to be the effect of another substance, (5) is infinite (proposition 7 and 8) and (6) is eternal (proposition 19). (Letter 2 adds the qualification IN SUO GENERE to infinity which presupposes the Cartesian doctrine of an extended and thinking substance.) (7) A substance is indivisible, the corporeal substance included (proposition 13, cf. letter 12). (8) This infinite, necessarily existing substance of which the existence is included in its essence is God (proposition 14) and therefore unique. Apparently this identification of God and substance made the latter concept redundant as after proposition 15 the word is only used five times in the *Ethics*. Letter 12 of April 1663 exemplifies such redundancy, for no definition of substance is given, while the following three particular Spinozistic notions of substance are listed. 'First, that existence appertains to its essence. Secondly, as a consequence, that substance is not manifold, but single: there cannot be two of the same nature. Thirdly, every substance must be conceived as infinite'. Apparently Spinoza used substance in a Wittgensteinian manner: to make it superfluous.

TEXTS

Geen zelfstandigheid die als deze door zig zelfs is, hangt van iets buyten hem af (KV 1.1). Zoo moet dan alle zelfstandigheid onbepaald aan 't goddelyk wezen behooren (KV 1.2). De ene zelfstandigheid de ander niet kan voortbrengen (KV 1.3). Oneijndige zelfstandigheden van de welke een ieder des zelfs oneyndig volmaakt moet zijn (KV 1.7). *Omnis res ... cujus realis idea in nobis est vocatur 'substantia'* (PPC 1def5–8, 10). *Substantia plus realitatis habet quam accidens vel modus* (PPC 1ax4). *'Substantiam'... id quod ad existendum solo Dei concursu indigent* (PPC 2def2); CM 1.2, CM 1.3, CM 2.1. *Substantia ipsa generari non potest, sed tantum a solo Omnipotente creari* (CM 2.12). *Primo, quod in rerum natura non possunt existere duae substantia, quin tota essentia different. Secundo substantia non posse produci; sed quod sit de ipsius essentia existere. Tertio quid omnis substantia debeat esse infinita, sive summe perfecta in suo genere* (Ep 2). *Per substantiam intelligo id, quod per se concipitur, hoc est cujus conceptus non involvit conceptum alterius rei ... Hinc clare constat primo quod substantia sit prior natura suis accidentibus. Secundo quod praeter*

substantias et accidentia nihil detur realiter, sive extra intellectum (Ep 4); Ep 6. *Me non demonstrare substantiam (sive ens) plura habere posse attributa ... Ipsa enim definitio sic sonat: per substantiam intelligo id, quod in se est, et per se concipitur, hoc est, cujus conceptus non involvit conceptum alterius rei* (Ep 9). *Primo quod ad ejus essentiam pertinet existentia, hoc est, quod ex sola ejus essentia et definitione sequatur eam existere. Secundum quod substantia non multiplex, sed unica ... Tertium quod omnis substantia non nisi infinita posit intelligi* (Ep 12). *Finis et substantia revelationis* (TTP 2, G III, 42) *Per substantiam intelligo id quod a se est et per se concipitur hoc est cujus conceptus non indigent conceptu alterius rei a quo formari debet* (E1def3). *Substantia prior est natura affectionibus* (E1p1). *Ad naturam substantiae pertinet existere* (E1p7) *Omnis substantia est necessario infinita* (E1p8). *Quamvis duo attributa realiter distincta concipiantur ... non possumus tamen inde non concludere ipsa dua entia sive duas diversas substantias constituere* (E1p10s). *Corpora ratione motus...et non ratione substantiae ab invicem distinguuntur* (E2lem1 post p13).

BIBLIOGRAPHY
Primary Sources
Descartes, R., *Principia philosophiae.*

Secondary Literature
Della Rocca, M., *Spinoza* (London: Routledge, 2008).
Gueroult, M., *Spinoza I. Dieu (Éthique I)* (Hildesheim: Olms, 1968).
Melamed, Y. 'Spinoza's Metaphysics of Substance: the Substance-Mode Relation as a Relation of Inherence and Predication', *Philosophy and Phenomenical Research*, no. 78 (2009), pp. 17–82.

Nyden-Bullock, T., *Spinoza's Radical Cartesian Mind* (London: Continuum, 2007).

Robinson, L., *Kommentar zu Spinozas Ethik* (Leipzig: Meiner, 1928).

Richter, G.T., *Spinozas philosophische Terminologie I: Grundbegriffe der Metaphysik* (Leipzig: Barth, 1913).

H. Krop

Superstitio

The word *superstitio* occurs no less than twenty-six times in the *Tractatus theologico-politicus*, six times both in the *Ethics* and the letters and only once in the *Tractatus politicus*. Two texts in particular explain the meaning of *superstitio* in Spinoza's thought, namely the appendix of *Ethics* 1 and the preface to the TTP. Although in the first passage the word superstition is only used once, it contains a general explanation of its origin, being the prejudice of finalism, the illusion of a free self and anthropocentrism, related to such passions as pride and self-abasement. This genealogical approach towards superstition seems to be a novelty, although Hobbes in *Leviathan* chapter 11 and *De Cive* 16.1 following Lucretius denounced fear as the source of superstition. For contrary to Spinoza both tradition and Hobbes opposed superstition to religion and simply identified it with false religion; see for example Micraelius's definition: 'superstition is a vicious cult' or *Leviathan* chapter 11: 'True Religion – Feare of power invisible, feigned by the mind, or imagined from tales publiquely allowed; not allowed, superstition. And when the power imagined is truly such as we imagine, true religion'.

According to Hobbes superstition is religion, which is both morally *and* intellectually wrong.

A slightly different explanation of the origin of superstition is given in the second text. In the preface to the TTP the word superstition occurs fourteen times. It is argued there that superstition is based on insecurity of fortune, ignorance, passions such as hope and especially fear, and an immoderate desire for uncertain goods. For all this it is postulated that human nature in general is inclined to superstition. Moreover, its false nature makes superstition detrimental to man and society. It is an appropriate means in the hands of rulers and kings to manipulate the multitude. As far as the passionate component of superstition is concerned, there is a domination of the passions of sadness, such as fear, hatred, jealousy, wrath and humility, over those of gladness, such as pride and ambition. So Spinoza calls superstition 'gruff and sad' (E4p45s2).

According to Spinoza superstition is false religion as well. It is false, however, not on account of its erroneous creed or doctrines, but since it is based on illusions and leads to wrong social practices. If the word superstition is used in relation to positive religions, especially Judaism or Christianity, Spinoza refers to their degeneration and decay. Such a degeneration manifests itself in forms of idolatry, for example in veneration of the letter of the Bible, or in a fixation on external ceremonies and rituals at the cost of inner morality (TTP 12). Superstition is characterized by a contempt of reason and (knowledge of) nature. See for example TTP chapter 7: 'To these evils is added superstition, which teaches men to despise reason and nature, and to admire and venerate only that which is opposed to both.' According to Spinoza's letters super-stition is based on prejudice and ignorance as well. See for example letter 73: 'Here I will add only this, that the chief distinction I make between religion and superstition is that the latter is founded on ignorance, the former on wisdom.' Hence contrary to reli-gion superstition has always a negative connotation. Superstition is an important cause of discord and civil strife in the soci-ety and the state. No wonder that Spinoza at the end of chapter 11 of the *Tractatus* expresses the wish 'to see religion freed again from all superstition'. Superstition is a politically dangerous phenomenon, par-ticularly if the civil authority by favouring one sect detracts from the 'freedom to philosophize' and turns religion into super-stition (TTP 17). Hence superstition means serfdom.

TEXTS

Hoc tamen hic addo, me inter religionem et superstitionem hanc praecipue agnoscere differentiam, quod haec ignorantiam, illa autem sapientiam pro fundamento habeat (Ep 73). *Causa a quo superstitione oritur, conservatur et fovetur metus est* (TTP praef., G III, 6). *Ad haec mala accessit superstitio, quae homines rationem & naturam contem-nere docet, & id tantum admirari ac vener-ari, quod huic utrique repugnat* (TTP 7, G III, 97–8). *Iam autem felix profecto nostra esset aetas, si ipsam etiam ab omni supersti-tione liberam videremus* (TTP 11, G III, 158). *Praejudicium in superstitionem versum* (E1app). *Nihil profecto nisi torva et tristis superstitio* (E4p45s2). *Cavendum est ne ipsi Patricii ... superstitione capti libertatem sub-ditis dicendi ea quae sentiunt, adimere stu-deant* (TP 8.46).

BIBLIOGRAPHY

Primary Sources

Hobbes, Th., *De Cive, Leviathan.*

Secondary Literature

Juffermans, P., *Drie perspectieven op religie in het denken van Spinoza. Een onderzoek naar de verschillende betekenissen van religie in het oeuvre van Spinoza* (Budel, Damon, 2003).

Samely, A., *Spinozas Theorie der Religion* (Würzburg: Köningshausen-Neumann, 1993).

Strauss, L., *Die Religionskritik Spinozas als Grundlage seiner Bibelwissenschaft* (Berlin: Akademie-Verlag, 1930).

P.C. Juffermans

Theocratia

Following Hugo Grotius's *Defensio fidei catholica* (1617) and Cunaeus's *De republica Hebraeorum* (1617), Spinoza called the Hebrew state a theocracy. The term had been coined by Flavius Josephus (*Contra Apion*, 2.17), and the Jewish historian added theo-cracy as a fourth regime to the ancient three forms. Unlike Josephus, however, he uses this concept not primarily as a reference to what is effectively a rule of priests, but indeed to a regime in which God rules. Spinoza deliber-ately interpreted the biblical idea of theocracy in a democratic fashion, while rejecting on exegetical grounds a hierocratic reading. The object of his criticism is precisely the rule of priests (TTP 18–19). According to the Pentateuch a theocratic regime prevailed in the period prior to Moses's election as medi-ator between God and the people, and during a limited period after Moses died. After the

Hebrews escaped from Egypt and became a free people, they decided to choose God as their ruler (TTP 17). Religion and state were one. But Spinoza adds to this that God's rule was mere opinion. In fact, Moses ruled as an absolute monarch. However, he did not designate someone as his successor. So, after his death power was divided. This excellent regime (see the *praestantia* in the title of chapter 17) can also be called a theocracy, because the temple served as court, the people were loyal to God as their judge and lawgiver, and a leader was only chosen by God himself.

Two reasons can be given for adding theocracy to the theory of regimes. The first reason is that all regimes are constituted by a transfer of power from the people to a supreme power (TTP 19). Spinoza even sees a similarity between democracy and theocracy, because in both regimes power is transferred without accepting a mediator. The second reason is that this supreme power has an absolute right to rule, and to choose those representing him. In both cases, however, Spinoza is fully aware that it is only through popular imagination that a theocracy can be an effective political order.

eligebatur (TTP 17, G III, 206, 211). *Vel in theocratia, qualis Hebraeorum civitas olim fuit* (TP 7.25).

BIBLIOGRAPHY
Primary Sources
Cunaeus, P., *De republica Hebraeorum* (Leiden, 1617).
Flavius Josephus, *Contra Apion.*
Grotius, H., *Defensio fidei catholica* (1617).

Secondary Literature
Balibar, É., *Spinoza et la politique* (Paris: Presses Universitaires de France, 1985), pp. 55–63.
Taubes, J. (ed), *Religionstheorie und politische Theologie. Bd. 3: Theokratie* (Munich: Fink, 1987).
Terpstra, M., 'De betekenis van de oudtestamentische theocratie voor de politieke filosofie van Spinoza. Een hoofdstuk uit de geschiedenis van de politieke theologie', *Tijdschrift voor filosofie,* no. 60 (1998), pp. 292–320.

M. Terpstra

TEXTS
Videlicet religionis dogmata non documenta, sed jura et mandata erant ... qui a religione deficiebat, civis esse desinebat et absolute jus civile et religio nullo prorsus discrimine habebantur. Et hac de causa hoc imperium theocratia vocari potuit. ... Imperium ab obitu Mosis uti diximus theocraticum, 1. quia imperii domus regia templum erat et sola ejus ratione omnes tribus concives erant, 11. quia omnes cives in fidem Dei supremi sui judicis jurare debebant. Et denique quia summus omnium imperator a nemine nisi a solo Deo

Theologia

From his first published writing in 1663 onwards, Spinoza warned against confusing theology, a kind of (pseudo-)knowledge based on revelation, with philosophy. Their separation, defended in letter 23 as well, is one of the declared main objectives of the *Tractatus theologico-politicus* (chapter 2). Moreover Spinoza attempted to eliminate the prevailing theological prejudices with respect to the Bible, the nature of faith and religion, which tended to transform reason and philosophy into a handmaiden of theology.

In accordance with Christian tradition Spinoza equates theology with the Word of God and Scripture. However, the unique principle of both is merely obedience, he argues, so in opposition to tradition, which distinguished between the distinct knowledge of God acquired by the theologian and the simple, implicit knowledge of God of the proverbial uneducated widow (Voetius, *Selectae disputationes* II, p. 516 and 523), Spinoza identifies theology with simple faith and a purely moral doctrine.

The theme of the basic distinction between theology and philosophy is addressed in TTP 15 where Spinoza argues that neither is reason subjected (*ancillari*) to theology nor theology to reason – in opposition to both Maimonides, who asserts that at least in some cases Scripture has to adapt to reason, and to Jehudah Alfakhar, who wants reason to submit to Scripture. The last view was advanced by at least some orthodox Reformed theologians such as Maresius in his *Systema* 1.16–19 and note to *ancillari*. Maresius accused Cartesian theologians (such as C. Wittich in his *Dissertatio* I) of refusing to accept the complete subservience of philosophy to theology, by assigning to each a different object and a different method: nature to philosophy and salvation to theology. However, sound Christian theology requires a dependence of philosophy which 'of old' was observed in the universities where the study of philosophy prepared students for the study of law, medicine and theology: 'the whole of philosophy remains subservient to theology in a *political* and *despotic* servitude'. Moreover, although theology is based on Scripture alone, 'orthodox' theologians underlined its cognitive nature. Maresius, for example, in his *Systema*

1.16–19 as well as Voetius acknowledged a theoretical dimension of theology alongside the practical one. The latter wrote in *Disputationes selectae I*, disp. 3: 'Faith and our whole theology may be called rational ... for it proves conclusions with scriptural authority and with arguments derived from Scipture among those men who acknowledge some of the divinely revealed truths.' According to Verbeek (2003, p. 108) the view of Maimonides is the view of mainstream Christian tradition, and in the modern period of Descartes and Hobbes. However, recent French scholarship has identified Maimonides's view with Lodewijk Meyer's.

Spinoza rejects the views of Maimonides and Alfakhar and contends that the object of philosophy is truth whereas theology is concerned with piety and obedience only. The first principle of theology (obedience is the salvation of man) cannot be demonstrated rationally; but it is nonetheless the constant object of moral certainty, which means that, at bottom, biblical morality complies with reason without being dependent on it.

To a certain extent Spinoza thus radicalized the non-orthodox view of theology. According to Meyer in *Interpres* 8, p. 58, there is no conflict between philosophical truth and theological truth since both originate from God. Also Arminius (*Opera*, p. 26) and other Remonstrants, such as Episcopius in *Institutiones theologiae* 1.2, underlined the basically practical nature of theology.

TEXTS

CM 2.11–12. *Velim notari, nos, dum philosophice loquimur, non debere phrasibus theologiae uti* (Ep 23). *Vulgus ... putant rationem theologiae ancillari* (TTP praef). *Ad separandam philosophiam a theologia*

327

(TTP 2, G III, 44). *Communia theologiae praejudicia tollere* (TTP 8, G III, 118). *Inter fidem sive theologiam et philosophiam nullum esse commercium* (TTP 14, G III, 179). *Qui philosophiam a theologia separare nesciunt, disputant an num Scriptura rationi, an contra rationem Scripturae debet ancillari ... theologiam sive verbum Dei ... theologiae fundamentale dogma ... hoc totius theologiae et Scripturam fundamentum* (TTP 15, G III, 180–8).

BIBLIOGRAPHY

Primary Sources

Arminius, J., *Opera theologica* (Frankfurt, 1635).

Episcopius, S., *Institutiones theologiae*, in *Opera theologica* I (Amsterdam, 1650).

Maresius, S., *Systema theologicum* (Groningen, 1673).

[Meyer, L.], *Philosophia S. Scripturae interpres* ([Amsterdam], 1666).

Voetius, G., *Selectae disputationes theologicae*, 5 vols (Utrecht, 1648–69).

Wittich, C., *Dissertationes duae* (Amsterdam, 1653).

Secondary Literature

Adler, J., 'Letters of Judah Alfakhar and David Kimhi', *Studia Spinozana*, no. 12 (1996), pp. 141–67.

Lagrée, J., 'Déraisonner avec ou sans la raison. Commentaire du chap. XV du *Traité théologico-politique*', in *Nature, Croyance, Raison. Mélanges offerts à Sylvain Zac* (Fontenay: Publications de l'ENS, 1992), pp. 81–100.

Verbeek, Th., *Spinoza's Theologico-Political Treatise. Exploring 'the Will of God'* (Aldershot: Ashgate, 2003).

R. Bordoli

Tolerantia

Spinoza uses the term *tolerantia* only once, in the Stoic sense of the virtue of constancy in the midst of evil and torture. In the past, therefore, he has rarely been included among the major early modern theorists of toleration along with Locke and Bayle, both because he does not employ the term and because the expression he employs in its place ('freedom to philosophize') is open to being rather narrowly defined. The subtitle of the *Tractatus theologico-politicus* states that the work aims to 'demonstrate that freedom to philosophize may not only be allowed without danger to piety and the stability of the republic but cannot be refused without destroying the peace of the republic and piety itself'. Recently, this has persuaded most commentators that Spinoza both defines LIBERTAS PHILOSOPHANDI broadly and sees it as a vital priority for society, although some commentators still interpret the expression narrowly or even construe it to signify just toleration of Spinoza's own philosophy in particular.

In any case, liberty of worship, conceived as something separate from freedom of thought, is clearly marginal in Spinoza's toleration, so much so that unlike Locke, for whom religious freedom was the crucial aspect of toleration, he scarcely discusses this question in the *Tractatus theologico-politicus* where he chiefly expounds his theory of toleration, though he says more about religious freedom in the *Tractatus politicus*. This marginality of freedom of worship in Spinoza was undoubtedly due to his regarding it as subordinate to what seemed to him the more important question of freedom of judgement. Religious freedom is thus treated as something comprised in but subsidiary to toleration in the wider sense of liberty of thought and expression.

Furthermore, Spinoza is reluctant to allow organized ecclesiastical structures to expand their influence and assert their spiritual authority over individuals, or engage in politics, in the way Locke's theory of toleration encourages churches to do. For Spinoza felt that toleration so structured can have deeply ambivalent results with regard to individual freedom and liberty of expression. He thus establishes a broad distinction between toleration of individual worship which he sees as one thing and empowering churches to extend their authority and following freely which he sees as something altogether different and less desirable. While granting that everyone must be free to express their beliefs no matter what faith they profess, Spinoza simultaneously urges the need for institutionalized constraints on the pretensions and activities of organized religion.

Freedom of expression, then, is what, for Spinoza, principally safeguards individual liberty under the state, leading him to criticize and oppose what he sees as the intolerance of the societies of his time. Here, book censorship posed a particular problem and one which hindered Spinoza in practice and in his private aspirations constantly in his later years. A key aim of his toleration theory, consequently, was to ground freedom for anyone to publish their views however much these may be decried by theologians and by the majority. Indeed, no other early Enlightenment theory of toleration clears a comparably broad path for liberty of the press. For Spinoza, the principle that society may rightly demand of the individual submission with respect to actions but not regarding thoughts, judgement and opinions, meant that men should also be free to express their views in discussion and print. All efforts to curb expression of opinion, he holds, not only subvert legitimate freedom but threaten the stability of the state.

TEXTS
Homines ... ad necem ducantur et quod castata malorum formido pulcherrimum fiat theatrum ad summam tolerantiae et virtutis exemplum (TTP 20, G III, 245).

BIBLIOGRAPHY
Secondary Literature
Israel, J., *Radical Enlightenment. Philosophy and the Making of Modernity* (Oxford: Oxford University Press, 2001).
———, *Enlightenment Contested. Philosophy, Modernity and the Emancipation of Man* (Oxford: Oxford University Press, 2006).

J.I. Israel

Transcendentale

Spinoza sometimes refers to the scholastic doctrine of transcendental terms, such as 'one', 'true', 'good'. 'Metaphysicians', he observes, call them the 'most general affections of being'. Spinoza, however, refrains from presenting a definition and he does not, as was usual, contrast them with the categorical terms, such as 'horse', 'white' and 'big'. In the *Cogitata metaphysica* 1.6 he merely lists them, discussing one by one their origins. Spinoza observed that the 'metaphysicians' falsely believe that 'one' signifies something real outside the intellect. They pretended that 'one' *adds* something to the real thing, but he rejects this position, for they mix up the real with the mere rational being. The transcendental 'one' only denotes a way of thinking (*modus cogitandi*) 'by which we separate one thing from another, when they are similar or for some reason occur together'. 'True' is an extrinsic

DENOMINATIO of a thing as well and 'is neither a name of a quality in the things themselves nor attributes at all except rhetorically'.
Its primary meaning is derived from its use in
ordinary language. Philosophers applied the
term to denote a true idea and only metaphorically a quality of a thing. Hence 'those
who believe that true is a transcendental
term, or an affect of being, are plainly
deceived'. The same applies to the last of the
three transcendental terms dealt with by
Spinoza: 'good'. 'Good' cannot be applied to
a thing as such, but we call a thing 'good'
because it is useful to us. Good expresses a
relation; so God cannot be called 'good'
before he created the world. Apparently
Spinoza refers to the theory of the transcendental terms in order to refute it and underline his overall 'nominalist' stance.

A comparable 'archeological' theory of the
transcendental is outlined in E2p40s1, where
Spinoza also discusses the origin of the 'common notions', which are the basis of our reasoning, the 'secondary notions' and the
universals. Here he lists the transcendentals
'being', 'thing' and 'something'. The
transcendentals, the secondary notions and
the universals are 'confused', he says, because
they concern a number of images, too large
for the limited capacity of the human body,
and 'inadequate' (which refers to their problematic relation to the nature of things), in
contradistinction to the common notions,
which are adequate. All these common
notions are useful, but whereas the transcendentals and the other notions originate in
imagination, the common notions are produced by reason.

In the seventeenth-century dictionaries the
transcendentale plays only a minor part.
Goclenius, for example, does not deal with
the term at all. Alsted defined: 'a
transcendental is a term which transcends

the categories either due to its great generality or because of its dignity'. Chauvin adds
that such general beings are only dealt with
in metaphysics and observes in a seemingly
cavilling manner that a definition like Alsted's might seem blasphemous to some, for
God, the object of the most eminent part of
metaphysics, is assimilated to the most
abstract beings. Moreover the most general
beings are the most abstract, which are conceived by the most confused and imperfect
concepts. Apparently Spinoza criticized a
theory already in disrepute among his contemporaries, perhaps with the exception of
the teachers in the schools.

The doctrine of the transcendental terms
originated in the Middle Ages. Philip the
Chancellor in his *Summa* dating from 1225
to 1228 was the first to develop a theory: the
transcendental terms refer to the 'most general things', viz. being, one, true and good.
One is primary, and negatively defined as
'lacking division'. Already Thomas Aquinas's
metaphysics focused in part on the doctrine.
We find his conception primarily in his *Dis-
puted Questions on Truth*, qu. 1, art. 1. When
we ask what something is, Thomas says, we
cannot go on infinitely. We have to arrive at
something which is first, viz. being, the end of
our intellectual reduction. All other conceptions are additions to being, not extrinsically,
but in as far as they express a mode which is
not contained in 'being'. These modes may be
either special, which are the ten categories, or
general, which are 'thing', 'one', 'something',
'good', 'true'. Aquinas underlined that a transcendental can imply a relation, e.g. 'true'
implies a relation of some thing to the intellect. A new chapter in the history of the
theory of the transcendentals was written by
John Duns Scotus (1265–1308/9). According
to him a transcendental term does not need
to be applicable to every category. Duns

Scotus accepts the transcendental terms as listed by Philip the Chancellor and Aquinas, but extends this list to include the 'disjunctive attributes of being', such as 'infinite or finite', 'capable of causing or capable of being caused', 'necessary or contingent'.

After the Middle Ages Suarez in *Disputationes metaphysicae* III questions the Scotist doctrine and argued that the transcendental terms are only created by the intellect and do not 'truly and really convene with being'. He observed 'that being as such cannot have true, completely real and positive passions' which are 'by nature' distinct from 'being'. Hence, he refuted the traditional premise that a transcendental term refers to an entity added to a thing. What is more, Suarez and Fonseca reduced Aquinas's set of five transcendental terms to the three Spinoza mentioned in the *Cogitata metaphysica*, since *aliquid* and *res* are merely synonymous with being. Suarez's theory is reproduced by Burgersdijk in his *Institutiones metaphysicae* I, chapter 10 and although he deals with them in pairs – unity and plurality (chap. 11), truth and falsehood (chap. 17) and good and bad (chap. 19) – cf. CM 1.6 – he like Spinoza does not use the Scotist notion of 'disjunctive attributes'.

'New philosophers' either completely ignored the doctrine, like Descartes, or like Bacon attempted to construe a non-scholastic theory. According to *De dignitate et augmentis scientiarum* III, chapter 1 the study of transcendentals is part of first philosophy which is ancient in name but novel in substance. First philosophy is the mother of all sciences and deals with their common axioms. Moreover it studies the transcendental terms such as 'possible and impossible', 'more or less', 'much and little', 'prior and posterior', the 'same and diverse', which denote the concomitant conditions of being.

This part of first philosophy augments our ability to reason, but it does not teach us the 'existence of things'. It for example does not explain why the amount of gold in nature is not the same as the amount of iron. Like Spinoza later he maintains that their significance is only of an epistemological nature. Hobbes denies that the doctrine has any use. Like Spinoza in the *Cogitata metaphysica*, Hobbes in his *Computatio* 2.7 observed that 'truth is not an affection of the things, but of a proposition' and 'when metaphysicians say, that a thing, one thing and a very thing are equivalent to one another, it is but trifling and childish'. This censure of scholastic logic was shared by many Cartesians. In his *Cogitata de interpretatione* Johannes de Raey rejected the traditional doctrine that a universal concept denotes 'a thing which by its nature is capable of being predicated of many things' and 'there is no universal in being' (VII, p. 550). Hence the universal – and the *transcendentale* – is merely a mode of considering.

TEXTS

Ad vulgo dictos terminos transcendentales transeo ... Hi termini ab omne fere metaphysicis pro generalissimis entis affectionibus habentur; dicunt enim omne ens esse unum, verum et bonum, quamvis nemo de iis cogitet (CM 1.5–6). *Ne quid horum omittam quod scitu necessarium sit causis breviter addam, ex quibus termini 'transcendentales' dicti suam duxerunt originem, ut ens, res, aliquid. Hi termini ex hoc oriuntur, quod scilicet humanum corpus, quandoquidem limitatum est, tantum est capax certi imaginum numeri ... in se distincte simul formandi* (E2p40s1). *Termino aliquo transcendentali formam alicujus rei singularis explicare* (TTP 1, G III, 28).

BIBLIOGRAPHY

Primary Sources

Bacon, F., *De dignitate et augmentis scientiarum* (London, 1623).

Burgersdijk, F., *Institutiones metaphysicae* (Leiden, 1642).

Hobbes, Th., *Computatio sive logica*, in *Elementorum philosophiae sectio prima De Corpore*, (London, 1655).

Raey, J. de, *Cogitata de interpretatione* (Amsterdam, 1692).

Suarez, F., *Disputationes metaphysicae* (Mainz, 1597).

Secondary Literature

Aertsen, J.A. 'The Medieval Doctrine of the Transcendentals. The Current State of Research', *Bulletin de philosophie médiévale*, no. 33 (1991), pp. 130–47.

Hubbeling, H.G., *Spinoza's Methodology* (Assen: Van Gorcum, 1964).

Knittermeyer, H., *Der Terminus transszendental in seiner historischen Entwicklung bis zu Kant* (Marburg: Hamel, 1920).

Pickavé, M. (ed.), *Die Logik des Transcendentalen. Festschrift für Jan A. Aertsen zum 65. Geburtstag* (Berlin and New York: Springer Verlag, 2003).

Verbeek, Th., 'Zijn en niet-zijn in Spinoza's *Cogitata metaphysica*', in G. Coppens (ed.), *Spinoza en de scholastiek* (Leuven: Acco, 2003), pp. 91–103.

Vona, P. de, *Spinoza e i Trascendentali* (Naples: Morano, 1974).

E.P. Bos

Utile / Utilitas

According to scholastic tradition the useful denotes a secondary good. Chauvin observed that a useful thing, i.e. a commodity, is an extrinsic good or a means to some primary final good. He adds that the relation between means and end is an objective one existing 'by nature'. Hence, only for beings in need of something else a useful thing may exist. There is nothing that can be useful to the most perfect being.

Man, as a finite being, has limited powers to preserve himself and therefore there are many things of use to him. This ontology implies that Spinoza uses the term in particular with respect to man. Since the desire for self-preservation is the essence of man, the most fundamental needs for man are those that support him in the realization of this end. However, all individuals are different, therefore their strivings for self-preservation are different as well. Each individual attempts to persevere in its being according to 'the laws of his own nature' (E4p19).

Moreover, it is by reason that a man is able to distinguish between the things which are truly useful to him and those which are only seemingly useful. Since according to Spinoza reason does not demand anything 'contrary to nature', seeking one's own advantage and striving for what is really useful to him is rational (E4p18s). This naturalism implies that Spinoza is able to identify the useful both with the virtuous and the good. For just like the useful the good is what supports the striving for self-preservation (E4p19).

The useful bridges the gap between Spinoza's moral theory and his social philosophy. Although individuals are different in character, desires and affects, for example, the similarities are more important. That the nature of one human being is more akin to the nature of another human being than to the nature of, say, a dog or a horse, is obvious. Hence, men who share something in their natures can increase their power by joining each other. Since power is the most useful thing to us it follows that '[t]o man there is nothing more useful than man' (E4p18s), because agreement is most likely between men. But men agree with each other only insofar as they are reasonable (E4p35). Their affective lives may make them very different and therefore dangerous for each other. Therefore a free or reasonable person tries to avoid the dangers of unreasonable human beings and will even avoid their favours which are most likely not useful to him (E4p70).

TEXTS

Quae mihi cum ratione convenire videntur, eadem ad virtutem maxime esse utilia credo (Ep 68). *Cum melior pars nostri sit intellectus, verum est, si nostrum utile quaerere velimus, nos supra omnia debere conari ut eum perficiamus* (TTP 4, G III, 59). *Humana natura constitutum est, omnes suum utile quaerunt* (TTP 5, 73). *Unusquisque sibi utile vel ductu sanae rationis, vel ex affectuum impetu judicat* (TTP 16, 190). *[Leges] humanae rationis non nisi hominum verum utile et conservationem intendunt* (TP 2.8), E1app. *Unusquisque ex suo affectu rem aliquam bonam, aut malam, utilem, aut inutilem esse judicat* (E3p39s). *Actiones quae solum agentis utile intendunt ad animositatem refero* (E3p59s). *Per bonum id intelligam, quod certo scimus nobis esse utile* (E4def1). *Homini nihil homine utilius* (E4p18s). *Quo magis unusquisque suum utile quaerere, hoc est suum esse conservare conatur, et potest eo magis virtute praeditus*

(E4p20). *Ex virtute agere nihil aliud est, ... idque quam ex fundamento proprium utile quaerendi* (E4p24). *Homini liberi sibi invicem utilissimi* (E4p71). E4app4, 9, 12.

BIBLIOGRAPHY
Secondary Literature
De Dijn, Herman, 'Theory and Practice and the Practices of Theory', in Marcel Senn and Manfred Walther (eds), *Ethik, Recht und Politik bei Spinoza. Vorträge des 6. Internationalen Kongresses der Spinoza Gesellschaft* (Zürich: Schultess, 2001), pp. 47–58.
Jarrett, Ch., 'Spinoza on the Relativity of Good and Evil', in O. Koistinen and J. Biro (eds), *Spinoza: Metaphysical Themes* (Oxford: Oxford University Press, 2002), pp. 159–81.
Wolf, J.C., 'Menschliche Unfreiheit und Desillusionierung (4praef-4p18)', in M. Hampe and R. Schnepf (eds), *Baruch de Spinoza. Ethik* (Berlin: Akademie Verlag, 2006), pp. 197–214.

M. Hampe

Vacuum

There are two main texts in which Spinoza discusses the vacuum (Dutch, *ijdel*), which he defines as 'extension without corporeal substance' (PPC 2d5). The first is his summary of Descartes's *Principia philosophiae*, which includes the argument in that text for the impossibility of a vacuum. This argument proceeds from the premises that the nature of corporeal substance consists in extension and that space does not differ *in re* from space to the conclusion that there can be no space without corporeal substance, that is, no vacuum (2p3).

Spinoza no doubt had this argument in mind when he appealed in E1p15s to his discussion 'elsewhere' of the vacuum (though there is also a mention of the vacuum in the earlier unpublished *Korte verhandeling*). But whereas in the earlier argument Spinoza repeated Descartes's claim that the extension of corporeal substance that fills space is divisible without limit, in the *Ethics* he took the impossibility of a vacuum to show that corporeal substance is indivisible. The argument here is that given the impossibility of a vacuum, a part of extension cannot be annihilated with all the other parts remaining as they are. But then the parts cannot be 'really distinct' in the precise Cartesian sense of being able to exist without the others. Rather, 'all must concur' in such a way that there is no gap in the extension of corporeal substance. Though the parts of matter can be distinguished 'insofar as we conceive matter to be affected in different ways', this distinction is only a modal and not a real one. Extension itself remains absolutely indivisible 'insofar as it is substance'.

TEXTS

KV 1.2; *Repugnat ut detur vacuum* (PPC 2p3). *Vacuum est extensio sine substantia corporea* (PPC 2d5); PPC 2p8s. *Cum igitur vacuum in natura non detur (de quo alias), sed omnes partes ita concurrere debent, ne detur vacuum, sequitur hinc etiam, easdem non posse realiter distingui, hoc est substantiam corpoream, quatenus substantia est, non posse dividi* (E1p15s).

BIBLIOGRAPHY
Primary Sources
Descartes, R., *Principia philosophiae*.

Bayle, P., *Dictionnaire historique et critique*, art. 'Spinoza'.

Secondary Literature
Bennett, J., 'Spinoza's Vacuum Argument', *Midwest Studies in Philosophy*, no. 5 (1980), pp. 381–9.
Grant, E., *Much Ado about Nothing: Theories of Space and the Vacuum from the Middle Ages to the Scientific Revolution* (Cambridge: Cambridge University Press, 1981).
Gueroult, M., *Spinoza* I: *Dieu* (Hildesheim: Olms, 1968), app. 10.
Schmaltz, T.M., 'Spinoza on the Vacuum,' *Archiv für Geschichte der Philosophie*, no. 81 (1999), pp. 174–205.

T.M. Schmaltz

Veritas

Just like Descartes Spinoza at least nominally subscribed to the traditional correspondence theory of truth. In axiom 6 of *Ethics* 1 he defines: 'a true idea must agree with its object (*ideatum*)'. In this axiom he implicitly identified the abstract concept 'truth' with a true idea. For: 'If you inquire what truth is beyond a true idea, you do the same thing as to ask what whiteness is beyond a white object'. However, according to the same *Cogitata metaphysica* 1.6 such definitions or correspondence originated in ordinary language. In explaining the traditional philosophical concept of truth Spinoza adopted a genealogical approach by asking for its 'primary significance'. Apparently 'true' was first attributed to stories, he observed. 'A narration was true which was in accord with the facts which it concerned; that was false which was not in accord with the facts of the case'.

Only afterwards 'philosophers' usurped 'truth' for denoting the correspondence of an idea with the thing it represents. 'An idea is true which represents the thing, as it is in itself.... For ideas are nothing else than mental narratives or histories of nature'. Finally truth is only metaphorically attributed to things in the external world. 'As for example, when we speak of true or false gold, as if the gold which we perceive might tell us something about itself that was in it or not.' Accordingly truth in this ontological or 'transcendental' sense is merely a rhetorical device. Apparently from the very beginning of his philosophical career Spinoza rejected the traditional theories of truth, or considered them to be of minor significance, since the agreement of an idea with its object is only an extrinsic denomination or an accidental property (E2def4). In the *Tractatus de intellectus emendatione* he argues that an idea may be true although nothing in the world actually corresponds to it and it may be false even if an object is in agreement with the idea. 'If an artisan has duly conceived a machine his thought is true even if if there has never been nor will be such a machine, wheras if someone says, for example, that Peter exists but does not know that Peter exists, that thought is false.' Hence, truth denotes the intrinsic quality of ideas, which are perfect and adequate, that is clear and distinct. The truth of ideas is due to God's intellect in which they exist objectively (E1p17s). In the *Ethics* the distinction between adequate ideas (E2def4) and true ideas (E1ax6) is a minor one. As he explains in letter 60: 'Between a true and an adequate idea I recognise no difference but this, that the word "true" has regard only to the agreement of the idea with its object (*ideatum*) whereas the word "adequate" has regard to the nature of the idea in itself.' The perfection

of such an idea, Spinoza observed, being equivalent with its truth, guarantees the correspondence of the idea with the object conceived by the mind. In this sense the truth is the standard of itself (E2p43s).

The author of the *Ethics* opposes truth to falsehood which consists in the *privatio* of knowledge because there is nothing positive in the ideas whereby they can be said to be false (E2p33). False ideas are mutilated ones, which being confused are imperfect ones.

All knowledge of the human body (E2p19), the human mind (E2p23) and the external bodies (E2p26) begins for Spinoza with affections of the body. Simultaneously with these affections, the mind has inadequate ideas of the affecting bodies. On the other hand, the ideas of those bodies that are common to all bodies, and are equally in a part of any body as in the whole, are necessarily adequate (E2p38). These ideas are also true because they correspond with the ideas in God, which all completely agree with their objects (E2p32).

TEXTS

Patet quod ad certitudinem veritatis nullo alio signo sit opus quam veram habere ideam (TIE 35, G II, 15). *Veritas se ipsam patefacit* (TIE 44, G II, 17). *Quod formam veri constituit, certum est cogitationem veram a falsa non tantum per denominationem extrinsecam, sed maxime per intrinsecam distingui. Nam si quis faber ordine concepit fabricam aliquam, quamvis talis fabrica numquam existerit, nec etiam unquam existura sit, ejus nihilominus cogitatio vera est et cogitatio eadem est, sive fabrica exstat sive minus, et contra si aliquis dicit Petrum ex. gr. existere, nec tamen scit, Petrum existere, illa cogitatio respectu illius falsa est* (TIE 69, G II, 26). *Philosophi postea usurparunt ad denotandum convenientiam ideae cum suo ideato: quare idea vera dicitur*

illa quae nobis ostendit rem ut in se est. ...
Atque postea metaphorice translata est ad res
mutas, ut cum dicimus verum aurum, quasi
aurum nobis repraesentatum aliquid de sei
ipsum narret, quod in se est. Proprietates ver-
itatis aut ideae verae sunt: 1. quod sit clara et
distincta. 2. quod omne dubium tollat, sive
quod sit certa (CM 1.6). *Inter ideam veram et*
adaequatam nullam aliam differentiam agno-
sco, quam quid nomen veri respiciat tantum-
modo convenientiam ideae cum suo ideato;
nomen adaequati autem naturam ideae in se
ipsae; ita ut revera nulla detur differentia inter
ideam veram et adaequatam praeter illam rela-
tionem extrinsecam (Ep 60). *Veritas et forma-*
lis essentia (E1p17s). *Qui veram habet ideam,*
simul scit se veram habere ideam (E2p43).

BIBLIOGRAPHY
Primary Sources
Descartes, R., *Meditationes de prima*
  philosophia.

Secondary Literature
Ellsipen, Ch., 'Die Erkenntnisarten', in
  M. Hampe and R. Schnepf (eds), *Baruch*
  de Spinoza, Ethik (Berlin: Akademie-
  Verlag, 2006), pp. 133–50.
Verbeek, Th., *Spinoza's Theologico-Political*
  Treatise. Exploring 'the Will of God'
  (Aldershot: Ashgate, 2003).

F. Buyse

Virtus

Spinoza's use of the term *virtus* reflects
the ways in which traditional ethical
vocabulary changed as it was appropriated
in the philosophical reflection of the seventeenth century. According to Chauvin for
example, virtue is ambiguous. In a broad
sense it means the power or the perfection of
any thing whatsoever, be it either natural or
supernatural, either innate or acquired. In a
stricter sense it refers to the Aristotelian concept of a habit, which perfects a man by its
corresponding action.

Occasionally Spinoza uses the term in its
broad meaning of 'power' (as in the 'power
to prophesy' in the *Tractatus theologico-*
politicus or the infinite powers of God: in the
Cogita metaphysica he speaks of God five
times as being 'of infinite power'). Usually,
though, in all of the major works the term
connotes both power and the traditional
moral virtues – albeit moral virtues reinter-
preted in the light of Spinoza's systematic
account of human nature.

From the ancients (especially Aristotle and
the Stoics) Spinoza inherited a complex conception of virtue that combines elements of
strength and power with the notion of the
characteristic excellences that mark an individual as a good exemplar of its kind. Spinoza
is not very interested in different natural kinds
per se, for he has argued that all things are
naturally characterized by the same essential
conatic endeavour to persevere in being. Still,
there are differences among species and
among individuals that must be acknowledged. The definition of *virtus* in *Ethics* 4
seeks to do justice to the complexity of the
situation by identifying virtue and power, in
so far as both are related to man's essence, or
the nature of man. This definition is found at
the beginning of part four, and the term *virtus*
is used more than thirty times in the remainder of the *Ethics*. Since virtue is nothing but
acting from the laws of one's nature, and the
conatus principle is the most basic law of
one's nature, it follows that the striving to
persevere in being is the foundation of virtue
(E4p18s). In a passage reminiscent of the

early arguments of Aristotle's *Nicomachean Ethics* Spinoza reasons that virtue being an ultimate end is wanted for its own sake.

Spinoza's technical understanding of the terms ACTIO and IDEA ADEQUATA leads to the conclusion that one can only be said to act from virtue (or indeed to *act* at all) if one is determined to do something because one has adequate ideas. But for Spinoza reason is understood in terms of having adequate ideas, so virtue regains its traditional connection with reason – albeit in a characteristically Spinozistic fashion by identifying reason with seeking one's own advantage (E4p24). Since real knowledge is grounded in knowledge of God, 'the mind's greatest virtue' is knowledge of God (E4p28).

To the extent that people live in accordance with reason, they agree in nature. Moreover, since knowledge of God is not a zero-sum good, it might be shared on an equal basis with all lovers of virtue (E4p36). The phrase 'those who seek virtue' is used repeatedly, and is a somewhat surprising locution since, of course, everyone strives to persevere and everyone seeks the power (the virtue) to do so. Presumably Spinoza's phrase refers to those who rightly understand the centrality of reason for virtue and who 'seek virtue' under the guidance of reason.

Near the end of part four of the *Ethics* Spinoza explicitly considers the ethical status of certain emotions or character traits that have traditionally been reckoned as virtues. Using power as the measuring stick, he declares that pity, repentance and humility do not qualify as virtues. The description of the 'free man' that closes part four does not say much about virtue per se, but it can be read as an account of the truly virtuous person. In the end, blessedness (BEATITUDO) itself has been identified with the active knowledge of God and thus with virtue. So the final proposition of the *Ethics* states that such bliss is no reward, but is virtue.

TEXTS

Infinitae virtutis (CM 2.10). *Virtus ad prophetandum* (TTP 11, G III, 155). *Per virtutem et potentiam idem intelligo, hoc est (per Prop. 7, p. 3) virtus quatenus ad hominum refertur est ipsa hominis essentia, seu natura, quatenus potestatem habet, quaedam efficiendi, quae solas per ipsius naturae leges possunt intelligi* (E4def8). *Quandoquidem virtus nihil aliud est, quam ex legibus propriae naturae agere, et nemo suum esse conservare conetur, nisi ex propriae naturae agere* (E4p18s). *Ex virtute absolutè agere, nihil aliud in nobis est quam ex ductu rationis agere, vivere, suum esse conservare (haec tria idem significant) ex fundamento proprium utile quaerendi* (E4p24). *Summum mentis bonum est Dei cognitio, et summa mentis virtus Deum cognoscere* (E4p28). *Summum bonum eorum, qui virtutem sectantur, omnibus commune est, eoque omnes aeque gaudere possunt* (E4p36). *Beatitudo non est virtus praemium; sed ipsa virtus* (E5p42).

BIBLIOGRAPHY
Secondary Literature
Garrett, D., 'Spinoza's Ethical Theory', in D. Garrett (ed.), *The Cambridge Companion to Spinoza* (Cambridge: Cambridge University Press, 1996), pp. 267–314.
Wolfson, H. A., *The Philosophy of Spinoza: Unfolding the Latent Processes of His Reasoning* (Cambridge, MA: Harvard University Press, 1934; reprinted in 2 vols, New York: Schocken, 1969).

T. Cook

Voluntas

Expressed in his peculiar metaphysical terminology, Spinoza's doctrine of the will was a novelty in the history of philosophy. According to this theory, neither the divine infinite nor the human finite will are part of the unchanging essence of the mind. Even God's will belongs to 'natured nature'. In Spinoza's view they are only modifications of the attribute of Thought (E1p31s). Being a mode of thinking, an act of willing is always produced by another cause, which incites the will to act. Hence the will is not a free, but a necessary cause (E1p32). The fiction that our will is free results from a lack of insight into the causal order of nature (E1app). What is more, the will is constituted by specific acts of willing. Accordingly the Aristotelian faculty of the will is a fiction, since the will is merely a metaphysical 'abstract' entity, like the universal. It is a rational entity, with no reality beyond the particular acts of willing and the ideas contained in the human mind at a specific moment in time. The will does not exist as something real in nature. As real entities only individual volitions exist, for which the term 'will' is used as a general name (KV 2.16; E2p48; Ep 2). Typical of Spinoza is thirdly the notion that the will is not essentially different from the understanding (E2p49c). A volition is the affirmation of the negation entailed in an idea. In other words thinking is the formation of ideas and at the same time the making of judgements. This faculty of making judgements is distinguished by Spinoza from desire (E2p48s). However, the making of judgements is not a purely intellectual activity, but follows directly from the human essence which in all its operations strives for self-preservation. So also judging is an existential activity influencing the conatus. In calling the conatus in as far as we are conscious of it 'will', Spinoza reformulates the traditional notion of the will as 'the appetitive or aversive faculty'. Will is nothing but a tendency of the mind to retain ideas agreeable to it, and to reject those which are distasteful.

The tendency to identify will and intellect was apparently inherent in modern philosophy. Chauvin observed that 'since according to modern philosophers the intellect is the same as the knowing soul, the will is identical with the willing soul as well. Hence intellect and will are no more differentiated than by a modal distinction'. Apparently, in this respect Descartes, who assumed two distinct faculties and two corresponding categories of acts of the mind, was an exception (PP 1.33). Spinoza rejected Descartes's doctrine that, in order to turn an affirmation into a belief, it is necessary to resort to non-intellectual acts of will (Ep 21). Thought has no forms at all that do not consist solely of forming and retaining ideas. According to Spinoza, the origin of error is not the will – as in Descartes – but vague, inadequate knowledge (E2p49; cf. PPC praef).

As will and intellect are one and the same, it follows that the development of the one runs parallel with that of the other. To the imagination, which represents things according to our impressions, corresponds, in the practical sphere, passion, or the instinctive movement which impels us towards an object or makes us shrink from it. When what the imagination shows us is of such a nature as to give our physical and moral life a greater intensity, or, in other words, when a thing is agreeable and we strive for it, this wholly elementary form of willing is called desire, love, joy or pleasure. In the opposite case, it is called aversion, hatred, fear or grief.

To the higher understanding corresponds, in the practical sphere, the will enlightened by reason, and determined, not by what is agreeable, but by what is true. Man acts when anything happens either within him or outside of him of which he is the adequate cause. On the other hand, man is passive when something happens within him or follows from his nature of which he is but the partial cause (E3def2). However active man may seem in his passions, he is really passive in the proper sense of the term: i.e. limited, impotent, or the slave of things. He can be made free and become active only through the understanding. To understand the universe is to be delivered from it. To understand everything is to be absolutely free. Passion ceases to be a passion as soon as we form a clear idea of it (E3p59; E5p3). Hence, freedom is found in thought and thus our knowledge of things is the measure of our morality. That is morally good which is conducive to the understanding; that is bad which hinders and diminishes it (E4p26 and 27).

TEXTS

Te onderzoeken, wat bij die geene die de wille stellen, de wille is en waar ... dog aangezien de wil een idee is van dit of dat te willen ... de algemeene wille een wijze van denken (KV 2.16). Na Aristotelis beschrijving scheijnt de wille te zijn die lust of trek die men heeft onder scheijn van goet (KV 2.17). *Voluntatem distinctam ab intellectu, multo minus tali praeditam esse libertate* (PPC praef). *Voluntas differt ab hac et illa volitione, eodem modo ac albedo ab hoc et illo albo ... Cum igitur voluntas non sit, nisi ens rationis* (Ep 2). *Cum Cartesio dico si voluntatem nostram extra limites intellectus nostri valde limitati non possumus nos*

miserrimos futuros (Ep 21). *Voluntas non potest vocari causa libera, sed tantum necessaria ... Voluntas certus tantum cogitandi modus est sicuti intellectus ... adeoque unaquaeque volitio non potest existere neque ad operandum determinari, nisi ab alia causa determinetur* (E1p32). *In mente nulla absoluta sive libera voluntas* (E2p48). *Eodem hoc modo demonstratur in Mente nullam dari facultatem absolutam intelligendi, cupiendi, amandi, etc. Unde sequitur, has, et similes facultates, vel prorsus fictitias, vel nihil esse praeter entia metaphysica, sive universalia* (E2p48s). *Voluntas et intellectus unum et idem sunt* (E2p49c). *Voluntatem ens esse universale, sive ideam, qua omnes singulares volitiones, hoc est id quod iis omnibus commune est explicamus* (Ep49s). *Hic conatus ... cum ad mentem solam refertur voluntas appellatur* (E3p9s). *Unius hominis voluntas varia et inconstans est* (TP 7.3).

BIBLIOGRAPHY
Primary Sources
Descartes, R., *Principia philosophiae, Meditationes.*

Secondary Literature
Gueroult, M., *Spinoza II – L'âme* (Paris: Aubier-Montaigne, 1974).

L. Spruit

5

SHORT SYNOPSES OF SPINOZA'S WRITINGS

Works published by Spinoza

During his lifetime, Spinoza published two works: *Renati Des Cartes Principia philosophiae* with its appendix *Cogitata metaphysica*(1663), and *Tractatus theologico-politicus* (1670, anonymously). He made preparations to have the *Ethica* printed in 1675, but abandoned the publication in view of the increasingly hostile atmosphere. The work did not come out until after Spinoza died, as the *pièce de résistance* of his *Opera posthuma* (1677, henceforth OP). In that volume, the philosopher's friends also included three unfinished texts: the early *Tractatus de intellectus emendatione*, a concise Hebrew grammar (*Compendium grammatices linguae Hebraeae*) and the treatise he was working on when he died, the *Tractatus politicus*. In addition, the OP contains a collection of 75 letters (*Epistolae*), sent by and to Spinoza.

Texts subsequently discovered; lost and spurious works; manuscripts

Since the seventeenth century, only one major new find has been added to this quantitatively modest *oeuvre*: the *Korte verhandeling van God, de mensch en deszelvs welstand* (Short Treatise), two manuscripts of which were discovered in the 1850s. Apart from that, the annotations to the *Tractatus*

theologico-politicus and about a dozen previously unknown letters have come to the surface. No further works by Spinoza are extant. He is reported to have written (in Spanish) a vindication of his dissent from Judaism after his excommunication in 1656, often referred to as *Apologia*, but no traces of this have been found (Walther and Czelinski, 2006, vol. 1, p. 399, no. 186). According to the editors of the posthumous works Spinoza also wrote a small treatise on the rainbow, but had presumably burnt it (Walther and Czelinski, 2006, vol. 1, p. 4). At any rate, it is certainly not the *Stelkonstige reeckening van den regenboog* (Algebraic Calculation of the Rainbow) that was published in The Hague in 1687, together with the *Reeckening van kanssen* (Calculation of Probabilities). Though both texts are still to be found in editions and translations of Spinoza's works, they are spurious. Their author has now been identified with certainty as Salomon Dierquens (De Vet, 2005). Spinoza's early biographer Colerus also reports – on the authority of what he calls people of distinction, who had seen the manuscript – that Spinoza wrote a treatise on the rainbow, but burnt it in the summer of 1676. In addition, Colerus passes on the (prima facie rather implausible) story that Spinoza had begun a Dutch translation of the Old

Testament; the Pentateuch had been finished long since, but he burnt it some days before he died (Walther and Czelinski, 2006, vol. 1, p. 146). The bulk of Spinoza's works survived in printed versions only. Though we know that some letters and several of his works (KV, E) circulated in manuscript, the only remnant of this is the oldest KV apograph. The autographs and fair copies that served as copy for the typesetters were presumably thrown away. A few letters (beautifully reproduced by Meijer, 1903) and a TTP copy with annotations in Spinoza's handwriting (Van der Werf, 2006) are still extant.

Languages, translations

A child of Portuguese-Jewish parents in Amsterdam, Spinoza spoke Portuguese at home, Spanish at school and in the synagogue, and he received a solid training in Hebrew. He had enough Dutch to write some of his letters in Dutch (albeit reluctantly: Ep 19; G IV, 95:12). Spinoza attended the Latin School of Franciscus van den Enden in Amsterdam. His Latin style is sober, clear and effective (Leopold, 2005; Kajanto, 2005; Beyssade, 2005; Akkerman, 2013). He composed all his philosophical works in Latin, the international language of scholarly communication. The KV did come down to us in Dutch, but this is a contemporary translation of a lost Latin original. Dutch renderings of his works were in great demand: a translation of PPC/CM came out in 1664, the TTP was immediately translated into Dutch but remained unpublished for a long time (Akkerman, 2005), the instalments of the Latin *Ethics* that Spinoza sent to the Amsterdam circle of friends were translated upon arrival, at least initially (see Ep 28: G IV, 163:19–24). The OP came out simultaneously with a Dutch version, *De nagelate schriften van B.d.S.* (henceforth NS).

1. Treatise on the Emendation of the Intellect | Tractatus de intellectus emendatione (TIE)

Though published posthumously, the TIE was written much earlier. Scholarship is still divided as to the chronological order of TIE and KV, but there is general agreement that these two unfinished texts constitute Spinoza's earliest known works. Though the chronology proposed by Mignini (in Mignini, 1979, and elaborated since), according to which the TIE precedes the KV, is not entirely conclusive, it is the best hypothesis developed so far, and it has in practice been adopted by many recent translators and commentators. Mignini suggests that Spinoza may have started writing the TIE as early as the end of 1656 or the beginning of 1657.

The TIE is sometimes referred to in Spinoza's correspondence as a work in progress. Apparently he never abandoned the idea of finishing it, but towards the end of his life he seems no longer very keen on revising it, either (Ep 60; G IV, 271:8–9). The text as we have it was published in the OP in 1677, from a manuscript presumably found among Spinoza's papers. The Latin of the TIE appears to have been edited by the OP editors more heavily than his other texts (Akkerman, 1987, pp. 25–6).

The TIE is composed as one continual text, without any captions. In volume two (1844) of his edition of Spinoza's complete works, K.H. Bruder introduced a division into 110 numbered sections. This is now generally used. Halfway through the text, in § 49, Spinoza offers an outline, in which he presents the argument as consisting of seven parts. Three parts had already been dealt with in the preceding 48 sections: (1) an introduction, setting forth the end to which all our thoughts should be directed (§§ 1–17); (2) an analysis of the modes of perception, in order to find the best mode to reach perfection (§§ 18–29); (3) the mind must investigate nature proceeding from a given true idea as the norm (§§ 30–48). The treatise was to continue with: (4) the 'first part of the method', showing how a true idea differs from all other perceptions, which the mind should avoid (§§ 50–90); (5) the 'second part of the method', setting down the rules for perceiving unknown things with the help of the norm of the given true idea (§§ 91–8); (6) establishing an order so as not to be waylaid by trifles (§§ 99–110, unfinished); (7) the most perfect method, which relies on the idea of the most perfect being (not realized).

(1) §§ 1–17. The opening pages of the TIE are justly famous for their vivid (and purportedly autobiographical) presentation of the author's quest for the *summum bonum* (see Zweerman, 1993; De Dijn, 1996, pp. 30–41): would it be possible, through a change in one's life plan, to attain a true and highest good, one from which eternal joy would follow? The only good that will fill the mind with a joy exempt from sadness, is (as Spinoza will substantiate later) knowledge of the mind's union with nature as a whole (§ 8), and love for something eternal and infinite (§ 10). Though good and bad, perfect and imperfect are relative notions, we know that we can become more perfect, i.e. acquire a stronger and more enduring human nature. A 'true good' is then defined as something that can be a means to attaining such a more perfect human nature; the 'highest good' is to enjoy such perfection (§ 13). The aim, then, is to acquire this nature, and to stimulate as many other people as possible to strive to attain it, too. This requires an understanding of the laws of nature as well as a reorganization of society (§ 14). First and foremost, however, we must work out a way

of healing the intellect, and that is what this treatise intends to do (§ 16). In the meantime, however, we need provisional rules for living. Spinoza formulates three such rules: speak to the understanding of the people; enjoy pleasure only insofar as it will preserve health; seek money and goods only insofar as they are necessary for self-preservation or socially inevitable (§ 17).

(2) §§ 18–29. The distinction between four modes of perception or cognition is manifestly akin to – though not identical with – the tripartite classification of the kinds of cognition in KV 2.1–2 and E2p40s2. The TIE has the following division (§ 19): (1) perception from hearsay or from signs; (2) perception from random experience; (3) perception that results from an inadequate inference to a thing's essence from an effect or from some universal; (4) perception of a thing either through its essence or through its proximate cause. Spinoza recommends using mainly the fourth mode of perception (§ 29), as being the most suitable for understanding nature and reaching perfection.

(3) §§ 30–48. So how do we attain this type of perception? Certain knowledge is possible only if a true idea is given from the outset. That idea will serve as the standard of truth. The true method is then defined (§ 36) as knowledge reflecting upon itself; or in other words, as the search, in the proper order, for truth itself, or for the objective essences of things (i.e. their essences as grasped in the mind), or for the ideas – all these are the same. The most perfect method is that which will show how the mind must be directed according to the standard of the given true idea of the most perfect being (§ 38), which underlies all being and knowing. In the following sections, Spinoza disposes of the objection that such a foundation

of the method would fall into an infinite regress, and explores how this method can be used to investigate nature in the proper order, without prejudices.

(4) §§ 50–90. After having provided an outline of the argument (§ 49), Spinoza embarks upon what he calls the 'first part' of method, or its initial task, viz. the separation of true ideas from all other perceptions, i.e. from false, fictitious and dubious ideas. How are we to get rid of these? The remedy is to perceive clearly and distinctly (§ 62), and to establish the investigation of nature on cognition of its source and origin. At its origin we find a unique, infinite being, which is thereby the standard of truth (§ 76). Doubt can arise only as long as we have no clear and distinct idea of God (§ 79). Spinoza then deals with the imagination: this is the source of errors, since it is passively determined by fortuitous corporeal motions (§ 84).

(5) §§ 91–8. The 'second part of the method' teaches that clear and distinct ideas can be produced only by the active, pure intellect, not by the imagination (§ 91). Since the process is a genetic one, it must start from a good definition. The ensuing sections are therefore devoted to the requirements of definitions. Spinoza distinguishes between a created thing, whose definition must include its proximate cause, and a thing that is cause of itself and on that account uncreated; it will have to be explained entirely through itself (§ 96, cf. also § 92).

(6) §§ 99–110. Is there a being that is the cause of all things? If so, its 'objective essence' (i.e. the idea of its essence as an object in our mind) will be the cause of all our other ideas, so that the concatenation of ideas in our mind will reflect the essence, order and unity of nature itself (§ 99; cf. § 42). If the method is to be successful, we must establish the order in which to proceed, and avoid wasting our time with trifles. Deducing our ideas from the 'series of things' (the way they are connected to each other) does not mean that we grasp the series of all mutable singular things – that would be far beyond our capacities. Instead, we should concentrate on the series of fixed and eternal things. How are we to go about this? At this stage Spinoza finally starts his investigation of the powers of the intellect – which was to constitute the chief part of his method (§ 106). After having detailed eight clearly perceived features of the intellect, however, the text grinds to a halt. Laconically, the editors of the OP remark: 'The rest is lacking.' Spinoza's fundamental claim, that all knowledge depends on the given true idea of God as the source of all that exists, will be elaborated in the *Ethica*.

2. Short Treatise of God, Man and His Well-Being | Korte verhandeling van God, de mensch en deszelvs welstand (KV)

Spinoza wrote the KV presumably in the years 1660–2, but he then abandoned it, to convert the material into a completely different text, which would eventually become the *Ethica*. What has come down to us as the text of the KV is not the original Latin work, but a contemporary Dutch translation, preserved in two manuscripts, A and B, both kept in the Royal Library in The Hague. The oldest manuscript, A, dates from the end of the seventeenth century. It is bound with a Dutch translation of the TTP and of the *Adnotationes*. Neither the translator nor the scribe have been identified. The manuscript contains many later additions by the Amsterdam physician Johannes Monnikhoff (1707–87; see Jensen, 2003b), who was a follower of the lay philosopher and mystic Willem Deurhoff (1650–1717; see Jensen, 2003a). In the middle of the eighteenth century, Monnikhoff also produced the manuscript now known as B, which is an apograph of A. In addition, Monnikhoff (or perhaps Deurhoff) produced an abstract of the text, which survives in Monnikhoff's hand as the 'Korte Schetz der Verhandeling van Benedictus de Spinoza over God, den Mensch, en deszelfs wel-stand' (Short Outline of Spinoza's Treatise on God, Man and His Well-Being). The outline was discovered in 1851; soon afterwards the two manuscripts of the KV turned up. The text of B was published in 1862, of A in 1869.

In its transmitted form, the KV consists of two parts, comprising ten and twenty-six chapters respectively. To this general structure Spinoza added, in different stages of the composition of the work, several subsidiary texts: two dialogues in part one, two appendices at the end, and a huge number of extensive explanatory notes. Though it is not always clear where the subsidiary texts belong, nor when and why they were added, they must have been part of Spinoza's initial attempt to revise the work (Mignini, 1986, pp. 63–6; cf. also pp. 821–64, about the series of numbers in manuscript A). In the process, however, he decided to abandon it altogether, and started recasting the material in what was eventually to become the *Ethica*. Though not presented in the geometric order, the KV resembles the *Ethica* in its general plan. The KV is couched in a more religious language than Spinoza's other works. Thus we encounter terms like creatures and creation (1.2), God's providence (1.5), predestination (1.6), immortality of the soul (2.23; app2), rebirth (2.22), son of God (1.9; 2.22, n. 4), devil (2.25). Spinoza gives these words a philosophical rather than a religious denotation.

Part One is about God and what pertains to him, that is to say: God's attributes, properties and modes. The first chapter offers proofs for the existence of God, who is then (KV 1.2) described as a single, unique substance of whose attributes only two are known to us, viz. thought and extension. The argument is interrupted by two dialogues that comment upon the preceding chapters and anticipate the epistemology and theory of the passions of Part Two. Chapters 3–6 deal with God's properties: causality, necessity, providence and predestination. Other features commonly attributed to God, such as eternity, infinity, immutability, omniscience, mercifulness, wisdom are modes rather than attributes of God (1.7). In chapters 8–9, Spinoza reformulates the distinction between God (substance and attributes) and the modes produced by God as a distinction between *natura naturans* and *natura naturata*. The use of scholastic terminology here is intentional. The KV offers the most extensive discussion of these notions; they reappear in CM (2.7; 2.9), Ep 9 and E1p29s – always in the context of his view that certain features of God (notably God's understanding) are modes rather than attributes. The concluding chapter of Part One defines good and evil as *entia rationis*, 'beings of reason', mental constructs that have no existence in nature.

Part Two then treats of man and what pertains to him, or, as the table of contents specifies, 'of a perfect man, capable of uniting himself with God'. Man, so the preface to this part emphasizes, is not a substance, but a finite mode produced by God. Spinoza immediately concentrates on the human mind and its three kinds of cognition (KV 2.1–2): opinion (also called imagination), true belief (or reason), and clear knowledge. (In E2p40s2, they reappear as imagination or opinion, reason, and intuitive knowledge.) The first kind is the source of error and of the passions (2.3), the second of good desires (2.4), the third of genuine love of God (2.5).

Spinoza then deals in more detail with the passions (2.6–14) and with the way reason can handle them. In the KV, the theoretical framework in which he analyses the passions is still basically that of Descartes's *Passions de l'âme*. His own mature theory of the affects as set forth in E3 is markedly different. In chapters 14–21, Spinoza elaborates specific aspects of reason: it can distinguish between good and evil passions, between truth and falsehood, and it can show us what the well-being of a perfect man consists in. The will is an illusory notion, which cannot account for human actions. Spinoza explicitly rejects fatalism, though: in fact the doctrine of necessity will help us to overcome evil passions and to advance society (KV 2.18; a similar passage is to be found in E2p49s, end). The final chapters deal with clear knowledge and the love of God. There are no devils: being completely opposite to God, the devil would have nothing from God and therefore cannot possibly exist, since everything owes its existence to him (2.25). Human freedom is the state we acquire through the union of the intellect with God (2.26).

After the main text, the KV has two appendices, whose relation to the rest is unclear. They apparently belong to a late stage in the revision of the work. The first appendix presents Spinoza's views on substance, attributes and God in the geometric order, with seven axioms, four propositions and a corollary. It is closely related to the (lost, but reconstructed) appendix to Ep 2 (Hubbeling, 1977; Saccaro del Buffa Battisti, 1990). The corresponding passages in E1 (definitions, axioms, propositions 1–8) constitute an elaboration of this material. In the second appendix of the KV, Spinoza unfolds his theory of the soul as the idea of the body, which will receive fuller treatment in E2.

3. Parts I and II of Descartes's *Principles of Philosophy* and *Metaphysical Thoughts* | *Renati Des Cartes Principiorum philosophiae pars I et II, Cogitata metaphysica* (PPC, CM)

PPC is a geometrically demonstrated digest of Parts One and Two (and a fragment of Part Three) of Descartes's *Principia philosophiae* (henceforth PP). CM, a series of reflections on metaphysical issues, was added to it as an appendix. Together these two closely related works constitute the only book Spinoza published under his full name. In 1663, when he was living in Rijnsburg, Spinoza taught a young student, Johannes Casearius, the basics of Descartes's philosophy. For this purpose, he had adapted selections from PP 2 and 3, supplemented with a discussion of some metaphysical questions Descartes had not dealt with. When his friends heard about this, they urged Spinoza to publish this digest in an extended version, expanding it with a geometric adaptation of PP 1, too (Meyer, PPC praef; G I, 129:32–130:13). PPC, Spinoza's version of Descartes's PP, is often referred to as 'the principles of Cartesian philosophy', but strictly speaking that is incorrect: it is a presentation of Descartes's book entitled 'Principles of Philosophy', rather than of Cartesian philosophy in general.

In Ep 12A (26 July 1663), Spinoza gives Lodewijk Meyer instructions for subediting the manuscript. Meyer also wrote the preface, in which he explicitly states that Spinoza does not present his own views here, but faithfully reproduces Descartes's arguments instead. Thus, Spinoza does not share Descartes's view that the will is a faculty distinct from the intellect, nor that the human mind or soul is a substance, nor that certain things (e.g. infinity) surpass the human understanding (Meyer, PPC praef; G I, 131:23–133:4).

Spinoza follows Descartes's arguments closely, though he freely changes the order of the exposition, and does not limit himself to PP. Especially PPC 1 draws on a variety of Cartesian sources, including the single text in which Descartes himself had geometrically rephrased the foundation of his metaphysics, the 'Arguments proving the existence of God and the distinction between the soul and the body arranged in geometrical fashion' (*Rationes Dei existentiam & animae a corpore distinctionem probantes, more geometrico dispositae*, AT VII, pp. 160–70), at the end of the Replies to the Second Set of Objections to the *Meditationes*.

The PPC starts with an introductory chapter to Part One, entitled 'Prolegomenon', not arranged geometrically. Here Spinoza expounds Descartes's radical doubt, his discovery of a solid foundation in the *cogito*, and the subsequent elimination of the initial doubt.

The demonstrations of PPC 1 rest on definitions and axioms, which Spinoza cites from Descartes's geometric exposition in the Second Replies. Propositions 1–4 derive the nature of the mind from the *cogito*. Mind and body are really distinct (1p8), and the mind is better known than the body (1p4c). In a painstaking reconstruction of Descartes's argument, Spinoza offers a deduction of God's existence from the idea the mind has of him (1p5–7, with scholia, corollaries and lemmas). Propositions 9–13 and 16–20 elaborate God's perfections: he is the creator and preserver of everything, understands in the highest degree, is supremely truthful, unique, incorporeal, immutable, constant and eternal, and he has preordained everything. In between, Spinoza elucidates Descartes's theory of truth and error: what we perceive clearly and distinctly is true, since God is not a deceiver (1p14), and error is caused by

misuse of the will, which assents to perceptions that are not clear and distinct. The final proposition of this part (1p21) is a transition to the subject matter of Part Two. It contains the Cartesian proof for the reality of matter, or, as Spinoza expresses it, of extended substance. As a thinking thing, I am closely united to a portion of this extended substance, viz. my body.

PPC 2 offers a survey of the foundations of Cartesian physics: the nature and properties of matter, motion and particles. It starts with nine definitions and as many as twenty-one axioms, culled from various articles in PP 2. Propositions 1–6 elaborate the nature of matter or body – crucial to Cartesianism is that matter coincides with extension. This rules out the existence of atoms, for when there is matter, there is extension and hence divisibility, too. Then the nature and the rules of motion are dealt with (2p7–23). This part of the argument includes the Cartesian formulation of the principle of inertia (2p14). God, who is the principal cause of motion (2p12), preserves the quantity of motion and rest that he initially imparted to matter (2p13). On the basis of these laws of motion, the rules of collision are presented (p24–31). Towards the end Spinoza introduces the changes in bodies surrounded by other bodies (2p31s). The five final propositions discuss the behaviour of fluids (p32–37), i.e. of bodies divided into many small particles, moving in all directions with equal force (2p37s).

Part Three is fragmentary indeed: apart from some preliminary material (preface, postulate, two definitions), it has only two propositions. In this rudimentary section, Spinoza deals with Descartes's theory of the shapes matter successively goes through on account of the laws of nature. It starts from the hypothesis that in the beginning God had divided matter into equal particles, and imparted motion to them. The result of this mechanical interaction is that celestial matter organizes itself into vortices. Thus, all heavenly bodies come into being (3post). In the vortices, the initially rough and irregular particles would gradually wear off, and become smooth and round (3p1–2).

CM is presented as an appendix to PPC. According to its subtitle, it deals with problems of the general and the special parts of metaphysics. Spinoza drew his material from contemporary neo-scholastic textbooks as well as from the works of Descartes. The connection between PPC and CM is difficult to assess. Since the work as a whole is intended as an introduction to Descartes's PP, it is not surprising that CM should counter neo-scholastic views with arguments taken from Descartes.

CM 1.1 is about being: real and fictitious beings, *entia rationis* ('beings of reason': mental constructs), and modes of thought. Crucial for Spinoza's own philosophy is the conclusion that being must be divided into substance (which exists necessarily) and modes (whose essence does not involve existence), rather than into substance and accidents. In CM 2, this is applied to God: his essence cannot be distinguished from his existence. The remainder of Part One is devoted to what Spinoza here calls the affections of being: necessity, contingency and (im)possibility (1.3), duration and time (1.4), and modes of thought such as order, difference and agreement, that arise from comparison (1.5). The final chapter (1.6) is a critique of the so-called transcendental terms: the one, the true and the good. In his discussion of truth and falsity, Spinoza defends a nominalist view: truth is nothing but a true idea, just as whiteness has no existence outside white bodies. Good and bad are relative notions only: things are neither good nor bad in themselves. God may be considered the supreme good, but there is no absolute evil. In CM 1.6, Spinoza also touches upon the *conatus*, the striving of every single thing to persevere in its being.

The special metaphysics dealt with in CM 2 is mainly about God's attributes, as Spinoza here calls them: eternity, unity, immeasurability, immutability, simplicity, God's life, intellect, will and power, creation, and concurrence. Chapter 12, the conclusion of the work, then discusses the human mind, more particularly the issues of the immortality of the soul and the freedom of the will. Though Spinoza in CM 2 unfolds several views that he maintains elsewhere, too (e.g. his critique of creation *ex nihilo* in 2.10), he also defends positions incompatible with his own philosophy – notably his arguments, borrowed from Descartes, for the freedom of the will (2.12). In CM he is no longer under the obligation to render faithfully Descartes's views, but Spinoza nevertheless expounds ideas (e.g. on the immortality of the soul and the freedom of the will) that are incompatible with what he maintains elsewhere. His aim is not to develop his own philosophy, but to show what sort of arguments Descartes could have produced against several neo-scholastic concepts.

4. *Theologico-Political Treatise and Annotations* | *Tractatus theologico-politicus, Adnotationes ad Tractatum theologico-politicum* (TTP, Adn)

Spinoza wrote the TTP in the years 1665 to 1669 (see Steenbakkers, 2010). The work is first referred to in Ep 30 (to Oldenburg, October 1665), and it was published early in 1670 or late in 1669. In view of its explosive contents, both the author and his publisher, the Amsterdam bookseller Rieuwertsz, thought it wiser not to reveal their names: the book was published anonymously, and under a false imprint (Künraht, Hamburg). In the autumn of 1675, Spinoza informs correspondents of his plan to supply some explanatory notes to the TTP, and in 1676 he presented a certain Klefmann with a copy of the book into which he had entered five handwritten notes. The total number of *Adnotationes* eventually rose to thirty-nine – some of them readers' comments rather than Spinoza texts (see Akkerman, 2005). The *Adnotationes* are too modest in size for an abstract.

In its subtitle, the TTP presents itself as a compound work, 'containing several dissertations, in which it is shown that the freedom to philosophize not only can be granted without harm to piety and the peace of the republic, but also cannot be abrogated without abrogating piety and the peace of the republic as well.' Spinoza's intention is clear: the TTP is a plea for the freedom to philosophize, and as such an intervention in the political debates of the period, at a time when the pressure on the authorities to muzzle free thought was increasing. But the TTP is also a pivotal text in the history of biblical criticism, and a classic of political thought.

In the Preface Spinoza explains the object of the work. Superstition is rampant, and it causes political instability. Everybody is prone to superstition, as the cause of superstition is fear, to which all people are subject. Christians are divided by hatred, churches have become corrupted, faith has turned into superstition and prejudice, reason is despised, Scripture is misunderstood. Spinoza will investigate the Bible anew, firmly resolved to accept as its teaching only what is drawn from Scripture itself. His conclusion will be that there is no conflict between revealed and natural knowledge. Everyone should be allowed freedom of judgement, and faith should be judged by works. In its second

part, the book will demonstrate that freedom can be allowed without endangering public peace and piety. The author will analyse the ancient Hebrew commonwealth, in order to show that the authority over both religious and civil law rests with the government. Its right and power are best maintained by allowing everyone to think what they want and to say what they think. Spinoza offers his book to the philosophical reader. The people (*vulgus*) and those subject to the same affects should rather not read it: they will only misinterpret it.

Chapter 1 is about prophecy. In keeping with his guiding principle, Spinoza accepts as prophecy only what is explicitly presented as such in Scripture. He defines it as certain knowledge revealed by God. Prophets perceived God's revelations only with the imagination, i.e. through (real or imaginary) words and images (1.27; section numbers according to TTP, ed. F. Akkerman [Paris, 1999]). The only person to whom God's decrees were ever directly revealed, without words or images, was Christ (1.18). Of prophets it is often said that the Spirit of the Lord is upon them. Spinoza examines the way in which the Hebrew word for spirit is used in Scripture, and concludes that prophets excelled in virtue and piety, and perceived the mind of God (1.25). We are ignorant of the laws of nature behind this phenomenon.

Chapter 2 argues that prophets were endowed with a lively imaginative faculty, not with any philosophical insight. Their certainty, then, is of a moral rather than of a mathematical nature (2.3). They never taught anything of interest about God's attributes (2.13): the teaching of the prophets did not extend beyond relatively simple, moral issues. God accommodated his revelations to the comprehension of the prophets. The only thing we should accept from prophecy is that which constitutes its purpose and substance (2.19). Spinoza's aim is to separate philosophy from theology (2.20).

Chapter 3 deals with the Hebrews as God's chosen people. Divine vocation means that somebody's choice for a way of living is determined by the laws of nature, i.e. God's decree and guidance (3.3) There are three honourable goals in life: understanding things through their first causes, taming the passions or acquiring virtue, and living in security and good health. Security can obtain only in a well-ordered society (3.5). Nations differ in order and laws, and it was herein that the Hebrews stood out. Other nations may have been divinely elected, too, but apparently this was not revealed to them prophetically. The divine vocation of the Hebrews consisted in the strength of their commonwealth, and lasted only as long as that endured (3.11). If the Hebrews could re-establish their state, God may elect them again (3.12).

Since everything is determined by nature's laws, all laws – both natural and ordained by human institutions – are ultimately divine (4.1) Yet it is relevant to distinguish between human law, promulgated for the protection of life and society, and divine law regarding only the supreme good, viz. the true knowledge and love of God (4.3). To direct one's life towards this supreme good may well be called the divine law (4.4). Its sum and first commandment is to love God. It is universal, does not require ceremonies nor belief in stories, and it is its own reward (4.6). God's laws are eternal truths. He is described as legislator and prince only to accommodate the inadequate comprehension of the people (4.10). Scripture recommends both the natural light and natural divine law (4.12, end).

In chapter 5 Spinoza explains, from Scripture, why ceremonies were instituted and why belief in biblical stories is useful. The ceremonies contributed to strengthening the Hebrew state (5.12) and have no validity beyond that; the same is true for Christian ceremonies (5.12). Historical narratives serve to propagate the message of Scripture among the common people (*plebs*), but whoever has sound opinions and a right way of living will be blessed without knowing them (5.19).

Chapter 6 is devoted to miracles, commonly believed to occur against the laws of nature. But nothing happens contrary to nature (6.3–5). If miracles could happen, they would subvert the belief in God (6.6–11). Scripture, too, presents God's decrees as the natural order (6.12–15). In interpreting miracles as related in Bible books, the opinions, prejudices and idioms of their authors must be taken into account (6.16–20). It is ignorance that makes people consider miracles as unusual events.

Chapters 7–15 expound Spinoza's interpretation of the Bible, and the conclusions he draws from this for the relation between faith and philosophy. He explains the principles of his method in Chapter 7. Knowledge of Scripture is to be sought only from Scripture itself (7.3). Its divinity resides exclusively in the truth of its moral teachings (7.4). Spinoza draws up three fundamental requirements for interpreting the Bible: (1) knowledge of the languages in which it was written, notably Hebrew; (2) a full inventory of the statements of each book; (3) a historical account of the vicissitudes of the books and their authors (7.5). In biblical interpretation, the Jewish tradition and the Roman Catholic magisterium are unreliable. The right approach is to study Scripture's words (7.9). This is beset with difficulties, as the historical and linguistic evidence is deficient. Still, the Bible's basic moral message is not affected (7.17). Spinoza rejects other methods: no supernatural light is needed (7.19), and Scripture should not be subordinated to reason (7.20–1).

In Chapter 8, Spinoza disproves Moses' authorship of the Pentateuch. Several other books, too, were written long after the events they relate: Joshua, Judges, Samuel and Kings. Spinoza suggests that the author or compiler of all these books may have been Ezra (8.12). That the books of the Bible are compilations is argued in Chapter 9. It is impossible to render biblical chronology coherent (9.7–12). Corrupt readings were introduced in the text in the process of scribal transmission (9.13–21). Chapter 10 investigates the status and transmission of a number of books in the Old Testament, and the establishment of the canon. It is clear that the authority of each Bible book must be examined separately (10.17).

Chapter 11 deals with the question whether the apostles wrote as prophets. Spinoza concludes that in the Epistles they appear as teachers, guided by the natural light (11.7). Since they had different audiences in mind, this gave rise to disputes subsequently (11.10).

In Chapter 12, Spinoza explains in what sense the Bible is God's sacred word. A text is divine only insofar as it inspires people to obey God, i.e. to live piously (12.5). Scripture is the word of God because, and as long as, it teaches the divine law (2.7). In spite of textual corruptions, its sum has come down to us without difficulty or ambiguity, viz. to love God above all else, and to love your neighbour as yourself (12.10).

Chapters 13–14 argue that Scripture teaches no philosophy, but simple matters (13.1). It requires no scientific understanding, only obedience to the divine commandment of justice and charity (13.3, 13.8, 14.1–3). All its other teachings about God are irrelevant (13.9), and everyone is free to interpret these

as he sees fit (14.1). From the Bible we can extract the seven tenets of universal faith: (1) God, the supreme being and model of true life, exists; (2) God is one; (3) God is omnipresent; (4) he has the supreme right and dominion over everything; (5) worshipping and obeying God consists in practising justice and charity; (6) only those who thus obey God will be saved; (7) God pardons those who repent (14.10). There is no connection between theology and philosophy: the latter's object is truth, whereas the goal of faith is obedience and piety. Faith therefore allows complete freedom to philosophize (14.13).

Chapter 15 concludes Spinoza's discussion of the Bible by emphatically stating that it cannot be subordinated to reason (as Maimonides would have it), nor reason to Scripture (Alpakhar's position). Philosophy is not subservient to theology, nor the other way around. The Bible, i.e. revelation, offers comfort to very many people, for whom living under the guidance of reason is unattainable.

The remaining five chapters constitute the political part of the treatise, exploring the extent to which the freedom to philosophize can be granted. Chapter 16 lays the foundations. The right of nature is defined as the right of every individual thing to exist and act in a determined way: right is co-extensive with power (16.2), and what reason considers evil, is so only with regard to our laws, not to those of nature at large (16.4). The passionate constitution of men makes the establishment of commonwealths necessary (16.5–7). The best form of government is a democracy, because it comes closest to natural liberty (16.8–11). Spinoza then defines private civil right, injury, justice, ally, enemy and treason (16.12–18). The supreme right to legislate in religious matters rests with the civil authorities (16.21).

Chapter 17 maintains that no one can transfer his power and right completely: the power of the state is never absolute (17.1–3). In a lengthy analysis of the foundation, organization and downfall of the Hebrew commonwealth, Spinoza argues that it was ruined by the unruliness of the priestly tribe of the Levites (17.27). The lessons from this are drawn in Chapter 18: the clergy should not be charged with political power, and it is dangerous to make opinions an offence (18.5). If political sovereignty, in whatever form of government, is tampered with, it will come to ruin (18.10).

Chapters 19–20 summarize the results of the investigation. Religion has force of law only if it has been granted by the civil authorities, and religious worship must submit to the interest of the state (19.2–11). Spinoza adduces historical examples to substantiate this. In Chapter 20, he addresses the main issue of the TTP: in a free state, everyone is allowed to think what he wants and to say what he thinks. Minds cannot be governed; the state, then, does not have the power to repress opinions, and consequently not the right to do so either. The ultimate end of politics is not subjection, but freedom (20.6). This is not without its drawbacks, but these must be accepted (20.10). The best form of government is democracy – a point Spinoza illustrates with a eulogy of Amsterdam (20.15). In conclusion the fundamental importance of the freedom of philosophizing is set forth once more, in six theses (20.16).

5. Ethics, Demonstrated in Geometric Order | Ethica ordine geometrico demonstrata (E)

Spinoza started writing the *Ethics* in the early 1660s, and completed it in 1675 (for the textual history, see Steenbakkers, 2009). Publication was postponed, however, because Spinoza feared the book would be prohibited

(Ep 68). Recently Leen Spruit discovered an early manuscript copy (1675) of the complete text in the Vatican Library (Spruit and Totaro, 2011; Totaro, Spruit and Steenbakkers, 2011). After his death (21 February 1677), a number of friends, presumably under the direction of Lodewijk Meyer, saw to it that the Latin manuscript was edited, translated into Dutch and published in two versions: Latin (OP) and Dutch (NS). The *Ethics* started as an elaboration of the KV, his earlier, abortive attempt to expound his system. The most conspicuous difference between the two expositions is that the early text is not presented 'in geometric order'. The geometric presentation is modelled on Euclid's *Elements*. Spinoza's use of it has become the paradigmatic specimen of this style of philosophizing. Yet for Spinoza it does not have a demonstrative value of itself: as the *Ethics* exemplifies, geometric deduction will yield true results only if the philosophy is developed in the right order. This means that the exposition must take its starting point in the fountainhead of all there is: God.

The *Ethics* is divided into five parts. Part One, 'Of God', presents Spinoza's metaphysics and ontology. God appears to be only one of the issues in the very beginning of the text, which focuses on the notions of 'cause of itself' and substance, but soon he turns out to be the point of departure: 'Except God, no substance can be or be conceived' (E1p14); 'God is unique, and … in Nature there is only one substance' (E1p14c1). The argument of Part One proceeds in two large strides: propositions 1 to 20 offer a deduction of substance as unique and all-embracing, that is, Nature as a dynamic and infinitely productive force (*natura naturans*), or God; propositions 21 to 28 then carry on the deduction by showing the effects of this productivity, the so-called modes or manifold configurations of the one substance.

By the term modes (also called affections in E1), Spinoza designates everything that exists in (and as an effect of) substance, from infinite natural phenomena such as motion and rest to finite and very limited forms of existence such as particular bodies (including human beings), ideas or affects. The global term for all these modes taken together is *natura naturata*, i.e. nature as the sum total of the workings of Nature's laws. Part One then culminates (propositions 29 to 35) in a forceful account of the thoroughgoing causality of God, i.e. nature, and a refutation of prejudices that prevent people from accepting this. Spinoza explicitly rejects contingency, free will, (im)perfection and teleology. The critique of finalism and of the related fallacies of anthropocentrism and anthropomorphism is set forth in the justly famous appendix to Part One, often read as an essay in its own right. We think that nature acts for an end, because *we* do so; and we think that nature was made for our sake: this is the root of all prejudice. But God or nature is indifferent to human needs, and there are no absolute values: good and evil are human projections.

Part Two, 'Of the Nature and Origin of the Mind', drastically limits the scope to 'those things that can lead us to the knowledge of the human mind and its highest blessedness'. Henceforth, the focus will be on human salvation. Part Two begins with a general examination of the nature of finite modes, which present themselves under two attributes, viz. thought and extension. Though God must necessarily have infinitely many attributes, only these two are accessible to us, because we are the sort of finite modes for which these two attributes are constitutional: under the attribute of extension we are bodies, under the attribute of thought we are minds. Body and mind are one and the same individual thing, seen under different attributes

(E2p21s). After a brief excursion on the nature of bodies (between p13 and p14), Spinoza examines what the mind is capable of. Through its physical counterpart, the body, it has access to external bodies. Its knowledge of this external environment is, however, inadequate, since it reflects the way our body is affected rather than the nature of the external body. Spinoza's term for this indispensable but limited kind of cognition is imagination. It follows from the common order of nature, and human beings could not possibly exist without it. The imagination thus conceived accounts for all experience and hence for empirical knowledge, and it provides us with memory. As a source of inadequate knowledge, the imagination is contrasted with two other kinds of knowledge in p40s2: reason and intuitive knowledge. From proposition 37 onwards, Part Two deals with reason, as the kind of knowledge that rests upon common notions, thus yielding adequate knowledge of universal laws. The discussion of the third kind, intuitive knowledge, is deferred to the second half of Part Five. The final propositions of Part Two offer another deconstruction of the mistaken notion of free will. Will and understanding are the same (p49c). Spinoza rejects the Cartesian division between the understanding as the source of ideas (wrongly taken to be a sort of mental pictures) and the will as the source of activity: ideas are dynamic, and do not require an impetus from a separate faculty such as the will. Part Two concludes with an enumeration of the moral and practical advantages of this new view of the human mind: it will allow a truly rational life. This theme will be taken up again in Part Four. First, however, Spinoza elaborates a complex theory of the mind's affective life.

Part Three, 'Of the Origin and Nature of the Affects', shows what it means that man is part and parcel of nature and hence subject to nature's laws like anything else. Human emotions, too, are natural phenomena that deserve examination: we must try to understand rather than scorn them (E3praef; cf. E2p49s towards the end, E4p50s, E4p73s, KV 2.18, TP 1.1, Ep 30). Spinoza's technical term for the emotions is affects, which he defines as those particular affections of body and mind that increase or diminish, aid or restrain our power of acting. They reflect the way our body is affected by the world around us. Since our experience is mediated by the imagination, this first kind of knowledge is pivotal in Spinoza's account of the affects: our emotional life is determined by the way we experience the world around us, rather than by the actual state of affairs. The notion of affect is a dynamic one, indicating rising and falling levels of activity or energy, both physical and mental. The motor of all dynamics in finite modes is the *conatus* (endeavour, striving): 'Each thing...strives to persevere in its being' (E3p6). The conatus is an expression of the power with which God exists and operates. It implies development, expansion, growth; not a mere conservation of the status quo. In human beings, this endeavour takes on different shapes: will, appetite, desire. The striving itself is involuntary: we do not strive for something because it is good, but we judge a thing to be good because we strive for it (E3p9s, end). The affects fall into two groups (E3def3exp). Those that we undergo or suffer are passions: they diminish our power of acting; these constitute by far the largest part of the affects. Those we are the active cause of are actions: they increase our power of acting. Into this dynamic scale Spinoza then introduces a further dynamism, viz. of degrees of perfection. God is most perfect (E2p1s), and God's modes display an infinite array of levels of perfection, reflecting the extent to which they share in God's power. As human beings are characterized by their minds, their level of perfection depends on what their minds can achieve. Joy (*laetitia*) is the transition to a greater degree of perfection, sadness (*tristitia*) the transition to a lesser degree of perfection. Together with desire (*cupiditas*) – the affective manifestation of the *conatus* – these are the three primary affects (E3p11s; aff2–4, aff4exp). All other affects are basically varieties of joy, sadness and desire. Spinoza then deduces the other affects in the scholia of E3 and in the appendix to Part Three, 'Definitions of the Affects'. The analysis investigates the mechanisms that give rise to an infinite variety of emotions. Thus affects can be modified by being joined with certain objects or by adding a temporal perspective; or again by mechanisms such as association and transfer, or by imitating the affects we perceive in others. Among the many affects Spinoza deduces in E3 we find love and hate, hope and fear, pity and envy, pride and shame. Some combined affects are inherently unstable and vacillating; here again, Spinoza has a particular interest in the dynamics of the process. The final scholium (E3p59s) is devoted to the mind's actions. These turn out to constitute a very small, but crucial subset of affects. Actions are always a matter of joy and desire, never of sadness: on account of the *conatus*, no one can be the adequate cause of his own transition to a lesser degree of perfection. Consequently, sadness is always a passion, something that happens to us. Joy and desire, on the other hand, can be due either to causes outside us, and then they are passions; or to ourselves, in which case they are actions. Actions result from adequate ideas, passions from inadequate ideas. Spinoza comprises the human active affects under 'strength of character' (*fortitudo*), which he divides into 'tenacity' (*animositas*; cf. *animosus* 'spirited, courageous') and 'nobility' (*generositas*; cf. *generosus* 'high-born, i.e. noble-spirited'). The appendix to Part Three is exclusively about passive affects: it offers a survey of 48 different species and concludes with a general definition, in which the physical and mental aspects are treated as a unity.

Part Four, 'On Human Bondage, or the Powers of the Affects', develops a perspective on the human condition from the point of view of our 'bondage', i.e. our subjection to passions. Paradoxically, a considerable portion of this part of the book is taken up by an extensive treatment of the life of the free man (p67–p73, and appendix), but this is part of Spinoza's strategy. In the Preface, Spinoza defines perfection and imperfection as mere 'modes of thought', i.e. as subjective valuations. Yet 'perfection' is a useful notion: it denotes a model of human nature that allows us to measure the extent to which we approach a rational way of life. Part Four deals with the rational or free man not as a real-life phenomenon, but as a model. It shows what our behaviour would be like if we were fully in command of our own lives. Man, however, will necessarily follow and obey the common order of nature (E4ax, p1–p4c). The perspective of Part Four brings out the normal situation (i.e. the common order of nature) by contrasting it with a hypothetical one, in which human beings are rational. The comparison reveals that being in command is not a matter of mere understanding. Our power of acting is to be increased not through insight alone, but by manipulating the opposing dynamics of the affects in order to keep them in check. Many of the precepts for a rational, virtuous life in Parts Four and Five aim at balancing the affects rather than getting rid of them. Against Descartes (*Passions de l'âme* § 48)

Spinoza argues that true knowledge of good and evil does not operate by means of truth as such (p14): in order to influence our affects, knowledge must itself have an affective side (p8). Indeed, insight does not of itself prevent us from acting wrongly: Spinoza repeatedly quotes Ovid's line 'I see and approve the better, but follow the worse' (*Metamorphoses* 7.20–1). The central notion of this part is virtue, which is based on our *conatus*, the striving to preserve our being. For Spinoza 'virtue' denotes qualities that are related to virility: courage, determination, power and strength (cf. p59s). In definition 8, virtue is defined as equal to power (*potentia*). Acting from virtue means: acting, living, preserving one's being by the guidance of reason, i.e. seeking one's own advantage (p24). Part Four introduces a societal perspective (p18s, p29–p37): nothing is more useful to a human being than another human being (p18s), preferably a rational one (p35c1), since they agree in nature and thus mutually enhance their powers of acting. Only in a society can morality be defined: there is no good or evil in the state of nature. Freedom can only emerge in society – any society (p73). Part Four is concluded by a list of precepts for the right way of living.

Part Five, 'Of the Power of the Intellect, or on Human Freedom', is the only part without definitions of its own. Its first half (to p20 inclusive) develops the strategy of a rational management of the affects. In the Preface Spinoza explicitly demarcates his position from the Stoics, since these, too, advocate a rational life. In this context, Spinoza also presents his devastating critique of Descartes's hypothesis of the pineal gland as the point of contact between body and mind. This speculative theory fails to explain not only the quantitative mechanics involved (motion, force, velocity), but also the interaction between body and mind. The mind's power is not to be explained in pseudo-physical terms – for Spinoza this is an ontological confusion, for substance is one – but in terms of mental capacities (knowledge, understanding, cognition), i.e. nature's power as seen from the perspective of the attribute of thought. Spinoza's strategy comes down to a reform or re-education of the imagination through training. In this therapy, cognition is a prerequisite: the imagination must be educated so as to take causality into account, which means that we gradually come to understand more things as necessary (p6). To understand nature is to increase one's power, which in turn is a transition to a higher degree of perfection, i.e. joy. As God (or nature) is the cause of this joy, it results in a love toward God (*amor erga Deum*, p15–16). In p20s, Spinoza summarizes what the mind can do to control the affects: cognition of the affects, rationally redistributing their causes, and several strategies of re-ordering their connections. The perspective is a temporal one, since Spinoza is dealing with the mind in connection with the body. At the end of that scholium, however, he announces a shift to a different level of analysis: he abandons the temporal perspective in order to pass to an examination of the mind's essence 'without relation to the body', that is to say: as it is in God, eternal. For our mind, being eternal is to conceive things under the aspect of eternity (*sub specie aeternitatis*), i.e. as necessary, or as they are in God (p31). This is where the third kind of knowledge, intuition, comes into its own: it is an immediate understanding of singular things as they are in God (p24–7). The love *toward* God now becomes an intellectual love *of* God (p32c), in a double sense: as the distinction between subject and object disappears together with the imagination, the

love of God is both our love for God and the love with which God loves himself (p36). This is, ultimately, what constitutes human salvation, blessedness or freedom (p36s). It allows a mitigation (not an elimination) of the fear of death (p38–9s). The more we understand things with the third kind of knowledge, the more our mind is eternal. This eternity is not an individual immortality of the soul: when the body dies, the mind ceases to function, and there will be no memory of one's individual existence. Memory belongs to the imagination and the body, and individuality lasts only as long as the body is alive. In p40s, Spinoza concludes his discussion of intuition and the eternity of the mind, and resumes his ethical argument, which is not, as he explicitly states, dependent upon the third kind of knowledge. In the final scholium of the book Spinoza stresses the difficulty of the philosophical road to salvation, in a paraphrase of Cicero's dictum *omnia praeclara rara*: 'All things excellent are as difficult as they are rare.'

6. Political Treatise | Tractatus politicus (TP)

After having completed his *Ethics*, in 1675, Spinoza embarked upon a new project: a treatise on politics. He died on 21 February 1677. By that time, he had finished ten chapters, and had begun composing chapter 11. The manuscript is lost: the Latin text as we have it is the version printed in the OP. A Dutch rendering (with some variant readings) came out simultaneously in the NS.

The TP is a classic *politica*: a theory of the nature and foundations of the state, followed by a discussion of the three forms of government (*status civilis*) traditionally considered as providing the basic patterns into which all varieties of states will fit: monarchy, aristocracy and democracy (TP 2.17). These basic forms are thought of as cyclic, succeeding one another in history (8.12). The TP as we have it comprises a part on politics in general and a part on the forms of government. From Ep 84 (to an unknown friend, second half of 1676) it appears that Spinoza had intended to write a third part, on laws and other particular questions regarding politics. The chapters have no captions, but these can in part be supplied from Ep 84. Each chapter is divided into short sections (called 'articles'). In developing his argument, Spinoza refers to preceding articles in a fashion reminiscent of the geometric order in the *Ethics*.

Chapter 1, the introduction, argues that the foundations of political rule are to be derived from common human nature rather than from reason (1.7). Human beings are driven first and foremost by their passionate nature. Rather than trying to understand these passions philosophers deride and bewail them. They consider men not as they are, but as they would want them to be (1.1). Politicians have been more to the point, since they know the practice of human behaviour from experience. Spinoza here has in mind Machiavelli, whose political realism he endorses in the TP. Spinoza's theory of politics starts from the laws of nature demonstrated in the *Ethics*, viz. that men are necessarily subject to passions (1.5). Reason can, to some extent, control the passions, but not sufficiently to make a rationally ordered state possible. Government must be so organized that rulers and ruled will do what contributes most to the security and stability of the state, whatever their motives. Security is the virtue of a state, as freedom and fortitude of spirit is the private virtue (1.6).

Chapter 2, on natural right, offers an outline of Spinoza's philosophy as presented in TTP and E. The power each thing has is the power of God, and its natural right extends as far as its power to exist and to act (2.3).

Since men are led by blind desire rather than by reason, their natural power and right is to be defined by their affective striving to persist in their being (2.5). For human beings, freedom consists in living according to reason (2.7; 2.11). This is not within everyone's reach, but whatever an individual does, whether wise or ignorant, he does by the supreme right of nature (2.8). To the extent that they are governed by anger and hatred, men are by nature enemies (2.14). When people join forces, their power increases (2.13) and they are guided as if by one mind (2.16). This collective right, as defined by the power of the multitude, is sovereignty (*imperium*): when exercised by the multitude as a whole, the government is a democracy; when by a selection of people, an aristocracy; and when it is in the hands of one person, a monarchy (2.17). In the state of nature, there is no sin (2.18) nor injustice (2.23): sin and injustice is that which is prohibited by law, and this is only possible in a state.

Chapter 3 analyses the right of the supreme civil authorities, in relation to its subjects (3.2–11) and to other states (3.12–17). The most fundamental feature of human nature is the universal endeavour of self-preservation (3.18). Even in society the natural right of each person does not cease to exist (3.3), but the more the commonwealth exceeds the individual in power, the less right he has (3.2). The most powerful commonwealth will be that which is based on and guided by reason (3.7). Sovereign states relate to one another like two people in the state of nature (3.11): they are enemies by nature (3.12). Commonwealths can become allies by concluding treaties, which will last as long as they have something to gain from them (3.14).

In Chapter 4, Spinoza discusses the tasks of the supreme authorities, such as legislation, criminal justice, the army, war and

356

peace, diplomacy and levying taxes (4.2). The commonwealth (*civitas*) can do no wrong, since it defines right and wrong, but it is bound by the natural law of self-preservation (4.5). In TP 4.6 Spinoza briefly mentions the social contract.

In the short but focal Chapter 5, Spinoza considers the ultimate purpose of the state: peace and security. The best state is where people live together in concord. Men will be passionate: to what extent this fact will affect the state's stability depends on the quality of its organization (5.2). Against Hobbes, Spinoza maintains that peace is not absence of war, but a virtue arising from strength of character (*animi fortitudo*) (5.4). Human life is defined not just by an uninterrupted functioning of the body, but most of all by reason, which is the true virtue and life of the mind (5.5). The best state is a state of free people (5.6).

In Chapters 6–7 Spinoza deals with monarchy. Its organization must ensure that rulers and ruled will act for the general interest, irrespective of their personal motives (6.3). A prince, who is after all just a human individual, cannot be expected to be unselfish. Therefore the proper way of organizing a monarchy is to ensure that the king will gain most by being concerned for the welfare of all (6.8). There must be a large council (6.15), that must be heard before the king can take any decision (6.17). The remainder of Chapter 6 and the whole of Chapter 7 are devoted to a detailed description of the arrangements required for a good monarchy, i.e. a monarchy established by a free people (7.26), specifying rules for the composition and functioning of the king's council, royal marriage, the education of the king's children, succession to the throne, the administration of justice, winning the people's support, avoiding corruption, property of land, the army, etc. Spinoza is aware that no state

actually meets all these requirements (7.30). In his conclusion, Spinoza rejects absolute monarchy: the king's power depends on the multitude (7.31).

Spinoza turns to aristocracy, whose rulers are called patricians, in Chapters 8–10. He distinguishes two forms: the most common is that the state coincides with or is organized exclusively around its capital (8.3–49), as in ancient Rome or in Venice in Spinoza's day; the other model is that of Holland, where sovereignty is held by several cities (Chapter 9). The number of patricians may vary from two to all, as long as they are enrolled in the supreme council by co-option. The ideal number of patricians will depend on the size of the state: Spinoza calculates a ratio of about 1 to 50 (8.13). Again, Spinoza is interested in the mechanisms that will prevent aristocratic rule from becoming absolute. The supreme council is supported by two subordinate bodies: the syndics who must control the laws (8.20) and the senate, charged with the daily affairs (8.29). Spinoza gives an extremely meticulous account of the exact arrangements that will make an aristocracy stable (8.11–49). Yet the one-city model of aristocracy remains a precarious form of government: the balance of power is easily disturbed if the patriciate fails to keep the multitude in check (8.39). Spinoza favours the second model, an aristocracy based on a number of cities. The balance of power this entails is conducive to co-operation and peace (9.14–5). Chapter 10 sums up the results of Spinoza's analysis: the foundations of aristocracy preclude equality (10.8). A state can survive only if its legal institutions remain inviolate (10.9), and this will succeed only if its laws are based on reason and simultaneously take into account the passionate nature of men (10.10). Spinoza claims that his two models can attain an optimum of stability, if they meet the conditions he has specified.

The embryonic Chapter 11 marks the transition to Spinoza's discussion of democracy – a form of government he labels 'absolute', since all political power ultimately depends on the multitude (11.1, cf. 8.3). The only topic he deals with is political participation. Since his criterion is being independent (*sui juris*, 11.3), he excludes women and *servi* (servants or slaves): they depend on men and masters respectively. It is by nature rather than by convention that men dominate women: equal female participation would imperil peace (11.4).

7. Concise Grammar of the Hebrew Language | Compendium grammatices linguae Hebraeae (CG)

Spinoza's unfinished 'Concise Grammar of the Hebrew Language' was published late in 1677 as part of the *Opera posthuma*. According to the 'Notice to the Reader' supplied by the editors of the OP, Spinoza wrote it 'at the request of certain of his friends who were diligently studying the Sacred Tongue'. It is unknown when and for what particular purpose (if any) it was written. It has been suggested that Spinoza may have taught Hebrew when he attended Van den Enden's Latin School, which would situate the origins of this grammar around 1657. Or again, given the affinity of the work with Spinoza's treatment of the Hebrew language in the TTP 7, Gebhardt (I, 626; IV, 444) assigned it to the period when Spinoza wrote the TTP, i.e. 1665–70. Recently, Proietti proposed a later date: between 1670 and 1675 (Proietti, 1989 and 2001).

Apparently, Spinoza had in mind a work in two parts: one about the inflection of nouns and verbs, another about syntax. The projected first part was nearly finished: in its final form, it has 33 chapters. Spinoza never started on the second part.

After four introductory chapters on the Hebrew letters, vowel points and accents, Spinoza devotes eight chapters to the nouns (*nomina*), of which he distinguishes six kinds: substantive, adjective, relative or preposition, participle, infinitive and adverb (CG 5). He starts with nouns rather than with verbs, as grammarians before him did, because Spinoza's distinctively original insight is that in Hebrew verbs are basically nouns. The remaining twenty-one chapters of CG are devoted to verbs, classified by Spinoza in eight conjugations.

8. Correspondence | Epistolae (Ep)

Among the texts Spinoza's editors published in 1677, after his death, they included a section with 74 letters from and to the philosopher, under the title 'Letters from Some Learned Men to B. d. S., and the Author's Replies, Greatly Contributing to an Elucidation of His Other Works' (*Epistolae Doctorum Quorundam Virorum ad B. d. S. et Auctoris Responsiones, ad Aliorum Ejus Operum Elucidationem Non Parum Facientes*, OP, pp. 393–614). Philosophical relevance, then, was their selection criterion: letters from Spinoza's correspondents were included only to bring his answers into relief, and messages that dealt with matters they considered trivial were omitted. This explains the absence of Oldenburg's last letter (Ep 79), to which Spinoza had not replied, and of Ep 12A (a short note to Meyer, giving him instructions for subediting PPC) and Ep 28, a very personal letter to Bouwmeester. Ep 28 provides precious details about the genesis of the *Ethics*, but Spinoza's friends (among them Bouwmeester) rejected it: on the manuscript, someone scribbled a note: 'Is of no value'. Apart from the 74 items in the section

Epistolae, OP contains one more letter, which serves as a preface to the TP (OP, p. 266). Since the seventeenth century, thirteen items have been added to Spinoza's correspondence. Of these 88 letters, 50 were written by Spinoza. As can be gathered from the letters that have come down to us, there must have been more (at least 117). Nevertheless, in comparison with such prolific letter-writers as Descartes and Leibniz, the volume of Spinoza's correspondence was relatively modest. A striking feature of it is that Spinoza politely and sometimes cordially replied to messages he received, but apparently never initiated an exchange.

The arrangement of the letters in the OP is by correspondent, which has the advantage of thematic coherence. Nineteenth-century editions of Spinoza's works stuck to this classification, until Van Vloten and Land, in their critical edition of 1882–3, introduced a purely chronological order, to document Spinoza's philosophical development. This also implied a radical renumbering of the letters. This is now generally used to refer to the letters (as 'Ep', followed by the number in Van Vloten and Land; later additions have been inserted in their chronology with letters added: Ep 12A, 48A, 48B, 67A).

The letters are an invaluable source of information about Spinoza's life, his network of friends and acquaintances, and his works. The reason for writing the TTP is explained in Ep 30, and in many later letters (Ep 43, 69, 73, 75, 77) Spinoza responds to criticisms of or queries about his views on religion. Of special interest are Spinoza's replies to his friends, who had access to his work in manuscript and sometimes ask for elucidations, e.g. Ep 9 to De Vries, and Spinoza's correspondence with Schuller and Tschirnhaus. Occasionally, we see glimpses of Spinoza's work in progress (TIE: Ep 6, 37, 60; PPC: 12A, 13; E: Ep 23,

28, 68; Adn: Ep 68, 69; TP: Ep 84), and samples of his critique of other modern philosophers (Bacon: Ep 2; Descartes: Ep 2, 15, 21, 26, 30, 32, 81, 83, Hobbes: Ep 50). The correspondence also reflects how Spinoza's contemporaries worried about the ethical and religious implications of his philosophy, and documents the variety of subjects that were discussed under the heading of philosophy: planets (Ep 26), hydrostatics (Ep 41), nitre (Ep 6, 13), probability calculus (Ep 38). Spinoza's expertise in lens-grinding is apparent in discussions of lenses, telescopes, optics and dioptrics (Ep 26, 32, 36, 39, 40, 46). His view on how to read the Bible, one of the crucial issues in the TTP, is set forth in several letters (Ep 19, 21, 75). Spinoza reacts to the accusation of atheism in Ep 43, and deals with a range of theological and religious questions: Christ (Ep 73, 75, 78), miracles (same letters) the relationship between philosophy and religion (Ep 76).

Two clusters of themes that turn up again and again, conferring philosophical coherence to the correspondence, are (1) the metaphysics of God, substance, attributes and modes, and (2) the ethical issues involved in problems of causality, necessity, freedom of the will and the existence of evil.

(1) From the beginning (Ep 2, with its lost appendix), Spinoza offers explanations of his definition of God as substance consisting of infinite attributes, and the difference between substance and modes – the groundwork of his philosophical system. We can see him trying to work out the distinguishing features – if any – of substance and attribute (Ep 9). When the *Ethics* is finished, Spinoza answers metaphysical questions still left unsolved: why we have access only to two attributes, extension and thought, of the infinitely many that God must necessarily have, what the immediate

and mediate infinite modes mentioned in E1p23dem are (Ep 64). A related metaphysical issue is that of infinity. Ep 12, to Meyer, circulated as a separate essay, 'On Infinity' (cf. Ep 81). Spinoza distinguishes three kinds: the infinity of that which exists from its own nature (substance); the infinity of that which has no bounds owing to its cause (infinite modes); the infinity (more properly called indefiniteness) of that which cannot be expressed in any number. In connection with this cluster of ontological questions, Spinoza also deals with epistemological and methodological matters in the letters. Thus, Ep 12 includes a discussion of the way our understanding handles notions like time, measure and number; Ep 17 is about the working of the imagination, Ep 37 about the right method, Ep 60 about true and adequate ideas. A question that Spinoza repeatedly addresses is that of definition (Ep 4, 9, 10, 60). Justly famous is his discussion of whole and parts, with the striking thought experiment of a tiny worm with our blood for its habitat (Ep 32).

(2) Several of Spinoza's correspondents were uneasy about his view on causality, necessity and freedom. The issues involved are intricately tied up with the metaphysics of his system, but the problems raised in the letters often have to do with the ethical aspects: if everything is determined, there is no moral responsibility, and evil ultimately derives from God. Both implications were unacceptable to Spinoza's contemporaries; so his theory must be wrong. Spinoza takes great pains to clarify his position. He points out that chance does not exist, that necessity is not the opposite of freedom, but of coercion (Ep 54, 56); freedom does not consist in free decision, but in free necessity (Ep 58, quoting E1def7). Man's moral responsibility resides in having to undergo the consequences of one's behaviour (Ep 78). This does not make God responsible for evil, for in nature there is no evil (Ep 23).

BIBLIOGRAPHY
Secondary Literature

Akkerman, F., 'La Latinité de Spinoza et l'authenticité du texte du Tractatus de intellectus emendatione', *Revue des sciences philosophiques et théologiques*, no. 71 (1987), pp. 23–9.

———, '*Tractatus theologico-politicus*. Texte latin, traductions néerlandaises et *Adnotationes*', in F. Akkerman and P. Steenbakkers (eds), *Spinoza to the Letter. Studies in Words, Texts and Books* (Leiden and Boston: Brill, 2005), pp. 209–36.

———, *Taal en tekst van Spinoza* (Voorschoten: Uitgeverij Spinozahuis, 2013).

Beyssade, M., 'Deux latinistes. Descartes et Spinoza', in F. Akkerman and P. Steenbakkers (eds), *Spinoza to the Letter. Studies in Words, Texts and Books* (Leiden and Boston: Brill, 2005), pp. 55–67.

De Dijn, H., *Spinoza. The Way to Wisdom* (West Lafayette, IN: Purdue University Press, 1996).

Hubbeling, H.G., 'The Development of Spinoza's Axiomatic (Geometric) Method: the Reconstructed Geometric Proof of the Second Letter of Spinoza's Correspondence and its Relation to Earlier and Later Versions', *Revue internationale de philosophie*, no. 31 (1977), pp. 53–68.

Jensen, L., 'Deurhoff, Willem', in W. van Bunge et al. (eds), *The Dictionary of Seventeenth and Eighteenth-Century Dutch Philosophers* (Bristol: Thoemmes, 2003), pp. 260–5.

———, 'Monnikhoff, Johannes', in W. van Bunge et al. (eds), *The Dictionary of Seventeenth and Eighteenth-Century Dutch Philosophers* (Bristol: Thoemmes, 2003), pp. 707–9.

Kajanto, I., 'Spinoza's Latinity', in F. Akkerman and P. Steenbakkers (eds),

Spinoza to the Letter. Studies in Words, Texts and Books (Leiden and Boston: Brill, 2005), pp. 35–54.

Leopold, J.H., 'Le langage de Spinoza et sa pratique du discours', trad. M. Beyssade, in F. Akkerman and P. Steenbakkers (eds), *Spinoza to the Letter. Studies in Words, Texts and Books* (Leiden and Boston: Brill, 2005), pp. 9–33.

Meijer, W., *Nachbildung der im Jahre 1902 noch erhaltenene eigenhändigen Briefe des B. de Spinoza, mit Erläuterungen und Übersetzungen* (The Hague: Meijer, 1903).

Mignini, F., 'Per la datazione e l'interpretazione del *Tractatus de intellectus emendatione* di B. Spinoza', *La cultura*, no. 17 (1979), pp. 87–160.

——— (ed./trans.), Spinoza, *Korte verhandeling van God, de mensch en deszelvs welstand/Breve trattato su Dio, l'uomo e il suo bene* (L'Aquila: Japadre, 1986).

Proietti, O., 'Il Satyricon di Petronio e la datazione della Grammatica Ebraica Spinoziana', *Studia Spinozana,* no. 5 (1989), pp. 253–72.

———, 'Per la cronologia degli scritti postumi di Spinoza. Terenzio e il Petronius di M. Hadrianides (Amsterdam, 1669)', *Quaderni di storia,* no. 53 (2001), pp. 105–54.

Saccaro del Buffa Battisti, G., 'La dimostrazione dell'esistenza di Dio dall'abbozzo del 1661 e dalla *Korte verhandeling* al De Deo', in F. Mignini (ed.), *Dio, l'uomo, la libertà. Studi sul Breve trattato di Spinoza* (L'Aquila: Japadre, 1990), pp. 95–118.

Spruit, L. and P. Totaro (eds), *The Vatican Manuscript of Spinoza's Ethica* (Leiden/Boston: Brill, 2011).

Steenbakkers, P., 'The Textual History of Spinoza's Ethics', in O. Koistinen (ed.), *The Cambridge Companion to Spinoza's Ethics* (Cambridge: Cambridge University Press, 2009), pp. 26–41.

———, 'The Text of Spinoza's *Tractatus theologico-politicus*', in Y. Melamed and M. Rosenthal (eds) *Spinoza's Theological-Political Treatise. A Critical Guide* (Cambridge: Cambridge University Press, 2010), pp. 29–40.

Totaro, P., L. Spruit and P. Steenbakkers, 'L'Ethica di Spinoza in un manoscritto della Biblioteca Apostolica Vaticana (*Vat. Lat. 12838*),' *Miscellanea Bibliothecae Apostolicae Vaticanae* 18 (2011), pp. 583–610.

Vet, J.J.V.M. de, 'Salomon Dierquens, auteur du Stelkonstige reeckening van den regenboog et du Reeckening van kanssen', trad. I. Salien, J. Ganault et D. van Mal-Maeder, in F. Akkerman and P. Steenbakkers (eds), *Spinoza to the Letter. Studies in Words, Texts and Books* (Leiden and Boston: Brill, 2005), pp. 169–88.

Walther, M. and M. Czelinski, *Die Lebensgeschichte Spinozas. Lebensbeschreibungen und Dokumente. Zweite, stark erweiterte und vollständig neu kommentierte Auflage der Ausgabe von Jakob Freudenthal 1899* (Stuttgart-Bad Cannstatt: Frommann-Holzboog, 2006).

Werf, Th. Van der, 'Klefmann's Copy of Spinoza's Tractatus Theologico-Politicus', *Studia Rosenthaliana*, no. 39 (2006), pp. 247–53.

Zweerman, Th., *L'Introduction à la philosophie selon Spinoza. Une analyse structurelle à l'introduction du Traité de la réforme de l'entendement, suivie d'un commentaire de ce texte* (Leuven/Assen: Presses Universitaires de Louvain/Van Gorcum, 1993).

P. Steenbakkers

6

SPINOZA SCHOLARSHIP

The history of Spinoza scholarship starts as early as the seventeenth century: soon after Spinoza's death in 1677 the first biographies were composed, while philosophers across the length and breadth of Western Europe rose to the challenge of deciphering the contents of his works, the *Tractatus theologico-politicus* and the *Ethics* in particular. Today, dozens of academics in Europe and the United States as well as in South America, Australia, New Zealand and Japan have made it their business to come to terms with the many intellectual challenges his writings continue to present us with. A selection from several of the most important early commentaries dealing with Spinoza's philosophy has been included in this volume. The chapter on Spinoza's life also reflects some of the impact his life and work had on his surroundings. After the publication of Jonathan Israel's *Radical Enlightenment* and *Enlightenment Contested*, it makes little sense to list once more all the late seventeenth and eighteenth-century authors involved in the assessment of Spinozism. For our purposes it seems more suitable to start this survey of the continuing tradition of Spinoza scholarship in the mid nineteenth-century, also because it would seem that it was only after the flowering of German Idealism and the subsequent emergence of the History of

Philosophy as a proper discipline that modern Spinoza scholarship came into its own. Spinoza owes his position in the canon of Western philosophy to the historiography developed by German scholars in the Hegelian tradition. An important landmark was Kuno Fischer's *Geschichte der neuern Philosophie* (1854).

One of the main reasons for situating the rise of modern Spinoza scholarship in the nineteenth century is the publication of several important editions of Spinoza's works (see Steenbakkers, 2007). During the eighteenth century no editions appeared, only a handful of translations. In 1802–3, the theologian and Orientalist H.E.G. Paulus (1761–1851), who held chairs at Jena, Würzburg and Heidelberg, brought out the first modern edition of Spinoza's *Opera*, which consists of a reprint of the seventeenth-century editions, adding an important section *Collectanea de vita B. de Spinoza*. This collection of the early biographies (Colerus, Lucas, Jelles, Kortholt) turned it into a treasure trove of Spinozana. In 1788 Paulus travelled to Amsterdam to collect further data, but over a century after Spinoza's death he was not able to add new findings to the facts uncovered already by Colerus. Though disappointing from a critical point of view, Paulus's edition had an enormous impact. It appeared at the right time in the right place: as a result of the German debates on Spinoza at the end of the eighteenth century, the so-called *Pantheismus-Streit*, Spinoza's works were in great demand. This was the edition used by Fichte, Schelling, Hegel (who contributed to it, if only modestly) and Schopenhauer. After two minor editions (Gfrörer's in 1830 and Riedel's in 1843), another important and influential edition of Spinoza's complete works appeared in 1843–6, published by the Lutheran minister K.H. Bruder (1812–92). Unlike Paulus, who merely reprinted the seventeenth-century editions, Bruder did independent editorial work, and his edition enjoyed considerable success: it went through a number of reprints and served as the basis for most of the commentaries and translations in the nineteenth and early twentieth centuries.

In 1862 the most important addition to the seventeenth-century corpus of Spinoza's texts was published by Johannes van Vloten (1818–83) as a *Supplementum* to the Bruder edition: in the 1850s two manuscript copies of the *Korte Verhandeling*, now held by the Koninklijke Bibliotheek in The Hague, had been discovered. Van Vloten also added several newly found letters and the anonymous *Stelkonstige reeckening van den regenboog*, which today however is no longer regarded as a work by Spinoza (De Vet, 2005). In addition Johannes van Vloten was instrumental in turning Spinoza into an icon of nineteenth-century freethinking. He wrote several fine monographs on Spinoza as well as dozens of highly polemical essays emphasizing the topicality of Spinoza's atheism and materialism, and in 1880, after a long and difficult campaign to raise funds, he could finally unveil Frédéric Hexamer's celebrated statue of Spinoza, still standing at the Paviljoensgracht

in The Hague. Together with the philosopher and Orientalist J.P.N. Land (1834–97), subsequently professor at Amsterdam and at Leiden, Van Vloten was also responsible for the last major edition of Spinoza's works published in the nineteenth century: the *Opera quotquot reperta sunt* (1882–3). Furnished with a (slender) apparatus criticus and rigorously based on the original editions, Van Vloten and Land's *Opera* were a major step forward in Spinoza scholarship. It was succeeded in the twentieth century by the monumental edition by Gebhardt, though in some cases Gebhardt's tendency to interfere with the text made it less reliable than the conservative edition offered by Van Vloten and Land. Regrettably, the subsequent printings (1895, 1914) are increasingly inferior, each adding new misprints to the ones copied from the preceding. The third printing, unfortunately most widely available, is very sloppy indeed.

Carl Gebhardt (1881–1934) had written his PhD on the *Tractatus de intellectus emendatione* (1905), made a living as director of the Schopenhauer Archives in Frankfurt, and made his name by producing a four-volume edition of Spinoza's works, which he claimed to be 'definitive' – an assessment that was widely accepted. Gebhardt was also a pioneer in situating Spinoza in the context of the Portuguese community of Amsterdam: as early as 1922 he edited the collected works of Uriel da Costa and the following year he published an important paper on Juan de Prado. Following earlier efforts such as most notably Manuel Joel's (1826–90), a definite 'tradition' was established of regarding Spinoza as an essentially Jewish philosopher. During the 1970s, research into the textual history of Spinoza's works, which had important but isolated forerunners like the Dutch poet J.H. Leopold, was rekindled by

363

Fokke Akkerman (see Akkerman and Steen-bakkers (eds), 2005, for an inventory of recent philological work on Spinoza). For the early works, important scholarly work has been done by Filippo Mignini. Recently a team of French, Italian and Dutch scholars has set out to produce yet another edition in the original Latin and Dutch, with French translations. This edition intends to succeed Gebhardt's in the twenty-first century. Three volumes have now appeared, containing the TTP, TP, KV, PPC and CM.

Research into the life and times of Spinoza also was rejuvenated during the nineteenth century, in particular in the latter half. Besides Van Vloten no other historian produced so many new details concerning Spinoza's biography as K.O. Meinsma (1865–1929) did, a teacher at the local grammar school of Zutphen. In 1896 he published his *Spinoza en zijn kring*, which was to be translated into German and French, containing a wealth of archival findings relating to Spinoza's Amsterdam 'circle', including Franciscus van den Enden (1602–74) and Adriaan Koerbagh (1632–69). During the twentieth century new data were added to the sources brought together by the Breslau professor of philosophy Jakob Freudenthal (1839–1907; Freudenthal 1899) by the remarkable figure of Stanislaus von Dunin-Burkowski (1864–1934). Born in Austria, this Polish count became a Jesuit in the Netherlands and spent most of his life in Germany studying early modern anti-Trinitarianism as well as Spinoz-ism. Willem Gerard van der Tak (1885–1958), a professional librarian and secretary to the Dutch Spinoza Society (Vereniging Het Spinozahuis), discovered many details relating to Spinoza's youth. Israel Révah (1917–73), hispanist at the Collège de France, unearthed new documents relating to Spinoza's excommunication from the

Jewish community in 1656. Odette Vlessing has been working for quite some time now on the legal aspects of Spinoza's excommuni-cation. During the early 1990s Marc Bedjai and Wim Klever claimed to have found evi-dence of the pre-eminent role Van den Enden played in Spinoza's entourage (see, however, Mertens, 1994). The most complete *status quaestionis* is now to be found in Steven Nadler's *Spinoza* (1999). Recently Manfred Walther re-edited Freudenthal's collection of documents relating to Spinoza's life, includ-ing many twentieth-century findings.

As far as the interpretation of Spinoza's philosophy is concerned, it should first be emphasized that not only many nineteenth-century freethinkers, such as Van Vloten, but also the eminent legal scholar Sir Frederick Pollock (1845–1937) appear to have regarded Spinozism first and foremost as an alterna-tive to German Idealism, which by the mid-dle of the century had lost much of its initial appeal and was starting to give way to vari-ous kinds of positivism. For most of his life, Van Vloten was locked in battle with Kan-tians in particular, while Pollock as a student felt uncomfortably surrounded by Hegelians dominating intellectual life in Oxford in par-ticular. His first paper on Spinoza dealt with 'the scientific character of Spinoza's philoso-phy'. Seven years later, in 1880, just before he was named professor of jurisprudence at the University of London, he published his highly influential *Spinoza: His Life and Philosophy*. A few years before his death, he returned to Spinoza once more, summarizing the main attraction of the Dutchman's philosophy as follows: 'Spinozism, as a living and construct-ive force, is not a system, but a habit of mind. There have been Kantians, who maintained, however they might differ in their interpret-ations, that Kant had said the final word in philosophy. Within my own memory there were many Hegelians who claimed no less of Hegel. But there is no such thing as a Spinozist school in that sense, and for my part I trust there never will be' (Pollock, 1935, pp. 135–6).

Van Vloten and Pollock were no academic philosophers, but in France several of the most prominent nineteenth-century academic philosophers shared a deep interest in Spinoza's philosophy: the eclectic idealist Victor Cousin (1792–1867) as well as the positivists Hyppolite-Adolphe Taine (1828–93) and Joseph-Ernest Renan (1823–93) all paid tribute to the formative influence Spinoza's work had on their own thought. It goes without saying that French philosophers have always been particularly concerned to assess the precise nature of Spinoza's relationship to Descartes. In 1877 Renan held a much quoted address in the The Hague at the commemoration of Spinoza's death. It would seem, however, that Victor Delbos (1862–1916) had a more decisive impact on the continuing presence of Spinoza in the philosophy curriculum in France: Delbos wrote two books on Spinoza, and especially his *Le spinozisme* is still being referred to to this day. This book was based on a series of lectures held at the Sorbonne in 1912–13, and it has been suggested that the anti-idealist emphasis of these lectures on the eve of the First Wold War was closely related to increasing suspicion among the French concerning Germany's political intentions.

After the turn of the century, however, increasingly rigorous scholarship was to replace much of the ideological strife characteristic of the nineteenth-century rediscovery of Spinozism as a comprehensive philosophy. The most accomplished attempt to represent Spinoza as the last major medieval thinker of the early modern age, rather than as a representative of the Cartesian breakthrough, was the impressive study by H.A. Wolfson (1934).

Wolfson (1887–1974) was born in Lithuania, but took his BA as well as his PhD from Harvard University, which he never left. He was professor of Judaic Studies for half a century and published seminal studies on the entire range of Jewish and Arabic philosophy. To his mind, Spinoza was essentially heir to Maimonides and Crescas, and he also made much of the traces to be found in Spinoza's earliest publications of neo-Platonism. Although the interpretation Wolfson ultimately presents us with is reminiscent of both Joel's and Gebhardt's previous work, the range and audacity of his scholarship continue to exert considerable influence. His interpretation of Spinoza as a Jewish mystic, and his attempt to reduce Spinozism to its alleged ancient and medieval sources, was to be criticized severely by post-war experts, most notably Martial Gueroult (1968), yet he would remain an important source of inspiration to several more recent authors arguing in favour of a Jewish interpretation of Spinozism, including Steven Nadler.

Moreover, the twentieth-century rediscovery of the early modern Hispanic cultural heritage of the 'marranos' inevitably gave rise to several attempts to include Spinoza into this tradition of forced subterfuge and dissimulation: independently, the Spanish philosopher Gabriel Albiac and the Israeli scholar Yirmiyahu Yovel argued that in particular the *Tractatus theologico-politicus* testifies to Spinoza's deliberate use of ambiguity. Thus, in a sense, they reiterated Leo Strauss's (1899–1973) insistence to take heed of Spinoza's 'strategic' authorship: according to Strauss Spinoza's 'exoteric' text should be sharply distinguished from its 'esoteric' message. Important though Wolfson's and Strauss's contributions no doubt were, it should be added that until the 1960s interest in Spinoza among professional philosophers and historians was fairly limited both in the US and Britain and on the European continent. As long as such schools of thought as phenomenology and existentialism dominated the practice of philosophy in Europe and while logical positivism set the agenda for most Anglophone philosophers, interest in Spinozism among academics remained sporadic and largely historical.

This situation changed drastically in the course of the 1960s. Within a few months in 1968 and 1969, three books appeared in Paris that altered Spinoza scholarship for good. First Martial Gueroult (1891–1976) issued the first part of his massive commentary on the *Ethics*, unimaginatively entitled *Spinoza I: Dieu*. It consists of a stunning reconstruction of the 'logic' of the first part of the *Ethics*. Gueroult had already established a formidable reputation as a historian of philosophy. His approach largely ignored the historical context of such authors as Fichte, Malebranche and Descartes, and attempted instead to capture inner 'reasoning' at work in e.g. the latter's *Meditations* (1953). He was mainly concerned with reconstructing the inner structure of the philosophical texts he was working on. As it turned out, Spinoza's *Ethics* proved a perfect subject for this approach. The unmatched rigour of Gueroult's analysis made it appear as if he had actually succeeded in improving the *Ethics*: in several cases he supplied additional demonstrations for its propositions, adding moreover the reasons Spinoza must have had not to include these alternative lines of reasoning.

Several of Gueroult's findings have been questioned in subsequent scholarship, but the way in which he demonstrated the basis of Spinoza's 'rationalism', as well as his destruction of any idealist reading of the *Ethics*, are still widely shared. Spinoza's

'rationalism', so Gueroult argued, can be fully appreciated only by comparing it to Descartes's, and more in particular to Descartes's insistence on the 'création des vérités éternelles'. According to Descartes, the most fundamental truths of logic and mathematics ultimately derive from God's will. They are true because God wanted them to be true, but in view of his sovereignty, God could clearly have wanted different truths to hold. As a consequence, Descartes's 'rationalism' should be deemed conditional since the ultimate truths of reality depend upon God's will, which in itself is perfectly incomprehensible. Spinoza on the other hand, Gueroult continued, removes God's will from his metaphysics by simply denying that such a faculty exists in the first place. Next, Gueroult delivered a lethal blow to any attempt to regard the *Ethics* as part of the idealist tradition in philosophy, by demonstrating that Spinoza's (infinite and finite) modes do not 'emanate' from the substance he calls 'God or nature', and subsequently by insisting on the necessity to remain loyal to the logic it entails: reality can in no way be regarded as the product of any 'constructive' creation on the part of the subject. Instead, 'subjects' should always be taken as products of substance. In short: man does not 'create' nature in any way, it is the other way around, for man is not a substance: he is always a product of nature.

Gueroult's approach to the history of philosophy inspired many French philosophers, including the young Alexandre Matheron, who largely independently had set out to write a thesis on the third, fourth and fifth parts of the *Ethics*. He defended his thesis in 1968 and published it the following year. He demonstrated how Spinoza, on the basis of the metaphysics and the epistemology delivered in the first two parts of the *Ethics*, had construed a social and an essentially political philosophy, largely ignored in the history of Spinoza scholarship. By a meticulous reconstruction of Spinoza's 'genealogy' of affects he succeeded in showing how according to Spinoza the emergence of political communities was a natural effect of the specific constitution of the human 'mode' and the specific way in which it interacted with the rest of reality. While the motivation behind Gueroult's efforts appears to have been largely esthetical, Matheron's reading of Spinoza was strongly informed by his Marxist sympathies. Over the next few decades, this particular approach would be further bolstered by former students of the neo-Marxist Louis Althusser (1918–90) such as Étienne Balibar and Pierre Macherey.

A third book which testified to the deep impact Spinoza apparently had on many French intellectuals during the 1960s was Gilles Deleuze's *Spinoza et le problème de l'expression* (1968). Gueroult, Matheron and Deleuze did not at all agree on every aspect of Spinoza's philosophy, but together they succeeded in delivering an interpretation characterized by a 'horizontal' ontology: according to their reading Spinoza's universe consists essentially of modes permanently interacting with and affecting each other. The collective appeal of their work unleashed a renaissance of scholarship, which has continued to this day and turned Paris into the unofficial 'capital' of Spinoza scholarship. The 'Association des Amis de Spinoza' is by far the most active group of scholars around today. Especially under the tutelage of Pierre-François Moreau, professor at the École normale supérieure de Lyon and a former student of Matheron, scores of up-and-coming French historians of philosophy, including Chantal Jaquet, Charles Ramond, Laurent Bove, Lorenzo Vinciguerra, and

Yves Citton are continuing a tradition first established in the late 1960s. Several Italian philosophers also play a prominent role in the 'Association', as is evident, for instance, from Antonio Negri's persistent reflection on the topicality of Spinoza's 'anomalous' thought. Difficult as it is to characterize the collective nature of their efforts, a number of themes clearly hold a special fascination for this latest revival of Spinoza scholarship; on the basis of a meticulous reading of Spinoza's texts, the precise nature of his 'rationalism' and his 'naturalism' have been questioned in depth, but also more specific notions such as individuality, the body, imagination and eternity have been addressed by the members of the 'Association', while the social and political dimensions of his thought have duly been emphasized with special attention to Spinoza's comments on democracy and what has been termed the 'liberating' potential of the multitude. The resistance to any Platonist reading of the *Ethics* seems to suit an essentially political agenda.

An important aspect of recent Spinoza scholarship is the emergence of new generations of translations such as those by Akkerman and Krop (Dutch), Curley and Shirley (English), Moreau, Lagrée and others (French), Bartuschat (German), Dominguez (Spanish), Mignini, Proietti, Cristofolini and Scribano (Italian). Italy has a remarkably high production in Spinoza studies, covering a wide range of approaches. One of the driving forces behind Italian scholarship was Emilia Giancotti (1930–92). In the past decades, many Italian students of Spinoza contributed to the lively debates on all aspects of his life, work and philosophy, among them Mignini, Cristofolini, Emilia Scribano, Pina Totaro, Daniela Bostrenghi, Roberto Bordoli and Omero Proietti.

The French-Italian 'New Spinoza' has drawn considerable attention in South America and in the United States as well. In the English-speaking world, Spinoza scholars take their cue from the analytical tradition in which they are trained. In Britain, the moral philosopher Stuart Hampshire (1914–2004) produced an elegant and influential introduction to Spinoza's philosophy (1951). There is no British school of Spinoza scholarship in the twentieth century, but among several important individual contributions Parkinson's monograph on epistemology (1954) should be noted. In recent times the remarkable study by Richard Mason (1951–2006) of *The God of Spinoza* (1999), and Susan James's work stand out. In the USA, Edwin Curley took the lead by delivering in 1969 a new interpretation of Spinoza in which he focused on Spinoza's Cartesian background. Jonathan Bennett, Alan Donagan (1925–91), Don Garrett, Steven Nadler, Thomas Cook and Michael DellaRocca followed suit. In general, most US philosophers writing on Spinoza tend to concentrate on his metaphysics and his epistemology. They prefer writing on Spinoza's views concerning substance and causality, and on (the impossibility of) mind-body interaction, but interest in his theological and political views appears to be on the increase in the Anglophone community of philosophers worldwide, as is demonstrated, for instance, by the writings of the Australian scholars Moira Gatens and Genevieve Lloyd. The Portuguese born neuroscientist Antonio Damasio, professor at the University of Southern California, enjoyed considerable success with his attempt to demonstrate the topicality of Spinoza's philosophy of mind. In the Netherlands and Belgium Hubertus Hubbeling (1925–86) and Herman de Dijn were instrumental in the post-war rediscovery of Spinoza just as Manfred Walther, until recently editor in chief of the annual *Studia Spinozana*, and Wolfgang Bartuschat were in Germany. In the Netherlands, Germany and France, meanwhile, from the 1980s onwards the reception of Spinoza's philosophy has also been studied with a new vigour. The British historian Jonathan Israel, however, composed by far the most comprehensive synthesis of the impact Spinozism had during the Enlightenment. His concept of an essentially Spinozist 'Radical Enlightenment' will no doubt be discussed by Spinoza scholars as well as Enlightenment specialists for many years to come.

Finally, it should be stressed that Spinoza turned out to be a philosopher who throughout the centuries also inspired 'laymen', including many artists and literary authors. In Western Europe and the US the rapid process of secularization during the 1960s and 1970s probably played an important role in the late twentieth-century rediscovery of Spinoza among a wider public. Apparently, the highly technical passages and often very abstract discussions to be found in the *Ethics* hardly diminish its appeal among readers without a professional background in philosophy. This seems to suggest Spinoza has a particular ability to affect his readers in a way few canonical philosophers have been able to do. Nobody knows to what extent the Spinozist 'habit of mind' Pollock referred to will continue to inspire academics and laymen in the way that it has over the past few centuries. Neither can we be sure that the currently prevailing 'horizontal' and 'liberating' reading of Spinoza will continue to dominate. Only a few years ago, Theo Verbeek presented us with a conservative analysis of Spinoza's political philosophy and in a recent British collection of papers the debate on Spinoza's indebtedness to neo-Platonism has been carefully reopened (Ayers (ed.), 2007), which only seems to confirm that at the moment there are no signs of any imminent waning of interest in the life and thought of Benedict de Spinoza.

BIBLIOGRAPHY
Primary Sources

Colerus, J., *Korte dog waar-achtige levens-beschryving van Benedictus de Spinoza. Uit autentique stukken en mondeling getuigenis van nog levende personen, opgestelt* (Amsterdam, 1705).

Lucas, M., 'La vie de feu Monsieur Spinoza', *Nouvelles Littéraires*, no. 10 (1714), pp. 40–74.

Spinoza, B. de, *Opera quae supersunt omnia*, 2 vols, ed. H.E.G. Paulus (Jena: In Bibliopolo Academico, 1802–3).

———, *Optimae notae qui ab restauratione litterarum ad Kantium usque floruerunt*, Tomus III, Sectio I et II. *Benedicti de Spinoza Opera philosophica omnia*, ed. A. Gförer (Stuttgart: Mezler, 1830).

Descartes, R. and B. de Spinoza, *Praecipua opera philosophica*, 2 vols, ed. C. Riedel (Leipzig: Hartung, 1843).

Spinoza, B. de, *Opera quae supersunt omnia*, 3 vols, ed. K.H. Bruder (Leipzig: Tauchnitz, 1843–6).

———, *Benedicti de Spinoza Opera quae supersunt omnia supplementum*, ed. J. van Vloten (Amsterdam: Muller, 1862).

———, *Opera quotquot reperta sunt*, 2 vols, ed. J. van Vloten and J.P.N. Land (The Hague: Nijhoff, 1882–3).

———, *Opera*, 4 vols (Heidelberg: Winter, 1925).

———, *Oeuvres* III: *Tractatus theologico-politicus/Traité théologico-politique*, ed. F. Akkerman, trans. J. Lagrée and

P.-F. Moreau (Paris: Presses Universitaires de France, 1999).

———, *Oeuvres* V: *Tractatus politicus/Traité politique*, ed. O. Proietti, trans. Ch. Ramond (Paris: Presses Universitaires de France, 2006).

———, *Oeuvres* I: *Premiers écrits*, ed. F. Mignini, trans. M. Beyssade (Paris: Presses Universitaires de France, 2009).

Secondary Literature

Akkerman, F., *Studies in the Posthumous Works of Spinoza. On Style, Earliest Translation and Modern Edition of Some Texts* (Meppel: Krips Repro, 1980).

———, and P. Steenbakkers (eds), *Spinoza to the Letter. Studies in Words, Texts and Books* (Leiden and Boston: Brill, 2005).

Albiac G., *La sinagoga vacía. Un estudio de las fuentes marranas del espinosismo* (Madrid: Hiperión, 1987).

Ayers, M. (ed.), *Rationalism, Platonism and God* (Oxford: Oxford University Press, 2007).

Balibar, É., *Spinoza et la politique* (Paris: Presses Universitaires de France, 1985).

Bartuschat, W., *Spinozas Theorie des Menschen* (Hamburg: Meiner, 1992).

Bedjai, M., 'Métaphysique, éthique et politique dans l'oeuvre du docteur Franciscus van den Enden (1602–1674)', *Studia Spinozana*, no. 6 (1990), pp. 291–301.

Bennett, J., *A Study of Spinoza's Ethics* (Cambridge: Cambridge University Press, 1984).

Bloch, O. (ed.), *Spinoza au XVIIIe siècle* (Paris: Méridiens Klincksieck, 1990).

———, *Spinoza au XXe siècle* (Paris: Presses Universitaires de France, 1993).

Bordoli, R., *Ragione e Scrittura tra Descartes e Spinoza. Saggio sulla 'Philosophia S. Scripturae Interpres' di*

Lodwijk Meyer e sulla sua recezione (Milan: Franco Angeli, 1997).

Boucher, W.I. (ed.), *Spinoza. Eighteenth and Nineteenth-Century Discussions*, 6 vols (Bristol: Thoemmes Press, 1999).

Bove, L., *La Stratégie du conatus. Affirmation et résistance chez Spinoza* (Paris: Vrin, 1996).

Bunge, W. van, *From Stevin to Spinoza. An Essay on Philosophy in the Seventeenth-Century Dutch Republic* (Leiden and Boston: Brill, 2001)

———, 'Spinoza Past and Present', in G.A.J. Rogers, T. Sorrell and J. Kraye (eds), *Insiders and Outsiders in Seventeenth-Century Philosophy* (New York and London: Routledge, 2009), pp. 223–37.

———, '"Geleerd spinozisme" in Vlaanderen en Nederland, 1945–2000', *Tijdschrift voor Filosofie* no. 71, (2009), pp. 11–36.

Citton, Y., *L'Envers de la liberté. L'invention d'un imaginaire spinoziste dans la France des lumières* (Paris: Éditions Amsterdam, 2006).

Cook, Th.J., *Spinoza's Ethics* (London and New York: Continuum, 2007).

Curley, E., *Spinoza's Metaphysics. An Essay in Interpretation* (Cambridge, MA: Harvard University Press, 1969).

———, *Behind the Geometrical Method. A Reading of Spinoza's Ethics* (Princeton: Princeton University Press, 1988).

Damasio, A., *Looking for Spinoza. Joy, Sorrow an the Feeling Brain* (Orlando: Harcourt, 2003).

De Dijn, H., *Spinoza. The Way to Wisdom* (West Lafayette: Purdue University Press, 1997).

———, *Spinoza. De doornen en de roos* (Kapellen: Pelckmans-Klement, 2009).

Delbos, V., *Le problème moral dans la philosophie de Spinoza et dans l'histoire du spinozisme* (Paris, Alcan, 1893).

———, *Le spinozisme* (Paris: Société Française d'Imprimerie, 1916).

Deleuze, G., *Spinoza et le problème de d'expression* (Paris: Minuit, 1969).

———, *Spinoza. Philosophie pratique* (Paris: Minuit, 1981).

DellaRocca, M., *Representation and the Mind-Body Problem in Spinoza* (Oxford: Oxford University Press, 1996)

———, *Spinoza* (New York: Routledge, 2008).

Donagan, A., *Spinoza* (Chicago: Chicago University Press, 1989).

Duffy, S., 'Spinoza Today. The Current State of Spinoza Scholarship,' *Intellectual History Review,* no. 19 (2009), pp. 111–32.

Dunin-Borkowski, S. von, *Spinoza*, 4 vols (Münster: Aschendorff. 1933–6).

Fischer, K., *Geschichte der neuern Philosophie*, vol. I (Mannheim: Bassermann and Mathy, 1854).

Freudenthal, J., *Die Lebensgeschichte Spinoza's in Quellenschriften, Urkunden und nichtamtlichen Nachrichten* (Leipzig: Von Veit, 1899).

Garrett, D. (ed.), *The Cambridge Companion to Spinoza* (Cambridge: Cambridge University Press, 1996).

Gatens, M. and G. Lloyd, *Collective Imaginings. Spinoza, Past and Present* (London and New York: Routledge, 1999).

——— (ed.), *Feminist Interpretations of Benedict de Spinoza* (University Park: The Pennsylvania State University Press, 2009).

Gebhardt, C., *Spinozas Abhandlung über die Verbesserung des Verstandes. Eine entwicklungsgeschichtliche Untersuchung* (Heidelberg: Winter, 1905).

Gebhardt, C. (ed.), *Die Schriften des Uriel da Costa* (Heidelberg: Winter, 1922).

——, 'Juan de Prado', *Chronicon Spinozanum*, no. 3 (1923), pp. 269–91.

Giancotti Boscherini, E., *Lexixon Spinozanum*, 2 vols (The Hague: Nijhoff, 1970)

Gueroult, M., *Descartes selon l'ordre des raisons*, 2 vols (Paris: Aubier, 1953).

——, *Spinoza I. Dieu (Éthique I)* (Hildesheim and New York: Olms, 1968).

——, *Spinoza II. L'âme (Éthique II)* (Hildesheim and New York: Olms, 1974).

Hampe, M. and R. Schnepf (eds), *Baruch de Spinoza. Ethik* (Berlin: Akademie Verlag, 2006).

Hampshire, S., *Spinoza* (Harmondsworth: Penguin, 1951).

Hubbeling, H.G., *Spinoza's Methodology* (Assen: Van Gorcum, 1964).

——, *Spinoza* (Baarn: Ambo, 1978).

Israel, J.I., *Radical Enlightenment. Philosophy and the Making of Modernity, 1650–1750* (Oxford: Oxford University Press, 2001).

——, *Enlightenment Contested. Philosophy, Modernity, and the Emancipation of Man, 1670–1752* (Oxford: Oxford University Press, 2006).

James, S., *Passion and Action. The Emotions in Early Modern Philosophy* (Oxford: Oxford University Press, 1997).

Jaquet, Ch., *Sub specie aeternitatis. Étude des concepts de temps durée et éternité chez Spinoza* (Paris: Éditions Kimé, 1997).

Joel, M., *Zur Genesis der Lehre Spinozas, mit besonderer Berücksichtigung des kurzen Traktats von Gott, dem Menschen und derselben Glückseligkeit* (Breslau: Schletter'sche Buchhandlung, 1871).

Juffermans, P., *Drie perspectieven op religie in het denken van Spinoza. Een onderzoek naar de verschillende betekenissen van religie in het œuvre van Spinoza* (Budel: Damon, 2003).

Kingma, J. , 'Spinoza Editions in the Nineteenth Century', in F. Akkerman and P. Steenbakkers (eds), *Spinoza to the Letter. Studies in Words, Texts and Books* (Leiden and Boston: Brill, 2005), pp. 273–81.

Klever, W.N.A. , 'Proto Spinoza Franciscus van den Enden', *Studia Spinozana, no. 6* (1990), pp. 281–9.

——, *Mannen rond Spinoza. Portret van een emanciperende generatie, 1650–1700* (Hilversum: Verloren, 1997).

Koistinen, O. and J.I. Biro (eds), *Spinoza. Metaphysical Themes* (Oxford: Oxford University Press, 2002).

Laerke, M., *Leibniz lecteur de Spinoza. La genèse d'une opposition complexe* (Paris: Champion, 2008).

Macherey, P., *Hegel ou Spinoza* (Paris: Maspero, 1979).

——, *Avec Spinoza. Études sur la doctrine et l'histoire du spinozisme* (Paris: Presses Universitaires de France, 1992).

——, *Introduction à l'Éthique de Spinoza*, 5 vols (Paris: Presses Universitaires de France, 1994–8).

Mason, R., *The God of Spinoza. A Philosophical Study* (Cambridge: Cambridge University Press, 1999).

——, *Spinoza: Logic, Knowledge and Religion* (Aldershot: Ashgate, 2007).

Matheron, A., *Individu et communauté chez Spinoza* (Paris: Éditions de Minuit, 1969).

——, *Le Christ et le salut des ignorants chez Spinoza* (Paris: Aubier-Montaigne, 1971).

——, *Anthroplogie et politique au XVIIe siècle (Études sur Spinoza)* (Paris: Vrin, 1986).

Mertens, F., 'Franciscus van den Enden: tijd voor een herziening van diens rol in het ontstaan van het spinozisme?', *Tijdschrift voor Filosofie*, no.56 (1994), pp. 717–38.

Montag, W. and T. Stolze (eds), *The New Spinoza* (Minneapolis: The University of Minnesota Press, 1997).

Meinsma, K.O., *Spinoza en zijn kring. Historisch-kritische studiën over Hollandsche vrijgeesten* (The Hague: Nijhoff, 1896).

Moreau, P.-F., *Spinoza. L'exprérience et l'éternité* (Paris: Presses Universitaires de France, 1995).

———, 'Spinoza's Reception and Influence', in Don Garrett (ed.), *The Cambridge Companion to Spinoza* (Cambridge: Cambridge University Press, 1996), pp. 408–33.

———, *Problèmes du spinozizme* (Paris: Vrin, 2006).

Nadler, S., *Spinoza. A Life* (Cambridge: Cambridge University Press, 1999).

———, *Spinoza's Heresy. Immortality and the Jewish Mind* (Oxford: Clarendon Press, 2001).

———, *Spinoza's Ethics. An Introduction* (Cambridge: Cambridge University Press, 2006).

Negri, A., *L'anomalia selvaggia. Saggio su potere e potenza in Baruch Spinoza* (Milan: Feltrinelli, 1981).

Norris, C., *Spinoza and the Origins of Modern Critical Theory* (Oxford: Blackwell, 1991).

Nyden-Bullock, T., *Spinoza's Radical Cartesian Mind* (London and New York: Continuum, 2007).

Otto, R., *Studien zur Spinozarezeption in Deutschland im 18. Jahrhundert* (Frankfurt: Lang, 1994).

Pollock, Sir F., *Spinoza. His Life and Philosophy* (London: Kegan Paul, 1880).

———, *Spinoza* (London: Duckworth, 1935).

Ramond, Ch., *Spinoza et la pensée moderne. Constitutions de l'Objectivité* (Paris: L'Harmatan, 1998).

Reijen, M. van, *Het Argentijnse gezicht van Spinoza. Passies en politiek* (Kampen: Klement, 2010).

Révah, I.S., *Des marranes à Spinoza*, ed. H. Méchoulan, P.-F. Moreau and C.L. Wilke (Paris: Vrin, 1995).

Schröder, W., *Spinoza in der deutschen Fühaufklärung* (Würzburg: Königshausen und Neumann, 1987).

Scribano, M.E., *Da Descartes a Spinoza. Percorsi della teologia razionale nel Seicento* (Milan: Franco Angeli, 1988).

Secrétan, C., T. Dagron and L. Bove (eds), *Qu'est-ce que les Lumières 'radicales'? Libertinage, athéisme et spinozisme dans le tournant philosophiqie de l'âge classique* (Paris: Éditions Amsterdam, 2007).

Steenbakkers, P., *Spinoza's Ethica from Manuscript to Print. Studies on Text, Form and Related Topics* (Assen: Van Gorcum, 1994).

———, 'Les éditions de Spinoza en Allemagne au XIXe siècle', in A. Tosel, P.-F. Moreau and J. Salem (eds), *Spinoza au XIXe siècle* (Paris: Publications de la Sorbonne, 2007), pp. 21–32.

Strauss, L., *Die Religionskritik Spinozas als Grundlage seiner Bibelwissenschaft. Untersuchungen zu Spinozas Theologisch-politischem Traktat* (Berlin: Akademie-Verlag, 1930).

Thissen, S., *De spinozisten. Wijsgerige beweging in Nederland, 1850–1907* (The Hague: SDU, 2000).

Tosel, A., P.-F. Moreau and J. Salem (eds), *Spinoza au XIXe siècle* (Paris: Publications de la Sorbonne, 2007).

Totaro, P. (ed.), *Spinoziana. Ricerche di terminologia filosofica e critica testuale* (Florence: Olschki, 1997).

Vaz Dias, A.M., and W.G. van der Tak, 'Spinoza. Merchant and Autodidact', *Studia Rosenthaliana*, no. 16 (1982), pp. 105–71.

——, 'The Firm of Bento y Gabriel de Spinoza', *Studia Rosenthaliana*, no. 16 (1982), pp. 178–89.

Verbeek, Th., *Spinoza's Theological-political Treatise. Exploring 'the Will of God'* (Aldershot: Ashgate, 2003).

Vernière, P., *Spinoza et la pensée française avant la Révolution* (Paris: Presses Universitaires de France, 1954).

Vet, J. J.V.M. de, 'Salomon Dierquens, auteur du *Stelkonstge reeckening van den regenboog* et du *Reeckening van* kansen', in F. Akkerman and P. Steenbakkers (eds), *Spinoza to the Letter. Studies in Words, Texts and Books* (Leiden and Boston: Brill, 2005), pp. 169–88.

Vinciguerra, L., *Spinoza et le signe. La genèse de l'imagination* (Paris: Vrin, 2005).

——, 'The Renewal of Spinozism in France, 1950–2000', *Historia Philosophica*, no. 7 (2009), pp. 133–55.

Vlessing, O. , 'The Excommunication of Baruch Spinoza. The Birth of a Philosopher', in J. Israel and R. Salverda (eds), *Dutch Jewry. Its History and Secular Culture (1500–2000)* (Leiden, Boston and Cologne: Brill, 2002), pp. 141–72.

Vloten, J. van, *Baruch d'Espinoza. Zijn leven en schriften, in verband met zijnen en onzen tijd* (Amsterdam: Muller, 1862).

Walther, M. and M. Czelinski (eds), *Die Lebensgeschichte Spinozas. Zweite, stark erweiterte und vollständig neu kommentierte Auflage der Ausgabe von Jakob Freudenthal 1899*, 2 vols (Stuttgart-Bad Cannstatt: Frommann Holzboog, 2006).

Walther, M. (ed.), *Spinoza in der deutsche Idealismus* (Würzburg: Königshausen und Neumann, 1997).

Werf, Th. van der (ed.), *Herdenking van de 375ste geboortedag van Benedictus de Spinoza, Mededelingen vanwege Het Spinozahuis*, no. 93 (2007).

Wielema, M., *The March of the Libertines. Spinozists and the Dutch Reformed Church (1660–1750)* (Hilversum: Verloren, 2004).

Wolfson, H.A., *The Philosophy of Spinoza. Unfolding the Latent Processes of his Reasoning*, 2 vols (Cambridge, MA: Harvard University Press, 1934).

Yovel, Y., *Spinoza and Other Heretics*, 2 vols (Princeton: Princeton University Press, 1988).

W. van Bunge

INDEX OF NAMES

The page numbers in bold denote where the main entry for an individual falls